Meet the *Southern Living* Foods Staff

On these pages we show the Foods Staff (left to right in each photograph) at work as they compile, test, taste, and photograph the recipes that appear each month in *Southern Living*.

Susan Payne, Foods Editor; Helen Anne Dorrough, Associate Foods Editor

Jean Wickstrom Liles, Senior Foods Editor

Susan Dosier, Phyllis Cordell, and Dana Adkins Campbell, Assistant Foods Editors

Cathy Dunklin, Julie Vaillancourt, and Karen Brechin, Editorial Assistants

Kaye Adams, Test Kitchens Director; Patty Vann, Assistant Test Kitchens Director

Diane Hogan and Judy Feagin, Test Kitchens Home Economists

Jane Cairns, Test Kitchens Home Economist; Peggy Smith, Marketing Manager

Leslie Byars, Assistant Photo Stylist; Charles Walton IV, Senior Foods Photographer; Jan Wyatt, Photographer; Beverly Morrow Perrine, Senior Photo Stylist

Southern Living®

1989 ANNUAL RECIPES

Library of Congress Catalog Number: 79-88364
ISBN: 0-8487-0796-6
ISSN: 0272-2003

Manufactured in the United States of America
First printing 1989

Southern Living®
    Senior Foods Editor: Jean Wickstrom Liles
    Foods Editor: Susan Payne
    Associate Foods Editor: Helen Anne Dorrough
    Assistant Foods Editors: Dana Adkins Campbell,
        Phyllis Young Cordell, Susan Dosier
    Editorial Assistants: Karen Brechin, Cathy Dunklin,
        Julie Vaillancourt
    Test Kitchens Director: Kaye Adams
    Assistant Test Kitchens Director: Patty Vann
    Test Kitchens Staff: Jane Cairns, Judy Feagin, Diane Hogan,
        Peggy Smith
    Senior Photo Stylist: Beverly Morrow Perrine
    Assistant Photo Stylist: Leslie Byars
    Senior Foods Photographer: Charles E. Walton IV
        Additional photography by *Southern Living* photog-
        rapher Jan Wyatt, pages 2 and 3.
    Production Manager: Clay Nordan
    Assistant Production Manager: Wanda Butler

Oxmoor House, Inc.
    Executive Editor: Ann H. Harvey
    Production Manager: Jerry Higdon
    Associate Production Manager: Rick Litton
    Art Director: Bob Nance
    Production Assistant: Theresa Beste

Southern Living® 1989 Annual Recipes

    Senior Editor: Olivia Kindig Wells
    Copy Editor: Mary Ann Laurens
    Editorial Assistant: Pam Beasley Bullock

    Designer: Carol Middleton
    Illustrator: Barbara Ball

Cover: *Roast Turkey and Cornbread Dressing (page 322) boasts a
simple garnish of orange slices, celery leaves, and fresh sage.*

Back cover: *Chocolate-Strawberry Shortcake (page 216) looks much like
the old classic Grandmother used to make, but chocolate is added to the
cake in this recipe.*

Page 1: *Alternate red and green apple wedges around the sides of
Four-Cheese Pâté (page 284).*

Page 4: *Fresh produce, as well as canned fruits and vegetables, stars in
these salads: (clockwise from top) Salade Riviera; Tropical Waldorf
Salad; Endive, Bacon, and Pecan Salad; Blue Cheese Coleslaw.
(Recipes, pages 12 and 13.)*

To find out how you can receive *Southern Living* magazine, write to
Southern Living®, P.O. Box 830119, Birmingham, AL 35283.

Table of Contents

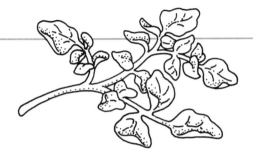

9

Our Year
At
Southern Living

The highlight this year for all of us at *Southern Living* was the move to our new corporate headquarters building in Birmingham. For the foods staff the excitement centered around moving into four spacious, well-equipped test kitchens, a photography studio, and new offices.

Beyond the packing and unpacking, there was a flurry of activity as the staff worked diligently to meet deadlines for our final 1989 issues.

Early in the year we surveyed the cooking interests and habits of many of our readers to stay attuned to current food needs and preferences. We learned that most of you enjoy cooking but are looking for recipes with short preparation time. Many of you continue to be concerned about good nutrition and cutting calories.

In anticipating your need for quick-and-easy recipes, we started the year with our new "QUICK!" feature. With a different food spotlighted each month, the aim is to keep the ingredient list short and keep total preparation time less than 30 minutes.

We're responding to your desire for more low-calorie and low-sodium recipes. Prepared by our registered dietitian, *On the Light Side* recipes prove that low-calorie eating can be enjoyable and that you don't have to give up all the foods you love. Each of these recipes includes an analysis of six nutrients along with the calorie count, taking the guesswork out of nutritious eating.

In contrast to quick-and-easy recipes, we know you want special recipes for entertaining and you look to

Southern Living when planning these occasions. Through our entertainment stories, you visit some of the South's best parties. Variety abounds in this year's Florida beachside brunch, Louisiana summer buffet, Georgia chili party, Tennessee holiday feast, and North Carolina cookie swap.

From your letters we know our party and menu stories are some of your favorites. In fact, many of you tell us of your successes with our menus and even send snapshots of *Southern Living* parties you've duplicated.

Because you continue to ask for more menus, the foods staff has created *Seasonings*, a monthly menu planner, designed around recipes in *1989 Annual Recipes*. The first issue of *Seasonings* will give you a complete menu for each day of January 1990 and help you make better use of your *1989 Annual Recipes*. These menus will offer ideas for special occasions, weekend lunches, and weekday family suppers. Subscribers to *Seasonings* will receive the menu planner on a monthly basis. You'll find additional information for ordering *Seasonings* on page 368.

After a busy but rewarding year, we present our *1989 Annual Recipes*. We think we've handpicked some of the South's most treasured recipes to share with you.

Jean Wickstrom Liles

JANUARY

*Wind down from the hustle and bustle of the holidays
with a leisurely gathering. Invite the ladies for lunch and
serve one of our simple but elegant menus. Or select a
crisp, bright salad from our sampling of winter salads
and plan a meal around it.*

A Winter Salad Sampler

Salads enhance meals with color, texture, and refreshing flavor, as well as important nutrients. Fortunately, improved growing techniques and modern transportation provide a large cast of interesting salad ingredients throughout the year.

Embellishing fresh produce with canned fruits and vegetables offers versatility and quick preparation.

TROPICAL WALDORF SALAD
(pictured on page 74)

1 (8-ounce) can crushed
  pineapple, undrained
1 red apple, unpeeled and
  chopped
¼ cup flaked coconut
¼ cup thinly sliced celery
¼ cup chopped macadamia nuts
  or toasted pecans
3 tablespoons chopped dried
  papaya
⅓ cup mayonnaise or salad
  dressing
1 green apple, unpeeled and
  sliced
1 red apple, unpeeled and
  sliced
Lettuce leaves

Drain pineapple, reserving juice; set juice aside. Combine pineapple and next 6 ingredients; stir well. Cover and chill.

Combine green and red apple slices and reserved pineapple juice, tossing to coat. Arrange apple slices and pineapple mixture on individual lettuce-lined plates. Yield: 6 servings.
Vivian Levine
Oak Ridge, Tennessee

MANDARIN TOSSED SALAD

1 head leaf lettuce, torn
1 cup sliced celery
6 green onions, chopped
3 tablespoons chopped fresh
  parsley
2 (11-ounce) cans mandarin
  oranges, drained
½ cup slivered almonds,
  toasted
Dressing (recipe follows)

Combine first 6 ingredients in a large bowl; toss with dressing. Yield: about 8 servings.

Dressing

½ cup vegetable oil
¼ cup tarragon wine vinegar
¼ cup sugar
½ teaspoon salt
¼ teaspoon pepper
½ teaspoon hot sauce

Combine all ingredients in a jar. Cover tightly, and shake vigorously. Chill. Shake again before serving over salad. Yield: 1 cup.
Sharron Kay Johnston
Fort Worth, Texas

SALADE RIVIERA
(pictured on page 74)

1 (14-ounce) can hearts of palm,
  drained and sliced
1 (14-ounce) can artichoke
  hearts, drained and quartered
½ cup chopped green pepper
½ cup chopped sweet red pepper
10 pimiento-stuffed olives, halved
10 ripe olives, halved
Vinaigrette Dressing
1 head Boston lettuce
2 hard-cooked eggs, cut into
  quarters
12 cherry tomatoes, halved

Combine first 6 ingredients in a bowl. Add Vinaigrette Dressing, and mix well; refrigerate at least 1 hour.

To serve, place salad on a bed of lettuce, and garnish with eggs and tomatoes. Yield: 4 to 6 servings.

Vinaigrette Dressing

3 tablespoons olive oil
3 tablespoons vegetable oil
3 tablespoons wine vinegar
½ teaspoon Dijon mustard
½ teaspoon salt
½ teaspoon pepper

Combine all ingredients in a jar; cover tightly, and shake vigorously. Yield: ⅓ cup.
Jennifer B. Lewis
Columbia, South Carolina

ENDIVE, BACON, AND PECAN SALAD
(pictured on page 74)

3 cups loosely packed Boston
  lettuce
3 cups loosely packed curly
  endive
1 medium purple onion, sliced
¾ cup coarsely chopped pecans,
  toasted
6 slices bacon
1½ teaspoons brown sugar
¼ cup red wine vinegar
¼ teaspoon salt
¼ teaspoon pepper

Combine first 4 ingredients in a large bowl; set aside.

Cook bacon until crisp; remove bacon, reserving 2 tablespoons drippings in skillet. Crumble bacon, and set aside. Add brown sugar, vinegar, salt, and pepper to skillet; cook over low heat until thoroughly heated. Pour over lettuce; toss gently. Sprinkle with bacon; serve immediately. Yield: 6 servings.

Kay Castleman Cooper
Burke, Virginia

BLUE CHEESE COLESLAW
(pictured on page 74)

1 medium cabbage
4 green onions with tops, sliced
1 cup mayonnaise
¼ cup prepared horseradish
½ cup (4 ounces) crumbled blue cheese, divided
Green onion flower (optional)

Reserve outer leaves, and shred remaining cabbage. Combine shredded cabbage and green onions in a large bowl; stir well. Cover and chill.

Combine mayonnaise, horseradish, and ¼ cup blue cheese, stirring well. Just before serving, spoon mayonnaise mixture over cabbage, and toss gently to coat.

Serve in cabbage-lined bowl. Garnish with remaining blue cheese and, if desired, a green onion flower. Yield: about 7 cups.

Sharon McClatchey
Muskogee, Oklahoma

Gather The Ladies For Lunch

Now that the holiday calendar is cleared, there's no better time to invite the ladies for a leisurely lunch or perhaps a relaxing supper.

The menu needn't be elaborate or lengthy; the two presented here each contain four recipes, many of which can be prepared ahead of time.

Rolled Cheese Soufflé
Orange Salad
With Honey Dressing
Marinated Vegetable Medley
Commercial croissants
Amaretto Chantilly

ROLLED CHEESE SOUFFLÉ

¼ cup plus 2 tablespoons all-purpose flour
¾ teaspoon salt
⅛ teaspoon red pepper
⅓ cup butter or margarine
1¼ cups milk
½ cup (2 ounces) shredded Cheddar cheese
½ cup freshly grated Parmesan cheese
7 eggs, separated
¼ teaspoon cream of tartar
1 to 2 tablespoons grated Parmesan cheese
Crab Filling
3 (1-ounce) slices Cheddar cheese

Lightly oil bottom and sides of a 15- x 10- x 1-inch jellyroll pan. Line with wax paper, allowing paper to extend beyond ends of the pan; lightly oil wax paper.

Combine flour, salt, and red pepper; stir well.

Melt butter in a large heavy saucepan over low heat; add flour mixture, stirring with a wire whisk until smooth. Cook 1 minute, stirring constantly with whisk. Gradually add milk; cook over medium heat, stirring constantly, until very thick and mixture leaves sides of pan. Remove from heat; add ½ cup each of Cheddar cheese and Parmesan cheese, stirring until cheeses melt.

Beat egg yolks in a large mixing bowl at high speed of an electric mixer until thick and lemon colored. Gradually stir about one-fourth of hot cheese mixture into egg yolks; add remaining cheese mixture to egg yolk mixture, beating well.

Combine egg whites (at room temperature) and cream of tartar in a large mixing bowl; beat at high speed of electric mixer until stiff peaks form. Fold one-third of egg whites into cheese mixture; carefully fold in remaining egg whites.

Pour cheese mixture into prepared pan, spreading evenly. Bake on center rack of oven at 350° for 18 minutes or until puffy and firm to the touch (do not overcook).

Overlap 2 lengths of wax paper (longer than jellyroll pan) on a smooth, slightly damp surface. Sprinkle 1 to 2 tablespoons Parmesan cheese over wax paper.

Loosen edges of soufflé with a metal spatula. Quickly invert jellyroll pan onto wax paper, with long side nearest you; remove pan, and carefully peel top wax paper from soufflé. Spoon Crab Filling over surface, spreading to edge. Starting at long side, carefully roll soufflé, jellyroll fashion, using wax paper to help support it as you roll it up.

Carefully slide the roll, seam side down, onto a large lightly greased ovenproof platter or baking sheet. Arrange cheese slices on top. Place 3 inches from broiler, and broil until cheese melts and roll is browned. Cut into slices. Yield: 8 servings.

Crab Filling

1½ cups fresh crabmeat, drained and flaked
¼ cup mayonnaise
¼ cup commercial sour cream
¼ teaspoon lemon juice

Combine all ingredients; stir well. Yield: 2 cups.

Note: Rolled Cheese Soufflé may be covered with plastic wrap and chilled 8 hours prior to broiling. Uncover and broil before serving.

Carol Barclay
Portland, Texas

ORANGE SALAD WITH HONEY DRESSING

⅓ cup sugar
2½ tablespoons lemon juice
2½ tablespoons honey
2 tablespoons vinegar
½ teaspoon dry mustard
½ teaspoon paprika
⅛ teaspoon salt
⅛ teaspoon celery seeds
½ cup vegetable oil
Boston lettuce
5 oranges, peeled and sliced

Combine first 8 ingredients in container of an electric blender; process until smooth. While blender is running, slowly pour oil into blender through opening in top; continue to process a few seconds until blended. Cover and chill.

Line individual salad plates with lettuce; arrange orange slices on lettuce, and drizzle dressing over top. Yield: 8 servings. *Nancy Matthews*
Norcross, Georgia

MARINATED VEGETABLE MEDLEY

⅔ cup vinegar
⅔ cup vegetable oil
⅓ cup chopped onion
1 teaspoon sugar
1 teaspoon salt
1 teaspoon dried whole basil
1 teaspoon dried whole oregano
⅛ teaspoon garlic powder
1 (14-ounce) can artichoke
  hearts, drained and quartered
1 cup broccoli flowerets
1 cup cauliflower flowerets
1 cup sliced carrot
1 cup sliced fresh mushrooms

Combine first 8 ingredients in a small saucepan. Bring mixture to a boil; cover, reduce heat, and simmer 12 minutes.

Combine vegetables and vinegar mixture. Cover and chill at least 3 hours. To serve, use a slotted spoon. Yield: 8 servings.
Mrs. Richard T. Hoehn
Memphis, Tennessee

AMARETTO CHANTILLY

3¾ cups miniature marshmallows
⅔ cup amaretto
1 tablespoon lemon juice
¼ teaspoon almond extract
½ cup chopped maraschino
  cherries
2 cups whipping cream
2 tablespoons finely chopped
  pistachios or almonds

Combine miniature marshmallows and amaretto in top of a double boiler; bring water to a boil. Cook until marshmallows melt, stirring occasionally. Stir in lemon juice, almond extract, and cherries. Cool slightly.

Beat whipping cream until soft peaks form; fold into marshmallow mixture. Spoon into individual serving dishes, and sprinkle with pistachios. Cover and freeze. Yield: 8 servings.
Aileen Wright
Nashville, Tennessee

Zucchini Soup
Walnut-Chicken Salad
Cheddar Muffins
Raspberry-Strawberry
Bavarian

ZUCCHINI SOUP

1 medium onion, chopped
1 cooking apple, peeled, cored,
  and chopped
2 tablespoons butter or
  margarine, melted
4 cups chicken broth
3 cups unpeeled, diced zucchini
  (about 3 medium)
1 cup milk
¼ cup whipping cream
¼ teaspoon pepper

Sauté onion and apple in butter in a Dutch oven until tender. Add broth and zucchini; bring to a boil. Cover, reduce heat, and simmer 30 minutes

or until zucchini is tender. Spoon mixture into container of an electric blender, and process until smooth.

Return zucchini mixture to Dutch oven; stir in milk, whipping cream, and pepper. Cook over low heat, stirring constantly, until well heated. Yield: about 8 cups.
Connie Jo Robinson
Bryan, Texas

WALNUT-CHICKEN SALAD
(pictured on page 4)

4 cups cubed cooked chicken
1⅓ cups chopped toasted walnuts
½ cup finely chopped celery
¼ cup chopped green onions
¼ cup raisins
½ cup mayonnaise
¼ cup lemon juice
¼ cup chutney, chopped
½ teaspoon salt
Lettuce leaves
8 carrot curls
16 slices tomato
16 slices pineapple
Additional mayonnaise (optional)
8 toasted walnut halves (optional)

Combine first 5 ingredients in a large bowl. Combine ½ cup mayonnaise, lemon juice, chutney, and salt; stir well. Pour over chicken mixture; toss gently. Cover and chill chicken mixture at least 2 hours.

Arrange lettuce leaves on 8 individual plates; place carrot curls and 2 slices each of tomato and pineapple on lettuce. Spoon about ¾ cup chicken mixture to the side of fruit. If desired, top each serving with a dollop of mayonnaise and a walnut half. Yield: 8 servings.
Cathy Williams
Vale, North Carolina

CHEDDAR MUFFINS
(pictured on page 4)

2 cups all-purpose flour
3½ teaspoons baking powder
½ teaspoon salt
1 teaspoon paprika
1 cup (4 ounces) shredded
   Cheddar cheese
1 egg, beaten
1 cup milk
¼ cup butter or margarine,
   melted

Combine first 5 ingredients in a large bowl; make a well in center of mixture. Combine egg, milk, and butter; add to dry ingredients, stirring just until moistened. Spoon into greased muffin pans, filling two-thirds full. Bake at 425° for 20 minutes. Remove from pans immediately. Yield: 1 dozen. *Maggie Cates*
Orlando, Florida

RASPBERRY-STRAWBERRY BAVARIAN

2 (3-ounce) packages
   strawberry-flavored gelatin
1½ cups boiling water
1 (8-ounce) carton commercial
   sour cream
1 pint strawberry ice cream,
   softened and cut into 1-inch
   pieces
2 (10-ounce) packages frozen
   raspberries in syrup, thawed
   and undrained
1 (10-ounce) package frozen
   strawberries in syrup, thawed
   and undrained
1 tablespoon lemon juice
1 cup whipping cream
¼ cup sifted powdered sugar
Chocolate curls

Dissolve gelatin in boiling water; stir in sour cream with a wire whisk. Add ice cream, and stir until melted. Add raspberries, strawberries, and lemon juice, stirring until blended. Pour mixture into twelve 6-ounce parfait glasses. Cover and chill.

Just before serving, combine whipping cream and powdered sugar in a small mixing bowl; beat at medium speed of an electric mixer until stiff peaks form. Top each parfait with whipped cream and chocolate curls. Yield: 12 servings. *Louise Fuller*
Eros, Louisiana

Stir Cheese Into The Soup

It takes a thick, rich soup to tame robust winter appetites, and any one of these versions will do the job with flair. When making these soups, be sure to cook with low heat after adding the cheese, as high heat can make it tough and stringy. To help the cheese melt evenly and the soup thicken smoothly, be sure to cube or shred the cheese as directed.

HAM-AND-CHEESE CHOWDER

2½ cups water
2 cups frozen hash brown
   potatoes
1½ cups thinly sliced carrot
½ cup chopped green pepper
¼ cup chopped sweet red pepper
2 cups chopped cooked ham
1 (17-ounce) can cream-style corn
1 (11-ounce) can Cheddar cheese
   soup, undiluted
½ cup water
Dash of white pepper

Combine first 5 ingredients in a Dutch oven; bring to a boil. Cover, reduce heat, and simmer 15 minutes or until vegetables are tender. Add ham and remaining ingredients; cook until thoroughly heated, stirring often. Yield: about 2 quarts.
Louise Holmes
Winchester, Tennessee

VEGETABLE-CHEESE SOUP

2 stalks celery, chopped
2 carrots, scraped and diced
1 medium onion, chopped
1 cup chopped cauliflower
½ cup chopped broccoli
1 clove garlic, minced
½ cup butter or margarine,
   melted
½ cup all-purpose flour
3 cups chicken broth
1 tablespoon Worcestershire
   sauce
½ teaspoon pepper
2½ cups milk
2 cups (8 ounces) shredded sharp
   Cheddar cheese
¼ cup sliced almonds, toasted

Sauté first 6 ingredients in butter in a Dutch oven until crisp-tender; add flour, stirring until smooth. Cook 1 minute, stirring constantly. Gradually add chicken broth; cook over medium heat, stirring constantly, until mixture is thickened and bubbly. Cover, reduce heat, and simmer 20 minutes or until vegetables are tender. Add Worcestershire sauce, pepper, milk, and cheese. Cook over low heat 10 minutes, stirring occasionally. Garnish individual servings with sliced almonds, and serve immediately. Yield: 2 quarts. *Patricia Pashby*
Memphis, Tennessee

Cheese Tips

■ Brush oil on a grater before shredding cheese for an easy cleanup.

■ Shred Cheddar or Swiss cheese and freeze; whenever you need some for cooking, just measure and use.

■ When you use cheese in a recipe, do not overcook it as it will become stringy.

CHEESY POTATO-AND-WILD RICE SOUP

½ cup uncooked wild rice
5 slices bacon
¼ cup chopped onion
2 (10¾-ounce) cans cream of
  potato soup, undiluted
4 cups milk
8 ounces American cheese, cubed

Wash wild rice in 3 changes of hot water; drain. Cook rice according to package directions, omitting salt; set rice aside.

Cook bacon in a Dutch oven until crisp; remove bacon, reserving 1 tablespoon drippings in Dutch oven. Crumble bacon, and set aside.

Sauté onion in bacon drippings until tender. Add soup, milk, cheese, and rice; cook over medium heat until cheese melts, stirring constantly. Garnish individual servings with bacon, and serve soup immediately. Yield: 9 cups.   *Natalie Lund*
Glasgow, Kentucky

HOT CHEESE CHOWDER

½ cup chopped celery
½ cup chopped onion
½ cup chopped green pepper
¼ cup butter or margarine,
  melted
3 cups chicken broth
1 medium potato, cubed
½ cup chopped carrot
½ cup all-purpose flour
2 cups milk, divided
12 ounces sharp American
  cheese, cubed
1 tablespoon chopped fresh
  parsley

Sauté celery, onion, and green pepper in butter in a Dutch oven until tender. Add chicken broth, potato, and carrot; bring to a boil. Cover, reduce heat, and simmer 20 minutes or until vegetables are tender.

Combine flour and ¾ cup milk, stirring until flour dissolves. Stir flour

mixture, remaining milk, cheese, and parsley into vegetable mixture. Cook over low heat, stirring constantly, until thickened and bubbly. Serve immediately. Yield: 2 quarts.
Jodie McCoy
Tulsa, Oklahoma

Good-For-You Legumes

It's believed that eating black-eyed peas on New Year's Day brings good luck, so try a Southern favorite, Black-Eyed Peas With Ham Hocks. And that's only one of the serving options with peas and beans that we offer here.

Dried peas and beans, which are both rich in nutrients, require soaking to rehydrate. If soaking 8 hours isn't possible, there's a quicker method. Combine 1 pound dried peas or beans and 6 to 8 cups water in a Dutch oven. Bring to a boil; cover and cook 2 minutes. Remove from heat, and let stand 1 hour. Drain and proceed as directed in each recipe.

BLACK-EYED PEAS WITH HAM HOCKS

3 cups dried black-eyed peas
6 cups water
3 pounds smoked ham hocks
1¼ cups chopped onion
1 cup chopped green pepper
2 bay leaves
1 teaspoon salt
1 (16-ounce) can stewed
  tomatoes, chopped

Sort and wash peas; place in a large Dutch oven. Cover with water 2

inches above peas; let soak 8 hours. Drain peas, and return to Dutch oven. Add 6 cups water and next 5 ingredients. Bring to a boil; cover, reduce heat, and simmer 45 minutes, stirring occasionally. Add tomatoes; cover and simmer an additional 15 minutes or until peas are tender.

Remove ham hocks and bay leaves. Cut ham from ham hocks, and chop; return to peas. Yield: 12 to 16 servings.   *Mildred Bickley*
Bristol, Virginia

SOUTHWESTERN BEANS

1 (16-ounce) package dried pinto
  beans
6 cups water
1 meaty ham bone
2 medium onions, chopped
1 green pepper, chopped
3 cloves garlic, minced
1 (10-ounce) can tomatoes with
  chiles, chopped and undrained
2 teaspoons brown sugar
1 teaspoon salt
1 teaspoon chili powder
1 teaspoon dried whole basil
1 teaspoon dried whole oregano
1 teaspoon Worcestershire sauce
½ teaspoon pepper
½ teaspoon ground cumin
½ teaspoon dried whole thyme
½ teaspoon dry mustard
Dash of ground red pepper
2 bay leaves

Sort and wash beans; place in a Dutch oven. Cover with water 2 inches above beans, and bring to a boil; cover and cook 2 minutes. Remove from heat, and let stand 1 hour. Drain beans, and return to Dutch oven.

Add 6 cups water, ham bone, and remaining ingredients. Bring to a boil; cover, reduce heat, and simmer 2 hours or until beans are tender. Remove ham hock and bay leaves. Cut ham from hock; chop. Return ham to beans. Yield: 8 servings.
Linda E. Whitt
Missouri City, Texas

SPICY-HOT BEANS

1 (16-ounce) package dried pinto
  beans
6 cups water
1 pound bacon, cut into ½-inch
  pieces
1 pound smoked link sausage, cut
  into ½-inch slices
2 medium onions, chopped
½ cup chopped green pepper
4 cloves garlic, minced
¼ cup Worcestershire sauce
¼ to ⅓ cup firmly packed brown
  sugar
2 tablespoons ground cumin
1 tablespoon chili powder
1 tablespoon pepper
1 tablespoon celery seeds
1 to 2 teaspoons hot sauce
1 teaspoon salt
1 bay leaf
1 (16-ounce) can tomatoes,
  undrained and chopped

Sort and wash beans; place in a large
Dutch oven. Cover with water 2
inches above beans; let soak 8 hours.
Drain beans, and return to Dutch
oven. Add 6 cups water.

Combine bacon and next 4 ingredients in a skillet; cook over medium
heat until bacon is browned and vegetables are tender. Drain. Add to
beans. Add Worcestershire sauce
and remaining ingredients except tomatoes, and bring mixture to a boil.
Cover, reduce heat, and simmer 2
hours or until beans are tender, stirring occasionally. Add tomatoes;
cook an additional 30 minutes. Remove bay leaf. Yield: 10 servings.
Laurie McIntyre
Lake Jackson, Texas

Tip: *Onions offer outstanding nutritive value. They are a good source of
calcium and vitamins A and C.
They contain iron, riboflavin, thia-
mine, and niacin; have a high per-
centage of water; and supply
essential bulk. They are low in calories and have only a trace of fat.*

THREE-BEAN SOUP

2 cups dried navy beans
1 cup dried red beans
1½ cups dried garbanzo beans
3 (10¾-ounce) cans chicken
  broth, undiluted
3⅔ cups water
2 onions, chopped
1 cup sliced carrot
1 cup sliced celery
1 large clove garlic, minced
2 tablespoons parsley flakes
1 teaspoon salt
2 teaspoons dried whole basil
1 teaspoon dried whole oregano
½ teaspoon pepper
3 cups chopped fresh spinach
  (about 4 ounces)
Grated Parmesan cheese
  (optional)

Sort and wash beans; place in a large
Dutch oven. Cover with water 2
inches above beans; let soak 8 hours.
Drain beans, and return to Dutch
oven. Add chicken broth and next 10
ingredients. Cover and bring to a
boil; reduce heat, and simmer 2
hours or until beans are tender, stirring occasionally. Add spinach, and
cook 10 to 15 minutes, stirring occasionally. Sprinkle each serving with
Parmesan cheese, if desired. Yield: 3
quarts.
Rebecca Pinckney
Atlanta, Georgia

SPLIT PEA SOUP

1 (16-ounce) package dried green
  split peas
2¾ quarts water
4 small hot peppers
3 medium onions, chopped
2 medium carrots, diced
2 bay leaves
1 large ham hock
¼ cup chopped celery leaves
2 tablespoons chopped parsley

Sort and wash dried green split peas;
place in a Dutch oven. Add 2¾
quarts water; cover and bring to a

boil. Cook 2 minutes. Remove from
heat, and let stand 1 hour.

Add hot peppers and remaining ingredients to peas. Bring to a boil;
cover, reduce heat, and simmer 1
hour. Remove ham hock, peppers,
and bay leaves. Cut ham from ham
hock, and chop; add to peas. If desired, spoon mixture into container of
an electric blender, and process until
smooth. Yield: about 2½ quarts.
Marian Parsons
Hurricane, West Virginia

PASSION PEAS

1 cup chopped green pepper
1¼ cups chopped celery
1⅓ cups chopped onion
6 jalapeño peppers, chopped
1 teaspoon salt
1 teaspoon freshly ground black
  pepper
¼ teaspoon ground nutmeg
¼ teaspoon ground cinnamon
2 tablespoons hot sauce
3 chicken-flavored bouillon cubes
½ cup catsup
2 (16-ounce) cans black-eyed
  peas, undrained
1 cup chopped tomatoes,
  undrained
1 teaspoon garlic powder
3 tablespoons all-purpose flour
½ cup water
Corn chips

Combine first 11 ingredients in a
large saucepan. Bring to a boil over
medium heat; add black-eyed peas,
tomatoes, and garlic powder. Reduce
heat, and simmer 30 minutes, stirring occasionally.

Combine flour and water, stirring
until flour dissolves; add to pea mixture, and cook, stirring constantly,
10 minutes. Serve hot with corn
chips. Yield: 4 cups.

Note: For nachos, spoon hot dip
onto corn chips, and sprinkle with
shredded Cheddar cheese.
Willard Chancellor
Athens, Texas

MEXICAN CHILI

2 pounds ground beef
¾ cup chopped green pepper
1 cup chopped onion
1 clove garlic, minced
1 (16-ounce) can kidney beans,
    drained
2 (8-ounce) cans tomato sauce
1 (16-ounce) can tomatoes,
    undrained and chopped
1 fresh or canned green chile,
    seeded and chopped
1 tablespoon plus 1 teaspoon chili
    powder
2 teaspoons ground cumin
½ teaspoon dried whole basil
½ teaspoon salt
¼ teaspoon pepper
¼ teaspoon hot sauce
Shredded Cheddar cheese
    (optional)
Corn chips (optional)

Combine beef, green pepper, onion, and garlic in a Dutch oven; cook over medium heat until meat is browned, stirring to crumble meat. Drain off drippings. Add kidney beans and next 9 ingredients; cover, reduce heat, and simmer 20 minutes, stirring occasionally. If desired, serve with shredded Cheddar cheese and corn chips. Yield: 7 cups.

Vicki L. Brown
Mount Sterling, Kentucky

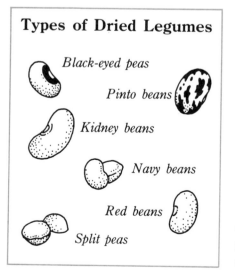

Types of Dried Legumes

Black-eyed peas

Pinto beans

Kidney beans

Navy beans

Red beans

Split peas

QUICK!

Bake Some Chicken

With the start of a new year, we found it fitting to offer a new, exciting column, "QUICK!" This will be a monthly feature offering a variety of quick recipes with few ingredients, all designed for busy folks who still yearn for good food.

You can build a menu around any of these chicken specialties. Side dishes or accompaniments may be as simple as a green salad or steamed vegetables.

LEMON CHICKEN BREASTS

3 tablespoons olive oil
4 chicken breast halves, skinned
1 teaspoon dried parsley flakes
½ teaspoon dried whole thyme
¼ teaspoon salt
1 cup Chablis or other dry white
    wine
3 tablespoons lemon juice
¼ teaspoon pepper
¼ teaspoon paprika
Fresh parsley sprig (optional)
Lemon slices (optional)

Heat oil in a heavy skillet until hot; add chicken, and cook 5 minutes on each side. Place chicken in an 8-inch square baking dish; discard drippings.

Add parsley flakes and next 3 ingredients to skillet; bring to a boil. Pour over chicken. Sprinkle with lemon juice, pepper, and paprika. Cover and bake at 400° for 25 minutes or until tender. If desired, garnish with parsley sprig and lemon slices. Yield: 4 servings.

Jean Pashby
Memphis, Tennessee

Tip: Browning the chicken in a skillet before baking shortens the overall cooking time.

BAKED CHICKEN NUGGETS

½ cup fine, dry breadcrumbs
¼ cup grated Parmesan cheese
¼ teaspoon salt
½ teaspoon dried whole basil
½ teaspoon dried whole thyme
4 chicken breast halves, skinned
    and boned
¼ cup butter or margarine,
    melted

Combine first 5 ingredients in a plastic bag; shake well.

Cut chicken into 1-inch pieces; dip chicken pieces in butter, and shake a few at a time in breadcrumb mixture. Place on a lightly greased baking sheet. Bake at 400° for 20 minutes or until tender. Yield: 4 servings.

Thelma Peedin
Newport News, Virginia

Tip: It will take about 3 minutes to cut chicken into nuggets with kitchen shears or a sharp knife. Use a plastic bag for dredging chicken to make cleanup a snap.

CHICKEN SALAD ITALIAN

3 cups diced cooked chicken
1 cup chopped celery
1 (11-ounce) can mandarin
    oranges, drained
1 (15¼-ounce) can pineapple
    chunks, drained
¼ cup slivered almonds, toasted
½ cup commercial Italian
    dressing
Lettuce leaves

Combine first 6 ingredients; toss. Cover and chill. Serve on lettuce. Yield: 6 servings. *Lorraine Bennett*
Virginia Beach, Virginia

Tip: Use canned chicken, or microwave 4 chicken breast halves in ¼ cup water. Cover and microwave at HIGH 9 to 10 minutes, turning once; drain. Bone and chop chicken.

Calorie-Crunching Snacks

Most commercial snacks are high in fat, and high-fat foods seem to be more fattening than once thought. Recent studies have found that during digestion the body is able to convert dietary fat into body fat much easier than it does carbohydrate. In fact, almost one-fourth of carbohydrate calories are burned while being converted to body fat, leaving only 77 out of 100 calories to be stored as fat. But it takes just 3 calories to turn 100 calories of dietary fat into body fat, and that leaves 97 calories that will be stored.

Snacking itself isn't bad or fattening; it's the types of food eaten for snacks that are the problem. The snack recipes below will convince you that light-and-healthy snacks are something to cheer about.

SNACK MIX

2 cups toasted oat cereal
2 cups bite-size crispy wheat squares
2 cups bite-size crispy rice squares
2 cups stick pretzels
1½ cups bite-size shredded whole wheat cereal biscuits
Butter-flavored vegetable cooking spray
1½ teaspoons onion powder
1 teaspoon garlic powder
1 teaspoon ground celery seeds
1½ tablespoons reduced-sodium Worcestershire sauce
1 teaspoon hot sauce

Combine first 5 ingredients in a large roasting pan; spray thoroughly with cooking spray. Combine onion powder and next 4 ingredients; crumble over cereal mixture, tossing to coat. Bake at 250° for 2 hours, stirring and spraying with cooking spray every 15 minutes. Cool and store in airtight containers. Yield: 18 servings (68 calories per ½-cup serving).

□ *1.7 grams protein, 0.6 gram fat, 14 grams carbohydrate, 0 milligrams cholesterol, 88 milligrams sodium, and 11 milligrams calcium.*

PITA PIZZAS

1 cup thinly sliced zucchini
¾ cup sliced fresh mushrooms
½ cup sliced green onions
½ cup diced green pepper
1 cup commercial pizza sauce
8 (6-inch) whole wheat pita bread rounds
Vegetable cooking spray
3 tablespoons grated Parmesan cheese

Combine first 5 ingredients in a medium bowl; toss gently. Place pita rounds on baking sheets coated with cooking spray. Spread ¼ cup zucchini mixture on each pita round; sprinkle evenly with Parmesan cheese. Bake at 400° for 10 minutes. Cut each round into 8 wedges. Serve hot. Yield: 64 wedges (13 calories per wedge).

□ *0.4 gram protein, 0.3 gram fat, 2.2 grams carbohydrate, 0 milligrams cholesterol, 5 milligrams sodium, and 7 milligrams calcium.*

PITA CHIPS

4 (6-inch) whole wheat pita bread rounds
⅓ cup no-oil Italian dressing
½ cup grated Parmesan cheese
1½ tablespoons sesame seeds

Separate each pita bread into two rounds; cut each into 8 wedges to make 64 triangles. Brush inside of each triangle with dressing. Place on ungreased baking sheets, dressing side up. Combine Parmesan cheese and sesame seeds; sprinkle evenly over triangles. Bake at 425° for 10 minutes or until lightly browned. Cool on wire racks. Store in an airtight container. Yield: 64 chips (12 calories per chip).

□ *0.5 gram protein, 0.4 gram fat, 1.7 grams carbohydrate, 0 milligrams cholesterol, 25 milligrams sodium, and 13 milligrams calcium.*

PESTO TORTILLA SNACKS

1½ cups packed fresh basil, trimmed
⅔ cup grated Parmesan cheese
¼ cup pine nuts or walnut pieces, toasted
¼ teaspoon salt
¼ teaspoon pepper
¼ cup olive oil
4 (10-inch) flour tortillas
Vegetable cooking spray
2 cups (8 ounces) shredded part-skim mozzarella cheese

Position knife blade in food processor bowl; add first 5 ingredients. Top with cover, and process until smooth. With processor running, pour oil through food chute in a slow, steady stream until combined.

Place tortillas on a baking sheet coated with cooking spray. Spread pesto mixture evenly on tortillas; sprinkle with cheese. Bake at 425° for 8 minutes. Cut each tortilla into 8 wedges. Yield: 32 servings (76 calories per wedge).

□ *3.3 grams protein, 4.9 grams fat, 5.8 grams carbohydrate, 5 milligrams cholesterol, 84 milligrams sodium, and 102 milligrams calcium.*

WHOLE WHEAT PRETZELS

1 package dry yeast
1 tablespoon sugar
¾ teaspoon salt
1½ cups warm water (105° to 115°)
2¼ cups all-purpose flour
1½ cups whole wheat flour
1 cup (4 ounces) shredded sharp Cheddar cheese
Vegetable cooking spray
1 egg white
2 tablespoons water

Dissolve yeast, sugar, and salt in 1½ cups warm water; let yeast mixture stand 5 minutes.

Combine flours and cheese in a large mixing bowl. Add yeast mixture; beat at low speed of an electric mixer until mixture is well blended. Turn dough out onto a lightly floured surface, and knead until smooth (about 5 minutes).

Using kitchen shears dipped in flour, cut dough into 32 pieces; shape each into a ball. Roll each ball on a lightly floured surface to form a rope 14 inches long. Twist each into a pretzel shape; place on baking sheets coated with cooking spray.

Combine egg white and water; mix well. Brush each pretzel with egg white mixture. Bake at 425° for 12 to 15 minutes or until lightly browned. Yield: 32 pretzels (71 calories each).

☐ *2.8 grams protein, 1.4 grams fat, 11.8 grams carbohydrate, 4 milligrams cholesterol, 79 milligrams sodium, and 30 milligrams calcium.*

CHEESE-HERB DIP

1 cup reduced-calorie mayonnaise
⅓ cup light process cream cheese product, softened
1 tablespoon minced parsley
1 tablespoon grated onion
2 teaspoons capers, drained
1 teaspoon fines herbes
½ teaspoon reduced-sodium Worcestershire sauce
¼ teaspoon salt

Combine all ingredients, and mix well. Chill. Serve as a dip with carrot sticks, celery sticks, zucchini, or radishes. Yield: 1⅓ cups (39 calories per tablespoon).

☐ *0.4 gram protein, 3.7 grams fat, 1.2 grams carbohydrate, 4 milligrams cholesterol, 134 milligrams sodium, and 8 milligrams calcium.*

Joyce Andrews
Washington, Virginia

Snacks For Children

Sometimes it's hard to find snack recipes that please both parents and children. These recipes are easy to prepare and combine flavors no one can resist.

APPLESAUCE SNACK CAKES

1 cup butter or margarine, softened
2 cups sugar
2 eggs
2 teaspoons baking soda
1 teaspoon vanilla extract
1 (16-ounce) can applesauce
4 cups all-purpose flour
1½ teaspoons ground cinnamon
1 teaspoon ground allspice
½ teaspoon ground cloves

Cream butter; gradually add sugar, beating well at medium speed of an electric mixer. Add eggs, one at a time, beating well after each addition.

Stir soda and vanilla into applesauce. Combine flour and spices; add to creamed mixture alternately with applesauce mixture, mixing after each addition. Cover batter, and store in refrigerator up to 2 weeks.

When ready to bake, spoon batter into paper-lined muffin pans, filling two-thirds full. Bake at 400° for 17 to 19 minutes or until a wooden pick inserted in center comes out clean. Remove from pans, and let cool on wire racks. Yield: 2½ dozen.

Evelyn Howell
Orange, Texas

BANANA-BERRY FLIP

1 cup strawberry-flavored carbonated beverage
1 cup vanilla ice cream
1 medium-size ripe banana, quartered
1 teaspoon vanilla extract

Combine all ingredients in container of an electric blender; process mixture until smooth. Serve immediately. Yield: about 3½ cups.

Cathy Williams
Vale, North Carolina

No-Recipe Snacks

■ Spread peanut butter on slices of apple, pear, or banana.

■ Freeze juice in popsicle molds.

■ Toast English muffin halves, and melt cheese on top.

■ Spread cream cheese or shredded cheese on a flour or corn tortilla, and heat. Roll up like a jellyroll.

■ Combine cereal, nuts, and raisins, and keep the mixture in zip-top plastic bags.

■ Spread applesauce over graham crackers.

Breakfast Sandwiches

Serve these breakfast treats, and watch them become family favorites. Young children in particular enjoy Sausage in a Bun, our version of a breakfast hot dog. The halved hot dog buns and small link sausages are easy for children to handle. Keep in mind that cooking times vary slightly for different brands of sausage, so it's best to check sausage for doneness by cutting one in half and examining the color.

BREAKFAST PITA POCKETS

½ **pound bulk pork sausage**
4 **eggs**
¼ **cup milk**
½ **teaspoon dried whole oregano**
⅛ **to ¼ teaspoon salt**
¼ **teaspoon pepper**
4 **slices Provolone cheese (about
   1 ounce each)**
4 **(6-inch) pita bread rounds**

Crumble sausage into a shallow 1-quart casserole. Cover tightly with heavy-duty plastic wrap; fold back a small edge of wrap to allow steam to escape. Microwave at HIGH 3 to 4 minutes or until sausage is browned, stirring once. Drain well on paper towels. Set aside.

Combine eggs, milk, oregano, salt, and pepper in a shallow 1-quart casserole, mixing well. Microwave at HIGH 2 to 4 minutes, pushing cooked portion to center at 1-minute intervals.

Cut cheese and pita bread rounds in half. Line each bread half with one piece of cheese. Combine sausage and egg mixture; spoon about ¼ cup sausage-egg mixture into pita pockets. Wrap each pita pocket in a paper towel. Place 4 pita pockets on a paper plate or glass pizza plate, and microwave at MEDIUM (50% power) 1 to 2 minutes or until warm. Repeat process with remaining sandwiches. Yield: 4 servings.

Note: Sandwiches may be prepared in advance. Wrap each in a paper towel, and place in a zip-top plastic bag. Refrigerate. **To reheat,** remove from plastic bag, and place wrapped pita pockets on a plate. Microwave according to chart, giving plate a half-turn after cooking time is half over.

Amount (halves)	Microwave at MEDIUM (50% power)
1	1 minute and 30 seconds
2	3 minutes
3	4 minutes
4	5 minutes

FRUIT-AND-CHEESE BREAKFAST SANDWICHES

2 **tablespoons chopped pecans**
1 **apple, cored and cut into 12
   wedges**
2 **tablespoons orange juice**
½ **(8-ounce) package cream
   cheese**
⅛ **teaspoon ground cinnamon**
Pinch of ground allspice
2 **tablespoons raisins**
1 **tablespoon orange marmalade**
8 **slices raisin bread, toasted**

Spread pecans in a pieplate; microwave at HIGH 2 minutes or until lightly toasted. Set aside.

Toss apple wedges in orange juice. Set aside.

Place cream cheese in a 2-cup glass measure, and microwave at HIGH 30 to 45 seconds or until softened. Add toasted pecans, cinnamon, allspice, raisins, and orange marmalade, mixing until blended. Spread about 1 tablespoon mixture on each slice of toast.

Arrange 3 apple wedges on each of 4 slices of toast. Top with remaining slices of toast. Wrap sandwiches individually in paper towels. Place sandwiches on a paper plate, and microwave at HIGH 45 seconds or until warm. Serve sandwiches immediately. Yield: 4 servings.

Note: Sandwiches may be prepared in advance. Wrap each in a paper towel, and place in a zip-top plastic bag. Refrigerate. **To reheat,** remove from plastic bag, and place wrapped sandwiches on a plate. Microwave according to chart, giving plate a half-turn after cooking time is half over.

Amount	Microwave at HIGH Power
1	20 seconds
2	40 seconds
3	1 minute
4	1 minute and 15 seconds

SAUSAGE IN A BUN

8 link sausages
4 hot dog buns
8 (⅔-ounce) slices process
 American cheese
Apple jelly (optional)

Arrange sausage in a spoke fashion in a pieplate. Cover with paper towels, and microwave at HIGH 3 minutes, giving the dish a half-turn after 1½ minutes. Drain on paper towels.

Cut hot dog buns in half crosswise. Fold cheese slices in half; place one folded slice and one sausage in each bun half. Individually wrap two sandwich halves in paper towels, and place on a 12-inch glass pizza plate. Microwave at HIGH 1 to 1½ minutes or until heated. Serve with apple jelly, if desired. Yield: 4 servings.

Note: Sandwiches may be prepared in advance. Wrap each in a paper towel, and place in a zip-top plastic bag. Refrigerate. **To reheat,** remove from plastic bag, and place wrapped sandwiches on a plate. Microwave according to chart, giving plate a half-turn after cooking time is half over.

Amount (halves)	Microwave at HIGH Power
2	30 seconds
4	1 minute and 15 seconds
6	1 minute and 30 seconds
8	2 minutes

Breakfast On The Run

If your schedule requires a quick breakfast, these recipes offer practical, home-baked alternatives to restaurant fast foods. Many of these items can be started the night before or mixed up quickly in the morning. For instance, roll up Sausage-Cheese Turnovers the night before, using commercial biscuits. Bake them in the morning and you've got a quick breakfast.

SAUSAGE-CHEESE TURNOVERS

10 (1-ounce) link sausages
2 ounces sharp Cheddar cheese
1 (11-ounce) can refrigerated
 biscuits
2 tablespoons cornmeal

Cook sausage in a skillet until browned; drain well. Set aside.

Cut cheese into 2- x ½- x ¼-inch strips; set aside.

Roll each biscuit to a 4-inch circle on wax paper sprinkled with cornmeal. Place a cheese strip and sausage in center of each biscuit. Fold over, and pinch edges to seal. Press edges with a fork dipped in flour. Place on a lightly greased baking sheet; bake at 400° for 10 minutes. Yield: 10 servings. *Nita Brown Oklahoma City, Oklahoma*

BREAKFAST SCONES

⅓ cup currants
¾ cup buttermilk
2 cups all-purpose flour
2 teaspoons baking powder
¼ teaspoon baking soda
2 tablespoons sugar
1 tablespoon grated orange rind
Pinch of salt
¼ cup plus 1 tablespoon butter
 or margarine
Milk
Sugar

Soak currants in buttermilk.

Combine flour and next 5 ingredients, mixing well. Cut in butter with a pastry blender until mixture resembles coarse meal. Gradually add currants and buttermilk, stirring just until dry ingredients are moistened. Turn dough out onto a lightly floured surface, and knead lightly 4 or 5 times.

Roll dough to ½-inch thickness; cut with a 3-inch biscuit cutter. Place on a lightly greased baking sheet. Brush scones with milk, and sprinkle with sugar. Bake at 400° for 16 minutes or until lightly browned. Yield: 10 scones. *Ella C. Stivers Houston, Texas*

MINCEMEAT-SPICE BARS

1 cup shortening
½ cup firmly packed brown sugar
½ cup sugar
2 eggs
2¼ cups all-purpose flour
1 teaspoon baking soda
1 teaspoon salt
¼ teaspoon ground cinnamon
¼ teaspoon ground nutmeg
⅛ teaspoon ground mace
2 cups commercial mincemeat
 with rum and brandy
1 cup chopped pecans
1 cup quick-cooking oats,
 uncooked
1 teaspoon vanilla extract

Cream shortening; gradually add sugars, beating well at medium speed of an electric mixer. Add eggs, one at a time, beating after each addition. Combine flour, soda, salt, and spices; gradually add to creamed mixture. Stir in mincemeat and remaining ingredients. Spoon batter into a greased and floured 15- x 10- x 1-inch jellyroll pan. Bake at 350° for 25 to 30 minutes or until lightly browned. Cool and cut into bars. Yield: 4 dozen. *Mary Ellen Springer Springfield, Virginia*

FRUITED HONEY-YOGURT SMOOTHIE

1 (8-ounce) carton plain or
 flavored yogurt
1 (6-ounce) can frozen orange
 juice concentrate, thawed and
 undiluted
1 cup water
⅓ cup honey
1½ teaspoons vanilla extract
Ice cubes

Combine first 5 ingredients in container of an electric blender; add enough ice cubes to bring mixture to 5-cup level. Process until frothy. Yield: 5 cups.
Frieda Harris
Leesville, Louisiana

Favorite High-Fiber Muffins

Mary Mertins of Milton, Florida, combined two of her favorite muffin recipes and came up with Blueberry-Bran Muffins. She makes a batch and freezes the extras to have on hand for a quick breakfast.

BLUEBERRY-BRAN MUFFINS

1¼ cups morsels of wheat bran
 cereal
1 cup milk
3 cups all-purpose flour
2 tablespoons baking powder
1 teaspoon salt
½ cup sugar
2 eggs, beaten
½ cup butter or margarine,
 melted
½ cup milk
2 cups fresh or frozen
 blueberries, thawed

Combine cereal and 1 cup milk; let stand 5 minutes.

Combine flour and next 3 ingredients in a large bowl; make a well in center of mixture.

Combine eggs, butter, and ½ cup milk; add to dry ingredients, stirring just until moistened. Gently stir in cereal mixture and blueberries. Spoon into greased muffin pans, filling two-thirds full. Bake at 400° for 20 to 25 minutes. Yield: 2 dozen.

A Catch Of Fresh Shrimp Ideas

Fresh shrimp can fit into the menu for any occasion, as you can see with the recipes here.

For a special family dinner, try the Polynesian Shrimp Curry. It's an easy entrée that stretches a pound of shrimp to serve four. Just add a crisp vegetable salad to round out a complete meal.

POLYNESIAN SHRIMP CURRY

2 cups milk
1 (3½-ounce) can flaked coconut
1 pound unpeeled medium-size
 fresh shrimp
1 (15¼-ounce) can pineapple
 chunks, drained
½ cup butter or margarine,
 melted and divided
1 teaspoon curry powder
⅓ cup chopped green onions
⅓ cup chopped celery
½ cup all-purpose flour
½ teaspoon garlic salt
1¼ cups chicken broth
Hot cooked rice

Combine milk and coconut in a small saucepan; bring to a boil. Reduce heat, and simmer 2 minutes. Strain mixture; set milk and coconut aside.

Peel and devein shrimp. Sauté shrimp and pineapple chunks in ¼ cup butter in a large skillet 3 to 5 minutes or until shrimp turn pink, stirring frequently. Drain shrimp mixture, and discard liquid. Set shrimp mixture aside.

Combine remaining ¼ cup butter and curry powder in a large skillet; cook over low heat, stirring constantly, 2 minutes. Add green onions and celery; cook, stirring constantly, until crisp-tender. Combine flour and garlic salt; add to onion mixture. Cook 1 minute, stirring constantly.

Gradually add reserved coconut milk and chicken broth; cook over medium heat, stirring constantly, until thickened and bubbly. Stir in shrimp mixture and reserved coconut. Serve over rice. Yield: 4 servings.
Doris Garton
Shenandoah, Virginia

COCONUT-BEER SHRIMP

½ pound unpeeled medium-size
 fresh shrimp
¾ cup pancake mix
¾ cup beer
¼ cup all-purpose flour
1 cup flaked coconut
Vegetable oil

Peel and devein shrimp, leaving tails intact; rinse well, and set aside.

Combine pancake mix and beer in a small bowl, mixing well; set aside. Dredge shrimp in flour; shake off excess. Dip shrimp into beer batter; dredge batter-coated shrimp in coconut. Pour oil into a heavy saucepan to a depth of 2 to 3 inches; heat to 350°. Fry shrimp, 5 or 6 at a time, in oil about 45 seconds on each side or until shrimp are golden brown. Drain on paper towels, and serve immediately. Yield: 4 appetizer servings.
Linda Keith
Dallas, Texas

PRAWNS FLAMBÉ

2 pounds unpeeled large fresh
  shrimp
1 tablespoon vegetable oil
2 tablespoons brandy
White Wine Sauce
Hollandaise Sauce

Peel and devein shrimp; sauté in oil.
Cook, stirring constantly, 3 to 5 minutes; drain off liquid. Add brandy,
turn heat to low, and ignite when
brandy is heated; stir well. Add
White Wine Sauce and Hollandaise
Sauce to shrimp, mixing well. Serve
immediately. Yield: 4 servings.

White Wine Sauce

2 cloves minced garlic
¼ cup chopped onion
¼ cup chopped green pepper
1 tablespoon vegetable oil
1 tablespoon diced pimiento
¼ teaspoon pepper
2 tablespoons white wine
Dash of Worcestershire sauce
Dash of hot sauce
2 tablespoons commercial sour
  cream
1 tablespoon chopped fresh
  parsley

Sauté garlic, onion, and green pepper
in oil until crisp-tender. Add pimiento
and next 4 ingredients, stirring well.
Cover and simmer 5 minutes. Stir in
sour cream and chopped fresh parsley. Yield: ⅓ cup.

Hollandaise Sauce

3 egg yolks
⅛ teaspoon salt
Dash of white pepper
2 tablespoons lemon juice
½ cup butter or margarine,
  divided

Beat egg yolks, salt, and pepper in
top of a double boiler; gradually add
lemon juice, stirring constantly. Add
about one-third of butter to egg mixture; cook over hot (not boiling)
water, stirring constantly, until butter melts.

Add another third of butter, stirring constantly; as sauce thickens,
stir in remaining butter. Cook until
thickened. Yield: ¾ cup.

Mrs. J. W. Riley, Jr.
Kingsport, Tennessee

An Easy Appetizer

Celeste Thompson of Lubbock,
Texas, knows how to turn simple,
everyday ingredients into a special
appetizer.

SESAME CHEESE BITES

1 (9-inch) refrigerated piecrust
1½ cups (6 ounces) shredded
  sharp Cheddar cheese
½ cup sesame seeds, toasted
½ teaspoon red pepper
1 to 2 teaspoons ice water

Position knife blade in food processor
bowl. Add first 4 ingredients; top
with cover, and process 30 seconds.
With processor running, slowly add
water (1 teaspoon at a time); process
just until dough begins to form a ball
and leaves sides of bowl. Cover and
chill 30 minutes.

Shape dough into 1-inch balls.
Place about 2 inches apart on ungreased baking sheets. Flatten each
ball with a fork dipped in flour. Bake
at 450° for 8 to 10 minutes or until
lightly browned. Cool on wire racks.
Yield: 3½ dozen.

Fresh Ginger For Pungent Flavor

All over the world, ginger has left its
mark on the cuisines and cultures of
those who have savored its tingly,
fresh-hot flavor.

Ginger may be used in several
forms. The most familiar is dried
ground ginger, found on grocery
shelves and used mostly in baked
goods. Gingerroot, the knobby, firm,
gray-beige form of the spice, is available in most large grocery stores.
Many varieties exist and can be easily interchanged in recipes for dips,
meat marinades, and beverages.

To use fresh ginger, peel the root
and slice, mince, dice, or grate. It's
best to cut the ginger into very thin
slices, and then cut across the fibers
if a recipe calls for slices. The dry
root will keep for a week in the vegetable crisper of the refrigerator. For
longer periods, store it in a paper
bag inside a plastic bag, and refrigerate. It can also be pickled in sherry
to be grated or minced as needed.

CHICKEN-FRIED WILD RICE

4 chicken breast halves, skinned
  and boned
¼ cup teriyaki sauce
¼ cup soy sauce
¼ cup Chablis or other dry white
  wine
2 cloves garlic, minced
½ teaspoon grated fresh
  gingerroot
¼ teaspoon Chinese five-spice
  powder
1 (4-ounce) package uncooked
  wild rice
¼ teaspoon salt
1 teaspoon vegetable oil
1 green pepper, sliced
⅔ cup sliced carrot
⅔ cup chopped onion
⅔ cup sliced fresh mushrooms
½ cup frozen English peas,
  thawed
¼ cup slivered almonds, toasted

Cut chicken into 1-inch pieces; place
in a small bowl. Add teriyaki sauce
and next 5 ingredients; stir well.
Cover and refrigerate at least 1 hour.

Cook wild rice according to package directions, using ¼ teaspoon
salt; keep warm.

Heat oil in a heavy skillet at medium high (325°) for 1 minute. Add green pepper, carrot, and onion; stir-fry 3 minutes. Add mushrooms and peas; stir-fry 2 minutes. Stir vegetable mixture into rice.

Add chicken and marinade to skillet, and stir-fry for 4 to 5 minutes or until chicken is tender. Add rice-and-vegetable mixture; stir-fry 1 to 2 minutes or until thoroughly heated. Sprinkle with almonds. Yield: 6 servings.

Marise Meier
Kennesaw, Georgia

MONGOLIAN BEEF STIR-FRY

1 (¾-pound) flank steak
2 tablespoons water
1 tablespoon reduced-sodium soy
  sauce
2 teaspoons sesame oil
1½ teaspoons cornstarch
¼ cup peanut oil
2 dried red peppers, chopped
3 cups coarsely chopped broccoli
1 bunch green onions, cut into
  1½-inch pieces
1 (7-ounce) jar baby corn ears,
  drained
1 (8-ounce) can sliced water
  chestnuts, undrained
2 (⅛-inch-thick) slices fresh
  gingerroot, diced
1 tablespoon reduced-sodium soy
  sauce
¼ cup water
1 tablespoon sweet rice cooking
  wine
1 tablespoon cornstarch
1 teaspoon sugar
½ teaspoon salt
½ teaspoon pepper
1 teaspoon sesame oil
Hot cooked rice

Partially freeze steak; slice diagonally across grain into 2- x 1-inch strips, and set aside. Combine 2 tablespoons water, 1 tablespoon soy sauce, sesame oil, and cornstarch in a shallow dish, mixing well; add beef. Cover and refrigerate at least 15 minutes.

Pour peanut oil around top of preheated wok, coating sides; heat at medium high (325°) for 1 minute. Add steak and marinade; stir-fry until steak browns. Remove steak. Add red peppers; stir-fry 30 seconds. Add chopped broccoli and next 4 ingredients; stir-fry 2 minutes.

Combine 1 tablespoon soy sauce and remaining ingredients except rice; mix well. Add soy sauce mixture and steak to wok; stir-fry 1 to 2 minutes or until mixture is thickened and bubbly. Serve over hot cooked rice. Yield: 4 servings.

Michelle Marsh
Birmingham, Alabama

GINGER-MARINATED FLANK STEAK

½ cup soy sauce
¼ cup sugar
2 tablespoons vinegar
1 clove garlic, minced
1 teaspoon ground ginger
1 (1-pound) flank steak

Combine all ingredients except steak in a shallow dish, stirring well. Place steak in dish; cover and refrigerate 8 hours, turning steak occasionally.

Drain steak, reserving marinade. Grill over medium-hot coals 8 to 10 minutes on each side or to desired degree of doneness, basting often with marinade. To serve, slice steak across grain into thin slices. Yield: about 4 servings.

Joan M. Nowell
Fort Worth, Texas

Indulge In Mississippi Mud

Any Southerner worth his or her grits knows what you mean when you talk about Mississippi Mud. The words are identified with layered chocolate desserts often found at Southern dinner tables and covered-dish dinners. Here, we offer two versions of Mississippi Mud.

MISSISSIPPI MUD BROWNIES

½ cup butter or margarine
1 cup sugar
2 eggs, slightly beaten
¾ cup all-purpose flour
⅛ teaspoon salt
¼ cup cocoa
1 teaspoon vanilla extract
½ cup chopped pecans
1½ cups miniature marshmallows
Chocolate frosting (recipe follows)

Place butter in a 2-quart mixing bowl; microwave at HIGH 1 minute or until butter melts. Stir in sugar and eggs; set aside.

Combine flour, salt, and cocoa; stir well. Stir dry mixture into egg mixture. Stir in vanilla and pecans.

Spread batter in a greased and floured 8-inch square baking dish. Shield corners with triangles of aluminum foil, keeping foil smooth and close to dish. Place baking dish on a microwave-safe cereal bowl inverted in the oven. Microwave at MEDIUM (50% power) 6 to 7 minutes, giving dish a half-turn after 3 minutes. Remove shields; microwave at HIGH 2 to 3 minutes or until top is almost dry. Remove from oven, and place directly on countertop to cool.

Sprinkle marshmallows over brownies; cover with aluminum foil. Let stand 2 minutes. Remove aluminum foil. Spread with chocolate frosting; cool completely on a wire rack. Cut brownies into squares to serve. Yield: 16 brownies.

Chocolate Frosting

¼ cup butter or margarine
3 tablespoons milk
3 tablespoons cocoa
½ teaspoon vanilla extract
2 cups sifted powdered sugar

Combine butter and milk in a large microwave-safe mixing bowl; microwave at HIGH 1½ to 2 minutes or until butter melts. Stir in cocoa and vanilla. Gradually add powdered sugar, beating at medium speed of an electric mixer until smooth. Yield: 1¼ cups.

MISSISSIPPI MUD PIE

3 (1-ounce) squares unsweetened
   chocolate
1½ cups sifted powdered sugar
½ cup whipping cream
⅓ cup butter or margarine
3 tablespoons light corn syrup
Dash of salt
1 tablespoon vanilla extract
1 (9-inch) graham cracker crust
1 cup chopped pecans, divided
3 cups coffee-flavored ice cream,
   softened and divided
Sweetened whipped cream

Melt chocolate in a heavy saucepan over low heat; add powdered sugar and next 4 ingredients. Cook, stirring constantly, until mixture is smooth. Remove from heat; stir in vanilla, and let cool.

Spread ½ cup chocolate sauce in graham cracker crust; sprinkle with ¼ cup pecans. Freeze 10 minutes. Remove from freezer, and spread 1 cup ice cream over pecans; freeze 20 minutes. Repeat layers twice.

Cover pie, and freeze at least 8 hours. Drizzle remaining chocolate sauce over pie. Pipe whipped cream onto pie, and sprinkle with remaining pecans. Yield: one 9-inch pie.

Edith Askins
Greenville, Texas

From Our Kitchen To Yours

News updates and bulletins are sent to our Foods staff from a number of agencies, including the USDA Food and Drug Administration, the American Egg Board, and the Cooperative Extension Services. After reading and studying the recent information concerning food poisoning and the use of raw egg yolks, the home economists in our Test Kitchens have taken a close look at how egg yolks are used in our recipes.

Food poisoning outbreaks have been linked to the bacteria *Salmonella enteritidis*. Studies by federal health experts report egg yolks to be the most frequent culprit, and the source of most of these cases was restaurant, deli, or catered food. Food poisoning may result when raw or undercooked egg yolks are eaten. The possibility of food poisoning from this bacteria is probably extremely low; however, our Foods staff encourages caution when eating egg yolks and foods containing yolks.

Recipes using raw egg yolks published in *Southern Living Annual Recipes* pass the test of either minimal cooking temperature or pH balance. Egg yolks and yolk-containing recipes are cooked to 165°. Sauces, salad dressings, and frostings using uncooked egg yolks are tested for a pH balance of 5 or less. When mixed in proper amounts, citrus juice, vinegar, and chocolate, all containing acid, can make the food safe without cooking. For example, the high acid content of lemon juice and baking the meringue of lemon icebox pie prevent bacterial growth, making the popular dessert safe if it is properly refrigerated.

Pasteurized Egg Substitute

If you question whether your favorite recipes are safe or if you are concerned with thoroughly cooking eggs, try substituting a pasteurized egg product. Pasteurization destroys salmonella bacteria, but these products must be handled carefully to avoid contamination.

An egg substitute can replace eggs in most recipes, and the added bonus is that the product is cholesterol free. Use ¼ cup of egg substitute for 1 egg or 1 egg yolk. This liquid egg product is purchased frozen and can be stored in the refrigerator up to seven days after thawing. Do not refreeze. Remove the amount of egg product needed at one time. Do not put any unused portion back into the original container; pour any leftover product into a clean container, tightly seal, and refrigerate.

Cooking With Eggs

■ Refrigerate eggs in their original carton at a temperature that is below 40°.

■ Use Grade AA or A eggs, and discard cracked ones.

■ Use raw eggs within five weeks, hard-cooked eggs within one week, and leftover yolks and whites within four days.

■ Do not purchase eggs that are unrefrigerated.

■ Never leave eggs or egg dishes at room temperature for more than one hour.

■ Cook egg yolks thoroughly until there is no visible liquid; cook hard-cooked eggs 7 minutes; poach eggs 5 minutes; and fry eggs 3 minutes on each side.

■ Promptly refrigerate foods containing eggs, such as cream pies, custards, and puddings; use within three to four days.

■ When making homemade ice cream, heat milk-and-egg mixtures to a temperature of 165°, or use a cooked custard as the ice cream base.

■ Avoid milkshakes that contain raw egg yolks.

■ When refrigerating a large amount of a hot egg dish, divide the food into several shallow containers to cool quickly.

■ Be sure to thoroughly wash hands, equipment, and work areas with hot, soapy water before and after handling raw eggs.

■ Never mix the eggshell with the contents of the egg.

■ Resist sampling cake batter or raw cookie dough.

■ Serve cooked eggs and food containing eggs immediately after cooking, or refrigerate immediately for serving later.

FEBRUARY

Take the chill out of winter with a pot of old-fashioned soup or stew. While it simmers, enjoy our special section, "On the Light Side," packed full of tempting, light recipes to help you discover just how delicious healthy eating can be.

Soups Of The South

Southern soups have always been filled with the ingredients of the land. Georgians, however, didn't take much to George Washington Carver's idea of peanut soup. But in Virginia, the creamy combination of chicken broth and peanut butter caught on. Today, you can still find it served as a specialty of the house at inns and eating establishments nestled in the rolling Virginia countryside.

Another Southern specialty, Brunswick stew, has many variations. The stew is represented here with a mouth-watering version from Virginia called Strader Stew.

In Florida, Cuban influences have expanded the Southern repertoire of foods to include black bean soup. The recipe presented here calls for hot peppers and garlic, which typify traditional black bean soup recipes, as well as a few extra touches, such as feta cheese and sherry.

STRADER STEW

2 (3- to 3½-pound) broiler-fryers
5 quarts water
2 (16-ounce) cans whole tomatoes, undrained and chopped
4 cups frozen whole kernel corn
2 cups frozen lima beans
3 medium potatoes, peeled and cubed
2 cups frozen cut okra
2 large onions, chopped
1 tablespoon sugar
1 tablespoon salt
1 teaspoon pepper
½ cup butter or margarine

Combine chicken and water in a large Dutch oven; bring to a boil. Cover, reduce heat, and simmer 1 hour. Remove chicken from broth, reserving broth. Cool chicken completely. Skin, bone, and shred cooked chicken.

Combine 4 quarts reserved broth, chicken, and remaining ingredients in Dutch oven; return to a boil. Reduce heat, and simmer, uncovered, 4 to 5 hours, stirring often. Add additional reserved broth or water to stew for a thinner consistency, if desired. Yield: about 1 gallon.

Philip L. Strader
Lynchburg, Virginia

BLACK BEAN SOUP
(pictured on page 40)

1 (16-ounce) package dried black beans
7 cups water
2 (14½-ounce) cans diluted chicken broth
1 small ham hock
1 tablespoon butter or margarine
2 cloves garlic, crushed
1 small hot pepper, chopped
1 medium onion, chopped
1 stalk celery, chopped
1 bay leaf
½ teaspoon salt
½ teaspoon dry mustard
½ teaspoon pepper
¼ cup dry sherry
Feta cheese (optional)

Sort and wash beans; place in a Dutch oven. Add 7 cups water. Bring to a boil; cover and cook 2 minutes. Remove from heat, and let stand 1 hour. Add chicken broth and remaining ingredients except sherry and feta cheese. Bring to a boil; cover, reduce heat, and simmer 2 to 2½ hours, stirring occasionally. Discard bay leaf. Remove ham hock; dice meat, and set aside. Discard bone.

Measure 4 cups soup, and pour into container of an electric blender; cover and process until mixture is smooth. Return mixture to Dutch oven. Add diced ham and sherry. Bring mixture to a boil; reduce heat, and simmer 10 minutes. Sprinkle each serving with feta cheese, if desired. Yield: 9 cups.

Note: Seeds in small hot pepper make the soup very hot. For a milder soup, remove seeds before chopping pepper. *Georgie O'Neill*
Welaka, Florida

PEANUT BUTTER SOUP
(pictured on page 40)

1 stalk celery, coarsely chopped
1 medium carrot, coarsely chopped
2 tablespoons chopped onion
¾ cup water
2 chicken-flavored or beef-flavored bouillon cubes
2 cups water, divided
½ cup creamy peanut butter
¼ teaspoon pepper
1 tablespoon cornstarch
½ cup half-and-half
Carrot strips (optional)
Chopped peanuts (optional)

Combine first 4 ingredients in a saucepan; cover and cook over low heat 10 minutes or until tender. Add bouillon cubes and 1½ cups water; cook, uncovered, until bouillon cubes dissolve. Pour mixture into container of an electric blender, and add peanut butter and pepper; process until mixture is smooth. Return mixture to saucepan.

Combine cornstarch and remaining ½ cup water, stirring until blended; stir into soup mixture. Bring to a boil; reduce heat to low, and cook 1 minute. Stir in half-and-half; cook over low heat, uncovered, stirring constantly, until thoroughly heated. If desired, garnish individual servings with carrot strips and chopped peanuts. Yield: 3 cups. *Cleo Jackson Whispering Pines, North Carolina*

QUICK!
Breads For Soup

With cold weather here, there's nothing like crusty bread and steaming soup to warm the body and thaw the soul. Our easy recipes rely on ready-made breads or refrigerated doughs for beginnings.

MAYONNAISE BREAD

2 cups self-rising flour
1 cup milk
¼ cup plus 2 tablespoons
 mayonnaise
2 tablespoons vegetable oil
½ teaspoon yellow cornmeal

Combine flour, milk, and mayonnaise in a bowl, stirring just until dry ingredients are moistened.

Grease a 10-inch cast-iron skillet with oil; place in a 400° oven for 4 minutes or until hot. Remove from oven; sprinkle with cornmeal. Spoon batter evenly into skillet. Bake at 400° for 25 minutes or until lightly browned. Yield: 6 to 8 servings. *Donna Hill Belden, Mississippi*

Tip: Leavenings such as baking powder or baking soda are commercially mixed into self-rising flour so you don't have to spend time measuring these additional ingredients.

SESAME KNOTS

1 (11-ounce) package refrigerated
 soft breadsticks
2 tablespoons butter or
 margarine, melted
½ teaspoon sesame seeds or
 poppy seeds

Separate dough, and loosely tie each piece of dough into a knot. Arrange rolls 1 inch apart on an ungreased baking sheet. Brush with butter; sprinkle with sesame seeds. Bake at 350° for 15 minutes or until golden brown. Yield: 10 servings. *Janet M. Filer Arlington, Virginia*

Tip: Embellish this recipe by sprinkling rolls with dried herbs, ground spices, or seasoning salts. With a spicier coating, this bread can double as an appetizer.

ONION-CHEESE
FRENCH BREAD

¼ cup butter or margarine,
 softened
¾ cup (3 ounces) shredded
 Cheddar cheese
½ cup mayonnaise
¼ cup chopped green onions
1 (16-ounce) loaf French bread

Combine first 4 ingredients; mix well. Slice bread in half lengthwise. Spread cheese mixture on bread. Broil 6 inches from heat 2 minutes or until bubbly. Yield: 8 to 10 servings. *Sharon McClatchey Muskogee, Oklahoma*

Tip: Try this recipe for a crowd. Spread topping on bread ahead of time, wrap tightly, and refrigerate. Unwrap and broil bread just before serving time.

CHIVE-GARLIC
FRENCH BREAD

¼ cup butter or margarine,
 softened
1 tablespoon minced chives
1 large clove garlic, minced
1 teaspoon lemon juice
10 (1-inch) slices French bread

Combine first 4 ingredients; spread on one side of bread slices. Place buttered side up on a baking sheet. Broil 6 inches from heat 2 to 3 minutes or until lightly browned. Yield: 10 servings. *Maggie Cates Orlando, Florida*

Tip: The butter mixture may be served on baked potatoes or other vegetables. Make an extra batch to keep on hand.

Bread Tips

■ To thaw frozen bread or rolls, wrap in aluminum foil and heat at 325° for 5 minutes.

■ Bread will stay fresher longer at room temperature or frozen. It is best not to store bread in the refrigerator.

QUICK BISCUITS

2 cups self-rising flour
⅔ cup buttermilk
⅓ cup corn oil

Combine all ingredients in a medium bowl, stirring just until dry ingredients are moistened. Turn dough out onto a floured surface, and knead dough 3 or 4 times.

Roll dough to ½-inch thickness; cut with a 2-inch biscuit cutter. Place biscuits on an ungreased baking sheet. Bake at 425° for 10 to 12 minutes or until biscuits are golden. Yield: 1 dozen.

Edna Ginn
Columbia, Mississippi

Tip: Mix up a powdered buttermilk blend if you don't have fresh buttermilk on hand.

From Our Kitchen To Yours

A simmering pot of soup or stew is a welcome sight on a dreary winter day. The secret of flavorful soups, such as Strader Stew in "Soups of the South" on page 28, is the broth or stock. Broth is a thin, clear liquid in which vegetables, herbs, meat, poultry, or seafood is simmered. When making stock (also a thin clear liquid), bones are added to extract additional flavor and gelatin. Brown stock, a richer flavored stock, is created by browning the bones before adding water.

A tasty broth can be prepared with very little effort in about an hour. Although it takes longer to achieve a stock, either procedure is easy because it's not necessary to peel or trim the vegetables; simply strain the stock, removing the vegetables. After bringing the ingredients to a boil, reduce the heat, and let the mixture simmer slowly; if the liquid is allowed to boil, the broth or stock will be cloudy. As the mixture simmers, remove any scum (which also causes clouding) that collects on the surface.

Because the mixture is cooked slowly, bones from roasted turkey, chicken, ham, pork, or beef—and those saved from deboning a chicken—can be used, making the stock economical. Add vegetables and herbs for extra flavor; carrot and onion deepen the color and add sweetness.

If the broth or stock is not part of a recipe, strain it through a sieve lined with several thicknesses of cheesecloth to remove meat, bones, vegetables, and small particles. Rinse the cheesecloth before straining to remove any starch that could cause clouding. After the broth or stock is strained, remove surface fat to make it lighter and healthier.

Because chilling to degrease takes time, broth and stock are ideal for making ahead. To prevent bacterial growth, quickly cool the hot mixture by placing the container in a large pan filled with ice water. Partially cover and refrigerate the mixture within 30 minutes; tightly covering the warm mixture will cause it to sour. It's best to first cover with plastic wrap because aluminum foil traps the heat. When thoroughly chilled, cover tightly.

All solidified fat should be removed before reheating. The easiest and most effective way is to refrigerate the broth or stock for eight hours so that you can lift the congealed layer of fat from the surface. To quickly remove some of the fat, use ice cubes or skim the surface with a large metal spoon, removing the fat globules. Wrapping an ice cube in rinsed cheesecloth and skimming it over the surface or adding ice cubes directly to the mixture causes the fat to congeal on contact with the ice; then it's easily removed.

Homemade broth or stock may be refrigerated up to four days. For longer storage, cool completely and freeze up to six months, with the exception of fish stock, which can be frozen only up to two months. Degrease broth and stock before freezing; frozen fat can turn rancid. Ladle the mixture into containers for convenient quantities, such as ice cube trays. Each cube yields approximately 2 tablespoons, making it handy to substitute for part of the milk in a cream sauce or for part of the cooking liquid in rice, pasta, or vegetables.

With today's busy schedules, it is sometimes more convenient when making soup to use commercial broths. They are usually saltier than homemade so remember to adjust your seasonings.

Soup and Stew Tips

■ Be sure to save your celery leaves. The outer leaves can serve as seasonings in soups, stuffings, and other cooked dishes. The inner leaves add a nice flavor to tossed salads.

■ For an informal appetizer, offer soup in mugs in the living room. It will spark appetites and the party.

■ Use a bulb baster to remove fat from broth, stew, or soup.

■ If you've added too much salt to soup or stew, simply drop in a peeled raw potato and cook a few minutes. Then remove the potato before serving the soup.

■ Reduce calories in meat dishes by trimming away visible fat before cooking the meat.

ON THE LIGHT SIDE

Wholesome Eating With Grains

Whole grains are making a comeback after being ignored for a number of years. Cracked wheat, millet, brown rice, barley, oats, wild rice, and many more of the lesser known whole grains are showing up on restaurant menus and supermarket shelves.

Why all the increased interest in whole grains? Nutritionally, they are a harvest of healthy components: dietary fiber, complex carbohydrates, protein, vitamins, and minerals. And because they aren't refined, they still contain their original bran, germ, and endosperm. Nothing has been added or taken away from them.

Grains contain a nondigestible fiber that moves along the digestive tract absorbing water and providing bulk.

BEEF-AND-BARLEY VEGETABLE SOUP
(pictured on page 40)

Vegetable cooking spray
1 pound lean ground chuck
5 cups water
1 (14½-ounce) can no-salt-added stewed tomatoes
1 (6-ounce) can low-sodium cocktail vegetable juice
⅓ cup barley
⅓ cup dried green split peas
½ cup chopped onion
1 tablespoon beef-flavored bouillon granules
¼ teaspoon pepper
¼ teaspoon dried whole basil
¼ teaspoon dried whole oregano
1 bay leaf
¾ cup chopped celery, with leaves
½ cup sliced carrot

Coat a large Dutch oven with cooking spray; place over medium-high heat until hot. Add ground chuck, and cook until browned, stirring to crumble meat. Drain and pat dry with paper towels. Wipe pan drippings from oven with a paper towel.

Return meat to Dutch oven; add water and next 10 ingredients. Bring mixture to a boil; cover, reduce heat, and simmer 30 minutes. Stir in celery and carrot; cover and simmer 30 minutes. Remove bay leaf, and serve. Yield: 8 servings (209 calories per 1-cup serving).

☐ *15 grams protein, 9 grams fat, 18.2 grams carbohydrate, 35 milligrams cholesterol, 443 milligrams sodium, and 40 milligrams calcium.*
Gail Comstock
Springfield, Missouri

"FRIED" CRACKED WHEAT

1 cup cracked wheat
1 egg
1 egg white
4 teaspoons vegetable oil, divided
1 cup diced uncooked chicken
½ cup chopped broccoli
½ cup diced carrot
¼ cup sliced green onions
1 clove garlic, minced
½ cup chopped water chestnuts
½ cup frozen English peas, thawed
¼ cup low-sodium soy sauce
⅛ teaspoon ground ginger

Place cracked wheat in a large bowl; cover with water 2 inches above wheat. Soak 1 hour; drain wheat thoroughly.

Combine egg and egg white, stirring until blended. Heat 2 teaspoons oil in a small skillet over medium heat, tilting pan to coat bottom. Pour in egg mixture. Cook without stirring until mixture begins to set; carefully flip egg over, and cook until done. Remove from pan, and let cool. Cut cooked egg into thin strips (about ¼ inch). Set aside.

Add remaining 2 teaspoons oil to wok or large Dutch oven. Add chicken, broccoli, carrot, onions, and garlic; stir-fry until chicken is done. Add cracked wheat, egg strips, and remaining ingredients; toss gently. Yield: 4 servings (335 calories per ½-cup serving).

☐ *21 grams protein, 7.5 grams fat, 43.7 grams carbohydrate, 102 milligrams cholesterol, 491 milligrams sodium, and 47 milligrams calcium.*

Tame Your Taste For Salt

Most of us eat too much salt or sodium (salt is 40% sodium). We learn at an early age that salt intensifies the flavor of food and believe that food without salt is bland and distasteful. But that's just not true. People on low-sodium diets for health reasons find that after two or three months they begin to taste the natural flavors of food and realize that foods they once enjoyed taste too salty. That's because the less salt that is eaten, the more sensitively taste buds will react to it.

Cutting down on the amount of salt eaten isn't harmful because Americans eat 10 to 30 times as much as they need. By simply avoiding the saltshaker and not cooking with salt, sodium intake can be cut in half.

The entrées presented here use a combination of ingredients to flavor food without using salt. Citrus juices, herbs, spices, and distinctly flavored wines and liquors enhance the natural flavor of food and contain no sodium. By combining several ingredients you won't miss the salt.

FRENCH-STYLE BEEF ROAST
(pictured on page 37)

1 (3-pound) boneless beef rump
   roast
1 large clove garlic, quartered
1 teaspoon dried whole thyme
½ teaspoon pepper
1 dried whole bay leaf
4 cups water
1 pound turnips, peeled and
   quartered
¾ pound onions, quartered
2 cups (2-inch pieces) carrots
1 cup (2-inch pieces) celery

Trim all visible fat from roast. Place roast in a large Dutch oven; add next 5 ingredients. Bring to a boil. Cover, reduce heat, and simmer 2½ hours.

Add turnips, onions, carrots, and celery to roast. Cover and cook an additional 30 minutes or until vegetables are tender.

Remove roast to a serving platter; let stand 10 minutes before slicing. Arrange vegetables around roast. Strain broth, and serve with roast. Yield: 10 servings (219 calories per 3-ounce serving with ½ cup vegetable mixture).

☐ *32.1 grams protein, 5.7 grams fat, 8.3 grams carbohydrate, 78 milligrams cholesterol, 120 milligrams sodium, and 41 milligrams calcium.*

Louise Ellis
Talbott, Tennessee

GRILLED PORK TENDERLOIN WITH BROWN SAUCE

8 cloves garlic, crushed
½ teaspoon pepper
¼ cup lime juice
1 tablespoon minced fresh
   oregano or 1 teaspoon dried
   whole oregano
2 (¾-pound) pork tenderloins
Brown Sauce
Steamed asparagus spears
   (optional)
Steamed baby carrots (optional)

Combine first 4 ingredients; stir well, and set aside.

Trim excess fat from tenderloins, and place pork in a large, shallow dish. Spread lime mixture over tenderloins; cover and chill 3 hours, turning occasionally.

Remove tenderloins from marinade, reserving marinade. Grill over medium-hot coals about 1 hour, turning occasionally and basting with reserved marinade. Meat is done when meat thermometer inserted in thickest part of tenderloin registers 160°. Serve tenderloins with Brown Sauce and, if desired, asparagus and carrots. Yield: 6 servings (177 calories per 3-ounce serving of meat and 3 tablespoons of sauce).

☐ *26.3 grams protein, 4.4 grams fat, 5.8 grams carbohydrate, 83 milligrams cholesterol, 160 milligrams sodium, and 22 milligrams calcium.*

Brown Sauce

2 tablespoons cornstarch
¾ teaspoon ground ginger
1½ cups canned low-sodium
   chicken broth
1½ tablespoons dry sherry
1½ tablespoons low-sodium soy
   sauce
½ teaspoon browning-and-
   seasoning sauce

Combine all ingredients in a heavy saucepan. Bring to a boil over medium heat; boil 1 minute, stirring constantly. Yield: 1½ cups (5 calories per tablespoon).

□ *0 grams protein, 0 grams fat, 0.8 gram carbohydrate, 0 milligrams cholesterol, 25 milligrams sodium, and 0 milligrams calcium.*
Mrs. Ruth A. Colosimo
Copperas Cove, Texas

SESAME FLOUNDER

8 (4-ounce) flounder fillets or other lean white fish fillets
Vegetable cooking spray
1 teaspoon lemon juice
¼ teaspoon pepper
½ cup diced onion
½ cup diced green pepper
½ cup diced celery
¼ cup frozen apple juice concentrate, thawed and undiluted
2 teaspoons toasted sesame seeds

Place fillets in a 13- x 9- x 2-inch baking dish coated with cooking spray. Drizzle with lemon juice; sprinkle with pepper.
Sauté onion, green pepper, and celery in apple juice concentrate until crisp-tender; spoon over fillets. Sprinkle with sesame seeds; bake at 350° for 20 to 25 minutes or until fish flakes easily when tested with a fork. Yield: 8 servings (130 calories per 3-ounce serving).

□ *21.8 grams protein, 1.9 grams fat, 5.4 grams carbohydrate, 54 milligrams cholesterol, 101 milligrams sodium, and 36 milligrams calcium.*
Mary Gervais
Matthews, North Carolina

CHICKEN CREOLE

Vegetable cooking spray
1 cup thinly sliced onion
1 cup chopped celery, with leaves
1 cup diced green pepper
3 cloves garlic, minced
2 cups sliced fresh mushrooms
2 cups diced uncooked chicken
1 (15½-ounce) can no-salt-added tomatoes
½ cup Chablis or other dry white wine
¼ to ½ teaspoon crushed red pepper flakes
¼ teaspoon pepper
1 bay leaf
2 cups hot cooked rice (cooked without salt or fat)
2 tablespoons chopped parsley

Coat a large nonstick skillet with cooking spray; place over medium-high heat until hot. Add onion and next 3 ingredients; sauté until crisp-tender. Add mushrooms, and cook about 3 minutes, stirring occasionally. Add chicken and next 5 ingredients; cook 25 minutes. Discard bay leaf. Serve over rice; sprinkle with parsley. Yield: 4 servings (303 calories per 1 cup chicken mixture and ½ cup rice).

□ *30.9 grams protein, 2.6 grams fat, 38.1 grams carbohydrate, 66 milligrams cholesterol, 122 milligrams sodium, and 93 milligrams calcium.*
Mrs. Robert S. Henderson
Virginia Beach, Virginia

Tip: *Use finely chopped fresh herbs whenever possible. Dried whole herbs are usually the next best choice since they maintain their strength longer than the commercially ground form. Remember to use 3 times more fresh herbs in a recipe if it calls for the more potent dried form.*

Salt—Cooking and Other Uses

■ Burned food can be removed from an enamel saucepan by using the following procedure: Fill the pan with cold water containing 2 to 3 tablespoons salt, and let stand overnight. The next day, cover the pan, and bring water to a boil.

■ When food boils over in the oven, sprinkle the burned surface with a little salt. This will stop smoke and odor and make the spot easier to clean. Also, rubbing damp salt on dishes in which food has been baked will remove brown spots.

■ When hard-cooking eggs, add 1 teaspoon salt to the water. This prevents a cracked egg from draining.

■ Salt can be eliminated from almost any recipe (except yeast bread and pickles) without affecting the quality of the product. (Salt is added to yeast breads for a smooth texture, and it is added to pickles for prevention of bacterial growth.)

■ Don't add salt to green salad until just before serving. Salt wilts and toughens salad greens.

■ Add salt to taste after microwaving vegetables to prevent dark spots from forming.

Fruit—Nature's Healthy Fast Food

Take advantage of succulent oranges and grapefruit, luscious pineapples and pears, and crunchy apples, which are especially delectable during the winter. Fruit is naturally low in calories, packed with vitamins, and a good source of dietary fiber, especially if it's eaten raw. Leaving the peel on apples and pears adds even more fiber.

WINTER FRUIT KABOBS

1 (8-ounce) can unsweetened pineapple chunks, undrained
3 tablespoons low-sugar orange marmalade
¼ teaspoon ground ginger
1 orange
1 medium apple, cut into 12 cubes
1 medium banana, cut into 12 slices

Drain pineapple chunks, reserving 2 tablespoons juice. Combine juice, marmalade, and ginger in a small saucepan; cook over low heat, stirring constantly, until hot. Remove from heat.

Peel orange; separate into sections, leaving membrane on orange. Combine orange sections and remaining fruit; spoon marmalade mixture over fruit. Toss gently, and arrange on 12 small skewers. Place on an ungreased baking sheet, and bake at 400° for 6 to 8 minutes or until thoroughly heated. Yield: 6 servings (78 calories per 2 kabobs).

□ *0.4 gram protein, 0.2 gram fat, 19.5 grams carbohydrate, 0 milligrams cholesterol, 1 milligram sodium, and 15 milligrams calcium.*

TANGY CITRUS SALAD

3 cups cubed fresh pineapple
3 cups grapefruit sections
1 teaspoon vanilla extract
1 (8-ounce) carton lemon low-fat yogurt
12 Boston lettuce leaves

Combine pineapple and grapefruit; cover and chill. Stir vanilla into yogurt. Line 6 individual plates with 2 lettuce leaves each; place 1 cup fruit on lettuce. Spoon 2 tablespoons yogurt mixture over each serving. Yield: 6 servings (109 calories per serving).

□ *3.1 grams protein, 1.1 grams fat, 23.5 grams carbohydrate, 2 milligrams cholesterol, 46 milligrams sodium, and 86 milligrams calcium.*

SANGRÍA FRUIT CUPS

1 medium-size red apple, unpeeled and chopped
1 medium pear, unpeeled and chopped
1 small tangerine, peeled and sectioned
1 tablespoon golden raisins
1 tablespoon chopped pecans
¼ cup white sangría
¼ cup orange juice

Combine first 5 ingredients in a large bowl. Combine sangría and orange juice; pour over fruit mixture, and toss. Cover and chill, stirring occasionally. Yield: 7 servings (64 calories per ½-cup serving).

□ *0.5 gram protein, 1 gram fat, 13.2 grams carbohydrate, 0 milligrams cholesterol, 1 milligram sodium, and 11 milligrams calcium.*

Swirl Bread With Herbs

The delightful combination of parsley, thyme, rosemary, and sage in Herbed Bread permeates the air. The scent will warm your home and beckon the entire household to the kitchen to wait until the bread comes hot from the oven.

HERBED BREAD

¼ cup margarine
1¼ cups water
2 cups whole wheat flour
1 package dry yeast
1 teaspoon onion powder
¼ teaspoon salt
¼ teaspoon white pepper
2 tablespoons instant nonfat dry milk powder
2 tablespoons honey
1¾ cups all-purpose flour, divided
Vegetable cooking spray
1 tablespoon margarine, melted
¼ cup minced fresh parsley or 2 tablespoons dried parsley flakes
1 tablespoon minced fresh thyme or 1 teaspoon dried whole thyme
¾ teaspoon minced fresh sage or ¼ teaspoon rubbed sage
¾ teaspoon minced fresh rosemary or ¼ teaspoon dried whole rosemary

Combine ¼ cup margarine and water in a saucepan; heat to 120° to 130°. Set aside.

Combine whole wheat flour and the next 6 ingredients in a large mixing bowl; add margarine-and-water mixture. Beat at medium speed of an electric mixer until smooth. Stir in 1½ cups all-purpose flour. Turn dough out onto a lightly floured surface. Knead 5 minutes, using remaining ¼ cup flour.

Place dough in a bowl coated with cooking spray, turning dough to coat top. Cover and let rise in a warm place (85°), free from drafts, 1 hour or until doubled in bulk.

Punch dough down; turn out onto a lightly floured surface. Roll into a 15- x 9-inch rectangle; brush with melted margarine. Combine parsley and remaining herbs; stir well. Sprinkle mixture over dough. Roll up, jellyroll fashion, starting with narrow end. Place seam side down in a 9- x 5- x 3-inch loafpan coated with cooking spray. Let rise in a warm place (85°), free from drafts, 45 minutes or until doubled in bulk.

Bake at 350° for 45 minutes or until golden. Remove from pan, and cool slightly. Yield: 16 servings (151 calories per ½-inch slice).

☐ *4.1 grams protein, 4.1 grams fat, 25.2 grams carbohydrate, 0 milligrams cholesterol, 85 milligrams sodium, and 26 milligrams calcium.*
Jean Burnett
Jefferson City, Tennessee

Low-Fat Dairy Coolers

Milk and other dairy products are important for people of all ages, not just children. Besides being major sources of calcium, dairy products provide vitamins A, D, and B-12, as well as phosphorus and riboflavin.

ORANGE-PINEAPPLE DRINK

1 (8-ounce) carton pineapple low-fat yogurt
½ cup unsweetened orange juice, chilled
Ice cubes

Combine yogurt and orange juice in container of an electric blender; process until smooth. Slowly add enough ice cubes to bring mixture to the 2-cup line. Process until smooth, and serve. Yield: 2 cups (76 calories per ½-cup serving).

☐ *2.3 grams protein, 0.5 gram fat, 15.8 grams carbohydrate, 0 milligrams cholesterol, 37 milligrams sodium, and 75 milligrams calcium.*
Melba B. Johnson
Shreveport, Louisiana

MOCHA MILKSHAKE

¾ cup evaporated skimmed milk, undiluted and chilled
¼ cup cold water
2 tablespoons chocolate-flavored syrup
½ teaspoon instant coffee granules
1 teaspoon vanilla extract
Ice cubes

Combine first 5 ingredients in container of an electric blender; process until foamy. Slowly add enough ice cubes to bring mixture to the 3-cup line. Process until smooth. Serve immediately. Yield: 3 cups (88 calories per 1-cup serving).

☐ *5.2 grams protein, 0.3 gram fat, 15.2 grams carbohydrate, 3 milligrams cholesterol, 82 milligrams sodium, and 188 milligrams calcium.*
Claudia Jeske
Chattanooga, Tennessee

CARROT COOLER

½ cup finely grated carrot
¾ teaspoon grated orange rind
¼ cup unsweetened orange juice
1½ cups vanilla ice milk

Combine all ingredients in container of an electric blender; process until smooth, and serve. Yield: 2 cups (82 calories per ½-cup serving).

☐ *2.2 grams protein, 2.1 grams fat, 14 grams carbohydrate, 7 milligrams cholesterol, 44 milligrams sodium, and 72 milligrams calcium.*
Alma B. Gudrian
Nashville, Tennessee

STRAWBERRY-BANANA SHAKE

2 cups fresh strawberries
2 cups nonfat buttermilk
1 small ripe banana, sliced (½ cup)
3 tablespoons honey

Wash and cap strawberries; drain well. Place a single layer of strawberries in a shallow pan; freeze.

Combine buttermilk and remaining ingredients in container of an electric blender. Process until smooth. Slowly add frozen strawberries; process until smooth. Serve immediately. Yield: 4½ cups (59 calories per ½-cup serving).

☐ *2.3 grams protein, 0.4 gram fat, 12.7 grams carbohydrate, 1 milligram cholesterol, 57 milligrams sodium, and 72 milligrams calcium.*
Kay Castleman Cooper
Burke, Virginia

Easy Entrées For Two

When it's just the two of you, these simple menu suggestions will fit the bill. Each entrée relies on a relatively short list of basic ingredients. And there's a quick menu suggestion for each recipe.

Cooking for two doesn't mean you can't take advantage of specials or bulk packaging. For example, when boneless pork chops are on sale, they can be wrapped individually in heavy-duty plastic wrap, packaged together in foil or a freezer bag, and frozen. The package should be dated and the chops used within three to six months.

If any of these recipes are doubled, remember that the greater quantity of food will increase the cooking time.

STUFFED PORK CHOPS WITH APRICOT GLAZE

2 tablespoons apricot preserves
1 tablespoon brown sugar
1 tablespoon brown mustard
⅛ teaspoon salt
¼ cup dried mixed fruit, chopped
2 tablespoons sliced green onions
1 egg, beaten
½ teaspoon ground ginger
2 tablespoons breadcrumbs
2 (1-inch-thick) boneless pork
   chops, cut with pockets
1 tablespoon vegetable oil

Combine first 4 ingredients in a 1-cup glass measure; microwave at HIGH 1 minute or until mixture is thoroughly heated. Stir and set aside.

Combine mixed fruit and next 4 ingredients, stirring well; stuff into pockets of chops, and secure openings with wooden picks.

Preheat a 10-inch browning dish at HIGH 8 minutes or according to manufacturer's directions. Add oil, and tilt to coat dish. Place chops on browning dish 1 minute or until sizzling stops. Spoon half of glaze over pork chops. Cover with wax paper; microwave at MEDIUM (50% power) 4 minutes. Turn pork chops over, and spoon remaining glaze over chops. Cover with wax paper; microwave at MEDIUM 4 minutes or until chops are done. Let stand, covered, 5 minutes. Yield: 2 servings.

Menu Suggestion: Serve with a green salad, commercial rolls, and a vegetable. (If the vegetable is microwaved, cook during the 5-minute standing time for pork chops.)

PEPPER-TOPPED LASAGNA ROLLS

2 lasagna noodles
1 tomato, peeled and chopped
1 small green pepper, cut into
   julienne strips
1 small sweet red pepper, cut
   into julienne strips
1 clove garlic, crushed
2 tablespoons olive oil
½ teaspoon dried whole basil
¼ teaspoon pepper
½ cup low-fat cottage cheese
1 egg
¼ cup grated Parmesan cheese,
   divided

Place lasagna noodles in a 10- x 6- x 2-inch baking dish; add 2½ to 3 cups water. Cover and microwave at HIGH about 10 minutes or until noodles are tender. Drain.

Combine chopped tomato and next 6 ingredients in a 1-quart casserole. Cover tightly with heavy-duty plastic wrap; fold back a corner of wrap to allow steam to escape. Microwave at HIGH 2 minutes. Drain.

Combine cottage cheese, egg, and 2 tablespoons Parmesan cheese; spread on lasagna noodles. Roll up jellyroll fashion, starting from end. Place lasagna rolls, seam side down, in a 1-quart casserole. Pour vegetable mixture over rolls. Cover and microwave at HIGH 6 to 8 minutes. Sprinkle with remaining Parmesan cheese. Yield: 2 servings.

Menu Suggestion: Serve with toasted garlic bread and a tossed green salad.

BREADED GROUPER FILLETS

½ cup nutlike cereal nuggets
2 tablespoons chopped fresh
   parsley
½ teaspoon dried whole rosemary
¼ teaspoon salt
2 (4-ounce) grouper fillets
⅓ cup low-fat plain yogurt
Lemon slices (optional)

Combine first 4 ingredients in a shallow dish; mix well. Brush fillets with yogurt on all sides; coat with cereal mixture. Place fillets in a 9-inch pie-plate. Microwave at HIGH 1½ minutes; give dish a half-turn. Microwave an additional 1½ to 2 minutes or until fish flakes easily when tested with a fork. Let stand 5 minutes. Garnish fillets with lemon slices, if desired. Yield: 2 servings.

Menu Suggestion: Serve with coleslaw and hot cornsticks.

Right: *French-Style Beef Roast (page 32) may be low in sodium, but it's not lacking in flavor.*

*These rich and beautiful desserts
boast chocolate throughout: (clockwise
from top) Chocolate Cheesecake With
Whipped Cream Frosting (page 42),
Chocolate-Pecan Torte (page 42),
and Chocolate Truffle Cake
(page 43).*

For Chocolate Truffle Cake, pipe frosting while moving decorating bag in a circular pattern to build a base for truffles.

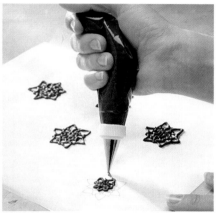

Cover the pattern with wax paper, and pipe Lacy Chocolate Garnishes for Chocolate Cheesecake With Whipped Cream Frosting; peel from wax paper when firm.

Paint a garnish directly onto Chocolate-Pecan Torte, using melted chocolate and an art brush.

Discover the wholesome, tasty goodness grain adds to Beef-and-Barley Vegetable Soup (page 31).

Even though Black Bean Soup has not been on Southern menus as long as Peanut Butter Soup, both merit the praise of discriminating cooks. (Recipes, page 28.)

Bring On The Citrus!

Adorn your winter menus with the beauty of fresh grapefruit and oranges. Low in calories yet bursting with flavor, citrus may be prepared in a variety of ways.

Grapefruit and oranges will hold their firmness and freshness for several weeks if stored properly. Citrus fruits maintain their juiciness at room temperature if eaten within several days. To store longer, place in refrigerator.

GRAPEFRUIT-AVOCADO SALAD

2 medium avocados, peeled and
　sliced
Lemon juice
2 large grapefruit, peeled and
　sectioned
Bibb lettuce leaves
½ cup chopped walnuts
¼ cup currants
Dressing (recipe follows)

Dip avocado slices in lemon juice, and set aside.

Alternate grapefruit sections and avocado slices in a circular pattern on lettuce leaves on individual salad plates. Spoon 2 tablespoons walnuts and 1 tablespoon currants in center of each salad. Serve with dressing. Yield: 4 servings.

Dressing

⅓ cup mayonnaise
2 tablespoons grapefruit juice
1 teaspoon honey
½ teaspoon grated grapefruit rind

Combine all ingredients, stirring with a wire whisk. Cover and chill before serving. Yield: ⅓ cup.　*C. Brandt*
Slidell, Louisiana

GRAPEFRUIT-APPLE SALAD

1 (8-ounce) can pineapple chunks,
　undrained
1 (3-ounce) package
　lemon-flavored gelatin
1 cup boiling water
¾ cup water
1 cup grapefruit sections
1 small unpeeled apple, chopped
½ medium-size green pepper,
　chopped
Lettuce leaves
Mayonnaise (optional)

Drain pineapple, reserving ¼ cup juice. Dissolve gelatin in 1 cup boiling water in a large bowl; add ¾ cup water and reserved pineapple juice. Chill until the consistency of unbeaten egg white.

Fold pineapple, grapefruit, apple, and green pepper into gelatin mixture. Pour into a lightly oiled 4-cup mold; cover and chill until firm. Unmold onto lettuce leaves; serve with mayonnaise, if desired. Yield: 6 to 8 servings.　*Violet Moore*
Montezuma, Georgia

ORANGE-ONION SALAD

½ cup olive oil
¼ cup vinegar
⅛ teaspoon salt
4 medium oranges, peeled and
　sliced
2 medium-size purple onions,
　sliced
Lettuce leaves

Combine oil, vinegar, and salt in a jar; cover tightly, and shake vigorously. Pour mixture over orange and onion slices in a shallow container, and toss gently. Cover and refrigerate at least 30 minutes; drain. Arrange orange and onion slices on lettuce leaves on individual salad plates. Yield: 4 to 6 servings.
Charlotte Pierce
Greensburg, Kentucky

BAKED ORANGES

6 navel oranges
1 cup orange juice
½ cup sugar
2 tablespoons butter or margarine
1 tablespoon cornstarch
Grated nutmeg (optional)

Wash oranges, and place in a large Dutch oven; cover with water. Bring to a boil; reduce heat, and simmer 5 minutes. Drain and set aside to cool.

Peel oranges, and cut into ½-inch-thick slices. Cut each slice in half, and arrange in a lightly greased 12- x 8- x 2-inch baking dish.

Combine orange juice and next 3 ingredients in a saucepan; bring to a boil, reduce heat, and simmer 1 minute. Pour hot mixture over orange slices; sprinkle with nutmeg, if desired. Bake at 350° for 15 minutes or until bubbly. Yield: 8 servings.
Sara M. Gaskins
Beckley, West Virginia

ORANGE-GINGER MUFFINS

2 cups all-purpose flour
2½ teaspoons baking powder
½ teaspoon salt
¼ teaspoon ground ginger
⅓ cup sugar
1 egg, beaten
⅔ cup milk
½ cup orange juice
¼ cup vegetable oil
2 teaspoons grated orange rind

Combine first 5 ingredients in a large bowl; make a well in center of mixture. Combine egg and remaining ingredients; add to dry ingredients, stirring just until moistened. Spoon batter into greased muffin pans, filling two-thirds full. Bake at 375° for 15 minutes. Remove muffins from pans immediately. Yield: 14 muffins.
Jodie McCoy
Tulsa, Oklahoma

A Chocolate Fantasy

Not only are these desserts filled with chocolate, they are frosted with it, too. And pretty garnishes on top carry out the color and flavor theme as well.

CHOCOLATE-PECAN TORTE
(pictured on pages 38 and 39)

4 eggs, separated
½ cup sugar
¾ cup ground pecans
⅓ cup cocoa
⅓ cup all-purpose flour
½ teaspoon baking soda
¼ teaspoon salt
¼ cup water
1 teaspoon vanilla extract
¼ cup sugar
Mocha Buttercream
½ cup finely chopped pecans
  (optional)
¼ cup semisweet chocolate
  morsels
1 teaspoon shortening
Chocolate leaves (optional)
1 semisweet chocolate morsel
  (optional)

Grease bottoms of two 9-inch round cakepans; line with wax paper, and grease paper.

Beat egg yolks at high speed of an electric mixer. Gradually add ½ cup sugar, beating until mixture is thick and lemon colored.

Combine ground pecans, cocoa, flour, soda, and salt; add to yolk mixture alternately with water, beginning and ending with pecan mixture. Stir in vanilla.

Beat egg whites (at room temperature) at high speed of electric mixer until foamy. Gradually add ¼ cup sugar, beating until stiff peaks form; fold into pecan mixture. Spread batter in prepared pans. Bake at 375° for 16 to 18 minutes. Cool in pans 10 minutes; remove layers from pans.

Remove wax paper; cool completely on wire racks.

Spread Mocha Buttercream between layers and on top and sides of torte; use a long metal spatula to smooth frosting on top of torte. Press ½ cup chopped pecans on sides of torte, if desired.

Place ¼ cup chocolate morsels and shortening in top of a double boiler; bring water to a boil. Reduce heat to low; cook until chocolate melts. Paint chocolate in desired design on top edge of torte. If desired, arrange chocolate leaves in center of torte, and cover center hole with chocolate morsel. Yield: one 9-inch torte.

Mocha Buttercream

1 tablespoon instant coffee
  granules
¼ cup hot water
½ cup butter or margarine,
  softened
3 tablespoons cocoa
4¼ to 4½ cups sifted powdered
  sugar
¾ teaspoon vanilla extract

Dissolve coffee granules in hot water; set aside to cool.

Cream butter and cocoa at medium speed of an electric mixer; add 4¼ cups powdered sugar to creamed mixture alternately with coffee, beginning and ending with powdered sugar. Add additional ¼ cup powdered sugar, if necessary, to make mixture a good spreading consistency. Stir in vanilla. Yield: 2 cups.

Note: For **chocolate leaves,** select such nonpoisonous leaves as mint or rose. Wash leaves, and pat dry with paper towels. Melt 1 or 2 (1-ounce) squares semisweet chocolate over hot water in a double boiler; let cool slightly.

Using a small spatula, spread a ⅛-inch layer of chocolate on the back of each leaf, spreading to edges. Place leaves on a wax paper-lined baking sheet, chocolate side up; freeze until chocolate is firm, about 10 minutes.

Grasp leaf at stem end, and carefully peel leaf away from chocolate. Chill until ready to use.

CHOCOLATE CHEESECAKE WITH WHIPPED CREAM FROSTING
(pictured on pages 38 and 39)

1⅓ cups semisweet chocolate
  morsels
3 (8-ounce) packages cream
  cheese, softened
1½ cups sugar
3 eggs
1 tablespoon cocoa
1½ teaspoons vanilla extract
1 (8-ounce) carton commercial
  sour cream
Chocolate Wafer Crust
Whipped Cream Frosting
Lacy Chocolate Garnishes

Place semisweet chocolate morsels in top of a double boiler; bring water to a boil. Reduce heat to low; cook until chocolate melts.

Beat cream cheese at high speed of an electric mixer until light and fluffy; gradually add sugar, mixing well. Add eggs, one at a time, beating well after each addition. Stir in melted chocolate, cocoa, and vanilla; beat until blended. Stir in sour cream, blending well. Pour into prepared Chocolate Wafer Crust. Bake at 300° for 1 hour and 40 minutes. Run knife around edge of pan to release sides. Let cool to room temperature on a wire rack; cover and chill at least 8 hours.

When ready to serve, spoon 2 cups Whipped Cream Frosting into a decorating bag fitted with large metal tip No. 2110. Set aside.

Remove cheesecake from pan, and place on a serving plate. Spread remaining frosting on top of cheesecake. Pipe reserved frosting as desired on top of cheesecake. Insert 12 Lacy Chocolate Garnishes equally around sides of cake, and place 1 in center. Yield: 12 servings.

Chocolate Wafer Crust

1½ cups chocolate wafer crumbs
⅓ cup butter or margarine,
  melted

Combine crumbs and butter, stirring well. Firmly press crumb mixture evenly into bottom and 1 inch up sides of a 9-inch springform pan. Bake at 350° for 6 to 8 minutes. Yield: one 9-inch crust.

Whipped Cream Frosting

1½ cups whipping cream
3 tablespoons cocoa
2 tablespoons powdered sugar
1 teaspoon vanilla extract

Combine all ingredients in a medium-size mixing bowl; beat until firm peaks form. Yield: 3 cups.

Lacy Chocolate Garnishes

½ cup semisweet chocolate morsels

Place chocolate morsels in top of a double boiler; bring water to a boil. Reduce heat to low; cook until chocolate melts. Let cool slightly, and spoon into a decorating bag fitted with metal tip No. 2.

Trace pattern for lacy garnishes onto white paper (see sketch, below). Cover pattern with a large sheet of wax paper. Pipe melted chocolate over wax paper-covered pattern, moving paper to position pattern in other places. Continue piping over pattern and moving paper to make 13 garnishes. Carefully transfer wax paper to a baking sheet, and chill until chocolate is firm. Carefully peel garnishes from wax paper. Yield: 13 garnishes.

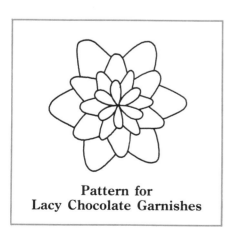

Pattern for Lacy Chocolate Garnishes

CHOCOLATE TRUFFLE CAKE
(pictured on pages 38 and 39)

Chocolate Truffles
2 to 3 tablespoons milk
Rich Chocolate Cake
Satiny Chocolate Frosting
2 (1.75-ounce) bottles chocolate sprinkles

Prepare Chocolate Truffles. Combine milk and reserved three-fourths of truffle mixture; beat at high speed of an electric mixer until mixture is spreading consistency. Spread between layers of Rich Chocolate Cake.

Spoon about 1 cup Satiny Chocolate Frosting into a decorating bag fitted with large tip No. 2110. Spread remaining frosting on top and sides of cake, spreading it smoothly with a long metal spatula. Pat chocolate sprinkles on sides of cake. Pipe 12 (1-inch) rosettes of frosting around top edge of cake. Place a truffle on each rosette. Chill until serving time. Yield: one 3-layer cake.

Chocolate Truffles

1 (12-ounce) package semisweet chocolate morsels
4 egg yolks
¼ cup plus 2 tablespoons butter or margarine, cut into cubes
¼ cup plus 2 tablespoons sifted powdered sugar
2 tablespoons chocolate sprinkles

Place chocolate morsels in top of a double boiler; bring water to a boil. Reduce heat to low; cook until chocolate melts. Remove container of chocolate from over boiling water.

Beat egg yolks until thick and lemon colored. Gradually stir about one-fourth of hot chocolate into yolks; add to remaining hot mixture, stirring constantly. Add butter and powdered sugar; beat at medium speed of an electric mixer until butter melts and mixture is smooth.

Place about one-fourth of truffle mixture in a small bowl; cover with a paper towel, and let stand in a cool dry place 1 hour (do not refrigerate). Set aside remaining truffle mixture to spread between layers of cake.

After one-fourth of truffle mixture has set for 1 hour, shape into 12 equal balls; roll balls lightly in chocolate sprinkles. Yield: 1 dozen truffles and filling for a 3-layer cake.

Rich Chocolate Cake

1 cup cocoa
2 cups boiling water
1 cup butter or margarine, softened
2½ cups sugar
4 eggs
1½ teaspoons vanilla extract
2¾ cups all-purpose flour
2 teaspoons baking soda
½ teaspoon baking powder
½ teaspoon salt

Combine cocoa and boiling water, stirring until mixture is smooth. Set aside, and let cool.

Cream butter, sugar, eggs, and vanilla at high speed of an electric mixer until light and fluffy, about 5 minutes.

Combine flour, soda, baking powder, and salt in a small bowl. Add to creamed mixture alternately with cocoa mixture; beat at low speed of electric mixer, beginning and ending with flour mixture.

Pour batter into 3 greased and floured 9-inch cakepans. Bake at 350° for 25 to 30 minutes. Cool in pans 10 minutes; remove from pans, and let cool completely on wire racks. Yield: three 9-inch cake layers.

Satiny Chocolate Frosting

1 (6-ounce) package semisweet chocolate morsels
½ cup milk
1 cup butter or margarine
2½ cups sifted powdered sugar

Combine semisweet chocolate morsels, milk, and butter in a large saucepan; cook over medium heat, stirring constantly, until melted and smooth. Remove from heat; blend in powdered sugar. Set pan in bowl of ice water; beat at medium speed of an electric mixer until frosting holds its shape. Yield: about 3 cups.

Be Their Valentine With A Menu For Six

Is the way to one's heart *really* through the stomach? Test the age-old adage with this scrumptious menu for six, and invite friends for a Valentine's Day celebration. Preparation is easy when you plan ahead.

Plan: Make the crêpes for Florentine Crêpe Cups up to a week ahead of time, and freeze. Combine ingredients for the crêpe filling, and bake Layered Flan early in the morning or perhaps even a day ahead.

About an hour before dinner, place Florentine Crêpe Cups and Buttered Carrots and Celery in a 350° oven; then you can end by cooking the Veal-and-Mushrooms Marsala.

Veal-and-Mushrooms Marsala
Buttered Carrots and Celery
Florentine Crêpe Cups
Layered Flan

VEAL-AND-MUSHROOMS MARSALA

½ cup all-purpose flour
¼ teaspoon salt
¼ teaspoon freshly ground pepper
6 veal cutlets (about 2¼ pounds)
¼ cup olive oil
½ pound fresh mushrooms, sliced
⅔ cup chopped green onions
2 tablespoons olive oil
6 medium tomatoes, peeled, seeded, and chopped
6 fresh basil leaves, chopped, or ½ teaspoon dried whole basil
1½ cups Marsala wine
⅓ cup freshly grated Parmesan cheese (optional)
⅓ cup chopped fresh parsley (optional)

Combine first 3 ingredients; dredge veal in flour mixture. Heat ¼ cup oil in a heavy skillet over medium heat. Add veal, and cook about 3 minutes on each side; drain on paper towels. Add mushrooms to skillet; sauté until tender, and remove from skillet.

Sauté green onions in 2 tablespoons oil in skillet. Stir in tomatoes and basil; cook 4 to 5 minutes or until most of liquid evaporates. Add wine, and simmer about 8 minutes. Return veal and mushrooms to skillet, and cook until thoroughly heated. If desired, sprinkle with Parmesan cheese and parsley. Yield: 6 servings.
Sue-Sue Hartstern
Louisville, Kentucky

BUTTERED CARROTS AND CELERY

5 medium carrots, scraped and cut into julienne strips
4 stalks celery, cut into julienne strips
½ cup water
2 tablespoons butter or margarine, melted
1½ teaspoons sugar
½ teaspoon salt
⅛ teaspoon pepper
2 tablespoons butter or margarine, melted

Combine first 7 ingredients in a 2-quart baking dish. Cover and bake at 350° for 45 minutes; drain. Add 2 tablespoons butter, tossing to coat. Yield: 6 to 8 servings.
Mrs. Earl L. Faulkenberry
Lancaster, South Carolina

FLORENTINE CRÊPE CUPS

1½ cups (6 ounces) shredded sharp Cheddar cheese
3 tablespoons all-purpose flour
1 (10-ounce) package frozen chopped spinach, thawed and drained
6 slices bacon, cooked and crumbled
3 eggs, beaten
⅔ cup mayonnaise
½ teaspoon salt
⅛ teaspoon pepper
6 (6-inch) crêpes

Combine cheese and flour; toss. Stir in spinach and remaining ingredients except crêpes, mixing well. Carefully place 6 crêpes into 6 lightly greased 6-ounce custard cups, and fill each with spinach mixture. Cover and bake at 350° for 35 to 40 minutes or until set. Yield: 6 servings.

Crêpes

⅔ cup all-purpose flour
½ teaspoon salt
1 cup milk
3 eggs
Vegetable oil

Combine flour, salt, and milk, beating at medium speed of an electric mixer until smooth. Add eggs, and beat well; let stand 20 minutes.

Brush bottom of a 6-inch crêpe pan or heavy skillet with oil; place over medium heat just until hot, but not smoking.

Pour 2 tablespoons batter into pan. Tilt pan in all directions so that batter covers pan with a thin film. Cook 1 minute or until lightly browned.

Lift edge of crêpe to test for doneness. Crêpe is ready for flipping when it can be shaken loose from pan. Flip crêpe, and cook about 30 seconds on other side. (This side is usually spotty brown and is the side on which filling is placed.)

Place crêpe on a towel to cool. Stack crêpes between layers of wax paper to prevent sticking. Repeat until all batter is used. Yield: 16 (6-inch) crêpes.

Note: Remaining crêpes may be frozen, if desired. Thaw at room temperature; fill as desired.

Suzanne McDonald
Monroeville, Alabama

LAYERED FLAN

¾ cup sugar
3 tablespoons water
1½ (1-ounce) squares semisweet
    chocolate
2 cups milk
4 eggs
½ cup sugar
½ teaspoon ground cinnamon
½ teaspoon vanilla extract
Pinch of salt
¾ cup flaked coconut
Chocolate leaves (optional)

Combine ¾ cup sugar and water in a heavy skillet; cook over medium heat, stirring constantly, until sugar dissolves and mixture turns light golden brown. Pour mixture into a lightly greased 6-cup ring mold or 9-inch round cakepan; set aside.

Place chocolate in container of an electric blender; process until finely ground. Add milk and next 6 ingredients; process at high speed 15 seconds or until mixture is well blended. Pour over caramelized sugar; cover pan with aluminum foil, and place in a large shallow pan. Pour hot water to a depth of 1 inch into larger pan. Bake at 350° for 50 minutes or until a knife inserted near center comes out clean.

Remove pan from water, and uncover; let cool on a wire rack at least 30 minutes. Loosen edges with a spatula. Invert flan onto a serving plate; cover and chill 8 hours. Garnish with chocolate leaves, if desired. (See page 42.) Yield: 6 servings.

Mary B. Quesenberry
Dugspur, Virginia

Salads Deserve Homemade Dressings

Natural flavors and easy preparation make these homemade dressings an easy way to set off the simplest green salads.

SOUR CREAM ITALIAN DRESSING

½ cup mayonnaise
½ cup commercial sour cream
2 tablespoons milk
1 tablespoon vinegar
1 clove garlic, minced
½ teaspoon dried whole oregano
½ teaspoon dried whole basil
½ teaspoon honey
¼ teaspoon salt
⅛ teaspoon pepper

Combine all ingredients in a small bowl, stirring well with a wire whisk. Cover and chill at least 2 hours before serving. Yield: 1 cup.

Cynda A. Spoon
Broken Arrow, Oklahoma

MAGNIFICENT SEVEN SALAD DRESSING

1 hard-cooked egg
⅔ cup mayonnaise
⅔ cup chili sauce
1½ tablespoons lemon juice
1 teaspoon tarragon vinegar
⅓ cup chopped green pepper
⅓ cup chopped sweet red pepper

Chop egg white, and reserve yolk for other uses. Set aside.

Combine mayonnaise, chili sauce, lemon juice, and vinegar; stir well with a wire whisk. Stir in chopped green and red pepper and chopped egg white. Chill at least 2 hours. Yield: 2¼ cups.

Irene R. Smith
Covington, Georgia

DIJON-HONEY DRESSING

1 cup mayonnaise
¼ cup Dijon mustard
¼ cup honey
2 tablespoons vegetable oil
¾ teaspoon cider vinegar
⅛ teaspoon onion salt
⅛ teaspoon red pepper

Combine all ingredients in container of an electric blender; process until smooth. Cover and chill thoroughly. Yield: 1¼ cups.

Lula Bell Hawks
Newport, Arkansas

BLUE CHEESE VINAIGRETTE

½ cup corn oil
3 tablespoons vinegar
½ teaspoon dried whole basil
¼ teaspoon dry mustard
½ cup (2 ounces) crumbled blue
    cheese

Combine all ingredients in container of an electric blender; process until cheese is finely crumbled. Cover and chill thoroughly. Stir well before serving. Yield: 1 cup. *Maggie Cates*
Greenville, Texas

WHITE WINE VINAIGRETTE

1 cup vegetable oil
¼ cup white wine vinegar
¼ cup lemon juice
2 teaspoons sugar
1 teaspoon salt
1 teaspoon dry mustard
½ teaspoon pepper
2 cloves garlic, peeled

Combine all ingredients in a jar; cover tightly, and shake vigorously. Chill 8 hours; remove garlic before serving. Yield: 1½ cups.

Yvonne M. Greer
Greenville, South Carolina

FRENCH DRESSING

1 cup vegetable oil
½ cup sugar
½ cup catsup
¼ cup vinegar
¼ cup chopped onion
1 teaspoon celery seeds
½ teaspoon salt

Combine all ingredients in container of an electric blender; process until smooth. Cover and chill thoroughly. Yield: 2 cups.

Sharon McClatchey
Muskogee, Oklahoma

Next Party, Serve "Mocktails"

These beverages are bubbly, tangy, and have exotic ingredients, such as cream of coconut, but they don't contain alcohol. They're part of a growing number of party punches called "mocktails" that are designed to delight all ages, especially adults limiting their consumption of alcohol.

VIRGIN SANGRÍA

1 (6-ounce) can frozen orange juice concentrate, thawed and undiluted
1 (6-ounce) can frozen unsweetened apple juice concentrate, thawed and undiluted
1 (33.8-ounce) bottle club soda, chilled
Decorative orange slices
Maraschino cherries

Combine orange juice and apple juice concentrates; stir well. Stir in chilled club soda. Serve over crushed ice. Garnish each serving with a decorative orange slice and a cherry. Yield: 5½ cups.

Romanza O. Johnson
Bowling Green, Kentucky

PARSON'S PIÑA COLADA

2 cups vanilla ice cream or ice milk
½ cup pineapple juice
¼ cup cream of coconut

Combine all ingredients in container of an electric blender; process until smooth. Serve immediately. Yield: about 2½ cups.

Bettye Cortner
Cerulean, Kentucky

PINK APPLE LIMEADE

1 (48-ounce) bottle cranberry juice, chilled
1 (32-ounce) bottle apple juice, chilled
2 (6-ounce) cans frozen limeade concentrate, thawed and undiluted
¼ cup lime juice

Combine all ingredients, stirring well; serve over crushed ice. Yield: about 3 quarts. *Elisabeth Weaver Winstead*
Nashville, Tennessee

MOCK PINK CHAMPAGNE

1 cup water
1 cup grapefruit juice
½ cup orange juice
¼ cup grenadine syrup
3½ cups ginger ale, chilled

Combine first 4 ingredients; stir well, and chill. Stir in ginger ale just before serving. Serve beverage over crushed ice. Yield: 6¼ cups.

Mrs. C. D. Marshall
Boston, Virginia

Party Tips

■ Slushes are refreshing beverages that can be made ahead and kept in the freezer. Immediately before serving slush, add carbonated beverage to the frozen base and stir.

■ To spruce up a punch bowl, add whole fruit and a fruit-filled ice ring of the same ingredients used in the punch.

■ Make ice cubes for a party ahead of time and store in plastic bags in the freezer. Count on 350 cubes for 50 people or 7 cubes per person.

■ Use muffin pans to make extra large ice cubes for punch.

■ The key to the best tasting coffee is buying fresh coffee beans and grinding them just before brewing.

■ When making coffee for your next party, allow 1 pound of coffee and 2 gallons of water for 40 servings.

Give Grits A Topping

You'll have to stay south of the Mason-Dixon line to enjoy these dishes. Our readers have paired two saucy entrées with grits, and the results are delicious!

GRILLADES AND GRITS

1 (4-pound) veal or beef boneless
    rump roast
½ cup bacon drippings, divided
½ cup all-purpose flour
1 cup chopped onion
2 cups chopped green onions
¾ cup chopped celery
1½ cups chopped green pepper
2 cloves garlic, minced
2 cups peeled and chopped
    tomatoes
½ teaspoon tarragon leaves
1 teaspoon dried whole thyme
1 cup water
1 cup Burgundy or other dry red
    wine
1 teaspoon salt
½ teaspoon pepper
2 bay leaves
½ teaspoon hot sauce
2 tablespoons Worcestershire
    sauce
3 tablespoons chopped fresh
    parsley
Garlic-Cheese Grits

Remove fat from meat; cut meat into ½-inch slices. Sauté 2 to 3 minutes on each side or until browned in ¼ cup bacon drippings in a heavy Dutch oven. Remove to platter, and repeat until all meat is browned. Set aside.

Add remaining ¼ cup bacon drippings to Dutch oven. Add flour; cook over medium heat, stirring constantly, until roux is the color of caramel. Add onion, green onions, and next 3 ingredients to roux, and cook until vegetables are tender. Add tomatoes, tarragon, and thyme.

Cook, stirring constantly, 3 minutes. Add water and next 6 ingredients, stirring until blended. Return meat to Dutch oven, stirring well. Bring mixture to a boil; cover, reduce heat, and simmer 1 hour, stirring occasionally. Uncover and simmer 30 minutes. Remove bay leaves; stir in parsley. Serve over Garlic-Cheese Grits. Yield: 12 servings.

Garlic-Cheese Grits

8 cups boiling water
1 teaspoon salt
2 cups uncooked quick-cooking
    grits
2 (6-ounce) rolls process cheese
    food with garlic

Bring water and salt to a boil in a Dutch oven; stir in grits. Return to a boil; reduce heat, and cook 4 minutes, stirring occasionally. Add cheese, stirring until melted. Yield: 12 servings.
Mary Hamblen
New Orleans, Louisiana

SHRIMP STEW OVER GRITS

2 (10¾-ounce) cans cream of
    celery soup, undiluted
1 medium-size green pepper,
    diced
1 medium onion, chopped
1 tablespoon Worcestershire
    sauce
1 tablespoon hot sauce
1 bay leaf
⅛ teaspoon pepper
1 (16-ounce) package peeled
    frozen small shrimp
Cooked buttered grits

Combine first 7 ingredients in a Dutch oven; stir well. Bring to a boil over medium heat; reduce heat, and simmer, uncovered, 20 minutes. Add shrimp, and cook 5 to 7 minutes, stirring occasionally. Remove bay leaf. Serve over buttered grits. Yield: 8 servings. *Harry M. Bayne*
Oxford, Mississippi

Tame Appetites With A Hearty Dip

Don't be caught defenseless when the family gathers after work or school and dinner's not ready yet; one of these hot-and-hearty dips will tame appetites and allow time to get supper on the table.

These recipes are just the right consistency for dipping immediately after they're cooked but will thicken a little as they cool. If you plan to keep them at room temperature very long, serve in a chafing dish to keep them warm.

CHILI DIP

1 pound ground beef
¼ cup chopped onion
1 (12-ounce) bottle chili sauce
1 (15-ounce) can chili without
    beans
2 (11¼-ounce) cans chili beef
    soup
½ cup (2 ounces) shredded
    Cheddar cheese

Cook ground beef and onion in a large skillet until meat is browned, stirring to crumble. Drain. Stir in chili sauce, chili, and soup. Spoon into a 1¾-quart baking dish; bake, uncovered, at 350° for 20 minutes. Sprinkle with cheese. Serve hot with tortilla chips. Yield: 6 cups.

Note: Dip thickens as it cools. Stir in a little boiling water to thin dip, if necessary. *Marilyn Campbell*
Orlando, Florida

HOT SPINACH-CHEESE DIP

2 (10-ounce) packages frozen
  chopped spinach
¼ cup butter or margarine
2 tablespoons all-purpose flour
½ cup evaporated milk
½ teaspoon pepper
¾ teaspoon garlic powder
¾ teaspoon celery salt
1 teaspoon Worcestershire sauce
2 tablespoons diced onion
1 (6-ounce) roll jalapeño cheese,
  cubed
½ cup soft breadcrumbs
1 teaspoon butter or margarine,
  melted

Cook spinach according to package directions, omitting salt. Drain spinach thoroughly, reserving ½ cup liquid. Set aside.

Melt ¼ cup butter in a saucepan over low heat; add flour, stirring until smooth. Cook 1 minute, stirring constantly. Add reserved spinach liquid, milk, and next 6 ingredients, stirring until cheese melts.

Spoon mixture into a lightly greased 1½-quart casserole. Combine soft breadcrumbs and 1 teaspoon melted butter; sprinkle over spinach mixture. Bake at 350° for 25 minutes or until thoroughly heated. Serve hot with crackers or raw vegetables. Yield: about 4½ cups.

Amy Godfrey
Houston, Texas

YELLOW SQUASH-ZUCCHINI DIP

4 medium-size yellow squash,
  chopped
4 medium zucchini, chopped
1 large onion, chopped
2 tablespoons butter or
  margarine, melted
1 (6-ounce) roll garlic cheese,
  cubed
1 (6-ounce) roll jalapeño cheese,
  cubed
1 (11-ounce) can Cheddar cheese
  soup, undiluted

Sauté first 3 ingredients in butter in a Dutch oven until crisp-tender. Add garlic cheese and remaining ingredients, stirring until blended and thoroughly heated. Serve dip warm with tortilla chips. Yield: 6 cups.

Pat Rush Benigno
Gulfport, Mississippi

HOT CLAM DIP

1 (6½-ounce) can minced clams,
  undrained
1 (8-ounce) package cream
  cheese, cubed
1 tablespoon butter or margarine
¼ teaspoon Worcestershire sauce
Dash of hot sauce

Drain clams, reserving juice. Set clams aside.

Combine clam juice and remaining ingredients in a saucepan; cook over low heat until cream cheese melts, stirring occasionally. Stir in minced clams. Serve dip hot with crackers. Yield: 1¼ cups.

Lestine Reeves
Belmont, North Carolina

HOT MUSHROOM DIP

1 pound fresh mushrooms, sliced
1 clove garlic, minced
¼ cup butter or margarine,
  melted
2 tablespoons dried whole parsley
1 tablespoon lemon juice
½ teaspoon salt
¼ teaspoon pepper
1 (8-ounce) carton commercial
  sour cream

Sauté mushrooms and garlic in butter in a large skillet until crisp-tender; continue cooking, stirring constantly, until all liquid evaporates. Add parsley and remaining ingredients; cook over low heat, stirring constantly, until thoroughly heated. Serve warm with crackers. Yield: 2 cups.

Marcia St. Clair
Hixson, Tennessee

Coleslaw Is Always A Southern Favorite

Coleslaw, often considered a summertime salad, is a good choice throughout the year. It's appreciated when served with barbecue and seafood as well as hot soups and stews. It's easily made in a food processor.

CONFETTI SLAW

1 small purple onion
3 cups shredded cabbage
1 cup shredded carrot
¼ cup thinly sliced radishes
½ cup commercial sour cream
¼ teaspoon garlic salt
1 whole radish with stem
  (optional)

Thinly slice onion, and separate into rings. Combine onion and next 3 ingredients in a medium bowl. Add sour cream and garlic salt; stir gently to coat. Serve immediately. Garnish with whole radish, if desired. Yield: 6 servings.

Jodie McCoy
Tulsa, Oklahoma

MEXICAN COLESLAW

3 cups shredded white cabbage
1 cup shredded red cabbage
¼ cup mayonnaise
¼ cup commercial sour cream
2 tablespoons vinegar
1 teaspoon sugar
1 teaspoon chili powder

Combine cabbages in a medium bowl. Combine mayonnaise and remaining ingredients in a small bowl; stir well. Pour dressing over cabbage; toss gently. Cover and chill before serving. Yield: 6 servings.

Betty Bierman
Brady, Texas

FREEZER COLESLAW

1 cup sugar
1 cup vinegar
1 cup water
½ teaspoon celery seeds
1 medium cabbage, shredded
  (about 8 cups)
1 large carrot, shredded
½ cup chopped green pepper
½ cup chopped sweet red pepper
1 medium onion, finely chopped
1 teaspoon salt

Combine first 4 ingredients in a saucepan; bring to a boil, stirring occasionally. Boil 1 minute. Cool to room temperature.

Combine shredded cabbage and remaining ingredients in a large bowl, and stir well. Pour dressing over cabbage mixture; toss gently. Pack coleslaw into 4 (1-pint) freezer containers, leaving ½ inch headspace. Cover and freeze. Store in freezer up to 1 month. Thaw coleslaw at room temperature 3 hours before serving. Yield: 4 pints.

Romanza O. Johnson
Bowling Green, Kentucky

CREAMY CUCUMBER SLAW

2 cups shredded cabbage
¼ cup sliced green onions
¼ cup sliced radishes
2 tablespoons chopped fresh
  parsley
1 small cucumber, peeled, seeded,
  and cubed
½ cup commercial sour cream
1 tablespoon lemon juice
1 tablespoon sugar
½ teaspoon prepared mustard
¼ teaspoon salt
½ teaspoon celery seeds
4 slices bacon, cooked and
  crumbled

Combine first 4 ingredients; cover and chill.

Combine cucumber and next 5 ingredients in container of an electric blender; process until smooth. Stir in celery seeds. Cover and chill.

Combine cabbage mixture and dressing just before serving. Sprinkle with bacon. Yield: 4 servings.

Carrie Treichel
Johnson City, Tennessee

HOT SLAW

4 slices bacon
1 teaspoon sugar
¼ teaspoon salt
¼ teaspoon pepper
3 tablespoons vinegar
6 cups shredded cabbage
1 cup chopped tomato
1 cup peeled and chopped
  cucumber
½ cup sliced green onions

Cook bacon in a skillet until crisp; remove bacon, reserving 3 tablespoons drippings in skillet. Crumble cooked bacon, and set aside. Add sugar, salt, pepper, and vinegar to pan drippings, stirring well; cook over medium heat until boiling.

Combine cabbage and remaining ingredients in a large bowl; add vinegar mixture, and toss gently. Sprinkle bacon over slaw, and serve immediately. Yield: 8 to 10 servings.

Olene Garrison
Johnson City, Tennessee

Add Old-Fashioned Buttermilk Flavor

Years ago when thick, slightly tart buttermilk was the by-product of churning butter from milk, thrifty Southerners soon found dozens of ways to use it.

If you don't use buttermilk often enough to keep it on hand, then use buttermilk powder. It comes in a can and will keep at least a year if stored in the refrigerator.

The powder can be stirred into recipes such as Whole Wheat Potato Rolls or used as a substitute for fresh buttermilk. To substitute buttermilk powder, use 1 cup of liquid, such as water, and ¼ cup of powder for 1 cup of fresh buttermilk. In baked recipes, add the powder with the dry ingredients and the additional liquid with the other liquids.

LEMON-BUTTERMILK CUSTARDS

¾ cup sugar
3 tablespoons cornstarch
1½ cups buttermilk
2 tablespoons butter or margarine
3 eggs, separated
1½ teaspoons lemon rind
¼ cup lemon juice
¼ cup sugar
Lemon twists

Combine ¾ cup sugar and cornstarch in a heavy saucepan; stir well. Add buttermilk, and cook over low heat, stirring constantly, until thickened. Stir in butter.

Combine egg yolks, lemon rind, and juice; beat well. Gradually stir about one-fourth of hot mixture into yolks; add to remaining hot mixture, stirring constantly. Cook over low heat, stirring constantly, 4 minutes or until smooth and thickened. Spoon mixture into four (10-ounce) ungreased custard cups.

Beat egg whites (at room temperature) in a large bowl at high speed of an electric mixer until foamy. Gradually add ¼ cup sugar, 1 tablespoon at a time, beating until stiff peaks form. Spread meringue over custard surface, making sure edges are sealed.

Bake at 400° for 2 to 3 minutes or until meringue peaks are lightly browned. Garnish with lemon twists. Yield: 4 servings. *Merle R. Downs*
Tryon, North Carolina

BUTTERMILK PANCAKES WITH FRUIT TOPPING

1 egg
1 cup self-rising flour
¼ teaspoon baking soda
1 tablespoon sugar
¾ cup buttermilk
2 tablespoons vegetable oil
Fruit Topping

Beat egg. Combine flour, soda, and sugar; add to egg. Add buttermilk and oil, beating until mixture is smooth.

For each pancake, pour about 2 tablespoons batter onto a hot, lightly greased griddle. Turn pancakes when tops are covered with bubbles and edges are cooked. Serve with Fruit Topping. Yield: 12 (3-inch) pancakes.

Fruit Topping

1 (8¾-ounce) can sliced peaches, undrained
½ cup apricot preserves
2 tablespoons butter or margarine
1 teaspoon lemon juice
¼ teaspoon vanilla extract
8 maraschino cherries, cut in half
1 banana, cut into ¼-inch slices

Drain peaches, reserving ¼ cup liquid. Combine peaches, ¼ cup peach liquid, and next 5 ingredients in a small saucepan. Bring mixture to a boil; reduce heat, and simmer 5 minutes. Remove from heat, and stir in banana slices. Yield: 2 cups.
Kim Shelton
Snow Camp, North Carolina

BUTTERMILK COFFEE CAKE

3 cups all-purpose flour
½ teaspoon salt
2 cups sugar
1 teaspoon ground cinnamon
1 teaspoon ground nutmeg
1 teaspoon ground cloves
¾ cup shortening
2 teaspoons baking soda
2 cups buttermilk
½ cup raisins
½ cup chopped pecans

Combine first 6 ingredients in a large mixing bowl; cut in shortening with a pastry blender until mixture resembles coarse meal. Reserve 1 cup crumb mixture for topping.

Dissolve soda in buttermilk; add to crumb mixture. Stir until smooth. Stir in raisins and pecans.

Pour batter into 2 greased and floured 9-inch round cakepans; sprinkle half of reserved crumb mixture over each. Bake at 350° for 30 to 35 minutes. Serve warm or cool. Yield: 2 (9-inch) cakes.
Ellen Davies
Richmond, Virginia

WHOLE WHEAT POTATO ROLLS

2 cups whole wheat flour
1 cup instant potato flakes
¼ cup buttermilk powder
1 package dry yeast
2 tablespoons sugar
2 teaspoons salt
2 cups warm water (120° to 130°)
¼ cup butter or margarine, softened
2 eggs
2½ to 3½ cups all-purpose flour
Melted butter

Combine first 6 ingredients in a large mixing bowl. Add water, ¼ cup butter, and eggs; beat at low speed of an electric mixer until moistened. Beat at medium speed 2 minutes. Gradually stir in enough flour to make a soft dough. Turn dough out onto a floured board, and let rest 5 minutes. Knead until smooth and elastic (5 to 8 minutes). Place dough in a well-greased bowl, turning to coat top. Cover and let rise in a warm place (85°), free from drafts, 1 hour or until doubled in bulk.

Punch dough down, and divide in half. Divide each half of dough into 12 pieces; shape each into a ball. Place 12 balls of dough in a lightly greased 9-inch round cakepan. Repeat procedure with remaining dough. Cover and let rise in a warm place, free from drafts, 30 minutes or until doubled in bulk. Bake at 400° for 20 to 25 minutes or until golden brown. Brush rolls with melted butter. Yield: 2 dozen.

Peanut Petits Fours

What makes Nutty Cakes special? It's the mingling of crunchy, toasted peanuts and creamy, coffee-flavored frosting that coats squares of mellow angel food cake.

NUTTY CAKES

1 (8-ounce) loaf angel food cake
2 teaspoons instant coffee granules
¼ cup hot water
½ cup plus 1 tablespoon butter, softened
1 (16-ounce) package powdered sugar, sifted
3 cups roasted peanuts, coarsely chopped

Using an electric knife, slice cake into 2 layers; cut each layer into 10 (1¼-inch) squares.

Dissolve coffee granules in hot water; set aside.

Cream butter at medium speed of an electric mixer; gradually add about one-third of powdered sugar, beating well. Add 2 tablespoons coffee mixture and remaining powdered sugar; mix well. Gradually add remaining coffee mixture, beating until spreading consistency.

Spread each side of cake squares with a thin layer of frosting; roll in peanuts. Yield: 20 (1½-inch) cakes.
Beth Hassey
Montgomery, Alabama

MARCH

Like good Southern cooks, this chapter offers a wide range
of recipes. Rich, lavishly frosted cake recipes passed from
generation to generation share top billing with an old
Southern favorite, catfish, served up new ways.

Catfish—Old Favorite, New Ways

No longer is the catfish solely assigned to the frying pan. Instead, it's lightly seasoned and baked, microwaved with a little butter and lemon juice, breaded with seasoned cracker crumbs, and more. Gone is the perception of catfish as a tough-skinned, flat-nosed scavenger.

Aquaculture, the practice of farming live fish in a controlled environment, pushed the farm-raised catfish to culinary prominence. George Williams, executive vice president of Catfish Farmers of America, says, "We're stressing the mild-flavored, textured white meat that's very versatile. The catfish are raised in a controlled environment of fresh water, where they eat grain and feed from the surface of the water."

This growing environment (in contrast to an uncontrolled pond or lake) lends a mild flavor and improved texture to the farm-raised catfish that can be harvested year-round. George says, "This way, we can produce a quality, nutritional product that is low in calories, fat, and cholesterol."

As a result, this mild-flavored, nutritious old favorite is popping up on restaurant menus across the country. And in homes, cooks are inspired to prepare it in fresh new ways.

SPICY CATFISH AMANDINE
(pictured on page 73)

¼ cup butter or margarine, melted
3 tablespoons lemon juice
6 (6-ounce) catfish fillets
1½ teaspoons Creole seasoning
½ cup sliced almonds

Combine butter and lemon juice; dip each fillet in butter mixture, and arrange in a 13- x 9- x 2-inch baking dish. Sprinkle fish with Creole seasoning and almonds. Bake at 375° for 25 to 30 minutes or until fish flakes easily when tested with a fork. Yield: 6 servings.   *Lucille James*
New Orleans, Louisiana

MICROWAVE CATFISH

4 (6-ounce) catfish fillets
2 tablespoons butter or margarine, melted
⅛ teaspoon garlic powder
1 tablespoon lemon-pepper seasoning

Brush fillets with butter; arrange in a 12- x 8- x 2-inch baking dish, placing meatier portions of fish toward outside edges of dish. Combine garlic powder and lemon-pepper seasoning; sprinkle over fillets. Cover tightly with heavy-duty plastic wrap; fold back a small edge of wrap to allow steam to escape. Microwave at MEDIUM HIGH (70% power) 4½ minutes. Rotate dish, and rearrange fish in dish. Cover and microwave at MEDIUM HIGH 4½ minutes or until fish turns opaque. Let stand, covered, 3 to 5 minutes. Yield: 4 servings.   *Jimmy Spencer*
Demopolis, Alabama

CATFISH WITH CREAM CHEESE STUFFING

4 (6- to 8-ounce) catfish fillets
1 teaspoon lemon juice
¼ teaspoon pepper
8 slices bacon
1 cup soft breadcrumbs
3 tablespoons cream cheese, softened
1 tablespoon lemon juice
1 tablespoon finely chopped celery
1 tablespoon finely chopped onion
1 tablespoon dried parsley flakes
1 teaspoon ground thyme
¼ teaspoon salt
¼ teaspoon pepper

Sprinkle fillets with 1 teaspoon lemon juice and ¼ teaspoon pepper; set fillets aside.

Cook bacon until limp but not crisp; set aside.

Combine breadcrumbs and remaining ingredients, stirring well. Spoon one-fourth of breadcrumb mixture onto each fillet. Carefully roll up. Wrap roll with 2 slices bacon, and secure with a wooden pick. Place seam side down in a lightly greased 8-inch baking dish.

Bake, uncovered, at 350° for 25 minutes or until fish flakes easily when tested with a fork. Remove all wooden picks before serving. Yield: 4 servings.
Beth MacMillan
San Antonio, Texas

CRACKERMEAL CATFISH FINGERS

1 pound catfish fillets
½ cup all-purpose flour
¼ teaspoon salt
¼ teaspoon coarsely ground pepper
2 eggs, beaten
2 tablespoons water
¾ cup round buttery cracker crumbs
¼ cup sour cream-onion cracker crumbs
¼ cup dry breadcrumbs
Vegetable oil
Commercial tartar sauce

Cut fillets into 3- x 1- x ½-inch strips; set aside.

Combine flour, salt, and pepper; set aside.

Combine eggs and water; beat well, and set aside.

Combine cracker crumbs and breadcrumbs.

Dredge fish strips in flour mixture, dip in egg mixture, and coat with crumb mixture. Pour oil to a depth of 1½ inches into a heavy skillet. Fry about one-fourth of fish strips in hot oil (375°) over medium-high heat 1 minute or until golden. Remove and drain on paper towels; set aside. Repeat with remaining fish strips. Serve with tartar sauce. Yield: 3 to 4 servings.
Jan Perrin
Fort Worth, Texas

ON THE LIGHT SIDE

Old-Time Breads Go Light

Freshly baked cornbread, biscuits, hush puppies, and yeast breads hold a special place on Southern menus.

Lard, butter, and bacon drippings were used in many old-time Southern breads to make them tender or flaky. But today we know that these particular fats can pose health problems because they contain cholesterol as well as saturated fat.

Saturated fats are a special concern because they stimulate the body's production of cholesterol. Most saturated fats come from animal products, but some, including tropical oils (such as coconut, palm, and palm-kernel oils) and vegetable shortening, are made from plants. Even though vegetable shortening does not contain cholesterol, its high saturated-fat content makes it unacceptable for light-and-healthy eating.

The growing awareness that 60% of the diet should be complex carbohydrates secures bread's place in healthy eating. You'll have a hard time telling the difference between these lightened-up recipes and old-time favorites. The fat used is either vegetable oil or reduced-calorie margarine, and both are low in saturated fats and cholesterol.

LIGHT BISCUITS
(pictured on pages 78 and 79)

2 cups all-purpose flour
1 tablespoon baking powder
¼ teaspoon baking soda
½ teaspoon salt
¼ cup reduced-calorie margarine
1 (8-ounce) carton plain low-fat yogurt
1 teaspoon honey

Combine first 4 ingredients in a medium bowl; cut in margarine with a pastry blender until mixture resembles coarse meal. Add yogurt and honey, stirring until dry ingredients are moistened. Turn dough out onto a lightly floured surface, and knead lightly 4 or 5 times.

Roll dough to ½-inch thickness; cut with a 2-inch biscuit cutter. Place on an ungreased baking sheet. Bake at 425° for 12 minutes or until lightly browned. Yield: 2 dozen (60 calories per biscuit).

☐ *1.7 grams protein, 1.5 grams fat, 9.9 grams carbohydrate, 1 milligram cholesterol, 120 milligrams sodium, and 45 milligrams calcium.*
Judy Williams
Lewisville, Texas

BAKED HUSH PUPPIES
(pictured on pages 78 and 79)

½ cup yellow cornmeal
½ cup all-purpose flour
1½ teaspoons baking powder
½ teaspoon salt
½ teaspoon sugar
⅛ teaspoon red pepper
1 egg, beaten
⅓ cup evaporated skimmed milk
¼ cup thinly sliced green onions
2 tablespoons vegetable oil
Vegetable cooking spray

Combine first 6 ingredients in a medium bowl; make a well in center of mixture. Combine egg, milk, green onions, and oil; add to dry ingredients, stirring just until moistened. Spoon about 1 tablespoon batter into miniature (1½-inch) muffin pans coated with cooking spray. Bake at 425° for 15 to 20 minutes or until lightly browned. Remove from pans immediately. Yield: 1½ dozen (51 calories per hush puppy).

☐ *1.4 grams protein, 2.1 grams fat, 6.4 grams carbohydrate, 15 milligrams cholesterol, 100 milligrams sodium, and 33 milligrams calcium.*

CORN STICKS

(pictured on pages 78 and 79)

½ cup yellow cornmeal
½ cup all-purpose flour
2 teaspoons baking powder
¼ teaspoon salt
1 tablespoon sugar
1 egg, beaten
½ cup evaporated skimmed milk
2 tablespoons vegetable oil
Vegetable cooking spray

Combine first 5 ingredients. Add egg, milk, and oil; stir until batter is smooth. Coat a cast-iron corn stick pan with cooking spray. Heat in a 425° oven 3 minutes or until hot. Remove pan from oven; spoon batter into pan, filling two-thirds full. Bake at 425° for 10 to 12 minutes or until bread is lightly browned. Yield: 1 dozen (81 calories per corn stick).

☐ *2.4 grams protein, 3.1 grams fat, 10.7 grams carbohydrate, 23 milligrams cholesterol, 117 milligrams sodium, and 66 milligrams calcium.*

CORNMEAL YEAST BREAD

(pictured on pages 78 and 79)

2 packages dry yeast
½ cup warm water (105° to 115°)
¾ cup warm evaporated skimmed milk (105° to 115°)
⅓ cup reduced-calorie margarine, softened
⅓ cup sugar
1 teaspoon salt
1 egg
1 cup all-purpose flour
¾ cup yellow cornmeal
3 to 3½ cups all-purpose flour
Vegetable cooking spray

Dissolve yeast in warm water in a large bowl; let stand 5 minutes. Add milk, margarine, sugar, and salt; stir until margarine melts. Add egg, 1 cup flour, and cornmeal; beat at medium speed of an electric mixer until well blended. Gradually stir in enough flour to make a stiff dough.

Turn dough out onto a lightly floured surface, and knead until smooth and elastic (about 10 minutes). Place in a bowl coated with cooking spray, turning to grease top. Cover and let rise in a warm place (85°), free from drafts, 1 hour or until doubled in bulk.

Punch dough down; divide in half. Shape dough into two loaves, and place in 8½- x 4½- x 3-inch loafpans coated with cooking spray. Cover and let rise in a warm place (85°), free from drafts, 45 minutes or until doubled in bulk. Bake at 350° for 30 to 35 minutes or until loaves sound hollow when lightly tapped. Remove loaves from pans; cool on wire racks. Yield: 2 loaves or 32 servings (109 calories per ½-inch slice).

☐ *3.1 grams protein, 1.7 grams fat, 20 grams carbohydrate, 9 milligrams cholesterol, 101 milligrams sodium, and 22 milligrams calcium.*
                    Dawn C. Hendricks
                    Harwood, Maryland

FRENCH BREAD

(pictured on pages 78 and 79)

½ cup warm skim milk (105° to 115°)
2 teaspoons sugar
2 packages dry yeast
1 cup boiling water
2 tablespoons sugar
2 tablespoons reduced-calorie margarine
2 teaspoons salt
1 cup cold water
6½ to 7 cups all-purpose flour
Vegetable cooking spray
1 egg white, beaten
2 tablespoons water
2 teaspoons sesame seeds, poppy seeds, dillseeds, or caraway seeds

Combine milk, 2 teaspoons sugar, and yeast in a small bowl; let stand 5 minutes. Combine boiling water and next 3 ingredients in a large mixing bowl; stir until margarine melts. Add 1 cup cold water; cool to lukewarm (105° to 115°). Stir yeast mixture into water mixture. Add 2½ cups flour; beat at medium speed of an electric mixer until blended. Gradually stir in enough remaining flour to make a soft dough.

Let dough stand in mixing bowl 10 minutes. Stir gently for a few seconds; cover. Repeat gentle stirring every 10 minutes for 40 minutes.

Turn dough out onto a lightly floured surface; divide into fourths. Roll each portion to a 17-inch rope. Tuck ends under to seal. Place in a French bread pan coated with cooking spray. Cover and let rise in a warm place (85°), free from drafts, 40 minutes or until doubled in bulk. Make diagonal slits about ¼-inch deep down the length of loaves, using a sharp knife. Combine egg white and 2 tablespoons water in a bowl, beating until blended. Brush gently over loaves after rising. Sprinkle loaves with seeds. Bake at 400° for 20 minutes or until loaves sound hollow when tapped. Yield: 4 loaves (54 calories per 1-inch slice).

☐ *1.6 grams protein, 0.4 gram fat, 10.7 grams carbohydrate, 0 milligrams cholesterol, 74 milligrams sodium, and 6 milligrams calcium.*

Cakes— Delicious Legacies

Southerners have a knack for whipping up high and handsome cakes. These labors of love grace both elegant sideboards and kitchen tables as trademarks of a good cook and as expressions of hospitality.

Tried-and-true family recipes have been passed on from generation to generation. Here are some of those delicious legacies.

NANNY'S LANE CAKE

1 cup butter, softened
2 cups sugar
3 cups sifted cake flour
1 tablespoon plus 1 teaspoon
  baking powder
¾ cup milk
1 teaspoon vanilla extract
8 egg whites
Lane Cake Filling
Seven-Minute Frosting
Pecan halves (optional)

Cream butter; gradually add sugar, beating well at medium speed of an electric mixer. Combine flour and baking powder; add to creamed mixture alternately with milk, beginning and ending with flour mixture. Mix after each addition. Stir in vanilla.

Beat egg whites (at room temperature) until stiff peaks form; fold into batter.

Pour batter into 4 greased and floured 9-inch round cakepans. Bake at 325° for 18 minutes or until a wooden pick inserted in center comes out clean. Cool in pans 10 minutes; remove from pans, and let cool completely on wire racks. (Layers are very tender and fragile, so handle them carefully.)

Spread Lane Cake Filling between layers and on top of cake. Spread Seven-Minute Frosting on sides. Garnish with pecan halves, if desired. Yield: one 4-layer cake.

Lane Cake Filling

8 egg yolks
2 cups sugar
1 cup butter
2 cups chopped pecans
1 cup currants or chopped raisins
1 (20-ounce) can crushed
  pineapple, well drained
¼ cup bourbon

Combine egg yolks, sugar, and butter in a heavy saucepan. Cook over medium heat, stirring constantly, until thickened (about 20 minutes). Remove from heat, and stir in pecans and remaining ingredients. Cool filling completely. Yield: 3¾ cups.

Seven-Minute Frosting

1½ cups sugar
¼ cup plus 1 tablespoon cold
  water
2 egg whites
1 tablespoon light corn syrup
1 teaspoon vanilla extract

Combine all ingredients except vanilla in top of a large double boiler. Beat at low speed of an electric mixer 30 seconds or just until blended.

Place over boiling water; beat constantly at high speed 7 minutes or until stiff peaks form. Remove from heat. Add vanilla. Beat 2 minutes or until frosting is thick enough to spread. Yield: 4¼ cups.

Elsie Young
Montgomery, Alabama

CARAMEL CAKE

1 cup commercial sour cream
¼ cup milk
1 cup butter, softened
2 cups sugar
4 eggs
2¾ cups all-purpose flour
2 teaspoons baking powder
½ teaspoon salt
1 teaspoon vanilla extract
1 teaspoon rum extract
Caramel Frosting
Pecan halves (optional)
Powdered sugar (optional)

Combine sour cream and milk; set mixture aside.

Cream 1 cup butter; gradually add 2 cups sugar, beating well at medium speed of an electric mixer. Add eggs, one at a time, beating well after each addition.

Combine flour, baking powder, and salt; add to creamed mixture alternately with sour cream mixture, beginning and ending with flour mixture. Mix after each addition. Stir in flavorings. Pour batter into 2 greased and floured 9-inch round cakepans; bake at 350° for 30 to 35 minutes or until a wooden pick inserted in center comes out clean. Cool in pans 10 minutes; remove from pans, and cool on wire racks. Spread Caramel Frosting between layers and on top and sides of cake. If desired, garnish with pecan halves, and sprinkle with powdered sugar. Yield: one 2-layer cake.

Caramel Frosting

3 cups sugar, divided
1 tablespoon all-purpose flour
1 cup milk
¾ cup butter or margarine
1 teaspoon vanilla extract

Sprinkle ½ cup sugar in a shallow, heavy 3½-quart Dutch oven; place over medium heat. Cook, stirring constantly, until sugar melts (sugar will clump) and syrup is light golden brown. Remove from heat.

Combine remaining 2½ cups sugar and flour in a large saucepan, stirring well; add milk, and bring to a boil, stirring constantly.

Gradually pour one-fourth of hot mixture into caramelized sugar, stirring constantly; add remaining hot mixture (mixture will lump, but continue stirring until smooth).

Return to heat. Cover and cook over low heat 2 minutes. Uncover and cook, without stirring, over medium heat until a candy thermometer registers 238°. Add butter, stirring to blend. Remove from heat, and cool, without stirring, until temperature drops to 110° (about 1 hour). Add vanilla, and beat mixture with a wooden spoon or at medium speed of an electric mixer, until frosting reaches spreading consistency. Yield: enough to frost a 2-layer cake.

Ethelwyn Langston
Birmingham, Alabama

Tip: *Tinted coconut makes a child's cake more festive. Fill a pint jar one-third to one-half full of coconut. Add a few drops of food coloring to 1 to 2 tablespoons water, and add to coconut; cover jar, and shake well.*

CHOCOLATE CAKE WITH FUDGE FROSTING

4 (1-ounce) squares unsweetened
  chocolate
1 cup shortening
2 cups sugar
2 eggs
2 cups all-purpose flour
2 teaspoons baking powder
½ teaspoon salt
1½ cups milk
1 teaspoon vanilla extract
1 cup chopped pecans
Fudge Frosting

Place chocolate in top of a double boiler; bring water to a boil. Reduce heat to low; cook until chocolate melts. Set aside, and let cool.

Cream shortening; gradually add sugar, beating well at medium speed of an electric mixer. Add eggs, one at a time, beating well after each addition. Stir in melted chocolate.

Combine flour, baking powder, and salt; add to chocolate mixture alternately with milk, beginning and ending with flour mixture. Stir in vanilla and pecans.

Pour batter into 2 greased and floured 9-inch round cakepans. Bake at 350° for 30 to 35 minutes or until a wooden pick inserted in center comes out clean. Cool in pans 10 minutes; remove from pans, and cool completely on wire racks.

Spread Fudge Frosting between layers and on top and sides of cake. Yield: one 2-layer cake.

Cake Tips

■ For best results in cake baking, let eggs, butter, and milk reach room temperature before mixing.

■ When filling a cake, place first two layers with bottom side up; place last layer top side up.

Fudge Frosting

2 cups sugar
½ cup cocoa
¼ teaspoon salt
½ cup milk
½ cup butter or margarine
1 teaspoon vanilla extract

Combine first 3 ingredients in a heavy saucepan; stir in milk. Add butter; bring to a boil. Cover and cook over medium heat 2 minutes. Remove from heat, and stir in vanilla. Beat at medium speed of an electric mixer until spreading consistency. Yield: 2¼ cups.

Paralee C. Patton
Athens, Alabama

SOUR CREAM POUND CAKE
(pictured on page 80)

¾ cup butter or margarine,
  softened
2¼ cups sugar
4 eggs
2¼ cups all-purpose flour
⅛ teaspoon baking soda
¾ cup commercial sour cream
1 teaspoon vanilla extract
¼ teaspoon almond extract
¼ teaspoon lemon extract
Powdered sugar (optional)
Lemon slices (optional)
Grated lemon rind (optional)
Fresh mint sprigs (optional)

Cream butter; gradually add sugar, beating well at medium speed of an electric mixer. Add eggs, one at a time, beating after each addition.

Combine flour and soda; add to creamed mixture alternately with sour cream, beginning and ending with flour mixture. Mix just until blended after each addition. Stir in flavorings.

Pour batter into a greased and floured 10-inch Bundt pan. Bake at 325° for 1 hour and 5 minutes or until a wooden pick inserted in center comes out clean. Cool in pan 10 to 15 minutes; remove from pan, and let cool completely on a wire rack. If desired, sprinkle with powdered sugar and garnish with lemon slices, grated lemon rind, and mint sprigs. Yield: one 10-inch cake.

Note: Cake may be baked in a greased and floured 2½-quart Turk's-head or Kugelhopf mold for 1½ hours or until a wooden pick inserted in center comes out clean.

Mrs. M. Dykes Barber
Birmingham, Alabama

COCONUT-PINEAPPLE CAKE
(pictured on page 80)

1 cup butter or margarine,
  softened
2 cups sugar
4 eggs
3 cups sifted cake flour
1 tablespoon baking powder
¼ teaspoon salt
1 cup milk
1 teaspoon vanilla extract
1 teaspoon almond extract
Pineapple Filling
2 cups grated coconut, divided
Seven-Minute Frosting

Cream butter; gradually add sugar, beating well at medium speed of an electric mixer. Add eggs, one at a time, beating well after each addition.

Combine flour, baking powder, and salt; add to creamed mixture alternately with milk, beginning and ending with flour mixture. Mix after each addition. Stir in flavorings.

Pour batter into 3 greased and floured 9-inch round cakepans. Bake at 350° for 25 to 30 minutes or until a wooden pick inserted in center comes out clean. Cool in pans 10 minutes; remove from pans, and cool completely on wire racks.

Spread 1 layer with half of Pineapple Filling; sprinkle ⅓ cup coconut over filling. Repeat procedure with second layer, filling, and coconut. Place third layer on top, and spread Seven-Minute Frosting on top and sides of cake; sprinkle with remaining coconut. Yield: one 3-layer cake.

To prepare coconut: Carefully pierce eyes of coconut with screwdriver or ice pick; drain liquid. Place coconut in pan. Heat at 350° for 15 to 30 minutes or until cracks appear. Remove from oven; cool. Tap with hammer to open. Pare off dark skin with vegetable peeler.

Pineapple Filling

1 cup sugar
3 tablespoons all-purpose flour
2 eggs, beaten
1 (8-ounce) can crushed pineapple, undrained
2 tablespoons lemon juice
1 tablespoon butter or margarine
1 teaspoon vanilla extract

Combine sugar and flour in a small saucepan; add remaining ingredients. Cook over medium heat, stirring constantly, until thickened (about 2 minutes). Cool. Yield: 1⅓ cups.

Seven-Minute Frosting

1½ cups sugar
¼ cup plus 1 tablespoon cold water
2 egg whites
1 tablespoon light corn syrup
Dash of salt
1 teaspoon vanilla extract

Combine all ingredients except vanilla in top of a large double boiler. Beat at low speed of an electric mixer 30 seconds or just until blended.

Place over boiling water; beat constantly at high speed 7 minutes or until stiff peaks form. Remove from heat. Add vanilla; beat 2 minutes or until frosting is thick enough to spread. Yield: 4¼ cups.

Note: For the flower garnish, weave a tiny ribbon in the center of a paper doily, gather it slightly, and place a flower, with its stem cut very short, in the center. The doily prevents the flower from touching the cake.

Susan Todd
Shreveport, Louisiana

From Our Kitchen To Yours

You'll glow with anticipation when you view the cakes on page 79. If you follow these procedures, techniques, and tips, baking these desserts will be easy.

A cake batter is easily thrown off balance. Factors crucial in cake baking include accurate measuring of ingredients, proper mixing procedure, and the use of specified ingredients. Cake flour, which is sifted before measuring, produces a soft, velvety cake. You can substitute all-purpose flour for cake flour by using 2 tablespoons less per cup. Special adjustments should be made when baking with corn oil margarine, whipped butter, or whipped margarine; don't randomly substitute these products in cake recipes.

Mixing Procedure

The conventional method of mixing a cake requires more time than other methods. If the batter is undermixed, the ingredients are not evenly distributed, causing the cake to fall. If the batter is overmixed, the cake will not rise properly and will be tough and dry. The solid fat, creamed until soft, is gradually mixed with sugar, beating at medium speed of an electric mixer about seven minutes to incorporate air.

Add large whole eggs or egg yolks one at a time, and blend into the creamed mixture after each addition; do not overbeat. The combined dry ingredients are added to the creamed mixture alternately with the liquid in about four portions; begin and end with the flour mixture, mixing about 10 seconds after each addition, until the mixture is smooth. Do not overbeat. Adding stiffly beaten egg whites to the batter is the last step in mixing many cakes. Using a rubber spatula, gently fold whites vertically down through the middle of the batter. Slide the spatula across the bottom of the bowl, bring some of the batter up, and then fold over the whites until evenly blended.

Baking Techniques

Shiny, metal cakepans produce the lightest, tenderest cakes; darkened metal or enamel pans can cause uneven and excessive browning. Use pans of the size specified in the recipe; incorrect pan size can cause the cake to be flat and shrunken or rise to a peak and fall. Grease bottom and sides of pans with shortening; do not use butter, margarine, or oil. Dust greased pan with flour.

Bake cake in a preheated oven with the rack positioned in the center. Stagger the pans so that they do not touch each other or the sides of the oven. Always keep the oven door closed until the minimum baking time has passed. Before removing the cake from the oven, test for doneness. When a wooden pick inserted in the center comes out clean, or the cake springs back when lightly touched, it is done. If the wooden pick is not clean, bake an additional five minutes, and check again for doneness. Let cake cool in the pan 10 to 15 minutes. Loosen edges with spatula, and invert the cake on a wire rack to cool completely before storing or frosting.

Frosting and Storing

Before frosting a cake, lightly brush loose crumbs from top and sides. Place three or four strips of wax paper over the edges of the cake plate. If the cake is two or more layers, place the first layer bottom side up. Spread on frosting or filling; place the last layer top side up. Spread a thin layer of frosting on the sides to set any remaining crumbs. Frost the sides, then the top. Carefully pull out wax paper.

Cut uniform slices with an electric knife or a serrated-edge knife.

Cool cakes thoroughly before storing; if covered while warm, cakes may become sticky. Cakes with fluffy frostings are best eaten the day they are made because this type frosting gradually disintegrates during storage. However, leftovers can be stored under a cake dome or a large inverted bowl with a knife under the edge keeping the dome slightly ajar

Cake Problems and Causes

If cake falls:
Oven not hot enough
Undermixing
Insufficient baking
Opening oven door during
    baking
Too much leavening, liquid,
    or sugar

If cake peaks in center:
Oven too hot at start of baking
Too much flour
Not enough liquid

If cake sticks to pan:
Cake cooled in pan too long
Pan not greased and floured
    properly

If cake cracks and falls apart:
Removed from pan too soon
Too much shortening, leaven-
    ing, or sugar

If crust is sticky:
Insufficient baking
Oven not hot enough
Too much sugar

If texture is heavy:
Overmixing when flour and
    liquid added
Oven temperature too low
Too much shortening, sugar,
    or liquid

If texture is coarse:
Inadequate mixing or creaming
Oven temperature too low
Too much leavening

If texture is dry:
Overbaking
Overbeaten egg whites
Too much flour or leavening
Not enough shortening
    or sugar

---

so that air can circulate. Store cakes with whipped cream or cream cheese frostings or fillings in the refrigerator. Unfrosted cakes and cakes with creamy-type frostings store easily under a cake dome, or they can be covered well with plastic wrap. Before using the plastic wrap, insert wooden picks into the cake in several places to prevent the wrap from marring the frosted surface.

Unfrosted cakes freeze up to five months. When completely cool, wrap in aluminum foil, and then in plastic wrap. Thaw cakes in their wrappers at room temperature about one hour.

A cake frosted with a creamy-type frosting will freeze up to three months. Place the cake, uncovered, in the freezer for several hours or until frozen. Loosely but thoroughly wrap with plastic wrap, and return to freezer. To thaw, unwrap the cake immediately when removed from freezer, and let stand at room temperature until thawed (two to three hours). A cake with a whipped cream or a cream cheese frosting is thawed unwrapped in the refrigerator for about four hours. Do not freeze cake batters and cakes with meringue-type frostings.

Raisins—Nature's Convenience Food

Clusters of grapes are picked and arranged on paper trays that are placed on the warm ground in the vineyard. Then nature does its magic to the fruit. The sun's rays transform juicy, green grapes into tangy, sweet, dark raisins.

Raisins, appreciated for their natural sweet flavor and abundant nutrients, are loaded with carbohydrates, the body's most efficient source of energy. They are perfect for nutritious snacks and easy to incorporate in recipes.

Once a package is opened, transfer raisins to an airtight container and refrigerate or store in a cool, dry place. If raisins form sugar crystals or become dry, place them in a colander; cover the colander, place it over boiling water, and steam raisins five minutes.

RAISIN SAUCE

½ cup golden raisins
½ cup water
⅓ cup red currant jelly
½ teaspoon grated lemon rind
¼ teaspoon salt
¼ teaspoon ground allspice
¼ cup orange juice
2 teaspoons cornstarch

Combine first 6 ingredients in a heavy saucepan; bring to a boil, stirring until jelly melts.

Combine orange juice and cornstarch, stirring until blended; gradually stir into raisin mixture. Bring to a boil over medium heat; cook 1 minute, stirring constantly. Serve with ham. Yield: 1 cup.   *Lenah Elliott*
Destin, Florida

APPLE-RAISIN BRANDY PIE

⅓ cup brandy
1 tablespoon lemon juice
1⅓ cups golden raisins
½ cup firmly packed brown sugar
3 tablespoons all-purpose flour
5 cups peeled, sliced cooking
    apples
1 unbaked 9-inch pastry shell
½ cup all-purpose flour
½ cup firmly packed brown sugar
½ teaspoon ground nutmeg
¼ cup butter, softened
Grapes (optional)
Lemon rind (optional)

Combine brandy and lemon juice in a saucepan; cook mixture until thoroughly heated. Add raisins, and simmer 3 minutes. Set aside, stirring occasionally.

Combine ½ cup brown sugar and 3 tablespoons flour in a large bowl, mixing well. Add apples, tossing to coat. Stir in raisin mixture. Spoon mixture into pastry shell.

Combine ½ cup flour, ½ cup brown sugar, and nutmeg; cut in butter with a pastry blender until mixture resembles coarse meal; sprinkle over pie. Bake at 375° for 45 minutes. Serve warm. If desired, garnish with grapes and lemon rind. Yield: one 9-inch pie.   *H. W. Asbell*
Leesburg, Florida

The Best Of Oatmeal Cookies

In this day of New American cuisine and fancy plates decked with food that looks like art, there's still something that's both secure and wonderful about a plain, brown oatmeal cookie.

But if you'd like a twist on this old Southern favorite, try Oat Brownies. Or how about adding a hint of citrus to the oatmeal flavor? That's what one of our readers did with her Oatmeal Sunshine Cookies.

GRANOLA GORP

3 cups natural granola cereal
1 (3-ounce) can chow mein noodles
1 cup salted peanuts
¼ cup butter or margarine, melted
1 cup raisins
½ cup dried banana chips
½ cup dried apple chips, chopped
½ cup semisweet chocolate morsels

Combine granola, chow mein noodles, and peanuts; stir well. Spread mixture evenly in a 15- x 10- x 1-inch jellyroll pan; pour butter over granola mixture.

Bake, uncovered, at 350° for 15 minutes, stirring every 5 minutes. Let cool. Stir in raisins, banana chips, apple chips, and chocolate morsels. Store mixture in an airtight container in a cool, dry place. Yield: about 7½ cups. *Mandy R. Williams*
Belton, South Carolina

OAT BROWNIES

½ teaspoon instant coffee granules
¼ cup water
½ cup butter or margarine
¼ cup cocoa
¼ cup quick-cooking oats, uncooked
2 eggs
¾ cup sugar
Dash of salt
1 tablespoon vanilla extract
¾ cup all-purpose flour
½ teaspoon baking powder

Combine coffee granules and water in a heavy saucepan; stir until granules dissolve. Add butter and cocoa; cook over low heat until butter melts and mixture is smooth, stirring constantly. Stir in oats; remove from heat. Cool.

Beat eggs; gradually add sugar, beating constantly with a wire whisk until smooth and slightly thickened. Stir in chocolate mixture, salt, and vanilla. Combine flour and baking powder; stir into chocolate mixture. Spoon batter into a lightly greased 9-inch square baking pan. Bake at 350° for 20 minutes or until a wooden pick inserted in center comes out clean. Cool and cut into squares. Yield: 20 brownies.
Ella C. Stivers
Houston, Texas

OATMEAL SUNSHINE COOKIES

½ cup butter or margarine, softened
1 cup firmly packed brown sugar
1 egg
1 cup all-purpose flour
½ teaspoon baking soda
½ teaspoon salt
1 tablespoon grated orange or lime rind
2 tablespoons orange or lime juice
1½ cups regular oats, uncooked
½ cup raisins
¼ cup chopped pecans

Cream butter; gradually add sugar, beating at medium speed of an electric mixer until light and fluffy. Add egg, and beat well.

Combine flour, soda, and salt; add to creamed mixture, mixing well. Stir in rind, juice, oats, raisins, and chopped pecans.

Drop dough by rounded teaspoonfuls onto greased cookie sheets. Bake at 350° for 10 to 12 minutes or until lightly browned. Let cool slightly on cookie sheets; remove cookies to wire racks to cool completely. Yield: about 4 dozen.
Charlotte Pierce
Greensburg, Kentucky

OATS-AND-PEANUT COOKIES

1 cup shortening
¾ cup sugar
¾ cup firmly packed dark brown sugar
2 eggs
2 teaspoons hot water
2 cups quick-cooking oats, uncooked
1¼ cups all-purpose flour
1 teaspoon baking soda
1 teaspoon salt
1½ cups raisins
1 (8-ounce) package candy-coated chocolate pieces with peanuts

Cream shortening; gradually add sugars, beating well at medium speed of an electric mixer. Add eggs and water, beating well.

Combine oats, flour, soda, and salt; add to creamed mixture, mixing well. Stir in raisins and candy.

Drop dough by rounded teaspoonfuls onto greased cookie sheets. Bake at 375° for 9 to 10 minutes or until lightly browned. Cool slightly on cookie sheets; remove to wire racks to cool completely. Yield: 6 dozen.

Opal Habeeb
Mobile, Alabama

Pralines
For Dessert

If you like the flavor of homemade pralines, don't just enjoy them as a sugary-flavored candy. Carol Barclay of Portland, Texas, crumbles the pecan-studded candy to serve in her recipe for Praline Freeze. Even without adding the homemade pralines, the ice cream mixture is a great dessert to have on hand for unexpected company.

Remember that it's important to cook the candy mixture in a heavy saucepan. Also, if it's a humid day, the candy may have a more sugary texture. Best results generally occur when the weather is dry.

PRALINE FREEZE

½ gallon vanilla ice cream, softened
½ cup praline liqueur
1 cup whipping cream
2 tablespoons sugar
Pralines (recipe follows)

Combine ice cream and liqueur in a large bowl. Spoon mixture into a 13- x 9- x 2-inch pan, and freeze.

Beat whipping cream until foamy; gradually add sugar, beating until soft peaks form.

Using an ice cream scoop, spoon ice cream mixture into individual compotes; sprinkle with crumbled pralines, and top with whipped cream. Yield: 8 servings.

Pralines

1½ cups sugar
¾ cup firmly packed brown sugar
¼ cup plus 2 tablespoons butter or margarine
½ cup half-and-half
2 cups pecan halves

Combine all ingredients in a large heavy saucepan. Cook over low heat, stirring gently, until sugar dissolves. Cover and cook over medium heat 2 to 3 minutes to wash sugar crystals from sides of pan. Uncover and cook to soft ball stage (235°), stirring constantly. Remove from heat, and beat with a wooden spoon just until mixture begins to thicken. Working rapidly, drop by tablespoonfuls onto greased wax paper; let stand until firm. Yield: 1½ dozen.

Appetizers
Invite A Party

Even if you buy the best wine or the finest sparkling water, guests will often judge a party by the food that's served. With the appetizers offered here, you can please even the pickiest guests. These recipes make tasty preludes to a casual dinner or an elegant party.

TANGY TAMALE BALLS

2 (16-ounce) cans tomatoes, undrained and pureed
1½ teaspoons chili powder
½ teaspoon salt
½ pound ground pork
½ pound ground beef
¾ cup cornmeal
2 tablespoons all-purpose flour
⅓ cup tomato juice
2 small cloves garlic, crushed
1½ teaspoons chili powder
1 teaspoon salt

Combine first 3 ingredients in a saucepan; bring mixture to a boil over medium heat.

Combine ground pork and remaining ingredients, mixing well. Shape into 1-inch balls, and add to sauce. Simmer meatballs 1 hour. Serve in a chafing dish. Yield: 4 dozen meatballs.

Sandy Hamilton
Kingwood, Texas

CRANBERRY FRUIT DIP

1 (6-ounce) carton vanilla yogurt
½ cup cranberry-orange relish
¼ teaspoon ground nutmeg
¼ teaspoon ground ginger

Combine all ingredients, mixing well. Cover and chill. Serve with fresh fruit. Yield: 1 cup.

Kathleen Schoenfelder
Bradenton, Florida

SESAME CHICKEN
APPETIZERS

½ cup soy sauce
2 tablespoons sesame oil
1 teaspoon ground ginger
3 green onions or scallions,
    sliced
2 cloves garlic, minced
4 chicken breast halves, skinned
    and boned
½ cup sesame seeds
Commercial sweet-and-sour sauce

Combine first 5 ingredients in a small
bowl; stir well. Cut each chicken
breast half into 4 strips. Add chicken
to marinade; cover and chill 1 hour.

Remove chicken from marinade;
weave 1 chicken strip on each of 16
skewers. Coat with sesame seeds;
place on rack in a broiler pan. Broil 4
to 5 inches from heat for 3 minutes;
turn skewers. Broil 3 minutes or
until done. Serve with sweet-and-
sour sauce. Yield: 16 appetizer
servings.   *Margee Striler*
                Kirkwood, Missouri

Wild About
Mushrooms

Horticulturists warn you not to pick
wild mushrooms that occasionally dot
your lawn, but you can have a lot of
fun picking those that are popping up
in supermarkets across the South.

The most popular varieties available in the South include enoki, shiitake, oyster, chanterelle, morel, and
cepe mushrooms. (See page 77 for
identification photographs.) The first
four are available fresh almost year-
round, and the latter two are almost
always found in the dried form.

When selecting fresh mushrooms,
be sure to touch and smell them.
Reject those that seem very moist or
that give off an unpleasant odor because their deterioration process has
probably begun.

Never wash fresh mushrooms
prior to storing them. Place different
varieties separately in paper sacks in
the refrigerator, as some types deteriorate faster than others. They'll
keep three to five days.

Dried mushrooms substitute nicely
for fresh in any dish that is to be
cooked. The cost of dried mushrooms may seem high, but their volume will increase greatly as they are
rehydrated; you won't have to use as
much of the dried. You can substitute
2 ounces of dried mushrooms for 6
ounces of fresh.

Dried mushrooms will keep their
quality for several months. Store in
airtight bags to keep them from re-
absorbing moisture.

Rehydrate dried mushrooms prior
to cooking by soaking them in warm
water 15 minutes. Then drain and
rinse the mushrooms well under running water to remove sand particles.
Cover them again with warm water,
and allow them to stand for five minutes. Drain and rinse well; pat dry
with paper towels.

CREAMED OYSTER
MUSHROOMS

1 pound fresh oyster mushrooms
⅓ cup finely chopped onion
1 clove garlic, minced
½ cup butter or margarine,
    melted
2½ tablespoons all-purpose flour
1 cup whipping cream
⅓ cup dry white wine
½ teaspoon salt
¼ teaspoon pepper

Cut mushrooms in halves or fourths,
if desired.

Sauté mushrooms, onion, and garlic in butter in a large skillet until
tender; remove mushroom mixture
with a slotted spoon, reserving drippings in skillet.

Add flour to drippings in skillet,
stirring until smooth. Cook 1 minute,
stirring constantly. Gradually add
whipping cream and wine; cook over
medium heat, stirring constantly,

until thickened and bubbly. Stir in
salt, pepper, and mushrooms; cook
until thoroughly heated. Yield: 6 to 8
servings.

SHIITAKE-CHICKEN STIR-FRY

1½ teaspoons cornstarch
2 tablespoons soy sauce
1 tablespoon peanut or vegetable
    oil
¼ teaspoon pepper
6 chicken breast halves, skinned,
    boned, and cut into 1-inch
    pieces
½ pound fresh shiitake
    mushrooms
2 tablespoons peanut or vegetable
    oil
1 medium onion, quartered and
    separated
1 large clove garlic, minced
1 (6-ounce) package frozen snow
    pea pods, thawed
2½ tablespoons cornstarch
¾ cup water
¾ teaspoon chicken-flavored
    bouillon granules
⅛ teaspoon ground ginger
Hot cooked rice

Combine first 4 ingredients in a medium bowl; stir until cornstarch dissolves. Add chicken; stir gently to
coat. Cover and chill 20 minutes.

Rinse mushrooms, and pat dry
with paper towels. Remove and discard stems, and halve or quarter
mushrooms, if desired.

Pour 2 tablespoons oil around top
of preheated wok, coating sides; heat
at medium high (325°) for 2 minutes.
Add mushrooms, onion, and garlic;
stir-fry 5 minutes. Add snow peas;
stir-fry 2 minutes. Remove vegetables from wok, and set aside.

Combine 2½ tablespoons cornstarch, water, bouillon granules, and
ginger in a small bowl; stir until cornstarch dissolves. Set aside. Add
chicken mixture to wok; stir-fry 4 to
5 minutes or until chicken is done.
Return vegetables to wok. Add
bouillon mixture; stir-fry 1 minute or
until thickened. Serve over hot
cooked rice. Yield: 6 servings.

VEAL-CEPE SAUTÉ
(pictured on page 76)

2 ounces dried cepe mushrooms
1 cup all-purpose flour
1 teaspoon salt
¾ teaspoon pepper
1½ pounds thin veal cutlets
  (about 12)
⅓ cup butter or margarine
1 tablespoon butter or margarine
2 cloves garlic, minced
¾ cup Chablis or other dry white
  wine
2 tablespoons chopped fresh
  parsley

Cover mushrooms with warm water; let stand about 15 minutes. Drain and rinse mushrooms well under running water to remove sand particles. Cover with warm water, and let stand 5 minutes. Drain and rinse; pat dry with paper towels. Coarsely chop mushrooms, if desired.

Combine flour, salt, and pepper; dredge veal in mixture. Melt ⅓ cup butter in a skillet over medium heat. Add veal; cook 1 minute on each side. Drain on paper towels.

Add 1 tablespoon butter to pan drippings; add garlic and mushrooms, and sauté until tender. Add wine; cook, uncovered, over high heat about 4 minutes. Return veal to skillet, and reheat about 3 minutes. Transfer veal to a serving platter; spoon mushroom mixture over veal, and sprinkle with parsley. Yield: 6 servings.

CHANTERELLE BROWN SAUCE

1 small onion, sliced
3 tablespoons butter or
  margarine, melted
6 ounces fresh chanterelle
  mushrooms, coarsely chopped
3 tablespoons all-purpose flour
2 teaspoons beef-flavored bouillon
  granules
2 cups water
¼ teaspoon pepper

Sauté onion in butter until tender; discard onion. Add mushrooms; sauté until mushrooms are tender and butter begins to brown. Add flour, stirring until smooth. Cook 1 minute, stirring constantly. Add bouillon granules; gradually stir in water. Cook over medium heat, stirring constantly, until thickened and bubbly. Stir in pepper. Serve with beef. Yield: 2½ cups.

SPINACH-ENOKI SALAD
(pictured on page 76)

1 pound fresh spinach
2 small heads Bibb lettuce
3½ ounces fresh enoki
  mushrooms, ends trimmed
½ red onion, sliced and separated
  into rings
½ cup coarsely chopped walnuts,
  toasted
Sweet-and-Sour Dressing

Tear spinach and lettuce into bite-size pieces in a bowl. Add next 3 ingredients. Toss with Sweet-and-Sour Dressing. Yield: 8 servings.

Sweet-and-Sour Dressing

¾ cup vegetable oil
⅓ cup vinegar
⅓ cup sugar
½ teaspoon salt
¾ teaspoon celery seeds
¾ teaspoon dry mustard
1 teaspoon grated onion
1 small clove garlic, minced

Combine all ingredients in a jar. Cover tightly, and shake vigorously. Chill several hours. Shake again just before serving. Yield: 1¼ cups.

WILD RICE WITH MORELS
(pictured on page 76)

2 ounces dried morel mushrooms
1 (6-ounce) package long-grain
  and wild rice mix
1 small onion, chopped
1 cup chopped pecans
¼ cup butter or margarine,
  melted
¼ teaspoon freshly ground pepper

Cover mushrooms with warm water; let stand about 15 minutes. Drain and rinse mushrooms well under running water to remove sand particles; cover with warm water, and let stand 5 minutes. Drain and rinse; pat dry with paper towels. Coarsely chop mushrooms, if desired.

Cook wild rice mix according to package directions. Set aside.

Sauté chopped onion, mushrooms, and pecans in butter until mushrooms are tender.

Combine rice, mushroom mixture, and pepper; toss gently. Yield: about 6 servings.

MIXED MUSHROOM SAUTÉ

2 ounces dried morel mushrooms
2 ounces dried cepe mushrooms
6 ounces fresh chanterelle
  mushrooms
3 green onions, sliced
1 clove garlic, minced
⅔ cup butter or margarine,
  melted
1 teaspoon dried Italian
  seasoning
¼ teaspoon salt
¼ teaspoon pepper

Cover dried mushrooms with warm water; let stand about 15 minutes. Drain and rinse mushrooms well under running water to remove sand particles. Cover with warm water, and let stand 5 minutes. Drain and rinse; pat dry with paper towels. Slice all mushrooms, if desired.

Sauté mushrooms, green onions, and garlic in butter in a large skillet until tender. Stir in seasonings. Yield: 8 servings.

Clever Ways
With Casseroles

Over and over again, the discerning cook turns to casseroles. Whether the occasion is a casual family dinner or an elegant dinner party, casseroles are a frequent selection for the Southern menu.

SEAFOOD CASSEROLE

6 cups water
2 pounds unpeeled medium-size
   fresh shrimp
1 pound fresh crabmeat, drained
   and flaked
¼ cup dry sherry
1 (4-ounce) can sliced
   mushrooms, drained
2 tablespoons chopped green
   onions
¼ cup plus 2 tablespoons butter
   or margarine, divided
¼ cup all-purpose flour
2 cups milk
1 teaspoon Worcestershire sauce
⅛ teaspoon salt
⅛ teaspoon white pepper
⅛ teaspoon celery salt
2 egg yolks
½ cup round buttery cracker
   crumbs
Green onion brushes (optional)

Bring water to a boil; add shrimp, and cook 3 to 5 minutes. Drain well; rinse. Peel and devein shrimp.

Combine shrimp, crabmeat, and dry sherry; cover and chill mixture 30 minutes.

Sauté mushrooms and chopped green onions in 2 tablespoons butter until tender; set aside.

Melt remaining ¼ cup butter in a large saucepan; add flour, and stir until smooth. Cook 1 minute, stirring constantly. Gradually add milk; cook over medium heat, stirring constantly, until mixture is thickened and bubbly. Stir in Worcestershire sauce and seasonings.

Beat egg yolks. Gradually stir about one-fourth of hot mixture into yolks; add to remaining hot mixture, stirring constantly. Stir in mushroom mixture and seafood; spoon into a lightly greased 13- x 9- x 2-inch baking dish. Sprinkle cracker crumbs over casserole. Bake at 350° for 20 minutes or until thoroughly heated. Garnish with green onion brushes, if desired. Yield: 8 to 10 servings.

Note: Casserole may be baked in greased individual baking shells; bake at 350° for 10 minutes or until thoroughly heated.
Alice K. Liles
Sylacauga, Alabama

MEXICAN LASAGNA

1 pound ground beef
½ cup chopped celery
½ cup chopped onion
¼ cup chopped green pepper
1 (14½-ounce) can tomatoes,
   undrained and chopped
1 (10-ounce) can enchilada sauce
¼ cup sliced pitted ripe olives
⅛ teaspoon salt
1½ cups (6 ounces) shredded
   process American cheese,
   divided
1 cup cream-style cottage cheese
1 egg, beaten
½ cup vegetable oil
8 corn tortillas

Combine first 4 ingredients in a skillet; cook over medium heat, stirring to crumble meat. Drain well. Add tomatoes and next 3 ingredients; stir well. Bring mixture to a boil; reduce heat, and simmer 10 to 15 minutes, stirring occasionally. Set aside.

Combine 1 cup American cheese, cottage cheese, and egg; stir well. Set aside.

Heat oil in a skillet. Cut 2 tortillas into quarters; cook in oil until crisp. Drain and set aside. Cook remaining whole tortillas; drain and crumble.

Spoon one-third of meat mixture into a lightly greased 12- x 8- x 2-inch baking dish. Spoon half of

cheese mixture over meat mixture; top with half of crumbled tortillas. Repeat layers, ending with meat mixture. Top with quartered tortillas. Bake at 350° for 30 minutes. Sprinkle with remaining ½ cup cheese; bake an additional 5 minutes. Let stand 5 minutes. Yield: 6 servings.
Shirley Mecca
Manchester, Missouri

Casserole Garnishing Tips

■ Experiment with a variety of serving dishes, such as ramekins (single-serving-size casserole dishes), baking shells, or uniquely shaped baking dishes. Dress up a simple 12- x 8-inch casserole by wrapping or draping a colorful napkin or cloth around the outside of the dish.

■ Mix up a creative topping. Combine breadcrumbs or cracker crumbs with butter and paprika for extra taste and color. Sprinkle crumbs in diagonal stripes or other patterns across the top of the casserole.

■ Rely on the ingredient listing for clues to quick and clever garnishes. Triangles of American cheese, lemon slices, cooked shrimp, cherry tomatoes, or carrot curls are just a few of the options.

■ Embellish with a fancier garnish—tomato roses, fluted mushrooms, or green onion fans—when the occasion calls for it.

CHICKEN-AND-SHRIMP FLORENTINE

1 pound unpeeled medium-size fresh shrimp
4 chicken breast halves, skinned and boned
¼ teaspoon garlic powder
¼ teaspoon pepper
2 tablespoons butter or margarine
½ cup dry white wine
2 (10-ounce) packages frozen chopped spinach
1 (8-ounce) package cream cheese, cubed
2 tablespoons butter or margarine
2 tablespoons grated Parmesan cheese
1 (10¾-ounce) can cream of mushroom soup, undiluted
1 (10¾-ounce) can cream of celery soup, undiluted
2 tablespoons fine, dry breadcrumbs
Lemon slices, halved (optional)
Additional cooked shrimp (optional)
Fresh parsley sprigs (optional)

Peel and devein 1 pound shrimp; set shrimp aside.

Sprinkle chicken with garlic powder and pepper, and place in a lightly greased 13- x 9- x 2-inch baking pan. Dot with 2 tablespoons butter, and pour wine over top. Broil 7 inches from heat 8 to 10 minutes or until lightly browned, turning once. Add shrimp; broil 5 to 8 minutes or until shrimp turns pink, stirring once. Remove from oven; cool slightly. Drain drippings, and reserve. Cut chicken into bite-size pieces; set chicken and shrimp aside.

Cook spinach according to package directions, omitting salt; drain well between layers of paper towels. Combine cream cheese and 2 tablespoons butter in a heavy saucepan; cook over medium heat, stirring constantly, until melted. Remove from heat; stir in Parmesan cheese and spinach.

Combine reserved drippings and soups; stir well. Gently stir in spinach mixture, chicken, and shrimp.

Spoon into a lightly greased 12- x 8- x 2-inch baking dish; sprinkle breadcrumbs on top. Bake at 350° for 35 to 40 minutes or until heated. If desired, garnish with lemon slices, cooked shrimp, and parsley. Yield: 8 servings.
Margaret Shook
Metairie, Louisiana

SPINACH-CHEESE CASSEROLE

2 (10-ounce) packages frozen chopped spinach, thawed and drained
2 (16-ounce) cartons cottage cheese
6 eggs
¼ cup butter or margarine, melted
1 (8-ounce) package sharp American cheese slices, cut into pieces
¼ cup plus 2 tablespoons all-purpose flour
¼ teaspoon dried whole thyme
¼ teaspoon pepper
Additional sharp American cheese slices

Drain spinach well between layers of paper towels. Combine spinach and next 7 ingredients, stirring until blended. Spoon into a lightly greased 13- x 9- x 2-inch baking dish. Bake at 350° for 35 minutes. Cut additional cheese in half diagonally; place on casserole, and bake an additional 10 minutes. Yield: 8 to 10 servings.

Note: Casserole may be baked in greased individual ramekins. Bake at 350° for 25 minutes. Top with American cheese slices, and bake an additional 5 minutes.
Judy Oosterhous
Texarkana, Texas

A Different Pizza

A pizza revolution has hit. Gourmet pizzas have the same crisp crust as traditional pizzas, but they are sporting nontraditional toppings.

VEGETABLE PIZZA

2 cups (8 ounces) shredded Monterey Jack cheese, divided
½ recipe Crispy Pizza Crust
1 cup sliced fresh mushrooms
½ cup small broccoli flowerets
1 small zucchini, thinly sliced
1 onion, sliced and separated into rings
½ red pepper, cut into strips
1 large clove garlic, minced
1 teaspoon dried Italian seasoning
2 tablespoons vegetable oil

Sprinkle half of cheese over Crispy Pizza Crust; set aside.

Sauté vegetables, garlic, and Italian seasoning in hot oil 3 to 5 minutes or until vegetables are barely crisp-tender. Spoon vegetables evenly onto pizza. Sprinkle with remaining cheese. Bake at 450° for 5 minutes or until cheese melts. Yield: one 12-inch pizza.

Crispy Pizza Crust

1 cup warm water (105° to 115°)
1 tablespoon olive or vegetable oil
1 teaspoon salt
1 package dry yeast
3 to 3¼ cups all-purpose flour, divided
1 to 2 teaspoons yellow cornmeal

Combine water, oil, and salt in a large mixing bowl; sprinkle yeast over water mixture, stirring to dissolve. Add 1½ cups flour; beat at medium speed of an electric mixer until blended. Gradually add enough flour to make a firm dough.

Turn dough out onto a lightly floured surface; knead until smooth (about 5 minutes). Shape into a ball, and place in a well-greased bowl, turning to grease all sides. Cover and let rise in a warm place (85°), free from drafts, 1 hour or until doubled in bulk.

Punch dough down, and divide in half. Roll one half to a 12-inch circle on a lightly floured surface. Transfer dough to an ungreased pizza brick or pizza pan sprinkled with cornmeal. Fold over edges of dough, and pinch to form crust. Prick bottom and sides of crust with a fork. Repeat with remaining dough. Bake at 450° for 10 minutes. Top and bake as desired. Yield: two 12-inch pizza crusts.

Note: Dough for second pizza may be greased on all sides, wrapped securely in plastic wrap, put into a plastic bag, and stored in refrigerator up to 3 days. Punch dough down daily. (Dough may also be frozen up to one month.) Let dough come almost to room temperature before shaping.

MICROWAVE COOKERY

Savvy Ways With Meat

With proper cooking techniques and a little microwave know-how, you can use your microwave oven to cook a variety of meats.

First, discard the myth that microwaves do not brown meat. They do brown some meats, especially ones that are high in fat, such as bacon and roasts. The fat comes to the surface of such meats, caramelizes, and browns. Easy Beef Roast takes advantage of the natural browning that occurs when microwaving a chuck roast. Other basic principles of meat

cookery are observed in this recipe. For instance, because chuck roast is a less tender cut of meat, it's cooked in a flavorful liquid of vegetable juice cocktail. The oven cooking bag holds flavor and heat in the roast, as a covered Dutch oven used in conventional cooking would.

Meats with a lower fat content will need help browning. Commercial products can be used, such as soy sauce, browning-and-seasoning sauce, Worcestershire sauce, barbecue sauce, coating mix, and breading, to render meats brown and tasty.

Browning dishes or browning units sear food much as a skillet does when food is cooked conventionally. A special substance enclosed in the base of the browning dish heats to very high temperatures (500° to 600°) when exposed to microwaves at HIGH power.

Browning dishes come in a variety of shapes and sizes, so follow the manufacturer's directions for heating.

VEGETABLE-STUFFED CHICKEN

1 small yellow squash, cut into ½-inch cubes
1 small zucchini, cut into ½-inch cubes
1 medium tomato, peeled and chopped
1 (6-ounce) jar marinated artichoke hearts, undrained and chopped
1 (3½-pound) broiler-fryer
1 tablespoon browning-and-seasoning sauce
1 tablespoon butter or margarine, melted
1 teaspoon dried whole basil
½ teaspoon grated lemon rind

Combine first 4 ingredients in a 1½-quart casserole. Cover tightly with heavy-duty plastic wrap; fold back a small edge of wrap to allow steam to escape. Microwave at HIGH 5 to 6

minutes or until vegetables are crisp-tender, stirring every 2 minutes; drain vegetables.

Spoon vegetables into cavity of chicken. Truss chicken, and place breast side down on a microwave roasting rack. Combine browning-and-seasoning sauce and butter; brush or rub half of mixture into skin. Combine basil and lemon rind; sprinkle half over chicken. Microwave at HIGH 10 minutes. Turn chicken, breast side up. Brush or rub remaining browning mixture into skin, and sprinkle with remaining basil mixture. Microwave at HIGH 18 to 22 minutes or until temperature of stuffing is 145° and meat at thigh registers 185°. Drumsticks will be easy to move. Yield: 4 servings.

EASY BEEF ROAST

⅓ cup all-purpose flour
1 (12-ounce) can vegetable juice cocktail
1 (3- to 3½-pound) boneless chuck roast

Combine flour and vegetable juice cocktail in a roasting bag. Close bag; shake to dissolve flour. Place bag in a 12- x 8- x 2-inch baking dish. Pierce roast with a fork at ½-inch intervals, and place in bag, turning to moisten. Tie bag securely with enclosed plastic tie (do not use a metal twist tie). Cut 6 (½-inch) slits in top of bag.

Microwave at MEDIUM LOW (30% power) 33 to 37 minutes per pound or to desired degree of doneness, giving dish a half-turn every 30 minutes. Let roast stand 10 to 15 minutes in bag before serving. Yield: 8 servings.

BLUE CHEESE BURGERS

1 pound lean ground beef
½ cup quick-cooking oats, uncooked
1 egg, beaten
1 tablespoon dried onion flakes
2 ounces blue cheese, crumbled
1 tablespoon browning-and-seasoning sauce
1 tablespoon water
4 hamburger buns, toasted

Combine first 4 ingredients, mixing well. Shape mixture into 8 patties, 4 inches in diameter. Sprinkle 1 tablespoon blue cheese onto 4 patties; top with remaining 4 patties, and press edges together to seal.

Place patties on a roasting rack in a 12- x 8- x 2-inch baking dish. Combine browning-and-seasoning sauce and water; brush tops of patties. Microwave at HIGH 3 minutes. Turn burgers; brush tops with browning-sauce mixture, and microwave at HIGH 3 minutes. Serve on hamburger buns. Yield: 4 servings.

SPICY-SEASONED CATFISH

2¼ teaspoons paprika
½ teaspoon chili powder
½ teaspoon ground red pepper
½ teaspoon black pepper
¼ teaspoon salt
¼ teaspoon ground cumin
¼ teaspoon onion powder
¼ teaspoon garlic powder
¼ cup butter or margarine, melted
2 tablespoons lemon juice
2 (½-pound) catfish, skinned and dressed
1 tablespoon vegetable oil
Chopped green onion tops

Combine first 8 ingredients; set mixture aside.

Combine ¼ cup butter and lemon juice. Dip each catfish in butter mixture. Place catfish on wax paper. Sprinkle catfish evenly on both sides with seasoning mixture, coating well; press seasonings into skin.

Heat microwave browning dish according to manufacturer's instructions. Pour oil on heated browning dish; tilt dish to coat bottom. Add fish; let stand in microwave about 1 minute or until sizzling stops. Microwave at HIGH 2 minutes. Turn fish over, and microwave at HIGH 1 minute. Remove fish to plates, and garnish with green onion tops. Yield: 2 servings.

Everyday Entrées

Whether you're cooking for the family or friends, you'll enjoy preparing recipes that are substantial enough to be a meal in themselves. For any of these entrées, all you'll need to add is salad and bread.

SWEET-AND-SOUR SHRIMP AND CHICKEN

¼ cup firmly packed brown sugar
2 tablespoons cornstarch
¾ teaspoon ground ginger
¼ teaspoon garlic powder
¼ teaspoon curry powder
1 tablespoon Worcestershire sauce
1½ cups pineapple juice
⅓ cup wine vinegar
¼ cup soy sauce
¼ cup catsup
1½ pounds unpeeled medium-size fresh shrimp
1 tablespoon butter or margarine, melted
1 tablespoon olive oil
2 cups cooked cubed chicken (about 3 breast halves)
1 cup unsalted cashew nuts
Hot cooked rice

Combine first 10 ingredients in a medium saucepan. Cook over medium heat 5 minutes or until mixture is clear and thickened, stirring frequently. Set mixture aside.

Peel and devein shrimp. Sauté in butter and oil in a skillet 3 minutes. Add chicken and nuts; sauté an additional 2 minutes. Add sauce to shrimp mixture, and cook until thoroughly heated, stirring occasionally. Serve over rice. Yield: 6 servings.
Beth R. McClain
Grand Prairie, Texas

SPICY CHICKEN DISH

2½ pounds chicken breast halves
2 cups chopped onion
1 large green pepper, chopped
4 cloves garlic, minced
1 tablespoon olive oil
2 tablespoons all-purpose flour
2 (16-ounce) cans whole tomatoes, undrained and chopped
1 (6-ounce) can tomato paste
1½ tablespoons Worcestershire sauce
1¼ teaspoons salt
¾ teaspoon pepper
½ teaspoon chili powder
¼ teaspoon dried whole basil
1 bay leaf
4 cups hot cooked rice
⅓ cup chopped fresh parsley
Gumbo filé

Cook chicken in boiling salted water to cover 30 minutes. Drain well, reserving 3 cups broth; let chicken cool. Skin, bone, and chop chicken; set aside.

Sauté onion, green pepper, and garlic in hot oil in a Dutch oven until tender. Stir in flour; cook 1 minute, stirring constantly. Gradually add reserved broth. Add tomatoes and next 7 ingredients; stir well. Bring to a boil, stirring constantly. Reduce heat, and simmer, uncovered, 1 hour. Add chicken; cook until heated. Remove and discard bay leaf.

Combine rice and parsley; stir well. Serve chicken mixture over rice; sprinkle with filé powder. Yield: 6 to 8 servings. *Mrs. Phillip Rose*
Harrisonburg, Virginia

THICK 'N' CRUSTY CHICKEN POT PIE

1 (2½- to 3-pound) broiler-fryer
1 onion, quartered
1 stalk celery, cut into large
  pieces
1 teaspoon salt
1 teaspoon dried whole basil
1 teaspoon dried whole thyme
1 teaspoon dried whole rosemary
  leaves, crushed
1 bay leaf
1 cup finely chopped celery
1 cup finely chopped onion
1 cup finely chopped carrot
1 cup finely chopped potato
⅓ cup butter or margarine,
  melted
½ cup all-purpose flour
1½ cups half-and-half
½ teaspoon salt
¼ teaspoon pepper
Pastry (recipe follows)
1 egg
1 tablespoon milk

Combine first 8 ingredients in a Dutch oven. Cover with water, and bring to a boil; cover, reduce heat, and simmer 1 hour or until chicken is tender. Remove chicken from broth; strain broth, reserving 1½ cups. Cool chicken. Remove chicken from bone; chop meat.

Sauté celery, onion, carrot, and potato in butter until crisp-tender. Add flour, stirring until smooth. Cook 1 minute, stirring constantly. Gradually add reserved broth and half-and-half; cook over medium heat, stirring constantly, until thickened and bubbly. Stir in ½ teaspoon salt, pepper, and chopped chicken.

Roll half of pastry to ⅛-inch thickness on a lightly floured surface. Fit pastry into a 9½-inch deep-dish pie-plate. Spoon chicken mixture into pastry.

Roll remaining pastry to ⅛-inch thickness, and place over chicken filling. Trim, seal, and flute edges. Roll out dough scraps, and cut into a chicken or desired shape. Dampen with water, and arrange over pastry, if desired. Cut slits in top of pastry to allow steam to escape.

Combine egg and milk; blend well. Brush over pastry. Bake at 400° for 30 minutes or until golden brown. Yield: 6 servings.

Pastry

3 cups all-purpose flour
1 teaspoon salt
1 cup shortening
1 egg, beaten
¼ cup plus 1 tablespoon ice
  water
1 tablespoon vinegar

Combine flour and salt; cut in shortening with a pastry blender until mixture resembles coarse meal.

Combine egg, ice water, and vinegar; sprinkle evenly over surface, and stir with a fork until dry ingredients are moistened. Shape into a ball. Yield: enough for one double-crust 9½-inch pie.   *Sally Murphy*
Allen, Texas

CAJUN CHICKEN OVER RICE

1½ pounds boneless chicken
  breast halves, cut into 1-inch
  pieces
⅛ teaspoon garlic powder
5 large tomatoes, peeled and
  chopped
2 large onions, chopped
1 large green pepper, chopped
¼ cup Worcestershire sauce
¼ cup soy sauce
1 to 2 teaspoons pepper
1 teaspoon dried whole basil
1 teaspoon dried whole marjoram
1 teaspoon dried whole oregano
Hot cooked rice

Sprinkle chicken with garlic powder; set aside.

Combine tomatoes and remaining ingredients except rice in a large Dutch oven. Bring to a boil; reduce heat, and simmer 15 minutes. Add chicken, and return to a boil. Cover, reduce heat, and simmer 30 minutes or until tender. Serve over rice. Yield: 6 servings. *K. Michelle Cobb*
Roxboro, North Carolina

ROYAL MEATBALLS

2 pounds ground beef
1 cup finely chopped onion
1½ teaspoons ground ginger
1½ teaspoons ground coriander
1 teaspoon salt
1 teaspoon chili powder
1 teaspoon paprika
1 teaspoon lemon-pepper
  seasoning
1 teaspoon chopped fresh parsley
1 (32-ounce) jar spaghetti sauce
2 cups finely chopped onion
2 cloves garlic, minced
1 tablespoon plus 1 teaspoon
  paprika
2 teaspoons chili powder
2 teaspoons grated fresh
  gingerroot
1½ teaspoons ground coriander
Hot cooked spaghetti

Combine first 9 ingredients in a large bowl; mix well. Shape mixture into 1½-inch balls; place meatballs on broiler pan, and bake at 300° for 20 minutes, turning after 10 minutes. Remove pan from oven, and drain meatballs on paper towels; set aside.

Combine spaghetti sauce and next 6 ingredients in a large Dutch oven. Cover and cook over medium heat 10 minutes. Add meatballs, and cook an additional 5 minutes. Serve meatballs with sauce over hot cooked spaghetti. Yield: 8 servings.
Sambhu N. Banik
Bethesda, Maryland

Tip: *Get in the habit of grocery shopping with a list. Watch newspapers for advertised "specials"; then plan a week's menus around bargains in foods the family enjoys.*

CHILI BEAN ROAST

1 (3- to 3½-pound) beef round tip
    roast
1½ teaspoons spicy brown
    mustard
2 tablespoons brown sugar
1½ teaspoons chili powder
½ teaspoon salt
¼ teaspoon pepper
1 (15½-ounce) can Mexican-style
    chili beans, undrained
1 cup chopped onion

Trim excess fat from roast. Spread mustard on all sides of roast. Combine sugar, chili powder, salt, and pepper in a small bowl; rub mixture on all sides of roast.

Place roast in a Dutch oven; top with undrained beans and chopped onion. Cover and bake at 350° for 2½ hours or until roast is done. Yield: about 8 servings.

Dorothy Nieman
Dunnellon, Florida

Frozen Vegetables, Always In Season

Fresh corn wouldn't be very creamy, fresh beans wouldn't be very tender, and fresh black-eyed peas probably wouldn't even be available at this time of year. But you can always depend on frozen vegetables, which have been harvested at their peak of flavor.

SQUASH FRITTERS

1 (10-ounce) package frozen
    sliced yellow squash
2 eggs, beaten
½ cup cracker crumbs
¼ teaspoon pepper
1 small onion, diced
Vegetable oil

Cook squash according to package directions; drain and mash. Combine squash and next 4 ingredients.

Pour oil to a depth of 2 inches in a heavy saucepan; heat to 375°. Drop squash mixture by tablespoonfuls into oil; fry until golden brown, turning once. Drain on paper towels. Serve immediately. Yield: 10 fritters.

Eileen Wehling
Austin, Texas

CORN-AND-GREEN CHILE CASSEROLE

2 (10-ounce) packages frozen
    whole kernel corn
2 tablespoons butter or margarine
1 (8-ounce) package cream cheese
1 tablespoon sugar (optional)
1 (4-ounce) can chopped green
    chiles, drained

Cook corn according to package directions; drain and set aside.

Melt butter in a heavy saucepan over low heat; add cream cheese, and stir until blended. Stir in corn, sugar, if desired, and green chiles. Spoon into a lightly greased 1-quart baking dish. Cover and bake at 350° for 25 minutes. Yield: 6 servings.

Clota Engleman
Spur, Texas

ENGLISH WALNUT BROCCOLI

2 (10-ounce) packages frozen
    chopped broccoli, thawed and
    drained
¼ cup butter or margarine
¼ cup all-purpose flour
2 teaspoons chicken-flavored
    bouillon granules
2 cups milk
⅓ cup water
3 tablespoons butter or margarine
1½ cups herb-seasoned stuffing
    mix
⅓ cup chopped walnuts

Arrange chopped broccoli in a lightly greased 10- x 6- x 2-inch baking dish, and set aside.

Melt ¼ cup butter in a heavy saucepan over low heat; add flour and bouillon granules, stirring until smooth. Cook 1 minute, stirring constantly. Gradually add milk; cook over medium heat, stirring constantly, until thickened and bubbly. Pour mixture evenly over broccoli.

Combine water and 3 tablespoons butter in a saucepan; cook over low heat until butter melts. Stir in stuffing mix and chopped walnuts. Spoon mixture on top of sauce. Bake, uncovered, at 350° for 30 minutes. Yield: 6 to 8 servings. *Diane Butts*
Boone, North Carolina

TASTY BLACK-EYED PEAS

2 (10-ounce) packages frozen
    black-eyed peas
1¼ cups chopped green pepper
¾ cup chopped onion
3 tablespoons bacon drippings
1 (7½-ounce) can whole
    tomatoes, undrained and
    chopped
½ teaspoon salt
¼ teaspoon pepper

Cook black-eyed peas according to package directions; drain well, and set aside.

Sauté green pepper and onion in bacon drippings until tender. Add peas, tomatoes, salt, and pepper; cook over low heat until thoroughly heated, stirring often. Yield: 6 servings. *Evelyn Snellings*
Richmond, Virginia

CREAMY SPINACH BAKE

4 slices bacon
2 (10-ounce) packages frozen
    chopped spinach, thawed and
    well drained
1½ cups commercial sour cream
1 (.25-ounce) envelope onion soup
    mix
⅓ cup grated Parmesan cheese

Fry bacon until crisp; drain on paper towels, and immediately wind 3 slices bacon to make curls while still warm. Let cool. Crumble other slice of bacon, and set aside.

Combine spinach, sour cream, and soup mix; stir well. Spoon into a lightly greased 1-quart casserole. Sprinkle cheese over spinach mixture. Bake at 350° for 30 minutes. Top with bacon curls and crumbled bacon. Yield: 6 servings.

Iris Brenner
Fort McCoy, Florida

Potatoes And Cheese: A Classic Combination

There's almost no limit to the recipes the creative cook can concoct using potatoes and cheese. Our files are filled with tasty combinations of these two popular foods.

ITALIAN-STYLE POTATOES

3 cups thinly sliced onion
2 cloves garlic, crushed
2 tablespoons olive oil
2 (16-ounce) cans tomatoes, undrained and chopped
¼ cup chopped fresh parsley
2 teaspoons dried whole basil
2 teaspoons dried whole oregano
½ teaspoon pepper
2½ pounds potatoes
¼ teaspoon salt, divided
1 cup (4 ounces) shredded Swiss cheese
3 tablespoons grated Parmesan cheese

Sauté onion and garlic in hot oil until crisp-tender. Add chopped tomatoes and next 4 ingredients, stirring well. Set aside.

Peel potatoes, and slice ⅛-inch thick. Spoon one-third of tomato mixture into a lightly greased 13- x 9- x 2-inch baking dish. Top with half of potatoes; sprinkle with ⅛ teaspoon salt and half of Swiss cheese. Spoon half of remaining sauce over cheese. Repeat layers to use remaining potatoes, salt, Swiss cheese, and sauce. Cover and bake at 375° for 45 minutes. Uncover and sprinkle with Parmesan cheese; bake an additional 35 minutes or until potatoes are tender. Yield: 10 servings. *Mary Valdrighi*
Knoxville, Tennessee

COTTAGE POTATOES

10 to 12 medium potatoes (4 pounds)
1¼ cups chopped onion
1 cup chopped green pepper
½ cup butter or margarine, melted
2½ teaspoons salt
½ cup milk
1 (4-ounce) jar diced pimiento, drained
1 (8-ounce) package process cheese, cubed

Cook potatoes in boiling water to cover 30 minutes or until done; drain. Allow potatoes to cool to touch. Peel and dice.

Sauté onion and green pepper in butter until tender. Combine potatoes, onion mixture, salt, and remaining ingredients; stir gently. Spoon into a lightly greased 13- x 9- x 2-inch baking dish; cover and bake at 400° for 30 minutes. Remove cover; bake an additional 10 minutes. Yield: 10 to 12 servings.

Nina L. Andrews
Tappahannock, Virginia

BLUE CHEESE-STUFFED POTATOES

3 (8-ounce) baking potatoes
Vegetable oil
¼ cup commercial sour cream
¼ cup commercial blue cheese salad dressing
¼ cup bacon-flavored bits
2 teaspoons chopped chives
¼ cup crumbled blue cheese

Wash potatoes, and rub skins with oil. Bake at 400° for 1 hour or until done. Allow potatoes to cool to touch. Cut potatoes in half lengthwise; carefully scoop out pulp, leaving shells intact.

Combine potato pulp, sour cream, and next 3 ingredients; stir well. Fill shells with potato mixture; sprinkle cheese over potatoes. Bake at 350° for 10 minutes or until thoroughly heated. Yield: 6 servings.

Pat Rush Benigno
Gulfport, Mississippi

SHREDDED POTATOES AU GRATIN

8 medium baking potatoes (3½ pounds)
2 cups (8 ounces) shredded sharp Cheddar cheese
2 cups whipping cream
1 teaspoon salt
¼ cup soft breadcrumbs
1 tablespoon butter or margarine, melted

Place potatoes in a Dutch oven, and cover with water. Bring to a boil; cover, reduce heat, and simmer 10 minutes. Drain and cool; peel and coarsely shred.

Alternate 2 layers of potatoes and cheese in a lightly greased 2½-quart casserole. Combine whipping cream and salt; pour over potatoes. Sprinkle with breadcrumbs, and drizzle with butter. Bake at 350° for 45 minutes. Yield: 8 to 10 servings.

Pearle E. Evans
Myrtle Beach, South Carolina

Down-Home Meat Loaf Supper

Outside the South, a meat loaf supper may be referred to as "diner" or "comfort" food. But south of the Mason-Dixon line, it's a fine example of our revered down-home cookin', the food Mama and Grandma specialize in. Lately, these "good-ole" foods have gained recognition and respect from coast to coast.

Special Meat Loaf
Savory Green Beans
Fix-Ahead Mashed Potatoes
Toasted Rolls With Herb Butter

SPECIAL MEAT LOAF

1 egg, beaten
½ cup soft breadcrumbs
1 teaspoon salt
½ teaspoon pepper
½ cup chopped onion
½ cup chopped green pepper
½ cup chopped celery
¼ cup chopped mushrooms
1 clove garlic, minced
1½ pounds ground beef
½ cup catsup
2 tablespoons tomato paste
1 tablespoon water

Combine first 9 ingredients in a large bowl, mixing well. Add ground beef; mix just until blended. Shape into an 8- x 4-inch loaf, and place in a 13- x 9- x 2-inch baking pan. Bake at 350° for 30 minutes. Combine catsup, tomato paste, and water, and spoon over loaf. Continue to bake 1 hour or until done. Yield: 6 servings.
Dee Buchfink
Lufkin, Texas

SAVORY GREEN BEANS

1½ pounds green beans
1 clove garlic, halved
2 tablespoons chopped onion
3 tablespoons vegetable oil
½ cup boiling water
½ teaspoon sugar
1 teaspoon dried whole basil
½ teaspoon salt
¼ teaspoon pepper

Wash beans; trim ends, and remove strings. Cut in half crosswise.

Sauté garlic and onion in vegetable oil; remove garlic, and discard. Add beans, boiling water, sugar, basil, salt, and pepper; cover and cook over medium heat 25 minutes or until beans are tender. Add 1 tablespoon additional water to mixture, if necessary. Yield: 6 servings.
Brenda Rohe
Charlotte, North Carolina

FIX-AHEAD MASHED POTATOES

3 pounds potatoes (about 4 large)
½ teaspoon salt
2 tablespoons butter or margarine
2 (3-ounce) packages cream cheese, softened
⅔ cup commercial sour cream
¼ cup milk
¾ teaspoon salt
1 tablespoon butter or margarine, melted
½ teaspoon paprika

Place potatoes in a saucepan; add water to cover and ½ teaspoon salt. Bring to a boil; cover, reduce heat to medium, and simmer 25 minutes or until potatoes are tender. Drain. Peel potatoes; place in a large mixing bowl, and mash with a potato masher. Add 2 tablespoons butter and next 4 ingredients, mixing until all ingredients are blended.

Spoon mixture into a lightly greased 12- x 8- x 2-inch baking dish. Brush top of mixture with melted butter; sprinkle with paprika.

Bake immediately, or cover and refrigerate. If refrigerated, let stand at room temperature 30 minutes before baking. Bake at 350°, uncovered, 30 minutes or until hot. Yield: 6 to 8 servings.
Dorothy Beckman
Springfield, Missouri

TOASTED ROLLS WITH HERB BUTTER

4 Kaiser rolls
¼ cup butter or margarine, softened
2 tablespoons minced fresh parsley
1½ tablespoons minced fresh chives
1½ teaspoons lemon juice

Slice rolls in half horizontally. Combine remaining ingredients, stirring well; spread evenly on cut side of rolls. Place rolls on a baking sheet. Broil 6 inches from heat 2 minutes or until golden. Serve hot. Yield: 8 servings.
Pat Koen
Austin, Texas

Special Entrées For Easter

Church bells ring out on Easter morning, tolling the religious holiday and welcoming the first buds and blossoms of spring. Families gather, often for the first time since Christmas, to celebrate the fresh, new season and anticipate warmer weather.

Such gatherings deserve special menu planning, and veal, lamb, and ham come to mind as superb entrée selections.

FROSTED HAM

1 (6- to 7-pound) boneless fully
  cooked ham
1 (10-ounce) bottle cola-flavored
  beverage
2 (8-ounce) packages cream
  cheese, softened
1 teaspoon prepared horseradish
¼ teaspoon white pepper
Radish roses (optional)
Carrot flowers (optional)
Green onion stems (optional)

Place ham, fat side up, on rack in a shallow roasting pan. (Do not score ham as it will have an uneven look when frosted.) Add cola-flavored beverage. Insert meat thermometer. Bake at 325° for 1½ hours or until meat thermometer registers 140°. Let cool.

Beat cream cheese at medium speed of an electric mixer until smooth and creamy. Add horseradish and pepper; beat well.

Place ham on a serving platter. Spread cream cheese mixture over cool ham. If desired, garnish with radish roses, carrot flowers, and green onion stems. Yield: 15 to 20 servings.   *Rebecca Benhard*
Palmetto, Louisiana

LEG OF LAMB
WITH MUSTARD SAUCE

½ cup Dijon mustard
1 teaspoon dried whole basil,
  crushed
¼ teaspoon ground ginger
1 clove garlic, minced
2 tablespoons olive oil
2 tablespoons Worcestershire
  sauce
1 (5-pound) leg of lamb

Combine first 6 ingredients, stirring well. Place lamb, fat side up, in a shallow roasting pan. Spread mustard mixture evenly over leg of lamb. Chill 2 hours.

Insert meat thermometer, making sure it does not touch fat or bone. Bake at 325° for 2 hours and 15 minutes or until meat thermometer registers 160°. Let stand 10 minutes before serving. Yield: 6 to 8 servings.   *Barbara Sherrer*
Bay City, Texas

VEAL ROAST
WITH VEGETABLES

1 (2½- to 3-pound) boneless veal
  sirloin roast
¼ cup plus 2 tablespoons butter
  or margarine, melted
½ cup chicken broth
½ cup Chablis or other dry white
  wine
1 cup pearl onions, peeled
5 carrots, cut into 1-inch pieces
3 stalks celery, cut into 1-inch
  pieces
½ pound fresh medium
  mushrooms
½ teaspoon salt
½ teaspoon pepper
Celery leaves (optional)

Brown roast on all sides in butter in a large Dutch oven. Add chicken broth and wine; cover, reduce heat, and simmer 1 hour and 15 minutes. Add onions and remaining ingredients except celery leaves; cover and cook 30 minutes or until vegetables are tender and meat thermometer registers 170°.

Place roast on a serving platter; arrange vegetables on platter, and spoon pan juices over roast. Garnish roast with celery leaves, if desired. Yield: 6 servings.
Sara A. McCullough
Broaddus, Texas

QUICK!

Scoop A Dessert

Dessert doesn't have to take hours to make to be good. Simple desserts, such as the ones you'll find here, will add a special touch to the meal without a big investment of time. These desserts are frozen, so you'll have them on hand for drop-in guests or when *you* have a craving for something sweet.

ICE CREAM CAKE

1 cup whipping cream
¼ cup cocoa
⅓ cup sugar
1 (8-ounce) loaf angel food cake
½ gallon butter pecan ice cream,
  softened

Combine whipping cream, cocoa, and sugar in a bowl; cover and chill. Beat chilled mixture at medium speed of an electric mixer until stiff peaks form. Set aside.

Slice cake horizontally into 3 layers. Place 1 layer of cake on a serving platter. Remove ice cream from container; slice horizontally into 3 pieces. Place 1 slice of ice cream on cake layer, spreading ice cream, if necessary, to cover entire surface. Repeat procedure with remaining cake layers and ice cream, ending with ice cream layer. Frost ice cream cake with chocolate whipped cream frosting. Freeze until firm. Yield: 8 servings.   *Mrs. P. J. Davis*
Drexel, North Carolina

Tip: Speed up the time it takes to chill the whipping cream mixture by setting the bowl in another bowl that's filled with ice.

CHOCOLATE ICE CREAM SANDWICHES

½ cup light corn syrup
½ cup chunky peanut butter
4 cups crispy rice cereal
1 pint chocolate or vanilla ice
    cream, softened

Combine corn syrup and peanut butter in a large bowl. Add rice cereal, and stir until cereal is well coated. Press cereal mixture into a 13- x 9- x 2-inch pan. Place in freezer until firm. Cut cereal into twelve 3-inch squares. Cut ice cream into 6 slices, and place between cereal squares. Freeze. Yield: 6 servings.

Charlotte Pierce
Greensburg, Kentucky

Tip: To keep cereal mixture from sticking to your hands, lightly grease hands with butter before pressing the mixture into the pan.

NUTTY ICE CREAM BALLS

2 pints vanilla ice cream
1 cup chopped walnuts, toasted
1 (4-ounce) package chocolate
    instant pudding mix
1 cup light corn syrup
2 tablespoons water
2 tablespoons butter or
    margarine, melted
Raspberries (optional)

Scoop ice cream into 6 balls; roll each ball in walnuts, and freeze. Combine pudding mix and next 3 ingredients, stirring well.

To serve, spoon about 3 tablespoons sauce in dessert dish, and place ice cream ball in sauce. Garnish with raspberries, if desired. Yield: 6 servings. *Ruth Chellis*
Easley, South Carolina

Tip: Make walnut-covered ice cream balls ahead of time, and keep them in the freezer until it's time for dessert.

DOUBLE-DELIGHT ICE CREAM PIE

1½ cups butter pecan ice cream,
    softened
1 (9-inch) frozen graham cracker
    crust
2 (1⅛-ounce) English
    toffee-flavored candy bars,
    crushed
1½ cups vanilla ice cream,
    softened

Spread butter pecan ice cream in graham cracker crust. Sprinkle with half of crushed candy bars; freeze. Spread vanilla ice cream over top, and sprinkle with remaining crushed candy bars; freeze until firm. Yield: one 9-inch pie. *Joy Garcia*
Bartlett, Tennessee

Tip: Soften solidly frozen ice cream by microwaving at HIGH 10 seconds or until soft.

New Twist For Angel Rolls

Many of our readers are familiar with angel rolls, the sweet-tasting dinner bread made from yeast dough that needs no rising. Try this recipe which uses an interesting pineapple topping variation.

PINEAPPLE ANGEL ROLLS

1 (15¼-ounce) can crushed
    pineapple, well drained
1 cup firmly packed brown sugar
¼ cup butter or margarine,
    softened
2 teaspoons ground cinnamon
1 recipe basic angel rolls dough
    (recipe follows)

Combine pineapple, brown sugar, butter, and cinnamon in a small bowl, mixing well. Spoon mixture evenly into 24 greased muffin cups.

Roll basic angel rolls dough to ½-inch thickness on a lightly floured surface; cut dough with a 2½-inch biscuit cutter. Place one roll over pineapple mixture in each muffin cup. Bake at 350° for 17 to 19 minutes or until rolls are golden brown. Cool in pan 5 minutes. Invert rolls onto a serving platter, and serve warm. Yield: 2 dozen.

Basic Angel Rolls

1 package dry yeast
¼ cup warm water (105° to 115°)
2½ to 3 cups all-purpose flour
2 tablespoons sugar
1 teaspoon baking powder
½ teaspoon baking soda
1 teaspoon salt
½ cup vegetable oil
1 cup buttermilk

Dissolve yeast in warm water in a bowl; let stand 5 minutes.

Combine flour, sugar, baking powder, soda, and salt in a large bowl; make a well in center of mixture. Combine oil, buttermilk, and yeast mixture; add to dry ingredients, stirring just until moistened. (Dough will be sticky.)

Roll dough to ½-inch thickness on a lightly floured surface; cut with a 2½-inch biscuit cutter. Use rolls as directed above, or place rolls on an ungreased baking sheet. Bake at 350° for 16 minutes or until golden brown. Yield: 2 dozen rolls.

Judy Grigoraci
Charleston, West Virginia

Right: *Enjoy Spicy Catfish Amandine (page 52), corn sticks, and coleslaw for a lazy springtime meal. Using few ingredients, this dish is sure to become a family favorite.*

Fresh produce, as well as canned fruits and vegetables, stars in these salads: (clockwise from top) Salade Riviera; Tropical Waldorf Salad; Endive, Bacon, and Pecan Salad; Blue Cheese Coleslaw. (Recipes, pages 12 and 13.)

Asparagus-Chicken Salad (page 83) with its delectable creamy dressing and Italian Chicken Cutlets (page 82) are examples of chicken cooked new ways with succulent fruits, tender vegetables, and aromatic cheese.

Oyster fans will enjoy the tasty blend of flavors in Baked Oysters Italiano (page 97) without having to worry about calories in this light recipe.

Wild mushrooms bring new life to traditional recipes: (from left) Wild Rice With Morels, Spinach-Enoki Salad, and Veal-Cepe Sauté. (Recipes, page 62.) At right are identification photographs of mushrooms available in supermarkets. Do not attempt to identify and pick mushrooms growing wild. Buy them only from experienced cultivators.

Fresh Oyster Mushrooms: *These cream-colored, fan-shaped mushrooms take their name from the shellfish they resemble in flavor and aroma. Both the stem and cap of this mushroom can be eaten.*

Fresh Chanterelle Mushrooms: *Trumpet-shaped chanterelles give off a faint aroma and flavor of apricots. Of these mushrooms, the large stems can be fibrous, although they and the caps are edible.*

Fresh Shiitake Mushrooms: *Distinguished by their smoky flavor and spongy texture, shiitakes can grow up to 8 inches in diameter. Discard the stems, as they are too tough to eat.*

Fresh Enoki Mushrooms: *The midgets of the mushroom family, enokis have tiny caps and matchstick stems. Enokis can be eaten raw, but be sure to trim away the lower part of the stem.*

Dried Morel Mushrooms: *Rarely available fresh, morels have a hollow cap with irregular pits. The stems of this mushroom are edible but they are often trimmed before drying because of toughness.*

Dried Cepe Mushrooms: *More frequently found in the dried form, cepes feature a strong mushroom flavor and a meaty texture; they are favorites for entrées. Both the stem and the cap are edible.*

Favorite Southern breads, (clockwise from top) Corn Sticks, Cornmeal Yeast Bread, Baked Hush Puppies, French Bread, and Light Biscuits (center), have been given the light touch. (Recipes, pages 53 and 54.)

The Sour Cream Pound Cake (in foreground) looks as elegant as the Coconut-Pineapple Cake. (Recipes, page 56.)

APRIL

It's spring—What better time to host a brunch? Festive menus, recipes, and ideas abound in the "Breakfasts & Brunches" special section. And for winning desserts, this chapter offers everybody's favorite, a classic cheesecake, along with five delicious variations.

Chicken—
Ever Changing, Always Good

Whenever Southerners think about chicken, most likely they imagine drumsticks sizzling in hot oil or a platter heaped high with fried chicken. Some folks might think of chicken and dumplings, while others might consider a brothy soup full of noodles or rice.

If you ask our readers about the chicken they ate last night, however, their answers may surprise you. Their recipes invite different, occasionally unexpected flavor combinations. Today's generation still loves fried chicken—but on a daily basis, their cooking style has changed.

Place each piece of chicken between 2 sheets of wax paper; flatten to ¼-inch thickness, using a meat mallet or rolling pin.

Combine breadcrumbs and next 5 ingredients; dip chicken in eggs, and dredge in breadcrumb mixture.

Heat vegetable oil in a large skillet over medium heat. Add chicken, and cook 3 to 4 minutes on each side or until golden brown, adding extra oil, if necessary. Drain on paper towels. Garnish with green onion strips, if desired. Yield: 6 servings.

Julie Earhart
St. Louis, Missouri

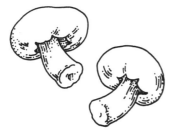

CHICKEN MURPHY

6 chicken breast halves, skinned
1 cup dry white wine
1 teaspoon dried whole basil
1 teaspoon dried whole oregano
½ teaspoon garlic powder
¼ teaspoon salt
⅛ teaspoon pepper
2 tablespoons butter or
  margarine, melted
1 (14-ounce) jar sweet cherry
  peppers, undrained
1 pound fresh mushrooms, halved

Place chicken breasts in a lightly greased 13- x 9- x 2-inch baking dish. Combine wine, basil, oregano, garlic powder, salt, and pepper in a small bowl; mix well, and pour over chicken. Cover and chill 8 hours.

Remove chicken from refrigerator; let stand 30 minutes. Brush butter on chicken; pour peppers and liquid over top. Cover and bake at 350° for 40 minutes. Uncover and add mushrooms. Bake, uncovered, an additional 20 minutes or until done. With a large slotted spoon, transfer chicken breasts, mushrooms, and peppers to a serving platter. Yield: 6 servings.

Merle Dunson
Greenville, South Carolina

ITALIAN CHICKEN CUTLETS
(pictured on page 75)

6 chicken breast halves, skinned
  and boned
1 cup Italian-seasoned
  breadcrumbs
½ cup freshly grated Romano or
  Parmesan cheese
¼ cup all-purpose flour
1 (0.8-ounce) envelope light
  Italian salad dressing mix
2 teaspoons dried whole oregano
¼ teaspoon garlic powder
2 eggs, beaten
⅓ cup vegetable oil
Green onion strips (optional)

CHICKEN IN HONEY SAUCE

1 cup all-purpose flour
1 teaspoon salt
1 teaspoon paprika
¼ teaspoon pepper
1 (3- to 3½-pound) broiler-fryer,
  cut up
½ cup butter or margarine,
  melted
Vegetable cooking spray
¼ cup butter or margarine,
  melted
¼ cup honey
¼ cup lemon juice

Combine first 4 ingredients in a plastic bag; shake to mix. Place 2 pieces of chicken in bag; shake well to coat chicken.

Dip floured chicken in ½ cup melted butter. Place chicken, skin side up, in a 13- x 9- x 2-inch baking dish coated with cooking spray. Repeat process with remaining flour mixture, chicken, and butter. Bake, uncovered, at 400° for 30 minutes.

Drain off pan drippings; turn chicken over. Combine ¼ cup butter, honey, and lemon juice; pour over chicken. Cover and bake an additional 30 minutes or until done, basting frequently with pan juices. Yield: 4 servings.

Terry L. Blake
Pittsboro, North Carolina

CHICKEN SUPERB CASSEROLE

1 (8-ounce) package medium egg
  noodles
1 (2½- to 3-pound) broiler-fryer,
  cut up
¼ cup plus 2 tablespoons butter
  or margarine
¼ cup plus 2 tablespoons
  all-purpose flour
2 cups half-and-half
2 tablespoons sherry
1 teaspoon salt
½ teaspoon celery salt
¼ teaspoon dried whole marjoram
⅛ teaspoon Beau Monde
  seasoning
1 (6-ounce) jar sliced mushrooms,
  drained
½ cup slivered almonds, toasted
3 tablespoons minced fresh
  parsley
½ cup (2 ounces) shredded
  Cheddar cheese

Cook egg noodles according to package directions, omitting salt. Drain and set aside.

Cook chicken in boiling water to cover 45 minutes; drain, reserving 2 cups broth. Set broth aside. Bone chicken; cut into bite-size pieces.

Melt butter in a large heavy saucepan over low heat; add flour, stirring until smooth. Cook 1 minute, stirring constantly. Gradually add 2 cups reserved chicken broth, half-and-half, and next 5 ingredients. Cook over medium heat, stirring constantly, until thickened and bubbly. Add noodles, chicken, mushrooms, almonds, and parsley, mixing well.

Spoon into a lightly greased 13- x 9- x 2-inch baking dish. Cover and bake at 350° for 35 minutes. Add cheese, and bake, uncovered, an additional 5 minutes or until cheese melts. Yield: 6 to 8 servings.

Rita W. Cook
Corpus Christi, Texas

ROAST CHICKEN WITH PINEAPPLE-MUSTARD GLAZE

2 (2½- to 3-pound) broiler-fryers,
  quartered
4 large cloves garlic, sliced
¼ cup butter or margarine,
  melted
¼ cup minced fresh parsley
1 teaspoon dried whole thyme
1 (20-ounce) can sweetened
  pineapple chunks, undrained
⅓ cup honey
¼ cup Dijon mustard
1 tablespoon cornstarch
Hot cooked rice
Fresh parsley sprigs (optional)

Place chicken, skin side up, on a rack in a roasting pan. Place garlic slices under skin of chicken.

Combine butter, parsley, and thyme; brush over chicken. Bake at 350° for 45 minutes.

Drain pineapple, reserving juice. Combine ¼ cup pineapple juice, honey, and mustard. Brush over chicken, and bake an additional 15 to 20 minutes.

Combine cornstarch, remaining honey mixture, pineapple chunks, and remaining juice in a heavy saucepan; cook over medium heat, stirring constantly, until thickened and bubbly. Boil 1 minute, stirring constantly. Serve chicken and sauce over cooked rice. Garnish with parsley sprigs, if desired. Yield: 8 servings.

Barbara E. Bach
Clearwater, Florida

ASPARAGUS-CHICKEN SALAD
(pictured on page 75)

1 pound fresh asparagus
1½ cups chopped cooked chicken
3 cups iceberg lettuce, torn into
  bite-size pieces
¼ cup slivered almonds, toasted
¼ cup chopped parsley
1½ tablespoons raisins
1 red apple, unpeeled
Lettuce leaves (optional)
Italian Cream Dressing

Snap off tough ends of asparagus. Remove scales with a knife or vegetable peeler, if desired. Cook asparagus, covered, in a small amount of boiling water 3 minutes. Plunge in ice water. Drain well.

Cut asparagus into 1½-inch pieces. Reserve 8 pieces for garnish. Combine remaining asparagus and next 5 ingredients in a large bowl. Cut half of apple into ½-inch cubes; stir into chicken mixture. (Reserve remaining apple for garnish.) Arrange salad in a lettuce-lined bowl, if desired. Garnish with reserved asparagus and apple slices. Pour Italian Cream Dressing over salad. Yield: 4 servings.

Italian Cream Dressing

¾ cup commercial sour cream
¼ cup crumbled Gorgonzola
  cheese or blue cheese
1 tablespoon lemon juice
¼ teaspoon garlic powder
Freshly ground pepper

Combine all ingredients; stir well. Yield: 1 cup.

Cathy Darling
Grafton, West Virginia

How to Bone a Chicken Breast

If you're in a hurry, boned, skinned chicken breast halves make cooking quick and easy. If you have time, however, you may appreciate the economy of boning the breasts at home.

Step 1: Pull the skin from the chicken, and discard. Split the breast in half lengthwise.

Step 2: Starting at the breastbone side of the chicken, slice meat away from the bone, using a thin, sharp knife, cutting as close to the bone as possible.

MICROWAVE COOKERY

Timesaving Barbecue

Say goodbye to a frequent barbecue problem—the charred outside and underdone inside of chicken and pork. It's easily and quickly solved by precooking in the microwave and then grilling for the final browning and crisping. This cooking method preserves moisture in the meat and saves time without sacrificing good barbecue flavor.

PORK LOIN ROAST WITH RED CURRANT SAUCE
(pictured on page 116)

1 teaspoon dried whole rosemary
½ teaspoon salt
¼ teaspoon pepper
⅛ teaspoon dried whole thyme
1 (3½- to 4-pound) rolled boneless pork loin roast
1 cup apple juice
¼ cup soy sauce
2 tablespoons lime juice
1 small onion, finely chopped
1 tablespoon butter
1½ tablespoons grated orange rind
⅓ cup orange juice
2 teaspoons grated lime rind
2 tablespoons lime juice
¼ cup plus 1 tablespoon red currant jelly
2 teaspoons cornstarch
2 tablespoons water
Orange rind (optional)
Lime rind (optional)
Fresh parsley sprigs (optional)

Combine first 4 ingredients; rub on roast. Place roast, fat side down, in a 12- x 8- x 2-inch baking dish. Combine apple juice, soy sauce, and 2 tablespoons lime juice; pour in dish around roast. Cover with heavy-duty plastic wrap; fold back a small edge of wrap to allow steam to escape. Microwave at MEDIUM (50% power) 20 minutes. Uncover and turn roast over; cover and microwave at MEDIUM 20 to 30 minutes or until internal temperature of roast reaches 140°, giving dish a half-turn every 10 minutes.

Grill roast over medium coals 25 to 30 minutes or until internal temperature reaches 160°, basting frequently with pan drippings. Set aside.

Place onion and butter in a 2-cup glass measure. Microwave at HIGH 1 minute or until onion is tender. Add 1½ tablespoons grated orange rind and next 4 ingredients, stirring well. Microwave at HIGH 2½ minutes. Combine cornstarch and water; add to sauce. Microwave at HIGH 1 minute or until mixture boils. If desired, garnish with orange and lime rinds and parsley. Serve sauce over sliced pork loin. Yield: 12 servings.

SWEET-AND-SOUR RIBS

¼ cup chopped green onions
1 tablespoon vegetable oil
¼ teaspoon dried red pepper flakes
1 cup commercial barbecue sauce
½ cup peach preserves
2 tablespoons white wine vinegar
2½ to 3 pounds country-style ribs
1 teaspoon pepper
½ teaspoon seasoned salt
½ teaspoon garlic powder
1 (12-ounce) can beer

Combine first 3 ingredients in a 2-cup glass measure. Microwave at HIGH, uncovered, 1 minute. Add barbecue sauce, preserves, and vinegar; microwave at HIGH 2 to 3 minutes or until preserves melt.

Sprinkle ribs with pepper, seasoned salt, and garlic powder; place meaty side down in a 12- x 8- x 2-inch baking dish. Pour beer over ribs. Cover with heavy-duty plastic wrap; fold back a small edge of wrap to allow steam to escape. Microwave at HIGH 30 minutes, rearranging ribs after 15 minutes. Drain well, reserving pan drippings.

Grill ribs, meaty side up, over medium coals 20 minutes, basting ribs frequently with barbecue sauce mixture. Yield: 3 servings.

CHICKEN WITH WHITE BARBECUE SAUCE

1½ cups mayonnaise
⅓ cup apple cider vinegar
¼ cup lemon juice
2 tablespoons sugar
2 tablespoons freshly ground pepper
2 tablespoons white wine Worcestershire sauce
1 (2½- to 3-pound) broiler-fryer, quartered

Combine first 6 ingredients in a small bowl; stir well. Arrange chicken in a shallow dish. Pour 1 cup sauce over chicken, turning to coat. Cover and chill remaining sauce. Cover and chill chicken 6 to 8 hours, turning occasionally. Remove chicken, reserving marinade, and arrange in a 12- x 8- x 2-inch baking dish with skin side down and thicker portion of chicken toward outside of dish. Cover with wax paper, and microwave at HIGH 10 to 12 minutes; turn and rearrange chicken after 5 minutes.

Grill chicken over medium-hot coals 20 minutes or until done, turning once and basting with reserved marinade. Serve with reserved sauce. Yield: 4 servings.

BREAKFASTS & BRUNCHES®

Off To A Shining Start

Breakfast, usually a family meal, also lends itself deliciously to Southern hospitality and entertaining.

Here we join Harriet and Philip Plyler of Tampa, Florida, and their party crew for brunch on the beach.

The menu has been designed so that it can be enjoyed anywhere. The omelet is cooked and the kabobs are easily reheated on a camp stove, but instructions are included for cooking these recipes in the kitchen, too. And best of all, these recipes are great for entertaining because everything except the omelet can be made ahead of time.

Tortilla Campesina
Fruit Kabobs
Almond Braid
Peach-Almond Pound Cake
Yacht Club Milk Punch
Orange juice   Champagne

TORTILLA CAMPESINA

1 cup olive oil
2 cups diced potato
1 cup diced onion
1 cup diced green pepper
½ pound smoked link chorizo
   sausage, chopped
12 eggs, beaten
¼ cup water
½ teaspoon salt
½ teaspoon pepper
Sliced smoked chorizo sausage
   (optional)
Avocado slices (optional)
Fresh parsley sprigs
   (optional)

Heat oil in a 9-inch nonstick skillet over medium heat until hot. Add diced potato, and cook, stirring often, until tender. Drain potatoes, reserving 3 tablespoons oil in skillet. Set potatoes aside. Add onion and green pepper to skillet; cook, stirring often, until vegetables are tender. Add chopped sausage and potatoes; cook 3 to 5 minutes.

Combine eggs, water, salt, and pepper; stir briskly with a wire whisk until blended. Pour egg mixture into skillet. Cover and cook until mixture starts to set; uncover and gently lift edges of omelet with a spatula, and tilt pan so that uncooked portion flows underneath. (Keep skillet covered as much as possible.) When eggs have set and are firm underneath, place a large plate over skillet and turn omelet upside down onto plate. Slide omelet back into skillet, uncooked side down; cover and cook until omelet is set. Turn out onto a serving plate. If desired, garnish with sliced sausage, avocado, and parsley. Yield: 8 servings.

FRUIT KABOBS

8 (12-inch) wooden skewers
16 slices bacon
1 fresh pineapple, peeled and
   cored
2 Granny Smith apples
2 Rome apples
1 (6-ounce) can pineapple juice
⅓ cup firmly packed brown sugar

Soak wooden skewers in water, and set aside.

Cook bacon until limp but not crisp; drain and set aside.

Cut pineapple into 1-inch pieces. Core all apples, and cut into 1-inch pieces. Combine pineapple, apple, and pineapple juice, tossing to coat fruit. Thread end of a piece of bacon on skewer; alternate pieces of Granny Smith apple, pineapple, and Rome apple, weaving bacon around each, adding another slice of bacon when needed. Repeat with remaining skewers, bacon, and fruit. Reserve remaining fruit for other uses.

Sprinkle each kabob with brown sugar. Broil 6 inches from heat 6 minutes, turning once, or until fruit begins to brown around edges. Yield: 8 servings.

Note: If desired, fruit kabobs can be individually wrapped in foil and reheated for 10 minutes on a baking sheet placed on a camp stove; turn kabobs frequently.

ALMOND BRAID

1 package dry yeast
1 teaspoon sugar
¼ cup warm water (105° to 115°)
½ cup milk
¼ cup butter or margarine
⅓ cup sugar
1 teaspoon salt
1 teaspoon ground nutmeg
1 egg, beaten
2¾ to 3¼ cups all-purpose flour,
   divided
1 tablespoon butter or margarine
1 teaspoon grated orange rind
1 tablespoon orange juice
1 tablespoon lemon juice
1¼ to 1½ cups sifted powdered
   sugar
¼ cup sliced almonds

Dissolve yeast and 1 teaspoon sugar in warm water in a large bowl; let stand 5 minutes.

Combine milk and next 4 ingredients in a saucepan; heat until butter melts. Cool to 105° to 115°. Add to yeast mixture. Stir in egg and 1 cup flour, mixing well. Gradually stir in enough remaining flour to make a soft dough.

Turn dough out onto a lightly floured surface, and knead 5 minutes or until smooth and elastic. Place dough in a well-greased bowl, turning to grease top. Cover and let rise in a warm place (85°), free from drafts, 1½ hours or until doubled in bulk. Punch dough down; cover and let rise in a warm place, free from drafts, 1 hour or until dough is doubled in bulk.

Punch dough down, and divide into 4 portions. Shape 3 portions of dough into 14-inch-long ropes. Place ropes on a greased baking sheet (do not stretch); pinch ends together at one end to seal. Braid ropes; pinch loose ends to seal. Tuck ends under, and spread braids apart in center.

Divide remaining portion of dough into thirds. Shape each third into a 12-inch rope; braid loosely. Pinch ropes together at ends to seal, and tuck ends under. Place braid on top of first braid. Cover and let rise in a warm place, free from drafts, 45 minutes or until doubled in bulk.

Bake at 350° for 20 minutes or until a wooden pick inserted in center comes out clean. Cool braid on a wire rack.

Combine 1 tablespoon butter and next 3 ingredients in a small saucepan; heat until butter melts. Stir in enough powdered sugar to reach glaze consistency; drizzle over braid, and sprinkle with almonds. Yield: one (14-inch) braid.

PEACH-ALMOND POUND CAKE

1 cup butter or margarine,
   softened
3 cups sugar
6 eggs
3 cups all-purpose flour
¼ teaspoon baking soda
½ teaspoon salt
½ cup commercial sour cream
1 cup mashed peaches
1 teaspoon vanilla extract
1 teaspoon almond extract

Cream butter; gradually add sugar, beating well at medium speed of an electric mixer. Add eggs, one at a time, beating after each addition.

Combine flour, soda, and salt. Combine sour cream and peaches. Add flour mixture to creamed mixture alternately with peach mixture, beginning and ending with flour mixture. Mix just until blended after each addition. Stir in flavorings.

Pour batter into two greased and floured 9- x 5- x 3-inch loafpans.

Bake at 350° for 1 hour and 5 minutes or until a wooden pick inserted in center comes out clean. Cool in pans 10 to 15 minutes; remove from pans, and let cool completely. Yield: two loaves.

YACHT CLUB MILK PUNCH

2 cups sugar
2 cups water
2 quarts milk
2 cups half-and-half
2 cups brandy
Freshly grated nutmeg

Combine sugar and water in a saucepan; bring to a boil, and cook 5 minutes. Cool. Chill at least 2 hours.

Combine chilled syrup, milk, and remaining ingredients except nutmeg. Stir well; serve over ice. Sprinkle with nutmeg. Yield: 3½ quarts.

ON THE LIGHT SIDE

Light Breakfast To Go

If breakfast at your house means grabbing a bite on the way out the door, you can enjoy these quick-to-serve recipes without giving up nutrition. Breakfast should account for one-third of the day's caloric and nutrient needs and consist of complex carbohydrates, such as cereal or bread; fruit, juice, or another source of vitamin C; and a protein-rich food, such as milk.

Calorie-Saving Tips

■ A calorie-saving trick for mealtime is to eat from a small luncheon plate instead of a large dinner plate. Smaller portions will look larger.

■ Choose dairy products made from skim or low-fat milk to keep fat and calories lower.

STUFFED PITA

2 (6-inch) whole wheat pita bread rounds
Vegetable cooking spray
1 tablespoon diced onion
1 tablespoon diced green pepper
¼ cup diced lean cooked ham
2 eggs, beaten
½ cup (2 ounces) shredded low-fat Swiss cheese
8 tomato slices

Cut pita bread in half; seal in aluminum foil, and heat in oven at 350° for 5 minutes. Remove from oven, and keep warm.

Coat a nonstick skillet with cooking spray; place over medium-high heat until hot. Add onion and green pepper; sauté until vegetables are tender. Stir in ham, and cook until thoroughly heated. Add eggs, and cook, stirring frequently, until eggs are set. Stir in shredded Swiss cheese; remove from heat.

Place 2 tomato slices inside each pita half; fill with ¼ cup egg mixture. Yield: 4 servings (135 calories each).

□ *10.7 grams protein, 5.1 grams fat, 11.2 grams carbohydrate, 148 milligrams cholesterol, 464 milligrams sodium, and 132 milligrams calcium.*

QUICK QUESADILLAS

6 (6-inch) corn tortillas
¾ cup (3 ounces) shredded low-fat Monterey Jack cheese
¾ cup (3 ounces) shredded sharp Cheddar cheese
1 (4-ounce) can chopped green chiles, undrained
1 cup chopped tomato

Place tortillas on ungreased baking sheets. Combine cheeses, and sprinkle 4 tablespoons on each tortilla; spread green chiles evenly on top. Broil 6 inches from heat for 2 to 3 minutes or until cheese melts. Remove from oven, and top with chopped tomato; fold in half. Yield: 6 servings (166 calories per serving).

□ *10.8 grams protein, 7.3 grams fat, 15.4 grams carbohydrate, 19 milligrams cholesterol, 195 milligrams sodium, and 295 milligrams calcium.*

TORTILLA ROLLUPS

4 (6-inch) whole wheat flour tortillas
¼ cup chunky peanut butter
½ cup unsweetened applesauce
¼ cup raisins
⅛ teaspoon ground cinnamon

Seal tortillas in aluminum foil, and bake at 325° for 15 minutes. Spread each tortilla with 1 tablespoon peanut butter, 2 tablespoons applesauce, and 1 tablespoon raisins. Sprinkle with cinnamon, and roll up tortillas jellyroll fashion. Yield: 4 servings (246 calories per serving).

□ *6.7 grams protein, 10.4 grams fat, 36.3 grams carbohydrate, 0 milligrams cholesterol, 80 milligrams sodium, and 40 milligrams calcium.*

BREAKFAST-IN-A-BOWL

¼ cup low-fat cottage cheese
½ cup vanilla low-fat yogurt
½ medium banana, sliced
2 tablespoons granola

Place cottage cheese in a cereal bowl; top with yogurt. Add banana slices; sprinkle with granola. Yield: 1 serving (265 calories per serving).

□ *15.4 grams protein, 5.2 grams fat, 41 grams carbohydrate, 10 milligrams cholesterol, 334 milligrams sodium, and 245 milligrams calcium.*

FRUIT SMOOTHIE

2 medium bananas, sliced
1 (8-ounce) can crushed pineapple in juice, undrained
½ cup orange juice
1 teaspoon sugar
1 cup crushed ice
1 (8-ounce) carton plain low-fat yogurt

Combine all ingredients except yogurt in container of an electric blender; process until smooth. Add yogurt, and process mixture just until blended. Yield: 4 cups (142 calories per 1-cup serving).

□ *4 grams protein, 1.2 grams fat, 31.1 grams carbohydrate, 3 milligrams cholesterol, 41 milligrams sodium, and 118 milligrams calcium.*

Fruit, Fresh As The Morning

The next time company gathers for breakfast or brunch, serve fruit with the meal. Nothing quite compares to the flavor and freshness of a juicy fruit side dish.

STRAWBERRIES IN CREAM

3 tablespoons sugar, divided
1 cup finely chopped fresh
  strawberries
1 (8-ounce) carton commercial
  sour cream
1 cup whipping cream
¼ cup dry white wine
Strawberry fans (optional)

Sprinkle 2 tablespoons sugar over chopped strawberries; let stand 15 minutes. Combine remaining 1 tablespoon sugar, sour cream, whipping cream, and wine; beat with a wire whisk until smooth. Fold in strawberry mixture. Cover and chill at least 1 hour. Spoon into bowls, and garnish each serving with a strawberry fan, if desired. Yield: 4 cups.
Pat Rush Benigno
Gulfport, Mississippi

BAKED ORANGE SLICES

6 oranges
1 tablespoon salt
2 cups sugar
½ cup light corn syrup
½ cup vinegar
Orange rind bows (optional)

Wash oranges; combine oranges and salt in a Dutch oven. Cover oranges with water, and boil 30 minutes; drain, reserving ¾ cup water. Set aside, and let cool.

Combine sugar, corn syrup, vinegar, and reserved ¾ cup water in Dutch oven; boil 5 minutes.

Cut each orange into 5 slices; remove seeds. Boil slices in syrup mixture 15 minutes. Arrange slices in a lightly greased 12- x 8- x 2-inch baking dish. Cover with syrup mixture, and bake at 350° for 40 minutes. Garnish each serving with bows made from strips of orange rind, if desired. Yield: 10 to 12 servings.
DeLois Gates
Baldwyn, Mississippi

CHOCOLATE-TOPPED GRAPEFRUIT

4 pink grapefruit, halved
  crosswise
3 (1-ounce) squares semisweet
  chocolate, chopped
Fresh mint sprigs

Remove seeds, and loosen sections of grapefruit halves. Set aside.

Place chocolate in a heavy-duty zip-top plastic bag; seal bag. Submerge bag in hot water until chocolate melts. Snip a tiny whole in end of bag, using scissors; drizzle chocolate over grapefruit in a sunburst design. Bake at 350° for 5 to 7 minutes. Garnish with fresh mint. Serve immediately. Yield: 8 servings.

Note: Instead of piping chocolate, 2 teaspoons semisweet chocolate mini-morsels may be sprinkled over each grapefruit half, if desired. Bake as directed.
Joel Allard
San Antonio, Texas

Add Soufflés To The Menu

In French, soufflé means "puff," and that's a perfect description of these delicious vegetable-flavored egg dishes. Each would make an ideal addition to the menu for a fancy brunch. Beaten egg whites folded into the mixture just before baking make soufflés rise to dramatic heights and give them a characteristic lightness.

The traditional soufflé dish is round and straight-sided, but any oven-proof, straight-sided dish will work. A removable collar made of aluminum foil guides high-rising soufflés. (Refer to the recipes for directions for making a collar.)

Bake soufflés in the center of the oven to help them rise evenly. Be sure to remove the rack above the dish in case the soufflé rises more than anticipated.

Resist the urge to open the oven door before the end of the baking time, as a sudden loss of heat in the oven can cause a soufflé to fall. At the end of the baking time, insert a knife into the center of the soufflé to test for doneness; it's ready if the knife comes out clean.

Soufflés fall rapidly after removal from the oven, so have the rest of the meal ready when the soufflé is done. If you need to hold the soufflé a few minutes before serving, just turn the oven off, and leave the soufflé in the oven, watching it through the oven window to make sure it doesn't overbrown.

YELLOW SQUASH SOUFFLÉ

¼ cup butter or margarine
¼ cup all-purpose flour
1⅓ cups milk
½ teaspoon salt
Dash of red pepper
1 tablespoon minced onion
1¼ cups grated yellow squash
   (about 1 pound)
5 eggs, separated
1 teaspoon cream of tartar
½ cup (2 ounces) shredded sharp
   Cheddar cheese

Cut a piece of aluminum foil long enough to fit around a 1½-quart soufflé dish, allowing a 1-inch overlap; fold foil lengthwise into thirds. Lightly oil one side of foil and bottom of dish. Wrap foil around outside of dish, oiled side against dish, allowing foil to extend 3 inches above rim to form a collar; secure with string.

Melt butter in a heavy saucepan over low heat; add flour, stirring until smooth. Cook 1 minute, stirring constantly. Gradually add milk; cook over medium heat, stirring constantly, until thickened and bubbly. Stir in salt, pepper, and onion; remove from heat, and let cool.

Squeeze grated squash in paper towels to remove as much liquid as possible; stir squash into sauce.

Beat egg yolks until thick and lemon colored; add to squash mixture, and stir well.

Beat egg whites (at room temperature) and cream of tartar until stiff but not dry; fold into squash mixture. Pour into prepared dish.

Bake at 350° for 1 hour; sprinkle top evenly with Cheddar cheese, and bake an additional 5 minutes or until a knife inserted in center comes out clean. Remove collar from soufflé dish, and serve soufflé immediately. Yield: 6 to 8 servings.

Note: To omit collar, bake mixture in a 2-quart soufflé dish.

CARROT PUFF

4 large carrots, sliced
½ cup butter or margarine
½ cup all-purpose flour
1½ cups half-and-half
6 eggs, separated
½ teaspoon salt
½ teaspoon ground nutmeg

Cook carrots in boiling water to cover 8 to 10 minutes or until tender; drain.

Position knife blade in food processor bowl; add carrots, and process until smooth. Set aside 1 cup carrot puree; reserve remaining puree for other uses.

Cut a piece of aluminum foil long enough to fit around a 1-quart soufflé dish, allowing a 1-inch overlap; fold foil lengthwise into thirds. Lightly oil one side of foil and bottom of dish. Wrap foil around outside of dish, oiled side against dish, allowing foil to extend 3 inches above rim to form a collar; secure with string.

Melt butter in a heavy saucepan over low heat; add flour, stirring until smooth. Cook 1 minute, stirring constantly. Gradually add half-and-half; stir in 1 cup carrot puree. Cook over medium heat, stirring constantly, until thickened and bubbly. Beat egg yolks. Gradually stir about one-fourth of hot mixture into yolks; add to remaining hot mixture, stirring constantly. Stir in salt and nutmeg; cool.

Beat egg whites (at room temperature) until stiff but not dry; gently fold into carrot mixture. Pour into prepared dish. Bake at 350° for 1 hour or until puffed and set. Remove collar, and serve immediately. Yield: 6 servings. *Mrs. Harland J. Stone*
Ocala, Florida

ASPARAGUS SOUFFLÉ

1 (10-ounce) package frozen
   asparagus
¼ cup butter or margarine
¼ cup plus 2 tablespoons
   all-purpose flour
1½ cups milk
½ teaspoon salt
¼ teaspoon pepper
Dash of red pepper
1 cup (4 ounces) shredded
   mozzarella cheese
4 eggs, separated

Cook asparagus according to package directions, omitting salt; drain well. Position knife blade in food processor bowl; add asparagus, and process until smooth. Set aside.

Cut a piece of aluminum foil long enough to fit around a 1-quart soufflé dish, allowing a 1-inch overlap; fold foil lengthwise into thirds. Lightly oil one side of foil and bottom of dish. Wrap foil around outside of dish, oiled side against dish, allowing foil to extend 3 inches above rim to form a collar; secure with string.

Melt butter in a large saucepan over low heat; add flour, stirring until smooth. Cook 1 minute, stirring constantly. Gradually add milk; cook over medium heat, stirring constantly, until thickened and bubbly. Stir in salt and next 3 ingredients.

Beat egg yolks until thick and lemon colored. Gradually stir about one-fourth of hot mixture into yolks; add to remaining hot mixture, stirring constantly. Add asparagus puree, and stir well.

Beat egg whites (at room temperature) until stiff but not dry; gently fold into asparagus mixture. Pour into prepared dish. Bake at 350° for 50 to 55 minutes or until puffed and set. Remove collar, and serve immediately. Yield: 6 servings.

Note: To omit collar, bake mixture in a 1½-quart soufflé dish.

Butter— Shaped For Show

Butter and margarine sold in convenient block, stick, or tub forms are simple to serve for a routine breakfast, but consider shaping the spread for special occasions. You can shape butter several days in advance and keep it chilled until it is needed for the impressive presentation.

Making butter molds, curls, and fancy balls are three of the easiest and prettiest ways to shape butter or margarine. These particular designs require only a little preparation and a few simple tools that can be found at most large department stores or kitchen specialty shops.

Once you complete your butter designs, chill them until ready to serve. Remember that butter will soften and lose its shape rapidly at room temperature. Serve shaped butter in an icer or on a bed of crushed ice if you want it to hold its shape longer, such as when you set it out for buffet service.

Butter Curls

For making butter curls, you'll need a hook-shaped implement called a butter curler. Work with a stick of butter at refrigerator temperature. Place the butter on a flat surface, and pull the butter curler, ridged side down, lengthwise down the stick. The butter will curl up and over the curler. Place finished curls in ice water until all are made. Remove them from the water, and place on a serving dish. Cover and chill until ready to use. One stick yields about two dozen curls.

Butter Molds

For molding butter, we found that rubber, plastic, or porcelain molds unmold more easily than wooden ones. The molds come in both large and pat-size designs. To make butter molds, first soften the butter. Spread butter into cavity of the mold, scraping the back surface of the butter to level it. Freeze for 30 minutes or until the butter is firm. Then invert the mold, and pop the butter out. Cover and chill until ready to use. Yields for butter molds vary.

Butter Balls

Purchase a set of butter paddles to make butter balls. Dip paddles in boiling water for 30 seconds; then chill paddles in ice water. Slice a stick of butter (at refrigerator temperature) into eight equal pieces. Stand one slice of butter at a time on the ridged side of one paddle; place remaining paddle, ridged side down, on butter, and move paddles in opposite directions to roll butter around on the ridges. If butter clings to paddles, dip paddles again in boiling water and then in ice water, and continue rolling. Place butter balls in ice water until all are made. Then remove them from water, and place on a serving dish; cover and chill. One stick of butter yields eight balls.

Coffee Break Treats

When guests come for breakfast or brunch, it's a treat to have home-baked yeast rolls and flaky pastries. If you're expecting a crowd, you may want to offer an assortment.

BRIOCHE

1 package dry yeast
¼ cup warm water (105° to 115°)
2 tablespoons sugar
1 teaspoon salt
1 cup butter or margarine, softened
5 eggs
3½ cups all-purpose flour, divided
Vegetable oil
1 egg yolk
1 tablespoon milk

Dissolve yeast in warm water in a large mixing bowl; add sugar, salt, butter, 5 eggs, and 2 cups flour. Beat at medium speed of an electric mixer 3 to 4 minutes, scraping sides of bowl occasionally. Add remaining flour, and beat until smooth.

Place dough in a well-greased bowl. Lightly grease top of dough with vegetable oil. Cover and let rise in a warm place (85°), free from drafts, 1½ hours or until dough is doubled in bulk.

Punch dough down; cover and refrigerate 8 hours.

Punch dough down. Divide into 4 equal portions; reserve one portion. Divide each of the 3 portions into 8 pieces; shape each piece into a ball (total of 24 balls). Place in well-greased 3½-inch individual brioche or muffin pans. Using a floured finger, indent the center of each ball.

Divide reserved portion of dough into 24 pieces, and shape each piece into a ball; gently press one ball into each indentation. Place pans in a roasting pan; cover with a cloth so that it does not touch rolls. Let rise in a warm place, free from drafts, about 45 minutes or until rolls are doubled in bulk.

Combine egg yolk and milk; mix well. Lightly brush top of each roll with egg mixture. Bake at 375° for 15 minutes or until golden brown. Yield: 2 dozen.   *Sue-Sue Hartstern*
Louisville, Kentucky

ANISE ROLLS

1 package dry yeast
¼ cup warm water (105° to 115°)
¾ cup milk
¼ cup butter or margarine
⅓ cup sugar
2 teaspoons anise seeds, crushed
½ teaspoon salt
1 egg, beaten
2½ to 3 cups all-purpose flour
1 egg, beaten
1 teaspoon anise seeds

Dissolve yeast in warm water; let stand 5 minutes.

Combine milk, butter, sugar, 2 teaspoons anise seeds, and salt in a saucepan. Heat until butter melts and sugar dissolves. Cool to 105° to 115°. Add 1 egg and yeast mixture. Gradually stir in enough flour to make a soft dough.

Turn dough out onto a floured surface, and knead until smooth and elastic (about 8 to 10 minutes). Place in a well-greased bowl, turning to grease top. Cover and let rise in a warm place (85°), free from drafts, 1 hour or until doubled in bulk.

Punch dough down; turn out onto a lightly floured surface, and shape into 24 balls. Place balls about 2 inches apart on greased baking sheets. Brush with beaten egg; sprinkle with 1 teaspoon anise seeds. Cover and let rise in a warm place, free from drafts, 45 minutes or until rolls are doubled in bulk. Bake at 400° for 8 to 10 minutes or until browned. Yield: 2 dozen.
Sharon McClatchey
Muskogee, Oklahoma

SWEET PUFFS

2 cups all-purpose flour
1 cup butter or margarine
½ cup commercial sour cream
1 egg yolk
Cheese filling (recipe follows)
Powdered sugar

Position knife blade in food processor bowl. Add flour and butter; pulse 4 or 5 times until mixture resembles coarse meal. Add sour cream and egg yolk; process until dough forms a ball, leaving sides of bowl. Divide in half; cover and chill 8 hours.

Roll pastry on a lightly floured surface to ⅛-inch thickness. Cut pastry into 3-inch squares. Gently press each square into miniature (1¾-inch) muffin pans, leaving corners extending beyond edges. Spoon 1 teaspoon cheese filling into each prepared shell. Fold and seal corners over filling. Chill 30 minutes.

Bake at 375° for 20 to 25 minutes. Remove from pan, and cool on a wire rack. Sprinkle with powdered sugar. Yield: 3½ dozen.

Cheese Filling

1 (8-ounce) package cream
   cheese, softened
1 egg
½ cup sugar
1 teaspoon vanilla extract
1 teaspoon grated lemon rind

Combine all ingredients; beat at medium speed of an electric mixer until smooth and fluffy. Yield: 1½ cups.
Molly Hughes
Irmo, South Carolina

Baking Tips

■ A handy substitute for cake flour: 1 cup minus 2 tablespoons of all-purpose flour equals 1 cup cake flour.

■ Every time the door of the oven is opened, the oven temperature drops 25 to 30 degrees. Use the oven window so as not to waste energy.

■ To know when yeast is doubled in bulk, press dough flat in a bowl, mark level on outside of bowl. Make a mark on outside of bowl that is double the first.

■ Use shiny cookie sheets and cakepans for baking. Dark pans absorb more heat and cause baked products to overbrown.

Enticing Breakfast Beverages

Oh, what genteel, simple pleasure we find in a hot cup of coffee. Steaming and aromatic, coffee encourages us to greet the day.

Those who don't drink coffee need not despair. Fruity beverages also make excellent choices for morning.

SPICED-UP COFFEE

⅔ cup ground coffee
1 teaspoon vanilla extract
1 teaspoon almond extract
6 cups water

Place coffee in coffee filter or filter basket; spoon flavorings over coffee.

Add water to coffeemaker, and brew. Serve immediately. Yield: about 6 cups.   *Ruth Witoshynsky*
Pembroke Park, Florida

GRAPEFRUIT SANGRÍA

4 cups grapefruit juice, chilled
3 cups Rhine wine, chilled
1½ cups ginger ale, chilled

Combine ingredients in a large pitcher; stir gently. Serve over ice. Yield: 8½ cups.   *Laura Morris*
Bunnell, Florida

Breakfast and Beverage Tips

■ For a quick juice, place frozen concentrate in a glass or plastic pitcher in the microwave oven. Microwave at HIGH for 30 to 50 seconds or until concentrate is soft. Add water and stir.

■ Submerge an unpeeled lemon or orange in hot water for 15 minutes before squeezing to yield more juice.

■ Breakfast is the most important meal of the day. It doesn't have to be elaborate, but it should be high in nutritional value to get your day off to a healthy start.

■ For easy cleanup, fill your blender container with warm water, add a few drops of liquid detergent, and blend 30 seconds; rinse well.

■ If muffins are done ahead of serving time, loosen them from their cups, tilt slightly, and slide the pan back into the oven to stay warm. This keeps the muffins from steaming on bottom.

■ Try a little calorie-free club soda in grape or apple juice to add a bubbly sparkle and to make the fruit juice calories go further.

GINGER-MINT COOLER

1 cup water
½ cup sugar
¼ cup chopped fresh mint leaves
½ cup lemon juice
1 (33.8-ounce) bottle ginger ale, chilled

Combine water, sugar, and mint in a small saucepan; bring to a boil, stirring constantly until sugar dissolves. Remove from heat. Strain mint from mixture; discard mint. Let mixture chill thoroughly.

To serve, combine mint mixture, lemon juice, and ginger ale, stirring well; pour over crushed ice. Yield: 6 cups.   *Emma Prillhart*
Kingsport, Tennessee

VODKA-ORANGE SLUSH

1 (6-ounce) can frozen orange juice concentrate, thawed and undiluted
¾ cup vodka
¾ cup milk
1 tablespoon sugar
Ice cubes

Combine orange juice concentrate, vodka, milk, and sugar in container of an electric blender. Add enough ice cubes to make mixture measure 4½ cups. Blend beverage mixture to desired consistency.

Serve beverage in individual stemmed glasses. Yield: 4½ cups.
Wendy Rico
Marietta, Georgia

Cheesecakes Flirt With Flavor

No matter what flavor cheesecake is your favorite, chances are it's reflected in this recipe. It makes a near-flawless vanilla cheesecake and can be used as a springboard for other versions of this dessert.

The basic recipe adapts well to other flavors such as praline and chocolate marble. Experiment with the instructions given, and use your imagination to create other flavors that satisfy your cravings. Just be sure to keep the basic proportions of ingredients about the same as the examples given. If you do try a new variation, keep in mind that the length of baking time can vary with any changes you make.

Bake the cheesecake until it's almost firm in the center but is still a little shaky. The cheesecake will firm up as it cools.

CREAMY VANILLA CHEESECAKE

5 (8-ounce) packages cream
   cheese, softened
1½ cups sugar
3 eggs
2½ teaspoons vanilla extract
Graham cracker crust (recipe
   follows)
Strawberry fans (optional)

Beat cream cheese at high speed of an electric mixer until light and fluffy; gradually add sugar, beating well. Add eggs, one at a time, beating well after each addition. Stir in vanilla. Pour into graham cracker crust.

Bake at 350° for 40 minutes; turn oven off, and partially open oven door. Leave cheesecake in oven for 30 minutes. Remove from oven, and let cool on a wire rack in a draft-free place. Cover cheesecake, and chill at least 8 hours. Garnish with strawberry fans, if desired. Yield: one 10-inch cheesecake.

Crème de Menthe Cheesecake: Use Chocolate Wafer Crust. Stir ¼ cup green crème de menthe into cheesecake mixture when vanilla is added. Bake at 350° for 45 minutes. Garnish with chocolate leaves, if desired.

Praline Cheesecake: Use graham cracker crust. Substitute dark brown sugar for white sugar in cheesecake mixture. Sauté 1 cup chopped pecans in 3 tablespoons melted butter or margarine; drain pecans on paper towel. Fold into cheesecake mixture when vanilla is added. Bake at 350° for 45 minutes. Garnish with toasted pecan halves, if desired.

Brown Sugar-and-Spice Cheesecake: Use Gingersnap Crust. For cheesecake mixture, substitute brown sugar for white sugar, and add 1 teaspoon ground cinnamon, ½ teaspoon ground cloves, and ½ teaspoon ground nutmeg when sugar is added. Bake at 350° for 45 minutes. Garnish with whipped cream, and sprinkle with nutmeg, if desired.

Chocolate Marble Cheesecake: Use Chocolate Wafer Crust. Prepare basic cheesecake mixture, and divide in half. Stir 6 ounces melted semisweet chocolate into half of cheesecake mixture. Pour half of plain cheesecake mixture into prepared crust; top with half of chocolate mixture. Repeat layers to use all of mixture. Gently swirl batter with a knife to create a marble effect. Bake at 350° for 40 minutes. Garnish with mint sprigs, if desired.

Black Forest Cheesecake: Use graham cracker or Chocolate Wafer Crust. Prepare basic cheesecake mixture; stir 6 ounces melted semisweet chocolate into cheesecake mixture. Pour about half of chocolate mixture into prepared crust; top with 1 cup canned dark, sweet, pitted cherries, drained and patted dry. Spoon remaining chocolate mixture evenly over cherries. Bake at 350° for 45 minutes. Garnish cheesecake with whipped cream and additional cherries, if desired.

Graham Cracker Crust

1⅔ cups graham cracker crumbs
⅓ cup butter or margarine,
   melted

Combine crumbs and butter, stirring well. Firmly press mixture evenly on bottom and 1 inch up sides of a 10-inch springform pan. Bake at 350° for 5 minutes. Yield: one 10-inch crust.

Chocolate Wafer Crust: Substitute 1⅔ cups chocolate wafer crumbs for graham cracker crumbs.

Gingersnap Crust: Substitute 1⅔ cups gingersnap crumbs for graham cracker crumbs.

Dates Make The Cake

The warm, spicy flavor of allspice accents sweet dates and crunchy walnuts in this light-and-airy Date-Nut Cake Roll. It's a welcome change to present this familiar flavor combination in something other than a dense fruitcake. The sponge cake is baked in a jellyroll pan and rolled into an elegant dessert that's just right to end a special meal.

DATE-NUT CAKE ROLL

1 (8-ounce) package whole pitted dates, chopped
1 cup water
¼ cup sugar
3 eggs
½ cup sugar
1 cup all-purpose flour
1 teaspoon baking powder
½ teaspoon ground allspice
Dash of salt
¾ cup finely chopped walnuts or pecans
1 to 2 tablespoons powdered sugar
2 (3-ounce) packages cream cheese, softened
¼ cup butter or margarine, softened
1 teaspoon vanilla extract
1 cup sifted powdered sugar
1 tablespoon powdered sugar
Additional walnuts or pecans

Grease and flour bottom and sides of a 15- x 10- x 1-inch jellyroll pan; set aside. Combine dates, water, and ¼ cup sugar in a saucepan. Cook over medium heat until thickened (about 10 minutes); cool.

Beat eggs in a large bowl at high speed of an electric mixer 5 minutes. Gradually add ½ cup sugar, beating until smooth. Add date mixture.

Combine flour, baking powder, allspice, and salt; fold into date mixture. Spoon batter into prepared pan, spreading evenly. Sprinkle with ¾ cup walnuts. Bake at 375° for 12 to 15 minutes.

Sift 1 to 2 tablespoons powdered sugar in a 15- x 10-inch rectangle on a towel. When cake is done, immediately loosen from sides of pan, and turn out onto sugared towel. Starting at narrow end, roll up cake and towel together; let cool completely on a wire rack, seam side down.

Combine cream cheese and butter in a medium bowl, and beat at medium speed of an electric mixer until fluffy. Add vanilla and 1 cup powdered sugar; beat until smooth.

Unroll cake; remove towel. Spread cake evenly with filling, reserving ⅓ cup filling for garnish, if desired. Reroll cake, without towel, and place on a serving plate, seam side down. Sprinkle with 1 tablespoon powdered sugar. If desired, pipe reserved filling lengthwise on top of cake roll, and top with walnuts. Store cake in refrigerator. Yield: 8 to 10 servings.

Bettylee Carmine
Lewes, Delaware

Dress Up Cake And Ice Cream In Minutes

Expect the unexpected. There are often drop-in guests and occasions when there just isn't time to make a special dessert as intended. For easy preparation, try the following recipes to embellish frozen pound cake and ice cream; you can keep both of these on hand.

You'll never go wrong with chocolate or nuts to top ice cream or cake. Toffee-Fudge Sauce is especially thick and yummy. Or you may already have pecans, brown sugar, and corn syrup to make Praline Sauce.

CHOCOLATE-ORANGE POUND CAKE

1 (16-ounce) loaf frozen pound cake, thawed
3 tablespoons orange juice
⅔ cup orange marmalade
1 (16-ounce) can ready-to-spread chocolate-fudge frosting

Cut cake horizontally into 4 layers. Place bottom layer, cut side up, on cake platter; brush with orange juice. Spread with ⅓ cup marmalade. Place another cake layer on top; brush with orange juice, and spread with ½ cup frosting. Place another cake layer on top; brush with orange juice, and spread with remaining marmalade. Top with remaining cake layer, cut side down. Spread remaining frosting on top and sides of cake. Chill. Yield: 8 to 10 servings. *Gizella C. Kolek*
Lakeland, Florida

PEAR WHIP

1 (16-ounce) can pear halves, drained and chilled
1 (8-ounce) carton plain yogurt
3 tablespoons honey

Combine all ingredients in container of an electric blender; blend at medium speed until smooth. Serve over pound cake or angel food cake. Yield: 2 cups. *Judy Grigoraci*
Charleston, West Virginia

BANANAS HAWAIIAN

¾ cup flaked coconut
3 tablespoons butter or margarine
½ cup firmly packed brown sugar
1 cup dark rum
¼ teaspoon ground cinnamon
6 firm bananas, peeled and sliced
2 quarts vanilla ice cream

Brown coconut in a skillet over medium heat, stirring constantly. Remove from pan; cool and set aside.

Combine butter, sugar, rum, and cinnamon in skillet; cook over medium heat, stirring often, until mixture boils. Add bananas; cook just until heated.

Spoon over ice cream; sprinkle with coconut. Serve immediately. Yield: 8 servings.

Margaret L. Hunter
Princeton, Kentucky

APPLE AMBROSIA SAUCE

½ cup frozen orange juice concentrate, thawed and undiluted
¾ cup water
1 (8-ounce) can crushed pineapple, undrained
3 cups shredded apple
½ cup flaked coconut

Combine orange juice concentrate and water in a large bowl; stir well. Add pineapple and remaining ingredients; toss gently. Serve over ice cream or pound cake. Store sauce in refrigerator. Yield: 4 cups.

Linda Gellatly
Winston-Salem, North Carolina

PRALINE SAUCE

1 cup water
⅔ cup chopped pecans
½ cup firmly packed brown sugar
½ cup dark corn syrup
1 tablespoon butter or margarine

Bring water to a boil in a small saucepan; add chopped pecans, reduce heat, and cook 5 minutes. Drain and set aside.

Combine brown sugar, syrup, and butter in a heavy saucepan. Bring mixture to a boil; reduce heat, and

simmer 5 minutes, stirring constantly. Stir in pecans. Serve warm over ice cream. Yield: 1 cup.

Marion Gilmore
Lake Placid, Florida

TOFFEE-FUDGE SAUCE

1 (14-ounce) bag caramels
½ cup milk chocolate morsels
¼ cup strong coffee
¼ cup milk

Combine all ingredients in a saucepan; cook over medium heat, stirring occasionally, until chocolate morsels and caramels melt. Serve warm over pound cake or ice cream. Yield: about 2 cups.

Note: One (12.25-ounce) jar caramel sauce may be substituted for bag of caramels. *Mrs. J. David Stearns*
Mobile, Alabama

ON THE LIGHT SIDE

Shellfish Treasures From The Sea

New evidence shows that shellfish once thought to be high in cholesterol are no longer villains. Original testing on shellfish couldn't distinguish among the different kinds of sterols in food of which cholesterol is only one. So shellfish was wrongly tagged as a high-cholesterol food.

There are two groups of shellfish: mollusks (oysters, scallops, and clams) and crustaceans (shrimp, crab, and lobster). New testing

shows that mollusks are low in cholesterol. A 3½-ounce serving contains between 35 and 50 milligrams of cholesterol, which is comparable to levels in most fin fish and is one-half to one-third the amount in beef and poultry.

Crustaceans are higher in cholesterol than mollusks, about 60 to 180 milligrams per 3½-ounce serving. However, they're still low enough to fit into light and healthy eating.

Tomatoes Stuffed With Sea Slaw features seafood mix that is made from fish flakes. It can be found at most fish markets or in the frozen foods section of the grocery store.

CLAM CHOWDER

1 (10-ounce) can whole shelled clams, undrained
1 tablespoon reduced-calorie margarine
⅓ cup chopped celery
⅓ cup chopped onion
1¼ cups peeled, diced potatoes
1 tablespoon cornstarch
1 cup skim milk
1 (12-ounce) can evaporated skimmed milk
½ teaspoon salt
⅛ teaspoon white pepper
Dash of hot sauce
Dash of paprika

Drain clams; reserve ½ cup liquid. Set clams aside.

Combine clam liquid, margarine, celery, onion, and potato in a Dutch oven, and bring to a boil. Cover, reduce heat, and simmer 15 minutes or until potatoes are tender.

Combine cornstarch and milks; add to potato mixture. Add clams, salt, and remaining ingredients. Cook over medium heat, stirring constantly, until thickened. Yield: 8 servings (104 calories per ½-cup serving).

□ *9.4 grams protein, 1.4 grams fat, 13.1 grams carbohydrate, 14 milligrams cholesterol, 284 milligrams sodium, and 186 milligrams calcium.*

CRAB-AND-SHRIMP ÉTOUFFÉE

2 pounds unpeeled medium-size
    fresh shrimp
⅔ cup chopped onion
¼ cup chopped green pepper
¼ cup chopped celery
3 cloves garlic, minced
2 tablespoons reduced-calorie
    margarine
⅔ cup no-salt-added chicken
    broth
⅓ cup white wine
1 tablespoon no-salt-added tomato
    paste
¼ cup chopped green onions
2 tablespoons chopped fresh
    parsley
2 teaspoons low-sodium
    Worcestershire sauce
¼ teaspoon salt
¼ teaspoon pepper
⅛ teaspoon hot sauce
1½ tablespoons cornstarch
⅓ cup no-salt-added chicken
    broth
12 ounces fresh crabmeat,
    drained and flaked
2 cups hot cooked rice

Peel and devein shrimp; set aside.
Sauté ⅔ cup chopped onion and next 3 ingredients in margarine in a large skillet until tender. Stir in ⅔ cup chicken broth and next 8 ingredients. Add shrimp; cover and simmer 5 minutes, stirring occasionally. Combine cornstarch and ⅓ cup chicken broth; add to shrimp mixture. Cook, stirring constantly, until mixture boils; boil 1 minute, stirring constantly. Stir in crabmeat, and cook until thoroughly heated. Serve over hot cooked rice. Yield: 6 servings (248 calories per ⅔ cup étouffée and ⅓ cup rice).

□ *27.1 grams protein, 4.5 grams fat, 22.8 grams carbohydrate, 148 milligrams cholesterol, 429 milligrams sodium, and 87 milligrams calcium.*

TOMATOES STUFFED WITH SEA SLAW

6 cups water
1 pound unpeeled medium-size
    fresh shrimp
½ pound seafood mix
1½ cups chopped red cabbage
1½ cups chopped green cabbage
½ cup grated carrot
¼ cup minced parsley
1 teaspoon celery seeds
½ teaspoon sugar
¼ teaspoon dry mustard
¼ teaspoon pepper
1 tablespoon cider vinegar
¼ cup reduced-calorie
    mayonnaise
1 (8-ounce) carton plain low-fat
    yogurt
6 medium tomatoes

Bring water to a boil; add unpeeled shrimp, and cook 3 to 5 minutes. Drain well, and rinse with cold water; chill. Peel and devein shrimp. Set aside 18 shrimp. Cut remaining shrimp in half, and combine with seafood mix, cabbages, grated carrot, and minced parsley.
Combine celery seeds and next 6 ingredients. Pour over cabbage mixture; toss gently.
Core tomatoes. Cut each into 6 wedges, cutting to, but not through, base of tomato. Spread wedges apart slightly.

Spoon cabbage mixture into tomatoes; top each with 3 shrimp. Yield: 6 servings (160 calories per serving).

□ *16.3 grams protein, 4.4 grams fat, 13.2 grams carbohydrate, 86 milligrams cholesterol, 463 milligrams sodium, and 360 milligrams calcium.*
Ginny Munsterman
Garland, Texas

CRAB-AND-MUSHROOM CASSEROLE

¼ cup finely chopped onion
¼ cup finely chopped celery
¼ cup finely chopped green
    pepper
2 tablespoons reduced-calorie
    margarine, melted
1 pound fresh mushrooms, sliced
¼ cup all-purpose flour
2 cups low-sodium chicken broth
½ cup egg substitute
1 pound fresh crabmeat, drained
    and flaked
1 tablespoon salt-free
    herb-and-spice blend
¾ teaspoon salt
⅛ teaspoon ground ginger
Vegetable cooking spray
¼ cup (1 ounce) shredded
    40%-less-fat sharp Cheddar
    cheese

Seafood Tips

■ When frozen, crabmeat becomes tough and watery, losing flavor. It's best to use crabmeat in a recipe and then freeze it. To serve, thaw crabmeat in the refrigerator and then follow recipe cooking instructions.

■ Count on 2 servings per ½ to 1 pound of shucked or shelled crab, lobsters, scallops, oysters, and shrimp.

■ When purchasing scallops, count on 40 to the pound. Since they are highly perishable, cook scallops within two days of purchase. Before cooking, always wash scallops well to remove sand and grit.

■ To make a modest amount of shrimp go further in a casserole or creamed dish, split large fat shrimp horizontally.

Sauté onion, celery, and green pepper in margarine in a large skillet until tender. Add mushrooms, and cook 10 minutes. Add flour, stirring until smooth. Cook 1 minute, stirring constantly. Gradually add chicken broth; cook over medium heat, stirring constantly, until mixture is thickened and bubbly. Gradually stir about one-fourth of hot mixture into egg substitute; add to remaining hot mixture, stirring constantly. Stir in crabmeat and next 3 ingredients.

Spoon mixture into a 12- x 8- x 2-inch baking dish coated with cooking spray. Bake at 350° for 35 minutes; sprinkle with cheese, and bake an additional 5 minutes. Yield: 6 servings (166 calories per serving).

☐ *18.7 grams protein, 4.4 grams fat, 12.7 grams carbohydrate, 45 milligrams cholesterol, 595 milligrams sodium, and 84 milligrams calcium.*
Hilda L. Brown
Winston-Salem, North Carolina

BAKED OYSTERS ITALIANO
(pictured on page 75)

Rock salt
3 tablespoons commercial Italian dressing
2 teaspoons lemon juice
¼ teaspoon hot sauce
2 tablespoons Italian-seasoned breadcrumbs
1 tablespoon grated Parmesan cheese
⅛ teaspoon garlic powder
⅛ teaspoon dried whole Italian seasoning
12 medium-size fresh raw oysters on the half shell
1 tablespoon minced fresh parsley

Sprinkle a thin layer of rock salt in a shallow baking pan.

Combine Italian dressing, lemon juice, and hot sauce; set aside. Combine breadcrumbs and next 3 ingredients; set aside. Place oysters (in shells) over rock salt. Sprinkle each oyster evenly with Italian dressing mixture and breadcrumb mixture. Bake at 425° for 6 to 8 minutes or until edges of oysters begin to curl. Sprinkle with fresh parsley. Yield: 1 dozen (17 calories per oyster).

☐ *1.4 grams protein, 0.5 gram fat, 1.6 grams carbohydrate, 8 milligrams cholesterol, 105 milligrams sodium, and 14 milligrams calcium.*

QUICK!
Grab A Snack

When the urge for a snack hits, there's no time to spare—you want it now. If your craving is for something a little out of the ordinary yet easy, try one of these tasty treats.

By simply stirring together a few ingredients and heating, you can create a quick, satisfying snack.

OPEN-FACED CHEESE-AND-OLIVE SNACK

1 (8-ounce) jar process cheese spread
1 (4¼-ounce) can chopped ripe olives, drained
½ cup mayonnaise
4 slices bacon, cooked and crumbled
6 hamburger buns, split

Combine cheese spread, chopped olives, mayonnaise, and crumbled bacon; spread about 2 tablespoons evenly over each bun half. Broil about 2 inches from heat until hot and lightly browned. Yield: 1 dozen.
Juanita Meece
Waco, Texas

BUTTERY CEREAL BITES

¼ cup butter or margarine
¼ teaspoon salt
6 cups crispy rice cereal squares
⅓ cup grated Parmesan cheese

Melt butter in a skillet; stir in salt. Add crispy rice cereal squares, stirring to coat; cook over low heat until cereal is lightly toasted, stirring constantly. Sprinkle with cheese; toss to coat. Spread mixture on paper towels, and let cool completely. Yield: 6 cups.
Wanda Bishop
Little Rock, Arkansas

TEX-MEX NACHOS

32 to 40 tortilla chips
2 cups (8 ounces) shredded Monterey Jack cheese
2 tablespoons sliced jalapeño peppers
⅛ teaspoon chili powder
Bean Dip

Arrange chips on a broiler-safe 15- x 9-inch platter, and sprinkle with cheese. Top cheese with jalapeño peppers; sprinkle with chili powder. Broil 4 inches from heat for 1 minute or until cheese melts. Serve with Bean Dip. Yield: about 3 dozen.

Bean Dip

1 (15½-ounce) can Mexican-style chili beans
½ teaspoon ground cumin
½ teaspoon chili powder
¼ teaspoon dried whole oregano

Drain beans, reserving 2 tablespoons liquid. Combine beans, reserved liquid, cumin, chili powder, and oregano in container of electric blender or food processor; pulse several times until beans are partially chopped.

Transfer mixture to a small saucepan; cook over low heat, stirring constantly, until mixture is thoroughly heated. Serve immediately. Yield: about 1 cup. *Becky Bradshaw*
Bedford, Texas

QUICK CHEESE SNACK

2 cups (8 ounces) shredded
    American cheese
1 stalk celery, chopped
¼ cup chopped onion
½ cup mayonnaise
¼ teaspoon pepper
48 slices party rye bread, toasted
    on both sides

Combine first 5 ingredients in a medium bowl; spread 1½ teaspoons of cheese mixture over each slice of bread. Broil 6 inches from heat about 2 minutes or until cheese melts. Yield: 4 dozen.

CHUNKY ARTICHOKE SPREAD

1 (6-ounce) jar marinated
    artichoke hearts, drained and
    chopped
2 tablespoons chopped green
    onions
1½ tablespoons mayonnaise
1 teaspoon lemon juice
1 teaspoon Worcestershire sauce
Dash of pepper

Combine all ingredients. Serve with melba toast. Yield: ¾ cup.

Mike Ginn
Columbia, Mississippi

Canned Salmon, Convenience Plus

Busy cooks know the value of canned salmon as a pantry staple with right-from-the-can convenience. It's a tasty and nutritious natural food with only salt added for flavor.

Canned salmon is available in a 15½-ounce can containing about 2 cups, a 7¾-ounce can containing 1 cup, and a 3¾-ounce can, which holds about ½ cup and is perfect for an individual serving.

If you've pondered over which variety of salmon to buy, the red or sockeye salmon has a firmer texture and is ideal for salads, hors d'oeuvres, and eating right from the can. The lighter colored pink varieties are an economical choice for casseroles, soups, sandwiches, or any cooked dishes.

SCALLOPED SALMON FOR TWO

1 (7¾-ounce) can salmon,
    undrained
¼ teaspoon chicken-flavored
    bouillon granules
¼ cup boiling water
¼ cup milk
1 egg, lightly beaten
1 tablespoon chopped fresh
    parsley
1 tablespoon finely chopped onion
1 cup herb-seasoned stuffing mix
½ cup (2 ounces) shredded
    Cheddar cheese
Vegetable Sauce

Drain salmon, reserving liquid; remove skin and bones, if desired. Flake salmon with a fork.

Dissolve bouillon granules in boiling water in a medium bowl. Add salmon liquid, milk, egg, parsley, and onion; mix well. Add salmon, stuffing mix, and cheese, mixing well. Place in 2 greased 10-ounce custard cups or 2 greased au gratin dishes. Bake at 350° for 30 minutes. Serve with Vegetable Sauce. Yield: 2 servings.

Vegetable Sauce

1 tablespoon butter or margarine
1½ teaspoons all-purpose flour
½ cup milk
⅛ teaspoon salt
⅛ teaspoon pepper
½ cup cooked English peas

Melt butter in a heavy saucepan over low heat; add flour, stirring until smooth. Cook 1 minute, stirring constantly. Gradually add milk; cook over medium heat, stirring constantly, until mixture is thickened and bubbly. Stir in salt, pepper, and peas. Yield: ¾ cup. *Ranaé Phelps*
Balch Springs, Texas

SALMON BURGERS

1 (15½-ounce) can salmon,
    undrained
¼ cup chopped onion
2 tablespoons butter or
    margarine, melted
1 egg, beaten
3 tablespoons fine, dry
    breadcrumbs
2 tablespoons chopped fresh
    parsley
½ teaspoon dry mustard
¼ teaspoon salt
¼ cup fine, dry breadcrumbs
Vegetable oil
4 hamburger buns, split and
    toasted
⅓ cup mayonnaise
1 tablespoon chopped sweet
    pickle

Drain salmon, reserving 2½ tablespoons liquid; set liquid aside. Remove skin and bones from salmon, if desired; flake salmon with a fork.

Sauté onion in butter in a skillet until tender. Stir in reserved salmon liquid, salmon, egg, and next 4 ingredients. Remove from heat; let cool to touch. Shape into 4 patties. (Mixture will be moist.) Dredge patties in ¼ cup breadcrumbs. Pour oil to a depth of ⅛ inch into a large heavy skillet. Cook patties in hot oil over medium heat 5 to 7 minutes on each side or until done. Drain. Place one patty on bottom half of each bun. Top with remaining bun halves.

Combine mayonnaise and chopped sweet pickle; serve with burgers. Yield: 4 servings. *Charlotte Pierce*
Greensburg, Kentucky

CHEESY SALMON PATTIES

1 (15½-ounce) can pink salmon,
    drained
1 egg, beaten
¼ cup buttermilk
⅓ cup self-rising flour
¾ cup (3 ounces) shredded sharp
    Cheddar cheese
Vegetable oil

Remove skin and bones from salmon,
if desired; flake salmon with a fork.
Add egg, buttermilk, flour, and
Cheddar cheese, stirring well. Shape
salmon mixture into 6 patties. (Mixture will be moist.) Pour oil to a
depth of ⅛ inch into a large heavy
skillet. Cook patties in hot oil over
medium heat 8 minutes or until
golden brown, turning once. Yield: 4
to 6 servings.   *Sharron Wright*
                        Austell, Georgia

SALMON SALAD

1 (7¾-ounce) can salmon, drained
1 (10-ounce) package frozen
    English peas
1 hard-cooked egg, chopped
½ teaspoon curry powder
3 tablespoons mayonnaise
1½ cups loosely packed
    watercress
1 (29-ounce) can sliced peaches,
    drained

Remove skin and bones from salmon,
if desired; flake salmon with a fork.
Set aside.
Cook English peas according to
package directions, and drain well.
Combine salmon, peas, chopped egg,
curry powder, and mayonnaise in a
medium bowl, tossing until all ingredients are coated. Cover salad, and
chill thoroughly.
Place watercress on 4 salad plates.
Arrange peach slices on watercress,
and spoon salmon mixture on
peaches. Yield: 4 servings.
                Mrs. Earl L. Faulkenberry
                Lancaster, South Carolina

Turn Rice Into Something Special

Versatile rice complements all kinds
of foods—meats, vegetables, and
even fruit. To set off your favorite
entrée, use one of these spruced-up
rice side dishes, all of which contain
a variety of flavorful ingredients.

CHEESE-PARSLIED RICE

3 cups cooked long-grain rice
2 cups milk
2 eggs, beaten
1 cup finely chopped fresh parsley
1 cup (4 ounces) shredded
    Cheddar cheese
¼ cup chopped onion
¼ cup butter, softened

Combine all ingredients; spoon into a
greased 2-quart casserole. Bake, uncovered, at 350° for 45 minutes.
Yield: 8 servings.   *Irene R. Smith*
                       Covington, Georgia

PORK FRIED RICE

1 (5-ounce) boneless pork chop,
    diced
½ cup diced carrot
½ cup finely chopped broccoli
½ cup frozen tiny English peas,
    thawed
¼ cup chopped green onions
2 tablespoons butter or
    margarine, melted
3 cups cooked long-grain rice
2 eggs, beaten
3 to 4 tablespoons soy sauce
¼ teaspoon garlic powder
⅛ teaspoon ground ginger

Sauté first 5 ingredients in butter in a
large skillet 3 to 4 minutes or until
pork is cooked. Remove from skillet,
and set aside. Cook rice in skillet
until thoroughly heated. Push rice to

sides of skillet, forming a well in center. Pour eggs into well, and cook
until set, stirring occasionally. Stir
rice into eggs; add vegetables, soy
sauce, and remaining ingredients,
stirring well. Yield: 4 to 6 servings.
                Betty Zickefoose
                Dahlonega, Georgia

RICE-AND-CHEESE CON CHILES

3 cups cooked long-grain rice
1 cup (4 ounces) shredded sharp
    Cheddar cheese
1 cup (4 ounces) shredded
    Monterey Jack cheese
2½ cups milk
1 (4-ounce) can chopped green
    chiles, drained
1 jalapeño pepper, minced
4 eggs, slightly beaten
1 teaspoon pepper
½ teaspoon salt
½ teaspoon dry mustard
1 tablespoon chopped fresh
    cilantro
1 teaspoon hot sauce
½ teaspoon ground cumin

Layer half of rice and half of each
cheese in a lightly greased 12- x 8- x
2-inch baking dish. Repeat layers.
Combine milk and remaining ingredients, mixing well. Pour over layers
in dish. Cover and bake at 325° for
30 minutes. Uncover and bake an additional 30 to 40 minutes or until set.
Let stand 10 minutes before serving.
Yield: 8 servings.

Note: To prepare ahead, cover and
refrigerate 8 hours. Remove from refrigerator; let stand 30 minutes.
Bake as directed.   *Sally Murphy*
                        Grapevine, Texas

ALMOND RICE

¼ cup chopped almonds
3 tablespoons butter or
    margarine, melted
3 cups cooked long-grain rice
⅓ cup minced fresh parsley
⅛ teaspoon curry powder

Sauté almonds in butter. Remove from heat; add rice and remaining ingredients. Yield: 4 to 6 servings.

T. O. Davis
Waynesboro, Mississippi

No-Fuss Fajitas

When Jan Ramsey of Quitaque, Texas, wants to fix something quick and easy, she makes Chicken Fajitas. "I put the chicken in to marinate before I go to work, then it's ready to cook when I get home," she says.

CHICKEN FAJITAS

2 tablespoons lemon juice
½ teaspoon salt
½ teaspoon liquid smoke
¼ teaspoon coarsely ground
    pepper
¼ teaspoon garlic powder
3 chicken breast halves, skinned,
    boned, and cut into strips
6 (6-inch) flour tortillas
2 tablespoons vegetable oil
1 green or sweet red pepper, cut
    into strips
1 medium onion, sliced and
    separated into rings

Combine first 5 ingredients in a small bowl. Add chicken; stir to coat. Cover and chill at least 30 minutes. Drain chicken, reserving marinade.

Wrap tortillas in aluminum foil; bake at 350° for 15 minutes.

Heat oil in a heavy skillet. Add chicken; cook 2 to 3 minutes, stirring constantly. Add marinade, pepper strips, and onion; sauté until vegetables are crisp-tender. Remove from heat. Divide mixture evenly, and spoon a portion onto each tortilla. If desired, top with any of the following: chopped tomato, green onions, lettuce, guacamole, sour cream, shredded cheese, and picante sauce; then wrap. Yield: 3 servings.

From Our Kitchen To Yours

Adding a special garnish turns any food into an appealing work of art. It can be as simple as a sprig of fresh herb or as elaborate as a celery rose. Whatever garnish you choose, it should be edible and complementary to the food in color, texture, size, and flavor. For a tasteful natural garnish, simply select an ingredient that is used in the recipe. However, if a usable garnish isn't in the recipe, then create one using one of the following: celery leaves, broccoli leaves, grated carrots, parsley sprigs, chopped green onions, or red or green pepper rings.

In preparing the garnishes illustrated at left, our test kitchens' home economist used only two kitchen utensils—a sharp knife and a vegetable peeler. For cutting the vegetables, use a small, sharp paring knife or a garnish knife, both of which have a very short blade, allowing for more control. This type knife is available from many kitchen shops and mail-order companies.

To curl and keep fresh those garnishes made from leeks, green onions, celery, carrots, and chile or jalapeño peppers, place them in ice water for at least one hour. Or these garnishes may be made ahead and stored in water in the refrigerator for one or two days.

Celery rose: *Hold a sharp knife at an angle and cut the outermost rib 1 to 2 inches above the base; arc cut to form a petal shape. Continue removing ribs, working toward the center. Put in ice water 30 minutes.*

Chile or jalapeño pepper flower: *Trim off chile end, keeping stem end about 2 inches; jalapeño is right size. Using a small knife, cut several slits in chile or jalapeño, beginning ¼ inch from stem end; remove seeds.*

Leek brush: *Select a small leek. Cut off a 1½- to 2-inch section from the bulb end; using a sharp knife, slice lengthwise into ⅛-inch strips, cutting almost to, but not through, bulb end. Place in ice water at least 1 hour.*

Cherry tomato flower: *Cut one small tomato into 6 pointed petals to within ¼ inch of stem end. Cut two medium tomatoes into 8 pointed petals. Open petals; remove seeds and pulp, and discard. Stack tomatoes.*

MAY

Strawberries, beautiful to look at and delicious to eat, are in season. Their rich taste flavors a wide range of recipes, from pies and tarts to sorbets and ice creams. Also fresh from the garden come bell peppers and other vegetables to highlight spring menus.

Fresh Vegetables, Simple Dining

In May, the sun's rays stretch longer across the South, gently coaxing fresh vegetables from carefully tended gardens.

Try one of these fresh vegetable recipes for easy preparation and quick menu planning. Each vegetable side dish complements a different grilled entrée—pork, chicken, beef, or fish. To complete the meal, serve a tossed salad or chilled soup and French bread.

MINT-GLAZED BABY CARROTS

8 medium carrots or 2 (12-ounce)
   packages baby carrots
3 tablespoons butter or margarine
2 tablespoons sugar
2 tablespoons finely chopped fresh
   mint leaves
Fresh mint sprigs (optional)

Scrape carrots; cut into 3-inch pieces. Arrange carrots in a vegetable steamer. Place over boiling water; cover and steam 12 minutes. Drain well.

Melt butter in a large skillet; stir in sugar and chopped mint. Add carrots, and cook over low heat about 8 minutes, stirring until well glazed. Garnish with fresh mint sprigs, if desired. Yield: 4 to 6 servings.

Heather Riggins
Nashville, Tennessee

LEMONY CUCUMBERS

2 medium cucumbers
¼ cup vinegar
2 tablespoons sugar
2 tablespoons chopped onion
1 tablespoon lemon juice
1 teaspoon celery seeds
¾ teaspoon salt
⅛ teaspoon pepper

Score cucumbers with a fork, and thinly slice.

Combine vinegar and remaining ingredients, stirring well. Pour over cucumbers; cover and chill 4 hours. Yield: 6 servings. *Brenda Rohe*
Charlotte, North Carolina

MARINATED ZUCCHINI

3 medium zucchini, thinly sliced
   (about 1¼ pounds)
¼ cup chopped onion
¼ cup chopped green pepper
¼ cup chopped celery
1 tablespoon chopped pimiento
⅓ cup cider vinegar
¼ cup sugar
¼ cup vegetable oil
1 tablespoon white wine vinegar
½ teaspoon salt
¼ teaspoon pepper
⅛ teaspoon hot sauce
Green onion fan (optional)

Combine first 5 ingredients; toss lightly. Combine cider vinegar and next 6 ingredients; mix well, and pour over zucchini mixture. Cover and chill 8 hours, stirring occasionally. Garnish with green onion fan, if desired. Yield: 4 to 6 servings.

Clota Engleman
Spur, Texas

SAUTÉED SWEET PEPPERS

1 large sweet red pepper
1 large sweet yellow pepper
1 large green pepper
1 tablespoon butter or margarine,
   melted
1 teaspoon chopped fresh thyme
   or ⅓ teaspoon dried whole
   thyme
Fresh thyme sprigs (optional)

Seed peppers, and cut into ½-inch pieces. Sauté peppers in butter in a large skillet about 8 minutes or until crisp-tender; stir in chopped thyme. Garnish with thyme sprigs, if desired. Yield: 6 servings.

Doris T. Ramsey
Martinsville, Virginia

Tip: *When you are selecting peppers, size is not an indication of quality. Look for peppers with smooth, slick skin that has not shriveled.*

Peppers Pack A Rainbow Of Colors

You're probably familiar with the distinctively sharp but pleasant flavor of green pepper. Red pepper offers a similar but milder flavor, and the yellow has a flavor even more delicate than the red. Both red and yellow peppers add a touch of sweetness to the dishes in which they're used, in contrast to the bolder flavor of green pepper.

If you've ever seen green peppers growing in a backyard garden, you might have noticed how some turn red if left on the vine past their prime. That's not the way red peppers sold in markets get their color, however. The red and yellow peppers sold commercially start out green, but they promptly take on their brilliant hues based on the seed variety. The best quality red and yellow peppers are actually cultivated in greenhouses. They are now being grown in greater volume to meet the increased demand by consumers.

Whether you're choosing peppers for soups, side dishes, or sauces, pick a color and flavor to complement the rest of the menu. For example, the look and taste of Bell Pepper Soup and Pepper Pesto vary depending on which color is chosen. After blending the pepper with other ingredients in the recipe, the color of the prepared dish is often not as vibrant as the color of the vegetable in its fresh form but rather a lighter shade of the pepper used.

peppers, discarding seeds and charred skin.

Sauté onion and garlic in butter in a Dutch oven until onion is tender. Add flour, stirring until smooth. Cook 1 minute, stirring constantly. Gradually add chicken broth; cook over medium heat, stirring constantly, until thickened. Stir in freshly ground pepper.

Pour half of soup mixture into container of an electric blender; add half of skinned peppers, and process until smooth. Return mixture to Dutch oven; repeat procedure with remaining ingredients. Simmer over low heat 10 minutes. Yield: 5 cups.

MIXED PEPPER SALAD
(pictured on page 114)

¼ cup sugar
3 tablespoons vinegar
2 tablespoons vegetable oil
¼ teaspoon freshly ground pepper
⅛ teaspoon salt
1 medium-size sweet red pepper
1 medium-size sweet yellow pepper
1 medium-size green pepper

Combine first 5 ingredients in a medium saucepan; bring to a boil, stirring until sugar dissolves. Remove from heat; cool.

Cut peppers into ½-inch squares. Add vinegar mixture; stir gently. Cover and chill 8 hours. Yield: about 4 servings.

BELL PEPPER SOUP
(pictured on page 114)

2 large red, yellow, or green peppers
½ cup chopped onion
2 cloves garlic, minced
⅓ cup butter or margarine, melted
⅓ cup all-purpose flour
1 quart canned diluted chicken broth
⅛ teaspoon freshly ground pepper

Place whole peppers on their sides on a large baking sheet. Bake at 500° for 20 minutes or until skin is blackened and charred. Transfer peppers immediately to a paper bag, and seal the top. Refrigerate 10 minutes or until peppers cool. Peel and seed

PEPPER PESTO
(pictured on page 114)

3 medium-size red, yellow, or green peppers
½ cup grated Parmesan cheese
⅓ cup walnut pieces
2 small cloves garlic, cut in half
¼ teaspoon salt
¼ teaspoon freshly ground pepper
½ cup olive oil

Place whole peppers on their sides on a large baking sheet. Bake at 500° for 20 minutes or until skin is blackened and charred. Transfer peppers immediately to a paper bag; seal top. Refrigerate 10 minutes or until cool. Peel and seed peppers, discarding seeds and skin.

Position knife blade in food processor bowl; add peppers, cheese, and next 4 ingredients. Cover and process until smooth. With processor running, pour oil through food chute in a slow, steady stream until combined. Use pesto immediately, or refrigerate up to 1 week in an airtight container. Toss with cooked spaghetti to serve. Yield: 1¾ cups.

Note: Pepper Pesto made with green peppers is pale in color. Add green food coloring, if desired.

QUICK!

Sauté An Entrée

Family and guests will think you've done something extra special when you serve a sautéed entrée. Sautéing cooks food fast, keeping meats juicy and vegetables crisp-tender. And calories are kept low because only a small amount of fat is used. Simply heat oil or butter in a heavy skillet, add food, stir until done, and eat.

LEMON-PEPPER CHICKEN

4 chicken breast halves, skinned and boned
¼ cup all-purpose flour
¼ teaspoon salt
¼ teaspoon lemon-pepper seasoning
¼ cup butter or margarine
2 teaspoons lemon juice

Place each piece of chicken between 2 sheets of plastic wrap, and flatten to ¼-inch thickness, using a meat mallet or rolling pin.

Combine flour, salt, and lemon-pepper seasoning in a small bowl. Dredge chicken breast halves lightly in flour mixture.

Melt butter in a large skillet over medium heat. Add chicken, and cook 3 to 4 minutes on each side or until golden brown. Add lemon juice, and cook 3 minutes. Yield: 4 servings.
Susan Joyce Morgan
Charlotte, North Carolina

JULIENNE PEPPER SAUTÉ
(pictured on page 114)

1 large sweet red pepper
1 large sweet yellow pepper
1 large green pepper
1 small onion, chopped
1 clove garlic, minced
3 tablespoons olive oil
1 teaspoon dried whole basil
½ teaspoon salt
¼ teaspoon freshly ground pepper

Seed red, yellow, and green peppers, and cut into ¼-inch strips. Sauté peppers, onion, and garlic in hot oil in large skillet just until tender (about 5 minutes). Stir in basil, salt, and ground pepper. Yield: 4 to 6 servings.

SOLE ROYALE

3 tablespoons lemon juice, divided
½ pound sole or flounder fillets
1 tablespoon butter or margarine, melted
2 tablespoons plain yogurt
2 tablespoons commercial sour cream
1 teaspoon honey
½ teaspoon dried whole dillweed
Chopped fresh parsley (optional)

Sprinkle 1 tablespoon lemon juice over fish fillets.

Sauté fish fillets in melted butter in a large nonstick skillet 2 minutes on each side or until fish flakes easily when tested with a fork. Remove fillets from skillet, and place on a heated serving platter. Keep fillets warm until serving time.

Combine remaining 2 tablespoons lemon juice, yogurt, sour cream, honey, and dillweed in a small saucepan. Cook over low heat just until sauce is warm; do not boil. Pour sauce evenly over fish, and sprinkle with chopped parsley, if desired. Yield: 2 servings. *Angela Falkner*
Corpus Christi, Texas

SWEET PEPPER-CHICKEN SAUTÉ

1 pound boneless chicken breasts, skinned
½ teaspoon Creole seasoning
1 medium-size sweet yellow pepper, cut into strips
1 medium-size sweet red pepper, cut into strips
1 medium-size green pepper, cut into strips
3 tablespoons butter or margarine, melted
1 teaspoon soy sauce

Cut chicken into thin strips. Sprinkle with Creole seasoning.

Sauté chicken and peppers in butter in a heavy skillet 10 to 12 minutes or until chicken is done. Remove from heat; stir in soy sauce. Yield: about 4 servings.

Jo Ann Anderson
Lufkin, Texas

TURKEY SAUTÉ

2 tablespoons soy sauce
¼ cup water
2 teaspoons cornstarch
1 teaspoon sugar
2 tablespoons vegetable oil
1 clove garlic, minced
½ teaspoon grated fresh gingerroot
1 pound turkey breast cutlets, cut into bite-size pieces
1 (6-ounce) package frozen snow pea pods, thawed
1 (8-ounce) can sliced water chestnuts, drained
½ small sweet red pepper, sliced

Combine first 4 ingredients; set aside. Heat oil 1 to 2 minutes in a large heavy skillet. Add garlic and gingerroot; sauté until tender. Add turkey, and cook, stirring constantly, 3 minutes or until lightly browned. Add snow peas, water chestnuts, and red pepper slices; cook 1 minute, stirring constantly. Add soy sauce mixture, and cook 2 minutes or until thickened. Yield: 4 servings.

Carol S. Noble
Burgaw, North Carolina

PLUM DELICIOUS PORK SAUTÉ

1 pound boneless pork loin chops
1 small onion, chopped
½ medium-size green pepper, chopped
1 tablespoon vegetable oil
½ cup plum jam
¼ cup rice vinegar
¼ teaspoon crushed red pepper
2 teaspoons soy sauce
1 (3-ounce) can chow mein noodles

Slice pork diagonally across grain into thin strips; set aside. Sauté onion and green pepper in hot oil in a skillet 2 minutes. Add pork strips; sauté until brown. Stir in jam and next 3 ingredients; simmer, uncovered, 8 to 10 minutes.

Place noodles on a baking sheet; bake at 375° for 3 to 5 minutes. Serve pork over noodles. Yield: 4 servings.

Primavera Hints Of Spring

As asparagus appears in the garden and on produce stands, thoughts turn to spring and delicate combinations of tender, new vegetables.

PASTA PRIMAVERA

1 pound fresh asparagus
1 medium onion, chopped
1 large clove garlic, chopped
3 tablespoons unsalted butter, melted
½ pound fresh mushrooms, thinly sliced
1½ cups small cauliflower flowerets
1 medium zucchini, thinly sliced
1 carrot, cut into ⅛-inch slices
1 cup whipping cream
½ cup chicken broth
2 tablespoons chopped fresh basil or 2 teaspoons dried whole basil
1 (3-ounce) package prosciutto, chopped
5 green onions, chopped
¼ teaspoon pepper
1 (16-ounce) package fettuccine or linguine
½ teaspoon salt
1 cup freshly grated Parmesan cheese
Fresh basil sprigs (optional)

Snap off tough ends of asparagus. Remove scales from stalks with a knife or vegetable peeler, if desired. Cut asparagus diagonally into ¼-inch slices, leaving tips intact; set sliced asparagus aside.

Sauté onion and garlic in butter in a large skillet until tender. Add asparagus, mushrooms, cauliflower, zucchini, and carrot; stir-fry 2 minutes or until crisp-tender. Remove several pieces of asparagus tips, mushrooms, and zucchini; reserve for garnish. Stir whipping cream, broth, and chopped basil into vegetable mixture; bring to a boil, and cook 3 minutes. Stir in chopped prosciutto, green onions, and pepper; cook 1 minute.

Cook fettuccine with salt, according to package directions; drain.

Combine fettuccine, vegetable mixture, and Parmesan cheese in a large bowl, tossing to coat. Garnish with reserved vegetables and, if desired, basil sprigs. Serve immediately. Yield: 8 servings.

Depend On Carrots

These carrot recipes will make it easy for you and your family to heed nutritionists' advice to eat plenty of this vitamin A-rich vegetable.

CARROT-CARAWAY SALAD

4 cups shredded carrot
½ cup chopped celery
¼ cup sliced green onions
½ teaspoon caraway seeds
¼ teaspoon salt
⅛ teaspoon pepper
⅓ cup mayonnaise
¼ cup buttermilk
Lettuce leaves

Combine first 8 ingredients, and toss well. Cover and chill. Serve salad in a lettuce-lined bowl. Yield: 6 to 8 servings.

Iris Brenner
Fort McCoy, Florida

GLAZED CARROTS

1 pound carrots
1 tablespoon vegetable oil
½ cup water
2 teaspoons cornstarch
2 teaspoons brown sugar
¼ teaspoon salt
2 teaspoons vinegar
¼ cup water

Scrape carrots; cut into thin slices. Sauté carrots in oil in a large skillet 2 to 3 minutes. Add ½ cup water; bring to a boil. Cover, reduce heat, and simmer 3 minutes or until crisp-tender. Combine cornstarch and remaining ingredients; stir into carrots. Cook over medium heat, stirring constantly, until thickened. Yield: 4 servings. *Mrs. Thomas Lee Adams*
Kingsport, Tennessee

CARROT STICKS

1 pound carrots
¾ cup water
¼ cup firmly packed brown sugar
2 tablespoons butter or margarine
1½ tablespoons prepared mustard
1 teaspoon prepared horseradish
¼ teaspoon salt
¼ teaspoon paprika

Scrape carrots, and cut into julienne sticks. Combine carrots and water in a medium saucepan; bring to a boil. Cover, reduce heat, and simmer 10 minutes or until carrots are crisp-tender. Drain carrots, reserving 1 tablespoon liquid.

Combine reserved liquid, brown sugar, and remaining ingredients in a small saucepan. Bring mixture to a boil over medium heat, stirring constantly; pour over carrots. Yield: 4 servings.
Aleisha Humphrey Schoenfelder
Stanardsville, Virginia

ON THE LIGHT SIDE

Eat Oats; Lower Cholesterol

Oat bran and oats are getting high marks on the nutrition report card these days. They've been linked to lower cholesterol levels in people who follow a low-fat, low-cholesterol, high-fiber diet.

The substance in oats that lowers cholesterol is the water-soluble fiber. As it moves through the digestive system, it draws out LDL cholesterol (the one that sticks to artery walls and narrows the passageway for blood) but spares HDL cholesterol (the type that helps prevent heart disease). All sources of water-soluble fiber, not just oats, do a good job of lowering cholesterol levels (see chart on page 108).

That doesn't mean that a bowl of oatmeal or a serving of black-eyed peas can undo the effects of eating a high-fat diet. But if you eat light and healthy, chances are good that your cholesterol level can be lowered further simply by adding water-soluble fiber to your diet.

If eating oatmeal cereal every morning isn't your idea of a tasty treat, try Bette Hallgren's Oat Bran Muffins. Two muffins have about the same amount of water-soluble fiber as a serving of oatmeal cereal.

OAT BRAN MUFFINS

2¼ cups unprocessed oat bran
¼ cup firmly packed brown sugar
1 teaspoon baking powder
¼ teaspoon salt
¾ cup skim milk
½ cup egg substitute
2 teaspoons vegetable oil
Vegetable cooking spray

Combine first 4 ingredients in a large bowl; make a well in center of mixture. Combine milk, egg substitute, honey, and oil; add to dry mixture, stirring just until moistened.

Spoon batter into muffin pans coated with cooking spray, filling three-fourths full. Bake at 425° for 15 minutes. Yield: 1 dozen (121 calories per muffin).

☐ *4.7 grams protein, 2.6 grams fat, 20.1 grams carbohydrate, 4.2 grams fiber, 0 milligrams cholesterol, 100 milligrams sodium, and 53 milligrams calcium.*

Raisin Oat Bran Muffins: Add ⅓ cup raisins to batter. Yield: 1 dozen (133 calories per muffin).

☐ *4.8 grams protein, 2.6 grams fat, 23.3 grams carbohydrate, 4.5 grams fiber, 0 milligrams cholesterol, 100 milligrams sodium, and 55 milligrams calcium.*

Banana Oat Bran Muffins: Add ½ cup mashed ripe banana. Yield: 1 dozen (129 calories per muffin).

☐ *4.8 grams protein, 2.6 grams fat, 22.2 grams carbohydrate, 4.5 grams fiber, 0 milligrams cholesterol, 100 milligrams sodium, and 54 milligrams calcium.*

Blueberry Oat Bran Muffins: Add ½ cup fresh or frozen (thawed) blueberries to batter. Yield: 1 dozen (125 calories per muffin).

☐ *4.7 grams protein, 2.6 grams fat, 20.9 grams carbohydrate, 4.4 grams fiber, 0 milligrams cholesterol, 100 milligrams sodium, and 54 milligrams calcium.*

Apple-Cinnamon Oat Bran Muffins: Add ½ cup minced apple and 1 teaspoon ground cinnamon. Yield: 1 dozen (124 calories per muffin).

☐ *4.7 grams protein, 2.6 grams fat, 20.9 grams carbohydrate, 4.4 grams fiber, 0 milligrams cholesterol, 100 milligrams sodium, and 56 milligrams calcium.*

Cranberry Oat Bran Muffins: Add ¾ cup fresh or frozen (thawed) cranberries to batter. Yield: 1 dozen (124 calories per muffin).

☐ *4.7 grams protein, 2.6 grams fat, 20.9 grams carbohydrate, 4.3 grams fiber, 0 milligrams cholesterol, 100 milligrams sodium, and 53 milligrams calcium.* Bette Hallgren
Woodstock, Virginia

HONEY-OAT BREAD

1⅔ cups bread flour
1 cup regular oats, uncooked
½ cup unprocessed oat bran
1½ teaspoons salt
3 packages dry yeast
1¾ cups water
½ cup honey
½ cup vegetable oil
½ cup egg substitute
2½ cups whole wheat flour
¾ cup bread flour, divided
Vegetable cooking spray
1 egg white
1 tablespoon water

Combine flour, oats, oat bran, salt, and yeast in a large mixing bowl. Combine 1¾ cups water, honey, and oil in a saucepan; heat mixture to 120° to 130°.

Gradually add liquid mixture and egg substitute to flour mixture; beat at low speed of an electric mixer until blended. Beat an additional 3 minutes at medium speed. Gradually stir in wheat flour and ¼ cup bread flour to form a soft dough.

Turn dough out onto a lightly floured surface. Knead until smooth and elastic (about 10 minutes); add enough of remaining ½ cup bread flour, 1 tablespoon at a time, to prevent dough from sticking to hands. Place dough in a large bowl coated with cooking spray, turning to coat top. Cover and let rise in a warm place (85°), free from drafts, 1 hour or until doubled in bulk.

Punch dough down; let rest 15 minutes. Divide dough in half, shaping each portion into a loaf. Place in a 9- x 5- x 3-inch loafpan coated with cooking spray. Cover and let rise in a warm place, free from drafts, 15 to 20 minutes or until doubled in bulk.

Combine egg white and 1 tablespoon water, and brush tops of loaves. Bake at 375° for 35 to 40 minutes or until loaves sound hollow when tapped. (Cover loaves with foil the last 10 minutes to prevent overbrowning, if necessary.) Remove bread from loafpans immediately, and cool on wire racks. Yield: 2 loaves (120 calories per ½-inch slice).

☐ *3.4 grams protein, 3.6 grams fat, 19.1 grams carbohydrate, 0.6 gram fiber, 0 milligrams cholesterol, 104 milligrams sodium, and 9 milligrams calcium.*

OATMEAL WAFFLES

1½ cups whole wheat flour
2 teaspoons baking powder
½ teaspoon salt
2 cups evaporated skimmed milk
½ cup egg substitute
2 tablespoons vegetable oil
2 tablespoons honey
1 cup regular oats, uncooked
Vegetable cooking spray

Combine first 3 ingredients in a medium mixing bowl. Add milk and next 3 ingredients; beat at medium speed of an electric mixer until blended. Stir in oats.

Coat a waffle iron with cooking spray; allow waffle iron to preheat. Spoon ⅓ cup of batter per waffle onto hot waffle iron, spreading batter to edges. Bake 5 minutes or until steaming stops. Repeat procedure with remaining batter. Yield: 12 (4-inch) waffles (147 calories each).

☐ *7.3 grams protein, 3.3 grams fat, 23.2 grams carbohydrate, 0.4 gram fiber, 2 milligrams cholesterol, 212 milligrams sodium, and 169 milligrams calcium.*

OATMEAL PANCAKES

1½ cups regular oats, uncooked
½ cup whole wheat flour
1 teaspoon baking soda
⅛ teaspoon salt
2 teaspoons sugar
2 cups nonfat buttermilk
½ cup egg substitute
1 teaspoon vanilla extract
Vegetable cooking spray
Apple Topping

Combine first 5 ingredients in a medium bowl. Add buttermilk, egg substitute, and vanilla; stir well. Coat a nonstick skillet with cooking spray; place over medium heat until hot. For each pancake pour 2 tablespoons batter into hot skillet. Turn pancakes when tops are covered with bubbles and edges look cooked. Serve warm with Apple Topping. Yield: 26 pancakes (38 calories each).

☐ *2.1 grams protein, 0.6 gram fat, 6.1 grams carbohydrate, 0.3 gram fiber, 0 milligrams cholesterol, 69 milligrams sodium, and 35 milligrams calcium.*

Apple Topping

2 cups unsweetened applesauce
1½ tablespoons brown sugar
¼ teaspoon apple pie spice
¼ teaspoon maple flavoring

Combine all ingredients in a small saucepan. Cook until hot and bubbly, stirring occasionally. Yield: 2 cups (9 calories per tablespoon).

☐ *0 grams protein, 0 grams fat, 2.4 grams carbohydrate, 0.4 gram fiber, 0 milligrams cholesterol, 1 milligram sodium, and 1 milligram calcium.*
Cynda A. Spoon
Broken Arrow, Oklahoma

Tip: *When preparing a whole wheat flour recipe, be sure not to sift the flour. Instead, stir flour lightly before measuring.*

OATMEAL BISCUITS

1¾ cups all-purpose flour
½ cup regular oats, uncooked
1 teaspoon baking powder
½ teaspoon baking soda
½ teaspoon salt
¼ cup reduced-calorie margarine
¾ cup nonfat buttermilk
Vegetable cooking spray

Combine first 5 ingredients; cut in margarine with a pastry blender until mixture resembles coarse meal. Add buttermilk, stirring until dry ingredients are moistened. Turn dough out onto a lightly floured surface, and knead lightly 4 or 5 times.

Roll dough to ½-inch thickness; cut with a 2-inch biscuit cutter. Place on a baking sheet coated with cooking spray. Bake at 425° for 12 to 15 minutes or until lightly browned. Yield: 14 biscuits (96 calories each).

□ *2.7 grams protein, 2.5 grams fat, 15.6 grams carbohydrate, 0.5 gram fiber, 1 milligram cholesterol, 180 milligrams sodium, and 41 milligrams calcium.*

CORN-OAT MUFFINS

1¼ cups nonfat buttermilk
½ cup yellow cornmeal
½ cup regular oats, uncooked
¼ cup egg substitute
3 tablespoons brown sugar
2 tablespoons vegetable oil
1 cup whole wheat flour
1 teaspoon baking powder
½ teaspoon baking soda
¼ teaspoon salt
Vegetable cooking spray

Combine first 3 ingredients in a bowl; let stand 1 hour. Add egg substitute, brown sugar, and vegetable oil, and mix well.

Combine flour and next 3 ingredients in a large bowl; make a well in center of mixture. Add buttermilk mixture to dry ingredients, stirring just until moistened.

Spoon batter evenly into muffin pans coated with cooking spray. Bake at 400° for 20 minutes. Yield: 1 dozen (112 calories per muffin).

□ *3.7 grams protein, 3 grams fat, 18 grams carbohydrate, 0.7 gram fiber, 1 milligram cholesterol, 143 milligrams sodium, and 65 milligrams calcium.*

APPLESAUCE OATMEAL

1 cup skim milk
½ cup regular oats, uncooked
½ cup unsweetened applesauce
1 tablespoon brown sugar
⅛ teaspoon vanilla extract
Dash of ground cinnamon

Heat milk in a heavy saucepan until hot. Stir in oats, and cook 5 minutes or until thickened, stirring occasionally. Add applesauce and remaining ingredients. Cook 1 minute or until thoroughly heated, stirring occasionally. Yield: 2 servings (179 calories per serving).

□ *7.5 grams protein, 1.5 grams fat, 33.7 grams carbohydrate, 2.6 grams fiber, 2 milligrams cholesterol, 67 milligrams sodium, and 170 milligrams calcium.*
Kay Stubbs
Mauk, Georgia

OAT CRUNCH TOPPING

1½ cups regular oats, uncooked
½ cup unprocessed oat bran
½ cup wheat germ, toasted
1 tablespoon ground cinnamon
1 tablespoon reduced-calorie margarine
¼ cup honey

Combine all ingredients in a medium bowl; spread on a baking sheet, and bake at 350° for 10 minutes. Let cool completely. Serve as a topping on yogurt or fruit. Yield: 2½ cups (28 calories per tablespoon).

□ *1.1 grams protein, 0.7 gram fat, 5 grams carbohydrate, 0.6 gram fiber, 0 milligrams cholesterol, 3 milligrams sodium, and 5 milligrams calcium.*
Beverly Swan
Graham, North Carolina

GARDEN PIZZA

1 cup regular oats, uncooked
1 teaspoon sugar
¼ teaspoon salt
1 package dry yeast
2 tablespoons vegetable oil
½ cup plus 2 tablespoons warm water (120° to 130°)
½ cup whole wheat flour
½ cup all-purpose flour
Vegetable cooking spray
2 cups sliced fresh mushrooms
1½ cups shredded carrot
1 cup thinly sliced zucchini
½ cup chopped onion
1 cup commercial pizza sauce
2 cups (8 ounces) shredded part-skim mozzarella cheese, divided
¼ cup grated Parmesan cheese
½ teaspoon dried Italian seasoning

Place oats in container of an electric blender or food processor; cover and process until oats resemble flour. Combine oat flour, sugar, salt, and yeast in a large bowl; add oil and water, mixing well. Add remaining flours, stirring until blended.

Turn dough out onto a lightly floured surface, and knead until smooth and elastic (about 5 minutes). Place dough in a large bowl coated with cooking spray, turning to coat top. Cover and let rise in a warm place (85°), free from drafts, 1 hour or until doubled in bulk.

Punch dough down, and turn out onto a lightly floured surface. Roll dough to a 14-inch circle; place on a 12-inch pizza pan coated with cooking spray. Turn extra dough under to form a rolled rim. Bake at 425° for 15 minutes. Set aside.

Coat a large, nonstick skillet with cooking spray; place over medium-high heat until hot. Add mushrooms and next 3 ingredients; sauté until tender. Set aside.

Spread pizza sauce evenly over crust; top with 1 cup mozzarella cheese, sautéed vegetables, and Parmesan cheese. Bake at 400° for 12 minutes; sprinkle with remaining mozzarella cheese and Italian seasoning. Bake an additional 5 minutes or until cheese melts. Yield: 8 servings (259 calories per slice).

☐ *13.2 grams protein, 11.1 grams fat, 27.7 grams carbohydrate, 1.6 grams fiber, 18 milligrams cholesterol, 261 milligrams sodium, and 242 milligrams calcium.*

ITALIAN MEAT PIE

1 (16-ounce) package frozen raw ground turkey, thawed
8 ounces frozen raw Italian turkey sausage, thawed
⅔ cup regular oats, uncooked
½ cup no-salt-added tomato sauce
¼ cup egg substitute
½ teaspoon pepper
2 teaspoons dried Italian seasoning
½ cup grated Parmesan cheese, divided
Vegetable cooking spray
1 (10-ounce) package frozen chopped spinach, thawed and drained
8 (½-inch) slices tomato
2 cups (8 ounces) shredded part-skim mozzarella cheese

Combine first 7 ingredients and ¼ cup Parmesan cheese. Pat evenly into bottom of a 13- x 9- x 2-inch baking dish coated with cooking spray. Bake at 350° for 35 minutes.

Top meat mixture with spinach, remaining ¼ cup Parmesan cheese, tomato slices, and mozzarella cheese. Bake 5 minutes or until cheese melts and casserole is bubbly. Yield: 8 servings (282 calories per serving).

☐ *29.2 grams protein, 13.4 grams fat, 12.7 grams carbohydrate, 2.2 grams fiber, 20 milligrams cholesterol, 520 milligrams sodium, and 343 milligrams calcium.*

MEAT LOAF

Vegetable cooking spray
1½ pounds lean ground chuck
½ cup regular oats, uncooked
¼ cup unprocessed oat bran
½ cup chopped onion
¼ cup chopped green pepper
⅓ cup commercial barbecue sauce
¼ cup egg substitute
2 tablespoons dried parsley flakes
2 tablespoons low-sodium Worcestershire sauce
¼ teaspoon pepper

Coat a 9- x 5- x 3-inch two-piece loafpan with drain holes in the bottom with cooking spray. Combine remaining ingredients. Shape into a loaf, and place in loafpan. Bake at 350° for 1 hour or until done. Remove from pan, and let stand 5 to 10 minutes before serving. Yield: 8 servings (275 calories per serving).

☐ *17.5 grams protein, 18.5 grams fat, 8.1 grams carbohydrate, 1.2 grams fiber, 64 milligrams cholesterol, 170 milligrams sodium, and 19 milligrams calcium.*

RASPBERRY-PEAR CRISP

2 medium pears, unpeeled, cored, and thinly sliced
Vegetable cooking spray
1 (16-ounce) package frozen unsweetened raspberries, thawed
1 cup quick-cooking oats, uncooked
¼ cup honey
3 tablespoons reduced-calorie margarine, melted
1 teaspoon ground cinnamon
½ teaspoon ground nutmeg

Arrange pear slices in a 12- x 8- x 2-inch baking dish coated with cooking spray. Arrange raspberries evenly over pears.

Combine oats and remaining ingredients; sprinkle over raspberries. Bake at 375° for 35 minutes or until pears are tender. Yield: 7 servings (170 calories per ½-cup serving).

☐ *2.7 grams protein, 4.6 grams fat, 32.8 grams carbohydrate, 6.7 grams fiber, 0 milligrams cholesterol, 48 milligrams sodium, and 30 milligrams calcium.*

Foods Containing Water-Soluble Fiber

Grains	Vegetables
Barley	Beans
Grits	(kidney, pinto,
Oat bran	and white)
Oats	Broccoli
	Brussels sprouts
Fruits	Cabbage
Apples	Corn
Apricots	Peas
Bananas	(black-eyed, green,
Oranges	and split)
Pears	Potatoes
Plums	(sweet and white)
Tangerines	

Get A Headstart On The Beverage

If you enjoy having a cool drink at a moment's notice, mix one of these beverages to keep on hand. Each recipe makes a chilly refresher in ready-to-drink form after a little thawing or in concentrate form to store in the refrigerator or freezer.

The recipes for Lemonade Concentrate and Bloody Mary Mix make drinks in concentrate form that you can dilute and serve immediately. Both of these keep up to a week in the refrigerator.

LEMONADE CONCENTRATE

1½ cups sugar
1 quart water
1½ cups freshly squeezed lemon juice

Combine sugar and water in a saucepan; bring to a boil. Reduce heat, and simmer 5 minutes, stirring until sugar dissolves. Cool. Stir in lemon juice. Cover and chill.

To serve lemonade, use equal portions lemonade concentrate and water. Serve over ice. Yield: 11 cups lemonade.
Jo Ann Maupin
Fort Payne, Alabama

Beverage Tips

■ Create a nonalcoholic bubbly beverage by adding sparkling mineral water to nutritious fruit juice concentrates.

■ Ice will be clearer if you first boil the water and allow it to cool before freezing it.

BLOODY MARY MIX

1 (46-ounce) can tomato juice
1 (10½-ounce) can beef broth, undiluted
2 teaspoons seasoned salt
1 teaspoon instant minced onion
1 teaspoon freshly ground pepper
1 teaspoon celery salt
1 teaspoon celery seeds
¼ teaspoon hot sauce
3 tablespoons lime juice
¼ cup Worcestershire sauce
1 cup vodka (optional)

Combine all ingredients except vodka; stir well, and chill 8 hours. Stir in vodka, if desired, just before serving. Serve over ice. Yield: 2 quarts.
Rita W. Cook
Corpus Christi, Texas

HOOTENANNY FRAPPÉ

1½ cups sugar
3½ cups water
1 (6-ounce) can frozen orange juice concentrate, thawed and undiluted
2 (10-ounce) packages frozen sliced strawberries in syrup, thawed
1 (8-ounce) can unsweetened crushed pineapple, undrained
Ginger ale, chilled

Combine sugar and water in a large saucepan; cook over medium heat until sugar dissolves, stirring constantly. Remove from heat; stir in orange juice concentrate, strawberries, and pineapple. Pour mixture into a 13- x 9- x 2-inch pan; freeze until firm.

To serve, let fruit mixture thaw at room temperature about 30 minutes. For each serving, spoon ½ cup fruit mixture into a glass, and add 1 cup ginger ale; stir until slushy. Refreeze remainder of fruit mixture, and use as needed. Yield: 18 servings.
Katie Harville
Grenada, Mississippi

BRANDY SLUSH

2 cups boiling water
4 regular-size tea bags
2 cups sugar
7 cups water
2 (12-ounce) cans frozen lemonade concentrate, thawed and undiluted
2 (12-ounce) cans frozen orange juice concentrate, thawed and undiluted
2 cups brandy
Lemon-lime carbonated beverage

Pour 2 cups boiling water over tea bags; cover and steep 5 minutes. Remove tea bags, squeezing gently. Set tea aside to cool.

Combine sugar and 7 cups water in a saucepan; bring to a boil, and boil until sugar dissolves, stirring occasionally. Set aside to cool.

Combine tea, sugar mixture, lemonade and orange juice concentrates, and brandy in a large freezer-proof container, stirring well. Freeze until mixture is firm.

To serve, spoon about ½ cup fruit mixture into each glass, and add ¼ cup lemon-lime beverage; stir until slushy. Refreeze remainder of fruit mixture; use as needed. Yield: 32 servings.
Kathy Kern
New Orleans, Louisiana

Prime-Time Strawberries

During April, May, and June, fields from Gonzalez, Louisiana, to Pungoteague, Virginia, abound with vines laden with plump, ravishingly red strawberries. Festivals celebrating the harvest lure city folk to rural areas as well as generate a lot of good recipes.

We think you'll agree that the rich taste of sun-ripened strawberries is brought out in these recipes.

SUMMERTIME FROZEN FRUIT SALAD

1 (8-ounce) package cream
   cheese, softened
¼ cup honey
1½ cups sliced fresh strawberries
2 medium bananas, sliced
1 cup miniature marshmallows
1 cup fresh pineapple chunks or
   1 (15¼-ounce) can pineapple
   chunks, drained
1 cup fresh cherries, pitted and
   halved
1 cup whipping cream, whipped

Beat cream cheese at medium speed of an electric mixer until smooth. Add honey, and beat well. Gently stir in strawberries and next 4 ingredients. Fold in whipped cream. Spoon mixture into a 9-inch square pan, and freeze. Remove salad from freezer 30 minutes before serving. Yield: 9 servings.   *Della Taylor*
Jonesboro, Tennessee

STRAWBERRY MARGARITA SORBET

2 cups water
1 cup sugar
4 cups fresh strawberries
½ cup lime juice
¼ cup plus 2 tablespoons tequila
¼ cup Triple Sec
Strawberry fans (optional)

Combine water and sugar in a small saucepan; bring to a boil, stirring constantly until sugar dissolves. Let mixture cool.

Puree 4 cups strawberries in blender or food processor. Combine pureed strawberries, sugar syrup, lime juice, tequila, and Triple Sec, stirring well. Pour mixture into freezer can of a 6-cup electric ice cream freezer. Freeze according to manufacturer's instructions. Garnish each serving with a strawberry fan, if desired. Yield: 6 cups.

Note: To prepare in a 13- x 9- x 2-inch pan, pour mixture into pan, and freeze until almost firm. Break mixture into large pieces, and place in processor bowl; process several seconds or until fluffy but not thawed. Return to pan, and freeze until firm.   *Cathy Schroeder*
Taylor, Texas

FRESH STRAWBERRY ICE CREAM

4 cups milk, divided
2 cups miniature marshmallows
4 eggs, well beaten
2½ cups sugar
2 cups half-and-half
1 cup whipping cream
2 teaspoons vanilla extract
4 cups pureed fresh strawberries

Combine 2 cups milk and marshmallows in a heavy saucepan; cook over medium heat until marshmallows dissolve. Gradually stir about one-fourth of hot mixture into beaten eggs; add to remaining hot mixture, stirring constantly. Cook 2 minutes or until temperature reaches 165°. Remove from heat, and add remaining 2 cups milk, sugar, half-and-half, whipping cream, and vanilla. Chill.

Combine strawberries and milk mixture in freezer can of a 5-quart, hand-turned or electric ice cream freezer. Freeze according to manufacturer's instructions. Let ripen for about 1 hour before serving. Yield: 1 gallon.   *Rosa Marie Rudd*
Spotsylvania, Virginia

STRAWBERRY-LEMON TART

Pastry for a 9-inch pie
½ cup sugar
1 tablespoon plus 1 teaspoon
   cornstarch
½ cup water
3 tablespoons lemon juice
1 egg yolk, beaten
2 tablespoons butter or margarine
3 cups sliced fresh strawberries
2 (3-ounce) packages cream
   cheese, softened
¼ cup sifted powdered sugar
⅓ cup flaked coconut
¾ cup whipping cream, whipped
¼ cup flaked coconut, toasted

Roll pastry to a 12-inch circle; place in a 10-inch tart pan with removable bottom. Prick bottom of pastry with a fork. Bake at 450° for 10 to 12 minutes or until browned. Set aside.

Combine ½ cup sugar and cornstarch in a heavy saucepan, stirring well. Stir in water and next 3 ingredients. Cook over medium heat, stirring constantly, until mixture boils. Boil 2 minutes or until temperature reaches 165°. Spoon mixture into prepared pastry shell. Top with sliced strawberries.

Combine cream cheese and powdered sugar in a small mixing bowl; beat at high speed of an electric mixer until smooth. Stir in ⅓ cup coconut. Fold in whipped cream. Spread mixture evenly on strawberries, and sprinkle with toasted coconut. Chill at least 4 hours. Yield: one 10-inch tart.   *Lucille James*
New Orleans, Louisiana

STRAWBERRY-CHOCOLATE TRUFFLE PIE

1 (6-ounce) package semisweet chocolate morsels
1 (8-ounce) package cream cheese, cubed
2 tablespoons butter or margarine
¼ cup sifted powdered sugar
3 tablespoons Triple Sec or orange juice
1 baked 9-inch pastry shell
3 to 4 cups fresh strawberries, hulled
¼ cup red currant jelly, melted
½ cup whipping cream
2 tablespoons powdered sugar
½ teaspoon grated orange rind
Orange rind strips (optional)
Fresh mint leaves (optional)

Combine chocolate morsels, cream cheese, and butter in top of a double boiler; place over boiling water. Cook, stirring constantly, until melted. Remove from heat, and stir in ¼ cup powdered sugar and Triple Sec. Spread mixture evenly in pastry shell. Cool.

Place strawberries, stem side down, over chocolate mixture; brush with jelly. Refrigerate 2 to 3 hours.

Combine whipping cream and 2 tablespoons powdered sugar in a small mixing bowl; beat until soft peaks form. Fold in grated orange rind.

If desired, garnish pie with orange-rind strips and mint leaves. Top each serving with a dollop of whipped cream. Yield: one 9-inch pie.
Lorraine G. Bennett
Virginia Beach, Virginia

STRAWBERRY COOKIE TARTS

⅓ cup shortening
⅓ cup sugar
1 egg
1 teaspoon vanilla extract
1 cup all-purpose flour
1 teaspoon baking powder
½ teaspoon salt
1 egg white, slightly beaten
¼ cup red currant jelly
2 teaspoons water
1 pint fresh strawberries, sliced

Cream shortening; add sugar, beating well at medium speed of an electric mixer. Add egg and vanilla, and beat until blended.

Combine flour, baking powder, and salt; stir into creamed mixture, mixing well. Chill.

Roll dough to ⅛-inch thickness between two sheets of wax paper. Remove top sheet of wax paper. Cut dough with a 4- x 3-inch wedge-shaped cookie cutter, removing excess dough. Transfer cookies on wax paper to a baking sheet. Freeze 15 minutes. Remove cookies from wax paper, and place on a lightly greased baking sheet. Repeat procedure with remaining dough.

Brush cookies with beaten egg white. Bake at 375° for 10 to 12 minutes or until lightly browned. Cool on wire racks.

Combine red currant jelly and water in a small saucepan; cook over low heat until jelly melts, stirring constantly. Cool slightly.

Brush cookies with jelly mixture; arrange strawberry slices, slightly overlapping, on cookies. Brush strawberries with jelly mixture. Yield: 1 dozen.
Jan Worthey
Decatur, Alabama

STRAWBERRY PINWHEEL SHORTCAKE
(pictured on page 113)

4 cups sliced fresh strawberries
2 to 3 tablespoons sugar
1½ cups all-purpose flour
1½ teaspoons baking powder
½ teaspoon salt
½ cup shortening
⅓ to ½ cup milk
1 tablespoon butter or margarine, melted
⅓ cup firmly packed brown sugar
Whipped cream
Strawberry leaves (optional)

Combine sliced strawberries and 2 to 3 tablespoons sugar; stir gently, and chill 1 to 2 hours.

Combine flour, baking powder, and salt; cut in shortening with a pastry blender until mixture resembles coarse meal. Gradually add enough milk to form a soft dough, stirring just until dry ingredients are moistened. Turn dough out onto a lightly floured surface, knead 4 or 5 times; roll dough to an 11- x 8-inch rectangle on a lightly floured surface. Combine butter and brown sugar; spread evenly over dough. Roll up jellyroll fashion, starting at narrow edge. Pinch seams together; cut into 1-inch slices. Place on a lightly greased baking sheet. Bake at 425° for 18 minutes or until lightly browned. Serve with sliced strawberries and whipped cream. Garnish with strawberry leaves, if desired. Yield: 8 servings.
Mrs. H. D. Baxter
Charleston, West Virginia

PEACH-BERRY COMPOTE

2 cups cantaloupe or honeydew melon balls
2 cups fresh strawberries, halved
2 cups fresh blueberries
3 medium bananas, sliced
1½ cups sliced fresh peaches
1 (25.4-ounce) bottle sparkling white grape juice, chilled

Layer melon balls, strawberries, and blueberries in a bowl or compote; cover and chill until serving time. Top with sliced bananas and peaches; pour white grape juice over top. Use a slotted spoon to serve. Yield: 8 to 10 servings.
Emma Prillhart
Kingsport, Tennessee

Right: *Strawberries are beautiful to look at and delicious to eat. Try Strawberry Pinwheel Shortcake for a delectable dessert. (The recipe is on this page.)*

Far right: *Pesto Chicken and Pasta (page 132) needs only 8 ingredients and about 20 minutes cooking time.*

Right: *Make one batch of Bell Pepper Soup (page 103) with red peppers and another with yellow, then swirl the two together.*

Below: *Color and flavor abound in such dishes as (from left) green Pepper Pesto tossed with spaghetti, Julienne Pepper Sauté, and Mixed Pepper Salad. Yellow and red Pepper Pesto are shown in the background. (Recipes, pages 103 and 104.)*

Pork Loin Roast With Red Currant Sauce (page 84) is the perfect recipe for timesaving barbecue. It's precooked in the microwave and grilled over hot coals for a moist, succulent flavor.

Here's The Secret To Tender Pot Roasts

If you think that purchasing a beef tenderloin is the only way to be sure you'll cook up a tender roast, then you will be surprised. Other cuts of meat can be just as flavorful and tender as the most expensive cuts.

Roasts such as rump, chuck, Boston roll, eye-of-round, sirloin tip, or brisket are considered to be less tender than tenderloin or sirloin because they are leaner and have less marbling (layers of fat that occur evenly distributed in the meat). Marbling makes the meat tender, juicy, and flavorful after cooking. To compensate for marbling, the other roasts can be braised (cooked in a small amount of liquid, covered with a lid, for an extended period of time over low heat). The result is moist, tender, and delicious.

According to the National Meat Board, rump roasts that are cut from the bottom round are leaner and harder to tenderize. The roast may be labeled as a round rump and may be less expensive.

Labels on beef cuts at the meat counter are often confusing. For example, chuck roast is a common cut for use in pot roast recipes and definitely should be cooked by braising. An English cut, a specific type of chuck roast, is generally easier to tenderize.

The name of a specific cut of beef may vary with the grocery store or meat market. If you're ever in doubt, ask your butcher to identify specific cuts of beef for you and to specify the best method of cooking each particular cut.

CANARY SIRLOIN ROAST

1 (4- to 5-pound) boneless sirloin tip roast
2 tablespoons vegetable oil
1 cup chopped onion
1 clove garlic, crushed
¾ cup hot water
3 tablespoons catsup
2 tablespoons vinegar
1 tablespoon brown sugar
¾ teaspoon salt
1 bay leaf
About ¼ cup all-purpose flour
About ¼ cup water

Brown roast on all sides in hot oil in a large Dutch oven; remove meat, and set aside. Sauté onion and garlic in drippings. Add roast, hot water, catsup, vinegar, brown sugar, salt, and bay leaf to Dutch oven. If handles are not ovenproof, cover with heavy-duty aluminum foil. Cover and bake at 325° for 3 hours or until roast is tender.

Remove and discard bay leaf. Remove roast from Dutch oven; cut into serving pieces, and place on a warm serving platter.

Measure liquid in Dutch oven. For every 1 cup liquid, combine 2 tablespoons flour and 2 tablespoons water; stir well. Stir flour mixture into hot liquid in Dutch oven. Cook over medium heat, stirring constantly, until gravy is smooth and thickened. Serve with roast. Yield: 8 to 10 servings.
Jane Noe
Sandia, Texas

POT ROAST IN SOUR CREAM

1 (3½- to 4-pound) boneless rump roast
2 tablespoons vegetable oil
½ cup water
½ teaspoon beef-flavored bouillon granules
1 bay leaf
½ teaspoon salt
½ teaspoon coarsely ground pepper
2 onions, quartered
2 carrots, scraped and cut into pieces
2 tablespoons all-purpose flour
3 tablespoons water
1 (8-ounce) carton commercial sour cream
Hot cooked noodles

Brown roast on all sides in hot oil in a large Dutch oven. Combine ½ cup water and bouillon granules; add to Dutch oven. Add bay leaf, salt, and pepper. Cover, reduce heat, and simmer 2½ hours. Add onion and carrot; cover and cook 30 minutes or until vegetables and meat are tender.

Remove roast and vegetables from Dutch oven; keep warm. Remove and discard bay leaf. Combine flour and 3 tablespoons water; stir into pan drippings. Cook, stirring constantly, until gravy is smooth and thickened. Add sour cream and vegetables to gravy, and cook, stirring constantly, until vegetables are thoroughly heated. Place cooked noodles on a serving platter. Slice roast, and arrange over noodles. Serve with gravy. Yield: 6 to 8 servings.
Maggie Cates
Greenville, Texas

Tip: *At the grocery store, look for meat cuts that have the most lean meat for the money. When you buy less expensive cuts make sure you are not paying for large amounts of gristle, fat, and bone. Since labels on meat can be confusing, ask your butcher to identify cuts of meat and to suggest the best cooking method.*

SEASONED EYE-OF-ROUND ROAST WITH RICE GRAVY

1 (2-pound) boneless eye-of-round roast
2 tablespoons safflower oil
1 tablespoon butter or margarine, melted
2 cups water
1 teaspoon dried parsley flakes
¾ teaspoon celery salt
¼ teaspoon garlic powder
¼ teaspoon dried whole oregano
⅛ teaspoon dried whole thyme
1 tablespoon cornstarch
1 cup milk
1 cup cooked rice

Brown roast on all sides in hot oil and butter in a Dutch oven; drain off drippings. Add water and seasonings. Bring to a boil; cover, reduce heat, and simmer 1½ to 2 hours or until roast is tender. Transfer roast to a serving plate, reserving ⅓ cup broth in Dutch oven.

Bring broth to a boil. Combine cornstarch and milk; gradually add mixture to broth, stirring constantly until smooth and thickened. Stir in rice, and cook until thoroughly heated. Serve gravy with thinly sliced roast. Yield: 6 servings.

Joyce Dean Garrison
Charlotte, North Carolina

FAVORITE POT ROAST

1 (2½- to 3-pound) Boston rolled or chuck roast
2 tablespoons vegetable oil
1 onion, sliced
1 (10¾-ounce) can beef consommé, undiluted
½ cup water
½ teaspoon liquid smoke
¼ teaspoon garlic powder
⅛ teaspoon pepper
1 bay leaf
6 medium potatoes, peeled and quartered
6 carrots, peeled and quartered
2 stalks celery, cut into 1-inch slices

Brown roast on all sides in hot oil in a large Dutch oven; drain off drippings. Place sliced onion on top of roast. Combine consommé and next 5 ingredients; mix well, and pour over roast. Cover, reduce heat, and simmer 2½ hours. Add vegetables; cover and simmer 25 minutes or until vegetables are tender, adding water, if necessary. Remove and discard bay leaf. Yield: 4 to 6 servings.

Jenny Campbell Berg
South Charleston, West Virginia

MICROWAVE COOKERY

Fast Snacks

When you don't want to heat up your kitchen just to prepare a snack or appetizer, microwave recipes offer tasty options.

SPINACH-TENDERLOIN PINWHEELS

2 (1- to 1½-pound) pork tenderloins, cut into 1-inch slices
1 teaspoon celery seeds
1 teaspoon dried whole thyme
½ teaspoon salt
½ teaspoon ground nutmeg
½ teaspoon freshly ground pepper
1 tablespoon olive oil
1 (10-ounce) package frozen chopped spinach, thawed and drained
½ cup salsa
¼ cup grated Parmesan cheese

Place tenderloin slices between sheets of wax paper; flatten to ⅛-inch thickness, using a meat mallet or rolling pin.

Combine celery seeds and next 4 ingredients, stirring well. Sprinkle seasoning evenly on both sides of tenderloin slices.

Heat microwave browning dish according to manufacturer's instructions. Add oil and half of tenderloin slices; microwave at HIGH 30 seconds on each side. Repeat procedure with remaining tenderloin slices.

Combine spinach and salsa; microwave at HIGH 8 minutes. Spoon about 1 tablespoon spinach mixture on each tenderloin slice, spreading evenly to edges. Roll up tightly jellyroll fashion; secure with a wooden pick. Place tenderloin rolls on a glass plate, and microwave at HIGH 2 minutes. Cut each tenderloin roll into 3 pieces; sprinkle with Parmesan cheese. Yield: about 4 dozen appetizers. *Wes Fankhauser*
Spartanburg, South Carolina

APPETIZER PIZZAS

1 pound bulk pork sausage
½ cup chopped onion
½ cup chopped green pepper
1 teaspoon dried whole oregano
1 teaspoon fennel seeds
⅛ teaspoon garlic powder
2 cups (8 ounces) shredded process American cheese
2 cups (8 ounces) shredded mozzarella cheese
2 (8-ounce) loaves party rye bread, lightly toasted, or 1 (5½-ounce) package Melba rounds

Combine sausage, onion, and green pepper in a 2-quart casserole. Cover with wax paper, and microwave at HIGH 6 to 7 minutes, stirring after 3 minutes. Remove sausage mixture from casserole, and drain on paper towels. Return sausage mixture to casserole. Add oregano and next 4 ingredients, mixing well. Cover with wax paper, and microwave at MEDIUM HIGH (70% power) 4 minutes or until cheese melts, stirring after 2 minutes.

Spread 1 tablespoon sausage mixture on each toasted bread slice. Line a 12-inch glass platter with paper towels; arrange 10 pizzas around outer edge of platter. Microwave, uncovered, at HIGH 1 minute or until heated, rotating dish a half-turn after 30 seconds. Repeat procedure with remaining bread and sausage mixture. Yield: 3½ dozen.

To freeze: Place uncooked pizzas in a single layer on large baking sheets; freeze. When frozen, place pizzas in plastic bag, and keep frozen until needed.

To serve, thaw and microwave, uncovered, at HIGH 1 minute or until heated, giving dish a half-turn after 30 seconds.

CHEDDAR-BACON DIP

4 slices bacon
1 (8-ounce) package cream cheese
1½ cups (6 ounces) shredded
   sharp Cheddar cheese
¼ cup whipping cream
1 teaspoon Worcestershire sauce
¼ teaspoon dry mustard
⅛ teaspoon onion powder
⅛ teaspoon hot sauce
Fresh parsley sprig (optional)

Place bacon on a rack in a 12- x 8- x 2-inch baking dish; cover with paper towels. Microwave at HIGH 3½ to 4½ minutes or until crisp. Crumble bacon, and set aside.

Place cream cheese in a 1-quart casserole. Microwave at HIGH 1 minute or until melted. Stir in Cheddar cheese and next 5 ingredients. Microwave at MEDIUM HIGH (70% power) 2½ minutes or until cheese is melted and mixture is heated, stirring once. Stir in crumbled bacon, reserving 1 tablespoon to sprinkle on top. Garnish with a parsley sprig, if desired. Serve with apple wedges or crackers. Yield: 2 cups.

POTATO SHELL APPETIZERS

2 slices bacon
2 large baking potatoes
¼ cup commercial sour cream
1 teaspoon chopped fresh chives
   or frozen chives, thawed
½ cup (2 ounces) shredded
   Cheddar or Swiss cheese

Place bacon on a rack in a 12- x 8- x 2-inch baking dish; cover with paper towels. Microwave at HIGH 2 to 3 minutes or until bacon is crisp. Drain bacon; crumble and set aside.

Wash potatoes, and pat dry; prick several times with a fork. Arrange potatoes on paper towels in microwave oven, leaving at least 1 inch between potatoes. Microwave at HIGH 7 to 8 minutes, turning and rearranging potatoes after 4 minutes; let stand 2 minutes. (If potatoes are not done after standing time, microwave an additional 30 seconds at HIGH.) Cool.

Cut potatoes in half lengthwise; cut each piece in half lengthwise again. Carefully scoop out pulp, leaving ¼-inch shells. Reserve pulp for use in other recipes.

Combine sour cream and chives. Spoon about 1¼ teaspoons on each potato skin; sprinkle with bacon and cheese. Place on a microwave-safe plate; microwave at HIGH 2 to 3 minutes or until cheese melts, giving dish a half-turn after 1 minute. Yield: 8 appetizer servings.

Sweet On Vidalias

Some say it's love at first bite—and no wonder. The sweet, tame Vidalia onion has enticed many onion eaters to ponder whether any other variety has ever truly affected their taste buds quite the way a Vidalia does. Some folks will eat Vidalias just like apples. Others might prefer them lightly seasoned and sautéed, baked, fried, or marinated.

Vidalias are harvested once a year. Experts say the flat-topped, round-based onion gets its sweet flavor from the low-sulfur content of the soil of Vidalia, Georgia, and surrounding counties.

VIDALIA ONION SAUTÉ

5 medium Vidalia onions, sliced
¼ cup butter or margarine,
   melted
½ teaspoon sugar
½ teaspoon salt
½ teaspoon pepper
½ cup dry sherry
2 tablespoons grated Parmesan
   cheese

Sauté onion slices in butter in a Dutch oven 6 to 8 minutes or until crisp-tender. Sprinkle with sugar, salt, and pepper; stir gently. Add sherry; simmer 2 minutes. Spoon into a serving dish; sprinkle with cheese. Yield: 8 servings.

Eleanor K. Brandt
Arlington, Texas

MARINATED VIDALIAS

2 medium Vidalia onions
1 cup water
½ cup sugar
¼ cup white vinegar
1 tablespoon plus 1 teaspoon
   mayonnaise
1 teaspoon celery seeds
Lettuce leaves

Slice onions, and separate into rings. Combine water, sugar, and vinegar; stir until sugar dissolves. Pour over onion rings. Cover and chill at least 3 hours; drain. Stir in mayonnaise and celery seeds. Serve on lettuce leaves. Yield: 4 servings.

Nancy Hood
Atlanta, Georgia

VIDALIA DEEP DISH

2 cups water
1 cup uncooked long-grain rice
6 large Vidalia onions
½ cup butter or margarine
2 tablespoons minced fresh
  parsley
¼ teaspoon salt
¼ teaspoon white pepper
1 cup (4 ounces) shredded Swiss
  cheese
1 cup whipping cream
Paprika

Bring water to a boil in a medium saucepan; add rice. Cover, reduce heat, and simmer 10 minutes. Drain and set aside.

Peel and chop onions. Melt butter in a Dutch oven over medium heat; add onion, and cook 15 minutes, stirring frequently. Remove from heat; stir in rice, parsley, and next 4 ingredients. Spoon mixture into a lightly greased 13- x 9- x 2-inch baking dish. Cover and bake at 350° for 30 minutes. Sprinkle lightly with paprika. Yield: 10 to 12 servings.
Ethel Jernegan
Savannah, Georgia

Herbs Liven Up Chicken

The same herbs that hint of warm weather and spice the air with a fresh, clean scent also invite delectable dining. Chicken's versatility and agreeable taste make it a fine partner for the flavors of parsley, thyme, basil, chives, and more.

Dijon-Herb Chicken is both fast and flavorful—it requires 30 minutes or less to prepare. If time is really short, use dried herbs to make preparation even faster. In most recipes, you can substitute 1 teaspoon dried herbs for 1 tablespoon fresh.

CHICKEN BREASTS WITH HERB BUTTER

½ cup butter or margarine,
  softened
2 tablespoons chopped fresh
  parsley
1 tablespoon minced fresh chives
1 tablespoon minced fresh thyme
2 teaspoons lemon juice
½ teaspoon salt
⅛ teaspoon pepper
4 chicken breast halves
1 cup sliced mushrooms
¼ cup chopped green onions
2 tablespoons all-purpose flour
1 (10¾-ounce) can chicken broth,
  undiluted
½ cup white wine

Combine first 7 ingredients; mix well. Loosen skin on chicken. Spread 2 tablespoons butter mixture under skin of each piece. Arrange chicken in a 13- x 9- x 2-inch baking pan. Bake, uncovered, at 375° for 50 to 60 minutes, basting occasionally with pan drippings. Remove chicken to a platter, reserving 2 tablespoons drippings. Sauté mushrooms and green onions in pan drippings. Add flour, stirring until combined; cook 1 minute. Gradually add broth and wine; cook over medium heat, stirring constantly, until mixture is thickened and bubbly. Serve with chicken. Yield: 4 servings.
Laurie McIntyre
Lake Jackson, Texas

DIJON-HERB CHICKEN

8 chicken breast halves, skinned
  and boned
¼ cup butter or margarine,
  melted
¼ cup lemon juice
2 tablespoons Worcestershire
  sauce
1 tablespoon Dijon mustard
½ teaspoon salt
2 tablespoons chopped fresh
  chives
2 tablespoons chopped fresh
  parsley

Sauté chicken in butter in a skillet over medium heat 10 minutes on each side. Remove chicken to a serving platter, reserving pan drippings in skillet; keep chicken warm. Add lemon juice and next 3 ingredients to pan drippings. Bring to a boil, stirring occasionally. Stir in chives and parsley. Pour over chicken. Yield: 8 servings.
Joanne Kent
Austin, Texas

SAVORY CHICKEN SAUTÉ

4 slices bacon
2 chicken breast halves, skinned
  and boned
2 tablespoons all-purpose flour
⅛ teaspoon salt
⅛ teaspoon pepper
2 cloves garlic, minced
1 medium onion, chopped
1 (4-ounce) can sliced
  mushrooms, drained
¾ cup stewed tomatoes with
  juice
Dash of poultry seasoning
Dash of ground red pepper
1 teaspoon white wine
  Worcestershire sauce
3 tablespoons dry white wine
3 tablespoons chopped fresh basil
Hot cooked rice or pasta

Cook bacon in a heavy skillet until crisp; remove bacon, reserving 1 tablespoon drippings in skillet. Crumble bacon, and set aside.

Place each piece of chicken between 2 sheets of plastic wrap, and flatten to ¼-inch thickness, using a meat mallet or rolling pin. Combine flour, salt, and pepper, and dredge chicken in flour mixture.

Heat 1 tablespoon bacon drippings in skillet over medium heat. Add chicken, and cook 3 to 4 minutes on each side or until golden brown. Add garlic and onion; cook over medium heat, stirring constantly, until onion is crisp-tender. Add mushrooms and next 6 ingredients; simmer 5 minutes. Serve over hot cooked rice or pasta. Sprinkle with crumbled bacon. Yield: 2 servings. *Mary V. Farris*
Falls Church, Virginia

From Our Kitchen To Yours

Besides tantalizing your sense of smell with marvelous aromas, herbs add savory fresh flavor to food. These fragrant plants offer tasty alternatives to salt. For ultimate herb flavor, use fresh herbs, which can be purchased at supermarkets. Or you can grow your own.

To keep herbs fresh and to minimize flavor loss up to seven days, refrigerate all cut herbs. Basil, chives, cilantro, dill, mint, parsley, rosemary, and tarragon stay fresh with the stems placed in a jar filled one-third with water and the tops covered with a plastic bag. Change the water every few days; discard rotting sprigs. Oregano keeps best in sealed plastic bags with the stems wrapped in damp paper towels. Stored dry (unwashed) in an open plastic bag, thyme remains fresh. Here are some tips.

—Rinse herbs under cool, running water; shake excess water from leaves. Gently pat dry on paper towels.

—For six servings, use 1 teaspoon of a dominant-flavored herb, such as rosemary or tarragon.

—For six servings, use 1 to 2 teaspoons of a medium-flavored herb, such as basil, dill, mint, and oregano.

—Cut herbs with kitchen scissors.

—Before cutting thyme or rosemary, strip small leaves from stems.

—Substitute 1 teaspoon dried herbs for 1 tablespoon fresh.

Herb	Characteristics
Basil	Bright-green, delicate, oval-shaped leaf; sweet aroma; clovelike spiciness
Chives	Long, slender, hollow grasslike leaf; delicate onion flavor
Cilantro	Slightly scalloped broad leaf; distinctive, pungent flavor; resembles parsley in appearance
Dill	Delicate feathery fernlike leaf; unique spicy flavor
Mint	Oval, green leaf with pointed tip; sweet refreshing flavor
Oregano	Dark-green, peppery-flavored leaf; pungent, spicy flavor
Parsley	Flat or curly bright-green leaf; faint celery-like flavor
Rosemary	Spiky, needlelike leaf; dominant pinelike flavor
Tarragon	Slender, pointed, green shiny leaf; dominant bittersweet flavor
Thyme	Tiny gray-green leaf; sharp, slightly sweet flavor

Dress Up Ground Beef

Usually we sandwich ground beef between buns or stir it up with tomato sauces, but wrapping it in pastry offers a pleasant variation from the ordinary.

CHEESEBURGER PIE

Pastry for a 9-inch pie
1 pound ground beef
¼ cup chopped green pepper
¼ cup chopped onion
1 (8-ounce) can tomato sauce, divided
½ cup dry breadcrumbs
2 tablespoons chopped fresh parsley
½ teaspoon dried whole oregano
¼ teaspoon pepper
1 egg, beaten
¼ cup milk
1 teaspoon prepared mustard
1 teaspoon Worcestershire sauce
2 cups (8 ounces) shredded Cheddar cheese
½ cup chili sauce

Line a 9-inch pieplate with pastry. Trim excess pastry around edges. Prick bottom and sides of pastry with a fork. Bake at 400° for 3 minutes; remove from oven, and gently prick with a fork. Bake pastry an additional 5 minutes.

Cook ground beef, green pepper, and onion in a large skillet until meat is browned, stirring to crumble meat; drain. Add ½ cup tomato sauce and next 4 ingredients, stirring well. Spoon mixture into prepared crust.

Combine egg and next 4 ingredients, stirring well; spoon evenly over meat mixture. Bake at 375° for 30 minutes.

Combine remaining tomato sauce and chili sauce; serve with pie. Yield: 6 servings.
Mrs. Roy Nieman
Dunnellon, Florida

MEAT LOAF IN A WRAP

2 cups soft breadcrumbs
½ cup chopped onion
1 egg, beaten
½ cup milk
¼ cup catsup
1 teaspoon salt
¼ teaspoon pepper
2 pounds lean ground beef
4 hard-cooked eggs, peeled
2 whole dill pickles, sliced in
    half lengthwise
1 (11-ounce) package piecrust mix
1 egg yolk
1 tablespoon water
4 pimiento-stuffed olives
Mustard Sauce

Combine first 8 ingredients in a large bowl. Place half of mixture in a 9- x 5- x 3-inch loafpan. Gently press hard-cooked eggs lengthwise down center of mixture; place pickles lengthwise on each side of eggs. Top with remaining meat mixture, gently pressing until top is smooth. Bake, uncovered, at 350° for 1 hour; remove from pan. Cool and drain on a wire rack 30 minutes.

Prepare piecrust mix according to package directions. Roll pastry on a lightly floured surface to a 23- x 16-inch rectangle, reserving scraps. Place meat loaf in center of pastry; moisten edges with water. Fold opposite sides over meat loaf, pressing edges to seal. Place meat loaf, seam side down, on a lightly greased pan. Combine egg yolk and water; brush pastry lightly with mixture. Carefully cut 4 holes in top of pastry to release steam as meat loaf bakes.

Roll reserved scraps to ⅛-inch thickness; cut into 4 strips. Place strips diagonally across pastry, and brush with egg-yolk mixture. Bake at 425° for 30 minutes. Remove from oven; place olives in steam holes. Chill. Cut into slices, and serve with Mustard Sauce. Yield: 8 servings.

Mustard Sauce

½ cup prepared mustard
½ cup mayonnaise
1 tablespoon grated onion

Combine all ingredients in a small mixing bowl. Stir well, and refrigerate. Yield: 1 cup.   *Carrie Bartlett*
Gallatin, Tennessee

Make It Mexican

Most Mexican meals are characterized by bowlfuls of toppings and salsas, which are piled onto the main dish. In Baton Rouge, Louisiana, Mrs. David Williams combines all that great flavor in one with her recipe for Torta Mexican Style.

TORTA MEXICAN STYLE

1 pound ground beef
1 (1¼-ounce) package taco
    seasoning mix
¾ cup water
1 (10-ounce) package frozen
    chopped spinach, thawed
1 cup ricotta cheese or cottage
    cheese
1 (16-ounce) package hot roll mix
1 egg, beaten
Fresh parsley sprigs
Cherry tomatoes
Picante sauce

Cook ground beef in a skillet until meat is browned, stirring to crumble. Drain. Combine ground beef, taco seasoning, and water; bring to a boil, reduce heat, and simmer 15 minutes. Set aside.

Drain spinach, and press between paper towels to remove excess moisture. Combine spinach and cheese, and set aside.

Prepare hot roll mix according to package directions. Turn out onto a lightly floured surface, and knead 5 minutes. Cover dough with a large bowl, and let rest 5 minutes. Divide dough into 3 portions; cover 2 portions, and set aside. Roll out 1 portion to an 11-inch circle on a lightly

floured surface. Carefully place circle in a lightly greased 9-inch springform pan, pressing dough into bottom and up sides. Spread meat mixture evenly over dough to within ½ inch of edge. Roll out each remaining portion of dough to a 9-inch circle. Place 1 circle over meat mixture, and spread spinach mixture evenly over dough. Place remaining dough circle over spinach mixture. Cover and let rise in a warm place (85°), free from drafts, 40 minutes.

Make indentations in dough with a knife so that top is divided into 8 wedges. (Do not cut through dough.) Brush top with beaten egg. Bake at 350° for 35 to 40 minutes. Remove sides of springform pan, and transfer torta to a serving plate. Garnish with parsley and cherry tomatoes. Slice and serve warm with picante sauce. Yield: 8 servings.

Plan Pork
For An Appetizer

In Sesame Pork Rounds, pork tenderloin gives up its typical place on the menu as an entrée and assumes a new role as an appetizer.

SESAME PORK ROUNDS

2 (¾-pound) pork tenderloins
½ cup soy sauce
⅓ cup honey
¼ cup dry sherry
¼ teaspoon garlic powder
¼ teaspoon ground ginger
Fresh watercress
2 tablespoons dry mustard
⅓ cup sesame seeds, toasted

Place tenderloins in a 12- x 8- x 2-inch baking dish. Combine soy sauce and next 4 ingredients, stirring well. Set aside ½ cup soy sauce mixture; pour remaining mixture over tenderloins. Cover and chill 8 hours, turning pork occasionally.

Remove tenderloins from marinade, reserving marinade. Place tenderloins on lightly greased rack of a broiler pan; pour water into broiler pan, and place rack in broiler pan. Bake at 375° for 30 minutes. Turn tenderloins, and brush with reserved marinade. Insert meat thermometer in center of tenderloin. Bake an additional 30 minutes or until thermometer registers 160°. Let cool slightly, and thinly slice. Arrange sliced tenderloin on a serving platter; garnish with watercress.

Combine mustard and reserved ½ cup soy sauce mixture; pour into a small serving bowl. Place toasted sesame seeds in a small serving bowl. Dip each slice of tenderloin into soy sauce mixture, and then into sesame seeds, using a wooden pick. Yield: 12 appetizer servings.

Perk Up Meals With A Salad

Let your imagination go wild with the wide variety of salad greens available at your supermarket. A combination of several different ones can turn a plain green salad into a tasty assortment of textures, colors, and flavors.

WILTED SPINACH SALAD

1 pound fresh spinach
6 slices bacon, cut into bite-size
    pieces
½ cup sliced green onions
2 tablespoons white wine vinegar
1 tablespoon lemon juice
2 teaspoons sugar
½ teaspoon salt
Dash of freshly ground pepper
2 hard-cooked eggs, chopped

Remove stems from spinach; wash leaves thoroughly, and pat dry. Tear into bite-size pieces, and place in a large salad bowl; set aside.

Cook bacon in a skillet until crisp; drain bacon on paper towels, reserving drippings in skillet, and set aside.

Add green onions and next 5 ingredients to bacon drippings in skillet; stir well, and cook until bubbly. Immediately pour over spinach, tossing to coat. Sprinkle with bacon and chopped eggs. Serve immediately. Yield: 6 servings.   *Reba B. Wilson*
Jasper, Alabama

MAGNOLIA BLOSSOM SALAD

6 cups torn, mixed salad greens
½ medium-size purple onion,
    sliced and separated into rings
1 ripe avocado, peeled and sliced
2 seedless oranges, pared and
    sectioned
2 hard-cooked eggs
2 teaspoons sugar
½ to 1 teaspoon salt
¼ cup olive oil
2 tablespoons orange juice
2 tablespoons lemon juice
3 drops hot sauce

Place mixed salad greens in a large salad bowl. Arrange onion rings in a circle over salad greens. Alternate avocado slices and orange sections on onion rings.

Cut eggs in half, separating whites from yolks. Dice whites; arrange whites in center of orange and avocado slices.

Mash egg yolks in bottom of a deep, narrow bowl. Add sugar and remaining ingredients; beat at high speed of an electric mixer until well blended. Pour over salad just before serving. Yield: 4 to 6 servings.
Barbara Beacom
Kernersville, North Carolina

ROMAINE-SPINACH SALAD

1 head romaine lettuce, torn
4 cups torn spinach
¼ cup sliced radishes
¼ cup sliced green onions
4 slices bacon, cooked and
    crumbled
2 hard-cooked eggs, sieved
1 clove garlic, crushed
1 teaspoon dry mustard
½ teaspoon salt
½ teaspoon pepper
1½ teaspoons minced fresh basil
    or ½ teaspoon dried whole
    basil
¼ cup white wine vinegar
½ cup vegetable oil

Combine first 5 ingredients in a large bowl; toss gently.

Combine eggs and remaining ingredients in a jar. Cover tightly, and shake vigorously; pour over salad. Toss gently; serve immediately. Yield: 8 servings.   *Charleen Hickey*
Helena, Arkansas

SESAME-ALMOND SALAD

⅔ cup vegetable oil
⅓ cup red wine vinegar
1 tablespoon grated Parmesan
    cheese
1 teaspoon seasoned salt
1 teaspoon parsley flakes
1 teaspoon dried whole oregano
1 teaspoon dried Italian salad
    dressing mix
¼ teaspoon onion powder
⅛ teaspoon garlic powder
2 cups torn romaine lettuce
2 cups torn Bibb lettuce
2 cups torn red leaf lettuce
¼ cup slivered almonds, toasted
1 tablespoon sesame seeds,
    toasted

Combine first 9 ingredients in a jar. Cover tightly, and shake vigorously. Chill. Combine romaine lettuce and remaining ingredients in a large bowl. Serve with chilled dressing. Yield: 4 servings.   *Nancy Burgiss*
Laurel Springs, North Carolina

Serve Mom Dessert

With Mother's Day just around the corner, we've put together several dessert recipes for children to make for Mother on her special day.

BERRIED TREASURE

2 (3-ounce) packages cream
   cheese, softened
1 (8-ounce) carton commercial
   sour cream
⅓ cup firmly packed light brown
   sugar
1 quart fresh strawberries, halved
   and chilled
¼ cup firmly packed light brown
   sugar

Combine first 3 ingredients in a small mixing bowl; beat at medium speed of an electric mixer until smooth. Chill 1 to 2 hours.

Spoon strawberries into 8 individual compotes or dessert dishes. Top with cream cheese mixture; sprinkle each with 1½ teaspoons brown sugar. Yield: 8 servings.

Carrie Bartlett
Gallatin, Tennessee

CHOCOLATE ICE CREAM BROWNIES

1 (23.6-ounce) package fudge
   brownie mix
½ gallon vanilla ice cream,
   softened
2 cups sifted powdered sugar
⅔ cup semisweet chocolate
   morsels
1½ cups evaporated milk
½ cup butter or margarine
1 teaspoon vanilla extract
1½ cups chopped pecans or
   walnuts

Prepare brownie mix according to package directions in a lightly greased 13- x 9- x 2-inch baking pan. Let cool in pan.

Spread ice cream over brownies; freeze until firm.

Combine sugar and next 3 ingredients in a saucepan. Bring to a boil; reduce heat to medium, and cook 8 minutes. Remove from heat, and stir in vanilla and pecans. Cool. Spread frosting over ice cream. Freeze.

Remove from freezer 5 to 10 minutes before serving. Cut into squares. Yield: 12 to 15 servings.

Mildred Sheppard
Crawfordville, Florida

CRUSTY CREAM CHEESE POUND CAKE

1 cup butter or margarine,
   softened
½ cup shortening
3 cups sugar
1 (8-ounce) package cream
   cheese, softened
3 cups sifted cake flour
6 eggs
1 tablespoon vanilla extract

Cream butter and shortening; gradually add sugar, beating well at medium speed of an electric mixer. Add cream cheese, beating until light and fluffy. Alternately add flour and eggs, beginning and ending with flour. Stir in vanilla.

Pour batter into a greased and floured 10-inch tube pan. Bake at 325° for 1 hour and 15 minutes or until a wooden pick inserted in center comes out clean. Cool in pan 10 minutes; remove from pan, and let cool completely on a wire rack. Yield: one 10-inch cake.

Donice Rogers
Columbia, Mississippi

LEMON-PECAN SQUARES

1½ cups all-purpose flour
⅓ cup powdered sugar
1 tablespoon grated lemon rind,
   divided
¾ cup butter or margarine,
   softened
1 (7-ounce) can flaked coconut
1 (14-ounce) can sweetened
   condensed milk
1 cup chopped pecans

Combine flour, powdered sugar, and 1 teaspoon lemon rind in a mixing bowl. Cut butter into flour mixture with a pastry blender until mixture resembles coarse meal. Press firmly and evenly into an ungreased 13- x 9- x 2-inch baking pan. Bake at 350° for 15 minutes.

Sprinkle coconut over baked layer; set aside.

Combine condensed milk and remaining 2 teaspoons lemon rind; drizzle evenly over coconut. Sprinkle pecans on top, pressing down slightly. Bake at 350° for 20 minutes. Cool on a wire rack. Cut into squares. Yield: 3½ dozen.

Mary Pappas
Richmond, Virginia

Dessert Tips

■ Leftover thin pancakes can be spread with jelly or jam, rolled up, and frozen; reheat in oven, and sprinkle with powdered sugar for dessert.

■ Semisweet chocolate morsels and semisweet chocolate squares can be used interchangeably when a recipe calls for this type chocolate melted.

JUNE

As summer rolls in, thoughts turn to fresh garden fare. This month's special section, "Microwave Cookery," is filled with recipes and tips for cooking vegetables this quick way. Other June treasures, fruits and berries, can be served a variety of ways, even preserved the light way. Most Southerners agree it wouldn't be summer without pies and cobblers baked with fresh berries.

It's Corn-Shucking Time!

Ears of corn, plump with kernels of pastel yellow or buttercup gold, are at their best right now with a sweet flavor that's unmatched any other time of year.

It's best to keep the corn refrigerated, unwashed, and in the shuck until you have a chance to prepare it.

For the best corn flavor in the recipe you prepare, use the ears within 24 hours of picking.

The number of ears you'll need for each recipe will vary with the size of the corn. We find that you can generally cut about ½ to ⅔ cup of kernels from an average ear of corn.

If you are selecting fresh corn from the market, be sure to look for fresh green husks, dry silks, and even rows of plump kernels. When you pop a kernel with your fingernail, if it is watery, then the corn is immature. Thick and starchy milk in the kernels indicates the corn is old.

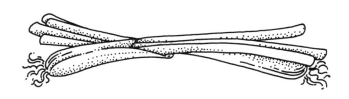

PIMIENTO-CORN SOUP
(pictured on page 149)

¾ cup diced onion
2 tablespoons butter or
    margarine, melted
2 cups white corn cut from cob
    (about 4 ears)
2 cups chicken broth
¼ teaspoon white pepper
1 (5-ounce) can evaporated milk,
    undiluted
1 (4-ounce) jar diced pimiento
Paprika

Sauté onion in butter in a large saucepan 3 minutes, stirring occasionally. Add corn; cook 3 minutes, stirring constantly. Stir in chicken broth and pepper. Cover, reduce heat to low, and simmer 5 minutes. Stir in milk; cook until thoroughly heated. (Do not boil.) Add pimiento; stir well. Ladle soup into bowls; sprinkle with paprika. Yield: 4 cups.
Kathleen D. Stone
Houston, Texas

MARINATED CORN SALAD
(pictured on page 149)

1¾ cups yellow corn cut from
    cob (about 4 ears)
¼ cup water
½ small green pepper, cut into
    ½-inch strips
½ cup chopped celery
2 tablespoons thinly sliced green
    onions
1 tablespoon chopped pimiento
1 tablespoon chopped fresh
    parsley
3 tablespoons vegetable oil
1 tablespoon cider vinegar
½ teaspoon salt
½ teaspoon dry mustard
⅛ teaspoon pepper

Combine corn and water in a medium saucepan. Bring to a boil; cover, reduce heat, and simmer 7 to 8 minutes or just until corn is tender. Drain. Combine corn, green pepper, and next 4 ingredients. Set aside.

Combine oil and remaining ingredients in a jar. Cover tightly; shake vigorously. Pour over salad; cover and chill 4 hours. Yield: 4 to 6 servings. *Mrs. James S. Stanton*
Richmond, Virginia

CORN CASSEROLE

About 4 ears fresh corn
4 eggs, separated
1 cup milk
⅔ cup (2.6 ounces) shredded
    Cheddar cheese
½ cup cracker crumbs
1 tablespoon butter or margarine,
    melted
½ teaspoon salt
¼ teaspoon pepper
¼ teaspoon dried whole dillweed
¼ teaspoon cream of tartar

Remove husks and silks from corn. Cut corn from cobs, scraping cobs to remove all milk. Measure 2 cups corn, and set aside.

Combine egg yolks, milk, cheese, cracker crumbs, butter, salt, pepper, and dillweed in a large bowl; add corn, and stir well.

Beat egg whites (at room temperature) and cream of tartar at high speed of an electric mixer until soft peaks form; fold whites into corn mixture. Spoon into a lightly greased 1½-quart casserole. Bake at 350° for 40 minutes. Yield: 4 to 6 servings.
Ruth K. Stevens
Sanford, North Carolina

SUMMER CORN RELISH

About 16 ears fresh yellow corn
4 cups chopped celery
2 cups diced sweet red pepper
2 cups diced green pepper
1 cup chopped onion
1 quart white vinegar (5% acidity)
1½ cups sugar
2 tablespoons pickling salt
2 tablespoons dry mustard
2 teaspoons celery seeds
1 teaspoon ground turmeric

Remove husks and silks from corn. Place ears in boiling water to cover. Return water to a boil; cook 5 minutes. Drain and immediately cover ears with ice water. Let stand until cool; drain. Cut corn from cob, measuring 8 cups of kernels.

Combine celery and remaining ingredients in a Dutch oven; bring to a boil. Boil, uncovered, 5 minutes, stirring occasionally. Add corn, and return to a boil. Cook 5 minutes, stirring occasionally. Spoon hot corn mixture into hot sterilized jars, leaving ½ inch headspace. Remove air bubbles; wipe jar rims. Cover at once with metal lids, and screw on bands. Process in boiling-water bath 15 minutes. Yield: 6 pints.

CORN-AND-OKRA CREOLE
(pictured on page 149)

1 cup chopped green pepper
½ cup chopped onion
2 tablespoons butter or margarine, melted
1½ cups white corn cut from cob (about 3 ears)
½ cup water
2 medium tomatoes, peeled, seeded, and chopped
1½ tablespoons tomato paste
½ teaspoon salt
¼ teaspoon pepper
¼ teaspoon dried whole thyme
¼ teaspoon paprika
1½ cups sliced okra

Sauté green pepper and onion in butter in a large skillet until crisp-tender. Add corn and water; cover and cook 10 minutes over medium heat, stirring occasionally. Add tomatoes and remaining ingredients except okra. Cover and simmer 10 minutes, stirring occasionally. Add okra; cover and simmer 5 to 7 minutes or until okra is done. Yield: 6 servings.
Harriet Crump
Collierville, Tennessee

FRESH CORN CUSTARD

2 tablespoons chopped green pepper
1 tablespoon butter or margarine, melted
2 cups corn cut from cob (about 4 ears)
3 eggs, slightly beaten
1 cup (4 ounces) shredded Cheddar cheese
¼ cup all-purpose flour
1 tablespoon sugar
½ teaspoon salt
⅛ teaspoon ground nutmeg
⅛ teaspoon pepper
2 cups half-and-half
2 tablespoons butter or margarine, melted
2 medium tomatoes, cut into ¼-inch slices
1 medium-size green pepper, cut into ¼-inch slices

Sauté chopped green pepper in 1 tablespoon butter. Combine green pepper, corn, eggs, and cheese in a large bowl, mixing well.

Combine flour and next 4 ingredients; add to corn mixture. Stir in half-and-half and 2 tablespoons butter. Pour mixture into a lightly greased 1½-quart baking dish. Arrange tomato slices and green pepper slices alternately around edge of dish. Place casserole in a 13- x 9- x 2-inch pan; pour hot water into pan to a depth of 1 inch. Bake, uncovered, at 325° for 1 hour and 10 minutes or until a knife inserted in center of custard comes out clean. Yield: 8 servings.
Louise Turpin
Birmingham, Alabama

FRIED CORN

12 ears fresh white corn
¼ cup butter or margarine
2 tablespoons bacon drippings
¾ cup water
1 teaspoon salt
¼ teaspoon pepper

Remove husks and silks from corn. Cut corn from cobs, scraping cobs to remove all milk. Heat butter and bacon drippings in a skillet until hot; add corn, water, salt, and pepper. Cook, uncovered, over medium heat until mixture comes to a boil. Cover, reduce heat, and simmer 10 to 12 minutes or until liquid is absorbed, stirring frequently. Yield: 10 to 12 servings.
Sharon Moulds
Largo, Florida

Corn Tips

■ If it is necessary to store fresh corn, buy it in the husks and store in the refrigerator. This prevents sugar in the corn from turning to starch.

■ To select fresh corn, look for fresh green husks, dry silks, and even rows of plump kernels.

■ To test the freshness of corn at the market, pop a kernel with your fingernail. If the milk is watery, then the corn is immature. If it is thick and starchy, the corn is old.

■ The yield of kernels cut from corn-on-the-cob will depend upon the size of the ears. Generally, two average-size ears of corn will yield about 1 cup of kernels.

QUICK!
Toss A Salad

Simple yet packed with variety, flavor, and nutrition, these salads can be made in minutes.

If calories are a concern, try replacing your favorite commercial salad dressing with its low-calorie counterpart. You'll save up to 80 calories a tablespoon.

QUICK CHEESY-MUSHROOM SALAD

2 cups torn Bibb lettuce
2 cups torn iceberg lettuce
6 slices bacon, cooked and crumbled
¼ pound fresh mushrooms, sliced
⅓ cup grated Parmesan cheese
¾ cup (3 ounces) shredded Swiss cheese
Commercial creamy Italian salad dressing

Combine all ingredients, except salad dressing; toss gently. Serve with salad dressing. Yield: 4 to 6 servings.
Mary Nell Livingston
Columbia, Mississippi

HARVEST CARROT SALAD

3 cups shredded carrot
1 (17-ounce) can apricot halves, drained and chopped
½ cup sliced celery
⅔ cup raisins
¼ cup chopped walnuts, toasted
½ cup salad dressing or mayonnaise

Combine all ingredients, tossing well. Cover and refrigerate. Yield: 6 to 8 servings.
Nancy Hall
Calvert City, Kentucky

SPINACH-PECAN SALAD

¾ cup sliced mushrooms
½ cup commercial Italian salad dressing
½ pound spinach
¼ cup golden raisins
¼ cup coarsely chopped pecans
1 hard-cooked egg

Toss mushrooms with salad dressing. Set aside.

Remove stems from spinach; wash leaves thoroughly, and pat dry. Tear into bite-size pieces. Combine spinach, mushrooms, raisins, and pecans in a bowl; toss gently. Grate egg over salad. Yield: 4 servings.
Mrs. Shaf Gregory
Naples, Florida

QUICK BEAN SALAD

1 (15-ounce) can garbanzo beans, drained
1 (16-ounce) can French-style green beans, drained
1 (14-ounce) can artichoke hearts, drained and quartered
½ cup commercial Italian salad dressing

Combine first 3 ingredients in a large bowl, tossing lightly. Pour dressing over vegetables; toss gently. If desired, cover and chill. To serve, use a slotted spoon. Yield: 6 to 8 servings.
Natalie Lund
Glasgow, Kentucky

TOMATO FLOWER SALAD

6 medium tomatoes, chilled
½ cup cottage cheese
½ cup chopped celery
½ cup chopped cucumber
1 tablespoon chopped green pepper
1 tablespoon chopped onion
2 tablespoons mayonnaise
¼ teaspoon salt
⅛ teaspoon pepper

Cut stems from tomatoes. Cut each tomato into 8 wedges, leaving wedges attached at bottom. Fan wedges slightly; set aside.

Combine cottage cheese and remaining ingredients; stir well. Spoon evenly into tomato flowers. Serve immediately. Yield: 6 servings.
Mrs. H. D. Baxter
Charleston, West Virginia

ZUCCHINI SALAD

7 small zucchini, thinly sliced diagonally
1 sweet red pepper, sliced into thin strips
1 green pepper, sliced into thin strips
3 stalks celery, thinly sliced diagonally
1 small red onion, thinly sliced and separated into rings
1 cup commercial Italian salad dressing
2 tablespoons sugar
1 tablespoon dried parsley flakes
½ teaspoon dried whole basil

Combine first 5 ingredients in a large bowl; stir well.

Combine salad dressing, sugar, parsley, and basil; add to vegetable mixture, tossing gently. Serve tossed, or arrange on individual plates as desired. Yield: 8 to 10 servings.
Mrs. Bill Anthony
Poteau, Oklahoma

Tip: *To speed up salad making, wash, trim, and dry all ingredients for the salad as soon as you buy them; tie the ingredients together in a plastic bag, and store them in the refrigerator. At mealtime, just pull out the bag, gently toss the ingredients, and serve with a variety of salad dressings.*

MICROWAVE
COOKERY

How The Experts Cook At Home

When it comes to easy cooking, Sally Stone Roberts and Carolyn Oswalt Bond are riding the wave to success. Their expertise in microwave cooking has not only earned them a weekly show on a Pensacola cable network, but it's made their cooking at home downright enjoyable.

"We've always done microwave recipes best," Carolyn explains. "Our strengths are in microwave cookery, and we decided that's what we wanted to feature on our shows." They bring extensive home economics coursework and years of cooking for their families to the microwave-cooking field.

EASY CHICKEN

2 tablespoons butter or
   margarine, melted
2 tablespoons olive oil
2 tablespoons lemon juice
2 tablespoons Chablis or other
   dry white wine
2 cloves garlic, minced
¼ cup sliced green onions
½ teaspoon salt
½ teaspoon dried whole marjoram
½ teaspoon paprika
¼ teaspoon pepper
6 chicken breast halves
1½ to 2 tablespoons
   browning-and-seasoning sauce
Hot cooked rice

Soak a 2-quart clay cooker in water 15 minutes; drain. Combine first 10 ingredients in a small bowl; set aside. Brush chicken on each side with browning-and-seasoning sauce, and place bone side up in prepared cooker. Cover with lid. Microwave at HIGH 15 minutes. Turn chicken; spoon sauce over chicken. Cover and microwave at MEDIUM (50% power) 15 minutes. Let stand, covered, 5 to 10 minutes. Serve over cooked rice. Yield: 6 servings.

Note: Chicken may be microwaved in an 8-inch square baking dish. Chicken will overlap slightly. Cover with heavy-duty plastic wrap; fold back a small corner of wrap to allow steam to escape.

ONE-STEP LASAGNA

1 pound lean ground beef
1 (15¼-ounce) jar commercial
   spaghetti sauce
½ cup water
¼ cup dry red wine
8 uncooked lasagna noodles
2 cups cottage cheese
3 cups (12 ounces) shredded
   mozzarella cheese
½ cup grated Parmesan cheese
Green pepper rings (optional)

Crumble beef into a microwave-safe colander; place colander in a 9-inch pieplate. Cover with wax paper; microwave at HIGH 5 to 6 minutes or until meat is no longer pink, stirring after 3 minutes.

Combine beef, spaghetti sauce, water, and wine. Spread one-third of mixture in a lightly greased 12- x 8- x 2-inch baking dish. Arrange 4 lasagna noodles on sauce. Layer 1 cup cottage cheese and 1 cup mozzarella cheese over noodles. Spoon half of remaining sauce over cheese. Top with 4 lasagna noodles and 1 cup cottage cheese, 1 cup mozzarella cheese, and remaining sauce; sprinkle with Parmesan cheese. Cover tightly with heavy-duty plastic wrap. Fold back a small corner of wrap to allow steam to escape.

Microwave at MEDIUM (50% power) 32 to 35 minutes, giving dish a half-turn after 15 minutes. Sprinkle with remaining 1 cup mozzarella cheese, and microwave, uncovered, at MEDIUM 2 minutes. Let stand 10 minutes. Garnish with pepper rings, if desired. Yield: 6 servings.

VEGETABLE MEDLEY

1½ cups broccoli flowerets
1½ cups sliced zucchini
½ cup sweet red pepper strips
½ cup sliced water chestnuts
¼ cup sliced green onions
2 teaspoons chicken-flavored
   bouillon granules
2 tablespoons butter or margarine

Combine first 5 ingredients in a shallow 2-quart casserole; sprinkle with bouillon granules, and toss. Dot with butter. Cover tightly with heavy-duty plastic wrap; fold back a small corner of wrap to allow steam to escape. Microwave at HIGH 4 minutes, giving dish a half-turn after 2 minutes. Let stand, covered, 5 minutes. Yield: 4 servings.

BLUEBERRY SAUCE

1 (16-ounce) package frozen
   blueberries
½ cup sugar
2 tablespoons cornstarch
⅛ teaspoon salt
½ cup water
1 tablespoon lemon juice
Fresh mint (optional)

Pierce blueberry package with a fork. Microwave at MEDIUM LOW (30% power) 6 to 8 minutes, rotating package after 4 minutes; drain blueberries. Set aside.

Combine sugar and cornstarch in a 1¾-quart casserole, mixing well. Add salt, water, and lemon juice, stirring until blended. Stir in blueberries.

Microwave at HIGH 6 to 7 minutes, stirring every 2 minutes until sauce is thickened and transparent. Serve over ice cream, pancakes, or cake. Garnish with mint, if desired. Yield: 2 cups.

EASY BLUEBERRY DESSERT

1 recipe Blueberry Sauce
1 (9-ounce) package yellow cake
   mix
¼ cup butter, thinly sliced
¼ cup chopped pecans
1 teaspoon ground cinnamon

Spoon hot Blueberry Sauce into a lightly greased 8-inch square baking dish. Sprinkle dry cake mix evenly over sauce; arrange butter slices over cake mix. Combine pecans and cinnamon; sprinkle over cake mix.

Microwave at HIGH 12 to 13 minutes, or until cake is firm and has a cobblerlike texture, giving the dish a quarter turn at 5-minute intervals. Serve warm with ice cream. Yield: 6 to 8 servings.

Homemade Pudding, A Microwave Favorite

Smooth, creamy pudding is a favorite dessert especially suited for cooking in the microwave. Because cooking occurs from all sides rather than only the bottom, the possibility of scorching is eliminated. For extra convenience, pudding can be measured, mixed, and cooked in a 4-cup glass measure.

CREAMY BANANA PUDDING

1 cup sugar
3 tablespoons cornstarch
3 cups milk
3 egg yolks, slightly beaten
2 teaspoons vanilla extract
½ cup commercial sour cream
Vanilla wafers
4 medium bananas
2 cups frozen whipped topping,
   thawed

Combine sugar and cornstarch in a 2-quart glass bowl. Gradually stir in milk; microwave at HIGH 9 minutes or until mixture is thickened, stirring every 3 minutes.

Gradually stir about 1 cup of hot mixture into yolks; add to remaining hot mixture, stirring constantly. Microwave at HIGH 1 to 2 minutes or until thickened, stirring twice. Fold in vanilla and sour cream.

Line bottom and sides of a 2-quart bowl with vanilla wafers. Slice 2 bananas, and layer over wafers. Pour half of custard over bananas. Repeat layers of vanilla wafers, bananas, and custard. Chill. Spread whipped topping over custard. Yield: 8 servings.

BREAD PUDDING

1 slice white bread, cut into
   cubes
2 tablespoons raisins
1 egg, beaten
½ cup evaporated milk
3 tablespoons water
2 tablespoons sugar
½ teaspoon ground cinnamon
¼ teaspoon ground nutmeg

Place half of bread cubes in each of 2 lightly greased 6-ounce custard cups; sprinkle each with 1 tablespoon raisins. Combine egg, milk, and water; mix well. Pour half of milk mixture into each cup. Combine sugar, cinnamon, and nutmeg; sprinkle 1 tablespoon mixture over each cup, reserving remaining mixture. Cover and microwave at MEDIUM (50% power) 3 minutes; stir and sprinkle each with remaining sugar mixture. Microwave at MEDIUM 3 to 4 minutes or until set. Yield: 2 servings.

Greta Alexander
Lenoir City, Tennessee

PECAN-MOCHA PUDDING

⅓ cup chopped pecans
⅓ cup sugar
⅓ cup firmly packed brown sugar
¼ cup all-purpose flour
2 cups milk
½ cup semisweet chocolate
   morsels
2 teaspoons instant coffee
   granules
3 eggs, beaten
2 tablespoons butter or margarine
1 teaspoon vanilla extract
Sweetened whipped cream

Spread pecans in a single layer on a 12-inch pizza plate. Microwave at HIGH 4 to 5 minutes or until toasted.

Combine sugars and flour in a 2½-quart glass bowl; gradually stir in milk. Microwave at HIGH 6 to 8 minutes or until thickened, stirring every 2 minutes. Add chocolate morsels and coffee granules; stir until chocolate melts.

Gradually stir about one-fourth of chocolate mixture into eggs; add to remaining hot mixture, stirring well. Microwave at HIGH 2 minutes or until thickened; stir after 1 minute.

Stir in butter and vanilla. Spoon mixture into 4 individual compotes. Cover and chill. To serve, top with whipped cream and toasted pecans. Yield: 4 servings.

Orange Rolls In A Jiffy

With conventional cooking, it usually takes too long to prepare fresh yeast rolls for breakfast. But with Easy Orange Rolls, the time is cut by more than half. You start with hot roll mix and let the bread rise and bake in the microwave.

Breads baked in the microwave have the same tender texture as those prepared conventionally, but they don't brown or develop that typical "oven-baked" crust. These orange rolls get a little color from their cinnamon filling and marmalade glaze.

EASY ORANGE ROLLS

1 (16-ounce) package hot roll mix
2 tablespoons butter or margarine
3 tablespoons sugar
1 tablespoon ground cinnamon
Glaze (recipe follows)

Prepare and knead roll mix according to package directions.

Place butter in a small custard cup. Microwave at HIGH 40 to 50 seconds or until melted. Set aside. Combine sugar and cinnamon.

Roll dough out on a floured surface to a 14- x 12-inch rectangle; brush with melted butter. Sprinkle with sugar mixture.

Roll dough jellyroll fashion, starting at long side. Pinch seam to seal (do not seal ends). Cut roll into 9 (about 1½-inch) slices; place slices, cut side down, in a greased shallow 2½-quart casserole. Cover with plastic wrap, and place in back of microwave. Place 1 cup water in a glass measure in front of rolls. Microwave at MEDIUM LOW (30% power) 1 to 2 minutes; let rolls stand in microwave 5 minutes. Repeat rising procedure 2 to 4 times or until rolls have doubled in bulk.

Remove cup of water from microwave. Uncover bread, and microwave at MEDIUM HIGH (70% power) 7 to 8 minutes or until done, giving dish a quarter-turn every 2 minutes. (Rolls are done when the top springs back when lightly pressed with a finger.) Spread with glaze while warm. Yield: 9 servings.

Glaze

1 cup sifted powdered sugar
¼ cup orange marmalade
½ teaspoon lemon juice

Combine all ingredients; stir well. Yield: about ½ cup.

Note: Rolls may be baked in a conventional oven at 325° for 30 minutes or until browned if a traditionally browned crust is desired.

Quick Dinner Options

It's 5 p.m.; do you know what you're having for dinner tonight? Maybe these microwave entrées will help. Most use only a handful of ingredients and require less than 30 minutes to prepare.

CRACKED PEPPER PATTIES

1¼ pounds ground sirloin
1 tablespoon cracked black pepper
1 tablespoon butter or margarine
1 clove garlic, minced
1 medium onion, sliced
½ cup beef broth
1 teaspoon Worcestershire sauce
1 teaspoon lemon juice

Shape meat into four ¾- to 1-inch-thick patties. Sprinkle both sides of patties with pepper; set aside.

Place a 10-inch browning skillet in microwave oven; preheat, uncovered, at HIGH 8 minutes or according to manufacturer's instructions. Add butter to hot skillet, tilting to coat surface. Place patties in hot skillet, and press with a spatula; turn and press until sizzling stops. Microwave, uncovered, at HIGH 3 minutes. Turn patties and microwave at HIGH 1 to 2 minutes. Transfer patties to a serving platter; keep warm.

Add minced garlic and onion slices to drippings; microwave at HIGH 1 minute or until onion is tender. Add beef broth, Worcestershire sauce, and lemon juice. Microwave at HIGH 1 minute or until mixture boils. Spoon onion mixture over patties; microwave at MEDIUM (50% power) 1 minute. Yield: 4 servings.

LEMON-HERB PORK CHOPS

2 tablespoons white wine
  Worcestershire sauce
2 tablespoons lemon juice
½ teaspoon browning-and-
  seasoning sauce
4 (¾-inch-thick) pork chops
1 teaspoon dried whole rosemary,
  crushed
½ teaspoon lemon-pepper
  seasoning
1 tablespoon vegetable oil

Combine first 3 ingredients; drizzle over each side of pork chops. Combine rosemary and lemon-pepper seasoning; sprinkle over each side of pork chops. Set aside.

Place a 10-inch browning skillet in microwave oven. Preheat, uncovered, at HIGH 6 to 8 minutes or according to manufacturer's instructions. Add oil to skillet, tilting to coat surface. Place chops and liquid in skillet with thickest portions toward outside of dish. Microwave at HIGH 1 minute. Turn chops, and microwave 1 minute. Cover skillet with lid; microwave at MEDIUM (50% power) 8 to 9 minutes or until chops are done, turning pork chops after 4 minutes. Yield: 4 servings.

PESTO CHICKEN AND PASTA
(pictured on page 115)

1 pound skinned and boned
  chicken breasts
1 tablespoon vegetable oil
1 cup sliced mushrooms
1 (14½-ounce) can tomato
  wedges, drained
1 cup chicken broth
1 tablespoon cornstarch
3 tablespoons commercial pesto
  sauce, divided
8 ounces fettuccine
Fresh basil sprig (optional)

Cut chicken into 1-inch pieces, and set aside.

Place a 10-inch browning skillet in microwave oven; preheat, uncovered, at HIGH 6 minutes or according to manufacturer's instructions. Add oil to hot skillet, tilting to coat surface. Add chicken, stirring well. Microwave, uncovered, at HIGH 3 to 4 minutes or until chicken is no longer pink, stirring every 2 minutes. Stir in sliced mushrooms and tomato wedges; microwave at HIGH 4 to 5 minutes or until mushrooms are tender.

Combine chicken broth and cornstarch; stir until smooth. Add to chicken mixture; microwave at HIGH 5 to 6 minutes or until slightly thickened. Add 1 tablespoon pesto sauce, stirring well.

Cook fettuccine according to package directions. Combine hot fettuccine and remaining pesto sauce, tossing gently. Serve chicken mixture over pasta. Garnish with basil sprig, if desired. Yield: 4 servings.

LEMON-GARLIC CHICKEN

2 tablespoons butter or margarine
¼ cup fresh lemon juice
½ teaspoon pepper
¼ teaspoon paprika
⅛ teaspoon garlic salt
4 (4-ounce) skinned and boned
  chicken breast halves

Place butter in a 12- x 8- x 2-inch baking dish. Microwave, uncovered, at HIGH 45 seconds or until butter melts. Stir in lemon juice and next 3 ingredients.

Pierce chicken breasts several times with a fork; place flesh side down in dish, turning to coat well.

Arrange chicken with thickest portions toward outside of dish. Cover with wax paper, and microwave at HIGH 10 minutes, giving dish a half-turn after 5 minutes. Microwave at MEDIUM HIGH (70% power) 6 to 8 minutes or until chicken is tender, turning and basting after 3 minutes. Yield: 4 servings.

Note: For 4 (6-ounce) bone-in, skinned chicken breast halves, arrange chicken with thickest portions toward outside of dish. Cover with wax paper, and microwave at HIGH 10 minutes, giving dish a half-turn after 5 minutes. Microwave at MEDIUM HIGH (70% power) 10 to 11 minutes or until chicken is tender, turning and basting chicken after about 5 minutes.

ON THE LIGHT SIDE

Healthy Microwave Cooking

Cooking in a microwave can actually improve the nutrition, healthiness, color, and texture of many foods. Vegetables are good examples of this because they cook in their own moisture, locking in vitamins, minerals, and flavor.

Microwaving also cuts calories in many dishes because little or no fat is needed. And the natural flavor of salt is enhanced in food so there's not as much temptation to reach for the salt shaker.

These stuffed vegetable recipes will enable you to create colorful, low-calorie accompaniments for almost any entrée.

SQUASH STUFFED WITH SPINACH PESTO

4 medium-size yellow squash (1 pound)
1 (10-ounce) package frozen chopped spinach
¾ cup (3 ounces) shredded part-skim mozzarella cheese, divided
¼ cup grated Parmesan cheese
1 small clove garlic, minced
2 tablespoons chopped onion
1 tablespoon pine nuts
1 teaspoon dried whole basil
¼ teaspoon dried whole marjoram
⅛ teaspoon white pepper
2 tablespoons Chablis or other dry white wine
1 tablespoon water
⅓ cup plain low-fat yogurt

Pierce squash several times with a fork. Arrange in microwave oven on paper towels. Microwave, uncovered, at HIGH 4 to 4½ minutes, rearranging after 2 minutes. Let stand 5 minutes.

Cut squash in half lengthwise; scoop out pulp, leaving ½-inch-thick shells. Set squash pulp aside for use in other recipes. Invert shells on paper towels, and set aside.

Remove wrapper from spinach package; place package in a small baking dish. Microwave at HIGH 3 minutes or until thawed. Drain spinach well, pressing between layers of paper towels to remove excess moisture. Combine spinach, ½ cup mozzarella cheese, and remaining ingredients in container of an electric blender. Process at medium speed until mixture is smooth.

Spoon spinach mixture into shells; sprinkle with remaining mozzarella cheese. Place in a 12- x 8- x 2-inch baking dish; cover with heavy-duty plastic wrap, and fold back a small edge of wrap to allow steam to escape. Microwave at HIGH 2 to 4 minutes or until thoroughly heated.

Yield: about 8 servings (76 calories per serving).

☐ *5.9 grams protein, 3.8 grams fat, 5.9 grams carbohydrate, 9 milligrams cholesterol, 136 milligrams sodium, and 187 milligrams calcium.*

STUFFED ZUCCHINI

4 medium zucchini (1½ pounds)
1 cup canned or frozen corn, thawed
1 cup (4 ounces) shredded low-fat Monterey Jack cheese
1 (2-ounce) jar chopped pimiento, drained
¼ cup chopped green pepper
2 teaspoons salt-free herb-and-spice blend
½ teaspoon onion powder

Pierce zucchini several times with a fork. Arrange in microwave oven on paper towels; microwave, uncovered, at HIGH 7 to 8 minutes, rearranging after 2 minutes. Let stand 5 minutes. Cut zucchini in half lengthwise; scoop out pulp, leaving ¼-inch-thick shells. Set squash pulp aside for use in other recipes. Invert shells.

Combine corn and remaining ingredients; spoon evenly into shells. Place in a 12- x 8- x 2-inch baking dish; cover with heavy-duty plastic wrap, and fold back a small edge of wrap to allow steam to escape. Microwave at HIGH 2 to 3 minutes or until thoroughly heated. Yield: 8 servings (64 calories per serving).

☐ *6.5 grams protein, 1.7 grams fat, 7.9 grams carbohydrate, 4 milligrams cholesterol, 38 milligrams sodium, and 160 milligrams calcium.*
                                    Joy L. Garcia
                              Bartlett, Tennessee

SPINACH-STUFFED MUSHROOMS

20 large mushrooms
1 (10-ounce) package frozen chopped spinach
¼ cup diced onion
⅓ cup plain low-fat yogurt
¼ cup (1 ounce) shredded 40%-less-fat Cheddar cheese
¼ cup (1 ounce) shredded low-fat Monterey Jack cheese
¼ cup grated Parmesan cheese
¼ teaspoon salt
¼ teaspoon garlic powder
¼ teaspoon dried whole oregano
1 tablespoon sherry
1 tablespoon grated Parmesan cheese

Clean mushrooms with damp paper towels. Remove and finely chop stems; set aside.

Place mushroom caps on a paper towel-lined pizza plate; set mushrooms aside.

Remove wrapper from spinach package; place package in a medium baking dish. Microwave at HIGH 3 minutes or until thawed. Drain spinach well, pressing between layers of paper towels.

Combine spinach, chopped mushroom stems, onion, and next 8 ingredients in a medium bowl; stir well.

Spoon spinach mixture into mushroom caps, and sprinkle evenly with 1 tablespoon Parmesan cheese. Microwave, uncovered, at HIGH 4 to 5 minutes or until mushrooms and stuffing are thoroughly heated, rotating a quarter-turn after each minute. Serve mushrooms immediately. Yield: 20 appetizer servings (26 calories per serving).

☐ *2.5 grams protein, 0.9 gram fat, 2.9 grams carbohydrate, 2 milligrams cholesterol, 72 milligrams sodium, and 72 milligrams calcium.*
                                    Susan Wright
                          Midlothian, Virginia

Microwave Shortcuts Save Time

Some foods are better cooked conventionally rather than in the microwave, but don't let that stop you from doing part of the cooking in the microwave. The techniques represented here are quicker to do in the microwave than in the conventional oven and yield good results.

Food	Temperature	Amount	Time
Melting Chocolate Morsels	Cook at MEDIUM (50% power)	½ to 1 cup 1½ cups 2 cups	2 to 3 minutes 3 to 3½ minutes 3½ to 4 minutes

Place chocolate morsels in a 1-quart mixing bowl; microwave at MEDIUM (50% power) until melted, stirring once.

Melting Chocolate Squares	Cook at MEDIUM (50% power)	1 to 2 squares 3 squares 4 to 5 squares 6 squares	1½ to 2 minutes 2 minutes 2 to 2½ minutes 2½ to 3 minutes

Place chocolate in a bowl; microwave at MEDIUM (50% power) until melted, stirring once.

Melting Butter or Margarine	Cook at HIGH	1 to 2 tablespoons 3 tablespoons ¼ to ½ cup ¾ cup 1 cup	35 to 45 seconds 50 to 55 seconds 1 minute 1 to 1½ minutes 1½ to 2 minutes

Place butter in a 2-cup glass measure; microwave at HIGH until melted.

Softening Butter or Margarine	Cook at LOW (10% power)	1 to 2 tablespoons 3 tablespoons ¼ to ½ cup 1 cup	15 to 30 seconds 30 to 45 seconds 1 to 1¼ minutes 1½ to 1¾ minutes

Place butter on a microwave-safe plate; microwave at LOW (10% power) until softened.

Rising Yeast Dough	Cook at MEDIUM LOW (30% power)	using 1 to 2 cups flour using 2 to 3 cups flour using 3 or more cups flour	1½ minutes 2 minutes 2½ minutes

Place dough in a large, greased, microwave-safe bowl, turning to grease all sides. Cover dough loosely with wax paper, and place in oven. Microwave at MEDIUM LOW (30% power) according to chart; let stand 5 minutes. Repeat microwaving and standing 2 to 4 times or until dough has doubled in bulk.

Hard-Cooked	Cook at	1 egg	1¼ to 1½ minutes
Eggs	MEDIUM	2 eggs	1¾ to 2¼ minutes
	(50% power)	3 eggs	3¾ to 4¼ minutes

Break eggs into lightly greased individual custard cups or microwave-safe coffee cups; pierce each yolk with a wooden pick. Cover with heavy-duty plastic wrap, and microwave at MEDIUM (50% power) to desired degree of doneness, turning cups halfway through cooking time. Let eggs stand, covered, 1 to 2 minutes. *Note:* While eggs prepared this way are not suitable for stuffing, they work well for egg salad or other dishes that use cooked eggs.

Toasting	Cook at	¼ cup chopped nuts	3 minutes
Nuts	HIGH	½ cup chopped nuts	3½ minutes
		1 cup chopped nuts	4 to 5 minutes

Spread nuts on a pieplate or a glass pizza plate. Microwave at HIGH until toasted; stir at 2-minute intervals.

Baking	Cook at	1 medium (6 to 7 ounces)	4 to 6 minutes
Potatoes	HIGH	2 medium	7 to 8 minutes
		4 medium	12 to 14 minutes

Rinse potatoes, and pat dry; prick several times with a fork. Arrange potatoes in microwave oven, leaving 1 inch between potatoes. (If microwaving more than 2 potatoes, arrange them in a circle.) Microwave at HIGH until done, turning and rearranging potatoes once. Let potatoes stand 5 minutes before serving.

Cooking	Cook at	1 slice	1 to 2 minutes
Bacon	HIGH	2 slices	2 to 3 minutes
		4 slices	3½ to 4½ minutes
		6 slices	5 to 7 minutes

Place bacon on a microwave-safe rack in a 12- x 8- x 2-inch baking dish; cover with paper towels. Microwave at HIGH 3 to 4 minutes or until bacon is crisp. Drain bacon.

Cooking	Cook at	½ pound	2 to 3 minutes
Ground Beef	HIGH	1 pound	4 to 6 minutes
		1½ pounds	6 to 8 minutes
		2 pounds	8 to 10 minutes

Crumble beef into a baking dish. Cover with wax paper, and microwave at HIGH until no longer pink, stirring at 2-minute intervals. Drain well.

Cooking	Cook at	1 skinned and boned chicken breast half (5 ounces)	3 to 4 minutes
Chicken	HIGH	2 skinned and boned chicken breast halves	4 to 5 minutes
		4 skinned and boned chicken breast halves	8 to 10 minutes
		1 (3-pound) broiler-fryer, cut up and skinned	9 to 10 minutes

Place chicken in a baking dish. Cover and microwave at HIGH until tender and done, giving dish a half-turn and rearranging chicken halfway through cooking time.

Serve A Slice Of Summer

With blackberries and several other fruits at their peak right now, there's practically no end to the goodies you can create. Treat your family to one of these summer delights.

PEACH PRALINE PIE

4 cups sliced fresh or frozen
   peaches, thawed
½ cup sugar
2 tablespoons tapioca
1 teaspoon lemon juice
½ cup all-purpose flour
¼ cup firmly packed brown sugar
¼ cup butter or margarine
½ cup chopped pecans
1 unbaked 9-inch pastry shell

Combine first 4 ingredients in a large bowl; let stand 15 minutes. Combine flour and brown sugar; cut in butter with a pastry blender until mixture resembles coarse meal. Stir in pecans. Sprinkle one-third of flour mixture in bottom of pastry shell. Spoon in peach mixture, and top with remaining flour mixture. Bake at 425° for 10 minutes. Reduce temperature to 350°, and bake 20 to 30 minutes or until pie is golden brown. Yield: one 9-inch pie.   *Sharon McClatchey*
Muskogee, Oklahoma

OLD-FASHIONED BLUEBERRY PIE

1 cup sugar
⅓ cup all-purpose flour
1 teaspoon grated lemon rind
⅛ teaspoon salt
4 cups fresh or frozen
   blueberries, thawed
Pastry for double-crust 9-inch pie
2 tablespoons butter or margarine

Combine first 4 ingredients, mixing well. Add blueberries, tossing gently. Set aside.

Roll half of pastry to ⅛-inch thickness on a lightly floured surface. Place in a 9-inch pieplate; trim off excess pastry along edges. Spoon blueberry mixture into pastry shell; dot with butter. Roll remaining pastry to ⅛-inch thickness; transfer to top of pie. Trim off excess pastry along edges. Fold edges under, and flute. Cut slits in top crust for steam to escape. Bake at 425° for 50 to 55 minutes or until golden. Cool before serving. Yield: one 9-inch pie.
Glyna Meredith Gallrein
Anchorage, Kentucky

CHILLED BLUEBERRY PIE
(pictured on pages 150 and 151)

4 cups blueberries, divided
2 tablespoons cornstarch
2 tablespoons water
½ cup light corn syrup
2 teaspoons lemon juice
1 cup whipping cream
2 tablespoons powdered sugar
   (optional)
1 (9-inch) graham cracker crust
Lemon slices (optional)
Fresh mint leaves (optional)

Puree 1 cup blueberries in an electric blender or food processor; set aside.

Combine cornstarch and water in a medium saucepan, stirring until blended. Add corn syrup, lemon juice, and blueberry puree. Bring mixture to a boil over medium heat, stirring constantly; boil 1 minute. Cool 1 hour. Fold remaining 3 cups blueberries into blueberry mixture, and set aside.

Beat whipping cream until foamy; gradually add powdered sugar, if desired, beating until soft peaks form. Spread whipped cream in bottom and on sides of piecrust, forming a 1-inch-thick shell. Spoon blueberry mixture into whipped cream shell. Chill at least 4 hours. If desired, garnish with lemon slices and mint leaves. Yield: one 9-inch pie.
Julie Earhart
St. Louis, Missouri

PEACH-AND-BLACKBERRY PIE
(pictured on pages 150 and 151)

⅔ cup sugar
1½ tablespoons quick-cooking
   tapioca
Pinch of salt
1 teaspoon grated orange rind
2 cups sliced fresh peaches
2 cups fresh blackberries
Cream Cheese Pastry

Combine first 4 ingredients in a bowl; mix well. Add peaches and blackberries; toss gently. Set aside.

Roll half of Cream Cheese Pastry to ⅛-inch thickness on a lightly floured surface. Place in a 9-inch pieplate. Trim off excess pastry along edges. Fold edges under, and flute. Spoon filling evenly into shell.

Roll remaining pastry to ⅛-inch thickness; cut pastry into ½-inch-wide strips. Twist each strip several times, and place on pie in a spiral design. Use extra pastry to shape leaf cutouts; place on outer end of spiral. Bake at 425° for 35 to 40 minutes or until crust is browned. Yield: one 9-inch pie.

Cream Cheese Pastry

2 cups all-purpose flour
½ teaspoon salt
½ cup shortening
2 (3-ounce) packages cream
   cheese
5 to 6 tablespoons cold water

Combine flour and salt; cut in shortening and cream cheese with a pastry blender until mixture resembles coarse meal. Sprinkle cold water (1 tablespoon at a time) evenly over surface; stir with a fork until dry ingredients are moistened. Shape into a ball; chill. Yield: pastry for one double-crust pie.
Mrs. Harland J. Stone
Ocala, Florida

Tip: *One pound of peaches equals 3 medium peaches or 2 cups sliced.*

COLOSSAL CHERRY COBBLER

½ cup butter or margarine
1 cup self-rising flour
1 cup sugar
1 cup milk
¾ teaspoon almond extract
4 cups pitted fresh sweet cherries

Melt butter in a 12- x 8- x 2-inch baking dish. Set aside. Combine flour and sugar; add milk and almond extract. Stir until blended. Spoon batter over butter; do not stir.

Spoon cherries over batter; do not stir. Bake at 375° for 35 minutes or until golden brown. Yield: about 8 servings.
Leslie Genszler
Roswell, Georgia

JUICY BLACKBERRY COBBLER
(pictured on pages 150 and 151)

4 cups fresh blackberries or 2 (16-ounce) packages frozen blackberries, thawed
1 cup sugar
½ cup water
Pastry (recipe follows)
2 tablespoons butter, melted and divided
2 tablespoons sugar, divided

Combine blackberries, 1 cup sugar, and water in a saucepan. Cook over medium heat 10 minutes; stir gently.

Pour half of berry mixture into a greased 12- x 8- x 2-inch baking dish. Roll pastry to ⅛-inch thickness on a lightly floured surface. Cut into 1-inch strips, and arrange half of strips in a lattice design over berry mixture. Brush with 1 tablespoon melted butter, and sprinkle with 1 tablespoon sugar. Bake at 375° for 10 to 12 minutes or until pastry is lightly browned.

Pour remaining berry mixture over baked pastry. Arrange remaining pastry strips in lattice design over berries. Brush with remaining butter, and sprinkle with remaining sugar. Bake at 375° for 20 to 25 minutes or until golden. Yield: 6 servings.

Pastry

1½ cups all-purpose flour
¾ teaspoon salt
½ cup shortening
¼ cup plus 1 tablespoon cold water

Combine flour and salt; cut in shortening with a pastry blender until mixture resembles coarse meal. Sprinkle water (1 tablespoon at a time) evenly over surface; stir with a fork until dry ingredients are moistened. Shape into a ball; chill. Yield: pastry for 1 cobbler.
Lurlene Crawford
Mayfield, Kentucky

Sweeten The Season With Blueberries

One of the pleasures of summer is blueberry patches swelling with little round berries. Take along a bucket to pick a bountiful supply, or bring home a basketful from local markets to use in all types of desserts and fruit salads.

Store fresh blueberries, covered, in the refrigerator up to two days. Wash them just before you're ready to use them, and rinse and blot carefully between paper towels to help prevent the bold color from bleeding onto the other ingredients with which they're mixed.

FRESH FRUIT BOWL

2 cups watermelon cubes
2 cups cantaloupe cubes
2 cups seedless green grapes
2 cups strawberries, hulled
2 cups fresh blueberries
Mandarin Dressing

Combine fruit in a large bowl; toss gently. Cover and chill, if desired. Serve with Mandarin Dressing. Yield: 12 servings.

Mandarin Dressing

1 cup mayonnaise
1 cup marshmallow cream
1 teaspoon grated orange rind
1 teaspoon grated fresh gingerroot

Combine all ingredients in a medium bowl, stirring gently. Yield: 2 cups.
Terri Farmer
West, Mississippi

FRESH BLUEBERRY STREUSEL PIE

1 (8-ounce) carton commercial sour cream
¾ cup sugar
1 egg
2 tablespoons all-purpose flour
1 teaspoon vanilla extract
¼ teaspoon salt
2½ cups fresh blueberries
1 unbaked 9-inch pastry shell
3 tablespoons all-purpose flour
2 tablespoons sugar
3 tablespoons butter or margarine
3 tablespoons chopped pecans

Combine sour cream, ¾ cup sugar, egg, 2 tablespoons flour, vanilla, and salt in a large mixing bowl; beat at medium speed of an electric mixer 5 minutes or until smooth. Fold in blueberries. Spoon into pastry shell. Bake at 400° for 25 minutes.

Combine 3 tablespoons flour and 2 tablespoons sugar; cut in butter with a pastry blender until mixture resembles coarse meal. Stir in pecans. Sprinkle mixture evenly over pie, and bake an additional 15 minutes. Yield: one 9-inch pie.
Mrs. Earl L. Faulkenberry
Lancaster, South Carolina

BLUEBERRY PANCAKES

1 cup all-purpose flour
1½ teaspoons baking powder
½ teaspoon salt
1 tablespoon sugar
¼ teaspoon ground cinnamon
1 egg, separated
2 tablespoons butter or
   margarine, melted
¾ cup milk
¾ cup fresh blueberries

Combine first 5 ingredients in a mixing bowl.

Beat egg yolk until thick and lemon colored; add butter and milk, stirring until blended. Add to dry ingredients, stirring just until moistened.

Beat egg white (at room temperature) until stiff peaks form; fold into batter. Gently fold in blueberries.

For each pancake, pour about ¼ cup batter onto a hot, lightly greased griddle. Turn pancakes when edges look cooked. Yield: 8 (4-inch) pancakes.
Cathy Williams
Vale, North Carolina

ON THE LIGHT SIDE

Preserve Fruit The Light Way

Enjoy fruit year-round by capturing its luscious flavor in jams, jellies, and preserves.

Traditional methods for making jams, jellies, and preserves depend on a reaction between pectin and large amounts of sugar to achieve a good gel. To lighten them, we reduced sugar, which can mean sacrificing consistency—but not always. We've worked with two methods for reducing sugar without having to give up the texture and appearance we're accustomed to.

One method uses a special low-methoxyl pectin and one-fourth to one-third the sugar that is normally needed for an assured set. Made from the inner rind of citrus fruit, low-methoxyl pectin reacts with calcium, instead of sugar, to gel fruit.

Lower calorie jams, jellies, and preserves that are prepared with low-methoxyl pectin should be processed in a boiling-water bath or stored in the freezer to prevent spoilage. Some of the spreads may not appear to be gelled after processing; however, if they are chilled before the jars are opened, this problem should be alleviated.

In our refrigerator jams, unflavored gelatin sets the fruit, and fruit juice concentrate sweetens it. Because these jams aren't processed and lack the preserving qualities of lots of sugar, they should be stored in the refrigerator.

DI-CALCIUM PHOSPHATE SOLUTION

½ teaspoon di-calcium phosphate
1 cup water

Combine ingredients in a jar. Cover tightly, and shake vigorously. Store in refrigerator. Yield: 1 cup.

Note: Di-calcium phosphate never completely dissolves, so it will have to be shaken before each use. The solution will keep indefinitely in the refrigerator.

STRAWBERRY JAM

1 quart crushed strawberries
⅓ cup water
1½ teaspoons lemon juice
1 cup sugar
1 teaspoon dry low-methoxyl
   pectin
1 tablespoon plus 1 teaspoon
   di-calcium phosphate
   solution

Combine first 3 ingredients in a Dutch oven. Bring mixture to a boil; cover, reduce heat, and simmer 10 minutes.

Combine sugar and low-methoxyl pectin; add to hot strawberry mixture, stirring until pectin is completely dissolved. Stir in di-calcium phosphate solution. Remove from heat, and place a spoonful of mixture in a measuring cup; chill until cool to touch to test thickness. If mixture is too thin, add 1 teaspoon di-calcium phosphate solution (shake before measuring), and retest; repeat testing procedure until jam thickens when chilled.

Bring mixture to a boil. Pour into hot sterilized jars, leaving ¼ inch headspace; wipe jar rims. Cover at once with metal lids, and screw on bands. Process in boiling-water bath 5 minutes. Chill before serving. Yield: 4½ half pints (13 calories per tablespoon).

Note: Store in refrigerator after 1 month to prevent color from fading. Opened jars keep 2 to 3 weeks in the refrigerator.

☐ *0.1 gram protein, 0 grams fat, 3.4 grams carbohydrate, 0 milligrams cholesterol, 0 milligrams sodium, and 1 milligram calcium.*

BLACKBERRY JAM

9 cups blackberries (about 4
   pounds)
¾ cup water
2 tablespoons lemon juice
1 cup plus 2 tablespoons sugar
1 tablespoon dry low-methoxyl
   pectin
2 tablespoons di-calcium
   phosphate solution

Sort and wash blackberries; remove stems and caps. Place blackberries in a Dutch oven; add water and lemon juice. Bring mixture to a boil; cover, reduce heat, and simmer 10 minutes. Crush blackberries, and return mixture to a boil.

Combine sugar and low-methoxyl pectin; add to hot berry mixture, stirring until completely dissolved. Stir in di-calcium phosphate solution. Remove from heat, and place a spoonful of mixture in a measuring cup; chill until cool to touch to test thickness. If mixture is too thin, add 1 teaspoon di-calcium phosphate solution (shake before measuring), and retest; repeat until jam thickens when chilled.

Bring mixture to a boil. Pour into hot sterilized jars, leaving ¼ inch headspace; wipe jar rims. Cover at once with metal lids, and screw on bands. Process in boiling-water bath 5 minutes. Chill before serving. Yield: 6 half pints (19 calories per tablespoon).

Note: Opened jars of jam keep 2 to 3 weeks in the refrigerator.

☐ *0.1 gram protein, 0.1 gram fat, 4.8 grams carbohydrate, 0 milligrams cholesterol, 0 milligrams sodium, and 6 milligrams calcium.*

BERRY REFRIGERATOR JAM

1½ teaspoons unflavored gelatin
3 tablespoons frozen sweetened grape juice concentrate, thawed and undiluted
¼ cup plus 2 tablespoons sugar
2 cups raspberries
1 cup blackberries

Sprinkle gelatin over grape juice concentrate in a saucepan; let stand 1 minute. Add sugar, raspberries, and blackberries; cook over low heat, stirring until sugar dissolves and berries are crushed. Let cool. Pour jam into airtight containers, and chill until set. Store jam in refrigerator. Yield: 1 pint (19 calories per tablespoon).

☐ *0.2 gram protein, 0.1 gram fat, 4.5 grams carbohydrate, 0 milligrams cholesterol, 0 milligrams sodium, and 3 milligrams calcium.*

BLUEBERRY REFRIGERATOR JAM

1½ teaspoons unflavored gelatin
⅓ cup frozen sweetened grape juice concentrate, thawed and undiluted
3 cups fresh blueberries

Sprinkle gelatin over grape juice concentrate in a large saucepan, and let mixture stand 1 minute. Add blueberries, and cook over low heat, stirring constantly, until gelatin dissolves and mixture thickens slightly. Let mixture cool.

Pour jam into airtight containers, and chill until set. Store jam in refrigerator. Yield: about 1 pint (14 calories per tablespoon).

☐ *0.2 gram protein, 0.1 gram fat, 3.5 grams carbohydrate, 0 milligrams cholesterol, 1 milligram sodium, and 1 milligram calcium.*

PLUM REFRIGERATOR JAM

1 envelope unflavored gelatin
⅓ cup frozen unsweetened apple juice concentrate, thawed and undiluted
3 tablespoons sugar
1½ teaspoons cornstarch
1 teaspoon lemon juice
3 cups chopped pitted unpeeled plums (about 1¼ pounds)

Sprinkle gelatin over apple juice concentrate in a large saucepan; let stand 1 minute. Add remaining ingredients. Bring to a boil, and simmer 3 minutes, stirring constantly.

Remove saucepan from heat; pour mixture into an airtight container. Chill until jam is set. Store jam in refrigerator. Yield: 1 pint (20 calories per tablespoon).

☐ *0.3 gram protein, 0.1 gram fat, 4.8 grams carbohydrate, 0 milligrams cholesterol, 1 milligram sodium, and 1 milligram calcium.*

CRABAPPLE JELLY

3 pounds crabapples, quartered
5 cups water
1 cup sugar
2 teaspoons dry low-methoxyl pectin
1 tablespoon plus 1 teaspoon di-calcium phosphate solution

Combine crabapples and water in a large Dutch oven; cover and bring to a boil. Reduce heat, and simmer 15 to 20 minutes or until crabapples are soft. Press mixture through a jelly bag, extracting 4 cups juice. Discard crabapple pulp.

Return juice to Dutch oven; bring to a boil. Combine sugar and low-methoxyl pectin; add to hot juice, stirring until completely dissolved. Stir in di-calcium phosphate solution. Remove from heat, and place a spoonful of mixture in a cup; chill until cool to test thickness. If mixture is too thin, add 1 teaspoon di-calcium phosphate solution (shake before measuring), and retest; repeat testing procedure until jelly thickens when chilled.

Bring mixture to a boil. Pour into hot sterilized jars, leaving ¼ inch headspace; wipe jar rims. Cover at once with metal lids, and screw on bands. Process in boiling-water bath 5 minutes. Chill jelly before serving. Yield: 5 half pints (21 calories per tablespoon).

Note: Opened jars keep 2 to 3 weeks in the refrigerator.

☐ *0.1 gram protein, 0 grams fat, 5.4 grams carbohydrate, 0 milligrams cholesterol, 0 milligrams sodium, and 3 milligrams calcium.*

Tip: *When you select blueberries at the market, look for those that are plump, firm, clean, and deep blue in color. A reddish tinge indicates immature berries.*

GRAPE JELLY

12 cups purple grapes (about 4
    pounds)
⅔ cup water
1½ tablespoons lemon juice
1 cup sugar
2 teaspoons dry low-methoxyl
    pectin
2 tablespoons plus 1 teaspoon
    di-calcium phosphate solution

Sort and wash grapes; remove
stems, and place in a large Dutch
oven. Crush grapes; add water and
lemon juice. Bring mixture to a boil;
cover, reduce heat, and simmer 10
minutes. Press mixture through a
jelly bag, extracting 4 cups juice.
Discard pulp. Cover; let stand 8
hours in a cool place.

Strain juice through a double thickness of damp cheesecloth into a large
Dutch oven. Place over high heat,
and cook, stirring constantly, until
mixture comes to a boil. Reduce
heat, and simmer 10 minutes. Combine sugar and low-methoxyl pectin;
add to hot juice, stirring until completely dissolved. Stir in di-calcium
phosphate solution.

Remove from heat, and chill a
spoonful of mixture until cool to
touch. If mixture is too thin, add 1
teaspoon di-calcium phosphate solution (shake before measuring), and
retest; repeat testing procedure until
jelly thickens when chilled.

Bring mixture to a boil. Pour into
hot sterilized jars, leaving ¼ inch
headspace; wipe jar rims. Cover at
once with metal lids, and screw on
bands. Process in boiling-water bath
5 minutes. Chill before serving.
Yield: 8 half pints (15 calories per
tablespoon).

Note: Opened jars keep 2 to 3
weeks in the refrigerator.

☐ *0.1 gram protein, 0 grams fat, 4
grams carbohydrate, 0 milligrams cholesterol, 0 milligrams sodium, and 2
milligrams calcium.*

PEACH PRESERVES

2 quarts peeled and coarsely
    chopped peaches (about 4¼
    pounds)
3 cups water
2 tablespoons lemon juice
1½ cups sugar
1 tablespoon plus 1 teaspoon dry
    low-methoxyl pectin
3 tablespoons di-calcium
    phosphate solution

Combine peaches, water, and lemon
juice in a large Dutch oven. Bring
mixture to a boil; cover, reduce heat,
and simmer 10 minutes.

Combine sugar and low-methoxyl
pectin; add to hot mixture, stirring
until completely dissolved. Stir in di-
calcium phosphate solution. Remove
from heat, and place a spoonful of
mixture in a measuring cup; chill until
cool to touch to test thickness. If
mixture is too thin, add 1 teaspoon
di-calcium phosphate solution (shake
before measuring), and retest; repeat
until preserves thicken when chilled.

Bring mixture to a boil. Pour into
hot sterilized jars, leaving ¼ inch
headspace; wipe jar rims. Cover at
once with metal lids, and screw on
bands. Process in boiling-water bath
5 minutes. Chill before serving.
Yield: 9 half pints (14 calories per
tablespoon).

Note: Opened jars keep 2 to 3
weeks in the refrigerator.

☐ *0.1 gram protein, 0 grams fat, 3.6
grams carbohydrate, 0 milligrams cholesterol, 0 milligrams sodium, and 1
milligram calcium.*

FIG PRESERVES

2 quarts fresh figs (about 3
    pounds)
¾ cup water
3 tablespoons lemon juice
1 cup sugar
2 teaspoons dry low-methoxyl
    pectin
1 tablespoon plus 1 teaspoon
    di-calcium phosphate solution

Pour enough boiling water over figs
to cover; let stand 10 minutes.
Drain, stem, and chop figs. Combine
figs, ¾ cup water, and lemon juice in
a large Dutch oven. Bring mixture to
a boil; cover, reduce heat, and simmer until mixture thickens.

Combine sugar and low-methoxyl
pectin; add to hot mixture, stirring
until completely dissolved. Stir in di-
calcium phosphate solution. Remove
from heat, and place a spoonful of
mixture in a measuring cup; chill until
cool to touch to test thickness. If
mixture is too thin, add 1 teaspoon
di-calcium phosphate solution (shake
before measuring), and retest; repeat
until preserves thicken when chilled.

Bring mixture to a boil. Pour into
hot sterilized jars, leaving ¼ inch
headspace; wipe jar rims. Cover at
once with metal lids, and screw on
bands. Process in boiling-water bath
5 minutes. Chill before serving.
Yield: 6 half pints (19 calories per
tablespoon).

Note: Opened jars keep 2 to 3
weeks in the refrigerator.

☐ *0.1 gram protein, 0 grams fat, 4.9
grams carbohydrate, 0 milligrams cholesterol, 0 milligrams sodium, and 5
milligrams calcium.*

Tips for
Preserving and Canning

■ In canning, jelly glasses may
be used for jelly only. For jam
and other products containing
fruit, standard canning jars and
lids must be used to ensure
proper processing.

■ Canning jars and metal bands
may be reused, but the lids
must always be new. Be sure to
sterilize the jars and metal
bands before using them again.

Sweet And Savory Chutneys And Relishes

A savory chutney or relish can add zest and variety to a meal by accenting meat dishes, adding flavor to stews, and spicing up dips.

Chutney is a relish seasoned with a blend of aromatic herbs and spices. It is particularly good with meat dishes and curries.

APPLE-CELERY RELISH

2 cups chopped celery
1½ cups peeled, chopped cooking apples
½ cup chopped green pepper
¾ cup cider vinegar (5% acidity)
¼ cup water
½ cup firmly packed brown sugar
½ teaspoon salt
½ teaspoon ground ginger

Combine all ingredients in a medium saucepan. Bring to a boil; cover, reduce heat, and simmer 45 minutes or until mixture thickens. Remove from heat, and cool. Cover and chill. Serve relish with pork or turkey. Yield: 2 cups.   *Cindy Murphy*
Cleveland, Tennessee

PEPPERY PEAR RELISH

15 pears, peeled, cored, and ground
12 medium onions, ground
6 sweet red peppers, ground
6 green peppers, ground
6 hot peppers, ground
2 tablespoons celery seeds
2 cups white vinegar (5% acidity)
2 cups prepared mustard
2 cups sugar
1 tablespoon salt

Combine all ingredients in a large kettle, mixing well. Bring to a boil;

reduce heat, and simmer, uncovered, 30 minutes, stirring occasionally.

Pour hot mixture into hot sterilized jars, leaving ¼ inch headspace. Remove air bubbles; wipe jar rims. Cover at once with metal lids, and screw on bands. Process relish in boiling-water bath 20 minutes. Yield: 12 pints.   *Alice McNamara*
Eucha, Oklahoma

PEAR-APPLE CHUTNEY

1½ teaspoons peppercorns
5 firm pears, peeled, cored, and chopped
3 cooking apples, peeled, cored, and chopped
3 fresh peaches, peeled and chopped
2 tomatoes, peeled, cored, and chopped
2 lemons, finely chopped
½ orange, finely chopped
2 cups cider vinegar (5% acidity)
1 (16-ounce) package brown sugar
1 (15-ounce) package raisins
1 (8-ounce) can sliced water chestnuts, drained
1 (2.7-ounce) jar crystallized ginger, chopped
1 clove garlic, crushed
3 tablespoons mustard seeds
1 tablespoon ground ginger
1 tablespoon Worcestershire sauce
1½ teaspoons salt
½ teaspoon ground cinnamon
¼ teaspoon red pepper
¼ teaspoon ground allspice

Tie peppercorns in a piece of cheesecloth. Combine peppercorns and remaining ingredients in a large kettle. Bring to a boil; reduce heat, and simmer, uncovered, 2 hours, stirring mixture occasionally.

Pour hot mixture into hot sterilized jars, leaving ¼ inch headspace. Remove air bubbles; wipe jar rims. Cover at once with metal lids, and screw on bands. Process chutney in boiling-water bath 10 minutes. Yield: 8 half-pints.   *Rita W. Cook*
Corpus Christi, Texas

MANGO CHUTNEY

4 cups peeled, chopped mangoes (4 mangoes)
3 medium onions, chopped
3 green peppers, chopped
1½ cups raisins
2 cloves garlic, minced
1 (2-inch) gingerroot, minced
2 cups cider vinegar (5% acidity)
2 cups sugar
1 (16-ounce) package brown sugar
1 tablespoon salt
1 tablespoon mustard seeds
1½ teaspoons ground cinnamon
¾ teaspoon ground cloves
½ teaspoon red pepper

Combine all ingredients in a large glass bowl, stirring well. Cover and let stand 8 hours.

Pour mixture into a Dutch oven; cook over medium heat, stirring occasionally, until mixture is the consistency of jam (about 1½ hours). Spoon hot mixture into hot sterilized jars, leaving ¼ inch headspace. Remove air bubbles; wipe jar rims. Cover at once with metal lids, and screw on bands. Process chutney in boiling-water bath 10 minutes. Yield: 4 pints.   *Hermine L. Hoffman*
Fort Lauderdale, Florida

From Our Kitchen To Yours

You can take advantage of summer's abundant supply of fresh fruits by stocking your pantry with delicious jams and jellies. "Preserve Fruit the Light Way," page 138, offers low-sugar recipes using updated processing recommendations.

Research tells us how long to process each food so that the contents in the jar reach the temperature necessary to destroy dangerous microorganisms. Whether food is processed in a boiling-water canner or in a pressure canner depends on its acidity. The time needed to safely process acid foods in a boiling-water canner ranges from 5 minutes to 1 hour and 25 minutes. USDA's new safety guidelines advise processing jam and jelly 5 minutes in a boiling-water canner. The open-kettle canning method and the use of paraffin are not considered safe for any home-canned food. When cooked food is placed in jars and sealed without processing, there is a risk of spoilage, especially in hot, humid climates. A paraffin seal when layered too thick is heavier than the jelly and pulls away from the jar sides allowing room for mold growth.

Processing Procedure

Wash empty jars in a dishwasher or in hot soapy water, rinsing well. Hard-water film on jars is easily removed by soaking jars for several hours in a solution of 1 cup vinegar and 1 gallon water.

Before filling, jars must be sterilized and lids heated. Place jars right side up on the rack in a boiling-water canner, and fill the canner with enough hot water so that the water level is 1 inch above the jar tops. Bring water to a boil, and boil 10 minutes. Carefully remove the hot jars with a jar lifter, and drain, saving the hot water for processing the filled jars. To heat the lids, follow the manufacturer's directions; some brands are brought to a boil and left in hot water; others need boiling for a certain period of time.

When filling jars with jam or jelly, leave ¼ inch of headspace. This space between the inside of the lid and the top of the food is needed for expansion of food as it is processed and for forming a vacuum in the cooled jars. Too much headspace can be caused when air bubbles trapped inside the jar rise to the top during processing; this can prevent proper sealing. To remove these air bubbles, run a plastic spatula around the edge of the jar, gently shifting the food, so that any trapped air escapes. Do not use a metal utensil; metal can scratch and weaken glass

causing breakage during processing. After removing the air bubbles, you may need to adjust the headspace.

To ensure an airtight seal, wipe the jar rim with a clean, damp cloth. Then place the lid on the jar rim, and screw on the metal band with your fingertips until tight, giving one last turn to make sure the band is snug. If the band is too loose, liquid can escape during processing and the seal can fail. If the band is too tight during processing, air cannot vent, causing food to discolor during storage. Overtightening also can cause the lid to buckle and the jar to break.

Using a jar lifter, position filled jars on rack in the canner, leaving space for water to flow evenly around them. If necessary, add more hot water so that the water level is 1 to 2 inches above the jar tops. Bring water to a boil; cover and reduce heat to maintain a gentle boil throughout correct processing time

(five minutes for jams and jellies). Carefully remove jars, placing right side up on a wire rack to cool at room temperature for 12 to 24 hours. Do not tighten the metal bands. As the jars cool, you might hear loud snaps indicating the contraction of the contents pulling the self-sealing lid firmly against the jar rim to form a vacuum.

When the jars are completely cooled, remove the bands and test each jar for a proper seal. The center of the lid should dip downward. Check each seal by looking for a dip; then press the lid with your fingers to be sure the center does not spring up when released. The lid can also be lightly tapped with a metal spoon; a sealed jar has a clear, ringing sound. Wipe off the processed jars; label and date. Store them in a cool, dry place. Most jams and jellies should keep for at least one year.

If a lid fails to seal, the food must be repacked and reprocessed within 24 hours with new, properly prepared lids. Or, if you don't have time to reprocess, store the jam or jelly in the refrigerator for up to 3 months. Low-sugar jams and jellies are an exception; these can be stored in the refrigerator up to 2 weeks.

Caution: Processing canned food in the microwave oven can be dangerous. To ensure that food has reached the proper internal temperature, a thermometer has to be placed in each jar. Therefore, the lid must be off, so a seal cannot be created and bacteria can grow.

Make-Ahead Meat Mix

Laura Norris of Charlotte, North Carolina, makes her Ground Meat Mix and freezes it to have when she needs a quick entrée. She prefers using turkey as the base, but some of her friends use beef.

GROUND MEAT MIX

3 pounds ground turkey or beef
2½ cups chopped onion
1 cup chopped green pepper
2 cloves garlic, minced
3 (15-ounce) cans tomato sauce
¾ cup water
1 tablespoon Worcestershire
    sauce
¼ teaspoon pepper

Combine first 4 ingredients in a Dutch oven; cook until meat is browned, stirring to crumble. Drain. Add tomato sauce and remaining ingredients; simmer, uncovered, 20 minutes, stirring occasionally. Cool. Put 3 cups mix each into 3 freezer containers, leaving ½ inch headspace; freeze. Yield: 9 cups.

Sloppy joes: Thaw 3 cups Ground Meat Mix, and heat thoroughly. Serve on buns. Yield: 6 servings.

Chili: Thaw 3 cups Ground Meat Mix, and add 1 (15½-ounce) can Mexican-style beans, undrained, and 2 teaspoons chili powder. Simmer 10 minutes. Yield: 4 cups.

Spaghetti: Thaw 3 cups Ground Meat Mix; add 1 (8-ounce) can tomato sauce, ½ teaspoon dried whole oregano, and ½ teaspoon dried whole basil. Simmer 10 minutes. Serve meat sauce over hot cooked spaghetti. Yield: 4 servings.

Savor Summer With A Bread

Take advantage of fresh produce to make one of these quick breads. They're called quick breads because they take less time to make than a bread leavened with yeast. Both recipes make two loaves, so you can keep one for yourself and share the other with a friend.

ZUCCHINI-HONEY BREAD

3 cups all-purpose flour
1 teaspoon baking powder
1 teaspoon baking soda
1 teaspoon salt
1 tablespoon ground cinnamon
1 cup chopped pecans
2 large zucchini
2 eggs, slightly beaten
1½ cups sugar
¾ cup honey
1 cup vegetable oil
2 teaspoons vanilla extract

Combine first 5 ingredients; stir in pecans. Peel zucchini, if desired; shred enough zucchini to measure 2 cups. Combine zucchini and remaining ingredients; add to flour mixture, stirring just until dry ingredients are moistened.

Spoon batter into 2 greased and floured 9- x 5- x 3-inch loafpans. Bake at 350° for 1 hour and 5 minutes or until a wooden pick inserted in center comes out clean. Cool in pans 10 minutes; remove from pans, and let cool on wire racks. Yield: 2 loaves.
                    Azine Rush
                    Monroe, Louisiana

CARROT BREAD

3 cups all-purpose flour
1 teaspoon baking soda
¾ teaspoon salt
2 cups sugar
1 teaspoon ground cinnamon
1 cup chopped pecans or walnuts
3 eggs, beaten
1 cup vegetable oil
2 cups grated carrot
1 (8-ounce) can crushed
    pineapple, drained
2 teaspoons vanilla extract

Combine first 5 ingredients; stir in pecans. Combine eggs and remaining ingredients; add to flour mixture, stirring just until dry ingredients are moistened.

Spoon batter into 2 greased and floured 8½- x 4½- x 3-inch loafpans.

Bake at 350° for 1 hour or until a wooden pick inserted in center comes out clean. Cool in pans 10 minutes; remove from pans, and let cool on wire racks. Yield: 2 loaves.

Chewy-Gooey Treats

When Ruth Tauzin of Opelousas, Louisiana, wants to make something special for her children and their friends, she always bakes Chocolate Chip Squares.

CHOCOLATE CHIP SQUARES

2 (20-ounce) rolls refrigerated
    chocolate chip cookie dough
2 (8-ounce) packages cream
    cheese, softened
1½ cups sugar
2 eggs

Freeze rolls of cookie dough; slice one roll of frozen cookie dough into 40 (⅛-inch) slices. Arrange cookie slices in a well-greased 15- x 10- x 1-inch jellyroll pan. Press cookie dough together to form bottom crust. Set pan aside.

Beat cream cheese at high speed of an electric mixer until light and fluffy; gradually add sugar, and mix well. Add eggs, one at a time, beating after each addition. Pour cream cheese mixture over cookie dough layer in pan.

Slice remaining frozen roll of cookie dough into 40 (⅛-inch) slices, and arrange over cream cheese mixture. Bake at 350° for 45 minutes. Let cool, and cut into squares. Yield: 4 dozen.

Wake Up To Breakfast For Two

Today, breakfast often consists of only a muffin or cereal, but when you have a little extra time in the morning, try this menu.

Tarragon Omelet
Potato Pancakes
Baking Powder Biscuits
Honey-Banana Smoothie

TARRAGON OMELET

6 eggs
3 tablespoons chopped fresh
  tarragon or 1 tablespoon dried
  whole tarragon
½ teaspoon salt
½ teaspoon white pepper
2 tablespoons water
2 tablespoons butter or margarine
1 medium tomato, peeled and
  chopped
½ cup (2 ounces) shredded
  Cheddar cheese
½ cup (2 ounces) shredded
  mozzarella cheese
2 tomato wedges (optional)
Fresh tarragon sprigs (optional)

Combine first 5 ingredients; stir with a wire whisk just until blended.

Heat an 8-inch omelet pan or heavy skillet over medium heat until hot enough to sizzle a drop of water. Add butter, and rotate pan to coat bottom. Pour egg mixture into skillet. As mixture starts to cook, gently lift edges of omelet with a spatula, and tilt pan so that uncooked portion flows underneath.

Sprinkle half of omelet with chopped tomato and cheeses; fold omelet in half, cut in half crosswise, and transfer to serving plates. If desired, garnish with tomato wedges and fresh tarragon sprigs. Yield: 2 servings.   *Susan Joyce Morgan*
Charlotte, North Carolina

POTATO PANCAKES

1 large potato, peeled and
  shredded
1 egg, slightly beaten
1½ tablespoons all-purpose flour
½ teaspoon salt
Vegetable oil

Combine first 4 ingredients, stirring well. Pour oil to a depth of ⅛ inch into a large heavy skillet. Drop potato mixture by 6 heaping tablespoonfuls into hot oil; press into 3-inch rounds with the back of a fork. Fry until golden brown, turning once. Drain well on paper towels. Yield: 2 servings.   *Gerry Snyder*
Port Richey, Florida

BAKING POWDER BISCUITS

½ cup all-purpose flour
1 teaspoon baking powder
⅛ teaspoon salt
1½ tablespoons shortening
¼ cup milk

Combine flour, baking powder, and salt; cut in shortening with a pastry blender until mixture resembles coarse meal. Add milk, stirring until dry ingredients are moistened. Turn dough out onto a floured surface, and knead lightly 4 or 5 times.

Roll dough to ½-inch thickness; cut with a 2-inch biscuit cutter. Place on a lightly greased baking sheet. Bake at 400° for 12 to 14 minutes or until lightly browned. Yield: 4 biscuits.   *Mrs. N. Burnes*
Midland, Texas

HONEY-BANANA SMOOTHIE

1 cup milk
2 tablespoons orange juice
2 tablespoons honey
1 banana, peeled, quartered, and
  frozen

Combine all ingredients in container of an electric blender; process mixture until frothy. Serve immediately. Yield: 2½ cups.   *Brenda Caston*
Covington, Louisiana

Don't Flip The Frittata

The name of the dish sounds fancy, but you'll be familiar with the techniques and flavors that make up a frittata. This thin egg patty is no more than an egg dish seasoned and cooked like an omelet, except that the cook forgoes the familiar "flip" at the end.

CORN-AND-SQUASH FRITTATA

3 to 4 medium ears fresh corn
2 eggs, beaten
2 tablespoons all-purpose flour
¼ teaspoon baking powder
¼ teaspoon salt
¼ teaspoon pepper
1 medium zucchini, unpeeled and
  coarsely grated
1½ tablespoons butter or
  margarine
Zucchini slices (optional)
Fresh parsley sprig (optional)

Cut corn from cobs, scraping cobs well to remove all milk; set aside 1 cup corn, and reserve remaining corn for other uses.

Combine eggs and next 4 ingredients; beat well with a wire whisk. Stir grated zucchini and corn into egg mixture; set aside.

Melt butter in an 8-inch nonstick skillet. Stir about 1 tablespoon melted butter into egg mixture, reserving remaining butter in skillet. Place skillet over medium heat until hot. Add egg mixture; cover, reduce heat to low, and cook 15 minutes or until set. If desired, garnish with zucchini slices and parsley sprig. Cut into wedges, and serve immediately. Yield: 4 servings. *Nell K. Gill* *Memphis, Tennessee*

POTATO FRITTATA

5 eggs, beaten
½ cup milk
3 tablespoons vegetable oil
1 cup peeled, cubed potato
¾ cup chopped onion
¼ teaspoon salt
⅛ teaspoon pepper
¼ cup grated Parmesan cheese
1 tablespoon chopped fresh
  parsley

Combine eggs and milk; mix well, and set aside.

Heat oil in a 10-inch nonstick skillet. Add cubed potato, onion, salt, and pepper; sauté 8 to 10 minutes or until tender and lightly browned. Add potato mixture, cheese, and parsley to egg mixture, stirring constantly.

Return skillet to heat; add egg mixture. Cover, reduce heat, and cook 12 to 15 minutes or until center is set. Cut into wedges, and serve immediately. Yield: 4 to 6 servings.
Ginny Whitt
Mount Washington, Kentucky

Try Tasty Blue Corn Muffins

If you see blue cornmeal on the shelves in specialty food stores and think that it's just another strange new food item, you'll be surprised to know that blue corn has long been a common food staple in the Southwest. The gray-blue meal is just beginning to find its way farther east.

Blue cornmeal, ground from speckled Indian blue corn, actually sports kernels of blackish purple, blue, and yellow. It's nuttier tasting than white or yellow meal; the corn is smoked and treated with lime before grinding. Blue meal is most often used in cornbreads, tortillas, and tamales. When you use the meal in this recipe, you'll notice the unique flavor.

BLUE CORN MUFFINS

½ cup diced sweet red pepper
½ cup diced sweet yellow
  pepper
¼ cup diced onion
1 tablespoon vegetable oil
¼ cup plus 2 tablespoons butter
  or margarine
½ cup shortening
1½ cups blue cornmeal
1 cup all-purpose flour
⅓ cup sugar
1 tablespoon baking powder
1 teaspoon salt
2 eggs, slightly beaten
1 cup milk
½ cup half-and-half
1 cup diced cooked ham

Sauté peppers and onion in hot oil in a large skillet until tender; set vegetables aside.

Combine butter and shortening in a small saucepan; cook over low heat until butter and shortening melt. Set mixture aside to cool.

Combine cornmeal, flour, sugar, baking powder, and salt; mix well, and set mixture aside.

Combine eggs, milk, half-and-half, and ham in a medium bowl. Stir in sautéed vegetables and melted butter mixture. Add vegetable mixture to dry ingredients, stirring just until dry ingredients are moistened.

Spoon batter into greased and floured muffin pans, filling three-fourths full. Bake at 350° for 20 to 25 minutes. Yield: 2 dozen.

Note: Regular white or yellow cornmeal may be substituted for blue cornmeal.

Zesty Chef's Salad

Lisa Grable Wallace of Raleigh, North Carolina, makes clever use of a popular Italian appetizer known as antipasto—an assortment of meats, olives, and cheeses—to create her special version of chef's salad.

ANTIPASTO SALAD

1 (0.6-ounce) package zesty
  Italian salad dressing mix
1 (12-ounce) jar whole mild
  banana peppers, drained
2 cups (8 ounces) shredded
  mozzarella cheese, divided
1 medium cucumber, thinly sliced
1 (6-ounce) can pitted ripe olives,
  drained
1 pint cherry tomatoes, halved
2 medium-size green peppers,
  coarsely chopped
1 bunch romaine lettuce, torn
  into bite-size pieces
2 carrots, coarsely grated
1 (3½-ounce) package sliced
  pepperoni
½ cup freshly grated Parmesan
  cheese (optional)

Prepare salad dressing mix according to package directions; set aside.

Reserve 3 banana peppers and ¼ cup mozzarella cheese for garnish. Layer cucumber, olives, tomatoes, green pepper, and remaining banana peppers in a 4-quart bowl; pour ½ cup dressing over vegetables. Top with layers of lettuce, carrot, 1¾ cups mozzarella cheese, and sliced pepperoni; cover and chill 2 to 6 hours. Garnish with reserved mozzarella cheese and banana peppers. Toss salad just before serving. If desired, serve with Parmesan cheese and remaining salad dressing. Yield: 8 to 10 servings.

Accent The Rice With Vegetables

If you're searching for new ways to serve rice, these combinations of rice and vegetables offer tasty options for salads, side dishes, and entrées.

CURRY RICE SALAD

1 (6-ounce) package long-grain and wild rice mix
2 cups chicken broth
1 cup raisins
1 cup hot water
½ cup sliced green onions
1 cup chopped pecans, toasted
1 (16-ounce) can garbanzo beans, drained
Lettuce leaves
Green onion fan (optional)
Dressing (recipe follows)

Combine rice mix and broth in a saucepan. Bring to a boil; cover, reduce heat, and simmer 20 to 25 minutes or until rice is tender and liquid is absorbed.

Combine raisins and water; let stand 10 minutes. Drain. Stir raisins, green onions, pecans, and beans into rice mixture. Serve on lettuce leaves. Garnish with a green onion fan, if desired. Serve with dressing. Salad may be served warm or cold and with or without dressing. Yield: 6 to 8 servings.

Dressing

⅔ cup mayonnaise
1 tablespoon curry powder
1 tablespoon honey
1 tablespoon vinegar
⅛ teaspoon red pepper
2 teaspoons prepared mustard
1 teaspoon Worcestershire sauce

Combine all ingredients; chill. Yield: ¾ cup.
Melanie Smith
Molena, Georgia

RICE-AND-AVOCADO SALAD

3 cups cooked rice
2 cups chopped cooked chicken
1 medium avocado, cut into ½-inch cubes
1 cup diagonally sliced celery
½ green pepper, cut into thin strips
¼ cup minced onion
3 tablespoons lemon juice
2 tablespoons vegetable oil
1 clove garlic, minced
Dash of hot sauce
1 teaspoon sugar
½ teaspoon salt
¼ teaspoon white pepper
Lettuce leaves
2 tomatoes, cut into wedges
1 medium avocado, sliced

Combine first 6 ingredients in a large bowl. Combine lemon juice and next 6 ingredients in a jar; cover tightly, and shake vigorously. Pour over rice mixture; toss gently. Cover. Chill at least 2 hours. Serve on lettuce with tomato wedges and avocado slices. Yield: 6 servings.
Sara A. McCullough
Broaddus, Texas

CARROT SOUP

1½ cups chopped onion
½ cup butter or margarine, melted
3 (10¾-ounce) cans chicken broth, diluted
1 pound carrots, thinly sliced
½ cup uncooked long-grain rice
1 sprig fresh thyme
¼ teaspoon white pepper

Sauté onion in butter in a Dutch oven until tender; add remaining ingredients. Bring to a boil; reduce heat, cover, and simmer 30 minutes, stirring occasionally. Remove from heat; cool 10 minutes.

Pour half of soup into container of an electric blender; blend until smooth. Repeat with remaining soup. Yield: 2½ quarts.
Mrs. Nels E. Johnson
McLean, Virginia

ZUCCHINI-RICE CASSEROLE ITALIANO

4 cups thinly sliced zucchini
1 pound ground beef
1 cup chopped onion
1 clove garlic, crushed
½ teaspoon salt
1 teaspoon dried whole basil
½ teaspoon dried whole oregano
¼ teaspoon pepper
2 cups cooked rice
1 (8-ounce) can tomato sauce
1 egg, beaten
1 cup cream-style cottage cheese
1 cup (4 ounces) shredded Cheddar cheese

Cook zucchini, covered, in a small amount of boiling water 2 minutes; drain well, and set aside. Combine beef and next 6 ingredients in a skillet. Cook until meat is browned, stirring to crumble meat; drain off pan drippings. Add rice and tomato sauce; set aside.

Combine egg and cottage cheese; stir well.

Layer half of zucchini in a lightly greased 13- x 9- x 2-inch baking dish; top with meat mixture and cottage cheese mixture. Top with remaining zucchini. Cover and bake at 350° for 20 minutes. Add Cheddar cheese; bake, uncovered, an additional 5 minutes. Yield: 6 servings.
Mrs. Raymond Allen
Opelousas, Louisiana

CONFETTI RICE

1 cup uncooked brown rice
½ cup frozen English peas, thawed
½ cup chopped carrot
4 slices bacon, diced
½ cup chopped onion
1 (4-ounce) can chopped green chiles, drained
1 tablespoon water
1 teaspoon salt
½ teaspoon pepper

Cook rice according to package directions; set aside.

Cook peas and carrot in a small amount of boiling water about 5 minutes or until tender. Drain.

Fry bacon in a large skillet; drain, reserving 2 tablespoons drippings. Set bacon aside. Sauté onion and green chiles in reserved bacon drippings. Add rice, peas, carrots, water, salt, and pepper. Cover and cook over low heat 5 to 10 minutes or until thoroughly heated. Stir in bacon. Yield: 6 servings.

Jan K. Sliwa
Temple, Texas

Great Flavor From A Bottle Of Dressing

Some recipes call for a lot of ingredients or a lengthy period of cooking to develop a rich flavor or full-bodied consistency, but not these. Each depends on commercial salad dressing as a key ingredient of the dish.

CHUNKY TUNA SPREAD

1 (6½-ounce) can chunk light
   tuna, drained and flaked
½ cup finely chopped cucumber
¼ cup finely chopped onion
⅓ cup commercial Thousand
   Island salad dressing
⅛ teaspoon salt
⅛ teaspoon pepper
Dash of garlic powder

Combine all ingredients, stirring well; cover and chill thoroughly. Serve with assorted crackers or thinly sliced cucumber. Yield: 1⅓ cups.

Tony Jones
Atlanta, Georgia

MUSHROOM-CHICKEN BAKE

1 (2½- to 3-pound) broiler-fryer,
   cut up and skinned
½ cup commercial Italian salad
   dressing
¼ teaspoon pepper
½ teaspoon paprika, divided
1 (4-ounce) can sliced
   mushrooms, drained
⅓ cup grated Parmesan cheese

Place chicken in a greased 13- x 9- x 2-inch baking dish. Pour dressing over chicken, and baste. Sprinkle with pepper and ¼ teaspoon paprika. Bake at 350°, uncovered, for 30 minutes. Turn chicken, and add mushrooms; sprinkle with Parmesan cheese and remaining ¼ teaspoon paprika. Bake an additional 30 minutes or until tender, basting occasionally. Yield: 4 servings.

Daisy Cotton
Karnes City, Texas

ZESTY BLACK-EYED PEAS

2 (16-ounce) cans black-eyed
   peas, rinsed and drained
1 cup chopped celery
1 green pepper, chopped
1 large tomato, peeled and
   chopped
1 clove garlic, minced
2 green onions, sliced
1 (4-ounce) jar sliced mushrooms,
   drained
1 (4-ounce) jar diced pimiento,
   drained
1 (8-ounce) bottle Italian salad
   dressing
Lettuce leaves
3 slices bacon, cooked and
   crumbled
3 green onions, thinly sliced

Combine first 9 ingredients in a large bowl, tossing gently. Cover and chill at least 8 hours, stirring occasionally. Drain, and spoon into a lettuce-lined bowl. Garnish with bacon and sliced green onions. Yield: 8 servings.

Joyce Whitehead
New Ulm, Texas

WILD RICE SALAD

1 (6¼-ounce) package long-grain
   and wild rice mix
1 (10-ounce) package frozen
   English peas, thawed and
   drained
1 (8-ounce) bottle commercial
   creamy cucumber salad
   dressing
2 tablespoons chopped onion

Cook rice mix according to package directions; cool slightly. Stir in peas and remaining ingredients; cover and chill at least 3 hours. Yield: 6 to 8 servings.

Edith G. Keenum
Hendersonville, North Carolina

New Ideas For Squash

Our readers enjoy squash with a variety of savory ingredients and seasonings. With so much fresh produce available, it's easy to experiment with new combinations.

ZUCCHINI AND TOMATOES BASIL

2 medium zucchini (¾ pound)
½ cup diced onion
1 teaspoon dried whole basil
2 teaspoons vegetable oil
2 medium tomatoes, peeled and
   chopped
½ teaspoon salt
⅛ to ¼ teaspoon pepper

Cut zucchini into ¼-inch slices; set aside. Sauté onion and basil in oil over medium heat 1 minute. Add zucchini, and cook 5 minutes, stirring occasionally. Add tomatoes, salt, and pepper; cook 3 minutes or until tender. Serve immediately. Yield: 4 to 6 servings.

Nora Henshaw
Okemah, Oklahoma

CRUMB-STUFFED SQUASH

6 medium pattypan squash
2 tablespoons diced celery
¼ cup thinly sliced green onions
1 tablespoon sliced green onion tops
¼ cup diced green pepper
½ teaspoon minced garlic
2 tablespoons butter or margarine, melted
½ teaspoon sugar
1 egg yolk, slightly beaten
½ to ¾ cup seasoned, dry breadcrumbs
⅛ teaspoon Worcestershire sauce
1 tablespoon sliced green onion tops
1 tablespoon minced parsley
½ teaspoon salt
⅛ teaspoon white pepper
⅛ teaspoon red pepper
2 or 3 drops hot sauce
1 tablespoon seasoned, dry breadcrumbs
1 tablespoon butter or margarine, melted

Cook pattypan squash in boiling salted water to cover 8 to 10 minutes or until tender but firm. Drain and let cool. Cut a ½-inch slice from stem end. Remove and discard seeds; scoop out pulp, leaving a ½-inch shell. Chop pulp.

Sauté celery and next 4 ingredients in 2 tablespoons butter in a large skillet until vegetables are tender. Add squash pulp, sugar, and egg yolk; stir well. Cover and cook over low heat 10 minutes. Add ½ cup breadcrumbs and next 7 ingredients. Add more breadcrumbs if mixture is too moist.

Place squash shells on an ungreased baking sheet; spoon stuffing mixture evenly into shells. Combine 1 tablespoon breadcrumbs and 1 tablespoon melted butter; sprinkle evenly over stuffing. Bake at 350° for 15 minutes or until squash and stuffing are thoroughly heated and breadcrumbs are browned. Yield: 6 servings.

Note: Large yellow squash may be substituted for pattypan squash.
Susie Pharr
New Iberia, Louisiana

SOUTH-OF-THE-BORDER SQUASH

4 yellow squash (1 pound)
1 medium onion, chopped
½ teaspoon salt
½ cup water
1 (4-ounce) can chopped green chiles, undrained
1 (2-ounce) jar chopped pimiento, drained
1 cup (4 ounces) cubed Monterey Jack cheese
2 hard-cooked eggs, sliced
¾ cup crushed corn chips

Cut squash into ¼-inch slices. Combine first 4 ingredients in a saucepan; cook 6 to 8 minutes or until squash is tender. Drain well. Add chiles, pimiento, and cheese. Spoon into a lightly greased 1¾-quart casserole. Place egg slices on top, and sprinkle with corn chips.

Bake at 350° for 20 minutes or until casserole is thoroughly heated. Yield: 4 servings.
Doris Phillips
Wichita, Kansas

SQUASH CON CREMA

2 small zucchini (½ pound)
2 yellow squash (½ pound)
6 green onions, sliced
3 tablespoons butter or margarine, melted
¾ cup whipping cream
2 fresh serrano chiles, chopped
1 (2-inch) stick cinnamon
4 whole cloves
¼ teaspoon salt
Dash of pepper

Cut each zucchini and yellow squash in half lengthwise; cut halves into ¾-inch slices.

Sauté zucchini, yellow squash, and green onion slices in melted butter in a large skillet about 4 minutes or just until vegetables are crisp-tender. Transfer vegetables to a colander to drain well.

Combine whipping cream, chopped chiles, cinnamon stick, and cloves in skillet. Bring mixture to a rapid boil; boil 2 minutes, stirring constantly, or until mixture thickens slightly. Remove and discard cinnamon stick and cloves; add vegetable mixture. Cook over medium heat, stirring constantly, until thoroughly heated. Stir in salt and pepper. Yield: 4 to 6 servings.
Connie Jennings
Houston, Texas

Above: *Savor such summer traditions as (clockwise from front) Corn-and-Okra Creole, Marinated Corn Salad, and Pimiento-Corn Soup. (Recipes, pages 126 and 127.)*

Right: *Fresh Corn Pudding (page 172) will jiggle a little when taken out of the oven but thickens as it cools.*

Savor seasonal fruits in these desserts
(from left) Chilled Blueberry Pie,
Peach-and-Blackberry Pie, and Juicy
Blackberry Cobbler. (Recipes, pages
136 and 137.)

Summer's golden fruit, the peach, shows off its good flavor in Peach Cardinale and Peach Frost. (Recipes, page 155.)

JULY

Fire up the grill! Our "Summer Suppers" special section
will help you plan cookouts, picnics, and parties, as well as
family meals. For grand finales, serve desserts made
from luscious fresh peaches, offered here in a wide
range of recipes.

Summer's Golden Fruit

It takes only one bite of a plump, ripe peach to send thoughts racing to the scrumptious desserts to come. These traditional recipes, as well as imaginative ideas for combining peaches and cream, will make the most of this juicy bounty.

For many folks, the season best not slip away without peach shortcake. The recipe featured here makes individual shortcakes, flavored with a hint of cinnamon and nutmeg and embellished with lots of sweet juices from the peaches.

mixture to peach mixture, stirring well. Bring to a boil; boil 1 minute, stirring constantly. Yield: 2 cups.

Whipped Cream Topping

½ cup whipping cream
1 tablespoon sugar
⅛ teaspoon lemon extract

Beat whipping cream until foamy; gradually add sugar and lemon extract, beating until stiff peaks form. Yield: 1 cup.   *Maggie Zimmer*
El Paso, Texas

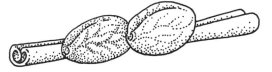

SPICY PEACH SHORTCAKES

1 cup all-purpose flour
1 teaspoon baking powder
¼ teaspoon salt
⅛ teaspoon ground nutmeg
3 tablespoons sugar
¼ cup shortening
⅓ cup milk
1 tablespoon butter or margarine, melted
1 tablespoon sugar
¼ teaspoon ground cinnamon
Peach Filling
Whipped Cream Topping

Combine first 5 ingredients in a medium bowl; cut in shortening with a pastry blender until mixture resembles coarse meal. Add milk; stir until dry ingredients are moistened. Turn dough out onto a floured surface, and divide into 4 portions. Shape each portion into a 3-inch round shortcake, and place on a greased baking sheet.

Brush tops of shortcakes with butter. Combine 1 tablespoon sugar and cinnamon; stir well. Sprinkle sugar mixture over tops of shortcakes.

Bake at 425° for 15 minutes or until golden brown.

Split shortcakes horizontally, and place bottom halves, cut side up, on serving plates. Spoon about ¼ cup Peach Filling over each half; place top half of shortcake over filling, cut side down. Spoon about ¼ cup filling over top half of shortcake. Top with a dollop of Whipped Cream Topping. Serve warm. Yield: 4 servings.

Peach Filling

2 cups sliced fresh peaches
   (about 1 pound)
½ cup sugar
¾ cup water
¼ cup sugar
⅛ teaspoon salt
⅛ teaspoon ground nutmeg
1 tablespoon cornstarch
¼ cup water
1 teaspoon lemon juice

Combine first 3 ingredients in a medium saucepan; cover and cook over medium heat 10 minutes or until peaches are tender.

Combine ¼ cup sugar, salt, nutmeg, and cornstarch in a small bowl; stir well. Add ¼ cup water and lemon juice; stir well. Add cornstarch

FRESH PEACH COBBLER

Pastry (recipe follows)
1 egg white, beaten
4 cups sliced fresh peaches
   (about 2 pounds)
2 tablespoons lemon juice
¾ cup sugar, divided
2 tablespoons all-purpose flour
¼ cup water
½ cup butter or margarine,
   divided

Roll pastry to a 14- x 10-inch rectangle on a lightly floured surface. Transfer pastry to a 10- x 6- x 2-inch baking dish, centering pastry lengthwise in dish, and allowing excess to hang over sides of dish. Brush pastry with egg white.

Combine peaches and lemon juice; toss gently. Add ½ cup sugar and flour, tossing until peaches are coated. Spoon peach mixture into prepared dish; sprinkle with remaining ¼ cup sugar and water. Dot peaches with ¼ cup butter. Fold excess pastry over peaches, leaving a 2-inch strip in center uncovered; dot pastry with remaining ¼ cup butter. Bake at 425° for 35 to 40 minutes. Yield: 6 servings.

Pastry

2 cups all-purpose flour
½ teaspoon salt
⅔ cup plus 2 tablespoons
   shortening
4 to 5 tablespoons cold water

Combine flour and salt; cut in shortening with a pastry blender until mixture resembles coarse meal. Sprinkle water (1 tablespoon at a time) evenly over surface; stir with a fork until dry ingredients are moistened. Shape dough into a ball, and chill. Yield: pastry for one cobbler.

Cathy Williams
Vale, North Carolina

PEACH CARDINALE
(pictured on page 152)

4 fresh peaches
3 cups water
1 cup sugar
1 tablespoon vanilla extract
1 (10-ounce) package frozen
    raspberries, thawed
1 tablespoon sugar
2 teaspoons cornstarch
¼ cup water
½ cup whipping cream, whipped
Fresh mint leaves (optional)

Place peaches in boiling water for 20 seconds. Remove with a slotted spoon, and plunge into ice water. Using the tip of a sharp knife, slip off skins. Cut peaches in half.

Combine 3 cups water and 1 cup sugar in a Dutch oven; bring to a boil, and cook 3 minutes, stirring occasionally. Reduce heat to low; add peach halves and vanilla. Simmer, uncovered, 10 to 15 minutes or until peaches are tender. Chill peaches in syrup at least 1 hour or up to 2 days.

Press raspberries through a food mill or sieve; discard seeds.

Combine 1 tablespoon sugar and cornstarch; stir in ¼ cup water. Add cornstarch mixture to raspberry puree, stirring well. Cook over medium heat until mixture boils. Boil 1 minute, stirring constantly. Chill.

Spoon whipped cream into 4 individual dessert dishes. Put 2 peach halves together, and place on top of cream in each dish. Pour about ¼ cup sauce around each peach. Garnish with fresh mint leaves, if desired. Yield: 4 servings.

Linda Corley
Sperry, Oklahoma

PEACH CHIFFON PIE

3 egg whites
1 cup sugar
⅔ cup saltine cracker crumbs
¼ teaspoon baking powder
½ cup chopped pecans
1 teaspoon vanilla extract
1 cup whipping cream
2 tablespoons sugar
2 cups sliced fresh peaches
    (about 1 pound)

Beat egg whites (at room temperature) at high speed of an electric mixer until foamy. Gradually add 1 cup sugar, 2 tablespoons at a time, beating until stiff peaks form. Fold in cracker crumbs, baking powder, pecans, and vanilla. Spoon meringue mixture into a buttered 9-inch pieplate. Bake at 325° for 30 minutes. Let cool.

Beat whipping cream at high speed until foamy; gradually add 2 tablespoons sugar, beating until soft peaks form. Fold in sliced peaches, and spoon evenly over meringue crust. Chill pie until ready to serve. Yield: one 9-inch pie.

Mrs. Clifford B. Smith, Sr.
White Hall, Maryland

PEACH FROST
(pictured on page 152)

3 ripe peaches, pitted, and
    quartered (about 1 pound)
¼ to ½ cup light corn syrup
¼ teaspoon ground ginger
1 cup pineapple or lemon sherbet
1 cup vanilla ice cream
½ cup ginger ale
Fresh peach slices (optional)
Fresh peach leaves (optional)

Combine first 3 ingredients in container of an electric blender; process until smooth. Add sherbet and ice cream; process until smooth. Add ginger ale; blend 30 seconds. If desired, garnish with fresh peach slices and leaves. Yield: 4 cups.

Betty Adams
Fort Payne, Alabama

PEACH-ALMOND ICE CREAM

2¼ cups milk
1¼ cups sugar
5 egg yolks
½ cup amaretto or other
   almond-flavored liqueur
7½ cups fresh peach slices
   (about 4 pounds)
1 tablespoon lemon juice
¼ cup sugar
2 cups whipping cream

Heat milk in a 3-quart saucepan over low heat. Combine 1¼ cups sugar and egg yolks; beat well. Stir about one-fourth of hot milk into yolk mixture. Return to remaining hot milk; stir well. Stir in amaretto; cook over low heat about 10 minutes, stirring constantly, or until mixture is no longer frothy and begins to curdle. Remove from heat; cover and chill at least 2 hours.

Place half of peach slices in container of an electric blender; blend until pureed. Pour into a large mixing bowl. Repeat with remaining peach slices; stir in lemon juice and ¼ cup sugar. Add chilled custard and whipping cream; beat at low speed of an electric mixer until smooth.

Pour into freezer can of a 5-quart hand-turned or electric freezer. Freeze according to manufacturer's instructions. Let ripen about 1 hour. Yield: about 1 gallon.

Marie Barrett Berry
Louisville, Kentucky

MICROWAVE COOKERY

Shortcuts To Jelly-Making

If you shy away from making jams and jellies because you don't like to cook the mixture a long time or process the jars, let your microwave and freezer simplify the procedure. These fresh-tasting jams and jellies cook quickly in the microwave and stay fresh up to a year when frozen.

In the microwave, most of these mixtures boil up high, so be sure to use deep containers when specified.

By storing the jellies in the freezer, you won't need to sterilize the jars or process them in a boiling-water bath. Just freeze the spread in traditional jelly jars or plastic containers made for freezer storage.

ORANGE-PINEAPPLE MARMALADE

2 medium oranges
1 (15¼-ounce) can crushed
   unsweetened pineapple, drained
4 cups sugar
2 tablespoons lemon juice

Wash oranges; cut into quarters. Remove seeds and membrane from each piece. Grind unpeeled fruit in food processor or meat grinder.

Combine ground fruit and remaining ingredients in a deep 2½-quart casserole. Microwave at HIGH 10 minutes or until mixture comes to a boil, stirring after 6 minutes. Microwave at HIGH 2 to 3 minutes.

Pour mixture into jelly jars or frozen food containers. Cover with lids; let stand 4 hours. Freeze marmalade up to 1 year, or refrigerate up to 3 weeks. Serve at room temperature. Yield: 4 cups.

FREEZER PLUM JAM

3 cups peeled, pitted, and mashed
   fresh plums
6 cups sugar
1 (1¾-ounce) package powdered
   pectin
¾ cup water

Combine plums and sugar, stirring well. Let stand 20 minutes, stirring occasionally.

Combine pectin and water in a 4-cup glass measure, stirring well. Microwave at HIGH 2 to 2½ minutes or until boiling. Boil 1 minute, stopping and stirring after 45 seconds. Stir well again, and pour pectin mixture over fruit. Stir 3 minutes.

Pour mixture into jelly jars or frozen food containers. Cover with lids; let stand 4 hours. Freeze jam up to 1 year, or refrigerate up to 3 weeks. Serve jam at room temperature. Yield: 7 cups.

QUICK GRAPE JELLY

2 cups bottled unsweetened grape
   juice
3 cups sugar
1 tablespoon lemon juice
1 (3-ounce) package liquid pectin

Combine first 3 ingredients in a deep 2-quart casserole. Microwave at HIGH 9 to 10 minutes or until mixture comes to a boil, stirring every 3 minutes. Stir in liquid pectin; microwave at HIGH 3 to 3½ minutes. Skim off foam with a metal spoon.

Pour mixture into jelly jars or frozen food containers. Cover with lids; let stand 4 hours. Freeze jelly up to 1 year, or refrigerate up to 3 weeks. Serve jelly at room temperature. Yield: 4 cups.

RED PEPPER JELLY

3¾ cups sugar
1 cup minced sweet red pepper
¾ cup white vinegar (5% acidity)
1½ teaspoons hot sauce
1 (3-ounce) package liquid pectin

Combine first 4 ingredients in a deep 2½-quart casserole. Microwave at HIGH 8 minutes, stirring after 6 minutes. Stir in pectin; microwave at HIGH 2 to 2½ minutes. Skim off foam with a metal spoon.

Pour mixture into jelly jars or frozen food containers. Cover with lids; invert 1 to 1½ hours to disperse minced pepper. Freeze jelly up to 1 year, or refrigerate up to 3 weeks. Allow jelly to come to room temperature before serving. Yield: 4 cups.

summer Suppers®

A Fancy For Summer Food And Fun

Our annual "Summer Suppers" special section will help you plan cookouts, picnics, and parties, as well as family meals with the greatest of ease. We offer recipes, menus, and suggestions to get you out of the kitchen and into the summer fun.

The festivities begin with a party in Shreveport, Louisiana, hosted by Mary Virginia and John Knight. Their scrumptious menu below comes complete with recipes and a schedule for preparing the meal with ease. Our hostess also offers advice for novice hostesses.

Mint Daiquiris   Iced tea
Mushroom Pâté
Shrimp Pizza Wedges
Pesto Chicken With Basil Cream
Squash Casserole
Sweet-and-Sour Asparagus
Toasted Crescent Rolls
Key Lime Tart in Coconut Crust
White Chocolate Mousse Cake
White wine

MINT DAIQUIRIS

2 (6-ounce) cans frozen limeade
   concentrate, thawed and
   undiluted
2 cups light rum
½ cup fresh mint leaves
Ice cubes
Fresh mint sprigs (optional)

Combine 1 can limeade concentrate, 1 cup rum, and ¼ cup mint leaves in container of an electric blender. Blend mixture 30 seconds. Add enough ice cubes to bring mixture to 4-cup level; blend until slushy. Pour into large freezer container. Repeat procedure with remaining limeade concentrate, rum, mint leaves, and ice. Freeze until serving time. Let thaw until slushy (about 20 minutes). Stir; serve immediately. Garnish with mint, if desired. Yield: 9 cups.

Note: Mint Daiquiris may be prepared one month in advance.

MUSHROOM PÂTÉ

1 pound mushrooms, chopped
2 tablespoons butter or
   margarine, melted
1 (8-ounce) package cream
   cheese, softened
½ teaspoon garlic salt
1 teaspoon seasoned pepper
Fresh rosemary (optional)
Sliced fresh mushrooms (optional)

Sauté chopped mushrooms in butter in a skillet over medium-high heat until liquid is absorbed (about 5 minutes). Let mushrooms cool to room temperature.

Position knife blade in food processor bowl. Add sautéed mushrooms, cream cheese, garlic salt, and pepper. Top with cover; process until smooth, scraping sides of bowl occasionally. Spoon into a greased 7½- x 3- x 2-inch loafpan. Chill.

Before serving time, toast French bread baguette slices at 300° for 10 minutes or until crisp.

Unmold pâté. If desired, garnish pâté with fresh rosemary and sliced fresh mushrooms. Serve with toasted French bread baguette slices. Yield: about 2 cups.

Schedule for Cooking

The recipes in this menu can all be prepared in advance. Mary Virginia Knight suggests the following timetable:

One Week to One Month Before the Party:
■ Prepare Mint Daiquiris, and freeze.
■ Prepare sponge cake (not filling and whipping cream) for White Chocolate Mousse Cake; wrap and freeze.

Two Days Before the Party:
■ Prepare Squash Casserole; cover and chill.
■ Prepare shrimp spread for Shrimp Pizza Wedges; cover and chill. Spread on tortillas just before baking.
■ Prepare Mushroom Pâté; cover and chill.
■ Prepare Key Lime Tart in Coconut Crust; cover and chill.

One Day Before the Party:
■ Make filling for and assemble White Chocolate Mousse Cake; cover and chill. (Frost cake day of the party.)
■ Assemble Pesto Chicken. Wait until day of the party to make the Basil Cream.
■ Prepare the Sweet-and-Sour Asparagus.
■ Cut and butter crescent rolls.

Day of the Party:
■ Make Basil Cream for Pesto Chicken.
■ Whip cream, and frost White Chocolate Mousse Cake.
■ Complete food preparation.

SHRIMP PIZZA WEDGES

1 (4¼-ounce) can medium shrimp, rinsed and drained
2 teaspoons lemon juice
1 (8-ounce) package cream cheese, softened
1 cup (4 ounces) shredded sharp Cheddar or Monterey Jack cheese
4 green onions, chopped
2 jalapeño peppers, seeded and chopped
2 cloves garlic, minced
2 tablespoons chopped fresh cilantro
1 teaspoon cumin
1 teaspoon chili powder
9 (6-inch) whole wheat flour tortillas
Fresh cilantro sprigs (optional)
Whole fresh shrimp (optional)

Combine medium shrimp and lemon juice; cover and refrigerate about 30 minutes.

Position knife blade in food processor bowl; add shrimp mixture, cream cheese, and next 7 ingredients. Top with cover; process about 1 minute or until smooth, scraping sides of bowl occasionally.

Place tortillas on ungreased baking sheets; spread about ¼ cup shrimp mixture on each tortilla. Bake at 350° for 10 minutes or until edges begin to brown. Cut each tortilla into 8 wedges. If desired, garnish with cilantro sprigs and whole shrimp. Serve hot. Yield: 72 wedges.

Note: Shrimp mixture may be refrigerated up to 2 days. Spread on tortillas just before baking.

PESTO CHICKEN WITH BASIL CREAM

8 chicken breast halves, skinned and boned
8 (1-ounce) slices prosciutto or ham
½ cup Pesto
¼ cup olive oil
2 cloves garlic, minced
¼ teaspoon pepper
Basil Cream
Fresh basil (optional)

Place each piece of chicken between two sheets of plastic wrap; flatten to ¼-inch thickness, using a smooth meat mallet or rolling pin. Place 1 slice of prosciutto and 1 tablespoon Pesto in center of each chicken piece. Roll up crosswise, and secure with a wooden pick. Place in a pan; cover and chill overnight, if desired. Let stand at room temperature 30 minutes before grilling.

Combine olive oil, garlic, and pepper. Grill chicken over medium coals 15 to 20 minutes or until done, turning and brushing occasionally with olive oil mixture. Serve with Basil Cream. Garnish with fresh basil, if desired. Yield: 8 servings.

Pesto

2 cups packed fresh basil
2 cloves garlic
¼ teaspoon salt
¼ teaspoon freshly ground pepper
½ cup freshly grated Parmesan cheese
½ cup freshly grated Romano cheese
½ cup olive oil

Remove stems from basil. Wash basil leaves thoroughly in lukewarm water, and drain well.

Position knife blade in food processor bowl. Add basil and next 5 ingredients, and top with cover; process until smooth. With food processor

running, pour oil through food chute in a slow, steady stream until combined. Yield: 1 cup.

Basil Cream

⅓ cup dry white wine
3 shallots, chopped (about ¼ cup)
1½ cups whipping cream
¼ cup minced fresh basil
1 cup chopped tomato

Combine wine and shallots in a saucepan; bring to a boil, and cook about 2 minutes or until liquid is reduced to about ¼ cup. Add whipping cream; return to a boil, and cook 8 to 10 minutes or until reduced to about 1 cup, stirring constantly. Stir in basil and tomato; cook just until heated. Yield: about 2 cups.

Note: Chicken may be grilled in advance and reheated. To reheat, reserve ¼ cup basting mixture, and chill. Place chicken rolls on jellyroll pan; cover with foil, and chill. Remove from refrigerator; let stand at room temperature 30 minutes. Reheat chicken rolls, covered, at 350° for 15 to 20 minutes. Uncover and brush chicken with reserved basting mixture. Bake, uncovered, an additional 5 to 10 minutes or until thoroughly heated.

SQUASH CASSEROLE

2 pounds yellow squash, cut into ¼-inch slices
½ cup water
½ teaspoon salt
1 cup chopped onion
1 cup chopped sweet red pepper
¼ cup butter or margarine, melted
1 egg, beaten
1 cup (4 ounces) shredded Cheddar cheese
1 (8-ounce) can sliced water chestnuts, drained
⅔ cup mayonnaise or salad dressing
2 teaspoons sugar
¼ teaspoon pepper
Sweet red pepper rings (optional)
Fresh parsley sprigs (optional)

Combine squash, water, and salt in a medium saucepan; bring to a boil. Cover, reduce heat, and simmer 10 minutes or until squash is tender. Drain well, and set aside.

Sauté onion and chopped red pepper in butter until crisp-tender (about 3 minutes). Combine vegetables, egg, and next 5 ingredients; spoon into a lightly greased 12- x 7- x 2-inch baking dish. Bake at 350° for 30 minutes or until bubbly. If desired, garnish with red pepper rings and parsley sprigs. Yield: 8 servings.

Note: To make ahead, prepare as directed but do not bake. Cover and chill up to 2 days. Remove from refrigerator; let stand 30 minutes. Bake as directed.

SWEET-AND-SOUR ASPARAGUS

2 pounds fresh asparagus spears
⅔ cup white vinegar
½ cup sugar
½ cup water
½ teaspoon salt
1 teaspoon whole cloves
3 (3-inch) sticks cinnamon
1½ teaspoons celery seeds
Lemon slices (optional)
Celery leaves (optional)

Snap off tough ends of asparagus. Remove scales from stalks with a knife or vegetable peeler, if desired. Arrange asparagus in steaming rack, and place over boiling water. Cover and steam 6 to 8 minutes or until crisp-tender. Drain.

Place asparagus in a 13- x 9- x 2-inch baking dish. Combine vinegar and next 6 ingredients in a small saucepan; bring to a boil. Pour mixture over asparagus. Cover; chill 24 hours. Drain; remove and discard cloves and cinnamon. Arrange asparagus on platter. If desired, garnish with lemon slices and celery leaves. Yield: 8 servings.

Reminders for a Novice Hostess

■ Organization and make-ahead recipes are the key. Make lists.
■ Start out with just two to four guests, a simple menu, and a casual and comfortable setting.
■ Recipes don't have to be difficult to be good. It's best to do a simple menu well. When you've gained confidence, work up to more complicated recipes.

■ Build a menu around easy, tried-and-true recipes that your family loves. For company, add to those familiar and reliable ones a couple of fun and unusual recipes you've been wanting to try.
■ It is important to keep in mind that guests are your friends and will understand if things aren't perfect.

July   159

KEY LIME TART
IN COCONUT CRUST

4 egg yolks
1 (14-ounce) can sweetened
    condensed milk
1 teaspoon grated lime rind
⅓ cup Key lime juice
Coconut Crust
Whipped cream
Fresh mint sprigs (optional)
Lime twist (optional)

Beat egg yolks with a wire whisk until lemon colored; add sweetened condensed milk, lime rind, and Key lime juice, stirring well. Spoon filling into Coconut Crust. Chill until firm.

Pipe or dollop whipped cream on pie. If desired, garnish with mint sprigs and lime twist. Yield: one 9-inch pie.

Coconut Crust

1 cup flaked coconut
½ cup gingersnap crumbs
½ cup graham cracker crumbs
¼ cup butter or margarine,
    melted

Combine all ingredients, mixing well. Firmly press mixture evenly over bottom and ¾ inch up sides of a 9-inch springform pan. Bake at 350° for 5 minutes. Chill thoroughly. Yield: one 9-inch crust.

Tip: *For an easy and attractive garnish, slice a lemon or lime into ¼-inch-thick slices; make a cut from the center of the slice to the outside edge, and gently twist the cut slice in opposite directions to a form an "S" shaped twist.*

WHITE CHOCOLATE
MOUSSE CAKE

5 eggs, separated
1 cup sugar
¼ cup boiling water
1 teaspoon vanilla extract
1 cup sifted cake flour
1½ teaspoons baking powder
¼ teaspoon salt
⅓ cup amaretto
¼ cup light corn syrup
White Chocolate Filling
1¾ cups whipping cream
¼ cup sifted powdered sugar
½ cup sliced almonds, toasted
Fresh raspberries (optional)
Fresh mint sprigs (optional)

Beat egg yolks at high speed of an electric mixer 4 minutes or until thick and lemon colored. Gradually add 1 cup sugar, beating well at medium speed of an electric mixer. Gradually add boiling water, beating well. Stir in vanilla.

Sift together flour, baking powder, and salt; add to egg yolk mixture, and stir until blended. Set aside.

Beat egg whites (at room temperature) until stiff peaks form; fold into egg yolk batter.

On outside of a 9-inch springform pan, cover bottom with heavy-duty aluminum foil. Pour cake batter into pan, and bake at 350° for 30 to 35 minutes. Cool completely.

Combine amaretto and light corn syrup, mixing well. Set aside.

Split cake horizontally into 3 layers. Brush amaretto mixture on each side of cake layers. Spread White Chocolate Filling between layers. Set aside.

Beat whipping cream until foamy; gradually add powdered sugar, beating until soft peaks form. Spread on top and sides of cake. Press sliced almonds into whipped cream on sides of cake. If desired, garnish with raspberries and mint sprigs. Yield: 1 (9-inch) cake.

White Chocolate Filling

9 ounces white chocolate,
    coarsely chopped
¼ cup whipping cream
3 egg yolks
⅓ cup sifted powdered sugar

Combine first 2 ingredients in top of a double boiler; bring water to a boil. Reduce heat to low; cook, stirring constantly, until chocolate melts.

Beat egg yolks until thick and lemon colored. Gradually stir about one-fourth of hot mixture into yolks; add to remaining hot mixture, stirring constantly. Add powdered sugar, and cook, stirring constantly, 5 minutes or until mixture reaches 165°. Cool until mixture reaches spreading consistency. Yield: enough filling for one 3-layer cake.

Note: Sponge cake may be baked in advance. Wrap and freeze. Thaw and slice into 3 layers. Spread with filling and whipped cream.

Picnic With A
New Menu

Outdoor entertaining is always fun, so round up the gang, head for the park, and take along this wonderful picnic. There's no better way to settle back and watch the sun go down.

Just fill your picnic basket and cooler with these foods for a delicious spread. Start by snacking on Hot-and-Spicy Pecans and tasty Liver Spread with crackers. Then team Croissant Sandwiches with Dilled Macaroni Salad and Honey-Sweet Carrot Salad for a filling meal.

Cookies are especially easy to pack for picnics, and we offer two

delightful choices—Crisp Coconut Cookies and Chocolate-Filled Bonbons. One is crisp and crunchy with cereal, and the other contains a chocolate kiss surprise.

Liver Spread
Hot-and-Spicy Pecans
Croissant Sandwiches
Dilled Macaroni Salad
Honey-Sweet Carrot Salad
Crisp Coconut Cookies
Chocolate-Filled Bonbons
Lemonade   Wine

LIVER SPREAD

½ pound chicken livers
4 hard-cooked eggs
½ cup pimiento-stuffed olives, drained
1 small onion
2 teaspoons prepared mustard
1 tablespoon mayonnaise or salad dressing
¼ teaspoon pepper
⅛ teaspoon Worcestershire sauce
Hard-cooked egg white (optional)
Green pepper (optional)
Whole pimiento (optional)

Cook chicken livers in a small amount of boiling water about 8 minutes; drain well. Cool.

Position knife blade in food processor bowl; add chicken livers, eggs, olives, onion, and mustard. Pulse 5 or 6 times. Add mayonnaise, pepper, and Worcestershire sauce; process until mixture is smooth.

Spoon into a serving container. Cover and chill. If desired, make a flower garnish with egg white, green pepper, and pimiento. Serve with crackers. Yield: 2 cups.
Joan Wegner
North Little Rock, Arkansas

HOT-AND-SPICY PECANS

1½ tablespoons butter or margarine
1½ tablespoons Worcestershire sauce
¼ teaspoon salt
¼ teaspoon ground cinnamon
⅛ teaspoon garlic powder
⅛ teaspoon red pepper
Dash of hot sauce
2 cups pecan halves

Melt butter in a large, heavy skillet or saucepan. Remove from heat; add remaining ingredients except pecans, stirring well. Add pecans, stirring to coat well.

Spread pecans evenly in a lightly greased 15- x 10- x 1-inch jellyroll pan. Bake at 300° for 20 minutes, stirring every 5 minutes. Place pecans on paper towels, and cool completely. Yield: 2 cups.
Diane Butts
Boone, North Carolina

CROISSANT SANDWICHES
(pictured on page 185)

1 (3-ounce) package cream cheese with chives, softened
1 teaspoon prepared horseradish
Dash of garlic powder
1 (6-ounce) package frozen croissants, baked and cooled
4 (1-ounce) slices cooked ham
½ medium cucumber, thinly sliced

Combine softened cream cheese, horseradish, and garlic powder; mix well. Split croissants lengthwise, and spread cut sides with cream cheese mixture.

Fold ham in half, and place on bottom halves of croissants; top with cucumber and remaining croissant halves. Yield: 4 sandwiches.

DILLED MACARONI SALAD
(pictured on page 185)

1 cup uncooked elbow macaroni
⅓ cup chopped onion
¼ cup chopped celery
¼ cup chopped green pepper
¼ cup shredded carrot
½ cup mayonnaise or salad dressing
1 tablespoon vinegar
½ to 1 teaspoon dried whole dillweed
¼ teaspoon garlic salt
¼ teaspoon onion salt

Cook macaroni according to package directions, omitting salt; drain. Rinse with cold water; drain again. Add onion, celery, green pepper, and carrot; toss well. Combine mayonnaise and remaining ingredients; gently stir mayonnaise mixture into macaroni mixture. Chill 1 hour. Yield: 4 to 6 servings.
Sharon Crider
Evansville, Wisconsin

HONEY-SWEET CARROT SALAD
(pictured on page 185)

1 pound carrots, scraped and shredded
1 (8-ounce) can crushed pineapple, drained
½ cup miniature marshmallows
½ cup flaked coconut
2 tablespoons sour cream
2 tablespoons lemon juice
2 tablespoons honey

Combine carrots, pineapple, marshmallows, and coconut; stir well.

Combine sour cream, lemon juice, and honey in a small bowl. Pour over carrot mixture, tossing well. Cover and refrigerate 8 hours. Yield: 4 to 6 servings.
Mrs. Robert L. Spence
Baton Rouge, Louisiana

CRISP COCONUT COOKIES
(pictured on page 185)

1 cup shortening
1 cup sugar
1 cup firmly packed brown sugar
2 eggs
2 cups flaked coconut
½ teaspoon vanilla extract
2 cups all-purpose flour
1 teaspoon baking soda
½ teaspoon baking powder
½ teaspoon salt
2 cups whole wheat flake cereal

Cream shortening; gradually add sugars, beating well. Add eggs, one at a time, beating well after each addition. Add coconut and vanilla. Combine next 4 ingredients. Add to creamed mixture; blend well. Stir in cereal. Roll into 1-inch balls; place on ungreased cookie sheets, and bake at 400° for 12 minutes. Yield: about 6 dozen.
Celesta McDonough
Hartford, Illinois

CHOCOLATE-FILLED BONBONS
(pictured on page 185)

¾ cup shortening
½ cup sugar
¼ cup firmly packed brown sugar
1 egg
2 teaspoons vanilla extract
½ teaspoon almond extract
1¾ cups all-purpose flour
½ teaspoon baking powder
½ teaspoon salt
½ cup finely chopped pecans
3 dozen milk chocolate kisses, unwrapped
Sifted powdered sugar

Combine first 3 ingredients; beat at medium speed of an electric mixer until light and fluffy. Add egg and flavorings; mix well. Combine flour, baking powder, salt, and pecans; add to creamed mixture, beating well.

Shape into 36 (1-inch) balls. Press each ball around a chocolate kiss, covering completely; place on ungreased cookie sheets. Bake at 350° for 12 to 14 minutes. Cool slightly on wire racks; roll in powdered sugar. Cool completely to store. Yield: 3 dozen.
Jana Dominguez
Navasota, Texas

Chill The Salad Until Suppertime

If company is coming for dinner in a couple of days, one thing you won't have to worry about is the salad. These recipes can be made ahead of time and kept chilled or frozen until time to eat.

LAYERED CHICKEN SALAD

3 cups chopped cooked chicken, divided
2 cups torn lettuce
1 cup cooked long-grain rice
1 (10-ounce) package frozen English peas, thawed
¼ cup chopped fresh parsley
2 large tomatoes, seeded and chopped
1 cup thinly sliced cucumber
1 small sweet red pepper, chopped
1 small green pepper, chopped
Dressing (recipe follows)
Red pepper rings

Layer 1½ cups chicken and lettuce in a 3-quart bowl. Combine rice, peas, and parsley; spoon evenly over lettuce. Layer tomatoes, cucumber, chopped red pepper, green pepper, and remaining 1½ cups chicken. Spoon dressing evenly over top of salad, sealing to edge of bowl. Top with red pepper rings; cover and chill 8 hours. Toss before serving. Yield: 8 servings.

Dressing

1 cup mayonnaise
½ cup sour cream
½ cup raisins
½ cup finely chopped onion
¼ cup sweet pickle relish
2 tablespoons milk
½ teaspoon celery seeds
½ teaspoon dillseeds
½ teaspoon dry mustard
½ teaspoon garlic salt

Combine all ingredients; stir well. Yield: about 2¾ cups.
Carrie Byrne Bartlett
Gallatin, Tennessee

CUCUMBER-ROAST BEEF SALAD

1 medium cucumber, sliced
1 cup (4 ounces) cubed Cheddar cheese
1 cup cubed cooked roast beef
½ cup sliced green onions
⅔ cup commercial creamy cucumber salad dressing
1 tablespoon white vinegar
1 tablespoon prepared horseradish
1 tablespoon chopped fresh dillweed
1 avocado
1 large tomato, cut into wedges
Lettuce leaves

Combine first 4 ingredients in a bowl. Combine cucumber dressing, vinegar, horseradish, and dillweed, stirring well. Pour over beef mixture, tossing well; cover and chill.

Just before serving, peel and slice avocado. Arrange beef mixture, tomato, and avocado on a lettuce-lined platter. Yield: 4 servings.

Mrs. H. D. Baxter
Charleston, West Virginia

LAYERED SPINACH SALAD

1 pound fresh spinach, torn into
  bite-size pieces
2 hard-cooked eggs, chopped
5 green onions, sliced
10 slices bacon, cooked and
  crumbled
1 (10-ounce) package frozen
  English peas, thawed
1 (8-ounce) carton sour cream
1 cup mayonnaise or salad
  dressing
¼ teaspoon lemon-pepper
  seasoning
⅛ teaspoon garlic powder
½ cup freshly grated Romano
  cheese (optional)

Layer spinach, eggs, green onions, bacon, and peas in a large deep bowl.

Combine sour cream and next 3 ingredients, stirring well; spoon evenly over peas, sealing to edge of bowl. Sprinkle with Romano cheese, if desired. Cover tightly, and chill 8 hours. Toss gently before serving. Yield: 8 servings. *Susan Todd*
Shreveport, Louisiana

Tip: *When buying spinach, remember that 1 pound fresh spinach yields about 1½ cups cooked.*

FROZEN
BLACK CHERRY SALAD

1 (20-ounce) can pineapple tidbits
1 (1.25-ounce) envelope whipped
  topping mix
1 (8-ounce) package cream
  cheese, softened
3 cups pitted fresh sweet
  cherries, halved (about 1½
  pounds)

Drain pineapple, reserving 3 tablespoons juice.

Prepare whipped topping mix according to package directions; set aside. Beat cream cheese and reserved pineapple juice at medium speed of an electric mixer until smooth. Add whipped topping; fold in pineapple and cherries. Pour into a lightly oiled 8-inch square dish or 8 lightly oiled individual molds; cover and freeze until firm. Remove from freezer 10 to 15 minutes before serving. Yield: 8 servings.

Mrs. Clifford B. Smith, Sr.
White Hall, Maryland

ON THE LIGHT SIDE

Lean, Tasty Burgers

Cookouts are one of the greatest pleasures of summer. And *the* most popular food at a cookout is hamburgers. The fat content can be kept low by using lean ground chuck and combining it with vegetables or breadcrumbs. This stretches the number of servings and adds fiber and flavor. Still another choice for those who prefer not to eat red meat is Walnut Burgers.

WALNUT BURGERS

⅔ cup regular oats, uncooked
1½ cups boiling water
Vegetable cooking spray
¼ cup diced onion
1 egg, slightly beaten
1 cup fine, dry breadcrumbs
1 cup chopped walnuts
½ teaspoon dried whole thyme
½ teaspoon dried whole oregano
½ teaspoon dried whole basil
½ teaspoon crushed red pepper
¼ teaspoon rubbed sage
¼ teaspoon pepper
1½ teaspoons tamari sauce
1 tablespoon vegetable oil
3 (6-inch) whole wheat pita bread
  rounds, halved
1½ cups shredded lettuce
1½ cups diced tomato
¼ cup plus 2 tablespoons plain
  low-fat yogurt

Cook oats in boiling water according to package directions; set aside.

Coat a nonstick skillet with cooking spray; place over medium-high heat until hot. Add diced onion, and sauté until tender. Combine cooked oatmeal, onion, egg, and next 9 ingredients; stir well. Shape mixture into 6 patties.

Heat oil in a large nonstick skillet over medium heat. Add patties, and cook 4 to 6 minutes on each side. Place in pita bread, and top each with ¼ cup lettuce, ¼ cup tomato, and 1 tablespoon yogurt. Yield: 6 servings (317 calories per serving).

☐ *11.8 grams protein, 17.1 grams fat, 31.3 grams carbohydrate, 47 milligrams cholesterol, 230 milligrams sodium, and 93 milligrams calcium.*

Amy B. Angert
Atlanta, Georgia

BURGERS WITH SPROUTS

1 pound lean ground chuck
1 (16-ounce) can bean sprouts, drained
⅓ cup minced green pepper
1 tablespoon brown sugar
1 teaspoon ground ginger
½ teaspoon garlic powder
½ teaspoon onion powder
¼ teaspoon salt
¼ teaspoon pepper
1 tablespoon low-sodium soy sauce
1 tablespoon reduced-calorie catsup
Vegetable cooking spray

Combine first 11 ingredients; shape into 6 patties. Coat grill rack with cooking spray; place on grill over medium-hot coals.

Place ground chuck patties on rack, and cook 8 minutes on each side or until done. Yield: 6 servings (157 calories per serving).

Note: To broil, place patties on broiler pan coated with cooking spray. Broil 6 inches from heat about 8 minutes on each side or until done.

☐ *20.6 grams protein, 6.2 grams fat, 3.5 grams carbohydrate, 61 milligrams cholesterol, 222 milligrams sodium, and 14 milligrams calcium.*
Anna Lundy
Fordoche, Louisiana

MUSHROOM BURGERS

1 pound medium-size fresh mushrooms
¼ cup reduced-calorie catsup
1½ pounds lean ground chuck
2 teaspoons chili powder
½ teaspoon salt
Vegetable cooking spray
8 (¼-inch-thick) onion slices

Remove stems from 8 mushrooms; fill caps with ½ tablespoon catsup, and set aside. Chop stems and remaining mushrooms. Add ground chuck, chili powder, and salt; stir well. Shape into 8 patties. Coat grill rack with cooking spray; place on a grill over medium-hot coals. Place patties on rack, and cook 5 minutes. Turn and top each patty with onion slice and reserved mushroom cap; cook 5 minutes or until done. Yield: 8 servings (135 calories per serving).

Note: To broil, place patties on broiler pan coated with cooking spray. Broil 6 inches from heat about 5 minutes on each side or until done. Top each burger with onion slice and mushroom cap.

☐ *16.6 grams protein, 5 grams fat, 6 grams carbohydrate, 46 milligrams cholesterol, 241 milligrams sodium, and 17 milligrams calcium.*
Lynn F. Wootan
Broussard, Louisiana

VEGETABLE BURGERS

1 teaspoon dry mustard
1 tablespoon warm water
1 pound lean ground chuck
1 cup diced tomato
1 cup diced mushrooms
2 teaspoons dried minced onion
¼ teaspoon salt
¼ teaspoon pepper
⅛ teaspoon garlic powder
Vegetable cooking spray

Combine mustard and water in a medium bowl; let stand 10 minutes. Add ground chuck and next 6 ingredients; stir well. Shape into 6 patties. Coat grill rack with cooking spray; place on grill over medium-hot coals. Place patties on rack, and cook 8 minutes on each side or until done. Yield: 6 servings (153 calories per serving).

Note: To broil, place patties on broiler pan coated with cooking spray. Broil 6 inches from heat about 8 minutes on each side or until done.

☐ *20.6 grams protein, 6.3 grams fat, 2.5 grams carbohydrate, 61 milligrams cholesterol, 142 milligrams sodium, and 12 milligrams calcium.*
Mrs. James L. Thomasson
Pine Bluff, Arkansas

BARBECUED BURGERS

1 pound lean ground chuck
1¼ cups soft breadcrumbs
¼ cup minced onion
½ cup part-skim ricotta cheese
¼ cup egg substitute
¼ cup reduced-calorie catsup
1 teaspoon prepared mustard
½ teaspoon low-sodium Worcestershire sauce
⅛ teaspoon pepper
Vegetable cooking spray
⅓ cup commercial barbecue sauce

Combine first 9 ingredients; shape into 8 patties. Place patties on broiler pan coated with cooking spray. Spread patties with half of sauce.

Broil patties 6 inches from heat 8 minutes; turn and brush with remaining barbecue sauce, and broil 8 minutes or to desired degree of doneness. Yield: 8 servings (219 calories per serving).

☐ *21.6 grams protein, 7.3 grams fat, 15.2 grams carbohydrate, 57 milligrams cholesterol, 329 milligrams sodium, and 72 milligrams calcium.*
Mary A. Larsh
Franklin, Virginia

TRIPLE-LAYER BURGERS

4 (1-inch-thick) unpeeled eggplant
    slices
1 tablespoon lemon juice
½ teaspoon salt
½ teaspoon dried whole marjoram
1 tablespoon vegetable oil
1 slice bread, torn
¼ cup egg substitute
1 pound lean ground chuck
¼ cup thinly sliced green onions
⅛ teaspoon pepper
Vegetable cooking spray
4 (½-inch-thick) tomato slices
Green onion fans (optional)

Brush eggplant with lemon juice;
sprinkle with salt and marjoram. Heat
oil in a large nonstick skillet over
medium heat. Add eggplant, and
cook 3 minutes on each side. Drain
well on paper towels.

Combine bread and egg substitute
in a medium bowl; let stand 3 minutes. Add ground chuck, green
onions, and pepper; stir well. Shape
into 4 patties. Coat grill rack with
cooking spray; place on grill over
medium-hot coals. Place patties on
rack, and cook 8 minutes on each
side or until done.

Place tomato slices on eggplant;
grill with patties the last 8 minutes.
To serve, place patty on top of tomato; garnish with green onion fans,
if desired. Yield: 4 servings (309 calories per serving).

☐ *33.9 grams protein, 12.9 grams
fat, 14.1 grams carbohydrate, 92 milligrams cholesterol, 416 milligrams
sodium, and 74 milligrams calcium.*
Linda Hampton
Waco, Texas

FAVORITE BURGERS

1¾ cups shredded potatoes
1 pound lean ground chuck
½ cup chopped mushrooms
¼ cup diced onion
¼ teaspoon salt
¼ teaspoon garlic powder
¼ teaspoon pepper
¼ teaspoon paprika
Vegetable cooking spray

Place potatoes between paper
towels, and squeeze until barely
moist; combine with next 7 ingredients. Shape into 8 patties. Coat
grill rack with cooking spray; place
on grill over medium-hot coals. Place
patties on rack, and cook 8 minutes
on each side or until done. Yield: 8
servings (137 calories per serving).

Note: To broil, place patties on
broiler pan coated with cooking
spray. Broil 6 inches from heat about
8 minutes on each side or until done.

☐ *15.9 grams protein, 4.6 grams fat,
7.1 grams carbohydrate, 46 milligrams cholesterol, 106 milligrams sodium, and 9 milligrams calcium.*

PIZZA BURGERS

1 (1-pound) package frozen raw
    ground turkey, thawed
½ cup diced celery
2 tablespoons diced onion
1 tablespoon low-sodium
    Worcestershire sauce
½ teaspoon dried whole basil
Vegetable cooking spray
⅓ cup tomato sauce
6 (⅔-ounce) slices 40%-less-fat
    sharp Cheddar cheese

Combine first 5 ingredients, mixing
well. Shape into 6 patties. Coat grill

rack with cooking spray; place on
grill over medium-hot coals. Place
patties on rack, and cook 5 minutes
on each side or until done.

Brush top of each cooked patty
with tomato sauce, and top with a
slice of cheese. Yield: 6 servings
(166 calories per serving).

Note: To broil, place patties on
broiler pan coated with cooking
spray. Broil 6 inches from heat about
5 minutes on each side or until done.

☐ *22.5 grams protein, 6 grams fat,
6.2 grams carbohydrate, 49 milligrams cholesterol, 146 milligrams sodium, and 153 milligrams calcium.*
Erma Jackson
Huntsville, Alabama

Burger Tips

■ Lightly mix and shape ground
meat or meat loaf mixtures,
keeping in mind that excessive
handling of the meat results in a
compact mixture.

■ When freezing meat patties,
steaks, or chops, separate with
two thicknesses of wrapping material between them so that the
pieces can be separated easily
without thawing more than
needed.

■ In most instances, count on 4
servings per pound when serving ground beef.

■ For a delicious aroma and flavor, add some red wine to the
skillet while frying hamburgers.

Treat Friends To A Casual Dinner

Long summer days lend themselves to casual suppers with friends. Serve a meal that's satisfying and attractive yet allows time for greeting guests.

Buttermilk-Pecan Chicken
Lemon Rice
Garden Salad
Cantaloupe Sundae
Coffee

BUTTERMILK-PECAN CHICKEN
(pictured on page 188)

⅓ cup butter or margarine
1 cup all-purpose flour
1 cup pecans, ground
¼ cup sesame seeds
1 tablespoon paprika
1½ teaspoons salt
⅛ teaspoon pepper
1 egg, slightly beaten
1 cup buttermilk
8 chicken breast halves, skinned and boned
¼ cup coarsely chopped pecans

Melt butter in a 13- x 9- x 2-inch baking dish; set aside. Combine flour and next 5 ingredients. Combine egg and buttermilk. Dip chicken in egg mixture, and dredge in flour mixture, coating well. Place in baking dish, turning once to coat with butter. Sprinkle with pecans. Bake chicken at 350° for 30 minutes or until done. Yield: 8 servings. *Thelma Peedin Newport News, Virginia*

LEMON RICE
(pictured on page 188)

1 medium onion, chopped
2 cloves garlic, minced
1 tablespoon vegetable oil
4 cups water
2 cups uncooked long-grain rice
4 chicken-flavored bouillon cubes
3 tablespoons lemon juice
½ cup chopped fresh parsley

Sauté onion and garlic in oil in a large saucepan until tender. Add water and next 3 ingredients. Bring to a boil; cover, reduce heat, and simmer 20 minutes or until rice is tender and liquid is absorbed. Stir in parsley. Yield: 8 servings. *Sally Murphy Grapevine, Texas*

GARDEN SALAD
(pictured on page 188)

4 cups torn iceberg lettuce
4 cups torn romaine lettuce
1 medium zucchini, thinly sliced
1 carrot, thinly sliced
½ cup sliced radishes
½ cup sliced fresh mushrooms
2 green onions, thinly sliced
Italian dressing (recipe follows)

Combine vegetables in a large bowl. Add Italian dressing, tossing well. Yield: 8 servings.

Italian Dressing

1 cup vegetable oil
½ cup white vinegar
¼ cup grated Parmesan cheese
1 teaspoon celery salt
½ teaspoon white pepper
½ teaspoon dry mustard
¼ teaspoon paprika
1 clove garlic, minced

Combine all ingredients in a jar; cover tightly, and shake vigorously. Chill thoroughly. Yield: 1¼ cups. *Daisy Cotton Karnes City, Texas*

CANTALOUPE SUNDAE
(pictured on page 188)

2 teaspoons cornstarch
2 tablespoons water
1 (10-ounce) package frozen raspberries, thawed and undrained
1 cantaloupe, peeled and cut into 8 wedges
1 quart vanilla ice cream, scooped into 8 balls
Fresh raspberries (optional)

Combine cornstarch and water in a saucepan; stir well. Add thawed raspberries; cook 1 minute, stirring constantly. Cool.

To serve, fill each cantaloupe wedge with a scoop of ice cream, and top with raspberry sauce. Garnish with raspberries, if desired. Yield: 8 servings. *Janie Wallace Seguin, Texas*

Attention, Outdoor Chefs

If the grilling competition has heated up in your neighborhood, invite friends over and woo them with the recipes here. You'll find additional tips for the road to grilling fame in our quick quiz. Test yourself!

SAUCY LAMB KABOBS

1 (8-ounce) can tomato sauce
¼ cup white wine
2 tablespoons ground coriander
2 tablespoons Worcestershire
  sauce
2 tablespoons vegetable oil
2 pounds (1-inch) lamb cubes
2 medium-size green peppers, cut
  into 1-inch pieces
2 large yellow onions, quartered
½ pound fresh mushrooms
1 pint cherry tomatoes
Hot cooked rice

Combine first 5 ingredients in a large
shallow container. Add lamb; cover
and marinate in refrigerator 4 hours.

Combine green pepper, onion, and
mushrooms in a small bowl; cover
with boiling water. Drain vegetables
after 5 minutes.

Remove lamb from marinade. Alternate lamb, green pepper, onion,
and mushrooms on skewers. Grill
over medium coals 8 to 10 minutes;
turn and add tomatoes to skewers.
Grill an additional 8 to 10 minutes or
to desired degree of doneness, basting frequently. Serve kabobs over
rice. Yield: 8 servings.

Elizabeth Williams
Clearwater, Florida

BARBECUED CHICKEN

1 cup vinegar
2 tablespoons butter or margarine
⅛ teaspoon garlic powder
1½ teaspoons Worcestershire
  sauce
¼ teaspoon lemon juice
Dash of red pepper
¼ teaspoon salt
¼ teaspoon freshly ground pepper
1 (2½- to 3-pound) broiler-fryer,
  split

Test Your Grilling IQ

Q. What's the difference between
grilling and smoking meat?
A. Grilling requires cooking about
4 to 6 inches from heat for a
relatively short time. Smoking involves imparting the flavor of
mesquite, hickory, or other wood
to the meat and cooking with in-
direct heat. The grill cover or lid
of the smoker is usually closed,
and a water pan is often placed
inside the grill or smoker to provide moist heat.

Q. What's a "dry rub"?
A. A dry rub is a mixture of
spices and seasonings used to flavor meats. Instead of a marinade,
the meat is sprayed with vinegar,
and then the dry seasoning mixture is rubbed on.

Q. What does a marinade contribute to grilled meat and poultry
other than flavor?
A. Tenderness—acids in vinegar,
wine, fruit juices, or commercial
marinades break down the protein
in the meat, thus tenderizing it as
it marinates.

Q. How can you tell if the coals
are hot?
A. If you can hold your hand over
the coals for only 2 seconds, they
are hot; for 3 seconds, they are
medium; and for 5 seconds, they
are low.

Did you know all the answers?
You're a four-star outdoor chef!
Less than three? These recipes
will build your confidence.

Combine vinegar, butter, garlic powder, Worcestershire sauce, lemon
juice, red pepper, salt, and freshly
ground pepper in a small saucepan.
Bring mixture to a boil; reduce heat,
and simmer 10 minutes. Set aside.

Place chicken, skin side up, in a
12- x 8- x 2-inch pan. Cover and
bake at 375° for 30 minutes.

Brush chicken with sauce. Place
chicken, skin side up, on grill; cook
over medium-hot coals 30 minutes or
until done, basting frequently with
sauce and turning chicken after 15
minutes. Yield: 2 servings.

Note: To microwave, place chicken,
skin side up, in a 12- x 8- x 2-inch
baking dish. Cover tightly with
heavy-duty plastic wrap; fold back a
small edge of wrap to allow steam to
escape. Microwave at HIGH 15 minutes, rotating dish after 7 minutes.

Brush chicken with sauce. Place
chicken, skin side up, on grill. Cook
over medium-hot coals 30 minutes or
until done, basting frequently with
sauce. Turn chicken after 15 minutes. Yield: 2 servings.

Ann Hall Harden
Pleasant Garden, North Carolina

Tip: *When using skewers, select
long sturdy ones that reach completely across the grill. Place food on
skewers, leaving space between each
piece to allow for heat penetration
and thorough basting. Unless some
types of vegetables are parboiled,
they may require a longer cooking
time than meat cubes.*

GRILLED TURKEY DRUMSTICKS

4 turkey drumsticks
¼ cup butter or margarine, melted
⅓ cup vegetable oil
⅓ cup dry sherry
⅓ cup soy sauce
1 clove garlic, minced
¼ cup chopped onion
¼ cup chopped fresh parsley
¼ teaspoon salt
¼ teaspoon pepper

Place turkey drumsticks in a large shallow dish. Combine remaining ingredients, stirring well. Pour over drumsticks; cover and marinate in refrigerator 8 hours, turning drumsticks occasionally.

Drain drumsticks, reserving marinade. Wrap each drumstick and ¼ cup marinade in heavy-duty aluminum foil. Grill over medium coals 1 hour, turning after 30 minutes. Remove foil, reserving marinade. Return drumsticks to grill, and continue cooking 30 to 40 minutes, basting frequently with reserved marinade. Yield: 8 servings.

Mrs. Homer Baxter
Charleston, West Virginia

SPICY SPARERIBS

¼ cup Hungarian paprika
1 tablespoon plus 1 teaspoon seasoned salt
1 tablespoon black pepper
2 teaspoons red pepper
2 teaspoons dry mustard
1½ teaspoons chili powder
1 teaspoon garlic powder
1 teaspoon ground oregano
1 teaspoon ground celery seeds
3 pounds spareribs
⅓ cup white wine vinegar

Combine first 9 ingredients in a small bowl, and set aside.

Cut ribs into serving-size pieces. Pour vinegar into a spray bottle, and mist ribs. Coat ribs with seasoning mixture.

Grill about 5 inches from medium coals 1 hour, misting with vinegar and turning frequently. Yield: 4 to 6 servings.

Rick Freeland
Helena, Arkansas

SMOKED BRISKET

Hickory chips
½ cup sugar
¼ cup paprika
2 tablespoons plus 2 teaspoons salt
2 tablespoons pepper
1 tablespoon plus ½ teaspoon garlic powder
1 (4- to 5-pound) beef brisket

Soak hickory chips in water for 1 to 24 hours.

Prepare charcoal fire by piling charcoal in one end of grill; let burn 15 to 20 minutes or until flames disappear and coals are white. Add 6 to 8 pieces of soaked hickory to coals.

Combine sugar and next 4 ingredients in a small bowl, stirring well. Rub brisket with dry mixture. Place brisket on rack away from coals on opposite end of grill; cover with grill hood. Open air vents halfway.

Cook brisket 1 hour; wrap in heavy-duty aluminum foil. Return brisket to grill; cover and cook an additional 30 minutes or to desired degree of doneness. Place additional hickory chips on coals, if necessary. Yield: 12 to 15 servings.

Alice McNamara
Eucha, Oklahoma

GRILLED FLANK STEAK

1 (1½-pound) flank steak
1 (10½-ounce) can consommé
1 cup red wine
⅔ cup soy sauce
½ cup sliced green onions
1 clove garlic, minced
2 tablespoons lime juice
2 tablespoons brown sugar

Trim excess fat from steak; score steak on both sides in 1½-inch squares. Place steak in a large shallow dish.

Combine remaining ingredients, stirring well. Pour over steak; cover and marinate in refrigerator 8 hours, turning occasionally.

Drain steak, reserving marinade. Grill over medium coals 7 to 9 minutes on each side or to desired degree of doneness, basting twice with reserved marinade. To serve, slice steak across grain into thin slices. Yield: about 6 servings.

Lana J. Tabb
Lakeland, Florida

Sweets On The Run

Amid summer's outdoor activity, who wants to stay inside cooking all day? There's no need to worry; now you can have your cake and eat it, too.

These terrific desserts can be made after the sun goes down and then taken along on the next day's outing to the pool or park.

For evening fun, pack a picnic basket to take along to the lake or to enjoy at a concert under the stars. Just be sure to include these portable desserts.

COCONUT-ORANGE CHESS PIE

1 cup sugar
1½ teaspoons all-purpose flour
1½ teaspoons yellow cornmeal
3 eggs, beaten
¼ cup butter or margarine,
  melted
¼ cup thawed, undiluted orange
  juice concentrate
2 tablespoons water
¼ cup flaked coconut
1 unbaked 9-inch pastry shell

Combine sugar, flour, and cornmeal, mixing well. Combine eggs and next 3 ingredients; add to sugar mixture, stirring well. Add coconut; pour into pastry shell. Bake at 350° for 35 minutes or until filling is set. Yield: one 9-inch pie.

Jodie McCoy
Tulsa, Oklahoma

YOGURT-LEMON-NUT CAKE

½ cup finely chopped walnuts
2 tablespoons sugar
1 teaspoon grated lemon rind
1 cup butter or margarine,
  softened
1 cup sugar
4 eggs
2½ cups all-purpose flour
1 teaspoon baking powder
1 teaspoon baking soda
½ teaspoon salt
1 (8-ounce) carton plain yogurt
2 teaspoons grated lemon rind
1 teaspoon vanilla extract
½ cup fresh lemon juice
½ cup sugar

Combine first 3 ingredients, stirring well; sprinkle in a greased and floured 10-inch tube pan. Set aside.

Cream butter in a large bowl; gradually add 1 cup sugar, beating well at medium speed of an electric mixer. Add eggs, one at a time, beating well after each addition.

Combine flour, baking powder, soda, and salt; add to creamed mixture alternately with yogurt, beginning and ending with flour mixture. Mix just until blended after each addition. Stir in 2 teaspoons lemon rind and vanilla.

Pour batter into prepared pan. Bake at 350° for 50 minutes or until a wooden pick inserted in center comes out clean. Cool in pan 10 minutes; remove from pan, and cool completely, sugar-nut side up, on a wire rack.

Combine lemon juice and ½ cup sugar in a small saucepan; bring to a boil, stirring until sugar dissolves. Pour hot glaze over cake. Yield: one 10-inch cake.

Peggy H. Amos
Martinsville, Virginia

WHITE CHOCOLATE BROWNIES

6 (1¼-ounce) white chocolate
  candy bars with almonds,
  divided
¼ cup butter or margarine
2 eggs
½ cup sugar
1 cup all-purpose flour
¼ teaspoon baking powder
⅛ teaspoon salt
1 teaspoon vanilla extract
¼ teaspoon almond extract
1 (1-ounce) square semisweet
  chocolate
1 teaspoon shortening

Combine 4 candy bars and butter in top of a double boiler; bring water to a boil. Reduce heat to low; cook until candy melts. Set aside to cool.

Beat eggs at medium speed of an electric mixer until thick and lemon colored; gradually add sugar, beating well. Combine flour, baking powder, and salt; add to egg mixture, mixing well. Stir in cooled candy mixture and flavorings.

Coarsely chop remaining 2 candy bars, and stir into batter. Pour batter into a greased 8-inch square pan. Bake at 350° for 25 minutes or until lightly browned. Cool on a wire rack.

Combine semisweet chocolate and shortening in a small saucepan; cook over low heat, stirring until chocolate melts. Drizzle over brownies; chill until chocolate hardens. Cut into squares. Yield: 16 brownies.

Elizabeth M. Haney
Dublin, Virginia

DOUBLE-CHIP PEANUT BUTTER COOKIES

1 cup butter or margarine,
  softened
1 cup creamy peanut butter
2 cups firmly packed brown sugar
2 eggs
1 teaspoon vanilla extract
1¼ cups all-purpose flour
1¼ cups whole wheat flour
1½ teaspoons baking soda
⅔ cup sesame seeds, toasted
½ teaspoon ground nutmeg
⅔ cup semisweet chocolate
  morsels
⅔ cup peanut butter morsels

Cream butter and peanut butter; gradually add brown sugar, beating well at medium speed of an electric mixer. Add eggs and vanilla, mixing well. Combine flours, soda, sesame seeds, and nutmeg; add to creamed mixture, and beat until smooth. Stir in morsels. Shape dough into 1-inch balls. Place on lightly greased cookie sheets. Bake at 350° for 11 to 13 minutes. Cool on wire racks. Yield: 7 dozen.

Vivian Levine
Oak Ridge, Tennessee

Try A Beverage For Dessert

These beverages satisfy your craving for something sweet, yet they're easier to make than a fussy dessert.

Brandy Velvet is as smooth as its name implies. Coffee ice cream, brandy, and coffee are combined with chocolate syrup. Bourbon gives Mocha Chocolate Fluff its flavor.

It's hard to refuse chocolate, but these fruit combinations may tempt you. Fresh strawberries lend luscious sweetness to Coco-Berry Calypso and Frozen Pink Vodka. Frozen raspberries and sherbet give rich flavor to Raspberry Cooler.

Because there is ice, ice cream, or sherbet in these beverages, it is best to prepare them just before serving. But if you have any left over, place the blender in the freezer for up to 45 minutes, and whirl the mixture again just before serving.

FROZEN PINK VODKA

1 (6-ounce) can frozen pink
    lemonade concentrate,
    undiluted
1 cup vodka
1 cup fresh whole strawberries
Ice cubes

Combine first 3 ingredients in container of an electric blender; add ice to make 5 cups. Process until smooth. Yield: 5 cups. *Terri Cohen*
Germantown, Maryland

CHOCOLATE MINT SHAKE

1 pint chocolate ice cream
½ cup milk
2 tablespoons white crème de
    menthe
1 teaspoon vanilla extract
½ teaspoon ground nutmeg

Combine all ingredients in container of an electric blender; blend until smooth. Serve immediately. Yield: 2½ cups. *Libby Winstead*
Nashville, Tennessee

BANANA-CHOCOLATE MALT

2 ripe bananas, chilled
¾ cup vanilla ice cream
¼ cup plus 2 tablespoons
    chocolate syrup
2 tablespoons malted milk powder
2 cups cold milk

Combine first 4 ingredients in container of an electric blender; blend until smooth. Add milk, and process until frothy. Serve immediately. Yield: 1 quart. *Barbara Devero*
Stroud, Oklahoma

MOCHA CHOCOLATE FLUFF

½ cup hot strong coffee
2 (1.65-ounce) bars milk
    chocolate, broken
⅓ to ½ cup bourbon
5 to 6 ice cubes
1 pint vanilla ice cream
Grated chocolate (optional)

Combine coffee and pieces of chocolate in container of an electric blender; blend mixture until smooth. Let cool.

Add bourbon and ice to coffee-chocolate mixture; blend until smooth. Add ice cream, and blend until mixture is smooth. Sprinkle individual servings with grated chocolate, if desired. Yield: 1 quart.

BRANDY VELVET

½ teaspoon instant coffee
    granules
¼ cup hot water
1 pint coffee ice cream
¼ cup brandy
¼ cup chocolate syrup
Grated chocolate (optional)

Combine coffee granules and hot water to make a strong coffee. Combine coffee, ice cream, brandy, and chocolate syrup in container of an electric blender; process until mixture is smooth. Pour into glasses; sprinkle each serving with grated chocolate, if desired. Serve immediately. Yield: 5 cups. *Zoe Newton*
Fort Smith, Arkansas

COCO-BERRY CALYPSO

3 cups fresh strawberries
1 (8.5-ounce) can cream of
    coconut
Ice cubes

Combine strawberries and cream of coconut in container of an electric blender; process until smooth. Add enough ice cubes to bring mixture to 4½-cup level. Blend until slushy. Serve immediately. Yield: 4½ cups.

Mrs. Grant Adkins
Wichita Falls, Texas

RASPBERRY COOLER

1 (10-ounce) package frozen
    raspberries, thawed
2 cups apple juice
1 cup raspberry sherbet

Combine raspberries and apple juice in container of an electric blender; process until smooth. Strain mixture; discard seeds. Return mixture to blender container; add sherbet, and process until smooth. Serve in glasses. Yield: about 4 cups.

Mrs. Grant Adkins
Wichita Falls, Texas

CITRUS FLOAT

1 pint orange or lemon sherbet
¼ cup frozen orange juice
    concentrate, undiluted
¾ cup cold water
1 (12-ounce) can ginger ale,
    chilled

Combine first 3 ingredients in container of an electric blender; blend.

Set A Summer Table Outdoors

You don't have to bring out the good china to set a fancy table. An outdoor table setting can have all the graciousness of formal dining, yet be as carefree as summer itself.

The Place Settings

Set the table on a shiny, brightly-colored plastic covering with coordinated picnic paraphernalia. Layer each place setting, starting with paper lace doilies. Then top with white plastic service plates that frame colored paper plates. Besides accenting the colored plates, the sturdier service plates lend support when the paper ones are filled.

Match plastic cups to the covering, and napkins to the plates. Nestle utensils inside napkins.

The Centerpiece

For a centerpiece, use three paper luminaries as vases. These bags with cutout designs are usually weighted with sand and illuminated with a candle for outdoor parties in the evening. However, for this centerpiece, their designs are highlighted with a contrasting sheet of tissue paper. Then flowers, in jars of water, can be put in the bags.

To give the table a festive look, sprinkle Mylar confetti, and drape curling ribbon. You can make the curling ribbon as thin as spaghetti with a shredder, an inexpensive tool usually available where party decorations are sold. Curl the ribbon; then clamp the shredder onto the ribbon, and pull it through.

Pour ½ cup sherbet mixture into each of 4 glasses; add one-fourth of ginger ale to each. Stir gently. Serve immediately. Yield: 3¼ cups.

Mrs. M. L. Shannon
Fairfield, Alabama

MOCHA POLKA

1 pint chocolate ice cream
2 cups cold coffee
1 tablespoon rum
Whipped cream
Ground nutmeg

Combine ice cream, coffee, and rum in container of an electric blender; blend until smooth. Pour into glasses, and top with whipped cream. Sprinkle with nutmeg, and serve immediately. Yield: 4 cups.

Doris T. Ramsey
Martinsville, Virginia

Tip: *For an interesting change, use fresh pineapple, cantaloupe, or other shells as containers for dips and spreads. Pineapple halves scooped out are beautiful for serving cheese dips or salads. Other fruit shells, such as melon, are nice containers for salads or appetizers.*

Light Ways With Summer Vegetables

Fresh vegetables—luscious green and red tomatoes, squash, okra, corn, peppers, green beans, butterbeans, and Vidalia onions—are some of the pleasures of summer's garden.

Today, nutrition-conscious Southerners have developed light methods of preparing favorite vegetables while preserving traditional flavor. One of the ways is through seasoning. A whole new world of flavor possibilities is opened up by seasoning favorite vegetables with low-calorie herbs and spices.

As you prepare fresh vegetables, keep the following recommendations in mind. Preserve the natural goodness of fresh vegetables by handling them properly from the time they are purchased or harvested until they're served. Store them in a cool, dry place away from light, and cook them as soon as possible to retain the most vitamins.

FRESH CORN PUDDING
(pictured on page 149)

2 cups corn cut from cob
 (about 4 medium ears)
1 tablespoon minced green
 pepper
1½ tablespoons all-purpose flour
2 teaspoons sugar
¼ teaspoon salt
¼ teaspoon mace
Dash of red pepper
½ cup egg substitute
1 cup evaporated skimmed milk
Vegetable cooking spray

Combine corn, green pepper, flour, sugar, salt, mace, and red pepper, stirring well. Combine egg substitute and evaporated skimmed milk; add to corn mixture.

Spoon mixture into a 1-quart casserole coated with cooking spray. Place dish in a large shallow pan; add water to a depth of 1 inch to pan. Bake at 350° for 1 hour or until a knife inserted in center comes out clean. Yield: 6 servings (102 calories per ½-cup serving).

□ *7.1 grams protein, 0.8 gram fat, 18.1 grams carbohydrate, 2 milligrams cholesterol, 185 milligrams sodium, and 133 milligrams calcium.*

VEGETABLE RAGOUT

Vegetable cooking spray
1½ cups chopped onion
1 cup chopped green pepper
3 cloves garlic, minced
4 cups peeled and cubed eggplant
 (about 1 medium)
2¾ cups sliced yellow squash or
 zucchini (about 4 medium)
1 cup chopped tomato
½ cup chopped mushrooms
½ teaspoon dried Italian
 seasoning
½ teaspoon salt
¼ teaspoon pepper
1 cup sliced okra

Coat a large Dutch oven with cooking spray; place over medium-high heat until hot. Add onion, green pepper, and garlic; sauté about 3 minutes. Stir in eggplant and next 6 ingredients; cook 5 to 8 minutes, stirring often. Add okra; cook about 5 minutes, stirring often. Yield: 6 servings (66 calories per 1-cup serving).

□ *2.9 grams protein, 0.7 gram fat, 14.4 grams carbohydrate, 0 milligrams cholesterol, 205 milligrams sodium, and 71 milligrams calcium.*
Candice Sanders
Nashville, Tennessee

STUFFED VIDALIA ONIONS
(pictured on pages 186 and 187)

4 medium-size Vidalia onions
 (about 1½ pounds)
2 tablespoons oil-free Italian
 dressing
½ cup diced sweet red pepper
1 cup diced zucchini
½ cup soft breadcrumbs
½ cup (2 ounces) shredded
 part-skim mozzarella cheese
2 tablespoons minced fresh
 parsley
¼ teaspoon dried whole oregano
Dash of hot sauce
Vegetable cooking spray
Paprika (optional)
Fresh parsley sprigs (optional)

Peel onions, and cut a slice from top and bottom; chop slices, and set aside. Cook onions in boiling water 15 to 20 minutes or until tender but not mushy. Cool. Remove center of onions, leaving shells intact; reserve onion centers for use in other recipes. Set onion shells aside.

Heat Italian dressing in a medium skillet until hot; add chopped onion, red pepper, and zucchini, and sauté until tender. Remove from heat; stir in breadcrumbs, cheese, minced parsley, oregano, and hot sauce.

Fill each onion shell with ½ cup vegetable mixture; place in an 8-inch square baking dish coated with cooking spray. Cover and bake at 350° for 20 minutes. Uncover and bake an additional 5 minutes. If desired, garnish with paprika and fresh parsley sprigs. Yield: 4 servings (111 calories per stuffed onion).

☐ *5.9 grams protein, 3.2 grams fat, 14.9 grams carbohydrate, 9 milligrams cholesterol, 245 milligrams sodium, and 128 milligrams calcium.*

SWEET-AND-SOUR SNAP BEANS

4 cups snapped fresh green beans (about 1 pound)
Vegetable cooking spray
¼ cup chopped onion
1 teaspoon cornstarch
¾ cup water, divided
¼ cup white vinegar
1 tablespoon sugar
¼ teaspoon salt
Dash of pepper
2 whole cloves
1 bay leaf

Place beans in a vegetable steamer over boiling water. Cover and steam 20 minutes.

Coat a nonstick skillet with cooking spray; place over medium-high heat until hot. Add onion, and sauté until tender. Combine cornstarch and ¼ cup water; add to onion mixture. Cook 1 minute, stirring constantly. Add remaining ½ cup water and remaining ingredients, stirring until smooth. Add beans; cover and cook over low heat 15 minutes or until beans are tender. Discard cloves and bay leaf. Yield: 6 servings (38 calories per ½-cup serving).

☐ *1.4 grams protein, 0.2 gram fat, 8.9 grams carbohydrate, 0 milligrams cholesterol, 102 milligrams sodium, and 31 milligrams calcium.*

STUFFED POTATOES

2 large baking potatoes (about 1¼ pounds)
Vegetable cooking spray
¼ cup plain nonfat yogurt
2 tablespoons minced chives
2 tablespoons grated Parmesan cheese
1 tablespoon skim milk
½ teaspoon salt
⅛ teaspoon garlic powder
Dash of pepper
¼ teaspoon paprika

Wash potatoes, and spray with cooking spray. Bake at 375° for 1 hour or until done. Let cool to touch. Cut potatoes in half lengthwise. Scoop out pulp, leaving a ¼-inch shell. Set shells aside. Combine potato pulp, yogurt, and next 6 ingredients in a medium bowl; mash until light and fluffy. Pipe or spoon potato mixture into shells. Place potatoes on an ungreased baking sheet. Sprinkle with paprika, and bake, uncovered, 10 minutes or until thoroughly heated. Yield: 4 servings (116 calories each).

☐ *4.8 grams protein, 1.1 grams fat, 22.4 grams carbohydrate, 2 milligrams cholesterol, 361 milligrams sodium, and 87 milligrams calcium.*
Susan Buckmaster
Charlotte, North Carolina

OKRA-AND-TOMATO BAKE

Vegetable cooking spray
3 cups sliced fresh okra
2 ounces chopped Canadian bacon
1 large tomato, chopped
1 medium onion, thinly sliced
¼ teaspoon salt
¼ teaspoon freshly ground pepper
2 tablespoons water

Coat a 1¾-quart casserole with cooking spray. Layer half of okra, Canadian bacon, tomato, and onion slices. Sprinkle evenly with ⅛ teaspoon salt

and ⅛ teaspoon pepper. Repeat layers. Sprinkle water over vegetables. Cover and bake at 350° for 40 to 45 minutes or until vegetables are tender. Yield: 6 servings (58 calories per ⅔-cup serving).

☐ *4.1 grams protein, 1.1 grams fat, 9.6 grams carbohydrate, 5 milligrams cholesterol, 239 milligrams sodium, and 61 milligrams calcium.*
Fran Ginn
Columbia, Mississippi

HERBED TOMATO SLICES
(pictured on pages 186 and 187)

15 (½-inch-thick) tomato slices
Vegetable cooking spray
⅓ cup Italian-seasoned breadcrumbs
2 tablespoons grated Parmesan cheese
¾ teaspoon finely chopped fresh basil or ¼ teaspoon dried whole basil
1 tablespoon reduced-calorie margarine, melted
Fresh basil sprigs (optional)

Arrange tomato slices in a 13- x 9- x 2-inch baking dish coated with cooking spray; set aside.

Combine breadcrumbs and next 3 ingredients; mix well. Sprinkle evenly over tomato slices; bake at 350° for 20 to 25 minutes. Garnish with basil sprigs, if desired. Yield: 5 servings (71 calories per 3-slice serving).

☐ *2.9 grams protein, 2.6 grams fat, 10.3 grams carbohydrate, 2 milligrams cholesterol, 280 milligrams sodium, and 44 milligrams calcium.*
Therese M. Golden
Wheaton, Maryland

"FRIED" GREEN TOMATOES

8 (½-inch-thick) green tomato
  slices
Butter-flavored vegetable cooking
  spray
1 tablespoon commercial oil-free
  Italian dressing
½ cup soft breadcrumbs
⅛ teaspoon salt
⅛ teaspoon onion powder
⅛ teaspoon pepper

Arrange tomato slices on a baking
sheet coated with cooking spray;
brush dressing on each slice. Combine remaining ingredients; spoon 1
tablespoon of crumb mixture on each
tomato slice. Spray each slice with
cooking spray. Bake at 400° for 18 to
20 minutes. Yield: 4 servings (81 calories per 2-slice serving).

□ 2.8 grams protein, 1.4 grams fat,
14.7 grams carbohydrate, 1 milligram
cholesterol, 219 milligrams sodium,
and 30 milligrams calcium.

Olive Oil Flatters Vegetables

Olive oil and herbs give these vegetable recipes pizzazz and offer many
tasty ways to enjoy the bounty of
summer vegetables. One combination, Fresh Basil Oil, provides many
options; you may even use the mixture on such vegetables as sweet red
peppers and squash.

FRESH BASIL OIL

1 clove garlic
½ small hot pepper, seeded
1 cup loosely packed fresh basil
1½ cups olive oil, divided
1 teaspoon salt

Position knife blade in food processor
bowl; add garlic and pepper. Pulse 2
or 3 times or until garlic and pepper
are minced. Add basil, ¼ cup olive
oil, and salt, and process until basil is
minced.
  Spoon mixture into a pint jar, and
add remaining 1¼ cups olive oil.
Cover tightly, and shake vigorously.
  Store mixture in refrigerator up to
1 week. To serve, toss a small
amount of flavored oil over steamed
yellow squash, red pepper, or carrots. Yield: 1¾ cups.   *Ann Kersey*
               Birmingham, Alabama

MARINATED TOMATOES

3 large tomatoes
⅓ cup olive oil
¼ cup red wine vinegar
1 teaspoon salt
¼ teaspoon pepper
½ clove garlic, crushed
1 tablespoon chopped parsley
1 tablespoon chopped fresh basil
  or 1 teaspoon dried whole basil
2 tablespoons chopped onion

Cut tomatoes into ½-inch-thick
slices, and arrange in a large shallow
dish; set aside.
  Combine remaining ingredients in a
jar; cover tightly, and shake vigorously. Pour over tomato slices.
Cover and marinate in refrigerator
several hours. Yield: 6 servings.
               Cheryl Keener
           Lenoir, North Carolina

GRILLED EGGPLANT

2 medium eggplants, unpeeled
  (about 2½ pounds)
¼ cup olive oil
2 tablespoons lemon juice
2 cloves garlic, crushed
2 teaspoons fresh thyme leaves
2 teaspoons fresh rosemary
  leaves
½ teaspoon salt
½ teaspoon pepper

Cut eggplants into ¾-inch slices.
Combine olive oil, lemon juice, and
garlic. Combine remaining ingredients. Brush oil mixture and sprinkle
herbs on each side of eggplant.
  Grill, covered, over medium-hot
coals 5 minutes; turn and grill an additional 5 minutes or to desired degree of doneness. Yield: 8 servings.

RATATOUILLE

1 small eggplant, peeled and
  cubed
3 medium zucchini, cut into
  ½-inch slices
2 large tomatoes, peeled and
  chopped
1 large onion, sliced
1 green pepper, cut into strips
¼ cup minced fresh parsley
1 tablespoon chopped fresh basil
½ teaspoon salt
¼ teaspoon pepper
3 tablespoons olive oil

Combine all ingredients in a large
Dutch oven. Bring to a boil; cover,
reduce heat, and cook 15 minutes,
stirring occasionally. Yield: 8
servings.   *Jeanne S. Hotaling*
               Augusta, Georgia

POTATOES ITALIANO

5 medium-size red potatoes (about
  2 pounds)
2 tablespoons chopped parsley
2 tablespoons chopped green
  onions
¼ cup olive oil
2 tablespoons tarragon vinegar
1 small clove garlic, minced
¾ teaspoon Worcestershire sauce
¾ teaspoon seasoned salt
½ teaspoon sugar
⅛ teaspoon dry mustard

Cook potatoes in unsalted water 25
minutes or until tender. Drain and
cool. Cut potatoes into ½-inch slices.

Combine potatoes, parsley, and green onions in a salad bowl. Combine remaining ingredients; pour over potatoes, tossing gently. Cover and let stand at room temperature 30 minutes. Yield: 4 to 6 servings.

Mrs. Farmer L. Burns
New Orleans, Louisiana

From Our Kitchen To Yours

Luminous, golden olive oil is becoming a Southern pantry staple. While lending distinctive flavor to many foods, this oil is also attracting attention for its health benefits. Not only is olive oil cholesterol free, but it is also a rich source of monounsaturated fat, which has the ability to lower blood cholesterol. Although there are advantages to substituting monounsaturated fat for other fats in the diet, olive oil, like all oils, has nine calories per gram. When using olive oil, follow nutritional guidelines to keep your fat intake down to 30% of your total daily calories.

Olive oil characteristics vary from heavy and robust to delicate and mild. Choosing an oil from the many varieties at the supermarket may be confusing. However, it can be simple when you understand the terminology on the manufacturer's label.

Varieties of Olive Oil

Olive oil is traditionally graded into categories based on its acidity—the lower the acidity, the stronger the olive flavor. The top category is extra virgin, which has the finest flavor, color, and aroma. You will probably find this lightest, most natural-tasting oil, with an acidity of less than 1%, to be the most expensive. Fine virgin olive oil, with an acidity rate of 1.5%, and virgin olive oil, with a higher acidity ranging up to 3%, are also quality oils.

When the acidity is greater than 3%, the oil must be refined. The refining process removes the extra acid; however, it also removes color, aroma, and flavor, leaving a tasteless product. To enhance the flavor and aroma, manufacturers blend virgin or extra virgin oil with the refined oil and label the product pure olive oil.

Light olive oil is a pure olive oil made with very little virgin oil. This product is for consumers who want to use olive oil with only a hint of the olive flavor. Less pungent and lighter in flavor, it is not lower in calories than other olive oils. But unlike extra virgin olive oil, it withstands higher temperatures without breaking down or smoking.

Selecting Olive Oil

When selecting an olive oil, consider its distinct flavor. Extra virgin or fine virgin olive oil offers richer olive flavor in marinades, salads, salad dressings, and pastas. Either is ideal for sautéing, grilling, and roasting; however, when olive oil is heated, the flavor becomes more subtle, making a less expensive oil a wiser choice for cooking.

Storing Olive Oil

Detecting "off" flavors can be difficult. It should be used within two years of pressing, but the manufacturers don't print pressing dates. It's best to buy in small quantities and keep tightly sealed and stored in a cool, dry place, protected from direct light. Under very hot, humid conditions, refrigeration may be necessary; however, chilled oil turns thick and cloudy. (These changes are not harmful.) To clear the oil, let it come to room temperature.

Flavored Olive Oil

To add an herbal taste to dressings, marinades, and sauces, use a flavored olive oil. When brushed on during grilling, these oils also enhance meat, fish, and vegetables. While available in some supermarkets, flavored olive oils can also be easily made. Loosely fill a clear jar with a fresh herb of your choice, and add enough mild-flavored olive oil to

cover the herb. (The herb must be submerged in the oil at all times.) Cover the jar tightly, and let stand at room temperature for two weeks. Carefully strain the oil, discarding the herb; then check the flavor. If a stronger flavor is desired, repeat the process, using fresh herbs. Pour into an airtight container; label and store in a cool, dark place. For gift-giving, add a fresh herb sprig to the oil, with suggestions for use.

Sweeten Meat Salads With Fruit

Spruce up your next luncheon or light supper by adding fruit to one of these meat salads featuring turkey, ham, or chicken. Pineapple, oranges, grapes, and apple add interesting textures, sweet flavors, and colorful garnishing.

TROPICAL HAM SALAD

1 large pineapple
2 cups cubed cooked ham
1 cup sliced celery
2 tablespoons chopped green pepper
½ cup mayonnaise
1 teaspoon prepared mustard
Lettuce leaves

Cut pineapple lengthwise into quarters, keeping leaves intact. Cut out pulp, leaving shells ½-inch thick; set shells aside.

Cut pineapple into bite-size pieces, discarding core. Combine pineapple and remaining ingredients except lettuce; toss gently. Chill.

Arrange pineapple shells on individual lettuce-lined plates. Spoon salad mixture into pineapple shells. Yield: 4 servings. *Alice M. Snyder*
Mount Rainier, Maryland

FRUIT-AND-TURKEY SALAD

2 cups chopped cooked turkey
½ cup sliced celery
½ cup plain low-fat yogurt
1 tablespoon mayonnaise
1 tablespoon honey
1 teaspoon grated orange rind
⅛ teaspoon salt
2 medium oranges, peeled and
    sectioned
Lettuce leaves
1 cup fresh strawberries, halved
1 small banana, sliced

Combine turkey and celery; set aside. Combine yogurt and next 4 ingredients; pour over turkey mixture, and toss gently. Cover and chill thoroughly.

Arrange orange sections on individual lettuce-lined plates. Just before serving, add strawberries and banana to turkey mixture; toss gently, and spoon onto plates. Yield: 4 servings.
Mildred Bickley
Bristol, Virginia

CHICKEN SALAD SUPREME

4 cups chopped cooked chicken
2 cups seedless grapes (about ¾
    pound)
½ cup slivered almonds, toasted
½ cup mayonnaise
¼ cup sour cream
1 tablespoon lemon juice
¼ cup chutney
½ teaspoon salt
⅛ teaspoon pepper
Lettuce leaves
Hard-cooked eggs, quartered
    (optional)

Combine chicken, grapes, and almonds. Combine mayonnaise and next 5 ingredients in a small bowl; add to chicken mixture, and toss well. Cover and chill.

Serve on lettuce leaves. Garnish with hard-cooked eggs, if desired. Yield: about 6 servings.
Mrs. E. O'Brien
Richmond, Virginia

CURRIED CHICKEN SALAD

1 (8-ounce) can pineapple chunks,
    undrained
4 cups diced cooked chicken
¼ cup chopped celery
2 tablespoons chopped green
    onions
⅓ cup toasted slivered almonds
⅓ cup raisins
⅔ cup mayonnaise
1 tablespoon Dijon mustard
¾ teaspoon curry powder
⅛ teaspoon salt
Lettuce leaves
Pineapple slices (optional)
Onion fans (optional)

Drain pineapple, reserving 2 tablespoons juice. Combine pineapple, chicken, and next 4 ingredients.

Combine reserved pineapple juice, mayonnaise, mustard, curry, and salt; add to chicken mixture, and toss well. Cover and chill. Serve on lettuce. If desired, garnish with pineapple slices and onion fans. Yield: 5 servings.
Sue Corhern
Tupelo, Mississippi

Sizzling Stir-Fry Creations

It's not just Chinese anymore. The wok has met growing acceptance as a versatile, enjoyable cooking tool, and more people are discovering the wonderful world of stir-frying.

Innovation is the key. Zucchini and tomatoes flecked with basil and oregano in Herb-Chicken Stir-Fry lend an Italian twist to the age-old art of stir-frying. It's an international culinary blend that your family is sure to love.

And as the cook, you'll love the quickness of this cooking method. One working wife and mother says she likes to serve her own creation, Shrimp and Refried Rice, to midweek dinner guests.

SHRIMP AND REFRIED RICE

1 pound unpeeled medium-size
    fresh shrimp
2 tablespoons vegetable oil
¼ cup chopped onion
2 tablespoons chopped sweet red
    pepper
1 (8-ounce) can sliced water
    chestnuts, drained
½ cup sliced fresh mushrooms
1½ cups fresh broccoli flowerets
3 tablespoons soy sauce
1 egg, beaten
1½ cups cooked rice

Peel and devein shrimp; set aside.
Pour oil around top of preheated wok or skillet, coating sides; heat at medium high (325°) for 1 minute. Add onion and pepper; stir-fry 2 minutes. Add shrimp, water chestnuts, and next 3 ingredients; cook, stirring constantly, 5 minutes. Push shrimp mixture up sides of wok, forming a well in center. Pour egg into well, and stir-fry until set. Stir shrimp mixture into egg. Add rice; stir-fry 1 to 2 minutes. Serve immediately. Yield: 4 servings.
Mrs. Billie Taylor
Wytheville, Virginia

PINEAPPLE-CHICKEN STIR-FRY

¼ cup soy sauce
2 tablespoons cornstarch
½ teaspoon ground ginger
1 tablespoon vegetable oil
4 chicken breast halves, skinned,
    boned, and cut into 1-inch
    pieces
1 clove garlic, minced
1 (20-ounce) can unsweetened
    pineapple chunks,
    undrained
1 pound fresh broccoli, cut into
    flowerets
1 large carrot, sliced
1 medium onion, sliced and
    separated into rings
Hot cooked rice

Combine soy sauce, cornstarch, and ginger in a small bowl; set aside.

Pour oil around top of preheated wok or skillet, coating sides; heat at medium high (325°) for 1 minute. Add chicken and garlic; stir-fry 2 to 3 minutes. Add pineapple, broccoli, carrot slices, and onion rings; cover and cook 3 to 4 minutes or until vegetables are crisp-tender. Add soy sauce mixture, and stir-fry until sauce bubbles and thickens. Serve pineapple-chicken mixture over hot cooked rice. Yield: 4 to 6 servings.

Mrs. Homer Baxter
Charleston, West Virginia

QUICK!

One-Dish Meals

One-dish meals make busy days easier. Add a green salad or toasted French bread to transform these recipes into complete meals. The ingredients for most of these recipes are shelf staples. Keep them on hand for fast entrées, or keep a copy of these recipes in a small notebook so that you can stop by the grocery store at day's end.

HERB-CHICKEN STIR-FRY

2 tablespoons all-purpose flour
2 teaspoons chicken-flavored bouillon granules
1 teaspoon seasoned salt
½ teaspoon dried whole basil
¼ teaspoon dried whole oregano
¾ cup water
2 tablespoons vegetable oil
1 small onion, chopped
1 clove garlic, minced
4 chicken breast halves, skinned, boned, and cut into 1-inch pieces
3 medium zucchini, thinly sliced
3 tomatoes, peeled and cut into eighths
Chow mein noodles (optional)

Combine first 6 ingredients.
Pour oil around top of preheated wok or skillet, coating sides; heat at medium high (325°) for 1 minute. Add onion and garlic; stir-fry until tender. Remove onion mixture from wok, and set aside.
Add chicken to wok; stir-fry 3 to 4 minutes. Remove from wok. Add zucchini to wok; cook, stirring constantly, 5 minutes. Add herb mixture and tomatoes; stir-fry until bubbly.
Return chicken and onion mixture to wok; stir-fry 1 minute. Serve with chow mein noodles, if desired. Yield: 4 to 6 servings. *Robert Macha*
Marlin, Texas

TACO PIZZA

2 cups biscuit mix
½ cup cold water
1 pound ground beef
1 cup water
1 (15½-ounce) can Mexican-style chili beans, undrained
1 (1¼-ounce) package taco seasoning mix
1 cup (4 ounces) shredded Cheddar cheese
1 cup crushed tortilla chips or corn chips
Shredded lettuce
Chopped tomatoes
Commercial taco sauce

Combine biscuit mix and ½ cup cold water; stir with a fork until a soft dough forms. Pat dough evenly into a lightly greased, 12-inch round pizza pan, forming ½-inch edge; prick bottom and sides with a fork. Bake at 425° for 10 minutes or until crust is lightly browned. Set aside.
Cook ground beef in a skillet until meat is browned, stirring to crumble. Drain off pan drippings; stir in 1 cup water, beans, and taco seasoning. Reduce heat, and simmer, uncovered, 5 minutes, stirring occasionally.
Spoon mixture over crust; top with cheese. Bake at 425° for 5 minutes.

Top with crushed corn chips, lettuce, and tomatoes. Serve immediately with commercial taco sauce. Yield: one 12-inch pizza.

Note: To microwave 1 pound ground beef, crumble into a microwave-safe colander; place colander in a 9-inch pieplate. Cover with wax paper, and microwave at HIGH 5 to 6 minutes or until meat is no longer pink, stirring once. *Barb Eyster*
Chapel Hill, North Carolina

CHICKEN CARUSO AND RICE

1 cup uncooked long-grain rice
4 skinned and boned chicken breast halves
¼ teaspoon garlic salt
¼ teaspoon pepper
2 cups sliced celery
2 tablespoons butter or margarine, melted
1 (15½-ounce) jar spaghetti sauce
1 teaspoon dried Italian seasoning
Grated Parmesan cheese (optional)

Cook rice according to package directions; set aside.
Cut chicken into ¼-inch strips; sprinkle with garlic salt and pepper. Sauté chicken and celery in butter in a nonstick skillet 4 to 5 minutes or until chicken is no longer pink. Stir in spaghetti sauce and Italian seasoning. Bring mixture to a boil; cover, reduce heat, and simmer 10 minutes. Serve over rice, and, if desired, sprinkle with grated Parmesan cheese. Yield: 4 to 6 servings.

Debbie Rendon
Pinellas Park, Florida

QUICK TURKEY DIVAN

12 thin slices baked turkey
(about 1¼ pounds)
2 (10-ounce) packages frozen
broccoli spears, thawed
1 (10¾-ounce) can cream of
chicken soup, undiluted
1 (4-ounce) package shredded
Cheddar cheese

Wrap turkey slices around broccoli spears; place in a lightly greased 12- x 8- x 2-inch baking dish. Spread soup over turkey rolls; cover with foil, and bake at 375° for 20 minutes. Uncover, top with cheese, and bake an additional 5 minutes. Yield: 6 to 8 servings.
Ranae Phelps
Dallas, Texas

BLACK BEANS AND RICE

1 (3½-ounce) bag pre-cooked
long-grain rice
1 (15-ounce) can black beans,
undrained
2 tablespoons salt-free
herb-and-spice blend
⅛ teaspoon pepper
½ cup (2 ounces) shredded sharp
Cheddar cheese
1 small onion, chopped
1 tomato, chopped (optional)

Cook rice according to package directions; set aside.
Combine beans, herb-and-spice blend, and pepper in a saucepan; bring to a boil, stirring constantly.
Spoon rice onto a serving platter. Pour bean mixture over rice. Top with cheese, onion, and, if desired, tomato. Yield: 3 servings.
Jan Griffin
Jacksonville, Florida

LINGUINE WITH CLAM SAUCE

1 (16-ounce) package linguine
2 cloves garlic, minced
½ cup butter or margarine,
melted
2 (6½-ounce) cans minced clams,
drained
½ teaspoon dried whole basil
½ teaspoon dried whole oregano
¼ teaspoon salt
¼ teaspoon pepper
½ cup chopped fresh parsley
1 cup grated Parmesan cheese

Cook linguine in a Dutch oven according to package directions. Drain and return to Dutch oven; set aside.
Sauté garlic in butter in a medium skillet; add clams and next 4 ingredients. Cook over low heat, stirring constantly, 5 minutes. Pour over hot cooked linguine; add parsley, and toss gently. Place on a warm platter, and top with Parmesan cheese. Yield: 4 to 6 servings.
Patricia Pashby
Memphis, Tennessee

Tomato Aspics
Rich With Flavor

When a Southerner mentions aspic, tomato is understood. And tomato aspic is one of the most popular side dishes served with chicken salad, especially for luncheons. We have several variations to give this favorite new appeal.

These recipes for tomato aspic offer a wide range of seasonings and vegetable combinations to embellish the tomato mixture. One of our favorites is Congealed Lemon-Tomato Salad, which is seasoned with dried sweet pepper flakes. Rubbed sage and garlic-flavored wine vinegar give this colorful salad an extra zing. Gazpacho Aspic is sure to please those who prefer to lace their aspic with a dash of hot sauce.

CONGEALED LEMON-TOMATO SALAD

1 (16-ounce) can tomatoes,
undrained
2 teaspoons dried sweet pepper
flakes
1 teaspoon dried minced green
onion
1 (3-ounce) package
lemon-flavored gelatin
⅓ cup chopped celery
⅓ cup chopped pimiento-stuffed
olives
2 tablespoons chopped purple
onion
1 tablespoon garlic-flavored wine
vinegar
¼ teaspoon dried parsley
¼ teaspoon dried basil
¼ teaspoon rubbed sage
⅛ teaspoon salt
Lettuce leaves

Pour tomatoes in container of an electric blender; process 5 seconds. Combine tomatoes, sweet pepper flakes, and green onion in a saucepan. Bring to a boil; remove from heat. Add gelatin, stirring until dissolved. Stir in celery and remaining ingredients except lettuce. Spoon mixture into 6 lightly oiled ½-cup molds or a lightly oiled 4-cup mold. Cover and chill. Unmold onto lettuce. Yield: 6 servings.
Joan E. Schultz
Maitland, Florida

ASPIC WITH
CUCUMBER-CURRY DRESSING

1 (14-ounce) can artichokes
1 (3-ounce) package
lemon-flavored gelatin
1¼ cups boiling water
1 (8-ounce) can tomato sauce
1 teaspoon celery seeds
1 tablespoon prepared horseradish
1 tablespoon white wine vinegar
Lettuce leaves
Cucumber-Curry Dressing
Cucumber slices (optional)
Artichoke wedges (optional)

Drain artichokes, reserving 2 artichokes for garnish, if desired. Coarsely chop remaining artichokes, and set aside.

Dissolve gelatin in boiling water; stir in tomato sauce and next 3 ingredients. Chill until the consistency of unbeaten egg white. Fold in chopped artichokes. Pour mixture into 8 lightly oiled ½-cup molds or a lightly oiled 4-cup mold. Cover and chill until firm. Unmold aspic onto lettuce leaves, and serve with Cucumber-Curry Dressing. If desired, garnish with cucumber slices and artichoke wedges. Yield: 8 servings.

Cucumber-Curry Dressing

1 cucumber, peeled and seeded
½ cup mayonnaise or salad
   dressing
¾ teaspoon lemon juice
¾ teaspoon curry powder

Grate cucumber, reserving ½ cup. Save remaining cucumber for other uses. Combine ½ cup cucumber and remaining ingredients. Chill thoroughly. Yield: ¾ cup.

Harry Evans Woodward
Richmond, Virginia

GAZPACHO ASPIC

1 (3-ounce) package
   lemon-flavored gelatin
1 cup boiling water
1 envelope unflavored gelatin
1¾ cups vegetable juice cocktail,
   divided
½ cup white vinegar
1 tablespoon lemon juice
½ teaspoon hot sauce
1 cup chopped celery
½ cup chopped green pepper
½ cup pimiento-stuffed olives,
   sliced
Lettuce leaves

Dissolve lemon gelatin in 1 cup boiling water.

Sprinkle unflavored gelatin over 1 cup vegetable juice cocktail in a saucepan; let stand 1 minute. Cook over low heat, stirring until gelatin dissolves. Add remaining vegetable juice, lemon gelatin mixture, vinegar, lemon juice, and hot sauce; chill until the consistency of unbeaten egg white. Fold in celery and remaining ingredients except lettuce; pour into a lightly oiled 5-cup mold. Cover and chill. Unmold onto lettuce leaves. Yield: 8 servings.

Bonnie Steele
Hagerstown, Maryland

Fish With Lively Flavor

If you're tired of bland-flavored fish, you'll appreciate these recipes that have pizzazz. Seasonings and vegetables as well as sour cream and buttermilk embellish the fish flavor.

GRILLED FISH
AND VEGETABLES

½ pound fresh mushrooms,
   sliced
3 medium tomatoes, peeled and
   cut into wedges
2 medium-size yellow squash,
   sliced
2 medium-size green peppers,
   chopped
1 medium zucchini, sliced
1 medium onion, chopped
½ cup butter or margarine
2 pounds amberjack fillets
½ cup soy sauce
1 clove garlic, pressed
¼ teaspoon pepper

Place vegetables on a 34- x 16-inch piece of heavy-duty aluminum foil, bending up edges to hold ingredients; dot with butter. Arrange fish over vegetables; top with soy sauce, garlic, and pepper. Fold foil over, sealing edges securely. Grill over hot coals 15 minutes. Pierce top side of foil at intervals with a fork; turn package over, and pierce. Grill 15 minutes. Remove from grill; serve immediately. Yield: 8 servings.

Rolinda Hans
Castroville, Texas

SPICY SNAPPER

2 medium onions, cut into ½-inch
   slices
1 sweet red pepper, cut into
   rings
1 or 2 jalapeño peppers, seeded
   and cut into thin strips
2 tablespoons vegetable oil
¼ cup seasoned or regular rice
   vinegar
¼ to ½ teaspoon dried whole
   oregano
6 red snapper fillets (about 2
   pounds)
½ teaspoon pepper
Lemon wedges (optional)
Jalapeño peppers (optional)

Sauté onion, red pepper rings, and jalapeño pepper strips in oil in a skillet until limp (about 5 minutes); add vinegar and oregano. Cook 1 minute; set aside.

Sprinkle fish fillets with pepper; place fillets in a single layer in a lightly greased 15- x 10- x 1-inch jellyroll pan, skin side down. Bake at 350° for 15 minutes.

Spoon onion and pepper mixture over fish, and bake an additional 5 minutes or until fish flakes easily when tested with a fork. Garnish with lemon wedges and jalapeño peppers, if desired. Yield: 6 servings.

Judi Grigoraci
Charleston, West Virginia

FILLET OF FISH À L'ORANGE

6 small green onions, chopped
½ pound fresh mushrooms, sliced
1 pound grouper or flounder
    fillets
¼ teaspoon salt
Freshly ground pepper
½ teaspoon dried whole Italian
    seasoning
2 tablespoons olive oil
¼ teaspoon soy sauce
½ cup white wine
¼ cup orange juice
3 tablespoons curaçao or other
    orange-flavored liqueur
Paprika
2 tablespoons minced parsley

Layer half each of green onions and mushrooms in a greased 9-inch baking dish. Add fish, and sprinkle with salt, pepper, and Italian seasoning. Add remaining green onions and mushrooms.

Combine olive oil and next 4 ingredients; pour over vegetables and fish. Cover and bake at 350° for 40 minutes or until fish is opaque. Sprinkle with paprika and parsley. Yield: 3 to 4 servings.   *Mary M. Hoppe*
Kitty Hawk, North Carolina

FISH WITH SOUR CREAM

½ cup all-purpose flour
1 teaspoon salt
¼ teaspoon pepper
6 orange roughy fillets (about
    2¼ pounds)
1½ cups buttermilk
¾ cup sour cream
1 tablespoon butter or margarine,
    melted
1 cup soft breadcrumbs
Fresh parsley sprigs

Combine flour, salt, and pepper; dredge fish in flour mixture. Arrange fish in a greased 13- x 9- x 2-inch baking dish; pour buttermilk over fish. Bake, uncovered, at 350° for 45 to 50 minutes or until fish is opaque.

Remove from oven; spread sour cream over fish. Combine butter and breadcrumbs; sprinkle over sour cream. Bake at 450° for 10 minutes or until browned. Garnish with parsley sprigs. Yield: 6 servings.
Azine G. Rush
Monroe, Louisiana

Entrées
With Convenience
In Mind

If you find yourself looking for a fast-to-fix entrée more times than you'd prefer, keep your pantry and freezer stocked with handy convenience items. Ready-to-use products can speed preparation for some tasty main dishes.

ROAST BEEF TURNOVERS

1 (10-ounce) package frozen patty
    shells, thawed
2 green onions, sliced
½ cup chopped celery
½ cup sliced mushrooms
2 tablespoons butter or
    margarine, melted
1¾ cups cubed cooked roast beef
½ cup chopped fresh parsley
¼ cup dry breadcrumbs
¼ teaspoon dried whole basil
⅛ teaspoon salt
¼ teaspoon pepper
1 egg, slightly beaten
1 tablespoon water
1½ teaspoons sesame seeds

Roll each patty shell to a 6-inch circle on a lightly floured surface.

Sauté green onions, celery, and mushrooms in butter until crisp-tender. Stir in roast beef and next 5 ingredients, mixing well. Place ¼ cup beef mixture in center of each pastry circle. Fold circle in half. Press edges of filled pastry firmly together, using a fork dipped in flour. Transfer to an ungreased baking sheet.

Combine egg and water, mixing well. Brush tops of turnovers with egg mixture; sprinkle with sesame seeds. Bake at 400° for 30 minutes or until golden brown. Serve immediately. Yield: 6 servings.
Sue-Sue Hartstern
Louisville, Kentucky

DOUBLE-CRUST TACO PIE

1 pound ground beef
1 (1¼-ounce) package taco
    seasoning mix
2 (8-ounce) cans refrigerated
    crescent dinner rolls
4 cups (16 ounces) shredded
    Monterey Jack cheese, divided
Sour cream
Commercial salsa
Jalapeño pepper slices

Cook ground beef in a skillet until browned, stirring to crumble meat. Drain well. Add taco seasoning mix, and prepare according to package directions. Set meat mixture aside.

Unroll one can of crescent rolls into two rectangles; press long sides together to make a 13- x 8-inch rectangle. Repeat process with second can of crescent rolls; set aside. Place one rectangle of dough on an ungreased baking sheet. Sprinkle with 2 cups cheese. Spread ground beef mixture evenly over cheese; sprinkle with remaining 2 cups cheese. Top with second rectangle of dough, pressing all edges to seal.

Bake at 400° for 15 minutes or until browned. Serve with sour cream, salsa, and jalapeño. Yield: 6 servings.
Joe F. Arnold
Birmingham, Alabama

PIZZA CASSEROLE

1 pound lean ground beef
1 large onion, chopped
1 green pepper, chopped
½ teaspoon garlic salt
¼ teaspoon pepper
¼ teaspoon dried whole oregano
¼ teaspoon dried whole basil
1 (14-ounce) jar commercial pizza
  sauce
1 (8-ounce) package uncooked
  macaroni
1 (3½-ounce) package sliced
  pepperoni
1 (4-ounce) package shredded
  mozzarella cheese

Combine first 3 ingredients in a large Dutch oven. Cook until meat is browned, stirring to crumble. Drain well. Return meat mixture to Dutch oven. Add garlic salt, pepper, oregano, basil, and pizza sauce, and stir well; cover, reduce heat, and simmer 15 minutes.

Cook macaroni according to package directions, omitting salt; drain. Add to meat mixture; stir well. Spoon into a lightly greased 12- x 8- x 2-inch baking dish; top evenly with pepperoni. Cover and bake at 350° for 20 minutes; top with cheese, and bake, uncovered, 5 minutes. Yield: 6 to 8 servings.   *Elizabeth M. Haney*
Dublin, Virginia

STROMBOLI

1 (16-ounce) loaf frozen bread
  dough, thawed
¼ pound thinly sliced ham
¼ pound sliced hard salami
½ teaspoon dried whole basil,
  divided
½ teaspoon dried whole oregano,
  divided
3 ounces sliced provolone cheese
1 cup (4 ounces) shredded
  mozzarella cheese
2 tablespoons butter or
  margarine, melted
1 teaspoon cornmeal

Place bread dough on a lightly greased baking sheet; pat to a 15- x 10-inch rectangle. Arrange ham slices lengthwise down center; place salami on top. Sprinkle with ¼ teaspoon basil and ¼ teaspoon oregano. Arrange provolone cheese over herbs, and top with mozzarella cheese; sprinkle with remaining herbs.

Moisten all edges of dough with water. Bring each long edge of dough to center; press edges together securely to seal. Seal ends.

Brush dough with 1 tablespoon butter. Sprinkle with cornmeal, and carefully invert. Brush top with remaining butter. Bake at 375° for 20 to 22 minutes. Yield: 4 servings.
Mrs. Robert Nesbit
Augusta, Georgia

HOT TUNA WAFFLE-WICH

1 (8½-ounce) can English peas,
  undrained
1 (10¾-ounce) can cream of
  mushroom soup, undiluted
1 (6½-ounce) can tuna, drained
  and flaked
⅛ teaspoon hot sauce
2 (5-ounce) packages frozen
  waffles
Cheese Sauce

Drain peas, reserving 2 tablespoons liquid. Combine peas, 2 tablespoons liquid, mushroom soup, tuna, and hot sauce in a saucepan. Cook over medium heat, stirring occasionally, until thoroughly heated.

Heat waffles according to package directions. Spoon about ½ cup tuna mixture on half of waffles; place remaining waffles over tuna. Top with Cheese Sauce. Yield: 4 servings.

Cheese Sauce

1 (11-ounce) can cheese soup,
  undiluted
¼ cup milk
1 teaspoon prepared mustard

Combine cheese soup and milk in a small saucepan; stir in mustard. Cook over medium heat until thoroughly heated. Yield: 1¼ cups.
Juanita Moye
West Helena, Arkansas

Take The Chill Off The Cheese

Don't wait until you dine in a restaurant to enjoy fried cheese, the popular appetizer that sports a crisp coating on the outside and warm, melting cheese oozing from the inside with each bite. It's easy to prepare this tasty delicacy at home.

The trick to frying cheese so that the crust turns golden before the inside melts through the crust is to coat the cheese with a crumb mixture and then chill it before frying. This ensures that the cheese is firm and cold before frying begins, and helps the final product turn out with the proper texture.

FRIED CHEESE BALLS

2 cups (8 ounces) shredded
  mozzarella cheese
2 egg whites
3 tablespoons all-purpose flour
½ teaspoon hot sauce
Vegetable oil

Combine cheese, egg whites, flour, and hot sauce; shape into 1-inch balls. Place cheese balls on wax paper, and chill 1 hour.

Pour oil to a depth of 2 inches into a Dutch oven; heat to 375°. Fry cheese balls in hot oil until golden brown. Drain on paper towels. Serve immediately. Yield: 2 dozen.
Mrs. H. D. Baxter
Charleston, West Virginia

FRIED CHEDDAR CHEESE

1¼ cups fine, dry breadcrumbs
1 tablespoon sesame seeds
1 (10-ounce) package sharp
  Cheddar cheese, cut into
  ½-inch cubes
2 eggs, beaten
Vegetable oil

Combine breadcrumbs and sesame seeds in a shallow dish.

Dip cheese cubes in beaten egg, and dredge in crumb mixture. Repeat procedure; place cheese on wax paper, and chill 1 hour.

Pour oil to a depth of 2 inches into a Dutch oven; heat to 375°. Fry cheese in hot oil until golden brown. Drain on paper towels. Serve immediately. Yield: 2 dozen.
Mrs. Bruce Fowler
Woodruff, South Carolina

HOT CHEESE CROQUETTES

2 cups (8 ounces) shredded sharp
  Cheddar cheese
2 cups (8 ounces) shredded Swiss
  cheese
3 tablespoons all-purpose flour
1 teaspoon salt
¼ teaspoon red pepper
4 egg whites
1¼ cups soft breadcrumbs
Vegetable oil

Position knife blade in food processor bowl. Combine first 5 ingredients in food processor bowl; process until smooth.

Beat egg whites (at room temperature) at high speed of an electric mixer until stiff peaks form. Fold beaten egg whites into cheese mixture. Shape into 1-inch balls, and roll in breadcrumbs; place cheese on wax paper, and chill 1 hour.

Pour oil to a depth of 2 inches into a Dutch oven; heat to 375°. Fry cheese balls in hot oil until golden brown. Drain on paper towels. Serve immediately. Yield: 3½ dozen.
Bobbie Trowbridge
Statesboro, Georgia

ITALIAN-STYLE
FRIED CHEESE

2 eggs, beaten
2 tablespoons soy sauce
2 tablespoons Worcestershire
  sauce
1 cup saltine cracker crumbs
2 tablespoons dried Italian
  seasoning
1 tablespoon granulated garlic
1 pound mozzarella or sharp
  Cheddar cheese, cut into
  1-inch cubes
Vegetable oil
Commercial marinara sauce
Lemon wedges (optional)
Fresh parsley sprigs (optional)

Combine first 3 ingredients; combine cracker crumbs, Italian seasoning, and garlic.

Dip cheese cubes in egg mixture; dredge in cracker mixture. Repeat procedure; place cheese on wax paper, and chill 1 hour.

Pour oil to a depth of 2 inches into a Dutch oven; heat to 375°. Fry cheese in hot oil until golden brown. Drain on paper towels. Serve immediately with marinara sauce. If desired, garnish with lemon wedges and fresh parsley sprigs. Yield: about 1½ dozen.
Susan A. Houston
Tucker, Georgia

Blend
A Healthy Shake

Toast the morning or the end of a workout with these icy-cold shakes. Yogurt (not the frozen variety) and fruit lend nutritious attributes.

These beverages are easy to prepare for a quick pick-me-up. Chilled fresh fruit may be used instead of frozen fruit, but the beverages will have a thinner consistency. You may want to buy frozen fruit to have on hand in the freezer or freeze fresh fruit—even bananas—when they are plentiful and at their finest.

TROPICAL DELIGHT

2 bananas, sliced and frozen
⅔ cup orange juice
⅔ cup plain yogurt
Ice cubes

Combine first 3 ingredients in container of an electric blender. Add enough ice cubes to bring mixture to 2½-cup level. Blend until smooth. Serve immediately. Yield: 2½ cups.

Note: Fresh fruit may be substituted, but the frozen fruit yields a thicker consistency.
Cheryl Richardson
Fairfax Station, Virginia

TWO-FRUIT SMOOTHIE

1 (8-ounce) carton plain yogurt
½ to ¾ cup milk
1 cup frozen unsweetened
  strawberries
2 bananas, sliced and frozen
1 tablespoon honey (optional)
Ice cubes

Combine first 5 ingredients in container of an electric blender. Add enough ice cubes to bring mixture to 4-cup level. Blend until smooth. Serve immediately. Yield: 4 cups.

Note: Fresh fruit may be substituted, but the frozen fruit yields a thicker consistency. *Denise Ray*
Hermitage, Tennessee

STRAWBERRY-PEACH
SMOOTHIE

1 cup frozen unsweetened
  strawberries
1 cup frozen sliced peaches
2 tablespoons strawberry jam
1 (8-ounce) carton plain yogurt
Ice cubes

Combine first 4 ingredients in container of an electric blender. Add enough ice cubes to bring mixture to 3-cup level. Blend until smooth. Serve immediately. Yield: 3 cups.

Note: Fresh fruit may be substituted, but the frozen fruit yields a thicker consistency.

Michelle D. Mueller
Seguin, Texas

RASPBERRY-AND-BANANA SHAKE

1 (8-ounce) carton raspberry yogurt
1 cup milk
1 large banana, sliced and frozen
¼ teaspoon vanilla extract
Ice cubes

Combine first 4 ingredients in container of an electric blender. Add enough ice cubes to bring mixture to 3-cup level. Blend until smooth. Serve immediately. Yield: 3 cups.

Note: Fresh fruit may be substituted, but the frozen fruit yields a thicker consistency. *Louise Ellis*
Baker, Florida

Freezing Bananas, Peaches, and Strawberries for Beverages

■ Select the ripest fruit for sweetest flavor.
■ Before freezing, peel and slice bananas and peaches. Wash and cap strawberries.
■ Freeze whole strawberries and peach and banana slices on a jellyroll pan. When frozen, transfer to freezer containers; cover and store in freezer.
■ The fruit will keep for several weeks without browning.

PEACH PICK-ME-UP

2 (8-ounce) cartons peach-flavored yogurt
1 (6-ounce) can frozen apple juice concentrate, unthawed and undiluted
⅛ teaspoon almond extract
Ice cubes

Combine peach-flavored yogurt, apple juice concentrate, and almond extract in container of an electric blender. Add enough ice cubes to bring mixture to 3-cup level. Blend until mixture is smooth. Serve beverage immediately. Yield: 3 cups.

Peggy Fowler Revels
Woodruff, South Carolina

A Dessert To Tempt Taste Buds

Chef John Wagner of the Flamingo Cafe in Destin, Florida, has created an unforgettable chocolate dessert that he has appropriately named Chocolate Decadence. Raspberry sauce, whipped cream, and fresh raspberries enhance the chocolate flavor of the brownie-like cake.

CHOCOLATE DECADENCE

16 (1-ounce) squares semisweet chocolate
⅔ cup butter or margarine
5 eggs, beaten
2 tablespoons sugar
2 tablespoons all-purpose flour
Raspberry Sauce
Whipped cream (optional)
Fresh raspberries (optional)

Line the bottom of a 9-inch springform pan with parchment paper; set pan aside.

Place chocolate and butter in top of a double boiler; bring water to a boil. Reduce heat to low; cook until chocolate and butter melt. Gradually add chocolate mixture to eggs, beating at medium speed of an electric mixer 10 minutes. Fold in sugar and flour. Pour into prepared pan. Bake at 400° for 15 minutes. (Cake will not be set in center.) Chill. Spoon about 3 tablespoons Raspberry Sauce on each dessert plate; place wedge of chocolate dessert on sauce. If desired, garnish with whipped cream and fresh raspberries. Yield: 10 to 12 servings.

Raspberry Sauce

2 cups fresh raspberries
2 cups water
¼ cup sugar
2 tablespoons cornstarch
2 tablespoons water

Combine fresh raspberries, 2 cups water, and ¼ cup sugar in a large saucepan, and bring to a boil. Reduce heat, and let mixture simmer 30 minutes. Put raspberry mixture through a food mill or sieve; discard seeds. Return raspberry mixture to saucepan, and set aside.

Combine cornstarch and 2 tablespoons water in a small bowl, stirring until mixture is smooth. Add cornstarch mixture to raspberry mixture. Cook over medium heat, stirring constantly, until mixture comes to a boil. Cook 1 additional minute, stirring constantly. Remove mixture from heat, and let cool thoroughly. Yield: 2 cups.

Luscious Strawberry Cake

Carol Plaster of Charleston, West Virginia, claims she's not a fancy cook, but after you taste her Rich White Cake With Strawberry Frosting, you'll think differently.

RICH WHITE CAKE WITH STRAWBERRY FROSTING

½ cup butter or margarine,
   softened
½ cup shortening
2 cups sugar
⅔ cup water
⅔ cup milk
3 cups sifted cake flour
1 tablespoon plus 1 teaspoon
   baking powder
1 teaspoon salt
2 teaspoons vanilla extract
1 teaspoon almond extract
6 egg whites
Strawberry Frosting
Whole fresh strawberries
   (optional)

Cream butter and shortening; gradually add sugar, beating at medium speed of an electric mixer.

Combine water and milk; set aside. Combine flour, baking powder, and salt; add to creamed mixture alternately with milk mixture, beginning and ending with flour mixture. Stir in flavorings.

Beat egg whites (at room temperature) until stiff peaks form. Gently fold into batter.

Pour batter into 3 greased and floured 9-inch round cakepans. Bake at 350° for 20 minutes or until a wooden pick inserted in center comes out clean. Cool in pans 10 minutes; remove from pans, and let cool completely on wire racks. Spread Strawberry Frosting between layers and on top and sides of cake. Garnish with whole strawberries, if desired.

Strawberry Frosting

2¼ cups whole unsweetened
   frozen strawberries
1 cup sugar
2 egg whites
Dash of salt

Thaw strawberries, and place in a strainer. Slightly mash strawberries, and let drain. Measure ⅔ cup strawberry pulp for frosting; reserve juice for other uses.

Combine pulp and remaining ingredients in top of a double boiler; place over boiling water. Beat at high speed of an electric mixer 7 minutes. Remove from heat. Yield: enough frosting for one 3-layer cake.

Rolls With A Southern Accent

It's no secret that Southerners love breads made from cornmeal, but Mrs. H. D. Baxter of Charleston, West Virginia, does more than prepare corn sticks and muffins. She tosses a little meal into her regular dough for dinner rolls and makes Cornmeal Rolls.

CORNMEAL ROLLS

2 cups milk
½ cup sugar
¼ cup shortening
¼ cup butter or margarine
2 teaspoons salt
1 package dry yeast
¼ cup warm water (105° to 115°)
2 eggs, beaten
5 to 5½ cups all-purpose flour,
   divided
1½ cups plain cornmeal
2 tablespoons butter or
   margarine, melted

Combine milk, sugar, shortening, ¼ cup butter, and salt in a saucepan; heat mixture until shortening and butter melt. Allow mixture to cool to 105° to 115°.

Dissolve yeast in warm water in a large bowl; let stand 5 minutes. Add milk mixture, eggs, and 3 cups flour; beat at medium speed of an electric mixer until smooth. Gradually stir in cornmeal and enough remaining flour to make a soft dough.

Turn dough out onto a lightly floured surface, and knead until smooth and elastic. Place in a well-greased bowl, turning to grease top. Cover and let rise in a warm place (85°), free from drafts, 1 hour or until dough is doubled in bulk.

Punch dough down; shape into 72 balls. Place 2 balls in each well-greased muffin cup. Cover and let rise in a warm place, free from drafts, 1 hour or until dough is doubled in bulk.

Bake at 375° for 15 minutes or until rolls are golden. Brush rolls with 2 tablespoons melted butter. Yield: 3 dozen.

Right: *Make a picnic of Dilled Macaroni Salad, Honey-Sweet Carrot Salad, and Croissant Sandwiches, followed with Crisp Coconut Cookies and Chocolate-Filled Bonbons. (Recipes, pages 161 and 162.)*

Page 188: *Entertain friends with a casual supper menu of Buttermilk-Pecan Chicken, Lemon Rice, Garden Salad, and Cantaloupe Sundae. (Recipes, page 166.)*

Reap the rewards of summer by serving your guests Stuffed Vidalia Onions (page 172) and Herbed Tomato Slices (page 173).

AUGUST

Succulent oysters, plump clams, and crabs with sweet,
tender meat are part of this month's seafood sampler from
Chesapeake Bay. In another feature, beef and pork are
served up leaner and easier than ever.

Pork And Beef: Leaner Than Ever

Southern agriculture and farming practices have changed, and one of the results is leaner, healthier beef and pork.

Leaner meat means two things. First, less cholesterol is consumed, which makes for healthier eating. Second, with less fat to absorb heat during cooking, meat cooks faster. Also, in response to consumer demand for quick, easy-to-prepare items, butchers are now offering a wider variety of meat cuts.

For example, pork tenderloin and top blade steak are available more often. The top blade steak is actually a smaller cut from the chuck. More familiar cuts such as pork chops are cooking faster, too. It takes approximately 15 minutes to broil a 1-inch-thick pork chop and the same amount of time to braise it.

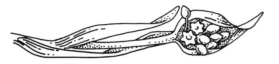

MEXICAN EYE ROUND ROAST

1 (2-pound) eye round roast
1 cup olive oil
⅔ cup lime juice
½ cup red wine vinegar
1 teaspoon coarsely ground pepper
1 teaspoon ground cumin
½ teaspoon onion powder
4 cloves garlic, crushed
Commercial salsa

Using a sharp knife, make a horizontal cut through center of roast to within ½ inch of other side. (Do not cut through.) Open roast like a book; place in a baking dish.

Combine olive oil and next 6 ingredients, stirring well; pour marinade over roast. Cover and marinate 8 hours, turning roast occasionally. Remove roast from marinade, and place on rack of a broiler pan. Bake at 425° for 45 minutes (140° rare) or to desired degree of doneness, basting with marinade occasionally.

Serve roast with salsa. Yield: 8 servings.

KOREAN STEAK

1 pound top round or top sirloin steak
¼ cup soy sauce
3 tablespoons vegetable oil
3 tablespoons sesame seeds
¼ teaspoon pepper
¼ teaspoon ground ginger
2 teaspoons brown sugar
1 clove garlic, minced
½ cup sliced green onions

Pound steak, using a meat mallet. Place steak in a large shallow dish. Combine soy sauce and remaining ingredients in a small bowl, stirring well. Pour mixture over steak; cover and allow to marinate in refrigerator 1 hour.

Remove meat from marinade, and place on lightly greased rack of a broiler pan. Broil 4 inches from heat 4 to 5 minutes; turn steak, and broil an additional 4 to 5 minutes. To serve, slice across grain into thin slices. Yield: 4 servings.

Judy R. Falls
Grapevine, Texas

Tips For Quick Meat Cookery

■ Kabobs or strips of meat cook faster than whole cuts. Marinate a beef or pork steak, and cut into strips for a stir-fry.

■ Avoid high heat for cuts that have little marbling or fat. Consider braising (cooking in a small amount of liquid) for cuts such as chuck, shoulder, and round.

■ Meat used for marinades should be about 1-inch thick. Use ⅓ to ½ cup marinade per pound of beef. You can refrigerate most meats with marinade in the morning, and they will be ready for cooking by suppertime.

■ Marinades serve two functions—to flavor and to tenderize. A tender cut, such as a sirloin steak or pork tenderloin, is often marinated to enhance flavor. A less-tender cut, such as a top round, needs marinating for tenderness. Acid—vinegar and lemon juice, for example—is what tenderizes the meat.

■ Try cooking frozen beef. Use tender cuts or ground beef, and allow one-third more cooking time. If you broil the meat, place the pan farther from the heat source (perhaps on the next rack down) to avoid burning the outside of the meat.

■ Cook your entire meal in a broiler pan by placing a vegetable brushed with Italian salad dressing or butter on the pan alongside the meat about 10 minutes before cooking is completed.

PEPPER STEAK STIR-FRY

1¼ pounds sirloin steak (1-inch thick)
½ cup canned diluted beef broth
¼ cup soy sauce
¼ cup water
1 tablespoon cornstarch
¼ cup vegetable oil
1 clove garlic, minced
1 teaspoon ground ginger
½ teaspoon salt
½ teaspoon pepper
1 large green pepper, cut into strips
1 large sweet red pepper, cut into strips
1 large onion, thinly sliced
1 (6-ounce) can sliced water chestnuts, drained
4 green onions, cut into 1-inch pieces
Hot cooked rice

Partially freeze steak; slice diagonally across the grain into 1½- x ⅛-inch strips. Set aside.

Combine beef broth, soy sauce, water, and cornstarch in a small bowl; set aside.

Heat oil in a skillet over medium-high heat; add garlic, ginger, salt, and pepper, and cook 1 minute, stirring constantly. Add steak, and cook 2 minutes or until browned; remove from skillet. Add pepper strips and onion, and cook 3 minutes or until crisp-tender. Add beef, water chestnuts, green onions, and broth mixture; cook 2 minutes or until thickened. Serve over rice. Yield: 4 to 6 servings.
Mary Waller
Winston-Salem, North Carolina

CURRIED APRICOT PORK CHOPS

4 (¾-inch-thick) pork loin chops
1 egg, beaten
¾ cup dry breadcrumbs
¼ cup vegetable oil
1 (16-ounce) can apricot halves in light syrup
2 tablespoons brown sugar
½ teaspoon curry powder
1 tablespoon butter or margarine

Dip chops in egg; dredge in breadcrumbs. Brown in hot oil; place in shallow 2-quart baking dish.

Drain apricots, reserving juice. Combine juice, brown sugar, and curry; pour over chops. Place apricots around chops. Dot with butter. Bake, uncovered, at 350° for 20 to 25 minutes or until tender. Yield: 4 servings.
Suzanne Bush
Dallas, Texas

OLIVE-PORK SCALOPPINE

½ cup all-purpose flour
½ teaspoon salt
¼ teaspoon pepper
1½ pounds pork tenderloin, cut into ½-inch slices
2 tablespoons vegetable oil
½ cup sliced green onions
½ cup dry sherry
½ cup water
½ teaspoon dried whole marjoram
½ teaspoon dried whole basil
2 cups sliced mushrooms
½ cup sliced pimiento-stuffed olives

Combine first 3 ingredients; dredge pork slices in mixture. Cook in hot oil in a large skillet until browned on both sides. Add green onions and next 4 ingredients; bring mixture to a simmer. Add mushrooms and olives; cook pork 4 minutes on each side or until tender. Yield: about 6 servings.
Beth Roaseau
Salem, Missouri

BROILED PORK CHOPS

½ cup tomato juice
2 tablespoons cider vinegar
1 tablespoon Worcestershire sauce
1 teaspoon prepared mustard
½ teaspoon sugar
¼ teaspoon salt
¼ teaspoon garlic salt
¼ teaspoon hot sauce
4 (1-inch-thick) pork chops

Combine first 8 ingredients in a small bowl, and set aside.

Place pork chops on lightly greased rack of a broiler pan; brush with tomato juice mixture. Broil 4 to 5 inches from heat 15 minutes, turning once and brushing occasionally with sauce. Yield: 4 servings.

Note: To braise pork chops, brown on both sides in 1 tablespoon vegetable oil in a large nonstick skillet; drain. Return pork chops to skillet; add tomato juice mixture. Bring mixture to a boil; cover, reduce heat, and simmer 15 minutes.
Bettye Cortner
Cerulean, Kentucky

From Our Kitchen To Yours

Slicing meat to look at the color of the juices or using an approximate cooking time in minutes per pound cannot accurately determine the degree of doneness for a large cut of meat. Suggested cooking times given in recipes and roasting charts are always approximations because the shape, thickness, and amount of fat and bone in meat vary, as will the temperature of the meat before it is cooked. Timetables are useful for estimating the total cooking time; however, reading the exact temperature is a more reliable guide. By using a meat thermometer, you can eliminate the guesswork and serve a tender, juicy entrée.

When using a dry-heat method to cook tender cuts, you should depend on a meat thermometer. Cook beef according to your preference—140° for rare, 150° for medium, or 160° for well-done. Boneless pork and veal need to be cooked to an internal temperature of 160°; cooking fully cooked hams to 140° brings out more flavor. Insert the thermometer at an angle into the thickest part of the meat. To prevent getting a distorted reading, make sure the bulb or probe doesn't touch fat, bone, or the bottom of the pan, and keep the top of the thermometer as far away from the heat source as possible. Shrinkage during cooking may cause the thermometer to shift; check occasionally to be sure it remains properly positioned.

For larger cuts, it is advisable to check the temperature more than once because the thermometer can conduct heat rapidly to the center of the meat. When the desired degree of doneness is indicated, push the thermometer into the meat a little farther, and then move it to a different area for another reading. If the temperature drops in either reading, the meat needs additional cooking. In our Test Kitchens, the home economists also use an instant-read meat thermometer, which is inserted periodically into the meat's center to check the temperature.

Because meat continues to cook slightly after it's removed from the heat source, remove it when the thermometer registers about 5 degrees lower than the desired temperature. Cover the meat loosely with aluminum foil, making sure the temperature rises to the desired level as it stands. This standing time also makes carving easier.

There are several good thermometers available. Whichever ones you choose, treat them with care. They are sensitive instruments, and in general, the more they cost, the more accurate and durable they are.

Never force the pointed probe into place, and do not wash in a dishwasher. Store your thermometer so it isn't knocked about in a drawer, and test it occasionally by putting the probe into boiling water to see if it registers 212°. If it isn't accurate, remember what allowance to make for the error. When using an instant-read thermometer, warm the probe in a little hot water before inserting it into hot meat.

The instant-read thermometer is tiny with an extremely strong, thin stem that is stored in an unbreakable nylon sheath. Unlike the roast/meat thermometer, the instant-read thermometer is never left in the meat during cooking. This thermometer will give a quick and accurate reading. It is also handy to use in testing the temperatures of egg-based sauces or steaks on the grill.

She Has A Crush On Herbs

Georgianne McGee of Waycross, Georgia, bends down in the herb garden right outside her kitchen door and gently picks a few tender, green leaves. She crushes just a portion in her palm to release the summer-fresh scent. "I can't stand to be without basil. I just keep some out, and even if I don't use it, I smell it as I walk out the door."

For fresh herb flavor, try one or more of her recipes.

SOURDOUGH DILL BREAD

Sourdough Starter

2 cups warm water (105° to 115°)
⅔ cup instant nonfat dry milk
¼ cup plus 2 tablespoons plain low-fat yogurt
2 cups all-purpose flour

Combine warm water and dry milk in a medium-size nonmetal bowl, and stir well. Stir in yogurt.

Cover starter loosely with plastic wrap or cheesecloth; let stand in a warm place (85°) 12 to 24 hours. (Mixture will be the consistency of yogurt.)

Gradually stir in flour, stirring until smooth and well blended. Cover starter loosely with plastic wrap; let stand in a warm place (85°) 2 to 4 days, stirring 2 or 3 times daily. (Mixture is ready to use when it bubbles and has a slightly sour smell.)

Place fermented mixture in refrigerator, and stir once a day. Use in 21 days. Yield: 2½ cups.

Primary Batter

1 cup Sourdough Starter
2 cups warm water (105° to 115°)
2½ cups all-purpose flour

Place 1 cup Sourdough Starter in a large nonmetal bowl; add water, and stir well. Gradually add flour, stirring until mixture is smooth. Beat at medium speed of an electric mixer about 4 minutes. Cover loosely with plastic wrap or cheesecloth; let stand in a warm place (85°) 12 hours. (A crust may form on mixture during this time. If this happens, stir mixture thoroughly.)

To use, remove 3 cups of Primary Batter for Sourdough Dill Bread. Return remaining Primary Batter to Sourdough Starter in the refrigerator. When Sourdough Starter is used again, repeat procedure for using Primary Batter. Yield: 4 cups.

Sourdough Dill Bread

3 cups Primary Batter
6 to 6½ cups all-purpose flour, divided
2 tablespoons sugar
1 cup small-curd creamed cottage cheese
1 cup milk
2 tablespoons butter or margarine
2 teaspoons salt
¼ teaspoon baking soda
2 tablespoons instant minced onion
2 to 3 teaspoons dillseeds

Place 3 cups Primary Batter in a large nonmetal bowl. Let stand at room temperature at least 1 hour. Stir in 1 cup flour and sugar. Set mixture aside.

Combine cottage cheese, milk, and butter in a saucepan; heat over low heat until butter melts, stirring occasionally. Cool to 105° to 115°. Add salt, soda, onion, and dillseeds, stirring well. Add cottage cheese mixture to Primary Batter mixture, stirring well. Add enough flour to make a soft dough. Turn dough out onto a lightly floured surface; knead 8 minutes or until dough is smooth and elastic. Place in a greased bowl, turning to grease top. Cover and let rise in a warm place (85°), free from drafts, 1 hour or until dough has doubled in bulk.

Punch dough down, and divide in half; shape each portion into a loaf. Place in two well-greased 9- x 5- x 3-inch loafpans. Cover and let rise in a warm place (85°), free from drafts, 45 minutes or until doubled in bulk. Bake at 375° for 45 minutes or until loaves sound hollow when tapped. Remove bread from pans; let cool. Yield: 2 loaves.

SPINACH-AND-HERB STUFFED PORK

1 (10-ounce) package frozen chopped spinach, thawed and drained
1 (3-ounce) package cream cheese, softened
4 green onions, chopped
¼ cup chopped fresh basil
2 to 3 cloves garlic, finely chopped
1½ teaspoons chopped fresh tarragon
¼ teaspoon red pepper
1 (3- to 4-pound) boneless pork loin roast
¼ teaspoon salt
⅛ teaspoon pepper
Fresh basil leaves (optional)

Combine first 7 ingredients, mixing until well blended; set aside.

Slice roast lengthwise, cutting to but not through one side. Open cut piece to enlarge roast; pound to ½-inch thickness, making a large rectangle. Sprinkle with salt and pepper. Spoon stuffing mixture evenly over pork. Beginning with long side, roll pork jellyroll fashion, and tie securely with heavy string at 2-inch intervals. Place roast on a greased rack in a shallow roasting pan. Insert meat thermometer into thickest part of roast, making sure it does not touch fat or stuffing.

Bake at 325° for 1 hour and 15 minutes or until meat thermometer registers 160°. Remove roast from oven; let stand 5 minutes.

Remove string; place roast on a serving platter, and garnish with basil leaves, if desired. Yield: 10 servings.

THYME-GRAPE JELLY

5 cups purple grape juice
2 teaspoons dried whole thyme
1 (1¾-ounce) package powdered pectin
7 cups sugar

Combine grape juice and thyme in a large kettle; bring to a boil. Remove from heat; let stand 15 minutes. Strain through a jelly bag or several thicknesses of cheesecloth. Return liquid to kettle; stir in pectin. Bring to a rolling boil, stirring constantly. Quickly stir in sugar. Bring to a full rolling boil. Boil 1 minute, stirring constantly. Remove from heat, and skim off foam with a metal spoon.

Quickly pour jelly into hot sterilized jars, leaving ¼ inch of headspace; wipe jar rims. Cover at once with metal lids, and screw on bands. Process in boiling-water bath 5 minutes. Yield: 8 half pints.

JELLY-GLAZED CORNISH HENS

1 cup Thyme-Grape Jelly or red currant jelly
½ cup Madeira wine
⅓ cup orange juice
2 tablespoons lemon juice
½ teaspoon vinegar
1½ teaspoons dried mustard
½ teaspoon grated orange rind
½ teaspoon grated lemon rind
¼ teaspoon salt
Dash of red pepper
1 tablespoon cornstarch
1 tablespoon water
4 (1- to 1½-pound) Cornish hens

Combine first 10 ingredients in a saucepan. Combine cornstarch and water; stir into sauce mixture. Cook over medium heat, stirring constantly, until mixture boils. Boil 1 minute, stirring constantly, until mixture is smooth and thickened. Remove from heat.

Remove giblets from Cornish hens. Rinse hens with cold water; pat dry.

Place hens, breast side up, on a rack in a shallow roasting pan. Bake at 325° for 1 to 1½ hours or until juices run clear when thigh is pierced with a fork, basting every 10 minutes during last 30 minutes of baking time. Serve with any remaining sauce. Yield: 4 servings.

FLAVORED OLIVE OIL

1 lemon
1 (4-inch) fresh rosemary sprig
2 large cloves garlic, halved
1 teaspoon whole peppercorns
2 cups olive oil

Peel lemon rind in long strips; place in a pint jar with tight-fitting lid. (Reserve lemon pulp for another use.) Add rosemary sprig and remaining ingredients to jar. Cover with lid; refrigerate 1 week.

Strain olive oil into an airtight container; store in refrigerator.

Note: To use as a salad dressing, combine 2 parts flavored olive oil to 1 part white wine vinegar.

TARRAGON VINEGAR

2 or 3 bunches fresh tarragon sprigs
3 to 3½ cups cider or red wine vinegar
Additional fresh tarragon sprigs (optional)

Slightly bruise tarragon; place in a 1-quart jar, packing firmly. Fill jar with vinegar; cover with lid. Let stand in bright light 1 week. Store in a dark place 2 to 4 weeks.

Strain vinegar into decorative jars, discarding herb sprigs. Add extra sprigs of fresh tarragon, if desired. Seal jars with a cork or other airtight lid. Yield: 3 to 3½ cups.

A Chesapeake Seafood Sampler

On the Chesapeake, crab feasts are relished like pig pickings in North Carolina and crawfish boils in Louisiana. And they occur as frequently as backyard cookouts. Mounds of steamed blue crabs are heaped on newspaper-covered picnic tables, and guests sit down determined to pick the meat from the shells.

All of these recipes were tested in our Test Kitchens with fresh seafood, just as Chesapeake residents would use. We've occasionally used canned or frozen seafood when appropriate, however, so that you can use whatever you prefer at home. For steamed crabs, you must always start with live ones.

CHESAPEAKE SOFT-SHELL CRABS

8 soft-shell crabs, fresh or frozen, thawed
1 cup all-purpose flour
3 tablespoons Old Bay seasoning
2 teaspoons pepper
1 teaspoon red pepper
1 teaspoon garlic powder
1 egg, beaten
½ cup milk
Vegetable oil

To clean crabs, remove spongy substance (gills) that lies under the tapering points on either side of back shell. Place crab on back, and remove the small piece at lower part of shell that terminates in a point. Wash crabs thoroughly; drain well.

Combine flour and next 4 ingredients; set aside. Combine egg and milk; stir well. Dip crabs into egg mixture; dredge in flour mixture.

Pour oil to a depth of 1 inch in a heavy Dutch oven; heat oil to 350°. Fry crabs 1 to 2 minutes; drain on paper towels. Yield: 4 servings.

CHESAPEAKE BAY CRAB CAKES

¼ cup minced onion
2 tablespoons minced green pepper
¼ cup butter or margarine, melted
1 pound fresh crabmeat, drained and flaked
¾ cup fine, dry breadcrumbs
1 egg, beaten
1 tablespoon mayonnaise or salad dressing
1 tablespoon dried parsley flakes
1 tablespoon lemon juice
1 teaspoon Worcestershire sauce
1 teaspoon Old Bay seasoning
1 teaspoon dry mustard
Dash of red pepper
¼ to ½ cup fine, dry breadcrumbs
Vegetable oil

Sauté onion and green pepper in butter until tender. Remove from heat; stir in crabmeat and next 9 ingredients. Mix well, and shape into 8 patties. Coat with additional breadcrumbs. Pour oil to a depth of ¼ inch into a heavy skillet. Fry cakes in hot oil (375°) for 4 to 5 minutes on each side. Yield: 8 servings.

Rheda Meekins
North East, Maryland

CRAB IMPERIAL

¼ cup butter or margarine
2 tablespoons all-purpose flour
1 cup milk
1 teaspoon dry mustard
½ teaspoon salt
⅛ teaspoon pepper
1 teaspoon Worcestershire sauce
½ cup diced green pepper
1 pound fresh lump crabmeat, drained
¼ cup soft breadcrumbs
2 teaspoons butter or margarine, melted
Paprika (optional)

Melt ¼ cup butter in a heavy saucepan over low heat; add flour, stirring until smooth. Cook 1 minute, stirring constantly. Gradually add milk; cook over medium heat, stirring constantly, until thickened and bubbly. Stir in mustard and next 4 ingredients. Fold in crabmeat. Spoon mixture into greased baking shells. Mix breadcrumbs and butter; sprinkle over crab mixture. Garnish with paprika, if desired. Bake at 425° for 15 to 20 minutes or until lightly browned. Yield: 6 servings.

Gail C. Nichols
Salisbury, Maryland

CHESAPEAKE CRAB SALAD

1 pound fresh lump crabmeat, drained
½ cup chopped celery
1 tablespoon chopped green pepper
1 tablespoon chopped fresh parsley
¼ teaspoon capers
¼ cup mayonnaise or salad dressing
2 tablespoons lemon juice
⅛ teaspoon salt
⅛ teaspoon seasoned pepper
Dash of garlic salt
⅛ teaspoon Worcestershire sauce
3 or 4 drops of hot sauce
Lettuce leaves

Combine all ingredients except lettuce; stir to mix. Cover and chill 1 to 2 hours. Serve on lettuce leaves. Yield: 4 servings.

Elizabeth T. Edmunds
Cambridge, Maryland

STEAMED BLUE CRABS

½ cup Old Bay seasoning
½ cup salt
3 cups white vinegar
3 cups beer
3 dozen live blue crabs

Combine seasoning and salt, and set mixture aside.

Combine vinegar and beer in a very large pot with a lid; bring to a boil. Place rack in pot over boiling liquid; arrange half of crabs on rack. Sprinkle with half of seasoning mixture. Top with remaining crabs, and sprinkle with remaining seasoning mixture.

Cover and steam 20 to 30 minutes or until crabs turn bright orange. Serve crabs immediately. Yield: 10 to 12 servings.

Lynne Hoot
Edgewater, Maryland

GRILLED OYSTERS MORNAY

2 dozen oysters in shell
1 shallot, minced
1 clove garlic, minced
2 tablespoons butter or margarine, melted
½ pound country ham, minced
½ pound fresh lump crabmeat, drained
Mornay Sauce

Scrub oysters. To open, insert an oyster knife into the hinge of shell, and twist. Discard top shells. Scrape a knife between the oyster and shell to free the meat from the shell.

Sauté shallot and garlic in butter 2 minutes. Stir in ham, and cook over low heat 2 minutes. Remove from heat. Spoon about 1 tablespoon ham mixture onto meat in each oyster shell; top each with crabmeat. Spoon about 1 tablespoon Mornay Sauce over crabmeat.

Cook oysters in a covered grill over hot coals 8 minutes, or bake oysters at 350° for 15 to 20 minutes. Yield: 2 dozen.

Mornay Sauce

2 tablespoons butter or margarine
2 tablespoons all-purpose flour
1 cup milk
½ cup (2 ounces) shredded Swiss cheese
½ cup (2 ounces) shredded Cheddar cheese
½ cup grated Parmesan cheese

Melt butter in a heavy saucepan over low heat; add flour, stirring until smooth. Cook 1 minute, stirring constantly. Gradually add milk; cook over medium heat, stirring constantly, until thickened and bubbly. Stir in cheeses. Yield: 1¼ cups.

Roland S. Ormrod
Towson, Maryland

OYSTERS ANNAPOLIS

20 oysters in shell
1 egg yolk, beaten
½ cup chopped green pepper
2 tablespoons chopped pimiento
1 teaspoon dry mustard
¼ cup mayonnaise or salad dressing
¼ teaspoon salt
¼ teaspoon white pepper
1 tablespoon Worcestershire sauce
1 pound fresh lump crabmeat
1 (4-pound) package rock salt

Scrub oysters. To open, insert an oyster knife into the hinge of shell, and twist. Discard top shells. Scrape a knife between the oyster and shell to free the meat from shell; set shells aside. Drain meat, and cut each oyster into 4 pieces. Combine oysters and next 8 ingredients, mixing well. Add crabmeat, and toss mixture gently.

Spoon about 3 tablespoons crab mixture into each oyster shell.

Sprinkle rock salt in bottom of a 15- x 10- x 1-inch jellyroll pan; arrange stuffed shells on rock salt. Bake at 350° for 20 to 25 minutes. Yield: 10 appetizer servings.

Tip: *The terms Select and Standard refer to oyster sizes. Select oysters are medium size, while Standard oysters are small.*

MARYLAND CLAMS CASINO

3 slices bacon
1 dozen cherrystone clams in
  shells
2 teaspoons Worcestershire sauce
1 teaspoon hot sauce
2 tablespoons seasoned
  breadcrumbs

Cut bacon slices into fourths, and partially cook; set aside.

Wash clams, discarding any open (dead) clams. Pry open shells; discard top shells. Scrape a knife between the clam and the shell to free the meat from the bottom shell. Place clams in shells on a shallow baking pan.

Sprinkle Worcestershire sauce and hot sauce evenly over clams. Top each with a piece of bacon and ½ teaspoon breadcrumbs. Broil stuffed clams 4 to 5 inches from heating element until edges of clams curl and bacon is done (about 2 to 3 minutes). Yield: 1 dozen.

STEAMED CLAMS
CHESAPEAKE

4 dozen small soft-shell clams in
  shell or 3 dozen cherrystone
  clams in shell
3 tablespoons Old Bay seasoning
½ teaspoon salt
¼ teaspoon pepper
1 cup water
Melted butter or margarine

Wash clams thoroughly; place in a large Dutch oven. Sprinkle lightly with seasonings. Add water; cover and bring to a boil. Reduce heat, and steam 10 to 15 minutes or until shells open wide. Drain clams, reserving liquid. Strain liquid.

Serve clams hot in shells with clam liquid and melted butter. Yield: about 2 servings.

MICROWAVE COOKERY

Few Ingredients, Lots Of Flavor

Team the microwave oven with recipes that contain only five ingredients and the phrase "quick and easy" takes on new meaning. These dishes require only a minute or two to assemble because of their short list of ingredients. And the cooking times range from 8 to 18 minutes for entrées that can feed a family.

BREADED CHICKEN BREASTS

4 chicken breast halves, skinned
¼ teaspoon garlic salt
½ teaspoon dried whole savory
¼ cup commercial ranch-style
  salad dressing
¼ cup Italian-seasoned
  breadcrumbs

Arrange chicken with thickest portion to outside in a shallow 10-inch round baking dish. Sprinkle with garlic salt and savory. Spread each side of breasts with dressing, and dredge in breadcrumbs. Cover with wax paper. Microwave at HIGH 15 minutes or until chicken is tender, giving dish a quarter-turn at 5-minute intervals. Serve immediately. Yield: 4 servings.
Joanne Wagner
Marietta, Georgia

FLOUNDER AMANDINE

3 tablespoons sliced almonds
2 tablespoons butter or margarine
2 tablespoons lemon juice
2 (8-ounce) flounder fillets
1 tablespoon chopped fresh
  parsley

Place almonds and butter in a 12- x 8- x 2-inch baking dish. Microwave at HIGH 6 minutes or until almonds are lightly toasted, stirring at 2-minute intervals. Stir in lemon juice. Place fillets over almonds, and cover tightly with heavy-duty plastic wrap; fold back a small corner of wrap to allow steam to escape. Microwave at HIGH 6 to 8 minutes or until fish flakes easily with a fork, giving dish a half-turn after 4 minutes.

Transfer fish to a serving platter, and drizzle almonds and butter over top. Sprinkle with fresh parsley. Yield: 2 to 4 servings.

MARMALADE-GLAZED HAM

½ cup orange marmalade
½ teaspoon ground ginger
½ teaspoon dry mustard
1½ teaspoons lemon juice
1 (1-pound) fully cooked ham
  slice

Combine first 4 ingredients in a 1-cup glass measure. Cover tightly with heavy-duty plastic wrap; fold back a small corner of wrap to allow steam to escape. Microwave at HIGH 1½ to 2 minutes. Set aside.

Place ham slice on a roasting rack in a 12- x 8- x 2-inch baking dish; cover with wax paper. Microwave at MEDIUM HIGH (70% power) 6 to 7 minutes or until ham is thoroughly heated, turning ham over after 4 minutes. Serve with marmalade sauce. Yield: 3 to 4 servings.

KIELBASA AND CABBAGE

½ medium cabbage (about 1
  pound)
1 pound kielbasa sausage, cut
  into 1-inch slices
1 teaspoon caraway seeds
¾ teaspoon seasoned salt
¼ cup commercial Italian salad
  dressing

Shred cabbage into thin strips. Combine cabbage, sausage, caraway seeds, seasoned salt, and salad dressing in a 4-quart casserole; toss gently. Cover with heavy-duty plastic wrap; fold back a small corner of wrap to allow steam to escape. Microwave at HIGH 8 to 10 minutes or until cabbage is crisp-tender, stirring at 4-minute intervals. Drain. Yield: 4 servings.

Pickles And Relishes With Flair

Tangy, crunchy, and out of the ordinary, these pickles and relishes add that special something to a menu. Fruits and vegetables are blended with spices, sugar, and vinegar to create crispness and a sweet-and-sour flavor.

JERUSALEM ARTICHOKE RELISH

2 quarts Jerusalem artichokes, well scraped and peeled
2 large onions, quartered
1½ cups white vinegar (5% acidity)
1¼ cups firmly packed brown sugar
1½ tablespoons salt
1 tablespoon celery salt
1½ teaspoons ground allspice
½ teaspoon ground turmeric
¼ teaspoon red pepper

Position knife blade in food processor bowl; add artichokes and onion. Top with cover; process until finely chopped.

Combine artichoke mixture and remaining ingredients in a Dutch oven, stirring well. Bring to a boil; reduce

heat, and simmer 30 minutes or to desired thickness.

Spoon into hot, sterilized half-pint jars, leaving ½-inch of headspace. Remove air bubbles; wipe jar rims. Cover at once with metal lids, and screw on bands. Process relish in boiling-water bath 10 minutes. Yield: 6 half pints.

CHAYOTE SQUASH PICKLES

8 quarts chayote squash (about 11 pounds)
½ cup salt
2 quarts crushed ice
5 cups sugar
5 cups white vinegar (5% acidity)
2 teaspoons mustard seeds
1½ teaspoons ground turmeric
1 teaspoon celery seeds
½ teaspoon ground cloves

Cut squash into thin strips; place in a large bowl, and sprinkle with salt. Place ice on top; cover and let stand 2½ to 3 hours. Rinse squash strips, and drain well.

Combine sugar and remaining ingredients in a large kettle; bring to a boil. Add squash, and cook until thoroughly heated. (Do not boil.)

Pack squash into hot, sterilized pint jars; cover with hot syrup, leaving ½-inch of headspace. Remove air bubbles; wipe jar rims. Cover at once with metal lids, and screw on bands. Process in boiling-water bath 10 minutes. Yield: about 9 pints.

PICKLED COCKTAIL ONIONS

4 cups pearl onions
3 tablespoons salt
¼ cup plus 2 tablespoons sugar
1 tablespoon whole mustard seeds
3 cups white vinegar (5% acidity)
4 small hot red peppers

Cover onions with boiling water; let stand 2 minutes. Drain. Rinse in cold

water, and peel. Sprinkle salt over onions in a medium bowl. Add water to cover onions. Cover and let stand 18 to 24 hours. Drain onions, and rinse well.

Combine sugar, mustard seeds, and vinegar in a heavy saucepan. Bring to a boil; reduce heat, and simmer, uncovered, 15 minutes.

Pack onions and 1 red pepper into hot, sterilized half-pint jars. Cover with hot liquid, leaving ½-inch of headspace. Remove air bubbles; wipe jar rims. Cover jars at once with metal lids, and screw on bands. Process in boiling-water bath 10 minutes. Yield: 4 half pints.

SWEET PICKLED CANTALOUPE

4 large firm cantaloupes (about 4 pounds each)
½ cup coarse salt
2 quarts water
2 tablespoons whole allspice
1 tablespoon whole cloves
5 (4-inch) sticks cinnamon
5 cups sugar
2 cups white vinegar (5% acidity)
2 cups water

Peel and seed cantaloupes, and cut into 1½- x ½- x ½-inch pieces to make 1 gallon. Dissolve salt in 2 quarts water; add cantaloupe. Let stand 2 hours. Drain and rinse cantaloupe. Set aside.

Tie spices in a cheesecloth bag. Combine spices and remaining ingredients in a large Dutch oven; bring to a boil. Cook 5 minutes. Add cantaloupe; return to a boil, and cook 3 to 5 minutes or just until cantaloupe is tender. Remove from heat; cover and let stand 8 hours.

Drain syrup from cantaloupe, and remove spice bag. Return syrup to Dutch oven; bring to a boil. Pack cantaloupe into hot, sterilized pint jars; cover with boiling syrup, leaving ½-inch of headspace. Remove air bubbles; wipe jar rims. Cover at once with metal lids, and screw on bands. Process in boiling-water bath 15 minutes. Yield: 4 pints.

MANGO RELISH

4 cups peeled, chopped green
   mangoes
3 medium-size green peppers,
   quartered
3 medium-size sweet red peppers,
   quartered
2 large hot peppers, seeded
2 large onions, quartered
4 cups sugar
2 cups raisins
1 cup white vinegar (5% acidity)
1 tablespoon salt
1 tablespoon mustard seeds
1 tablespoon celery seeds

Position knife blade in food processor bowl. Place mangoes in processor bowl, and pulse until fruit is coarsely ground. Repeat procedure with peppers and onion.

Combine mangoes, peppers, onion, and remaining ingredients in a large Dutch oven; bring to a boil. Reduce heat, and simmer, uncovered, 10 minutes. Cover and let stand 8 hours in a cool place.

Uncover and cook over low heat 30 minutes or until mixture is slightly thickened. Spoon into hot, sterilized half-pint jars, leaving ½-inch of headspace. Remove air bubbles; wipe jar rims. Cover at once with metal lids, and screw on bands. Process in boiling-water bath 10 minutes. Yield: 6 half pints.

ON THE LIGHT SIDE

Frosty, Light Desserts

There's nothing like the taste of an icy-cold dessert to finish off a meal or add refreshment to a sultry, summer day. And these fruity ice milks, whips, and fluffs satisfy cravings for ice cream without scooping up excess calories, fat, and cholesterol.

CANTALOUPE WHIP

2¼ cups cubed cantaloupe
1 tablespoon lemon juice
2 egg whites
¼ cup sugar

Place a single layer of cantaloupe in a shallow pan; freeze until firm. Drop cantaloupe through food chute of a food processor or blender with the motor running. Add lemon juice, and process until mixture is smooth.

Beat egg whites (at room temperature) in a small bowl at high speed of an electric mixer until foamy; gradually add sugar, 1 tablespoon at a time, beating until stiff peaks form. Fold into cantaloupe mixture. Spoon into an 8-inch square pan, and freeze until firm. Let stand at room temperature 10 minutes before serving. Yield: 4 servings (88 calories per ¾-cup serving).

☐ 2.4 grams protein, 0.3 gram fat, 20.5 grams carbohydrate, 0 milligrams cholesterol, 33 milligrams sodium, and 12 milligrams calcium.

RASPBERRY FLUFF

4 cups fresh raspberries
¼ cup sugar
1¼ cups orange juice
¼ cup lemon juice
¼ cup sugar

Place raspberries in a bowl, and mash slightly. Sprinkle with ¼ cup sugar, and let stand 30 minutes, stirring occasionally.

Combine orange juice and remaining ingredients in a small saucepan; cook over medium heat, stirring until sugar dissolves. Remove from heat, and let cool.

Place raspberry mixture in container of an electric blender or food processor; add orange juice mixture. Top with cover, and process until smooth. Pour into an 8-inch square pan, and freeze until almost firm. Spoon mixture into a large mixing bowl, and beat at medium speed of an electric mixer until smooth. Return mixture to pan, and freeze until firm. Let stand at room temperature 10 minutes before serving. Yield: 8 servings (122 calories per ½-cup serving).

☐ 0.9 gram protein, 0.4 gram fat, 30.6 grams carbohydrate, 0 milligrams cholesterol, 1 milligram sodium, and 18 milligrams calcium.
Nancy B. Vincent
Caneyville, Kentucky

STRAWBERRY WHIP

3 cups sliced strawberries
½ cup evaporated skimmed milk
2 egg whites
¼ cup sugar

Place strawberries in container of an electric blender or food processor. Top with cover, and process until smooth. Cover and chill.

Place milk in a small bowl; freeze until ice crystals form. With chilled beaters, beat milk at high speed of an electric mixer until stiff peaks form; fold into strawberries.

Beat egg whites (at room temperature) in a small bowl at high speed of electric mixer until foamy; gradually add sugar, 1 tablespoon at a time, beating until stiff peaks form. Fold into strawberry mixture. Serve immediately, or freeze until firm. If mixture is frozen, let stand at room temperature 10 minutes before serving. Yield: 5 servings (92 calories per 1-cup serving).

☐ 3.8 grams protein, 0.4 gram fat, 19.3 grams carbohydrate, 1 milligram cholesterol, 50 milligrams sodium, and 88 milligrams calcium.
Mary Jo Angelo
Birmingham, Alabama

LIME WHIP

1 envelope unflavored gelatin
1½ cups water, divided
¼ cup sugar
1 (6-ounce) can frozen limeade
   concentrate, thawed and
   undiluted
½ teaspoon grated lime rind
2 egg whites

Sprinkle gelatin over ¼ cup water in a medium saucepan; let stand 1 minute. Add sugar, and cook over medium heat, stirring until gelatin and sugar dissolve; remove from heat. Stir in remaining 1¼ cups water, limeade concentrate, and lime rind. Chill until the consistency of unbeaten egg white.

Beat egg whites (at room temperature) in a small bowl at high speed of an electric mixer until stiff peaks form. Fold into lime mixture; spoon into an 8-inch square pan, and freeze until firm. Let stand at room temperature 10 minutes before serving. Yield: 5 servings (113 calories per 1-cup serving).

☐ 2.6 grams protein, 0 grams fat, 27 grams carbohydrate, 0 milligrams cholesterol, 21 milligrams sodium, and 3 milligrams calcium.
Mrs. Dallas Collins
Swansboro, North Carolina

NECTARINE SHERBET

1 envelope unflavored gelatin
¼ cup evaporated skimmed milk
⅛ teaspoon salt
1 cup sugar
1 cup evaporated skimmed milk
3 cups peeled and chopped
   nectarines (about 1¾ pounds)
2 tablespoons lemon juice
1 egg white

Sprinkle gelatin over ¼ cup milk in a medium saucepan; let stand 1 minute. Cook over medium heat, stirring until gelatin dissolves; remove from heat. Add salt, sugar, and 1 cup milk; stir until sugar dissolves. Let mixture cool.

Place nectarines in container of an electric blender or food processor. Top with cover, and process about 1 minute or until smooth, scraping sides of container once. Combine nectarines, lemon juice, and gelatin mixture; stir well. Spoon into a 9-inch square pan; cover and freeze until firm.

Spoon frozen mixture into a large mixing bowl; add egg white. Beat at medium speed of an electric mixer until smooth and fluffy. Return to pan; cover and freeze 4 hours or until firm. Let stand at room temperature 10 minutes before serving. Yield: 10 servings (127 calories per ½-cup serving).

☐ 3.7 grams protein, 0.3 gram fat, 28.7 grams carbohydrate, 1 milligram cholesterol, 72 milligrams sodium, and 96 milligrams calcium.
Mrs. P. J. Davis
Drexel, North Carolina

BANANA YOGURT ICE MILK

1 envelope unflavored gelatin
3 tablespoons water
1 cup mashed ripe banana
1 cup evaporated skimmed milk
1 (8-ounce) carton plain low-fat
   yogurt
3 tablespoons honey
1 kiwifruit, peeled and thinly
   sliced
¼ cup blueberries
¼ cup raspberries
Fresh mint sprigs (optional)

Sprinkle gelatin over water in a saucepan; let stand 1 minute. Cook over medium heat, stirring until gelatin dissolves; remove from heat. Combine banana, milk, yogurt, and honey. Stir into gelatin mixture. Spoon into an 8-inch square pan; freeze until firm. Remove from freezer; break into chunks. Spoon mixture into a bowl; beat at medium speed of an electric mixer until smooth. Return mixture to pan; freeze until firm. Let ice milk stand at room temperature 10 minutes to soften. Serve with kiwifruit, blueberries, and raspberries. Garnish with fresh mint sprigs, if desired. Yield: 7 servings (120 calories per ½-cup serving).

☐ 5.9 grams protein, 0.8 gram fat, 23.8 grams carbohydrate, 3 milligrams cholesterol, 67 milligrams sodium, and 172 milligrams calcium.

PINEAPPLE SHERBET

1 envelope unflavored gelatin
¼ cup water
¼ cup sugar
2 (15¼-ounce) cans unsweetened
   crushed pineapple, undrained
2 tablespoons lemon juice
2 egg whites

Sprinkle gelatin over water in a small saucepan; let stand 1 minute. Add sugar, and cook over medium heat, stirring until mixture dissolves; remove from heat, and let cool.

Place pineapple in container of an electric blender or food processor. Top with cover, and process until smooth. Combine pineapple, lemon juice, and gelatin mixture; spoon mixture into an 8-inch square pan, and freeze until firm.

Break frozen mixture into chunks; return to blender or food processor, and process until smooth.

Beat egg whites (at room temperature) in a small bowl at high speed of an electric mixer until stiff peaks form. Fold beaten egg whites into pineapple mixture; return to pan, and freeze until firm. Let stand at room temperature 10 minutes before serving. Yield: 10 servings (77 calories per ½-cup serving).

☐ 1.6 grams protein, 0.1 gram fat, 18.9 grams carbohydrate, 0 milligrams cholesterol, 11 milligrams sodium, and 13 milligrams calcium.

QUICK!

Grill A Meal

Cooking on the grill is especially appealing for a summer evening. Here's a menu that can be assembled quickly and easily with a little planning. Use these steps to keep preparation organized.
— Place chicken in marinade.
— Prepare bread and corn; place on the grill.
— Slice zucchini into fans; mix oil and garlic powder.
— Place chicken on grill.
— Brush zucchini with oil mixture; place on grill.
— Slice bananas and strawberries for dessert.
— Turn chicken, bread, corn on the cob, and zucchini.
— Finish preparing dessert.
— Enjoy!

Grilled Chicken
Lemony Corn on the Cob
Grilled Zucchini Fans
Sliced Tomatoes
Greek Bread
Pound Cake With
Strawberry-Banana Topping

GRILLED CHICKEN

½ cup white vinegar
½ cup balsamic vinegar
½ cup water
1 teaspoon chili powder
½ teaspoon dried whole oregano
½ teaspoon freshly ground black pepper
1 bay leaf, crushed
4 chicken breast halves, skinned and boned

Combine first 7 ingredients in a zip-top heavy-duty plastic bag. Add chicken, and marinate 20 minutes; remove chicken from marinade, reserving marinade. Grill chicken, covered, over medium coals 8 to 10 minutes on each side, basting twice with marinade. Yield: 4 servings.
Fran Ginn
Columbia, Mississippi

LEMONY CORN ON THE COB

4 ears fresh corn
¼ cup butter or margarine, softened
½ to 1 teaspoon lemon-pepper seasoning

Remove husks and silks from corn just before grilling. Combine butter and lemon-pepper seasoning; spread on corn, and place each ear on a piece of heavy-duty aluminum foil. Roll foil lengthwise around each ear, and twist foil at each end. Grill corn, covered, over medium coals 20 minutes, turning after 10 minutes. Yield: 4 servings.

GRILLED ZUCCHINI FANS

3 tablespoons olive oil
¼ teaspoon garlic powder
4 small zucchini, cut into fans

Combine olive oil and garlic powder. Cut each zucchini into lengthwise slices, leaving slices attached on stem end. Fan slices out, and place on grill over medium coals; brush zucchini with olive oil mixture; cover and grill 5 minutes on each side, basting once with olive oil mixture. Yield: 4 servings.

GREEK BREAD

½ cup butter or margarine, softened
2 tablespoons mayonnaise or salad dressing
1 (2½-ounce) jar sliced mushrooms, drained
1 (4¼-ounce) can sliced black olives, drained
2 tablespoons chopped green onion tops
1 (16-ounce) loaf French bread
1 cup (4 ounces) shredded mozzarella cheese

Combine butter, mayonnaise, mushrooms, black olives, and green onion tops in a small bowl; set aside.
Slice French bread loaf in half lengthwise. Spread bottom side evenly with butter mixture; sprinkle evenly with shredded cheese. Place bread top over cheese. Wrap loaf in heavy-duty aluminum foil; grill over medium coals 20 to 25 minutes, turning after 10 minutes. Yield: 1 loaf.
Betty Haygood
Liberty, Mississippi

POUND CAKE WITH STRAWBERRY-BANANA TOPPING

2 tablespoons butter or margarine
2 tablespoons brown sugar
2 tablespoons lemon juice
¼ cup light rum
3 medium bananas, sliced
6 fresh strawberries, cut in half
Commercial pound cake

Melt butter in a skillet on grill. Add sugar, lemon juice, and rum; stir well. Cook until sugar dissolves (2 to 3 minutes), stirring constantly. Add bananas and strawberries, and cook until bananas are soft but not mushy (about 2 minutes). Serve over pound cake. Yield: 4 servings.

Note: Strawberry-Banana Topping may be served over vanilla ice cream instead of pound cake.

A Lovely Luncheon For 12

If your fancy for a luncheon leans toward something other than the traditional cold plate, try our summer menu for 12. Designed especially for memorable occasions, this menu offers suggestions for gatherings of bridesmaids, a bridge club, or a reunion of college friends.

The Day Before: Make the Marinated Tomatoes and Lime Sherbet, string the green beans, and chop the carrots for the rice.

The Day of the Luncheon: For a party of this size, you may want to ask a friend to assist you in the kitchen. About two hours before the luncheon, cook the Hearts of Palm Chicken Rolls, and cover with aluminum foil to keep hot.

Prepare Savory Rice and Green Beans With Cashews. Make the Béarnaise Sauce, which is a hollandaise sauce flavored with vinegar and tarragon, just before you're ready to serve your guests.

When Guests Arrive: Greet them at the door with a fluted glass of champagne or sparkling grape juice. And celebrate!

Champagne
Hearts of Palm Chicken Rolls
Savory Rice
Marinated Tomatoes
Green Beans With Cashews
Lime Sherbet

HEARTS OF PALM CHICKEN ROLLS

12 chicken breast halves, skinned and boned
½ teaspoon salt
½ teaspoon white pepper
¼ cup butter or margarine, melted
2 (14.4-ounce) cans hearts of palm, drained
Béarnaise Sauce
Fresh tarragon sprigs (optional)

Place each piece of chicken between 2 sheets of wax paper; flatten to ¼-inch thickness, using a meat mallet or rolling pin. Sprinkle with salt and pepper; brush with butter. Roll each piece of chicken around a heart of palm. Place seam side down on a lightly greased 15- x 10- x 1-inch jellyroll pan. Brush chicken rolls with remaining butter. Cover and bake at 350° for 1 hour. Spoon Béarnaise Sauce over chicken rolls. Garnish with fresh tarragon, if desired. Yield: 12 servings.

Béarnaise Sauce

3 tablespoons white wine vinegar
2 teaspoons minced shallots
1½ teaspoons chopped fresh tarragon or ½ teaspoon dried whole tarragon
3 egg yolks
⅛ teaspoon salt
⅛ teaspoon red pepper
2 tablespoons lemon juice
½ cup butter or margarine

Combine vinegar and shallots in a small saucepan; bring to a boil over medium heat. Reduce heat, and simmer until half of liquid evaporates. Strain, reserving liquid; discard solids. Let vinegar mixture cool slightly; stir in tarragon. Set aside.

Beat egg yolks, salt, and red pepper in top of a double boiler; gradually add lemon juice, stirring constantly. Add one-third of butter to egg mixture; cook over hot (not boiling) water, stirring constantly, until butter melts.

Add another third of butter, stirring constantly. As sauce thickens, stir in remaining butter; cook until thickened. Immediately remove from heat. Add vinegar mixture to sauce, stirring well. Serve immediately. Yield: ¾ cup.

SAVORY RICE

2 (10¾-ounce) cans chicken broth, undiluted
3½ cups water
½ teaspoon salt
2½ cups uncooked long-grain rice
2 carrots, finely chopped

Combine broth, water, and salt in a Dutch oven; bring to a boil. Add rice and chopped carrots. Cover, reduce heat, and simmer 20 minutes or until rice is tender and water is absorbed. Yield: 12 servings.

MARINATED TOMATOES

10 small tomatoes
½ cup sugar
½ cup white vinegar
2 tablespoons vegetable oil
1 tablespoon minced onion
1 tablespoon minced celery
1 tablespoon minced green pepper
1 teaspoon salt
½ teaspoon pepper
½ teaspoon Worcestershire sauce
Lettuce leaves

Dip each tomato into boiling water for 15 to 30 seconds; remove skin with paring knife. Core tomatoes, and place in an 8-inch square dish.

Combine sugar and next 8 ingredients in a jar; cover tightly, and shake vigorously. Pour over tomatoes. Cover and chill 8 hours, spooning marinade over tomatoes occasionally.

To serve, quarter tomatoes, and arrange 3 or 4 wedges on lettuce leaves. Yield: 12 servings.

Anne Dorrough
Birmingham, Alabama

GREEN BEANS WITH CASHEWS

3 pounds fresh green beans
3 cups water
¾ teaspoon salt
½ cup coarsely chopped cashews
2 tablespoons butter or
    margarine, melted

Wash beans, and remove strings. Combine beans, water, and salt in a Dutch oven. Bring to a boil; cover, reduce heat, and simmer 12 to 15 minutes. Drain.

Cook cashews in butter, stirring constantly, until toasted and lightly browned. Spoon over beans, and toss gently. Yield: 12 servings.

Note: 4 (9-ounce) packages frozen green beans, cooked according to package directions, can be substituted for fresh beans.

Mary Kay Menees
White Pine, Tennessee

LIME SHERBET

1 (12-ounce) can frozen limeade
    concentrate, undiluted
1⅓ cups sugar
½ gallon milk
4 egg whites
¼ cup sugar
8 drops green food coloring
    (optional)
4 drops yellow food coloring
    (optional)

Combine limeade concentrate and 1⅓ cups sugar in a Dutch oven; heat, stirring constantly, until sugar dissolves. Cool.

Add milk to limeade mixture. (Mixture will look curdled.)

Beat egg whites (at room temperature) until foamy. Gradually add ¼ cup sugar, 1 tablespoon at a time, beating until stiff peaks form. Fold into limeade mixture. Add food coloring, if desired. Pour into freezer can of a 5-quart hand-turned or electric freezer. Freeze according to manufacturer's instructions. Let ripen at least 1 hour. Yield: about ½ gallon.

Cathy Williams
Vale, North Carolina

Bake The Catch Of The Day

As more and more Southerners have turned to healthy eating, baked fish has become quite popular. Rich in protein and B vitamins, and low in calories and fat, fish is a natural choice for a healthy meal.

Overcooking is the biggest mistake made when preparing fish. It results in a dry, sometimes tough, piece of fish. To check for doneness, pierce the thickest part with a fork and twist to see if it flakes easily.

Easy-to-prepare Lemon Barbecued Catfish fits a busy lifestyle. Simply brush catfish fillets with lemon-dill barbecue sauce, and bake.

TROUT LAURIE

2 pounds trout fillets
1 cup lime juice
1 cup all-purpose flour
1 teaspoon garlic powder
1 teaspoon onion powder
½ cup butter or margarine,
    melted
⅔ cup water
¼ cup lemon juice
¼ cup sherry
1 (1⅛-ounce) package Hollandaise
    sauce mix
1 tablespoon chopped chives
1 teaspoon parsley flakes
½ teaspoon garlic powder
1 (6.5-ounce) can claw crabmeat,
    drained
1 (4-ounce) can sliced
    mushrooms, drained
¼ cup sliced almonds, toasted
½ teaspoon paprika

Place trout in a large shallow dish; pour lime juice over fish. Cover and marinate 2 hours in refrigerator, turning once. Drain.

Combine flour, 1 teaspoon garlic powder, and onion powder. Dredge fish in flour mixture. Brown fillets in butter in a large heavy skillet on each side, and place in a lightly greased 13- x 9- x 2-inch baking dish.

Add water and next 6 ingredients to drippings in skillet, stirring until blended. Cook over low heat until thickened, stirring constantly.

Stir in crabmeat, mushrooms, and almonds. Spoon mixture over fillets; sprinkle with paprika. Cover and bake at 350° for 30 minutes. Yield: 6 to 8 servings.

Laurie McIntyre
Lake Jackson, Texas

LEMON BARBECUED CATFISH

¼ cup commercial barbecue sauce
¼ teaspoon grated lemon rind
1½ tablespoons lemon juice
¼ teaspoon dried dillweed
1½ pounds catfish fillets

Combine first 4 ingredients; stir well. Brush each side of fillets with sauce, and place in a lightly greased 12- x 8- x 2-inch baking dish. Brush on remaining sauce. Bake at 350° for 25 minutes or until fish flakes easily when tested with a fork. To serve, place fillets on a serving platter. Yield: 6 servings. *Zelda T. Covey Birmingham, Alabama*

ALMOND BAKED FISH

1½ teaspoons lemon juice
1½ teaspoons butter or
 margarine, melted
¼ teaspoon salt
4 flounder fillets or other fish
 fillets (about 1 pound)
⅓ cup mayonnaise
½ cup saltine cracker crumbs
3 tablespoons butter or
 margarine, melted
2 tablespoons slivered almonds

Combine first 3 ingredients in a 12- x 8- x 2-inch baking dish. Arrange fish in dish; spread mayonnaise over fish.
 Combine cracker crumbs, 3 tablespoons melted butter, and almonds; sprinkle over fish. Bake at 400° for 10 to 15 minutes or until fish flakes easily when tested with a fork. Yield: 3 to 4 servings. *Kathleen Stone Houston, Texas*

ITALIAN FISH

1½ pounds flounder fillets or
 other fish fillets
¼ teaspoon dried whole oregano
⅛ teaspoon pepper
1 (15¼-ounce) jar spaghetti sauce
2 tablespoons minced fresh
 parsley
1 cup (4 ounces) shredded
 mozzarella cheese

Arrange flounder fillets in a lightly greased 13- x 9- x 2-inch baking dish; sprinkle with oregano and pepper. Pour spaghetti sauce over fillets; sprinkle with parsley. Bake, uncovered, at 350° for 20 minutes or until fish flakes easily when tested with a fork. Top with cheese; bake an additional 5 minutes. Yield: 6 servings. *Mary Pappas Richmond, Virginia*

Vegetable Side Dishes Complement The Cookout

Don't get in a rut serving plain baked potatoes every time you throw a steak on the grill. There are lots of ways to dress up this basic vegetable, as well as many other possibilities for vegetable side dishes.

DILLED GREEN BEANS

¾ pound fresh green beans
½ cup water
¼ teaspoon salt
1 medium onion, quartered and
 thinly sliced
2 tablespoons butter or
 margarine, melted
1 tablespoon chopped fresh
 dillweed or 1 teaspoon dried
 whole dillweed
1 tablespoon white wine vinegar
⅛ teaspoon ground savory

Wash beans; trim ends, and remove strings. Combine beans, water, and salt in a heavy saucepan. Bring to a boil; cover, reduce heat, and simmer 5 minutes or until crisp-tender. Drain and set aside.
 Sauté onion in butter in a skillet until tender. Stir in beans and remaining ingredients; cook over medium heat 5 minutes, stirring constantly. Yield: 3 servings. *Nell Gann Chattanooga, Tennessee*

SPINACH-STUFFED TOMATOES

4 small tomatoes
1 (10-ounce) package frozen
 chopped spinach
4 ounces process jalapeño
 pepper cheese spread,
 cut into cubes
⅛ teaspoon onion powder
⅛ teaspoon garlic powder
1½ tablespoons round buttery
 cracker crumbs
Paprika

Cut off top of each tomato; scoop out 1 inch of pulp. Set aside.
 Cook spinach according to package directions, omitting salt. Place cooked spinach on paper towels, and squeeze until barely moist. Combine spinach, cheese, onion powder, and garlic powder; cook over low heat, stirring until cheese melts. Spoon mixture into each tomato. Sprinkle with cracker crumbs and paprika; place tomatoes in a 13- x 9- x 2-inch pan. Bake at 300° for 15 minutes or until stuffed tomatoes are thoroughly heated. Yield: 4 servings.
 Frank Simpson, Jr. Bentonia, Mississippi

MUSHROOMS IN VERMOUTH

1 pound fresh mushrooms, sliced
1 tablespoon minced onion
¼ cup butter or margarine,
 melted
1 teaspoon cornstarch
1 teaspoon brown sugar
1 teaspoon soy sauce
⅓ cup dry vermouth

Sauté mushrooms and onion in butter 4 minutes. Set aside. Combine cornstarch and brown sugar; stir in soy sauce and vermouth. Add vermouth mixture to mushroom mixture, and bring to a boil over medium heat. Boil 1 minute. Serve with grilled meat. Yield: 4 servings.
 Maggie Cates Orlando, Florida

POTATOES ALFREDO

4 large baking potatoes
½ cup butter or margarine,
   melted
⅔ cup half-and-half
¾ cup grated Parmesan cheese,
   divided
1 tablespoon chopped fresh
   parsley

Scrub potatoes, and pat dry. Prick each potato several times with a fork. Arrange potatoes on a baking sheet; bake at 400° for 1 hour or until done. Let cool slightly.

Slice each potato in half lengthwise; carefully scoop out pulp, leaving shells intact. Mash pulp; add butter and half-and-half, and stir well. Add ½ cup Parmesan cheese, and stir until smooth. Stuff shells with potato mixture, and place on a baking sheet. Sprinkle potatoes evenly with remaining ¼ cup cheese. Broil 3 inches from heat 3 minutes or until lightly browned. Sprinkle with parsley. Yield: 8 servings.

Walter C. Lund
Miami, Florida

Cool, Refreshing Melons

Juicy, sweet melons are at their peak during the summer. Although it's hard to improve on their natural flavor, one of our readers has found a new way to make them extra special.

CANTALOUPE DELIGHT

1 tablespoon finely chopped
   crystallized ginger
1 teaspoon grated lime rind
2 tablespoons lime juice
4 cups cantaloupe balls
1 cup ginger ale, chilled
Fresh mint leaves (optional)

Combine ginger, lime rind, and lime juice; pour over cantaloupe balls. Cover and chill 8 hours. To serve, spoon into stemmed glasses, and pour ginger ale evenly over each serving. Garnish with mint, if desired. Yield: 4 to 6 servings.

Mrs. Richard L. Brownell
Salisbury, North Carolina

Dip Into Watermelon Punch

A large wedge of watermelon makes a great thirst quencher on a hot summer day, so when Deena R. Sharpe of Powell, Tennessee, sent us this recipe, it made sense to us that Watermelon Punch would be equally refreshing.

Serve the punch from the shell of the melon as Deena does. It makes a lovely presentation.

WATERMELON PUNCH

1 large watermelon
1½ cups sugar
1 cup water
1 (33.8-ounce) bottle ginger ale,
   chilled

Cut a thin slice from one end of melon, and slice top third from other end. Scoop pulp from melon, remove seeds, and mash pulp. Measure 1 gallon of juice, and set aside. Use a V-shaped knife or paring knife to make decorative cuts around edge of melon shell.

Combine sugar and water in a saucepan. Bring to a boil; reduce heat, and simmer 5 minutes. Add to 1 gallon watermelon juice, and chill. Just before serving, add ginger ale, stirring gently. Serve in watermelon shell. Yield: 5¼ quarts.

End The Meal With Waffles

Fire up the waffle iron just as you always do, but select accompaniments to serve with the waffles that will make them delicious desserts. Your family will enjoy the versatility these pretty patterned breads offer when ending the meal.

DESSERT PUMPKIN WAFFLES WITH MANDARIN ORANGE SAUCE

3 tablespoons shortening
½ cup sugar
1 egg
½ cup canned or cooked, mashed
   pumpkin
3 tablespoons water
¾ cup plus 2 tablespoons
   all-purpose flour
½ teaspoon baking soda
⅛ teaspoon baking powder
⅛ teaspoon salt
¼ teaspoon ground cinnamon
⅛ teaspoon ground cloves
⅓ cup milk
Mandarin Orange Sauce

Beat shortening well with a wooden spoon; gradually add sugar, beating well. Add egg, and beat well. Stir in pumpkin and water.

Combine flour, soda, baking powder, salt, and spices; add to creamed mixture alternately with milk, beginning and ending with flour mixture. Bake in preheated, oiled waffle iron. Cut waffles to make eight 4-inch squares. Serve waffles with Mandarin Orange Sauce. Yield: 8 servings.

Mandarin Orange Sauce

1 cup firmly packed brown sugar
2 teaspoons grated orange rind
½ cup orange juice
1 (11-ounce) can mandarin
   oranges, drained

Combine first 3 ingredients in a small saucepan, stirring well. Bring to a boil; reduce heat, and simmer until thickened (about 5 minutes), stirring frequently. Stir in oranges; serve warm. Yield: 1½ cups.

BANANA SPLIT WAFFLES

2 cups all-purpose flour
1 teaspoon baking soda
½ teaspoon salt
⅓ cup sugar
2 eggs, separated
2 cups buttermilk
¼ cup butter or margarine, melted
½ gallon vanilla ice cream
4 bananas
1 (20-ounce) can pineapple tidbits, drained
Commercial chocolate syrup

Combine flour, soda, salt, and sugar in a large bowl. Combine egg yolks, buttermilk, and butter; add to flour mixture, stirring until dry ingredients are moistened.

Beat egg whites (at room temperature) until stiff peaks form; carefully fold into batter. Bake in preheated, oiled waffle iron. Cut waffles to make 16 (4-inch) squares.

Slice ice cream into eight ½-inch-thick slices, shaping it to fit waffles; reserve remaining ice cream for other uses. Slice bananas. To assemble each serving, stack one 4-inch waffle, 1 slice ice cream, and another 4-inch waffle. Top with banana slices, pineapple tidbits, and chocolate syrup. Serve immediately. Yield: 8 servings.

Tip: *Ripe bananas can be refrigerated to keep them an additional 3 to 5 days. Or peel, mash, and freeze in airtight containers for use in baking.*

A Pleasant Wake-Up Call

The irresistible aroma of fresh-baked muffins is sure to get your family up on the right side of the bed. They'll think you've been awake for hours, and only you will know how quick and easy these treats really are.

BANANA-POPPYSEED MUFFINS

1 cup whole wheat flour
¾ cup all-purpose flour
2 teaspoons baking powder
½ teaspoon salt
1 tablespoon poppyseeds
2 ripe bananas
¾ cup sugar
¼ cup vegetable oil
2 teaspoons orange juice
1 egg
Citrus glaze (recipe follows)

Combine first 5 ingredients in a large mixing bowl; make a well in center of mixture.

Place bananas in container of an electric blender; process until smooth. Add sugar, oil, orange juice, and egg; blend thoroughly. Add liquid mixture to dry ingredients, stirring just until moistened. Spoon into greased muffin pans, filling two-thirds full. Bake at 375° for 20 minutes. Remove from pans immediately, and glaze. Yield: 1 dozen.

Citrus Glaze

1¼ cups sifted powdered sugar
1 teaspoon grated orange rind
¼ cup orange juice
1 teaspoon vanilla extract

Combine all ingredients; stir well. Yield: about ⅔ cup.
Mrs. Sina Carroll
Cave City, Kentucky

BACON-AND-CHEESE MUFFINS

1¾ cups all-purpose flour
2½ teaspoons baking powder
½ teaspoon salt
2 tablespoons sugar
10 slices bacon, cooked and crumbled
½ cup (2 ounces) shredded Cheddar cheese
½ teaspoon chopped fresh parsley
1 egg, beaten
¾ cup milk
⅓ cup vegetable oil

Combine first 7 ingredients in a large bowl; make a well in center of mixture. Combine egg, milk, and oil; add to dry ingredients, stirring just until moistened. Spoon into greased muffin pans, filling two-thirds full. Bake at 400° for 20 to 25 minutes. Remove from pans immediately. Yield: 1 dozen.
Eileen Wehling
Austin, Texas

ORANGE MUFFINS

1½ cups all-purpose flour
2 teaspoons baking powder
½ cup sugar
½ teaspoon ground cinnamon
½ teaspoon ground allspice
½ cup golden raisins
1 egg, beaten
½ cup milk
¼ cup vegetable oil
1 teaspoon grated orange rind
¼ cup orange juice
1 teaspoon orange extract

Combine flour, baking powder, sugar, cinnamon, allspice, and raisins in a large mixing bowl; make a well in center of mixture. Combine egg and remaining ingredients; add to dry mixture, stirring just until moistened. Spoon batter into greased muffin pans, filling two-thirds full. Bake at 400° for 20 minutes. Remove muffins from pans immediately. Yield: 13 muffins.
Ryan Williams
Fort Worth, Texas

Slice Into Fresh Pineapple

Years ago when sailors returned home with goodies from faraway ports, they would place a fresh pineapple on their gatepost as an invitation to visitors, thereby establishing the pineapple as a symbol of Southern hospitality. But the use of pineapple didn't stop at the gate. Southerners have been using it in recipes for generations.

Ripe pineapples, depending on the variety, vary in color from nearly all green to golden. If the fruit is soft at the base, it has begun to deteriorate.

FROZEN TROPICAL PARADISE

3 eggs, beaten
1 cup milk
¾ cup sugar
2 cups whipping cream
1¼ cups chopped fresh pineapple or 1 (20-ounce) can crushed pineapple, drained
½ cup flaked coconut, toasted
1 teaspoon vanilla extract
Fresh pineapple slices and leaves (optional)
Flaked coconut, toasted (optional)

Combine eggs, milk, and sugar in a heavy saucepan. Cook over medium heat, stirring constantly, until mixture thickens (about 15 minutes). Chill. Stir in whipping cream, chopped pineapple, ½ cup coconut, and vanilla. Pour into the freezer can of a 1-quart ice cream freezer. Freeze according to manufacturer's directions. If desired, serve scoops on fresh pineapple slices, and garnish with pineapple leaves and toasted coconut. Yield: 1 quart.

To prepare without an ice cream freezer: Prepare custard as directed above; chill. Beat whipping cream at high speed of an electric mixer until soft peaks form. Fold whipped cream, pineapple, coconut, and vanilla into chilled custard. Spoon mixture into a 9-inch square pan. Cover and freeze until firm. Let stand 20 minutes at room temperature before serving.

Mildred Bickley
Bristol, Virginia

PINEAPPLE AND FRESH CITRUS

1 fresh pineapple, peeled, cored, and cubed
3 oranges, peeled, seeded, and sectioned
2 pink grapefruit, peeled, seeded, and sectioned
½ cup honey
½ cup flaked coconut
¼ cup chopped pecans (optional)

Combine first 5 ingredients, and stir gently. Cover and chill several hours. Sprinkle with pecans before serving, if desired. Yield: 12 servings.

Maggie Cates
Greenville, Texas

PEACHY FRUIT SALAD

2 cups fresh strawberries, halved
1 orange, peeled, seeded, and sectioned
2¼ cups fresh pineapple chunks
1 (21-ounce) can peach pie filling
3 bananas, sliced

Combine first 3 ingredients in a large bowl. Add pie filling; stir gently to coat. Cover and chill 1 hour. Add bananas just before serving. Yield: 8 servings.

Pat Rush Benigno
Gulfport, Mississippi

Step 1: *Cut off the green crown and a thin slice from the bottom of the pineapple to level it. Slice away the shell using thin lengthwise cuts, leaving brown specks on the fruit.*

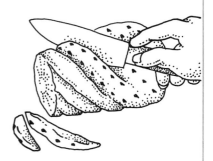

Step 2: *With a small knife, cut diagonal strips around the pineapple just deep enough to remove the brown specks or eyes.*

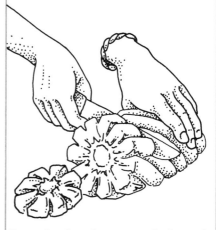

Step 3: *Cut the prepared pineapple into slices or, if you prefer, into lengthwise spears.*

A Southern Specialty

Through the years, pound cake recipes have taken on many variations, such as Mahogany Pound Cake offered here.

To ensure the best pound cake, precise measuring and careful mixing are important. A critical step is creaming the butter or shortening until it's light and fluffy. Using an electric mixer and ingredients that have been at room temperature for about 2 hours, this procedure takes at least 5 minutes. When adding the eggs, flour, and liquid as directed, mix just enough to blend. Overbeating at these stages can cause the cake to be tough.

GLAZED POUND CAKE

1 cup butter or margarine,
  softened
¼ cup shortening
3 cups sugar
5 eggs
3 cups all-purpose flour
½ teaspoon baking powder
½ teaspoon salt
1 cup milk
1 teaspoon rum extract
1 teaspoon coconut extract
1 cup sifted powdered sugar
½ cup water
1 teaspoon almond extract

Cream butter and shortening; gradually add sugar, beating well at medium speed of an electric mixer. Add eggs, one at a time, beating after each addition.

Combine flour, baking powder, and salt; add to creamed mixture alternately with milk, beginning and ending with flour mixture. Mix just until blended after each addition. Stir in rum and coconut extracts.

Pour batter into a greased and floured 10-inch tube pan. Bake at 325° for 1 hour and 30 minutes or until a wooden pick inserted in center comes out clean. Cool in pan 10 minutes. Remove from pan, and let cool completely on a wire rack.

Combine powdered sugar, water, and almond extract in a small saucepan. Bring to a boil over medium heat, and cook until sugar dissolves. Pour glaze slowly over cake. Yield: one 10-inch cake.   *Azine G. Rush*
Monroe, Louisiana

MAHOGANY POUND CAKE

1 cup butter or margarine,
  softened
2 cups sugar
1 cup firmly packed brown sugar
6 eggs, separated
2½ cups all-purpose flour
½ cup cocoa
1 cup commercial sour cream
¼ teaspoon baking soda
1 teaspoon vanilla extract

Cream butter; gradually add sugars, beating well at medium speed of an electric mixer. Add egg yolks, one at a time, beating after each addition.

Sift flour and cocoa together. Combine sour cream and baking soda. Add flour mixture to creamed mixture alternately with sour cream, beginning and ending with flour mixture. Mix just until blended after each addition. Stir in vanilla.

Beat egg whites (at room temperature) until stiff peaks form; fold into batter. Spoon batter into a greased and floured 10-inch tube pan. Bake at 325° for 1 hour and 15 minutes or until a wooden pick inserted in center comes out clean. Cool in pan 10 minutes; remove from pan, and let cool completely on a wire rack. Yield: one 10-inch cake.   *Glenda Marie Stokes*
Florence, South Carolina

SOUR CREAM-ORANGE PECAN POUND CAKE

1 cup shortening
3 cups sugar
6 eggs
3 cups all-purpose flour
¼ teaspoon baking soda
½ teaspoon salt
1 (8-ounce) carton sour cream
1 tablespoon plus 1 teaspoon
  orange extract
1 cup chopped pecans

Cream shortening; gradually add 3 cups sugar, beating well at medium speed of an electric mixer. Add eggs, one at a time, beating well after each addition.

Combine flour, soda, and salt in a small bowl; add to creamed mixture alternately with sour cream, beginning and ending with flour mixture. Mix just until blended after each addition. Stir in orange extract and chopped pecans.

Pour batter into a greased and floured 10-inch tube pan. Bake at 325° for 1 hour and 30 minutes or until a wooden pick inserted in center of cake comes out clean.

Allow cake to cool in pan 10 to 15 minutes; remove cake from pan, and let cool completely on a wire rack. Yield: one 10-inch cake.

Dora Hancock
Pottsboro, Texas

Tip: *To measure shortening, use the easy water-displacement method if the water that clings to the shortening will not affect the product. (Keep in mind this important point: Do not use this method for measuring shortening for frying.) To measure ¼ cup shortening using this method, put ¾ cup water in a measuring cup; then add shortening until the water reaches the 1-cup level. Just be sure that the shortening is completely covered with water. Drain off the water before using the shortening.*

Serve Cereal On The Side

It's hard to beat the convenience of shaking ready-to-eat cereal from a box in the morning, but don't limit your cereal consumption to quick breakfasts or this form of the grain. Cereals come in an assortment of grains and processing forms that can add interest to any meal.

For best results, follow the package directions for cooking times and amounts of water to use. These two factors vary, depending on the type of grain and its processing.

Most cereal side dishes are baked or stirred on the cook top, but Muesli doesn't require cooking.

PEAR-OATMEAL BAKE

1 (29-ounce) can pear halves, undrained
2 cups milk
2 tablespoons brown sugar
1 tablespoon butter or margarine
¼ teaspoon salt
¼ teaspoon ground cinnamon
1½ cups regular oats, uncooked
½ cup chopped pecans
¼ cup raisins

Drain pears, reserving 1 cup juice. Set aside 2 pears for garnish. Chop remaining pears; set aside.

Combine 1 cup reserved juice, milk, brown sugar, butter, salt, and cinnamon in a large saucepan; bring to a boil. Add chopped pears, oats, pecans, and raisins. Return mixture to a boil.

Spoon mixture into a lightly greased 2½-quart casserole. Bake at 350° for 20 minutes. Stir mixture, and bake an additional 5 minutes. Garnish dish with reserved pear halves. Yield: 8 to 10 servings.

Anne P. Thomas
Columbia, South Carolina

MUESLI

½ cup soft wheat berries
3 cups water
½ cup raisins
1 cup boiling water
2 apples, cored and chopped
¼ cup lemon juice
⅓ cup quick-cooking oats, uncooked
1 banana, sliced
1 cup seedless green grapes
¼ cup chopped prunes
⅓ cup chopped pecans
1 (8-ounce) carton plain or lemon yogurt
¼ cup honey

Soak wheat berries in 3 cups water 8 hours; drain. Soak raisins in 1 cup boiling water 15 minutes; drain. Combine chopped apple and lemon juice, tossing well.

Combine wheat berries, raisins, apple, lemon juice, oats, and next 4 ingredients, tossing well. Spoon mixture into bowls. Top with a dollop of yogurt, and drizzle with honey. Yield: 7 cups.

Debbie Esprey
Hickory, North Carolina

FULL-OF-FIBER HOT CEREAL

4 cups water
½ cup uncooked regular oats
½ cup uncooked bulgur
¼ cup uncooked hulled buckwheat groats
¼ cup uncooked triticale flakes
2½ tablespoons uncooked regular cream of wheat
2 tablespoons regular grits
⅓ cup raisins
¼ cup chopped cashews
¼ cup sunflower kernels, toasted
¼ cup honey
1 apple, cored and chopped
1 teaspoon ground cinnamon
2 teaspoons butter or margarine
1 cup milk

Bring water to a boil in a large saucepan; stir in oats and next 5 ingredients. Return to a boil; reduce heat, and cook 12 to 15 minutes, stirring occasionally. Stir in raisins and next 6 ingredients. Serve with milk. Yield: 6 to 8 servings.

Note: Additional water may be added, if needed, while cooking the oats mixture.

Mark A. Hopkins
Blacksburg, Virginia

Storing Staples

■ Arrange your kitchen storage area so that you can store food in coolest area of kitchen, away from oven and range.

■ Be sure to keep staples such as sugar, flour, and spices in tightly covered containers at room temperature. Staples that are frequently replenished should be rotated so that the oldest is always used first.

■ Keep staples and all dry foods in their original containers or airtight ones.

SEPTEMBER

Football season is here. Plan a pregame brunch, or pack a picnic basket for tailgating. And for work or school, try our updated versions of brown-bagging. Top it all off with a fancy variation of gingerbread or strawberry shortcake.

Hospitality Is The Common Thread In These Breads

Nothing warms the soul like the steam rising out of a hot-from-the-oven biscuit just opened for a generous pat of butter. And what could be more welcoming than the slightly sweet, savory blend of flavors and the moist, tender, melt-in-your-mouth texture? While everyone, no doubt, champions a personal favorite, all can probably agree that these outstanding variations of home-made quick breads are the epitome of Southern hospitality.

Be it breakfast, lunch, *or* dinner, a few crumbs left on the plate are a telltale sign that the short time in the kitchen was well spent. For hints on making delicious biscuits every time, see "From Our Kitchen to Yours" on the facing page.

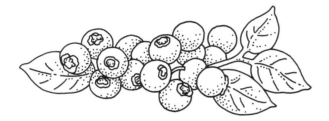

SWEET POTATO BISCUITS

2 cups self-rising flour
¼ cup sugar
3 tablespoons shortening
2 tablespoons butter or margarine, softened
1 cup cooked, mashed sweet potatoes (about 1 large sweet potato)
⅓ cup milk

Combine flour and sugar in a medium bowl; cut in shortening and butter with a pastry blender until mixture resembles coarse meal. Add mashed sweet potatoes and milk, stirring just until dry ingredients are moistened. Turn dough out onto a lightly floured surface; knead 4 or 5 times.

Roll dough to ½-inch thickness; cut with a 2-inch biscuit cutter. Place on lightly greased baking sheets. Bake at 400° for 15 minutes or until golden brown. Yield: 1½ dozen.

Ethel Jernegan
Savannah, Georgia

NUTTY TEA BISCUITS

2 cups all-purpose flour
1 tablespoon plus 1 teaspoon baking powder
½ teaspoon salt
¼ cup sugar
¼ cup shortening
½ cup chopped pecans
1 egg, beaten
⅓ to ½ cup milk

Combine first 4 ingredients in a medium bowl; cut in shortening with a pastry blender until mixture resembles coarse meal. Stir in pecans.

Place egg in a 1-cup measure, adding milk to measure ¾ cup. Add to flour mixture, stirring just until dry ingredients are moistened. Turn dough out onto a lightly floured surface, and knead 4 or 5 times.

Roll dough to ½-inch thickness; cut with a 2-inch biscuit cutter. Place on a lightly greased baking sheet. Bake at 400° for 12 to 15 minutes or until golden brown. Yield: 1½ dozen.

Becky Duncan
Leming, Texas

BLUEBERRY BUTTERMILK BISCUITS

2 cups all-purpose flour
1 tablespoon baking powder
¼ teaspoon baking soda
1 teaspoon salt
½ cup sugar
1 teaspoon grated orange rind
⅓ cup shortening
1 egg, beaten
¾ cup buttermilk
½ cup fresh or frozen blueberries
3 tablespoons butter or margarine, melted
3 tablespoons sugar
¼ teaspoon ground cinnamon
⅛ teaspoon ground nutmeg

Combine first 6 ingredients in a medium bowl; cut in shortening with a pastry blender until mixture resembles coarse meal.

Combine egg and buttermilk; add to flour mixture, stirring just until dry ingredients are moistened. Stir in blueberries. Turn dough out onto a heavily floured surface, and knead 4 or 5 times.

Roll dough to ½-inch thickness; cut with a 2½-inch biscuit cutter. Place on lightly greased baking sheets. Bake at 400° for 15 minutes or until golden brown.

Combine butter and remaining ingredients, stirring well; brush on warm biscuits. Yield: 15 biscuits.

Carolyn Rosen
Nashville, Tennessee

GLAZED RAISIN BISCUITS

2½ cups biscuit mix
2 tablespoons sugar
1 teaspoon ground cinnamon
½ cup raisins
1 egg, beaten
⅔ cup milk
Vanilla Glaze

Combine biscuit mix, sugar, cinnamon, and raisins in a medium bowl; add egg and milk, stirring just until dry ingredients are moistened. Turn dough out onto a lightly floured surface, and knead 4 or 5 times.

Roll dough to ½-inch thickness; cut with a 2-inch biscuit cutter. Place on lightly greased baking sheets. Bake at 350° for 15 minutes or until golden brown. Brush biscuits with Vanilla Glaze. Yield: 1½ dozen.

Vanilla Glaze

⅔ cup sifted powdered sugar
1 tablespoon water
¼ teaspoon vanilla extract

Combine all ingredients. Yield: about ¼ cup.   *Cathy Darling*
Grafton, West Virginia

CHEESE ANGEL BISCUITS

1 package dry yeast
1 teaspoon sugar
2 tablespoons warm water
  (105° to 115°)
1 cup buttermilk
3 cups self-rising flour
1 teaspoon baking powder
¾ teaspoon baking soda
2 tablespoons sugar
⅓ cup shortening
1 cup (4 ounces) shredded sharp
  Cheddar cheese

Combine first 3 ingredients; let stand 5 minutes. Add buttermilk to yeast mixture, and set aside.

Combine flour, baking powder, soda, and 2 tablespoons sugar in a large mixing bowl; cut in shortening with a pastry blender until mixture resembles coarse meal. Stir in shredded Cheddar cheese.

Add buttermilk mixture, stirring just until dry ingredients are moistened. Cover and chill 30 minutes. Turn dough out onto a lightly floured surface, and knead 4 or 5 times.

Roll dough to ½-inch thickness; cut with a 2½-inch biscuit cutter. Place on lightly greased baking

sheets. Cover and let rise in a warm place (85°), free from drafts, 30 minutes. Bake at 400° for 10 to 12 minutes or until golden brown. Yield: 20 biscuits.   *Doris T. Ramsey*
Martinsville, Virginia

RISE-AND-SHINE BISCUITS

1 tablespoon plus 2 teaspoons
  sugar
⅓ cup sour cream
⅓ cup club soda
2 cups biscuit mix

Combine first 3 ingredients in a medium bowl, stirring well. Add biscuit mix, stirring just until dry ingredients are moistened. Turn dough out onto a lightly floured surface, and knead 10 to 12 times.

Shape dough with hands into 6 biscuits about 1-inch thick. Place one biscuit in the center of a lightly greased 8-inch round cakepan. Arrange remaining biscuits in a circle surrounding center biscuit. Bake at 450° for 16 to 18 minutes or until golden brown. Yield: 6 biscuits.
Carol Noble
Burgaw, North Carolina

From Our Kitchen To Yours

Fresh from the oven, steaming, plump biscuits are almost impossible to resist. During breakfast, lunch, or supper, you'll find this tempting quick bread gracing Southern tables. Serve one or all of the varieties of good biscuits on these two pages.

A good biscuit has straight sides and a golden-brown, level top. The crust is crisp, tender, and free from excess flour, and the slightly moist and tender crumb peels off in layers.

Making a delicious biscuit is easier than you may think. The secret of light and flaky biscuits is to begin with a sticky, wet dough and handle it as little as possible. The most tender biscuits contain solid fat, such as shortening or butter. After the dry ingredients are combined, the fat is cut in with a pastry blender, using a chopping motion, until the flour absorbs the fat and the mixture looks like coarse meal. If you choose to use a food processor, combine the dry ingredients in the processor bowl by pulsing one or two times; add the fat, and process, pulsing six or seven times, until the mixture resembles coarse meal.

Biscuits are most often made with quick-acting leavening agents, such as baking powder and baking soda. These ingredients begin releasing bubbles of carbon dioxide as soon as they are moistened; therefore, the liquid is added all at once and stirred quickly with a fork until the mixture stiffens and leaves the sides of the bowl. Too much mixing makes biscuits tough and heavy. If using the processor, slowly add the liquid through the food chute with the processor running until the dough forms a ball leaving the sides of the bowl. (Caution: The processor can easily overwork the dough.) At this point, the dough should be soft and slightly sticky. Sprinkle a board or pastry cloth with only a little flour, and knead the dough lightly four or five times just until it feels soft and not sticky; don't work in too much flour.

In the oven, biscuits rise quickly and are double leavened by steam and gases formed by baking powder or baking soda; dough rolled ½-inch thick produces 1-inch-high, fluffy biscuits. To avoid lopsided biscuits, cut the dough by firmly pressing a floured cutter straight down without twisting. Biscuits should be cut close together, leaving as little dough as possible to reroll. Do not knead the scraps; simply press together, reroll, and cut.

If you like biscuits with crusty sides, place them 1 inch apart on a shiny baking sheet. For soft sides, arrange them close together in a shallow baking pan. After cutting, they should not stand longer than 15 minutes or the carbon dioxide will escape; cover unbaked ones with a cloth or wax paper to prevent drying.

Busy cooks can easily prepare hot biscuits to highlight any meal. Although biscuits taste best served immediately, leftovers can be reheated. Store any leftovers in an airtight container at room temperature up to two days. To reheat, wrap in aluminum foil, and bake at 400° for 10 to 15 minutes or until hot.

Biscuits can be frozen unbaked or partially baked. Bake until they have risen and begun to brown; let cool, package in an airtight container, and freeze. When ready to serve, do not thaw; simply bake in a hot oven until browned. To freeze unbaked biscuits, place on baking sheets, cover, and freeze; then place frozen biscuits in an airtight container. To serve, bake frozen biscuits according to recipe directions, increasing the baking time about 5 minutes or until they're golden brown.

Have Beverages, Will Travel

If fall activities, such as pregame picnics and football games, keep you on the run, take along a little something to quench your thirst on those busy, sunny days.

Each of these beverages can be made ahead, chilled, and then stored in an insulated container until you're hot and thirsty. Just pack ice in the cooler, and then pour the drinks when you're ready.

If you need some quick energy, try one of our simple fruit juice blends. Both Tropical Fruit Whisper and Apple Lemonade will make a hit with all ages. But if the party is strictly for adults only, Piña Colada Punch or Three-Fruit Sangría will surely satisfy.

THREE-FRUIT SANGRÍA

Juice of 1 large orange
Juice of 2 large lemons
Juice of 2 large limes
½ cup sugar
1 (750-milliliter) bottle Burgundy or dry red wine
⅓ cup cognac

Combine first 4 ingredients in a small saucepan. Cook over medium heat until sugar dissolves, stirring constantly; cool.

Combine juice mixture, wine, and cognac; chill beverage thoroughly. Yield: 5 cups.

Harriet O. St. Amant
Vienna, Virginia

PIÑA COLADA PUNCH

1 (46-ounce) can pineapple juice
1 (16-ounce) can cream of coconut
2 cups light rum
2 tablespoons lemon juice
Crushed ice

Combine pineapple juice, cream of coconut, rum, and lemon juice, stirring well. Serve punch over crushed ice. Yield: 9½ cups.

Marietta Marx
Louisville, Kentucky

TROPICAL FRUIT WHISPER

2 cups cranberry-apple drink, chilled
1 cup pineapple juice, chilled
1 cup orange juice, chilled
¼ teaspoon ground ginger

Combine all ingredients, stirring well. Serve over ice. Yield: 1 quart.

Alice McNamara
Eucha, Oklahoma

APPLE LEMONADE

¼ to ½ cup sugar
½ cup water
2 cups apple juice
½ cup lemon juice

Combine sugar and water in a saucepan; cook over medium heat until sugar dissolves.

Combine sugar mixture, apple juice, and lemon juice, stirring well. Let lemonade mixture chill thoroughly. Serve over ice. Yield: 3⅓ cups.

Sarah Bondurant
Hernando, Mississippi

ALMOND TEA

4 regular-size tea bags
2 cups boiling water
1½ cups sugar
⅓ cup lemon juice
1 teaspoon vanilla extract
1 teaspoon almond extract
2 quarts water

Warm teapot by rinsing with small amount of boiling water. Place tea bags in teapot; pour 2 cups boiling water over tea. Cover and steep 3 to 5 minutes.

Remove tea bags from teapot. Add sugar, lemon juice, and flavorings; stir until sugar dissolves. Add 2 quarts water to mixture, and stir well. Refrigerate tea mixture and let chill thoroughly. Serve tea over ice. Yield: 2½ quarts.

Rhonda G. Ford
Talbott, Tennessee

Game-Day Brunch

Friends will cheer when you serve this menu before the game. It's designed so that you can complete most of the cooking in advance.

You can welcome friends with Cranberry Spritzers and serve coffee or juice with the meal.

Cranberry Spritzers
Saucy Scrambled Egg Casserole
Grapefruit
With Pear-Berry Puree

CRANBERRY SPRITZERS

2 (12-ounce) cans frozen
   cranberry juice concentrate,
   thawed and undiluted
4 lemon slices
4 orange slices
4 lime slices
2 (750-milliliter) bottles
   champagne, chilled
Lemon, orange, and lime slices
   (optional)

Combine first 4 ingredients in a large pitcher; cover and refrigerate mixture 8 hours.

Use slotted spoon to remove fruit; add champagne to cranberry juice, stirring gently. Garnish with lemon, orange, and lime slices, if desired. Serve spritzers over crushed ice. Yield: about 9 cups.

Note: Two (23-ounce) bottles chilled sparkling mineral water may be substituted for the champagne.
Linda Keith
Carrollton, Texas

Tip: *To freshen air throughout the house, boil 1 tablespoon of whole cloves in a pan of water.*

SAUCY SCRAMBLED EGG CASSEROLE

¼ cup butter or margarine
½ cup all-purpose flour
4 cups milk
¼ teaspoon pepper
2 (2.5-ounce) jars sliced
   mushrooms, drained
1 (5-ounce) jar dried beef,
   chopped
4 slices bacon, cooked and
   crumbled
16 eggs, beaten
1 cup evaporated milk
¼ cup butter or margarine
Dried beef slices
   (optional)
Chopped fresh parsley
   (optional)

Melt ¼ cup butter in a heavy saucepan over low heat; add flour, stirring until smooth. Cook 1 minute, stirring constantly. Gradually add milk; cook over medium heat, stirring constantly, until thickened and bubbly. Stir in pepper, mushrooms, chopped dried beef, and bacon; remove from heat, and set aside.

Combine eggs and evaporated milk; mix well. Melt ¼ cup butter in a large nonstick skillet over medium heat. Add egg mixture, and cook, without stirring, until egg mixture begins to set on bottom. Draw a spatula across bottom of pan to form large curds. Continue until eggs are thickened but still moist; do not stir constantly. Remove from heat.

Layer half of egg mixture in a lightly greased 13- x 9- x 2-inch baking dish. Cover with half of sauce mixture; repeat procedure with remaining egg and sauce mixtures. Cover and chill 8 hours.

Remove from refrigerator; let stand 30 minutes. Cover and bake at 275° for 1 hour. If desired, garnish with sliced dried beef and chopped parsley. Yield: 12 servings.

To Microwave Bacon and Sauce:
Place bacon on a rack in a 12- x 8- x 2-inch baking dish; cover with paper towels. Microwave at HIGH 3½ to 4½ minutes or until bacon is crisp. Drain bacon; crumble and set aside.

Place ¼ cup butter in a 2-quart glass measure; microwave at HIGH 55 seconds or until butter melts. Add flour, stirring until smooth. Gradually add milk, stirring well. Microwave at HIGH 6 to 8 minutes, stirring every 3 minutes with a whisk until thickened and bubbly. Microwave at HIGH 3 to 4 minutes, stirring at 1-minute intervals. Add pepper, mushrooms, chopped dried beef, and bacon, stirring well. Set aside. Proceed as directed above.
Stanlay Perryman
Birmingham, Alabama

GRAPEFRUIT WITH PEAR-BERRY PUREE

1 (8-ounce) package dried pears
2 cups water
1 cup fresh or frozen blueberries
1 tablespoon light corn syrup
1 teaspoon lemon juice
7 grapefruits
Fresh mint leaves

Combine pears and water in a medium saucepan; cover and simmer 30 minutes. Drain pears, reserving 1 cup liquid.

Position knife blade in food processor bowl. Add pears and blueberries; process until pureed.

Combine fruit puree, reserved liquid, corn syrup, and lemon juice; cover and chill.

Peel and section grapefruits, and place sections on paper towels to drain. Arrange mint and 6 grapefruit sections on each plate, and serve with puree mixture. Yield: 12 servings.
Velma Kestner
Berwind, West Virginia

Appetizers For The Football Crowd

Don't be empty-handed when the crowd gathers at your house to watch a televised football game. Offer a couple of these snacks.

Let the health conscious try Tuna-Stuffed Cherry Tomatoes. Hearty eaters will enjoy meaty Pizza Horns.

BACON SWIRLS

6 slices bacon, cooked and crumbled
1 (4-ounce) can mushroom stems and pieces, drained and chopped
¼ cup mayonnaise or salad dressing
½ teaspoon garlic powder
1 (8-ounce) can refrigerated crescent dinner rolls
2 (3-ounce) packages cream cheese, softened
1 egg white, lightly beaten
Poppy seeds

Combine first 4 ingredients; stir well, and set aside.

Separate crescent dough into 4 rectangles; press perforations to seal. Spread one-fourth of cream cheese over each dough rectangle, leaving ¼-inch margin on one long side and no margin on other sides. Spread one-fourth of bacon mixture evenly over cream cheese. Roll dough, jellyroll fashion, starting at long sides with filling spread to edge; pinch seams to seal. Cut rolls into ½-inch slices; place cut side down on a lightly greased baking sheet.

Brush each slice with egg white, and sprinkle with poppy seeds. Bake slices at 375° for 9 minutes or until lightly browned. Serve warm. Yield: 3 dozen.
Eileen Wehling
Austin, Texas

TUNA-STUFFED CHERRY TOMATOES

36 medium-size cherry tomatoes
1 (6½-ounce) can tuna, drained and flaked
⅓ cup mayonnaise or salad dressing
½ cup chopped celery
¼ cup chopped fresh parsley
2 tablespoons minced green onions
¼ teaspoon pepper
Chopped fresh parsley (optional)

Cut top off each cherry tomato; scoop out pulp, reserving pulp for other uses. Invert tomatoes on paper towels to drain.

Combine tuna and next 5 ingredients; stir well. Cover and chill.

Spoon 1½ teaspoons tuna mixture into each tomato. Garnish with parsley, if desired. Yield: 3 dozen.
Miss C. A. Pierce
Greensburg, Kentucky

PIZZA HORNS

1 pound lean ground beef
1 tablespoon chopped onion
½ cup commercial pizza sauce
1 tablespoon chopped fresh parsley
¼ teaspoon dried whole oregano
Pastry (recipe follows)
1 egg, beaten

Cook ground beef and onion in a heavy skillet until meat is browned, stirring to crumble meat; drain well. Stir in pizza sauce, parsley, and oregano; set aside.

Divide pastry into 6 portions. Roll 1 portion into a 9-inch circle on a lightly floured surface; cut into 8 wedges. Place 1 heaping teaspoon meat mixture at wide end of wedge. Roll each wedge, beginning at wide end. Seal points, and place rolls on a lightly greased baking sheet. Repeat procedure with remaining dough and meat mixture. Brush with beaten egg. Bake at 375° for 20 minutes or until lightly browned. Yield: 4 dozen.

Pastry

2 cups all-purpose flour
½ teaspoon salt
½ cup butter or margarine
⅔ cup sour cream

Combine flour and salt; cut in butter with pastry blender until mixture resembles coarse meal. Stir in sour cream. Shape dough into a ball; cover and chill. Yield: pastry for 4 dozen appetizers.
Dorothy Nieman
Dunnellon, Florida

New Pizzazz For Traditional Desserts

Gingerbread, strawberry shortcake, and apple pie are tasty, old favorite desserts, but some cooks are tempted to try new recipes when company is coming. The recipes offered here, however, add a little intrigue to traditional desserts, turning them into real showstoppers.

GINGERBREAD CAKE ROLL
(pictured on page 224)

3 eggs, separated
1 tablespoon butter or margarine, melted
½ cup molasses
¼ cup sugar
1 cup all-purpose flour
¾ teaspoon baking powder
¾ teaspoon baking soda
⅛ teaspoon salt
½ teaspoon ground cinnamon
½ teaspoon ground cloves
½ teaspoon ground ginger
1 to 2 tablespoons powdered sugar
Spiced Cream
Pecan halves (optional)
Grated orange rind (optional)

Oil bottom and sides of a 15- x 10- x 1-inch jellyroll pan with vegetable oil; line with wax paper, and oil and flour wax paper. Set pan aside.

Beat egg yolks in a large bowl at high speed of an electric mixer until thick. Stir in butter and molasses.

Beat egg whites (at room temperature) until foamy. Gradually add ¼ cup sugar, beating until stiff but not dry. Fold egg whites into yolk mixture. Combine flour and next 6 ingredients; gradually fold flour mixture into egg mixture. Spread batter evenly in prepared pan. Bake at 350° for 8 to 10 minutes.

Sift powdered sugar in a 15- x 10-inch rectangle on a cloth towel. When cake is done, immediately loosen from sides of pan, and turn cake out onto sugared towel. Peel off wax paper. Starting at narrow end, roll up cake and towel together; let cool completely on a wire rack, seam side down.

Unroll cake; spread with half of Spiced Cream, and carefully reroll. Place cake on plate, seam side down. Spread remaining cream on all sides. Pull an icing comb or a fork down length of frosting, if desired.

If desired, garnish cake with pecan halves and grated orange rind. Yield: 10 servings.

Spiced Cream

1½ cups whipping cream
⅓ cup sifted powdered sugar
1 teaspoon ground cinnamon
¼ teaspoon ground cloves
1 teaspoon vanilla extract

Combine all ingredients in a medium bowl; beat until soft peaks form. Yield: 3 cups.

APPLE-AMANDINE PIE

Basic pastry (recipe follows)
¾ cup slivered almonds
½ cup sugar
1 egg
1 tablespoon butter or margarine, melted
2 cups water
2 tablespoons lemon juice
3 medium-size cooking apples, unpeeled
3 tablespoons sugar
3 tablespoons sliced almonds
2 tablespoons butter or margarine, melted
¼ cup apricot preserves
2 tablespoons water
1 tablespoon kirsch or other cherry-flavored liqueur

Roll pastry to ⅛-inch thickness on a lightly floured surface. Place pastry in a 9-inch pieplate; trim excess pastry from edges. Cut small leaves from pastry scraps; moisten edge of piecrust with water, and gently press cutouts around the edge, overlapping slightly. Set aside.

Position knife blade in food processor bowl. Add ¾ cup almonds; process 1 minute or until finely ground. Add ½ cup sugar, egg, and 1 tablespoon butter; process until blended. Spread evenly over pastry.

Combine 2 cups water and lemon juice. Core apples, and cut in half vertically. Cut apples lengthwise into ⅛-inch-thick slices, keeping slices in order as they are cut. Carefully dip each group of apple slices into lemon juice mixture, keeping slices in order; drain well.

Arrange apple slices over almond mixture in the shape of six apple halves, letting slices fan out slightly. Top with 3 tablespoons sugar; sprinkle 3 tablespoons almonds in center and around edge of pie. Drizzle with 2 tablespoons butter. Bake at 400° for 40 to 50 minutes or until pie is golden brown.

Combine preserves and 2 tablespoons water; cook over low heat until preserves melt. Press mixture through a sieve, discarding pulp. Stir kirsch into syrup. Carefully brush syrup over pie. Yield: one 9-inch pie.

Pie Pastry Tips

■ Unless otherwise specified, always preheat the oven at least 20 minutes before baking.

■ Roll pie pastry on a lightly floured surface, but remember that too much flour toughens the crust. A stockinette rolling pin cover minimizes the amount of flour needed during rolling.

■ Make a quick job of rolling pastry. Roll lightly; keep in mind that too much handling will result in a tough crust.

■ For an attractive pastry shell, brush the top with milk or slightly beaten egg white before baking. You may then sprinkle the top of the pastry with sugar for a special glaze.

■ Pans used for pastry never need greasing. The pastry shell or crumb crust will not stick to the sides of the pan.

Basic Pastry

1¼ cups all-purpose flour
½ teaspoon salt
⅓ cup plus 2 tablespoons shortening
3 to 4 tablespoons cold water

Combine flour and salt; cut in shortening with pastry blender until mixture resembles coarse meal. Sprinkle cold water (1 tablespoon at a time) evenly over surface; stir with a fork until dry ingredients are moistened. Shape into a ball; cover and chill. Yield: pastry for one 9-inch pie.

CHOCOLATE-STRAWBERRY SHORTCAKE
(pictured on back cover)

½ cup shortening
1¼ cups sugar
2 eggs, separated
1¼ cups sifted cake flour
2 teaspoons baking powder
¼ teaspoon salt
⅓ cup cocoa
⅔ cup milk
1 teaspoon vanilla extract
1 envelope unflavored gelatin
¼ cup cold water
2 cups whipping cream
½ cup sifted powdered sugar
3 cups fresh strawberries, sliced
3 whole strawberries (optional)

Cream shortening; gradually add 1¼ cups sugar, beating well at medium speed of an electric mixer. Add egg yolks, beating well.

Combine flour, baking powder, salt, and cocoa; add to creamed mixture alternately with milk, beginning and ending with flour mixture. Mix after each addition. Stir in vanilla.

Beat egg whites (at room temperature) until stiff peaks form. Gently fold into batter. Pour into 3 greased and floured 9-inch round cakepans. Bake at 350° for 18 minutes or until a wooden pick inserted in center comes out clean. Let cakes cool in pans 10 minutes; remove from pans, and cool.

Sprinkle gelatin over cold water in a small saucepan; let stand 1 minute. Cook over low heat, stirring until gelatin dissolves.

Beat whipping cream in a chilled bowl at low speed of an electric mixer, gradually adding dissolved gelatin. Increase to medium speed, and beat until mixture begins to thicken. Add powdered sugar, and beat at high speed until soft peaks form.

Place 1 cake layer on serving plate. Spread one-third of whipped cream over layer, and arrange half of sliced berries on top. Repeat procedure, ending with whipped cream. Garnish with whole strawberries, if desired. Yield: one 3-layer cake.

Tempting Lunchbox Treats

Brown bagging used to be for people on a budget—but no longer. Folks are realizing that packing a lunch allows them to choose light and healthy foods to eat when and where they want—in a park, at an outdoor concert, or at their desks.

Keeping lunch light helps prevent a midafternoon slump. Including complex carbohydrates (pasta, breads, starches) and lean protein, such as chicken or turkey, provides the nutrition that's needed to stay alert through the afternoon.

Airtight plastic containers and sealable sandwich bags make storing lunch easy. If refrigeration isn't available at your workplace, a minicooler or an insulated bag kept cool by a water-filled, frozen plastic container is a good idea. Or freeze small cans of juice, and pack them with lunch.

CREAMY TURKEY-BASIL PASTA
(pictured on page 221)

1 tablespoon chopped fresh basil
⅛ teaspoon garlic powder
⅛ teaspoon dry mustard
2 tablespoons egg substitute
1 teaspoon lemon juice
¼ cup olive oil
2 tablespoons nonfat yogurt
2 cups cooked rotini noodles
   (cooked without salt or fat)
1 cup fresh broccoli flowerets
1 cup cubed cooked turkey breast
2 ounces low-fat Swiss cheese,
   cut into thin strips
¾ cup chopped tomato
2 tablespoons sliced green onions
¼ teaspoon salt

Combine first 5 ingredients in container of an electric blender or food processor. Process 20 seconds. With motor running, gradually add olive oil in a slow, steady stream. Add yogurt (at room temperature), and process 5 seconds. Set aside.

Combine rotini noodles and remaining ingredients; add dressing, and toss gently. Cover and chill. Yield: 4 servings (285 calories per 1¼-cup serving).

☐ *16.8 grams protein, 15.4 grams fat, 21 grams carbohydrate, 22 milligrams cholesterol, 541 milligrams sodium, and 167 milligrams calcium.*

ORIENTAL CHICKEN PITA

2 (4-ounce) skinned, boned
   chicken breast halves
½ cup alfalfa sprouts
¼ cup diced water chestnuts
¼ cup sliced green onions
1 tablespoon rice vinegar
1 tablespoon reduced-sodium soy
   sauce
1 teaspoon sesame oil
1 (6-inch) whole wheat pita bread
   round, cut in half
2 lettuce leaves

Combine chicken and enough water to cover in a medium saucepan. Cook over medium heat 15 minutes or until tender; drain. Chop chicken into bite-size pieces.

Combine chicken and next 3 ingredients. Combine vinegar, soy sauce, and sesame oil; pour over chicken mixture, and toss gently. Line pita bread halves with lettuce; fill with chicken mixture. Yield: 2 servings (232 calories per serving with 1 cup chicken salad).

Note: Chicken mixture may be stored in an airtight container and chilled until ready to serve.

☐ *25.3 grams protein, 6.2 grams fat, 16.4 grams carbohydrate, 63 milligrams cholesterol, 303 milligrams sodium, and 47 milligrams calcium.*

HAM-AND-CHEESE LETTUCE ROLLS

2 teaspoons reduced-calorie
   mayonnaise
2 teaspoons prepared mustard
⅛ teaspoon celery seeds
⅛ teaspoon lemon juice
2 (¾-ounce) slices cooked ham
2 (⅔-ounce) slices low-fat Swiss
   cheese
2 large lettuce leaves
½ cup alfalfa sprouts

Combine first 4 ingredients, and set mixture aside.

Place 1 ham slice and 1 Swiss cheese slice on each lettuce leaf; spread evenly with mayonnaise mixture. Top with alfalfa sprouts, and roll up jellyroll fashion; secure with wooden picks. Wrap in plastic wrap, and chill. Yield: 2 servings (81 calories per roll).

☐ *9.5 grams protein, 4.1 grams fat, 2.1 grams carbohydrate, 15 milligrams cholesterol, 612 milligrams sodium, and 146 milligrams calcium.*
Frances Spedaliere
Virginia Beach, Virginia

PASTA SALAD

3 cups cooked tri-colored rotini
   noodles (cooked without salt
   or fat)
¼ cup commercial reduced-calorie
   Italian salad dressing
¾ cup sweet red pepper strips
½ cup sliced carrot
¼ cup sliced green onions
1 (14-ounce) can artichoke
   hearts, drained and quartered
¼ cup grated Parmesan cheese
¼ teaspoon dried whole basil
¼ teaspoon freshly ground pepper
¼ cup commercial reduced-calorie
   Italian salad dressing

Combine cooked rotini and ¼ cup Italian salad dressing; toss gently. Cover and chill.

Combine red pepper strips and remaining ingredients; add chilled rotini, and toss gently. Serve salad chilled. Yield: 5 cups (121 calories per 1-cup serving).

☐ *5.2 grams protein, 1.8 grams fat, 22 grams carbohydrate, 3 milligrams cholesterol, 416 milligrams sodium, and 87 milligrams calcium.*
Anne P. Pope
Chapel Hill, North Carolina

BLACK BEAN SALAD

2 (15-ounce) cans black beans,
   drained and rinsed
1 cup chopped tomato
¾ cup chopped sweet red pepper
⅔ cup sliced green onions
½ cup chopped celery
1 tablespoon lemon rind
1 clove garlic, minced
2 tablespoons chopped cilantro
   leaves (optional)
1 (0.7-ounce) envelope Italian
   salad dressing mix
¾ cup water
¼ teaspoon red pepper
2 tablespoons olive oil

Combine first 7 ingredients and, if desired, cilantro leaves; set aside. Combine dressing mix and remaining ingredients in a jar. Cover tightly; shake vigorously. Pour dressing over salad, and toss gently. Cover and chill. Toss gently before serving. Yield: 8 servings (140 calories per ¾-cup serving).

☐ *6.7 grams protein, 3.9 grams fat, 20.9 grams carbohydrate, 0 milligrams cholesterol, 236 milligrams sodium, and 33 milligrams calcium.*

Tip: *Add marinated vegetable salads to your next dinner party. They can be prepared in advance and chilled until serving time—an important bonus for the busy cook.*

TOMATO SOUP
(pictured on page 221)

1 (16-ounce) can reduced-sodium
   whole tomatoes, undrained
1 (14½-ounce) can stewed
   tomatoes, undrained
½ teaspoon dried whole basil
½ teaspoon dried whole oregano
¼ teaspoon freshly ground pepper

Combine all ingredients in container of an electric blender or food processor; process until smooth. Pour into a small saucepan, and cook over medium heat until mixture boils. Cover, reduce heat, and simmer 15 to 20 minutes. Serve hot. Yield: 4 cups (50 calories per 1-cup serving).

☐ *1.9 grams protein, 0.2 gram fat, 12 grams carbohydrate, 0 milligrams cholesterol, 276 milligrams sodium, and 78 milligrams calcium.*

STUFFED BAKED APPLES

4 medium-size baking apples,
   cored
¼ cup raisins
¼ teaspoon ground cinnamon
¾ cup water
1 teaspoon lemon juice

Peel top third of each apple; place in an 8-inch square baking dish. Place 1 tablespoon raisins in each cavity, and sprinkle evenly with cinnamon. Combine water and lemon juice; pour over apples. Cover and bake at 375° for 45 minutes; chill. Yield: 4 servings (109 calories per apple).

☐ *0.5 gram protein, 0.5 gram fat, 28.4 grams carbohydrate, 0 milligrams cholesterol, 1 milligram sodium, and 16 milligrams calcium.*
Alta M. Russell
Victoria, Texas

BANANA-RAISIN MUFFINS
(pictured on page 221)

1¼ cups all-purpose flour
½ cup whole wheat flour
1 teaspoon baking soda
¼ teaspoon salt
¼ cup vegetable oil
¼ cup egg substitute
⅓ cup honey
1 cup mashed ripe banana
⅓ cup raisins
1 teaspoon vanilla extract
Vegetable cooking spray

Combine flours, baking soda, and salt in a large bowl; make a well in center of mixture.

Combine oil and next 5 ingredients; add to dry ingredients, stirring just until moistened. Coat paper muffin pan liners with cooking spray; spoon batter into liners, filling two-thirds full. Bake at 350° for 15 minutes. Remove from pans immediately. Yield: 18 muffins (116 calories per muffin).

☐ *2 grams protein, 3.5 grams fat, 19.9 grams carbohydrate, 0 milligrams cholesterol, 84 milligrams sodium, and 16 milligrams calcium.*

QUICK!
Start With Soup

Think a moment. How many cans of soup are sitting on your pantry shelves? If you're like most of our readers, quite a few. Busy cooks know how easy it is to rely on soup for fast meals—and for more than just soup and a sandwich. Using soup eliminates time spent making sauces or thickening cooking liquids in more complicated recipes. Here, our readers make smart use of soup with a variety of entrées.

SHORTCUT VEGETABLE-BEEF STEW

3 large red potatoes
3 large carrots
1 quart water
1 (1.25-ounce) envelope onion
   soup mix
1 pound lean ground beef
1 (10¾-ounce) can cream of
   mushroom soup, undiluted

Cube potatoes. Scrape carrots, and cut into ½-inch slices. Combine potatoes, carrots, water, and onion soup mix in a large saucepan; bring to a boil. Cover, reduce heat, and simmer 15 minutes or until vegetables are tender. Do not drain.

Cook ground beef in a skillet until browned, stirring to crumble. Drain. Stir ground beef and mushroom soup into vegetable mixture. Cook until thoroughly heated. Yield: 4 servings.
Jennifer Cairns
Alabaster, Alabama

GOLDEN CHOPS WITH VEGETABLES

6 (½-inch-thick) pork chops
   (about 2¼ pounds)
1 (10¾-ounce) can golden
   mushroom soup, undiluted
¼ cup water
½ teaspoon rubbed sage
1 cup sliced carrot
½ cup chopped onion
1 medium-size green pepper, cut
   into strips

Brown pork chops in a large nonstick skillet; remove pork chops, and drain. Combine soup, water, and sage in skillet; add carrot and onion. Arrange pork chops over soup mixture; cover and simmer over medium heat 15 minutes, stirring and rearranging pork chops once. Add green pepper; cover and cook an additional 10 minutes. Yield: 6 servings.
Pamela Deutsch
Dallas, Texas

SHRIMP CHOWDER

8 slices bacon
1 medium onion, chopped
1 stalk celery, chopped
1 green pepper, chopped
2 (10¾-ounce) cans cream of
   potato soup, undiluted
1 (10¾-ounce) can cream of
   celery soup, undiluted
2 (4¼-ounce) cans small shrimp,
   drained and rinsed
4 cups milk
¼ teaspoon pepper

Cook bacon in a large Dutch oven until crisp; remove bacon, reserving 1 tablespoon drippings in Dutch oven. Crumble bacon, and set aside.

Sauté onion, celery, and green pepper in bacon drippings until tender. Add potato soup and remaining ingredients, stirring well. Cook over medium heat until thoroughly heated. Sprinkle each serving with bacon. Yield: 2½ quarts.
Letty Albritton
Athens, Alabama

EASY CHICKEN POT PIE

1 (5-ounce) can chicken, drained
1 (10¾-ounce) can cream of
   chicken soup, undiluted
1 (16-ounce) can mixed
   vegetables, drained
½ cup milk
¼ teaspoon pepper
1 (4.5-ounce) can refrigerated
   tender-layer buttermilk biscuits

Combine first 5 ingredients, mixing well. Spoon into a lightly greased 10- x 6- x 2-inch baking dish.

Separate biscuits; place on top of pie. Bake at 450° for 20 minutes, covering loosely with foil after 12 minutes. Yield: 4 to 6 servings.
Ranae Phelps
Dallas, Texas

QUICK CURRIED CHICKEN

1 pound boneless chicken breasts, cubed
1 medium onion, chopped
¼ cup butter or margarine, melted
1 (10¾-ounce) can cream of chicken soup, undiluted
1 to 2 teaspoons curry powder
1 (8-ounce) carton sour cream
Hot cooked rice

Sauté chicken and onion in butter in a skillet until chicken is tender. Stir in soup and curry powder; cook over medium heat until bubbly. Add sour cream; heat thoroughly. Serve over rice. Yield: 4 to 6 servings.
Sharon McClatchey
Muskogee, Oklahoma

Tip: You may purchase a whole, fully cooked roast chicken to substitute for the sautéed chicken breasts. Dice chicken, and add to soup mixture; cook as directed.

Curry, A Seasoning With Many Spices

For years, good cooks have flavored sauces with curry powder for a distinctive taste. Now many have discovered that curry powder's rich, heady flavor has a number of uses. For Curried Vegetables, there's no sauce at all; the recipe teams the unusual blend of spices to a medley of stir-fried vegetables. On the other hand, Chicken Curry is a traditionally thick curry-seasoned sauce with chunks of chicken served over rice.

The reader who sent us the recipe for Chicken Curry says that it is perfect for entertaining. With it, she serves a green salad or broccoli and cauliflower; then for dessert she offers her guests a selection of homemade cookies. The complete meal can be made the day before.

CHICKEN CURRY

6 chicken breast halves
2 cloves garlic
2 bay leaves
4 whole peppercorns
1 teaspoon salt
1 carrot, sliced
1 onion, sliced
½ cup chopped celery
1 apple, peeled, cored, and chopped
3 tablespoons butter or margarine, melted
1½ tablespoons curry powder
½ teaspoon chili powder
3 tablespoons all-purpose flour
¼ teaspoon ground mace
¼ teaspoon ground allspice
¼ teaspoon ground nutmeg
¼ teaspoon ground cinnamon
¼ teaspoon ground cloves
Celery leaves (optional)
Hot cooked rice
Assorted condiments

Place chicken, garlic, bay leaves, peppercorns, and salt in a Dutch oven; add water to cover. Bring to a boil over medium heat; cover, reduce heat, and simmer 45 minutes or until tender. Drain, reserving broth. Bone chicken; cut into bite-size pieces.

Sauté carrot, onion, celery, and apple in butter in a Dutch oven 15 minutes or until tender. Add curry and chili powder, and cook 5 minutes, stirring occasionally. Add ½ cup reserved chicken broth. Place mixture in container of an electric blender, and process until smooth. Add flour, and process until well blended. Return mixture to Dutch oven, and cook until thickened. Gradually add 2 cups reserved chicken broth, stirring constantly. Cook 5 minutes. Add mace and next 4 ingredients. Gently stir in chicken. Garnish with celery leaves, if desired. Serve over rice with several of the following condiments: flaked coconut, peanuts, chopped green pepper, chopped green onions, chopped hard-cooked egg, chutney, currants, and crumbled cooked bacon. Yield: 6 servings.
Edwina Foster Evans
Birmingham, Alabama

CURRIED VEGETABLES

1 cup chicken broth
1 tablespoon cornstarch
½ teaspoon salt
2 tablespoons vegetable oil
1 cup sliced carrot
1 cup cauliflower flowerets
⅓ pound fresh green beans, broken into 1-inch pieces
1 cup sliced zucchini
1 small sweet red pepper, coarsely chopped
1 cup broccoli flowerets
2 to 3 teaspoons curry powder

Combine first 3 ingredients; stir until cornstarch dissolves. Set aside.

Heat oil in a large skillet. Add vegetables; stir-fry 8 minutes or until crisp-tender. Add curry powder; stir-fry 15 seconds. Stir in cornstarch mixture, and stir-fry 1 minute or until thickened. Serve immediately. Yield: 6 to 8 servings.
Peggy Fowler Revels
Woodruff, South Carolina

Curry Tips

■ When seasoning foods with curry powder, keep in mind that it is a rich blend of turmeric, coriander, cumin, red pepper, and fenugreek.

■ For a wonderfully seasoned popcorn, add ½ to ¾ teaspoon curry powder to 4 cups buttered, salted popcorn. Serve with an ice-cold beverage.

The Simple Goodness Of Tomatoes

As brilliant as the red setting sun, tomatoes are the base of many elaborate soups and sauces. But for purists, simple recipes may offer the best treatment of the plump, juicy produce. In the following recipes, we chop or slice the tomatoes and add only a few ingredients to let the tangy flavor shine through.

CLASSY GAZPACHO

8 large tomatoes, peeled and
    diced
1 large cucumber, peeled, seeded,
    and diced
1 green pepper, diced
1 cup cold water
¼ cup olive oil
3 tablespoons red wine vinegar
2 small cloves garlic, crushed
¾ teaspoon salt
½ teaspoon pepper
¼ cup fine, dry breadcrumbs

Combine all ingredients except breadcrumbs. Stir well; cover and chill 8 hours. Ladle gazpacho into serving bowl; sprinkle with breadcrumbs. Yield: about 2 quarts.

Sharlyn Davis
Norfolk, Virginia

TOMATO-HERB SALAD

3 medium tomatoes, sliced
2 tablespoons vegetable oil
2 tablespoons white wine vinegar
½ teaspoon salt
¼ teaspoon pepper
2 tablespoons chopped fresh
    chives

Arrange tomatoes in a 13- x 9- x 2-inch dish. Combine oil, vinegar, salt, and pepper in a jar; cover tightly, and shake vigorously. Pour dressing over tomatoes. Sprinkle with chives. Cover and chill at least 2 hours. Yield: 4 to 6 servings.

Edith Wetherington
Valdosta, Georgia

TOMATO-MOZZARELLA SALAD

½ pound fresh mozzarella cheese,
    in brine or 1 (6-ounce) package
    chèvre cheese
1 head Boston lettuce
3 large tomatoes, sliced
¼ teaspoon salt
Vinaigrette dressing (recipe
    follows)

Remove cheese from brine; slice cheese with an electric knife into 12 slices, ⅛- to ¼-inch thick. Cut 12 rounds from cheese using a 2- to 2½-inch cutter. Reserve cheese scraps in brine for other uses. Set cheese rounds aside. If using chèvre cheese, slice roll into 12 (⅛- to ¼-inch) slices.

Line serving platter or 6 salad plates with lettuce. Arrange tomato slices on lettuce, and sprinkle tomatoes with salt. Top each tomato slice with a cheese round. Spoon dressing over salad, and serve immediately. Yield: 6 servings.

Vinaigrette Dressing

½ cup olive oil
⅓ cup white wine vinegar
1½ tablespoons chopped fresh
    basil or 1½ teaspoons dried
    whole basil
¼ teaspoon salt
⅛ teaspoon freshly ground pepper

Combine all ingredients in a jar; cover tightly, and shake vigorously. Chill thoroughly. Yield: about 1 cup.

Serve Summer Tomatoes All Year

The notion that tomatoes won't taste as good in a couple of months as they do now has been challenged. Years of research have provided improved winter tomatoes for consumers. If handled properly, these tomatoes should taste summer fresh.

Winter tomatoes have to be shipped pale pink in order to reach their destinations in good shape. But when you buy the dull-pink-looking tomatoes, let them ripen just as you would bananas or avocados.

Allow them to sit a few days at room temperature, and they'll redden and soften nicely. The length of time it takes depends on how red they are when you buy them. Placing these tomatoes in a fruit-ripening bowl may speed the process slightly.

The secret to making sure tomatoes ripen is keeping them at room temperature. *Never* put tomatoes in the refrigerator because the cold temperature stops the ripening process and kills tomato flavor. Once ripened, they'll still keep a few more days without refrigeration.

If you follow these directions yet the tomatoes never ripen, perhaps your merchant or his transporter chilled the tomatoes at some point.

Right: *For a special lunch that's also healthy, try Tomato Soup, Creamy Turkey-Basil Pasta, a Banana-Raisin Muffin, and fresh fruit. (Recipes begin on page 216.)*

Above: *Types of pasta are easily identified. (Top row) spinach mostaccioli, tri-colored rotini, bow ties, and ziti (bottom row) rigatoni, vegetable-colored elbow macaroni, spinach fettuccine, and seashells.*

Top: *These three pasta dishes with low-fat toppings are delectable treats for light and healthy eating: (from left) Marinara Sauce (page 239) over mostaccioli, Seafood Sauce (page 239) over spinach fettuccine, and Chicken Marsala (page 237) over linguine.*

Left: *Marinara Sauce (page 239) spooned over Meatballs (page 237) and a bed of linguine makes a stunning dish for a pasta bar. Round out the menu with a green salad, Parmesan cheese, and Caraway Breadsticks (page 239).*

Try a delightful variation on an old favorite. You'll hardly recognize Gingerbread Cake Roll (page 214); it tastes like the familiar single-layer cake topped with whipped cream, but it looks spectacular.

Pizza For Vegetable Lovers

If you're a vegetable-pizza fan but hate all the chopping, you'll want to try Vegetarian Processor Pizza. According to Margaret Clements of Alachua, Florida, even the crust is mixed in the food processor.

VEGETARIAN PROCESSOR PIZZA

1 (6.5-ounce) package pizza crust
　mix
½ small onion, quartered
1 clove garlic
1 cup Italian tomato sauce
¾ teaspoon dried whole basil
¼ teaspoon dried whole oregano
½ medium zucchini
½ medium-size sweet red pepper
½ medium eggplant, peeled
¼ pound fresh mushrooms
¾ cup ripe olives
2 tablespoons salad olives
4 ounces mozzarella cheese
½ cup grated Parmesan cheese

Combine ingredients for pizza crust according to package directions. Position plastic mixing blade or knife blade in food processor bowl; add pizza crust mixture. Process about 20 seconds or until mixture forms a ball. Place dough in a greased mixing bowl, turning to grease top. Cover and let stand in a warm place (85°), free from drafts, 5 minutes. With greased hands, spread dough in bottom and ½ inch up sides of a 13- x 9- x 2-inch baking dish; bake at 400° for 5 minutes.

Position knife blade in processor bowl; add onion and garlic. Process until finely chopped. Add tomato sauce, basil, and oregano; process 10 seconds. Spread half of sauce over crust; set remainder aside.

Position slicing disc in processor bowl; using medium pressure on food pusher, slice zucchini. Arrange half over pizza; set remainder aside.

Repeat slicing procedure with red pepper, eggplant, mushrooms, and olives. Layer half over zucchini, and set remainder aside.

Position shredding disc in processor bowl; process mozzarella cheese until shredded. Sprinkle half each of mozzarella cheese and Parmesan cheese over pizza; set remainder aside. Spread remaining sauce on top of cheeses.

Repeat layering procedure with remaining vegetables; bake at 425° for 10 minutes. Sprinkle with remaining cheeses; bake an additional 5 minutes or until melted. Yield: 4 servings.

No-Fret Family Supper

Your family will enjoy the taste of this easy-to-prepare meal. Not only have we created a worry-free, weeknight family supper, but we have also mapped out its preparation to make the most efficient use of your time and energy. With few ingredients, the recipes are easy, and together they make an attractive, delicious, nutritious meal.

Pretty Pear Plate
Mustard-Apricot Pork Chops
Oven-Steamed Rice
Lemon-Garlic Zucchini

Plan: Prepare rice. While it is baking, assemble pear salad, and place in refrigerator to chill. There's time to set the table before preparing the pork chops and zucchini.

PRETTY PEAR PLATE

1 (8-ounce) can jellied cranberry
　sauce, chilled
1 (16-ounce) can pear halves,
　drained
4 lettuce leaves
2 tablespoons whipped cream
　cheese
2 tablespoons sour cream
2 tablespoons chopped pecans

Cut cranberry sauce into 8 slices. Cut each pear half lengthwise into 2 pieces. Place lettuce on 4 individual salad plates. Arrange 2 slices of cranberry sauce on each lettuce leaf. Arrange pears evenly on cranberry sauce in spoke fashion.

Combine cream cheese and sour cream; spoon 1 tablespoon cream mixture in center of pears, and sprinkle with pecans. Yield: 4 servings.
Mrs. Thomas Lee Adams
Kingsport, Tennessee

MUSTARD-APRICOT PORK CHOPS

⅓ cup apricot preserves
2 tablespoons Dijon mustard
4 (¾-inch-thick) pork chops
3 green onions, chopped

Combine preserves and mustard in a small saucepan; heat until preserves melt, stirring occasionally. Set aside.

Trim excess fat from pork chops, and place chops on a lightly greased broiler pan. Broil 4 inches from heat for 5 minutes; brush chops with half of glaze, and turn. Broil 5 minutes, and brush with remaining glaze. Broil an additional 2 minutes, and sprinkle with green onions. Yield: 4 servings.
Carol Y. Chastain
San Antonio, Texas

OVEN-STEAMED RICE

1 cup uncooked long-grain rice
2 cups canned diluted chicken
   broth
1 (4-ounce) jar sliced mushrooms,
   drained
1 small onion, chopped
1 teaspoon parsley flakes
¼ teaspoon salt

Combine all ingredients; stir well. Pour into a lightly greased 1½-quart casserole. Cover and bake at 350° for 55 minutes or until rice is tender and liquid is absorbed. Yield: 4 servings.
Ginny Whitt
Campbellsville, Kentucky

LEMON-GARLIC ZUCCHINI

4 medium zucchini, diagonally
   sliced
1 clove garlic, crushed
2 tablespoons lemon juice
2 tablespoons olive oil
¼ teaspoon salt
¼ teaspoon pepper

Combine all ingredients in a skillet. Cook over low heat 5 to 7 minutes or until zucchini is tender, stirring frequently. Yield: 4 servings.
P. Keeney
Newark, Delaware

Tex-Mex For Two

These recipes for two servings of Tex-Mex dishes are great for singles and couples because there won't be a lot of leftovers.

Use fresh Anaheim green chiles or canned whole green chiles for Chiles Rellenos. Topped with spicy picante sauce, it's a dish with lots of zip.

Guacamole served on the side or spooned over Chicken Flautas adds color and flavor. Roll up each tortilla tightly, and secure with a wooden pick to hold in the filling.

CHICKEN FLAUTAS WITH GUACAMOLE

¼ cup chopped onion
1 clove garlic, minced
1 tablespoon vegetable oil
1½ teaspoons cornstarch
¼ cup chicken broth
1 cup cooked shredded chicken
½ teaspoon salt
¼ teaspoon pepper
2 tablespoons chopped green
   chiles
6 (6-inch) corn tortillas
Vegetable oil
Guacamole

Sauté onion and garlic in 1 tablespoon oil in a skillet until tender. Set aside. Combine cornstarch and chicken broth; add cornstarch mixture, chicken, and next 3 ingredients to onion mixture. Cook over medium heat, stirring constantly, until mixture thickens. Set aside.

Fry tortillas, one at a time, in ¼ inch hot oil (375°) about 5 seconds on each side or just until softened. Drain on paper towels. Spread about 2 tablespoons chicken mixture in center of each tortilla. Roll up each tortilla tightly, and secure with a wooden pick. Heat oil in skillet. Add flautas, and brown on all sides over high heat (375°). Drain on paper towels. Serve with Guacamole. Yield: 2 servings.

Guacamole

1 ripe avocado, peeled, seeded,
   and mashed
2 tablespoons chopped onion
1 medium tomato, peeled and
   chopped
1 clove garlic, minced
2 tablespoons lemon juice
¼ teaspoon salt
¼ teaspoon pepper

Combine all ingredients in a small serving bowl, stirring until blended. Yield: 1¾ cups.
Evelyn Giles
Conyers, Georgia

CHILES RELLENOS

4 fresh Anaheim green chiles
4 ounces Longhorn cheese or
   Monterey Jack cheese
1 egg, separated
1 teaspoon all-purpose flour
⅛ teaspoon baking powder
½ cup all-purpose flour
¼ teaspoon salt
Vegetable oil
Commercial picante sauce

Place chiles on a baking sheet; broil 5 to 6 inches from heat, turning often with tongs, until chiles are blistered on all sides. Immediately place in a plastic storage bag; fasten securely, and let steam 10 to 15 minutes. Remove peel of each chile (chiles will be limp). If desired, carefully remove seeds, leaving sides of chiles and stem ends intact.

Cut cheese into 4 strips; place inside chiles, trimming strips to fit chiles, if necessary. Secure with wooden picks, and set aside.

Beat egg white (at room temperature) until stiff peaks form. Combine egg yolk, 1 teaspoon flour, and baking powder. Fold yolk mixture into whites; set aside.

Combine ½ cup flour and salt; dredge chiles in flour mixture, coating well; dip in egg mixture. Pour oil to a depth of 2 inches into a skillet; heat to 375°. Fry chiles, turning once, until golden brown. Drain on paper towels. Serve immediately with picante sauce. Yield: 2 servings.
Mrs. Harry Zimmer
El Paso, Texas

Breakfast For A Pair

Weekend mornings are cherished times. Whether you rise with the sun or sneak out for the newspaper and crawl back under the covers with it, breakfast with your favorite person is a must on your day off.

Oven-Baked Pancake for Two tastes as good as it looks. Be sure to bring it straight to the table from the oven to enjoy the height of its presentation. It will soon fall, but the flavor will still be tops. Overnight French Toast gives morning convenience. The ingredients are combined the evening before; then they're cooked quickly in the morning.

PUFFED CHEESE OMELET

3 tablespoons butter or margarine
3 tablespoons all-purpose flour
⅛ to ¼ teaspoon salt
¾ cup milk
⅓ cup (1.3 ounces) shredded extra-sharp Cheddar cheese
3 eggs, separated

Melt butter in a heavy saucepan over low heat; add flour and salt, stirring until smooth. Cook 1 minute, stirring constantly.

Gradually add milk; cook over medium heat, stirring constantly, until thickened and bubbly. Add cheese, stirring until melted; remove from heat, and cool slightly.

Beat egg yolks until thick and lemon colored. Gradually stir about one-fourth of hot mixture into yolks; add to remaining hot mixture, stirring constantly. Beat egg whites (at room temperature) until stiff but not dry; fold into cheese mixture. Spoon into two 3-cup baking dishes. Bake at 350° for 20 minutes or until puffed and golden brown. Yield: 2 servings. *Mrs. William H. Smith*
Lynchburg, Virginia

OVERNIGHT FRENCH TOAST

2 eggs, beaten
½ cup milk
1 tablespoon orange juice
1½ teaspoons sugar
⅛ teaspoon salt
½ teaspoon ground cinnamon
¼ teaspoon vanilla extract
6 (¾-inch-thick) slices French bread
2 tablespoons butter or margarine, divided
Powdered sugar

Combine eggs, milk, orange juice, sugar, salt, cinnamon, and vanilla; beat well. Set aside.

Place bread in a single layer in a shallow dish. Pour egg mixture over bread; turn slices to coat evenly. Cover and refrigerate 8 hours.

Melt 1 tablespoon butter in a large skillet; arrange 3 slices bread in skillet, and cook 3 minutes on each side or until browned. Repeat procedure with remaining butter and bread slices. Sprinkle toast with powdered sugar. Yield: 2 to 3 servings.

Mary Kay Menees
White Pine, Tennessee

OVEN-BAKED PANCAKE FOR TWO

3 eggs
½ cup all-purpose flour
½ cup milk
2 tablespoons butter or margarine, melted
¼ teaspoon salt
2 tablespoons sugar
2 tablespoons sliced almonds, toasted
2 tablespoons butter or margarine
2 tablespoons lemon juice

Beat eggs at medium speed of an electric mixer until well blended. Gradually add flour, beating until smooth. Add milk, 2 tablespoons butter, and salt; beat until batter is smooth. Pour batter into a greased 10-inch skillet. Bake at 400° for 15 minutes or until pancake is puffed and golden brown.

Sprinkle with sugar and toasted almonds. Combine 2 tablespoons butter and lemon juice; heat until butter melts. Serve over hot pancake. Yield: 2 servings. *Ruth S. Roth*
Springfield, Virginia

OAT PANCAKES

1 cup all-purpose flour
2 teaspoons baking powder
¼ teaspoon salt
½ cup regular oats, uncooked
1 tablespoon sugar
1 egg, beaten
1 cup milk
½ cup grated apple
3 tablespoons butter or margarine, melted

Combine first 5 ingredients in a bowl; make a well in the center. Combine egg, milk, apple, and butter; add to dry ingredients, stirring just until moistened.

For each pancake, pour about ⅓ cup batter onto a hot, lightly greased griddle. Turn pancakes when tops are covered with bubbles and edges look cooked. Yield: 8 (4-inch) pancakes. *Helen Fraizer*
Lucedale, Mississippi

Fill Omelets
For Breakfast
Or Lunch

Don't wait until you go out for breakfast to enjoy an omelet. These egg rounds are simple to make at home and versatile enough to serve for any meal of the day.

Omelets are nothing more than a beaten egg mixture cooked in a skillet and folded—often around a filling. The variations in the fillings determine the time of day for which the omelet is appropriate.

Serve Omelets With Creole Sauce for lunch—the spicy sauce flavors them nicely for that time of day. For breakfast, consider Strawberry-Sour Cream Omelet. It's light and puffy because the egg whites are beaten and folded into the yolk mixture.

Egg Tips

■ Do not wash eggs before storing; washing removes the coating that prevents the entrance of bacteria. Wash just before using, if desired.

■ To maintain high quality in eggs, always be careful to store eggs large end up in their original container.

■ Serve egg dishes on warm plates to keep the eggs from cooling too quickly.

■ Raw eggs separate more easily while still cold from the refrigerator, but let whites reach room temperature in order to get maximum volume when beating.

OMELETS
WITH CREOLE SAUCE

¼ cup diced cooked ham
¼ cup (1 ounce) shredded
   Cheddar cheese
2 tablespoons sliced green onions
2 tablespoons diced mushrooms
4 eggs
⅛ teaspoon salt
⅛ teaspoon pepper
Dash of Worcestershire sauce
Dash of hot sauce
1 tablespoon butter or margarine,
   divided
Creole Sauce
Jalapeño pepper slices (optional)

Combine first 4 ingredients; toss gently. Divide mixture in half, and set aside. Combine eggs, salt, pepper, Worcestershire sauce, and hot sauce in a medium bowl; whisk just until blended.

Heat a 6- or 8-inch omelet pan or heavy skillet over medium heat until hot enough to sizzle a drop of water. Add ½ tablespoon butter, and rotate pan to coat bottom.

Pour half of egg mixture into skillet. As mixture starts to cook, gently lift edges of omelet with a spatula, and tilt pan so that uncooked portion flows underneath.

Sprinkle half of ham mixture on one side of omelet. Loosen omelet with a spatula; fold in half, and transfer to plate. Keep warm. Repeat procedure with remaining butter and omelet ingredients.

Spoon half of Creole Sauce over each omelet. Garnish, if desired. Yield: 2 servings.

Creole Sauce

¾ cup tomato puree
½ cup diced green pepper
½ cup sliced green onions
½ teaspoon salt
¼ teaspoon pepper
⅛ teaspoon hot sauce

Combine all ingredients in a small saucepan; stir well. Bring to a boil over medium heat. Reduce heat, and simmer 10 to 12 minutes, stirring often. Yield: about 1 cup.
Clairiece Gilbert Humphrey
Charlottesville, Virginia

ROLLED OMELET

6 eggs, separated
1½ teaspoons cream of tartar
1 (3-ounce) package cream
   cheese, softened
⅓ cup sour cream
2 green onions, thinly sliced
2 slices boiled ham, cut into thin
   strips
Cheese sauce (recipe follows)
4 slices bacon, cooked and
   crumbled

Grease a 9-inch square pan, and line bottom with wax paper. Grease top of wax paper; set pan aside.

Beat egg whites (at room temperature) and cream of tartar until foamy, using a wire whisk. Beat egg yolks until lemon colored; fold whites into yolks. Pour mixture into prepared pan. Bake at 350° for 10 minutes or until omelet is set. Broil 1 minute to lightly brown top of omelet. Loosen omelet with a spatula, and transfer to a warm platter.

Combine cream cheese and sour cream; mix well. Spread evenly over omelet; sprinkle evenly with green onions and ham. Roll up jellyroll fashion. Top with cheese sauce, and sprinkle with bacon. Serve immediately. Yield: 3 to 4 servings.

Cheese Sauce

2 tablespoons butter or margarine
2 tablespoons all-purpose flour
1 cup milk
¼ teaspoon salt
½ cup (2 ounces) shredded sharp
  Cheddar cheese

Melt butter in a heavy saucepan over low heat; add flour, and cook 1 minute, stirring constantly. Gradually add milk; cook over medium heat, stirring constantly, until thickened and bubbly. Add salt and cheese; stir until cheese melts. Yield: 1¼ cups.

Gene Lominac
Raleigh, North Carolina

STRAWBERRY-SOUR CREAM OMELET

5 eggs, separated
1 (8-ounce) carton sour cream,
  divided
½ teaspoon salt
2 tablespoons butter or margarine
1 pint fresh strawberries, sliced
Powdered sugar (optional)

Beat egg yolks until thick and lemon colored. Add ½ cup sour cream and salt; beat until blended.

Beat egg whites (at room temperature) until soft peaks form; fold into yolk mixture.

Heat a 10-inch ovenproof skillet over medium heat until hot enough to sizzle a drop of water. Add butter, and rotate pan to coat bottom. Pour egg mixture into skillet. Cook over low heat 8 to 10 minutes or until lightly browned on bottom. Remove from heat, and bake at 325° for 12 to 15 minutes or until golden brown. Loosen omelet with a spatula; fold in half, and gently slide omelet onto serving plate. Top with remaining sour cream and strawberries. Dust with powdered sugar, if desired. Yield: 6 servings. *Marie A. Davis*
Drexel, North Carolina

Morning Sweet Bread

Orange Butter Coffee Cake is special to Mrs. David Williams of Baton Rouge, Louisiana, for several reasons. "This recipe has been in our family for a long time," Mrs. Williams says. "It won my niece a blue ribbon at the state fair. The recipe makes two cakes, so I sometimes share one with a friend."

ORANGE BUTTER COFFEE CAKE

1 package dry yeast
¼ cup warm water (105° to 115°)
¼ cup sugar
1 teaspoon salt
2 eggs
½ cup sour cream
¼ cup butter or margarine,
  softened
2¾ to 3 cups all-purpose flour
¼ cup butter or margarine,
  melted and divided
¾ cup sugar
¾ cup flaked coconut
2 tablespoons grated orange rind
Glaze (recipe follows)
2 tablespoons flaked coconut,
  toasted
Citrus rind bows (optional)

Dissolve yeast in warm water in a large bowl; let stand 5 minutes. Add ¼ cup sugar, stirring until dissolved.

Add salt, eggs, sour cream, and ¼ cup butter to yeast mixture; beat at medium speed of an electric mixer until blended. Gradually stir in enough flour to make a soft dough. Place in a well-greased bowl, turning to grease top. Cover and let rise in a warm place (85°), free from drafts, 2 hours or until doubled in bulk.

Punch dough down; turn dough out onto a well-floured surface, and knead 15 times. Divide dough in half. Roll half of dough to a 12- x 10-inch rectangle on a lightly floured surface.

Brush about 1 tablespoon butter evenly over dough, leaving a 1-inch margin at sides.

Combine ¾ cup sugar, ¾ cup coconut, and orange rind in a small bowl; mix well. Sprinkle half the mixture evenly over dough, leaving a 1-inch margin.

Roll up dough, jellyroll fashion, beginning at long side; pinch seam to seal. Place roll on a large greased baking sheet, seam side down; shape into a ring, and pinch ends together.

Using kitchen shears, make cuts in dough at 1-inch intervals around ring, cutting two-thirds of the way through roll at each cut. Gently turn each piece of dough on its side, slightly overlapping the slices. Brush with about 1 tablespoon melted butter. Repeat with remaining dough.

Cover and let rise in a warm place, free from drafts, 55 minutes or until doubled in bulk. Bake at 350° for 20 to 25 minutes or until coffee cakes are golden brown. Transfer to a wire rack. Drizzle coffee cakes with glaze while warm, and sprinkle with toasted coconut. Garnish coffee cakes with citrus rind bows, if desired. Yield: 2 coffee cakes.

Glaze

¾ cup sugar
2 tablespoons orange juice
¼ cup butter or margarine
⅓ cup sour cream

Combine sugar, orange juice, and butter in a small saucepan; bring mixture to a boil, stirring constantly. Boil 3 minutes, stirring constantly. Remove from heat, and stir in sour cream. Yield: 1 cup.

Breakfast In Minutes

It takes only a few minutes in the morning to make Breakfast Sandwiches, thanks to the microwave oven. But if you can't squeeze in enough time to prepare them prior to racing out the door in the morning, make them the night before, and reheat them. This recipe is versatile enough to accommodate either schedule.

BREAKFAST SANDWICHES

4 slices bacon
4 eggs
¼ cup sour cream
4 English muffins, split and
 toasted
4 (⅔-ounce) slices process
 American cheese

Place bacon on a rack in a 12- x 8- x 2-inch baking dish; cover with paper towels. Microwave at HIGH 3½ to 4½ minutes or until bacon is crisp. Drain bacon, and set aside.

Crack 1 egg in each of four 6-ounce custard cups. Pierce each yolk one time with a wooden pick, and pierce egg whites several times. Cover cups with heavy-duty plastic wrap; fold back a small edge of wrap to allow steam to escape. Arrange cups in a circle on a microwave-safe round platter with 1-inch space between cups. Microwave on MEDIUM (50% power) 4 to 5 minutes or until whites are set, giving dish a quarter-turn every 2 minutes. Let stand 1 minute.

Spread sour cream over cut side of each muffin half. Place 1 slice of bacon (broken in half), an egg, and a slice of cheese on each of 4 muffin halves; top with remaining muffin halves. Place sandwiches on a paper plate, and cover with paper towels. Microwave at MEDIUM 1½ to 2 minutes or until sandwiches are heated. Yield: 4 servings.

Note: Sandwiches may be prepared in advance. Wrap each in a paper towel, and place in a zip-top plastic bag. Refrigerate. **To reheat,** remove from plastic bag, and place wrapped sandwiches on plate. Microwave according to the following chart, giving plate a half-turn after designated cooking time is half over.

Amount	Microwave at MEDIUM (50% power)
1	1½ minutes
2	2 to 3 minutes
3	3 to 4 minutes
4	4 to 5 minutes

Raisin Bread In The Round

If Round Raisin Bread's unique shape or appealing ingredients don't capture your attention, then maybe its convenience will. The recipe calls for the new fast-acting yeast instead of regular yeast, so the procedure is simplified and shortened.

The dough-rising ability of this yeast is up to 50% faster than regular yeast, and you'll need to let the dough rise only one time. If you use regular yeast for this recipe, the dough would rise twice, and it would take longer to double because it contains a little more sugar than usual, and the rye flour, almonds, and raisins make it heavy. Using rapid-rise yeast shortens the process by about an hour for this recipe.

Always add this type yeast directly to the dry ingredients before rehydration, setting aside about 1 cup of the flour to work into the dough after the liquid is added. Have the temperature of the liquid ingredients between 125° and 130° for maximum yeast action. Add enough of the remaining 1 cup flour to make the dough a good consistency, and knead the dough as the recipe directs. Cover the dough, and let it rest 10 minutes. Shape the dough, and place it in the container in which it will bake; cover it, and let it rise until doubled in bulk.

ROUND RAISIN BREAD

2¾ to 3¼ cups all-purpose flour,
 divided
1 cup rye flour
½ cup sugar
2 packages rapid-rise yeast
1 teaspoon salt
1 teaspoon ground cardamom
1 cup half-and-half
¼ cup plus 2 tablespoons butter
 or margarine
¼ cup water
2 egg yolks
1½ teaspoons grated orange rind
1½ teaspoons grated lemon rind
¾ cup golden raisins
½ cup chopped blanched almonds

Combine 2 cups all-purpose flour, rye flour, and next 4 ingredients in a large bowl; stir and set aside. Combine half-and-half, butter, and water in a saucepan; heat until butter melts, stirring occasionally. Cool to 125° to 130°. Gradually add half-and-half mixture to flour mixture; add egg yolks and orange and lemon rinds, stirring until smooth. Gradually stir in enough remaining flour to make a soft dough.

Turn dough out onto a lightly floured surface, and knead until smooth and elastic (about 8 minutes). Knead in raisins and almonds until evenly distributed. Cover dough, and let rest 10 minutes.

Shape into a ball; place in a well-greased 2½-quart soufflé dish. Cover and let rise in warm place (85°), free from drafts, 1 hour or until dough is doubled in bulk. Bake at 350° for 25 minutes; shield with foil to prevent excess browning. Bake 25 minutes or until loaf sounds hollow when tapped. Remove from dish; cool on wire rack. Yield: 1 loaf.

Velma Kestner
Berwind, West Virginia

MICROWAVE COOKERY

Treat Yourself To Apples and Pears

It's fun to buy apples and pears at an orchard or a roadside stand, but a grocery store will do fine, too—as long as you get the pick of this season's harvest. These recipes make quick use of apples and pears.

You won't have to wait long to enjoy crunchy Caramel Apples. Caramels melt in the microwave oven in just a few minutes. Experiment with a variety of coatings—we tried English toffee-flavored candy bars and almond brickle chips.

Our other recipes rely on the microwave to leave fruit succulent and tasty. Spiced Fall Pears is an easy side dish that highlights the natural goodness and firm texture of pears. Gingered Pears offers the same ease and a similar flavor in a dessert.

SPICED FALL PEARS

4 ripe pears, peeled and sliced
2 tablespoons brown sugar
½ to 1 teaspoon ground allspice
2 tablespoons butter or margarine
¼ cup orange juice
2 tablespoons honey

Place pear slices in an 8-inch square baking dish. Combine brown sugar and allspice; sprinkle over pears. Dot with butter. Pour orange juice into dish, and drizzle honey over pears.

Cover tightly with heavy-duty plastic wrap; fold back a corner of wrap to allow steam to escape. Microwave at HIGH 6 to 8 minutes or until tender, rotating dish halfway through cooking time. Yield: 4 servings.

CARAMEL APPLES

5 medium apples
1 (14-ounce) package caramels
2 tablespoons water
1 (6-ounce) package almond brickle chips or 1⅓ cups crushed English toffee-flavored candy bars

Wash and dry apples; insert wooden skewers into stem end of each apple. Set aside.

Combine caramels and water in a 1½-quart bowl; microwave at HIGH 2½ to 3½ minutes, stirring after each minute until sauce is smooth.

Dip apples into hot caramel sauce, turning until coated. Scrape excess sauce from bottom of apples; then roll them in brickle chips.

Place on greased wax paper. Store in refrigerator. Let stand at room temperature 15 minutes before serving to allow caramel to soften. Yield: 5 servings.

Note: If caramel sauce hardens during dipping, microwave at HIGH 10 seconds to soften.

GINGERED PEARS

3 pears
1 tablespoon butter or margarine
2 tablespoons honey
¾ teaspoon ground ginger
2 tablespoons light rum
¼ cup sliced almonds
Vanilla ice cream

Peel pears, cut in half lengthwise, and seed. Place pears, cut side down, in a 2-quart shallow casserole, and set aside.

Place butter in a 1-cup glass measure. Microwave at HIGH 35 seconds or until melted. Add honey, ginger, and rum; stir well. Pour over pears. Cover tightly with heavy-duty plastic wrap; fold back a corner of wrap to allow steam to escape. Microwave at HIGH 4 to 6 minutes or until pears are done.

Spread almonds in a pieplate; microwave at HIGH 4 to 5 minutes or until lightly toasted.

To serve, place a pear half in each individual serving dish; place scoop of ice cream on top of pears. Drizzle with pear sauce, and sprinkle with almonds. Yield: 6 servings.

Microwave Tips

■ To determine whether or not a dish is microwave-safe, pour 1 cup water into a glass measure. Place the measure in the microwave in the dish being tested. Then microwave at HIGH for 1 minute. If the dish being tested is warm and the water cool, the dish is unsafe.

■ Microwave casseroles will cook more evenly using ingredients of similar size and shape.

■ Remember—standing time is part of the cooking process in microwaving foods. It allows for the food to complete cooking.

Fancy Dessert Tarts

If you feel yourself falling into the rut of serving the same old thing for dessert, try one of these tarts for something a little different.

Tarts look especially attractive with their golden, freestanding crusts, but don't let their appearance fool you into thinking they're more difficult to prepare than they really are. If you can make a pie, you can make these tarts.

The key that gives these desserts their identity and appeal is the shallow pan with a removable bottom in which they are baked. It's called a tart pan, and its fluted edges give the crust a shapely finish.

When the tart is ready, just place one hand underneath the pan, and slip away the metal ring along the sides. Carefully remove the bottom plate with a spatula, if desired.

You can find tart pans at most large department stores or kitchen specialty shops. They're also available from many mail-order companies that carry cooking equipment.

ALMOND TART

1 cup all-purpose flour
1 tablespoon sugar
½ cup unsalted butter
1 tablespoon cold water
½ teaspoon vanilla extract
¼ teaspoon almond extract
½ cup ground almonds
¾ cup sifted powdered sugar
1 egg
1 egg white
2 tablespoons unsalted butter, melted
1 teaspoon grated lemon rind
1¼ cups sliced almonds
¾ cup sugar
1 cup whipping cream
2 teaspoons Grand Marnier or other orange-flavored liqueur
¼ teaspoon almond extract
Pinch of salt

Combine flour and 1 tablespoon sugar; cut in ½ cup butter with a pastry blender until mixture resembles coarse meal. Sprinkle water, vanilla, and ¼ teaspoon almond extract evenly over surface; stir with a fork until dry ingredients are moistened. Shape into a ball. Press pastry in bottom and up sides of a 10½-inch tart pan. Place a piece of aluminum foil over pastry; gently press into pastry shell. (This will keep the sides of pastry from collapsing.)

Cover foil with a layer of pastry weights or dried peas or beans. Bake at 400° for 6 minutes. Remove weights and foil; bake an additional 2 minutes. Remove from oven; cool 10 minutes.

Combine ground almonds, powdered sugar, egg, and egg white in container of an electric blender; process until smooth. Add 2 tablespoons butter and lemon rind; process 15 seconds. Spread mixture in pastry shell; bake at 400° for 5 minutes. (Mixture will not be firm.) Remove from oven, and set aside. Reduce oven temperature to 375°.

Combine sliced almonds and remaining ingredients; stir well. Spoon mixture over egg filling; bake at 375° for 35 to 40 minutes or until mixture is golden brown and set. Let tart cool before serving. Yield: one 10½-inch tart.
Betty Rabe
Plano, Texas

KIWIFRUIT TART

½ cup sugar
2 tablespoons plus 2½ teaspoons cornstarch
⅛ teaspoon salt
2 egg yolks, beaten
2 cups milk
1 tablespoon butter or margarine
¾ teaspoon vanilla extract
Tart pastry (recipe follows)
5 kiwifruit, peeled and sliced
4 or 5 strawberries, sliced
1 whole strawberry

Combine sugar, cornstarch, and salt in a medium saucepan, stirring until blended. Combine egg yolks and milk; stir into sugar mixture. Bring to a boil over medium heat; cook 1 minute, stirring constantly. Stir in butter and vanilla; pour into baked pastry shell. Cool 30 minutes. Top with sliced fruit as desired, and place whole strawberry in center for garnish. Yield: one 9-inch tart.

Tart Pastry

1¼ cups all-purpose flour
2 tablespoons sugar
½ teaspoon salt
⅓ cup plus 2 tablespoons shortening
3 tablespoons cold water

Combine flour, sugar, and salt; cut in shortening with pastry blender until mixture resembles coarse meal. Sprinkle cold water (1 tablespoon at a time) evenly over surface; stir with a fork until dry ingredients are moistened. Shape into a ball, and chill.

Roll dough to ⅛-inch thickness on a lightly floured surface. Place in a round 9-inch tart pan; trim excess pastry along edges.

Prick bottom and sides of pastry generously with a fork. Bake at 450° for 10 to 12 minutes or until pastry is golden brown. Yield: pastry for one 9-inch tart.
Jane Moore
Norfolk, Virginia

Fruit Tips

■ To prepare kiwifruit, first chill the fruit; then peel and thinly slice crosswise for use in recipes or as a garnish.

■ Remember to hull strawberries after washing so that they won't become mushy.

OCTOBER

As autumn leaves take on bright hues

of red and yellow, so thoughts naturally turn

to foods that reflect October colors.

Honey, nature's sweetener, is one such golden treat.

It glistens on the table or sweetens a variety

of dishes in our collection of honey recipes. Even pies

and cakes, featured in our "QUICK!" column

and in "Feast on Grandma's Cooking,"

wear the colors of the season.

Feast On Grandma's Cookin'

Do you remember family gatherings at Grandma's house? The best part came when the dinner bell rang and you sat down to the feast Grandma had so lovingly prepared. It seems like yesterday. The smells of the Sunday meal she served come back to us and with them, unforgettable childhood memories. The recipes chosen for this menu keep that tradition alive and help to create memories for today's grandchildren.

Best Ever Sunday Chicken   Pot Roast and Gravy
Old-Fashioned Mashed Potatoes
Glazed Carrots
Savory Green Beans
Fruit Medley
Crescent Rolls
Coconut Cream Pie   Spicy Jam Cake

BEST EVER SUNDAY CHICKEN

2 cups all-purpose flour
1½ teaspoons salt
2 teaspoons dried whole thyme
2 teaspoons paprika
2 eggs, beaten
⅔ cup milk
¼ cup lemon juice
5 pounds chicken pieces
Vegetable oil

Combine first 4 ingredients in a plastic bag; shake to mix, and set aside. Combine eggs, milk, and lemon juice; stir well.

Skin chicken, if desired. Place 2 or 3 pieces in bag; shake well. Dip in egg mixture; return to bag, and shake again. Repeat procedure with remaining chicken.

Pour oil to depth of ¾ inch into a large heavy skillet. Fry 4 or 5 pieces of chicken in hot oil (350°) over medium heat 15 minutes or until golden brown, turning to brown both sides. Drain on paper towels. Repeat procedure with remaining chicken. Yield: 8 servings.

Mrs. Earl L. Faulkenberry
Lancaster, South Carolina

POT ROAST AND GRAVY

1 teaspoon seasoned salt
½ teaspoon onion powder
¼ teaspoon seasoned pepper
⅛ teaspoon garlic powder
1 (5-pound) boneless chuck roast
1 tablespoon olive oil
¾ cup water
1 large onion, chopped
¼ cup chopped green pepper
2 cloves garlic, minced
2 bay leaves
2 teaspoons parsley flakes
¼ teaspoon dried whole thyme
All-purpose flour

Combine first 4 ingredients; rub mixture evenly on roast. Brown roast on both sides in hot olive oil in a large Dutch oven. Add water and next 6 ingredients. Cover and bake at 325° for 3 hours or until tender. Remove roast to serving platter, reserving liquid in Dutch oven. Remove bay leaves.

Skim fat; measure liquid, and return to Dutch oven. Combine 1 to 1½ tablespoons flour and 2 tablespoons water for each cup of liquid; stir well. Stir flour mixture into liquid. Cook over medium heat, stirring constantly, until thickened and bubbly. Serve gravy with roast. Yield: 8 to 10 servings.

OLD-FASHIONED MASHED POTATOES

8 medium potatoes, peeled and cut into eighths (about 3¼ pounds)
1 medium onion, finely chopped
½ to ⅔ cup milk, divided
⅓ cup butter or margarine
1 teaspoon grated Parmesan cheese
1 teaspoon salt
¼ teaspoon sugar
⅛ teaspoon pepper

Cook potatoes and onion in boiling water to cover 15 minutes or until tender. Drain and mash. Add ½ cup milk and remaining ingredients. Add more milk, if needed, for desired consistency. Yield: 8 servings.

Norma Cowden
Shawnee, Oklahoma

Tip: *Keep potatoes and onions in a cool, dark place with plenty of air circulation to prevent sprouting.*

GLAZED CARROTS

3 (12-ounce) packages small
   whole carrots, scraped
¼ cup honey
¼ cup butter or margarine,
   melted
¼ cup firmly packed brown sugar

Cook carrots in a small amount of boiling water about 10 minutes or until crisp-tender. Drain, reserving ¼ cup liquid. Combine reserved liquid, honey, butter, and brown sugar, stirring well. Pour over carrots, and cook over low heat until thoroughly heated. Yield: 6 to 8 servings.

Hazel Sellers
Albany, Georgia

SAVORY GREEN BEANS

2 pounds fresh green beans
¼ cup butter or margarine
½ cup chopped onion
4 green onions, sliced
2 cloves garlic, minced
1 teaspoon Creole seasoning
⅛ teaspoon freshly ground pepper
½ teaspoon chopped dillweed

Wash beans; trim ends, and remove strings. Add water to depth of 1 inch into a large Dutch oven; bring to a boil. Add beans. Cover, reduce heat, and simmer 10 minutes or until beans are crisp-tender. Drain beans. Plunge into ice water; drain and set aside.

Melt butter in Dutch oven; add chopped onion and remaining ingredients. Cook over medium heat, stirring constantly, until onions are crisp-tender. Add beans, and cook until beans are thoroughly heated. Yield: 8 servings.

Yolanda Trahan
Houma, Louisiana

FRUIT MEDLEY

2 apples, cored and sliced
½ cup pineapple juice or orange
   juice
3 bananas, sliced
4 oranges, peeled, seeded, and
   sectioned
¾ pound seedless green grapes,
   halved

Toss apple slices in pineapple juice; drain, reserving juice. Arrange apple slices in a glass bowl. Toss banana slices in reserved juice; drain. Layer banana slices on apple slices. Arrange orange sections over banana slices, reserving 5 sections for garnish. Top with grape halves. Garnish with reserved orange sections. Yield: about 12 servings.

CRESCENT ROLLS

¾ cup milk
¼ cup shortening
3 tablespoons sugar
1 teaspoon salt
1 package dry yeast
¼ cup warm water (105° to 115°)
1 egg
½ teaspoon grated orange rind
¼ teaspoon ground cardamom
3 cups all-purpose flour, divided

Place first 4 ingredients in a small saucepan; heat until shortening melts, stirring occasionally. Remove from heat, and cool to 105° to 115°.

Dissolve yeast in warm water in a large mixing bowl; let stand 5 minutes. Stir in milk mixture, egg, orange rind, and cardamom. Add 1 cup flour, stirring well. Gradually add remaining 2 cups flour, mixing well. Cover and refrigerate dough at least 8 hours.

Punch dough down, and divide in half. Roll each portion into a 9-inch circle on a floured surface. Cut each circle into 12 wedges; roll each wedge tightly, beginning at wide end. Seal points, and place rolls on lightly greased baking sheets with the point side down.

Cover and let rise in a warm place (85°), free from drafts, 1 hour or until doubled in bulk. Bake at 375° for 10 to 12 minutes or until golden. Yield: 2 dozen.

Mrs. Hugh F. Mosher
Huntsville, Alabama

Cooking with Onions and Carrots

■ The darker the orange color of carrots, the greater the content of vitamin A.

■ Remove the tops of carrots before refrigerating. Tops drain the carrots of moisture, making them limp and dry.

■ When selecting onions, consider all of the flavor possibilities. The large Spanish or Bermuda onion and the small white onion are usually mild in flavor; on the other hand, Globe types, such as red, brown, and small yellow onions, are stronger flavored.

■ For a small amount of grated onion, place in a garlic press.

■ To peel small white onions easily, pour boiling water over onions in a bowl and let stand 1 minute; drain and cover with cold water. Peel when cool.

COCONUT CREAM PIE

1 cup sugar
⅓ cup all-purpose flour
¼ teaspoon salt
1 (5-ounce) can evaporated milk
2¼ cups milk
3 eggs, separated
2 tablespoons butter or margarine
1 teaspoon vanilla extract
1 (3½-ounce) can flaked coconut
Pastry shell (recipe follows)
½ teaspoon cream of tartar
3 tablespoons sugar
¾ teaspoon cornstarch
3 tablespoons flaked coconut,
   toasted

Combine first 3 ingredients in a heavy saucepan; gradually add milks, stirring until blended. Cook over medium heat, stirring constantly, until mixture thickens and comes to a boil.

Beat egg yolks until thick and lemon colored. Gradually stir about one-fourth of hot mixture into yolks; add to remaining hot mixture, stirring constantly. Cook over medium heat, continuously stirring 1 minute. Remove from heat; stir in butter and next 2 ingredients. Spoon mixture into pastry shell.

Beat egg whites (at room temperature) and cream of tartar at high speed of an electric mixer just until foamy. Combine 3 tablespoons sugar and cornstarch; gradually add, 1 tablespoon at a time, to whites, beating until stiff peaks form and sugar dissolves (2 to 4 minutes). Spread meringue over hot filling, sealing to edge of pastry. Bake at 450° for 5 minutes or until lightly browned. Sprinkle with toasted coconut. Yield: one 9-inch pie.

Pastry Shell

1¼ cups all-purpose flour
½ teaspoon salt
½ cup shortening
3 tablespoons cold water

Combine flour and salt; cut in shortening with pastry blender until mixture resembles coarse meal. Sprinkle cold water, 1 tablespoon at a time, evenly over surface; stir with a fork until dry ingredients are moistened. Shape into a ball; chill.

Roll pastry to ⅛-inch thickness on a lightly floured surface. Place in a 9-inch pieplate; trim off excess pastry along edges. Fold edges under, and flute. Prick bottom and sides of pastry shell generously with a fork. Bake at 450° for 10 to 12 minutes or until golden brown. Yield: one 9-inch pastry shell.

Nancy W. Otto
Dayton, Texas

SPICY JAM CAKE

1 cup shortening
2 cups sugar
3 eggs
3 cups all-purpose flour, divided
1 teaspoon ground cloves
1 teaspoon ground cinnamon
1 teaspoon ground allspice
1 teaspoon ground nutmeg
1 teaspoon baking soda
1 cup buttermilk
1 cup strawberry preserves
2 cups chopped pecans
1 cup raisins
Caramel Frosting

Cream shortening; gradually add sugar, beating well at medium speed of an electric mixer. Add eggs, one at a time, beating well after each addition. Set aside.

Combine 2¾ cups flour and spices. Dissolve soda in buttermilk. Add flour mixture to creamed mixture alternately with buttermilk, beginning and ending with flour mixture. Mix after each addition. Stir in preserves.

Combine pecans, raisins, and remaining ¼ cup flour; stir into batter.

Pour batter into 3 greased and floured 9-inch round cakepans. Bake at 350° for 30 to 35 minutes or until a wooden pick inserted in center comes out clean. Cool in pans 10 minutes; remove from pans, and let cool completely on wire racks.

Spread Caramel Frosting between layers and on top and sides of cake. Yield: one 3-layer cake.

Caramel Frosting

3 cups sugar, divided
1 tablespoon all-purpose flour
½ teaspoon salt
1 cup milk
¾ cup butter or margarine
1 teaspoon vanilla extract

Sprinkle ½ cup sugar in a shallow, heavy 3½-quart Dutch oven; cook over medium heat, stirring constantly, until sugar melts (sugar will clump) and turns light golden brown. Remove from heat.

Combine remaining 2½ cups sugar, flour, and salt in a saucepan; stir in milk. Cook mixture over medium heat until sugar dissolves, stirring constantly. Add butter, and bring to a boil.

Gradually pour one-fourth of hot mixture into caramelized sugar, stirring constantly; add remaining hot mixture (mixture will lump, but continue stirring until smooth).

Return to heat; cook over medium heat, without stirring, until mixture reaches 230° (about 2 minutes); stir in vanilla. Remove from heat. Beat mixture with a wooden spoon or at medium speed of an electric mixer until spreading consistency (about 15 minutes). Yield: enough for one 3-layer cake.

Katherine Mabry
Athens, Alabama

ON THE LIGHT SIDE

Entertain With A Light Pasta Bar

Pasta bars, those buffets offering a variety of sauces and pastas, are a new way of entertaining with lighter fare for today's tastes. Usually two to three sauces are served with three or more shapes, colors, or flavors of pasta. A green salad and breadsticks complete the menu.

Most of the pasta eaten in this country is ordinary white spaghetti. But there are enough different kinds of pasta to boggle the mind. Following are a few basics to consider when deciding which pasta to use for a particular dish.

—Serve rich, thick sauces with a flat pasta that does not trap too much of the sauce.

—Thin sauces, such as Marinara Sauce or pesto sauce, should be served with thin pasta such as vermicelli or spaghetti.

—Tubular or shell pasta is designed to trap sauce. It particularly enhances meat and vegetable sauces.

—Chunky vegetable or meat sauces should be served with thick pasta: ziti, mostaccioli, rigatoni, or fettuccine.

—Good pasta is made from 100% durum semolina wheat, which is rich in B vitamins and iron.

CHICKEN MARSALA
(pictured on page 223)

6 (4-ounce) skinned and boned
  chicken breast halves
Vegetable cooking spray
1½ cups Marsala wine
2 tablespoons olive oil
1½ cups thinly sliced fresh
  mushrooms
1 cup sliced sweet red pepper
1 cup sliced sweet yellow pepper
½ cup sliced green onions
2 cloves garlic, minced
2¾ cups no-salt-added chicken
  broth
1 tablespoon lemon juice
½ teaspoon dried whole oregano
½ teaspoon dried whole basil
½ teaspoon salt
½ teaspoon pepper
1 tablespoon cornstarch
¼ cup no-salt-added chicken
  broth
Hot pasta (cooked without fat
  or salt)

Cut chicken into strips; set aside. Coat a Dutch oven with cooking spray; place over medium-high heat until hot. Add chicken strips, and sauté until tender; remove and set aside. Add wine to Dutch oven, and bring to a boil; pour over chicken.

Add olive oil to Dutch oven, and heat until hot. Add mushrooms and next 4 ingredients; sauté until crisp-tender. Add 2¾ cups chicken broth and next 5 ingredients; bring to a boil. Add chicken mixture, and return to a boil.

Combine cornstarch and ¼ cup chicken broth; stir into chicken mixture. Bring to a boil; boil 1 minute, stirring constantly. Serve mixture over cooked pasta. Yield: 7 cups (263 calories per 1-cup serving and ½ cup pasta).

□ 25.8 grams protein, 5.6 grams fat, 24.8 grams carbohydrate, 56 milligrams cholesterol, 237 milligrams sodium, and 34 milligrams calcium.

MEATBALLS
(pictured on page 222)

1 pound lean ground chuck
1 teaspoon dry mustard
¼ teaspoon salt
¼ teaspoon pepper
⅛ teaspoon garlic powder
1 teaspoon reduced-sodium
  Worcestershire sauce
Dash of hot sauce
Vegetable cooking spray

Combine first 7 ingredients; shape into 16 balls. Place meatballs on a rack that has been coated with cooking spray; place rack in a shallow roasting pan. Broil meatballs 4 inches from heat 3 to 5 minutes on each side or to desired degree of doneness. Drain on paper towels. Yield: 16 meatballs (60 calories each).

□ 5.2 grams protein, 4 grams fat, 0.1 gram carbohydrate, 17 milligrams cholesterol, 50 milligrams sodium, and 3 milligrams calcium.

Turkey Meatballs: Substitute 1 (1-pound) package frozen raw ground turkey thawed for ground chuck, and proceed with recipe. Yield: 16 meatballs (42 calories each).

□ 5.4 grams protein, 2.1 grams fat, 0.1 gram carbohydrate, 20 milligrams cholesterol, 61 milligrams sodium, and 15 milligrams calcium.
Barbara B. Hahn
Bethany, Oklahoma

TORTELLINI SALAD

1 (8-ounce) package cheese-filled
  spinach tortellini
½ cup chopped sweet red pepper
½ cup chopped green pepper
¼ cup chopped green onions
¼ cup sliced ripe olives
¼ cup olive oil
3 tablespoons wine vinegar
1½ tablespoons chopped fresh
  parsley
1½ tablespoons chopped fresh
  dillweed or 1½ teaspoons dried
  whole dillweed
2 teaspoons chopped fresh
  oregano or ½ teaspoon dried
  whole oregano
1½ teaspoons Dijon mustard
¼ teaspoon salt
¼ teaspoon freshly ground pepper

Cook tortellini in unsalted boiling water 15 to 20 minutes or until tender; drain. Combine tortellini and next 4 ingredients; toss gently.

Combine olive oil and remaining ingredients in container of an electric blender or food processor; process until blended. Pour dressing over tortellini mixture; toss gently. Cover and chill 8 hours. Toss gently before serving. Yield: 5 cups (115 calories per ½-cup serving).

□ 2.9 grams protein, 7.1 grams fat, 11.1 grams carbohydrate, 8 milligrams cholesterol, 153 milligrams sodium, and 33 milligrams calcium.
Fran Ginn
Columbia, Mississippi

Pasta Tips

- Uncooked pasta of similar sizes and shapes may be interchanged in recipes, but measure by weight and not volume. When cooked, noodles swell slightly; spaghetti and macaroni double in size. Cooked pasta, however, can be substituted cup for cup.

- Store pasta in a cool, dry place free from dust and moisture for up to one year; store egg noodles for up to 6 months.

- Allow 2 ounces of uncooked pasta and 1 to 1 ½ cups cooked pasta per person.

- Cook pasta until al dente (to the tooth); this means it's pliable but firm to the bite and no longer starchy.

- When cooked al dente, pasta can be reheated. To do this, drop cooked pasta in boiling water that has been removed from heat 1 to 2 minutes.

- To cook pasta, use 3 quarts of rapidly boiling water for every 8 ounces of dried pasta. To prevent the boil from subsiding, add pasta gradually in small amounts, and follow package directions for cooking times.

- Do not substitute Oriental-style noodles (cellophane or rice sticks) in pasta recipes.

- Drain pasta immediately after cooking, and transfer to a warmed serving bowl. No rinsing is necessary unless specifically stated in the recipe or unless preparing a cold pasta salad. Slightly undercook any pasta to be used as part of a recipe requiring further cooking.

- To store cooked pasta, toss it lightly with olive oil to prevent sticking together; cover and refrigerate until needed.

FETTUCCINE PRIMAVERA

2 cups thinly sliced broccoli
  flowerets
1 cup thinly sliced carrot
½ cup sliced green onions
2 cloves garlic, minced
3 tablespoons chopped fresh basil
¼ cup reduced-calorie margarine,
  melted
2 cups sliced fresh mushrooms
¼ teaspoon salt
¼ teaspoon pepper
½ cup Chablis or other dry white
  wine
3½ cups cooked fettuccine
  (cooked without salt or fat)
3 tablespoons grated Parmesan
  cheese

Sauté first 5 ingredients in margarine in a large skillet 5 minutes or until vegetables are crisp-tender, stirring often. Add mushrooms, salt, pepper, and wine; cook 2 minutes or until mushrooms are tender. Gently toss fettuccine and cheese. Yield: 7 servings (179 calories per 1-cup serving).

□ *5.8 grams protein, 5.8 grams fat, 25.3 grams carbohydrate, 2 milligrams cholesterol, 96 milligrams sodium, and 78 milligrams calcium.*
Laurie Gladstone
Wheaton, Maryland

WHOLE WHEAT MACARONI WITH PESTO

1 tablespoon olive oil
1 teaspoon water
⅛ teaspoon ground nutmeg
⅛ teaspoon salt
1 small clove garlic, minced
3 tablespoons minced fresh basil
3 tablespoons minced fresh
  parsley
¼ cup grated Parmesan cheese
2 cups cooked whole wheat
  macaroni (cooked without salt
  or fat)

Combine oil, water, nutmeg, salt, garlic, basil, parsley, and cheese in container of an electric blender. Cover and process until smooth pesto is formed.

Combine macaroni and pesto mixture in a medium bowl, and toss gently. Yield: 4 servings (158 calories per ½-cup serving).

□ *6.1 grams protein, 6.3 grams fat, 21.3 grams carbohydrate, 4 milligrams cholesterol, 169 milligrams sodium, and 115 milligrams calcium.*

SPICY SHERRIED MUSHROOM SAUCE

½ pound fresh mushrooms, diced
½ cup diced onion
¼ cup dry sherry
8 large cloves garlic, minced
2 tablespoons chopped fresh basil
½ teaspoon white pepper
½ teaspoon ground coriander
½ teaspoon ground allspice
½ teaspoon red pepper flakes
2 (14-ounce) cans Italian plum tomatoes, undrained and diced
Hot pasta (cooked without salt or fat)

Combine first 9 ingredients in a large saucepan; bring to a boil. Cover, reduce heat, and simmer 5 minutes. Add canned tomatoes, and cook, uncovered, 20 minutes.

Serve over pasta. Yield: 8 servings (117 calories per ½ cup sauce and ½ cup pasta).

☐ *4.2 grams protein, 0.5 gram fat, 24.8 grams carbohydrate, 0 milligrams cholesterol, 367 milligrams sodium, and 60 milligrams calcium.*
Marsha Littrell
Sheffield, Alabama

MARINARA SAUCE
(pictured on pages 222 and 223)

Vegetable cooking spray
1½ tablespoons olive oil
1 cup chopped onion
6 large cloves garlic, minced
2 tablespoons minced fresh parsley
1 teaspoon dried whole oregano
1 teaspoon dried whole basil
½ teaspoon dried whole thyme
1 teaspoon salt
¼ teaspoon freshly ground pepper
2 bay leaves
1 (28-ounce) can whole tomatoes, undrained and chopped
2 (6-ounce) cans tomato paste
¾ cup dry red wine
¾ cup water

Coat a Dutch oven with cooking spray; add oil. Place over medium-high heat until hot. Add onion and garlic; sauté until tender. Add parsley and next 5 ingredients; stir 1 minute. Add remaining ingredients; reduce heat, and simmer, uncovered, 30 to 45 minutes, stirring often. Remove bay leaves. Yield: 10 servings (78 calories per ½-cup serving).

☐ *2.3 grams protein, 2.5 grams fat, 13.6 grams carbohydrate, 0 milligrams cholesterol, 549 milligrams sodium, and 57 milligrams calcium.*

Marinara Sauce With Italian Turkey Sausage: Add 1 (16-ounce) package Italian turkey sausage; sauté with vegetables until done, and proceed with recipe. Yield: 12 servings (119 calories per ½-cup serving).

☐ *9 grams protein, 4.7 grams fat, 11.3 grams carbohydrate, 26 milligrams cholesterol, 488 milligrams sodium, and 67 milligrams calcium.*
Robin Edelman
Cumberland, Maryland

SEAFOOD SAUCE
(pictured on page 223)

1 cup diced green pepper
1 cup sliced fresh mushrooms
½ cup diced onion
2 cloves garlic, minced
2 tablespoons reduced-calorie margarine, melted
2 tablespoons all-purpose flour
1 cup evaporated skimmed milk
1 cup skim milk
3 tablespoons dry sherry
1 (8-ounce) package frozen, peeled, cooked shrimp, thawed
6 ounces seafood mix, chopped
¼ cup grated Parmesan cheese
Hot pasta (cooked without fat or salt)

Sauté first 4 ingredients in margarine until vegetables are tender. Add flour; cook, stirring constantly, 1 minute. Gradually add evaporated skimmed milk and skim milk, stirring constantly until mixture is thickened and bubbly. Stir in sherry, shrimp, seafood mix, and Parmesan cheese; cook sauce until thoroughly heated. Serve over pasta. Yield: 8 servings (282 calories per ½ cup sauce with 1 cup pasta).

☐ *18.5 grams protein, 3.9 grams fat, 41.9 grams carbohydrate, 63 milligrams cholesterol, 347 milligrams sodium, and 327 milligrams calcium.*

CARAWAY BREADSTICKS
(pictured on page 222)

1½ cups whole wheat flour
1 package dry yeast
¾ teaspoon salt
1 cup water (120° to 130°)
1 tablespoon vegetable oil
1 tablespoon honey
1½ teaspoons caraway seeds
1¼ to 1½ cups all-purpose flour
Vegetable cooking spray

Combine first 3 ingredients in a large bowl; add water, oil, and honey. Beat at medium speed of an electric mixer 2 minutes or until smooth. Gradually stir in caraway seeds and enough all-purpose flour to make a moderately stiff dough.

Turn dough out onto a lightly floured surface; knead until smooth and elastic (about 6 to 8 minutes).

Divide dough into fourths; cut each fourth into 10 equal pieces. Shape each piece into an 8-inch rope (cover remaining dough to prevent drying). Place ropes 1 inch apart on baking sheets coated with cooking spray. Cover and let rise in a warm place (85°), free from drafts, 50 minutes (dough will not double in bulk). Bake at 400° for 10 minutes or until lightly browned. Yield: 40 breadsticks (37 calories per breadstick).

☐ *1.1 grams protein, 0.6 gram fat, 7 grams carbohydrate, 0 milligrams cholesterol, 44 milligrams sodium, and 3 milligrams calcium.*

An Appetite For Food And Sport

Southern plantation and hunting preserve owners understand the lure of autumn woods for hunters. They are proud of the life they've sculpted and the recreation they offer at their lodges. They're also proud of the food they serve to the visiting hunters. Here some of the lodgekeepers offer their favorite recipes for wild-game lovers everywhere.

■ In Thomasville, Georgia, chef Richard Imel of Foxfire Hunting Preserve describes Foxfire Quail simply—a "standard quail recipe with a Cajun white sauce." The recipe is more involved than that, but it's worth the effort!

FOXFIRE QUAIL

1 teaspoon poultry seasoning
1 teaspoon dried whole thyme
1 teaspoon salt
1 teaspoon pepper
½ teaspoon garlic powder
12 quail, dressed
4 to 6 tablespoons butter or
  margarine
1 to 2 tablespoons peach brandy
2 tablespoons butter or margarine
2 (16-ounce) cans peach halves,
  drained
Seafood Cheese Sauce

Combine first 5 ingredients. Lightly sprinkle all sides of quail with ice water, and then with half of seasoning mixture. Repeat procedure; set quail aside.

Melt 4 tablespoons butter in a skillet. Add quail, and cook over low heat 30 to 35 minutes or until done, turning occasionally. Add extra butter, if necessary. Transfer to serving platter. Sprinkle with peach brandy; keep warm.

Melt 2 tablespoons butter in a skillet. Add peach halves; cook over medium heat, turning once, until lightly browned and thoroughly heated. Arrange peach halves around quail on platter; serve with Seafood Cheese Sauce. Yield: 6 servings.

Seafood Cheese Sauce

3 cups water
½ teaspoon salt
¼ teaspoon red pepper
¼ teaspoon garlic powder
1 bay leaf
1 pound unpeeled fresh shrimp
½ cup butter or margarine
½ cup all-purpose flour
2 cups half-and-half
2 cups milk
¼ teaspoon salt
⅛ teaspoon white pepper
⅛ teaspoon black pepper
⅛ teaspoon red pepper
2 egg yolks
1 cup (4 ounces) cubed process
  American cheese
½ cup (2 ounces) shredded Swiss
  cheese

Bring first 5 ingredients to a boil; add shrimp, and cook 3 to 5 minutes. Drain shrimp well, reserving seasoned liquid in pot. Rinse shrimp with cold water, and save for other use. Boil seasoned liquid 10 to 15 minutes or until reduced to 1 cup. Remove bay leaf. Measure ¼ cup stock; set aside. Save remainder for other uses.

Melt ½ cup butter in a large Dutch oven. Add flour; cook over low heat, stirring constantly, until roux is caramel colored (25 to 30 minutes). Gradually add half-and-half and milk to roux; cook over medium heat, stirring constantly, until mixture is thickened and bubbly. Stir in ¼ teaspoon salt, ⅛ teaspoon each white, black, and red peppers, and ¼ cup reserved shrimp stock.

Beat egg yolks until thick and lemon colored. Gradually stir about one-fourth of hot mixture into yolks; add to remaining hot mixture, stirring constantly, until thickened. Add cheeses to mixture; stir until melted. Yield: 4½ cups.

Note: One teaspoon chicken-flavored bouillon granules may be substituted for shrimp when preparing stock. If using bouillon granules, omit salt.

■ Jerry Waters, owner of Hawkeye Hunting Club in Center, Tennessee, created the recipe for J.W. Quail. It's his favorite entrée for small dinner parties.

J.W. QUAIL

2 cups water
2 tablespoons salt
4 quail, dressed
3 tablespoons butter, divided
4 cloves garlic
½ cup dry white wine
¼ teaspoon salt
¼ teaspoon pepper
Sugar

Combine water and 2 tablespoons salt in a large bowl. Add quail; soak 2 hours. Drain.

Arrange quail on a rack in a large saucepan with a tight-fitting lid. Add water to a depth of 1 inch in the pan, making sure the water does not touch the bottom of the rack. Cover and bring water to a boil; reduce heat, and simmer 30 minutes. Remove quail. Place 1 teaspoon butter, 1 clove garlic, and 2 tablespoons wine inside cavity of each quail; sprinkle each cavity with remaining salt and pepper. Place about 1 teaspoon butter and 2 pinches of sugar on breast of each quail. Wrap birds in aluminum foil, breast side down. Bake at 350° for 35 minutes. Remove foil, turn breast right side up, and broil 2 minutes or until breast is golden brown. Yield: 2 servings.

■ Hawkeye-Stuffed Quail is a favorite dish at the Hawkeye Hunting Club's lodge in Center, Texas. The recipe came from owner Jerry Waters's grandmother.

HAWKEYE-STUFFED QUAIL

12 quail, dressed
1 pound lean bulk pork sausage
12 slices bacon
¼ cup butter or margarine, divided
¼ cup all-purpose flour
2 cups red wine
2 tablespoons grape jelly
½ teaspoon salt
¼ teaspoon pepper

Rinse quail thoroughly with cold water; pat dry. Spoon sausage into body cavity of quail. Wrap 1 bacon slice around each quail, and secure with a wooden pick.

Melt 1 tablespoon butter in a skillet; add quail, 3 or 4 at a time. Cook until browned on both sides. Remove and place in a 13- x 9- x 2-inch baking dish. Repeat procedure with remaining quail. Drain pan drippings, reserving 1 tablespoon.

Combine remaining 3 tablespoons butter and pan drippings in skillet; add flour, stirring until smooth. Cook 1 minute, stirring constantly. Gradually add wine; cook over medium heat, stirring constantly, until mixture is thickened and bubbly. Stir in jelly, salt, and pepper. Pour over quail. Bake at 325° for 45 minutes or until done. Yield: 6 servings.

■ Mary Elizabeth Vaughn grew up in Thomasville, Georgia (where her husband, Jimmy Vaughn, now owns Foxfire Hunting Preserve), and learned how to cook game early on. Her recipe for Foxfire Duck is spiked with brandy and herbs. One duck will serve two.

FOXFIRE DUCK

1 (1-pound) wild duck, dressed
Vegetable oil
½ pound fresh mushrooms, cut in half
3 tablespoons all-purpose flour
3 cups water
¼ teaspoon dried whole basil
¼ teaspoon dried whole thyme
1 bay leaf
¼ teaspoon salt
¼ teaspoon pepper
1 medium onion, sliced
2 to 3 tablespoons brandy
Hot cooked wild rice

Wash duck, and cut in half at breast-bone; drain and pat dry. Heat ¼ inch of oil in a large skillet; add duck halves, and cook over medium heat 10 minutes or until brown, turning occasionally. Drain, reserving 3 tablespoons oil in skillet. Place duck on paper towels.

Sauté mushrooms in hot oil in skillet 3 minutes. Add flour; cook over low heat 1 minute, stirring constantly. Gradually add water; cook over medium heat, stirring constantly, until mixture comes to a boil. Add basil and next 5 ingredients, mixing well. Return duck to skillet; cover, reduce heat, and simmer 1½ hours. Add brandy, stirring well. Remove bay leaf. Serve over rice. Yield: 2 servings.

Serving Game

■ Serve brandied fruits as an elegant side dish with wild duck and other game. For more casual meals, serve fried apple slices.

■ Consider other classic game accompaniments that include cabbage, turnips, chestnuts, mushrooms, and onions, as well as hot buttered grits or rice.

■ Be sure to offer tangy relishes or chutneys with game.

■ To mix up a quick and easy sauce to serve with game, stir 2 tablespoons horseradish and ½ teaspoon dry mustard into ½ cup currant jelly.

■ Choose an appropriate bread to accompany platters of game, including hot buttered biscuits, French bread and garlic bread, cornbread and corn muffins, cornpone, and homemade rolls.

■ Lillie Bell's Venison Roast is a specialty served often at Bostick Plantation, Estill, South Carolina. Resident expert cook Lillie Bell Brooks wrote the recipe down for the first time so we could try it in our Test Kitchens. She soaks the venison in salted water and rinses it to enhance the flavor of the game.

■ Bostick Venison With Chutney-Mustard Sauce is another way to serve venison. Chef Ann Hollings occasionally works at Bostick Plantation, Estill, South Carolina, when they're entertaining special guests. This is her recipe.

You'll Hardly Recognize Oyster Stew

Mention oyster stew, and a buttery, creamy soup brimming with oysters comes to mind. But these three versions from our readers are a bit chunkier and spicier than the norm.

LILLIE BELL'S VENISON ROAST

1 (5- to 7-pound) venison roast
¼ cup salt
1 teaspoon seasoned salt
1 teaspoon garlic powder
1 teaspoon pepper
1 teaspoon soy sauce
1 onion, sliced
2 tablespoons all-purpose flour
¼ cup butter or margarine
1 to 2 quarts water, divided
All-purpose flour

Combine roast, water to cover, and ¼ cup salt in a large Dutch oven. Cover and let soak 2 hours. Drain, rinse, and pat dry.

Combine seasoned salt, garlic powder, and pepper; sprinkle on both sides of roast. Sprinkle with soy sauce. Place onion slices on top of roast, and sprinkle with 2 tablespoons flour. Place pats of butter on onion. Wrap roast twice in heavy-duty aluminum foil. Place in roasting pan; add 1 quart water. Cover and bake at 350° for 4 to 5 hours. Add water, if necessary, to roasting pan, but do not open foil.

Remove roast from pan. Carefully open foil, and measure liquid. Combine 1½ tablespoons flour and 2 tablespoons water for each cup of liquid; stir well. Stir into flour mixture. Cook over medium heat, stirring constantly, until thickened and bubbly. Serve gravy with roast. Yield: 6 servings.

Note: Remove as much fat as possible before cooking to eliminate any gamey flavor.

BOSTICK VENISON WITH CHUTNEY-MUSTARD SAUCE

1 pound venison tenderloin
¼ cup all-purpose flour
¼ teaspoon salt
¼ teaspoon pepper
¼ teaspoon paprika
¼ teaspoon garlic powder
Pinch of ground red pepper
2 to 3 tablespoons butter or margarine, melted
Chutney-Mustard Sauce

Cut venison tenderloin into ½- x ½-inch strips. Combine flour and seasonings in a plastic bag; add venison strips. Close bag securely, and shake vigorously.

Cook half of venison strips in 2 tablespoons butter in a large skillet until golden, turning once; drain on paper towels. Repeat with remaining venison strips, adding butter if necessary. Serve with Chutney-Mustard Sauce. Yield: 8 appetizer or 4 main-dish servings.

Chutney-Mustard Sauce

3 tablespoons coarse-grained mustard
1½ tablespoons Dijon mustard
2 tablespoons chutney

Combine all ingredients in a small bowl; stir well, and chill at least 2 hours. Yield: ⅓ cup.

OYSTER-SAUSAGE STEW

½ pound bulk pork sausage
⅓ cup diced onion
1 (12-ounce) container fresh Standard oysters
1½ cups milk
⅛ teaspoon hot sauce

Cook sausage and onion in a skillet until browned, stirring to crumble meat; drain well. Remove meat from skillet.

Drain oysters, reserving liquid. Place oysters in skillet, and cook over low heat until edges begin to curl; turn oysters, and add sausage mixture. Stir in reserved oyster liquid, milk, and hot sauce. Cook until mixture is hot. Yield: 3½ cups.

George Donigian
Clarksville, Virginia

OYSTER-BROCCOLI STEW

2 (11-ounce) cans Cheddar cheese soup, undiluted
3½ cups milk
2 cups diced potato
⅓ cup chopped onion
1 (10-ounce) package frozen chopped broccoli
1 (12-ounce) container fresh Standard oysters
¼ cup butter or margarine

Combine first 5 ingredients in a Dutch oven, stirring well. Bring to a boil; cover, reduce heat, and simmer

25 to 30 minutes or until potatoes are tender.

Drain oysters, reserving liquid. Using kitchen shears, cut through oysters 6 to 8 times. Set aside.

Melt butter in a small saucepan; add oysters and oyster liquid. Bring to a boil; reduce heat, and cook until edges curl, about 3 minutes. Add oyster mixture to broccoli mixture; simmer 5 minutes. Yield: 10 cups.

Judy D. Burner
Hayes, Virginia

POTATO-OYSTER STEW

1 (12-ounce) container fresh
  Standard oysters
1 medium-size red potato, peeled
  and cubed
3 cups water
½ teaspoon salt
1 medium onion, chopped
1 stalk celery, chopped
⅓ cup butter or margarine,
  melted
¼ cup all-purpose flour
2 cups half-and-half
¼ teaspoon garlic powder
¼ teaspoon pepper
2 teaspoons chopped fresh parsley
Chopped fresh parsley (optional)

Drain oysters, reserving liquid. Using kitchen shears, cut through oysters 6 to 8 times. Set aside.

Place potato in a medium saucepan; add water and salt. Bring to a boil; cover, reduce heat, and simmer 15 to 20 minutes or until tender. Drain, reserving liquid.

Sauté onion and celery in butter in a 3-quart saucepan until tender. Stir in flour, and cook 1 minute. Gradually add reserved potato liquid and half-and-half; cook over medium heat, stirring constantly, until mixture slightly thickens.

Stir in cubed potato, oysters, reserved oyster liquid, garlic powder, and next 2 ingredients. Simmer 8 to 10 minutes or until edges of oysters curl. Garnish with chopped parsley, if desired. Yield: 6½ cups.

Mary Helen Hackney
Greenville, North Carolina

Piped Potatoes Dress This Meat Loaf

Paula Griswold of Hendersonville, North Carolina, came up with the idea of topping meat loaf with the side dish that it's commonly served with—mashed potatoes. Her resulting recipe, Elegant Meat Loaf, is anything but common.

ELEGANT MEAT LOAF

1 clove garlic, minced
1 teaspoon butter or margarine,
  melted
1 pound ground round
½ pound ground pork
1 egg, beaten
2 slices rye bread, torn into
  small pieces
½ cup chopped onion
¼ cup chopped green pepper
¼ cup firmly packed brown sugar
¾ cup catsup
¼ cup white vinegar
2 teaspoons Worcestershire sauce
1 teaspoon dry mustard
½ teaspoon salt
¼ teaspoon pepper
¼ cup catsup
Mashed Potato Topping
½ cup (2 ounces) shredded
  Cheddar cheese
Ground nutmeg
Chopped fresh parsley (optional)

Sauté garlic in butter; combine with next 13 ingredients. Stir until blended. Shape into a 9- x 5-inch oval loaf, and place on a lightly greased rack in a broiler pan. Spoon ¼ cup catsup on top, cover with foil, and bake at 350° for 1 hour. Uncover and bake an additional 15 minutes. Place meat loaf on an ovenproof platter.

Spread Mashed Potato Topping over entire meat loaf. Using a pastry bag, pipe remaining topping around base of meat loaf. Bake at 375° for 10 minutes. Sprinkle with cheese and nutmeg, and bake an additional 5 minutes. Garnish meat loaf with chopped fresh parsley, if desired. Yield: 6 servings.

Mashed Potato Topping

4 large potatoes, peeled and
  cubed
½ cup sour cream
¼ cup butter or margarine
1 tablespoon grated onion
Salt and pepper to taste
Milk

Cook potatoes in water to cover until tender; drain well, and mash. Combine potatoes and next 4 ingredients. Stir in enough milk to make potato mixture a good consistency. Yield: 6 servings.

From Our Kitchen To Yours

Discover the bountiful selection of vegetables available at supermarkets and farmers markets this time of year. While adding color, variety, and flavor to menus, these fresh vegetables furnish abundant vitamins and minerals. They also contain no cholesterol and are good sources of dietary fiber. Because of modern marketing techniques, most vegetables are available year-round; however, now's the time to take advantage of some that are unfamiliar and often neglected.

The firm, white bulb and straight stalks of the crunchy, anise-flavored vegetable **fennel** are eaten like celery. The delicate, feathery green leaves make attractive garnishes.

When cooked, fennel's mildly sweet flavor is accentuated. Select fennel with fresh-looking green tops and plump, firm bulbs 3 to 4 inches in diameter; trim off stalks to within 1 to 2 inches of the bulb, discarding the tough outer stalks while reserving leaves for garnish.

Kohlrabi, a plump light-green or lavender stemmed vegetable, looks like a bulb but is grown above ground. Sometimes called "cabbage turnip," kohlrabi resembles a turnip but tastes like a mild cabbage. Served raw or cooked, kohlrabi can be substituted for turnips. Purchase unscarred bulbs about 2 to 3 inches in diameter with crisp leaves.

Similar in appearance, parsnips and salsify are root vegetables. **Parsnips,** good substitutes for carrots, look like dingy-white carrots. Sometimes called "oyster plant," **salsify,** with its elusive sweetness, is black on the outside. Both vegetables can be refrigerated in the crisper for several weeks. After peeling the vegetables, soak them in a solution of 1 teaspoon lemon juice to 1½ cups water before cooking them, to prevent discoloration. Select well-shaped, small- to medium-size roots without blemishes or soft spots.

Two other similar root vegetables are turnips and rutabagas. **Turnips** are round with whitish skin and a purple band. When turnips are eaten raw, the crunchy, bittersweet flavor is suggestive of radishes. For the best flavor, purchase ones not more than 3 inches in diameter. Often called yellow turnips, **rutabagas** differ in shape due to their elongated globes. During processing, a thin coating of paraffin is applied to the yellow-orange flesh to prevent moisture loss and improve the storing quality. The waxy surface is easily removed by peeling. Turnips and rutabagas can be used interchangeably in recipes; however, rutabagas have a stronger flavor. Select smooth, firm, and unblemished vegetables.

A round, brownish root with rough skin and a green top, **celeriac** (celery root) has a nutty-sweet celery flavor. An excellent choice for soups and purees, this vegetable is easier to peel if first cut into slices, but it darkens with exposure to air. To prevent discoloration, soak cut pieces in a solution of water and lemon juice for several minutes. When cooked, the crunchy texture becomes similar to the texture of a firm potato. Firm roots without deep cracks are the wisest selections.

Fresh **brussels sprouts** have a delicate taste if not overcooked. To ensure even cooking, make a cut with the tip of a paring knife in the shape of an X in the stem end. Select firm, compact, bright-green heads, with tight-fitting outer leaves free from black spots.

Hearty **kale** belongs to the cabbage family. The deeply frilled, green to greenish-purple leaves can be eaten raw but have an improved texture when steamed, sautéed, or stir-fried. Be sure to choose a small, deep-colored bunch with crisp, unbruised leaves. To wash, strip the leaves from the stems.

Vegetable Storage Guidelines

■ For maximum flavor and nutritive value, use fresh vegetables within a few days of purchase.
■ To prevent flavor and odor penetration and to minimize water loss, store different types of produce (except tomatoes, potatoes, and onions) in closed plastic bags in refrigerator.
■ To prevent wilting and flavor change, rinse green, leafy vegetables under cool water, and drain thoroughly. Wrap in paper towels, place in plastic bags, and refrigerate.
■ Corn, beans, peas, and other vegetables will lose sweetness as sugar in their tissues turns to starch. Store dry and unwashed in plastic bags in refrigerator.

Tasty Ideas For Turnips

Mention turnips and many folks think of a "mess of greens" to simmer and serve with cornbread and pot liquor. But don't forget the roots have many other serving options. Their crisp texture is highlighted in Turnip Slaw. Raw turnip slices or strips also provide a nice addition to relish trays.

Cooked turnips make an elegant side dish to serve as an alternative to potatoes. Try Turnips au Gratin for a nice accompaniment to pork. To enhance the flavor of soups and stews, add slices of turnip to simmer with the other vegetables.

Fresh turnips are available year-round. Look for roots that are smooth, firm, and heavy for their size. Store roots in a cool, moist area or in a plastic bag in the refrigerator crisper.

TURNIPS AU GRATIN

5 cups diced turnip (about 3 pounds)
1 teaspoon salt
1 teaspoon sugar
2 tablespoons butter or margarine
2 tablespoons all-purpose flour
1½ cups milk
1 teaspoon seasoned salt
⅛ teaspoon pepper
¾ cup (3 ounces) shredded Cheddar cheese
¼ cup fine, dry breadcrumbs

Combine first 3 ingredients in a Dutch oven; add water to cover. Bring to a boil; cover, reduce heat, and simmer 10 to 12 minutes or until tender. Drain well, and set aside.

Melt butter in a large heavy saucepan over low heat; add flour, stirring constantly. Gradually add milk; cook over medium heat, stirring constantly, until thickened and bubbly.

Add salt, pepper, and cheese, stirring until cheese melts. Remove from heat; stir in turnips.

Spoon turnip mixture into a lightly greased 1½-quart casserole; sprinkle breadcrumbs over casserole. Bake at 350° for 20 to 25 minutes or until hot and bubbly. Yield: 6 servings.

Clota Engleman
Spur, Texas

TURNIP SLAW

3 cups shredded turnip (about 2 pounds)
1½ cups shredded carrot
½ cup raisins
½ to ¾ cup mayonnaise or salad dressing
1 tablespoon lemon juice

Combine all ingredients in a large bowl; stir well. Cover and chill. Yield: 6 to 8 servings. *Doris Holly*
Tulia, Texas

Accent Vegetables With An Easy Sauce

If you're looking for new ways to serve vegetables, these recipes are interesting yet easy. Lemony Cucumber Sauce, for instance, takes just 10 minutes to make and is delicious served over the vegetable of your choice.

Two of the recipes, Asparagus Supreme and Broccoli With Lemon Cream, team a green vegetable with a tangy sauce. Both recipes offer quick alternatives to preparing a white sauce. And in both recipes, the sauces are spread over the vegetables and then baked, making them ideal for advance preparation.

ASPARAGUS SUPREME

2 pounds fresh asparagus
½ cup chopped onion
2 tablespoons butter or margarine, melted
2 tablespoons all-purpose flour
1 (8-ounce) carton sour cream
¼ teaspoon salt
⅛ teaspoon pepper
½ cup (2 ounces) shredded Cheddar cheese

Snap off tough ends of asparagus. Remove scales with a vegetable peeler or knife, if desired. Place asparagus in a vegetable steamer over boiling water; cover and steam 8 to 10 minutes or until crisp-tender. Arrange asparagus in a lightly greased 12- x 8- x 2-inch baking dish. Set dish aside.

Sauté onion in butter in a small saucepan over low heat; add flour, stirring until smooth. Cook 1 minute, stirring constantly. Add sour cream, salt, and pepper, stirring well. Cook over medium heat until thoroughly heated (do not boil). Spoon over asparagus. Bake at 350° for 15 minutes. Sprinkle top evenly with shredded cheese, and bake an additional 5 minutes or until cheese melts. Yield: 8 servings.

Lucy Persons
Macon, Georgia

BROCCOLI WITH LEMON CREAM

1½ pounds fresh broccoli
2 (3-ounce) packages cream cheese, softened
½ cup milk
1 teaspoon grated lemon rind
1 tablespoon lemon juice
½ teaspoon ground ginger
½ teaspoon ground cardamom
½ cup slivered almonds
1 tablespoon butter or margarine, melted

Trim off large leaves of broccoli, and remove tough ends of lower stalks.

Wash broccoli thoroughly, and cut into spears. Cook in a small amount of boiling water 8 to 10 minutes or just until crisp-tender. Drain and arrange in a greased 12- x 8- x 2-inch baking dish.

Combine cream cheese and next 5 ingredients; beat well. Spoon mixture over broccoli. Cover and bake at 350° for 15 minutes.

Sauté almonds in butter; spoon over broccoli. Yield: 6 servings.

Gayle Fleming
Northport, Alabama

LEMONY CUCUMBER SAUCE

2 egg yolks, beaten
½ cup butter or margarine, cut into slices
2 tablespoons lemon juice
1 cup finely chopped cucumber, well drained (1 large cucumber)

Combine egg yolks, butter, and lemon juice in a small saucepan. Cook over low heat, stirring constantly, about 10 minutes or until butter melts and sauce thickens. Stir in cucumber. Serve immediately over hot cooked asparagus, carrots, or other vegetables. Yield: 1 cup.

Merle R. Downs
Tryon, North Carolina

Tip: *When a sauce curdles, follow this procedure: Remove pan from heat and plunge into a pan of cold water to stop the cooking process. Beat sauce vigorously or pour into a blender and process until the sauce is smooth.*

Braid
A Bread

She first prepared it one Christmas morning because the recipe was so special, but Jam-and-Cheese Loaf is now a year-round choice for Anna Vintila of Churchville, Virginia.

JAM-AND-CHEESE LOAF

1 package dry yeast
½ cup warm water (105° to 115°)
2½ cups biscuit mix
1 tablespoon sugar
1 egg, beaten
1 (8-ounce) package cream
  cheese, softened
⅓ cup sugar
1 tablespoon lemon juice
¼ cup strawberry or other flavor
  preserves

Dissolve yeast in warm water; let stand 5 minutes. Add biscuit mix, 1 tablespoon sugar, and egg; stir well.

Turn dough out onto a floured surface, and knead until smooth and elastic. Place dough in a well-greased bowl, turning to grease top; cover and chill 8 hours. Punch dough down, and turn out onto a lightly greased baking sheet; roll dough into a 14- x 9-inch rectangle.

Combine cream cheese, ⅓ cup sugar, and lemon juice; beat at medium speed of electric mixer until smooth. Spread 2 inches wide lengthwise down center of dough. Make 3-inch cuts into dough at 1-inch intervals on long sides. Fold and overlap strips diagonally over filling in a braided fashion. Cover; let rise in warm place (85°), free from drafts, 45 minutes or until doubled in bulk. Bake at 350° for 20 minutes.

Remove from oven, and spoon preserves down center. Return to oven; bake an additional 5 minutes. Remove from oven, and let stand 10 minutes. Yield: one 14-inch loaf.

Cream Cheese
Spreads Burst
With Flavor

Cheese spreads get high marks from hostesses because of their popularity on the menu and their make-ahead potential. And some of the most flavorful of these appetizer spreads start with cream cheese.

Whether the recipes call for it or not, cream cheese spreads keep so well that you can always make them a day or two ahead of time, and then cover and refrigerate until serving time. For easier spreading, let them sit at room temperature about 15 minutes prior to serving.

PARMESAN-CREAM CHEESE BALL

2 (8-ounce) packages cream
  cheese, softened
½ cup mayonnaise or salad
  dressing
⅓ cup grated Parmesan cheese
10 slices bacon, cooked and
  crumbled
¼ cup sliced green onions
Green onion fan (optional)
Bacon curl (optional)

Beat cream cheese at medium speed of an electric mixer until smooth. Add mayonnaise and Parmesan cheese; beat until blended. Stir in crumbled bacon and green onions; cover and chill at least 3 hours. Shape mixture into a ball; if desired, garnish with green onion fan and bacon curl. Serve cheese ball with assorted crackers. Yield: 2¾ cups.
Camilla C. Hudson
Denton, Texas

HERBED CHEESE BALL

2 (8-ounce) packages cream
  cheese, softened
1 tablespoon minced onion
1 (0.4-ounce) package
  buttermilk-style salad
  dressing mix
1 cup chopped pecans

Combine first 3 ingredients in a mixing bowl; beat at medium speed of an electric mixer until smooth. Cover and chill several hours. Shape mixture into a ball, and roll in pecans. Serve with assorted crackers. Yield: 2 cups.
Nancy Morris
Salisbury, North Carolina

CARAWAY CHEESE

1 cup butter or margarine,
  softened
4 (3-ounce) packages cream
  cheese, softened
2 tablespoons caraway seeds
2 teaspoons paprika
2 teaspoons prepared mustard
Additional paprika

Combine butter, cream cheese, caraway seeds, 2 teaspoons paprika, and prepared mustard in a mixing bowl; beat at medium speed of an electric mixer until smooth. Shape mixture into a ball; sprinkle with additional paprika. Serve with crackers. Yield: 2⅔ cups.
Sue-Sue Hartstern
Louisville, Kentucky

HAWAIIAN CHEESE LOG

1 (8-ounce) package cream
  cheese, softened
2 cups (8 ounces) shredded
  Cheddar cheese
1 (8¼-ounce) can crushed
  pineapple, drained
¼ cup chopped dried apricots
1 teaspoon diced crystallized
  ginger
¾ cup chopped pecans

Combine first 5 ingredients, mixing well. Shape mixture into two 6-inch logs; roll each log in chopped pecans. Cover and chill. Serve with assorted crackers or sliced apples or pears. Yield: two 6-inch logs.

Mrs. John Rucker
Louisville, Kentucky

ROQUEFORT PECAN LOG

2 (3-ounce) packages cream cheese, softened
8 ounces Roquefort cheese, crumbled
2 tablespoons grated onion
1 small clove garlic, crushed
1 cup chopped pecans

Combine first 4 ingredients in a mixing bowl; beat at medium speed of an electric mixer until smooth. Shape mixture into a 10-inch log; roll in chopped pecans. Cover and chill at least 3 hours. Serve with assorted crackers. Yield: about 2 cups.

Norma Cowden
Shawnee, Oklahoma

One-Dish Dinners For Two

You can keep the cooking and dishwashing to a minimum when serving two people by preparing a one-dish dinner. Just add bread and perhaps a salad or dessert.

For starters, try Sausage Ratatouille. You make it ahead, chill to allow the flavors to blend, and then reheat it at dinnertime.

Prepare Chinese-Style Chicken Dinner just before serving it. After cutting the vegetables, it will take less than 15 minutes to sauté the ingredients.

CHINESE-STYLE CHICKEN DINNER

¼ small cabbage, shredded (about 2 cups)
1 large stalk celery, cut into julienne strips
1 small carrot, cut into julienne strips
1 small onion, sliced
1 tablespoon vegetable oil
2 chicken breast halves, skinned and boned
1 tablespoon cornstarch
2 tablespoons soy sauce
¾ cup chicken broth
Hot cooked rice

Sauté first 4 ingredients in hot oil in a skillet over high heat 5 minutes or until crisp-tender. Remove vegetables from skillet.

Cut chicken into bite-size pieces. Sauté chicken in drippings in skillet until tender. Combine cornstarch, soy sauce, and chicken broth, stirring until cornstarch dissolves. Add to chicken, and stir until mixture begins to bubble. Cook 1 minute; stir constantly. Return vegetables to skillet; stir until heated. Serve over rice. Yield: 2 servings.

Edna Baugh
Wilmington, North Carolina

SKILLET CHICKEN DINNER

2 chicken breast halves, skinned
1 tablespoon vegetable oil
½ cup diced carrot
½ cup (1½-inch pieces) green beans
½ cup (2-inch pieces) celery
½ cup chicken bouillon
2 teaspoons cornstarch
2 tablespoons water

Brown chicken on all sides in hot oil in a heavy skillet. Remove chicken; set aside. Add vegetables to skillet; stir-fry 2 minutes. Remove vegetables from skillet; set aside.

Add bouillon and chicken to skillet, and bring to a boil; cover, reduce heat, and simmer 20 minutes or until done. Remove chicken to serving dish; keep warm.

Combine cornstarch and water. Stir into drippings in skillet; cook over medium heat, stirring constantly, until thickened and bubbly. Add vegetables; cook until thoroughly heated. Spoon over chicken breasts. Yield: 2 servings.

Marguerite Schaeffer
Long Beach, Mississippi

CHILI MANICOTTI

4 manicotti shells
2 tablespoons minced onion
1 small clove garlic, minced
1 tablespoon vegetable oil
1 (11¼-ounce) can condensed chili beef soup with beans, undiluted
1 cup water
1 egg, beaten
¾ cup cottage cheese
½ cup (2 ounces) shredded Cheddar cheese, divided

Cook manicotti shells according to package directions, omitting salt. Drain shells, and set aside.

Sauté onion and garlic in hot oil in a large saucepan until tender. Stir in soup and water. Bring to a boil; reduce heat, and simmer 2 minutes. Remove from heat.

Combine egg, cottage cheese, and half of Cheddar cheese; stir well. Stuff manicotti shells with cheese mixture.

Spoon half of soup mixture into a lightly greased 1-quart casserole. Arrange stuffed shells over sauce. Spoon remaining sauce over shells. Cover and bake at 350° for 30 minutes; uncover. Sprinkle with remaining Cheddar cheese, and bake an additional 5 minutes. Let stand 5 minutes before serving. Yield: 2 servings.

Ashlyn Ritch
Forsyth, Georgia

SAUSAGE RATATOUILLE

½ pound Italian sausage
¼ cup olive oil
1 small onion, chopped
1 small eggplant (¾ pound), cut into ½-inch cubes
1 zucchini, sliced
1 clove garlic, minced
1 large tomato, peeled and chopped
½ teaspoon dried whole oregano
¼ teaspoon salt
¼ teaspoon pepper
Fresh parsley sprigs

Remove casings from sausage. Cook sausage in a large skillet over medium heat until meat is browned, stirring to crumble. Drain well, and set aside.

Heat oil in a large skillet; add onion, and sauté 2 minutes over medium heat, stirring constantly. Add eggplant, and sauté 3 minutes, stirring constantly. Add zucchini and garlic; reduce heat, and simmer 10 minutes. Add tomato, sausage, and seasonings; cover and simmer an additional 5 minutes, stirring once. Garnish with parsley. Yield: 2 servings.
Norma Miller
Sevierville, Tennessee

MICROWAVE COOKERY

Microwave The Main Dish

For a quick family supper, serve Microwave Pizza Casserole or Chicken-and-Broccoli Stroganoff. You may want to round out the menu with a green salad to go with either of these tasty selections.

If you prefer a one-dish meal that's not a casserole, try Fish-and-Potato Platter. The potatoes require the most cooking, so they are placed around the outside of the dish where the microwaves begin cooking first.

CHICKEN-AND-BROCCOLI STROGANOFF

1 (10-ounce) package frozen broccoli flowerets
1 tablespoon butter or margarine
½ cup chopped onion
3 tablespoons all-purpose flour
⅛ to ¼ teaspoon salt
¼ teaspoon white pepper
1 (14½-ounce) can ready-to-serve chicken broth
2 cups cubed cooked chicken
1 (2½-ounce) jar sliced mushrooms, drained
1 (8-ounce) carton sour cream
Hot cooked noodles

Cook broccoli according to package directions; drain and set aside.

Place butter in a 2-quart round casserole. Microwave at HIGH 35 seconds or until melted. Stir in onion. Cover tightly with heavy-duty plastic wrap; fold back a small edge of wrap to allow steam to escape. Microwave at HIGH 2 minutes. Add flour, salt, and pepper, stirring until smooth; gradually add chicken broth, stirring well. Microwave at HIGH, uncovered, 4 to 6 minutes or until thickened and bubbly, stirring at 2-minute intervals with a wire whisk. Stir in broccoli, chicken, and mushrooms; microwave at HIGH 2 minutes. Stir in sour cream; microwave at HIGH 1 minute.

Serve stroganoff over noodles. Yield: 6 servings. *Patricia Andrews McAlester, Oklahoma*

FISH-AND-POTATO PLATTER

1 (8-ounce) carton plain nonfat yogurt
¼ cup chopped fresh dillweed
2 tablespoons rice vinegar
2 tablespoons chopped chives
½ teaspoon salt
½ teaspoon pepper
¾ pound small red potatoes, unpeeled and cut into ⅛-inch slices
1 pound salmon or amberjack fillets, skinned and cut crosswise into 3- x 1½-inch pieces
1 cup broccoli flowerets
2 tablespoons lemon juice

Combine first 6 ingredients in a small bowl; cover and chill.

Overlap potato slices around edge of a microwave-safe, round 12-inch platter. Cover tightly with heavy-duty plastic wrap; fold back a small edge of wrap to allow steam to escape. Microwave at HIGH 3 minutes. Uncover and place fish in a ring inside potatoes with pieces end to end. Mound broccoli in center of platter. Sprinkle fish and potatoes with lemon juice; cover. Microwave at HIGH 8 minutes or until fish is cooked through and potatoes are tender, giving dish a half-turn at 4-minute intervals. Serve with dill sauce. Yield: 4 servings.

MICROWAVE PIZZA CASSEROLE

2 cups egg noodles
1 pound ground beef
⅓ cup chopped green pepper
1 small onion, chopped
1 (15½-ounce) jar pizza sauce
1 cup water
½ teaspoon garlic salt
1 (4-ounce) can sliced mushrooms, drained
⅓ cup sliced pepperoni, cubed ham, or Canadian bacon
1 cup (4 ounces) shredded mozzarella cheese

Cook egg noodles according to package directions. Drain and set aside.

Combine ground beef, green pepper, and onion in a 12- x 8- x 2-inch baking dish. Cover tightly with heavy-duty plastic wrap; fold back a corner of wrap to allow steam to escape. Microwave at HIGH 5 minutes or until done, stirring at 2-minute intervals; drain.

Add noodles, pizza sauce, and next 4 ingredients, mixing well. Cover and microwave at HIGH 17 to 19 minutes, stirring at 6-minute intervals. Sprinkle with cheese; cover and let stand 5 minutes. Yield: 6 servings.

Susan Hall
Russellville, Arkansas

with cold water. Split and clean tails. Cut meat into ½-inch pieces; press between layers of paper towels to remove excess water.

Combine lobster, French dressing, and sherry; stir gently. Cover and refrigerate 3 to 4 hours. Drain mixture, if necessary.

Combine lobster mixture, chopped celery, asparagus, mayonnaise, and pepper in a medium bowl; stir gently until coated.

If desired, serve on lettuce leaves, and top with tomato wedges. Yield: 6 servings.

in the microwave. Place a cup of honey in a microwave-safe container; then microwave on HIGH for 2 to 3 minutes or until crystals dissolve, stirring every 30 seconds. Be careful, though, not to scorch or boil the honey; just keep in mind that overheating destroys the delicate flavor of the honey.

The Best Of Seafood In A Salad

Mildred Sherrer of Bay City, Texas, was right when she said her Lobster Salad was special. We made it with lobster as well as a less expensive seafood mix and liked it both ways.

LOBSTER SALAD

2½ quarts water
4 (10-ounce) lobster tails, fresh or frozen, thawed, or 1 pound seafood mix
½ cup commercial French dressing
¼ cup dry sherry
1 cup chopped celery
⅓ pound fresh asparagus, cut into 1-inch pieces
½ to ¾ cup mayonnaise
¼ teaspoon pepper
Bibb lettuce leaves (optional)
Tomato wedges (optional)

Bring water to a boil; add lobster tails. Cover, reduce heat, and simmer 12 to 15 minutes. Drain. Rinse

Honey, Nature's Sweetener

Drizzled on a warm, tender biscuit or a thick slice of toast, honey glistens a rich, golden hue. Swirled in a cup of bracing tea, it lends distinctive flavor. And for cooking, honey presents many attributes beyond its unique sweet flavor.

The flavor, color, and aroma of the many varieties depend on the flowers from which the bees gather the nectar. As a rule, the lighter the color, the milder the flavor. Mildly flavored honey, such as clover and orange blossom, are best for cooking. Use strongly flavored types in spreads or other recipes where a distinct honey flavor is desired.

Honey's velvety, rich consistency makes it ideal for sweetening beverages and making shiny glazes and silky smooth sauces.

Honey is best stored in a dry place because it tends to absorb moisture and become granulated. To liquify granulated honey, remove the lid, and place the honey container in a bowl of warm (not hot) water until crystals dissolve. Or you can heat it

MARINATED PORK CHOPS

6 (1-inch-thick) pork chops (about 3 pounds)
¾ cup honey
½ cup white vinegar
¼ cup soy sauce
½ teaspoon ground ginger
1 clove garlic, minced

Place pork chops in a 13- x 9- x 2-inch baking dish. Combine remaining ingredients; pour over pork chops. Cover and refrigerate at least 8 hours.

Remove from refrigerator; let stand 30 minutes. Bake in marinade, covered, at 325° for 1 hour or until a meat thermometer registers 160°. Yield: 6 servings.

Susan Todd
Shreveport, Louisiana

Honey Tips

■ For cooking, measure any butter or oil first, and then the honey. This way, the honey slides right out of the cup.

■ Here's a quick tangy sauce to accompany baked ham or fried chicken fingers: Combine equal amounts of honey and prepared mustard; stir well.

■ Too much honey in a recipe may make the dish too brown.

ORANGE SALAD WITH HONEY-BERRY DRESSING
(pictured on page 262)

1 (8-ounce) can jellied cranberry sauce
¼ cup honey
1 tablespoon orange juice
6 large oranges, peeled, seeded, and sectioned
1 red Delicious apple, unpeeled and chopped
1 cup seedless green grapes, halved (about ½ pound)
1 medium banana, peeled and sliced
Orange cup (optional)
Fresh mint sprig (optional)

Heat cranberry sauce in a small saucepan until melted. Stir in honey and orange juice. Cool.

Combine oranges, apple, and grapes in a large bowl; refrigerate. Stir in banana before serving.

Serve with cranberry-honey mixture. If desired, serve mixture in an orange cup, and garnish with fresh mint. Yield: about 8 servings.

Marie A. Davis
Drexel, North Carolina

HONEY-CURRY BREAD
(pictured on page 262)

¼ cup butter or margarine
1 tablespoon curry powder
1¾ cups buttermilk
⅔ cup honey
2 packages dry yeast
½ cup warm water (105° to 115°)
7 to 8 cups unbleached all-purpose flour
2 teaspoons salt
1 egg
2 teaspoons water
2 tablespoons sliced almonds

Melt butter in a saucepan; stir in curry powder. Cook over low heat 1 minute. Add buttermilk and honey; heat to 105° to 115°. Dissolve yeast in ½ cup warm water in a large bowl; let stand 5 minutes. Stir in buttermilk mixture. Gradually add 4 cups flour and salt, beating at medium speed of an electric mixer until mixture is smooth. Gradually stir in enough of the remaining flour to make a soft dough.

Turn dough out onto a floured surface, and knead until smooth and elastic (about 5 minutes). Shape into a ball, and place in a well-greased bowl, turning to grease top. Cover and let rise in a warm place (85°), free from drafts, for 45 minutes or until doubled in bulk.

Punch dough down; turn out onto a lightly floured surface. Divide dough in half; divide each half into thirds. Shape each third into a 15-inch rope. Place 3 ropes, side by side, on a greased baking sheet (do not stretch); pinch ends together at one end to seal. Braid ropes; pinch loose ends to seal. Repeat with remaining dough.

Cover and let rise in a warm place, free from drafts, about 45 minutes or until doubled in bulk.

Combine egg and 2 teaspoons water; beat well. Gently brush dough with egg mixture. Sprinkle with almonds. Bake at 350° for 25 to 30 minutes or until done; cool on wire rack. Yield: 2 loaves.

Rublelene Singleton
Scotts Hill, Tennessee

HONEY-BRAN MUFFINS

1½ cups shreds of wheat bran cereal
1 cup milk
1 egg, beaten
⅓ cup honey
⅓ cup butter or margarine, melted
1¼ cups all-purpose flour
1 tablespoon baking powder
½ cup chopped pitted dates
½ cup raisins

Combine cereal and milk; let stand 5 minutes. Stir in beaten egg, honey, and butter.

Combine flour and remaining ingredients in a large bowl; make a well in center of mixture. Add cereal mixture, stirring just until moistened.

Spoon mixture into greased muffin pans, filling three-fourths full. Bake at 400° for 15 minutes or until done. Remove from pans immediately. Yield: 15 muffins.

Carole Madison
Paducah, Kentucky

HONEY CAKE SQUARES

1 cup chopped walnuts
¾ cup chopped pitted dates
3 tablespoons all-purpose flour
¾ cup butter or margarine, softened
¾ cup sugar
3 eggs
1 cup all-purpose flour
1½ teaspoons baking powder
¼ teaspoon salt
½ teaspoon ground cardamom
1 teaspoon grated orange rind
¼ cup milk
¼ cup honey
Powdered sugar

Combine walnuts and dates; dredge in 3 tablespoons flour, stirring to coat evenly. Set aside.

Cream butter in a large bowl; gradually add sugar, beating well at medium speed of an electric mixer. Add eggs, one at a time, beating after each addition until blended.

Combine 1 cup flour and next 4 ingredients; add to creamed mixture alternately with milk, beginning and ending with flour mixture. Mix after each addition. Stir in the walnut-date mixture.

Spoon mixture into a greased and floured 13- x 9- x 2-inch pan. Bake at 350° for 25 to 30 minutes or until a wooden pick inserted in center comes out clean. Drizzle with honey, and cool in pan. Cut into 1½-inch squares or diamonds. Sprinkle with powdered sugar. Yield: 4 dozen.

Jenny Heinzmann
Lothian, Maryland

SOUTHERN HONEY CAKE

¼ cup pineapple juice
¼ cup water
¾ teaspoon baking soda
1 cup sugar
3 eggs
1 cup vegetable oil
1 cup honey
2½ cups all-purpose flour
1 teaspoon baking powder
1 teaspoon salt
2 teaspoons ground cinnamon
½ teaspoon ground allspice
1 teaspoon vanilla extract
½ cup chopped pecans

Combine pineapple juice and water in a small saucepan; bring to a boil. Stir in soda; set aside.

Combine sugar, eggs, oil, and honey; beat at medium speed of an electric mixer until well blended. Combine flour and next 4 ingredients; add to creamed mixture alternately with pineapple juice mixture, beginning and ending with flour mixture. Mix after each addition. Stir in vanilla and pecans. Spoon batter into a greased and floured 12-cup Bundt pan. Bake at 325° for 1 hour or until a wooden pick inserted in center comes out clean. Cool in pan 10 minutes; remove from pan, and let cool completely on a wire rack. Yield: one 10-inch cake.   *Cathy Williams*
Vale, North Carolina

FROZEN BOURBON-PECAN PIE
(pictured on page 262)

⅓ cup bourbon
2 eggs, separated
½ cup honey
⅛ teaspoon salt
2 teaspoons vanilla extract
1½ cups whipping cream
¾ cup coarsely chopped pecans
Nutty Oat Crust
Honey-Chocolate Sauce
Pecan halves (optional)

Combine bourbon, egg yolks, honey, and salt in a small saucepan; stir well. Cook over low heat, stirring

constantly, until mixture thickens (do not boil). Remove from heat. Stir in vanilla; let cool completely.

Beat egg whites (at room temperature) until stiff but not dry; set aside. Beat whipping cream until soft peaks form. Fold whipped cream and chopped pecans into cooled mixture; then fold in beaten egg whites. Spoon into Nutty Oat Crust; freeze 8 hours or until firm. Drizzle pie with Honey-Chocolate Sauce; garnish with pecan halves, if desired. Serve pie with remaining sauce. Yield: one 9-inch pie.

Nutty Oat Crust

½ cup butter or margarine,
   softened
¼ cup firmly packed light brown
   sugar
1 cup all-purpose flour
¼ cup regular oats, uncooked
¼ cup finely chopped pecans

Cream butter; gradually add sugar, beating well at medium speed of an electric mixer. Add flour, oats, and pecans; beat at low speed until blended. Press on bottom and 1 inch up sides of a lightly greased 9-inch springform pan. Prick dough with a fork; bake at 350° for 20 to 25 minutes or until lightly browned. Cool. Yield: 1 (9-inch) crust.

Honey-Chocolate Sauce

¼ cup plus 2 tablespoons cocoa
1½ tablespoons cornstarch
½ cup water
¾ cup honey
Pinch of salt
¼ cup plus 2 tablespoons butter
   or margarine, melted
1 teaspoon vanilla extract

Combine cocoa and cornstarch in a small saucepan; stir in water, mixing well. Add honey and salt. Cook over medium heat, stirring constantly, until mixture boils; boil 1 minute. Add butter, 1 tablespoon at a time, stirring constantly until melted. Stir in vanilla. Serve at room temperature. Refrigerate leftover sauce for other uses. Yield: 1⅔ cups.

Chocolate Fit For A Queen

The next time you invite friends for a special occasion, roll out the red carpet—treat them like royalty by serving dainty Black-Bottom Goodies. If ever something should be offered on a silver platter, these elegant but easy creations are it.

Cream cheese filling sits atop a moist, chocolate base, and miniature chocolate morsels complement the tiny cakes.

BLACK-BOTTOM GOODIES

1½ cups all-purpose flour
1 teaspoon baking soda
½ teaspoon salt
1 cup sugar
¼ cup cocoa
1 cup water
⅓ cup vegetable oil
1 tablespoon vinegar
1 tablespoon vanilla extract
1 (8-ounce) package cream
   cheese, softened
1 egg
½ cup sugar
⅛ teaspoon salt
1 (6-ounce) package semisweet
   chocolate mini-morsels

Combine first 5 ingredients in a large bowl; make a well in center of mixture. Combine water, oil, vinegar, and vanilla; add to dry ingredients, stirring well. Spoon batter into paper-lined miniature muffin pans, filling two-thirds full.

Combine cream cheese and next 3 ingredients, stirring well. Stir in chocolate morsels. Spoon about 1 teaspoon cream cheese mixture over chocolate batter in each muffin cup. Bake at 350° for 10 to 15 minutes. Yield: 5 dozen.

QUICK!

A Pie For Dessert

Busy cooks have little time to prepare old-fashioned desserts. So instead of making elaborate pies from a long list of ingredients, they're combining commercial products for desserts that are equally tasty.

PEANUT BUTTER PIE

1 (8-ounce) package cream cheese
½ cup sugar
½ cup creamy peanut butter
1 teaspoon vanilla extract
1 cup whipping cream
1 (9-inch) commercial graham
  cracker crust
1 to 2 tablespoons chopped salted
  peanuts

Combine cream cheese and sugar; beat at medium speed of an electric mixer until smooth. Add peanut butter and vanilla; beat well. Set aside.

Beat whipping cream until soft peaks form; fold into peanut mixture. Spoon into crust; sprinkle with peanuts. Chill at least 3 hours. Yield: one 9-inch pie. *Betty Joyce Mills*
Birmingham, Alabama

QUICK PEACH PIE

1 (16-ounce) package frozen
  sliced peaches, thawed
½ cup light corn syrup
2 tablespoons water
2 tablespoons cornstarch
2 tablespoons lemon juice
1 (6-ounce) commercial graham
  cracker crust
1 cup whipping cream, whipped

Place 1 cup peaches in container of an electric blender or food processor; process until smooth. Pour pureed peaches into a saucepan; add corn syrup, water, and cornstarch. Cook over medium heat, stirring constantly, until mixture comes to a boil. Cook 1 minute, stirring constantly. Remove from heat; stir in remaining peach slices and lemon juice.

Spoon mixture into crust; top with whipped cream. Cover and chill 8 hours. Yield: one 8-inch pie.
Cindi Rawlins
Dunwoody, Georgia

PINEAPPLE PIE

1 (14-ounce) can sweetened
  condensed milk
½ cup lemon juice
1 (20-ounce) can crushed
  pineapple, drained
1 (8-ounce) carton frozen whipped
  topping, thawed
1 (9-ounce) commercial graham
  cracker crust

Combine condensed milk and lemon juice; stir well. Fold in pineapple and whipped topping. Spoon mixture into crust. Chill. Yield: one 9-inch pie.
Joanne R. Harper
Roswell, Georgia

DECADENT MUD PIE

½ gallon coffee ice cream,
  softened
1 (9-ounce) commercial graham
  cracker crust
1 (11.75-ounce) jar hot fudge
  sauce, heated
Commercial whipped topping
Slivered almonds, toasted

Spread ice cream evenly over crust; cover and freeze until firm. To serve, place pie slice on serving plate; spoon hot fudge sauce over each slice. Dollop with whipped topping, and sprinkle with toasted almonds. Serve immediately. Yield: one 9-inch pie. *Tami Summerour*
Little Mountain, South Carolina

FUDGE PIE

1 cup sugar
¼ cup all-purpose flour
¼ cup cocoa
½ cup butter or margarine,
  melted
2 eggs, beaten
¼ teaspoon vanilla extract
½ cup chopped pecans
1 unbaked 9-inch pastry shell
Ice cream (optional)

Combine first 6 ingredients; stir well. Stir in pecans. Pour mixture into pastry shell. Bake at 350° for 25 minutes or until a wooden pick inserted in center comes out clean. Serve with ice cream, if desired. Yield: one 9-inch pie.
Connie Reeves
McGregor, Texas

Finishing Touches

■ Add a finishing touch to pies: Garnish with an ingredient used in the pie, such as lemon slices on a lemon pie or peanuts on a peanut butter pie.

■ Here's a quick garnish: Use a vegetable peeler to make chocolate curls. Just pull the peeler firmly down the flat surface of a chocolate bar.

Have Treats Ready

When neighborhood goblins come calling, be prepared with a few extra goodies besides commercial candy for special little friends.

Our "treats" come in the form of tasty things to nibble on, such as Peppy Pumpkin Cookies. You can also wrap up little bags of Fancy Gorp, a blend of chocolate morsels, nuts, and raisins.

The "trick" is a collection of ghoulish little Green Pepper People you can scatter among the goodies to set the mood for Halloween.

PEPPY PUMPKIN COOKIES

1 cup butter or margarine,
    softened
1¼ cups sifted powdered
    sugar
1 egg
1½ teaspoons vanilla
    extract
½ teaspoon almond extract
2½ cups all-purpose flour
½ teaspoon salt
Green and orange paste
    food coloring
Pecan pieces
Chocolate morsels

Cream butter in a large mixing bowl at medium speed of electric mixer; gradually add powdered sugar, beating at medium speed of an electric mixer until mixture is light and fluffy. Add egg and vanilla and almond extracts, beating until blended.

Combine flour and salt in a medium mixing bowl; add flour mixture to creamed mixture, mixing well.

Color ⅔ cup cookie dough with green food coloring. Color remaining dough with orange food coloring.

Spoon orange dough into a pastry bag fitted with metal tip No. 2110. Pipe mixture into pumpkin shapes on ungreased cookie sheets. Spoon green mixture into a pastry bag fitted with metal tip No. 10. Pipe green stems on each pumpkin.

Bake cookies at 400° for 6 to 8 minutes. Immediately arrange pecan pieces and chocolate morsels to make pumpkin faces.

Remove decorated cookies to wire racks to cool completely. Yield: 3 dozen.
Elizabeth S. Bowman
Chattanooga, Tennessee

Halloween Decorations: Green Pepper People

It won't take anyone long to fall in love with these Green Pepper People—they're so ugly they're cute! Make a family of these forlorn creatures to decorate a holiday table, give to neighborhood children, or even stuff with chicken or tuna salad for Halloween supper.

To make these creatures, pick the shapeliest peppers from the store or garden. Wash the peppers, cut around the stem end, and remove core and seeds. At the opposite end, cut a mouth; the shape of each pepper will give a suggestion of a nose, chin, cheeks, and other facial features.

Carrot slices, radish slices, and whole cloves can be used to make eyes, and you can add shredded carrot, green onion fans, or cauliflower and broccoli flowerets for hair. Cut teeth from the white part of a radish; secure teeth and other features to pepper using wooden picks. Make a collar for each pepper "person" with leaf lettuce.

If you make them in advance, place each pepper "person" in a plastic bag, and refrigerate until needed. The peppers can be washed again and chopped up for cooking after Halloween. Just make sure they don't sit out at room temperature too long, or their quality will deteriorate.

FANCY GORP

1 (16-ounce) package
    candy-coated chocolate pieces
1 (12-ounce) jar unsalted roasted
    peanuts
1 (6-ounce) can salted natural
    almonds
1 (6-ounce) package semisweet
    chocolate morsels
1 (6-ounce) package butterscotch
    morsels
1 cup raisins

Combine all ingredients, stirring gently; store in an airtight container. Yield: 2 quarts.
Midge Finnerty
Washington, Virginia

A Cake
For Good Luck

Peppermint Candy Cake is a symbol of good luck in the Singleton family in Scotts Hill, Tennessee. Rublelene Singleton's grandmother started making the cake about 70 years ago. "I can still hear her beating the towel-wrapped peppermint candies with her hammer," says Rublelene.

PEPPERMINT CANDY CAKE

⅔ cup shortening
1¾ cups sugar
3 cups sifted cake flour
3½ teaspoons baking powder
½ teaspoon salt
1⅓ cups milk
1 teaspoon vanilla extract
4 egg whites
Peppermint Filling
¾ cup (5 ounces) crushed
   peppermint candy, divided
Fluffy Frosting

Cream shortening; gradually add sugar, beating well at medium speed of an electric mixer. Combine flour, baking powder, and salt; add to creamed mixture alternately with milk, beginning and ending with flour mixture. Mix after each addition. Stir in vanilla.

Beat egg whites (at room temperature) until stiff peaks form. Gently fold into batter.

Pour batter into 3 greased and floured 8-inch round cakepans. Bake at 350° for 25 to 27 minutes or until a wooden pick inserted in center comes out clean. Cool in pans 10 minutes. Remove from pans; cool 10 minutes on wire racks. While warm, prick cake layers at 1-inch intervals with a fork.

Place 1 cake layer on cake plate; spread with ⅓ cup Peppermint Filling, and sprinkle with crushed peppermint candy. Repeat with remaining layers. Frost top and sides with Fluffy Frosting; sprinkle top and sides with peppermint candy. Yield: one 3-layer cake.

Peppermint Filling

⅓ cup butter or margarine
1 cup sugar
⅓ cup milk
½ teaspoon peppermint extract

Melt butter in a small saucepan. Add remaining ingredients; bring to a boil, stirring constantly. Boil 1 minute, stirring constantly. Yield: 1 cup.

Fluffy Frosting

1 cup sugar
¼ teaspoon cream of tartar
⅓ cup water
2 egg whites
1 teaspoon vanilla extract

Combine sugar, cream of tartar, and water in a saucepan. Cook over medium heat; stir constantly until clear. Cook, without stirring, to soft ball stage (240°).

Beat egg whites until soft peaks form; continue beating, adding syrup in a slow, steady stream. Add vanilla; continue beating until stiff peaks form and frosting is thick enough to spread. Yield: 5 cups.

Please Pass
The Pancakes

The pancakes of today take on a different definition from the original mixtures of pounded grain and water spread on a rock to dry in the sun. Primitive men would hardly recognize our lighter versions cooked on heat-controlled griddles and flavored with such ingredients as fruit, ham, and cheese. Imagine their delight at the first taste of the sweet syrups and sauces drizzled over the top.

When mixing the batter for pancakes, stir just until the dry ingredients are moistened. Any small lumps that remain in the batter will disappear when the pancakes cook. If overbeaten, the pancakes will be tough and heavy.

Pancakes cooked on the griddle have a built-in indicator to tell you when to turn them. As soon as the top surface is filled with bubbles and the edges begin to look cooked, the pancakes are ready to turn. The second side will take only a minute or two to brown.

AMBROSIA PANCAKES
WITH ORANGE SYRUP

1 egg
1 cup milk
½ cup flaked coconut
1 tablespoon vegetable oil
1 teaspoon grated orange rind
1 cup pancake-and-waffle mix
Orange Syrup

Beat egg; add milk, coconut, oil, and orange rind, stirring well. Add pancake mix; stir just until dry ingredients are moistened.

For each pancake, pour about 2 tablespoons batter onto a hot, lightly greased griddle. Turn pancakes when tops are covered with bubbles and edges look cooked. Serve with Orange Syrup. Yield: 12 pancakes.

Orange Syrup

1 cup orange sections, coarsely
   chopped
1 cup maple-flavored syrup

Combine ingredients in a small saucepan. Cook until thoroughly heated. Yield: 1½ cups. *Linda H. Sutton
Winston-Salem, North Carolina*

MAPLE-BACON OVEN PANCAKE

2 eggs, slightly beaten
1½ cups biscuit mix
1 tablespoon sugar
¾ cup milk
¼ cup maple-flavored syrup
1½ cups (6 ounces) shredded
  Cheddar cheese, divided
12 slices bacon, cooked and
  crumbled
Maple-flavored syrup

Combine first 5 ingredients in a bowl; beat at medium speed of an electric mixer until smooth. Stir in ½ cup cheese. Pour into a greased and floured 13- x 9- x 2-inch baking dish. Bake at 425° for 12 minutes. Sprinkle pancake with remaining cheese and bacon; bake 3 to 5 minutes or until a wooden pick inserted in center comes out clean. Cut into squares, and serve with maple syrup. Yield: 8 servings.
Teresa Crow
Atlanta, Texas

HAM GRIDDLE CAKES

1 cup milk
1 cup quick-cooking oats,
  uncooked
2 tablespoons vegetable oil
2 eggs, beaten
½ cup all-purpose flour
2 tablespoons sugar
2 teaspoons baking powder
1 cup diced cooked ham
Maple-flavored syrup

Combine milk and oats in a large bowl; let stand 5 minutes. Add oil and eggs, stirring well. Combine flour, sugar, and baking powder; add to oat mixture, stirring just until moistened. Stir in ham.

For each pancake, pour about ¼ cup batter onto a hot, lightly greased griddle. Turn pancakes when tops are covered with bubbles and edges look cooked. Serve with maple syrup. Yield: 11 pancakes.
Mrs. A. Mayer
Richmond, Virginia

A Perfect Partner For Coffee

Date Dessert Squares drew plenty of compliments from Kathleen Stone's friends in Houston, Texas, but the first seal of approval came from her spouse. "My husband's a chocolate lover, a chocoholic," Kathleen explains. "He loved it, and if *he* loves it, then I know it's good!"

DATE DESSERT SQUARES

1⅓ cups cream-filled chocolate
  sandwich cookie crumbs (about
  18 cookies)
3 tablespoons butter or
  margarine, melted
2 (8-ounce) packages whole pitted
  dates
¾ cup water
¼ teaspoon salt
2 cups miniature marshmallows
½ cup chopped pecans
1 cup whipping cream
¼ cup sifted powdered sugar
½ teaspoon vanilla extract

Combine crumbs and butter, mixing well; set aside 1 tablespoon crumb mixture. Firmly press remaining crumb mixture evenly in bottom of a lightly greased 8-inch square baking dish. Bake at 350° for 8 minutes.

Combine dates, water, and salt in a large saucepan. Bring to a boil over medium heat; reduce heat, and simmer for 3 minutes or until dates are tender, stirring occasionally. Add marshmallows and pecans, and cook until marshmallows melt, stirring constantly. Cool. Spread mixture evenly over baked crust.

Beat whipping cream until foamy; gradually add powdered sugar and vanilla, beating until soft peaks form. Spread over date layer, and sprinkle with reserved crumb mixture. Chill at least 2 hours. Yield: 9 servings.

Toss Vegetables With Pasta

Pasta has worked its way into most Southern kitchens and hearts. It's especially good combined with a variety of vegetables.

Most people agree pasta should be cooked al dente—tender but chewy. To serve pasta cold, rinse it after cooking to prevent sticking.

PASTA AND VEGETABLES

¼ cup olive oil
2 cloves garlic, minced
1 teaspoon dried whole thyme
½ teaspoon dried whole oregano
½ teaspoon dried whole savory
½ teaspoon dried whole basil
½ teaspoon salt
½ teaspoon pepper
2 cups chopped onion
1 (12-ounce) package corkscrew
  macaroni
½ cup sliced celery
½ cup sliced green onions
3 ounces snow pea pods,
  blanched
2 cups green pepper strips
2 tomatoes, cut into wedges
½ cup salad olives
½ cup ripe olives, halved
¼ cup lemon juice
¼ teaspoon salt
¼ teaspoon pepper

Heat oil in a large Dutch oven. Remove from heat. Add garlic and next 6 ingredients, stirring well. Let mixture stand at room temperature 1 hour. Add onion to mixture, and sauté until tender. Set aside.

Cook macaroni according to package directions; drain. Rinse with cold water, and drain.

Add macaroni and remaining ingredients to onion mixture, tossing well. Spoon into a large salad bowl; cover and chill 8 hours. Toss before serving. Yield: 14 servings.
Adam G. Marsh
Lusby, Maryland

VEGETABLE PASTA SALAD

1 (8-ounce) package corkscrew
  macaroni
1 teaspoon salt
1 medium onion, chopped
1 cup sliced fresh mushrooms
1 clove garlic, minced
2 tablespoons olive oil
1 medium carrot, thinly sliced
1 cup broccoli flowerets
1 medium zucchini, thinly
  sliced
1 cup frozen English peas
2 tablespoons chopped fresh
  basil or 2 teaspoons dried
  whole basil
2 tablespoons chopped fresh
  parsley
1 pint cherry tomatoes, cut in
  half
Vinaigrette dressing (recipe
  follows)
Lettuce leaves
Grated Parmesan cheese
  (optional)

Cook macaroni according to package
directions, using 1 teaspoon salt;
drain. Rinse with cold water; drain.
Set aside. Sauté onion, mushrooms,
and garlic in 2 tablespoons olive oil in
a skillet until onion is tender. Add
carrot, broccoli, zucchini, and peas;
cook 2 minutes. Add macaroni, basil,
and parsley, mixing well. Stir in tomatoes. Toss with vinaigrette dressing, and serve on lettuce leaves.
Garnish with Parmesan cheese, if desired. Yield: 10 to 12 servings.

Vinaigrette Dressing

⅓ cup olive oil
¼ cup red wine vinegar
1 tablespoon water
1 teaspoon minced onion
1 clove garlic, minced
¼ teaspoon salt
¼ teaspoon sugar
¼ teaspoon paprika
¼ teaspoon pepper
⅛ teaspoon dry mustard

Combine all ingredients in a jar.
Cover tightly, and shake vigorously.
Yield: ⅔ cup.   *Julie Earhart*
                  St. Louis, Missouri

VERMICELLI WITH
FRESH SPINACH SAUCE

1 (8-ounce) package vermicelli
2 tablespoons butter or margarine
½ pound fresh chopped spinach
½ teaspoon salt
½ teaspoon pepper
1 cup part-skim ricotta cheese
¼ cup milk
½ cup grated fresh Parmesan
  cheese

Cook vermicelli according to package
directions; drain and set aside.
  Melt butter in a large skillet; add
spinach, and cook over medium heat
10 minutes, stirring constantly. Add
salt and next 3 ingredients to spinach; cook over low heat, stirring constantly, until mixture is heated (do
not boil). Add grated Parmesan
cheese, tossing well. Serve over hot
vermicelli. Yield: 4 servings.
                  Lenah Elliott
                  Destin, Florida

GARDEN PASTA MEDLEY

1 (8-ounce) package small shell
  pasta
1 cup broccoli flowerets
¾ cup sliced yellow squash
½ cup chopped sweet red pepper
½ cup thinly sliced radishes
¼ cup chopped celery
2 tablespoons chopped fresh
  parsley
4 ounces Cheddar cheese, cubed
1 (8-ounce) bottle commercial
  creamy cucumber salad
  dressing
Lettuce leaves
Fresh parsley sprigs (optional)
Radishes (optional)

Cook pasta according to package directions; drain. Rinse with cold
water; drain.
  Combine pasta and next 8 ingredients, tossing well; chill. Serve on
lettuce leaves. If desired, garnish
with parsley and radishes. Yield: 6 to
8 servings.   *Susan Wright*
              Midlothian, Virginia

Pan Rolls, Easy And Versatile

"Whole Grain Pan Rolls are tasty and
healthy," Susie Timmons of Winston-
Salem, North Carolina, comments.
They are easy homemade rolls with
the bonus of whole wheat.

WHOLE GRAIN PAN ROLLS

1 cup water
¼ cup honey
¼ cup butter or margarine
¾ cup whole wheat flour
½ cup regular oats, uncooked
2 packages dry yeast
1 teaspoon salt
1 egg
2¼ to 2½ cups all-purpose flour

Combine water, honey, and butter in
a small saucepan; heat until butter
melts. Cool to 120°.
  Combine wheat flour, oats, yeast,
and salt in a large bowl; stir well.
Gradually add hot liquid mixture,
beating at low speed of an electric
mixer 1 minute. Add egg, and beat 2
minutes at medium speed. Gradually
add enough all-purpose flour to make
a soft dough.
  Turn dough out onto a heavily
floured surface; knead until smooth
and elastic (about 8 minutes). Shape
into 24 balls; place in a lightly
greased 13- x 9- x 2-inch pan. Cover
and let rise in a warm place (85°),
free from drafts, 1 hour or until doubled in bulk. Bake at 375° for 20
minutes or until lightly browned.
Yield: 2 dozen.

Right: *The colorful flecks of red and
green in the dressing make Hearts of
Palm Salad (page 276) a nice choice
for holiday menus.*

Above: *Pull out the fine china to serve this menu: Stuffed Chicken Breasts, Glazed Sweet Potatoes, and Lemon Green Beans. (Recipes begin on page 274.)*

Left: *Mixed Greens With Blue Cheese Vinaigrette (page 274) makes a refreshing salad course.*

Above: *Serve Pots de Crème for Two (page 275) in wine glasses for an elegant ending to the meal.*

Above: *To lend an air of elegance to most any meal, serve Peppered Beef Tenderloin Bundles (page 272).*

Right: *Dazzle your guests with Stuffed Crown Pork Roast (page 272). This spectacular entrée is cooked the light way.*

Above: *Serve a rich dessert with the crunchy, pecan-filled flavor of pralines. Offer Old-Fashioned Pralines plain, or crumble into Praline Pastries or Praline Ice Cream. (Recipes, page 318.)*

Left: *Nature's golden sweetener shows off its versatility in (from front) Honey-Curry Bread, Frozen Bourbon-Pecan Pie, and Orange Salad With Honey-Berry Dressing. (Recipes begin on page 250.)*

Above: *Your guests will be pleasantly surprised to discover cake with lemon filling under this golden meringue.*
Lemon Meringue Cake (page 296) decorated with lemon slices makes a pretty dessert.

NOVEMBER

Celebrate Thanksgiving with a lavish feast of turkey and dressing, or give a stately crown roast the place of honor on your holiday table. These recipes and much more are part of our "Holiday Dinners" special section. You'll find the calories trimmed from traditional Thanksgiving fare in our "On the Light Side" buffet. And throughout the chapter the dessert offerings are appealing and varied, including golden strudel and rich, dark pots de crème, as well as luscious lemon cakes and spicy pies.

Breads And Pastries From Our Ancestors

The Southland is home to many vital ingredients of the great American melting pot—a vessel both cultural and culinary, at once historical and ever changing.

Our foods tell a lot about our heritage, and some of the most interesting lore lies behind the South's ethnic breads and pastries, born of both near- and far-lying lands.

■ One savory, spicy bite of these triangular, deep-fried party appetizers known as Samosas will take you on a culinary trip to India.

■ Jewish immigrants to this country brought us the bagel, or "water doughnut," called this because the dough is briefly boiled before it is baked. Bagels are intentionally bland and thus suitable for a myriad of spreads and toppings.

BAGELS

4 to 4½ cups all-purpose flour, divided
3 tablespoons sugar
2 teaspoons salt
2 packages dry yeast
1½ cups water
2 tablespoons butter or margarine
3½ quarts water
1 tablespoon sugar
2 teaspoons salt
1 egg white
1 tablespoon water
Coarse salt, sesame seeds, caraway seeds, or poppyseeds (optional)

Combine 1½ cups flour and next 3 ingredients in a large bowl; set aside.

Combine 1½ cups water and butter in a saucepan; heat until butter melts, stirring occasionally. Cool to 120° to 130°. Add to flour-yeast mixture. Beat at medium speed of an electric mixer 2 minutes. Gradually stir in enough remaining flour to make a stiff dough.

Turn dough out onto a floured surface, and knead 8 to 10 minutes or until smooth and elastic. Place in a well-greased bowl, turning to grease top. Cover and let rise in a warm place (85°), free from drafts, 1 hour or until doubled in bulk.

Punch dough down; cover and let rest 15 minutes. Shape dough into 12 balls. Cut center of each ball with a 1-inch cutter, or punch a hole with a floured finger. Gently pull dough away from center to make a 1- to 1½-inch hole.

Bring 3½ quarts water and next 2 ingredients to a boil in a large Dutch oven. Reduce heat; add bagels, and simmer 3 minutes on each side. Drain on paper towels.

Place bagels on lightly greased baking sheets. Combine egg white and 1 tablespoon water; brush mixture on bagels. If desired, sprinkle with coarse salt, sesame seeds, caraway seeds, or poppy seeds, and lightly press into bagels. Bake at 375° for 25 minutes or until golden brown. Yield: 1 dozen.

Sue-Sue Hartstern
Louisville, Kentucky

SAMOSAS

1 pound potatoes, peeled and diced
1 medium onion, chopped
1 tablespoon vegetable oil
¾ cup frozen chopped cauliflower, thawed
½ cup frozen English peas, thawed
2 tablespoons flaked coconut
2 tablespoons chopped peanuts
2 tablespoons raisins
1 tablespoon chopped cashews
1½ teaspoons salt
1½ teaspoons ground coriander
1½ teaspoons ground cumin
1 teaspoon ground ginger
½ teaspoon lemon-pepper seasoning
½ teaspoon ground cloves
¼ teaspoon red pepper
Pastry (recipe follows)
Vegetable oil
Chutney

Cook potatoes in boiling water to cover 5 minutes or until tender; drain well, and set aside.

Sauté onion in 1 tablespoon oil in a large skillet; stir in cauliflower and next 12 ingredients; cook over low heat 5 minutes, stirring constantly. Add potatoes, and mix well.

Divide pastry into 2 portions; divide each portion into 12 pieces. Roll each piece to ⅛-inch thickness on a lightly floured surface. Cut into a 5-inch circle, and cut in half. Place about 2 teaspoons potato mixture in center of each half-circle; brush edges of pastry with water, and fold in half. Seal edges. Repeat with remaining pastry and potato mixture.

Pour oil to a depth of 2 inches into a Dutch oven; heat to 375°. Fry pastries 1 to 2 minutes on each side or until golden brown; drain on paper towels. Serve pastries with chutney. Yield: 4 dozen.

Pastry

4 cups all-purpose flour
1 teaspoon salt
½ cup vegetable oil
1¼ cups water

Combine flour and salt; add oil, stirring until mixture resembles coarse meal. Sprinkle with water (1 tablespoon at a time), stirring quickly. Form dough into a ball. Yield: enough for 4 dozen pastries.

Note: Samosas can be frozen. To reheat, place deep-fried, frozen pastries on cookie sheets. Bake at 350° for 15 to 20 minutes or until thoroughly heated. *Sambhu N. Banik*
Bethesda, Maryland

■ Austria, Hungary, Czechoslovakia, and Germany all lay claim to strudel, a delicate, fruit-filled pastry. Traditionally, the dough is stretched on a tabletop, and fists are clenched to avoid tearing it with fingernails. Instead of following this procedure, Mrs. Jack Davis makes it with phyllo.

Baking Tips

■ Bread made with fruit or nuts should be tested with a straw or wire cake tester in the center. The tester should come out perfectly clean if the bread is done.

■ Clean, dry coffee cans make ideal baking containers to use for gift breads.

■ Bread will stay fresh in the freezer for two to three months; it's safe to eat after that time, but it will lose some of its flavor.

APPLE STRUDEL
(pictured on page 303)

¼ cup raisins
1 tablespoon rum extract
6 medium apples, peeled, cored, and thinly sliced
¾ cup sugar
½ cup blanched almonds, chopped
1 teaspoon ground cinnamon
½ teaspoon ground cloves
12 sheets commercial frozen phyllo pastry, thawed
⅔ cup butter or margarine, melted
½ cup fine, dry breadcrumbs, divided

Combine raisins and rum extract; let stand 2 hours. Combine raisin mixture, apples, and next 4 ingredients.

Place 1 sheet of phyllo on a damp towel (keep remaining phyllo covered). Lightly brush phyllo with melted butter. Layer 5 more sheets phyllo on first sheet, one at a time, brushing each sheet with butter. Sprinkle evenly with ¼ cup breadcrumbs. Spread half of apple filling over buttered phyllo, leaving a 3-inch border on 1 long edge of pastry and a 2-inch border on other 3 edges. Fold long edge with 3-inch border over apple filling. Fold short edges of phyllo over 2 inches; brush with melted butter. Fold other long edge of phyllo over 2 inches; brush with melted butter.

Starting at long side with 2-inch border, roll jellyroll fashion. Place pastry, seam side down, on a lightly greased 15- x 10- x 1-inch jellyroll pan. Brush with melted butter. Repeat procedure with remaining ingredients for second strudel. Bake at 375° for 45 minutes or until golden brown. Cool on wire racks. Yield: 2 strudels. *Mrs. Jack Davis*
Charlotte, North Carolina

■ Pecans and cinnamon are obvious in this cousin of Moravian Sugar Cake, but mashed potatoes are a surprise ingredient. RaNelle Simon adds a glaze of powdered sugar and milk for a Polish touch.

POLISH SUGAR CAKE
(pictured on page 303)

2 packages dry yeast
½ teaspoon sugar
½ cup warm water (105° to 115°)
¾ cup water
2 tablespoons instant nonfat dry milk powder
½ cup butter or margarine
2½ to 3 cups all-purpose flour, divided
¼ cup instant mashed potato granules
½ cup sugar
½ teaspoon salt
2 eggs, beaten
¾ cup firmly packed brown sugar
1½ teaspoons ground cinnamon
1 cup chopped pecans
⅓ cup butter or margarine, melted
¾ cup sifted powdered sugar
1 tablespoon milk

Dissolve yeast and ½ teaspoon sugar in ½ cup warm water in a large bowl; let stand 5 minutes.

Combine ¾ cup water, milk powder, and ½ cup butter in a saucepan; heat until butter melts, stirring occasionally. Add yeast mixture, 1 cup flour, and next 4 ingredients; stir until smooth. Stir in enough remaining flour to make a soft dough. Cover and let rise in a warm place (85°), free from drafts, 1 hour or until doubled in bulk.

Punch dough down; cover and let rise 30 minutes or until doubled in bulk. Punch dough down, and spread in a lightly greased 15- x 10- x 1-inch jellyroll pan.

Combine brown sugar, cinnamon, and pecans; sprinkle evenly over dough. Make shallow indentations in dough at 1-inch intervals, using the round handle of a wooden spoon. Drizzle dough with ⅓ cup melted butter; let rise 30 minutes or until doubled in bulk. Bake at 375° for 12 to 15 minutes or until done.

Combine powdered sugar and milk in a small bowl; drizzle mixture over warm coffee cake. Cut cake into squares. Yield: 15 servings.
RaNelle T. Simon
Lafayette, Louisiana

■ These Mexican pastries called Sopaipillas get their name from a word meaning "pillow" and are served as a dinner bread or a dessert.

SOPAIPILLAS
(pictured on page 303)

2 cups all-purpose flour
2 teaspoons baking powder
½ teaspoon salt
2 tablespoons shortening
¾ cup hot water (120°)
Vegetable oil
Honey (optional)
½ cup sugar and ½ teaspoon
    ground cinnamon (optional)

Combine flour, baking powder, and salt; cut in shortening with a pastry blender. Add water, stirring with a fork until blended. Turn dough out onto a lightly floured surface, and knead 10 to 12 times. Place dough in a plastic bag to rest for 20 minutes.

Roll dough to ⅛-inch thickness; cut dough into 3-inch squares. Cut each square in half diagonally to form 2 triangles.

Pour oil to a depth of 3 inches into a Dutch oven; heat to 360°. Fry a few triangles at a time in oil, lightly pressing down with the back of a fork until dough starts to puff. Release and continue cooking until golden brown, spooning oil over top of triangles and turning once. Drain.

If desired, serve with honey, or combine sugar and cinnamon and roll sopaipillas in sugar-cinnamon mixture. Yield: 28 sopaipillas.

Mrs. W. F. Smith
Lampasas, Texas

From Our Kitchen To Yours

The aroma of bread baking can summon happy memories of childhood. Remember how, after you helped Mother make bread, a light dusting of flour covered everything? Memories can be made today using one of these methods. Here are questions today's bakers ask.

What Kinds Of Yeast Are Available?

Yeast comes in granular form in individual packages labeled **active dry yeast** or **rapid-rise** or in cake form of moist **compressed** yeast. One package of dry yeast has 2½ teaspoons and can be interchanged with one 0.6-ounce cake.

Using rapid-rise yeast saves time. If you combine this yeast with the quick-mix method, your bread will rise up to 50% faster. With a change in the procedure, rapid-rise yeast can be used in traditional recipes.

Which Method Saves Time?

The **direct** or **rapid-mix** method streamlines the baking process by eliminating the need for the traditional step of dissolving the yeast in lukewarm water (105° to 115°). Adding the yeast directly to a small portion of the dry ingredients before adding hot liquid (120° to 130°) hastens rising by increasing the dough's temperature. Because the dry ingredients protect the yeast, warmer liquid can be added.

The **quick-mix** method using the faster rapid-rise yeast offers a solution to the time-management problem. By eliminating the dissolving step, adding warmer liquid (125° to 130°), and replacing the first rising period with a 10-minute resting time, 45 to 50 minutes can be saved.

Can Rising Be Hastened?

Bread dough needs a draft-free environment of 85° to rise properly. This is the method we use. Shape the dough into a ball, and place it in a well-greased bowl, turning to grease all sides; cover with plastic wrap.

Let the dough rise in a gas oven with a pilot light burning or in a cold electric oven containing a large pan of hot water. To test for proper rising, lightly press a finger ½ inch into the dough. When the indentation remains, the dough is ready for the next step. Let dough rise until this occurs, or it will yield a heavy, textured bread. Dough that has risen too long can have a sour flavor.

Using the microwave can cut the rising time in half. Place dough in a well-greased, nonmetallic bowl, turning to grease the top. Cover loosely with wax paper. Set the bowl in a 12- x 8- x 2-inch baking dish, and pour hot water to a depth of 1 inch in bottom dish.

Microwave at MEDIUM-LOW (30% power) 2 minutes; let stand in the microwave 5 minutes. Repeat microwaving and standing 3 times or until the dough is doubled in bulk, giving the dish a quarter-turn after each microwaving period. If the dough's surface appears to be drying out, carefully turn the dough over in the bowl. When the rising is complete, punch the dough down, and proceed with the recipe.

Does Bread Freeze Well?

Baked bread can be frozen up to 3 months, but raw dough should not be frozen unless specified in the recipe. The proportion of yeast to other ingredients must be tailored specially to freezing conditions.

To prepare baked bread for freezing, cool it on a wire rack away from drafts to prevent sogginess and shrinkage. Wrap cooled bread in aluminum foil, and seal tightly in a plastic bag; label and date. Thaw foil-wrapped bread at room temperature 2 to 3 hours, or bake wrapped at 350° for 20 to 30 minutes.

Bread Tips

■ Bread is done when an instant-read thermometer registers 190° and when the loaf sounds hollow when lightly tapped.

■ Ingredients such as whole grain flour, herbs, seeds, fruits, and nuts increase rising times.

Ring In The Holidays

This "Holiday Dinners" special section is our gift to you during this busy season. No matter what kind of occasion you are planning—a fancy affair, a casual gathering, or a night at home with the family—we've got you covered with the recipes and menus featured on the following pages. If the crowd is coming for supper at your house before or after a concert, church function, or busy day, you'll appreciate the quick after-work menu or one of the hearty soups to serve as an entrée.

Children delight in the festivities, so we've included recipes that they can handle, as well as lots of goodies they can share with friends.

We offer lots of options so that you can design your own menu. Start with one of the entrées with fewer calories; the savings will allow guests to splurge on one of the many luscious desserts we've included.

For a more formal celebration, you'll enjoy the menu below, served at Bill and Sharon Miller's dinner party in Knoxville, Tennessee.

Herb Vegetable Dip
Artichoke Soup
Hatcreek Quail
Goat Cheese Rosemary
Rack of Lamb
Gourmet Wild Rice
Cardamom Carrots
Mixed greens
Commercial dressing
Queen's Chocolate Cake
Strawberry Tart
Coffee   Wine

HERB VEGETABLE DIP

2 egg yolks
1 tablespoon lemon juice
½ teaspoon dry mustard
¼ teaspoon salt
¾ cup olive oil
½ cup sour cream
1 tablespoon minced fresh parsley
1 teaspoon minced fresh tarragon

Combine first 4 ingredients in container of an electric blender; process until mixture is thick and lemon colored. With blender running, gradually add olive oil in a slow, steady stream, mixing just until well blended and thickened. Transfer to a bowl; fold in sour cream and remaining ingredients. Cover and chill. Serve dip with vegetables. Yield: 1 cup.

ARTICHOKE SOUP

1 cup sliced green onions
¼ cup chopped onion
2 tablespoons butter or margarine, melted
2 tablespoons all-purpose flour
1 (14½-ounce) can ready-to-serve chicken broth
1 (14-ounce) can artichoke hearts, undrained and chopped
¼ teaspoon white pepper
2 tablespoons minced fresh parsley

Sauté onions in butter in a large saucepan until tender. Add flour, and cook 1 minute, stirring constantly. Gradually stir in chicken broth, and cook until thickened, stirring constantly. Stir in artichoke hearts with liquid and white pepper. Cook until thoroughly heated. Spoon into serving bowls; sprinkle with fresh parsley. Yield: 3 cups.

Note: To make recipe ahead, prepare as directed. Cover and chill. Reheat to serve.

Tip: *Read labels to learn the weight, quality, and size of food products. Don't be afraid to experiment with new brands. Store brands can be equally good in quality and nutritional value, yet lower in price than well-known brands. Lower grades of canned fruit and vegetables are as nutritious as higher grades. Whenever possible, buy most foods by weight or cost per serving rather than by volume or package size.*

HATCREEK QUAIL

6 quail (about 3 pounds)
2 cups orange juice
Olive oil
2 oranges
1 (33.8-ounce) bottle cola-flavored
   beverage

Place quail in a shallow dish; add orange juice. Cover and refrigerate 8 hours. Drain.

Brush quail with olive oil. Cut each orange into 3 slices.

Soak hickory chips in water at least 15 minutes. Prepare charcoal fire in smoker, and let burn 10 to 15 minutes. Place hickory chips on coals. Place water pan in smoker, and fill with cola-flavored beverage.

Place orange slices on food rack, and top with quail. Cover with smoker lid; cook 1 to 1½ hours or until quail is done.

Remove quail from food rack and place on platter; cover and chill. Thinly slice quail to serve. Yield: 6 appetizer servings.

GOAT CHEESE ROSEMARY

½ cup chopped fresh rosemary,
   divided
1 (3-ounce) package chèvre
   cheese, cut into 12
   (¼-inch-thick) slices
⅓ cup olive oil
12 (½-inch-thick) French bread
   baguette slices, lightly toasted
Fresh rosemary sprig

Sprinkle ¼ cup rosemary in a 10- x 6- x 2-inch baking dish; arrange cheese slices over rosemary. Pour olive oil over cheese; sprinkle with remaining rosemary. Cover and chill 8 hours.

Remove cheese slices from dish, reserving marinade; place one cheese slice on each piece of bread. Brush each slice lightly with reserved marinade, and top with a small sprig of rosemary. Place on a baking sheet; broil 6 inches from heat 1 minute or until cheese is warm. Yield: 12 appetizer servings.

RACK OF LAMB

¼ cup olive oil
3 tablespoons Dijon mustard
1 clove garlic, crushed
½ teaspoon salt
½ teaspoon dried whole
   thyme
2 (8-rib) lamb rib roasts
   (about 2¼ pounds each)
1 cup soft breadcrumbs
¼ cup butter or margarine,
   melted
Sauce (recipe follows)

Combine first 5 ingredients in a bowl; mix with a wire whisk.

Trim and discard exterior fat on lamb roasts to ¼ inch; spread with mustard mixture. Combine breadcrumbs and butter in a small bowl; pat over mustard mixture.

Place roasts, fat side up, on rack in roasting pan; insert meat thermometer in thickest part of roast, not resting in fat or on bone.

Bake roasts, uncovered, at 375° for 45 minutes or until meat thermometer registers 140° for rare, 160° for medium, or desired degree of doneness. Serve lamb with sauce. Yield: 6 to 8 servings.

Note: Be careful not to overcook the meat. Lamb that is cooked over 160° is less flavorful.

Sauce

1 (14½-ounce) can ready-to-serve
   beef broth, undiluted
3 tablespoons minced onion
3 tablespoons minced carrot
1 tablespoon minced celery
2 fresh parsley sprigs
1 large bay leaf
½ teaspoon dried whole rosemary
½ teaspoon dried whole thyme
1 tablespoon tomato paste
½ cup dry vermouth
1 tablespoon arrowroot
1 tablespoon water

Combine first 8 ingredients in a saucepan; bring to a boil over medium heat. Reduce heat to low; simmer, uncovered, 20 minutes. Strain broth; discard vegetables. Return broth to saucepan. Add tomato paste and vermouth.

Combine arrowroot and water, stirring until smooth; add to broth, stirring well. Cook over medium heat, stirring constantly, until thickened and bubbly. Yield: 1¼ cups.

Note: Lamb may be coated with mustard and breadcrumb mixture in advance. Cover and chill. Remove from refrigerator; let stand at room temperature 30 minutes.

Insert meat thermometer in roast, and bake as directed. Prepare sauce; cover and chill. Reheat sauce to serve.

Tip: *Fresh meat, poultry, and fish should be loosely wrapped and refrigerated; use in a few days. Loosely wrap fresh ground meat, liver, and kidneys; use in one or two days. Frankfurters, bacon, and sliced sandwich meats can be stored in original wrappings in the refrigerator. Store all meat in the coldest part of the refrigerator.*

GOURMET WILD RICE

⅓ cup currants
2 tablespoons brandy
⅔ cup wild rice
2 cups ready-to-serve chicken
  broth
2 tablespoons olive oil
⅓ cup pine nuts, toasted

Combine currants and brandy, and set aside.

Wash wild rice in 3 changes of hot water; drain. Combine rice and chicken broth in a medium saucepan; bring to a boil. Cover, reduce heat, and simmer 45 minutes or until rice is tender and liquid is absorbed. Stir in currant mixture, olive oil, and pine nuts. Yield: 6 servings.

CARDAMOM CARROTS

1½ pounds carrots, scraped and
  cut into julienne strips
½ cup butter
¼ cup honey
2 teaspoons grated lemon rind
¼ cup lemon juice
¼ cup orange juice
1 tablespoon cornstarch
⅓ cup dry vermouth
¾ teaspoon ground cardamom
¼ teaspoon salt
½ teaspoon pepper
2 tablespoons chopped fresh
  parsley

Cook carrots in a small amount of boiling water 4 minutes or until crisp-tender. Drain carrots, and plunge into cold water; drain again.

Melt butter in a large skillet over low heat; add honey and next 3 ingredients, stirring until blended.

Combine cornstarch and vermouth; stir into sauce. Cook over medium heat, stirring constantly, until mixture boils. Add carrots, cardamom, salt, and pepper to sauce. Cook over low heat until carrots are thoroughly heated. Stir in fresh parsley. Yield: 6 servings.

Note: To make ahead, cook carrots; plunge into cold water. Cover and chill. Prepare sauce; cover and chill. To serve, place sauce in a large saucepan. Drain carrots, and add to sauce. Let come to room temperature. Cook over low heat until carrots are thoroughly heated, stirring occasionally. Add fresh parsley.

QUEEN'S CHOCOLATE CAKE

⅔ cup semisweet chocolate
  morsels
2 tablespoons dark rum
3 eggs, separated
¼ teaspoon cream of tartar
Dash of salt
2 tablespoons sugar
½ cup butter, softened
⅔ cup sugar
⅓ cup ground almonds
¼ teaspoon almond extract
¾ cup sifted cake flour
Chocolate Butter Frosting
⅓ cup sliced almonds, toasted

Place chocolate morsels in top of a double boiler; bring water to a boil. Reduce heat to low; cook, stirring occasionally, until chocolate melts. Remove from hot water, and let cool completely. Stir in rum.

Combine egg whites, cream of tartar, and salt in a small mixing bowl; beat at medium speed of an electric mixer until foamy. Add 2 tablespoons sugar, 1 tablespoon at a time, beating at high speed until stiff peaks form. Cover and set aside.

Cream butter; gradually add ⅔ cup sugar, beating well. Add egg yolks, one at a time, beating until pale yellow (about 5 minutes). At low speed of mixer, add chocolate mixture; beat until smooth. Add ground almonds and almond extract; mix until blended. Fold in egg white mixture alternately with flour, beginning and ending with egg white mixture.

Spoon batter into a greased and floured 9-inch round cakepan. Bake at 350° for 20 to 22 minutes or until a wooden pick inserted 1½ inches from edge of pan comes out clean. (Center may be soft and will be creamy when cool.) Cool in pan 10 minutes; remove from pan, cover cake with a linen towel, and cool completely on a wire rack.

Spread Chocolate Butter Frosting on top and side of cake. Arrange almond slices on top of cake; cover and chill. Let stand at room temperature about 2 hours before serving. Yield: one 9-inch cake.

Chocolate Butter Frosting

½ cup semisweet chocolate
  morsels
2 tablespoons dark rum
¼ cup plus 2 tablespoons butter,
  softened

Combine chocolate morsels and rum in top of a double boiler; bring water to a boil. Reduce heat to low; cook, stirring occasionally, until chocolate melts. Remove from hot water. Add butter, 1 tablespoon at a time, and beat at high speed of an electric mixer. Place mixture over cold water, and beat until cool and of spreading consistency. (Frosting will lighten in color.) Yield: enough frosting for one 9-inch cake layer.

STRAWBERRY TART

¾ cup sugar
2 tablespoons cornstarch
1½ cups water
¼ cup strawberry-flavored gelatin
4 cups fresh strawberries
Crust (recipe follows)
Fresh whole strawberries
    (optional)
Whipped cream (optional)

Combine first 3 ingredients in a medium saucepan; bring to a boil over medium heat, stirring constantly. Boil 1 minute, stirring constantly. Remove from heat; add gelatin, and stir until smooth. Let cool.

Wash and hull 4 cups strawberries; cut in half lengthwise. Brush tart shell with glaze. Arrange strawberries, cut side down, in shell. Spoon remaining glaze over strawberries; chill until firm. If desired, garnish with whole strawberries and whipped cream. Yield: one 11-inch tart.

Crust

2 cups all-purpose flour
1 teaspoon salt
2 tablespoons sugar
⅔ cup plus 2 tablespoons
    shortening
4 to 5 tablespoons cold water

Combine first 3 ingredients; cut in shortening with a pastry blender until mixture resembles coarse meal. Sprinkle water evenly over surface of mixture; stir with a fork until dry ingredients are moistened. Shape into a ball.

Roll dough to ⅛-inch thickness on a lightly floured surface. Fit pastry into an 11-inch tart pan. Prick bottom generously with a fork. Bake at 450° for 12 to 15 minutes or until lightly browned. Cool before filling. Yield: one 11-inch tart shell.

ON THE LIGHT SIDE

Feast On Light Holiday Entrées

Holidays present something of a dilemma for health-conscious folks. After all, special occasions deserve special foods, but holiday foods are notorious for being laden with calories and fat. That's why we created some lavish yet light entrées that may become a holiday tradition at your home.

STUFFED CROWN PORK ROAST
(pictured on pages 260 and 261)

1 (12-rib) crown roast of pork,
    well trimmed (about 7 pounds)
½ teaspoon salt
½ teaspoon pepper
1 (6-ounce) package long-grain
    and wild rice mix
1 cup raisins
2 cups canned reduced-sodium
    chicken broth
½ cup canned garbanzo beans or
    chick-peas, rinsed and drained
½ cup chopped pecans, toasted
½ cup sliced green onions

Fold a piece of aluminum foil into an 8-inch square; place on a rack in a roasting pan. Season roast with salt and pepper; place roast, bone ends up, on foil-lined rack. Bake at 325° for 1 hour.

Combine rice mix, raisins, and chicken broth; bring to a boil. Cover, reduce heat, and simmer 20 to 25 minutes or until rice is tender and liquid is absorbed. Add garbanzo beans, pecans, and green onions; toss gently.

Cut a piece of foil long enough to fit around ribs; fold foil lengthwise into thirds. Wrap foil around ribs, and fold over tips of ribs. Spoon rice mixture into center of roast, and cover with foil. Insert meat thermometer into roast without touching bone or fat. Bake at 325° for 1½ hours or until meat thermometer reaches 160°. Remove foil from roast, and let stand 15 minutes before serving. Yield: 12 servings (355 calories per 3 ounces pork and ⅓ cup stuffing).

□ *28.4 grams protein, 16.1 grams fat, 23.6 grams carbohydrate, 71 milligrams cholesterol, 386 milligrams sodium, and 36 milligrams calcium.*

PEPPERED BEEF TENDERLOIN BUNDLES
(pictured on page 260)

Vegetable cooking spray
1 cup chopped zucchini
1 cup chopped mushrooms
½ cup chopped onion
1 clove garlic, minced
¼ teaspoon salt
8 (4-ounce) beef tenderloin steaks
2 tablespoons cracked black
    pepper
16 sheets commercial frozen
    phyllo pastry, thawed

Coat a nonstick skillet with cooking spray; place over medium-high heat until hot. Add zucchini and next 4 ingredients; sauté until tender.

Sprinkle both sides of steaks with pepper; set aside. Coat a nonstick skillet with cooking spray; place over high heat until hot. Add steaks, and cook 1½ minutes on each side. Remove from skillet; set aside.

Place 1 sheet of phyllo on a towel (keep remaining phyllo covered); spray with cooking spray. Fold phyllo in half lengthwise; place a steak 3 inches from the end. Spoon 2 tablespoons zucchini mixture on steak, and fold narrow end of phyllo over stuffing. Fold sides of pastry over steak, and roll up. Place a second sheet of phyllo on a towel; cut it into a 12-inch square, and coat with cooking spray. Place wrapped steak, stuffing side up, in center of phyllo square. Bring ends to the middle, gently pressing together in center, and pull ends up and out to resemble a package. Coat each bundle with cooking spray, and place on a baking sheet coated with cooking spray. Repeat with remaining steaks. Bake at 400° for 15 minutes for rare, 17 minutes for medium rare, or 20 minutes for medium. Yield: 8 servings (330 calories per bundle).

□ *28.3 grams protein, 10.6 grams fat, 29.5 grams carbohydrate, 73 milligrams cholesterol, 293 milligrams sodium, and 20 milligrams calcium.*

BAKED HAM WITH CRANBERRY-HONEY GLAZE

1 (8-pound) smoked fully cooked ham half, well trimmed
¾ cup frozen cranberry juice cocktail concentrate, thawed and undiluted
2 cups sparkling mineral water
Vegetable cooking spray
Cranberry-Honey Glaze

Place ham in a large zip-top, heavy-duty plastic bag. Pour cranberry concentrate and mineral water over ham. Seal bag securely. Place ham in a large bowl, and chill 8 hours, turning occasionally.

Remove ham from marinade, reserving marinade. Place ham on a rack coated with cooking spray; place rack in a shallow roasting pan. Insert meat thermometer, making sure it does not touch fat or bone. Bake at 325° for 2 hours; baste occasionally with marinade. Remove ham from oven; coat exposed portion of ham with Cranberry-Honey Glaze. Bake, uncovered, an additional 15 minutes or until meat thermometer registers 140°. Transfer ham to a platter, and let stand 10 minutes before slicing. Serve with Cranberry-Honey Glaze. Yield: 18 servings (128 calories per 3 ounces ham).

□ *18.1 grams protein, 4.8 grams fat, 2 grams carbohydrate, 46 milligrams cholesterol, 1,042 milligrams sodium, and 7 milligrams calcium.*

Cranberry-Honey Glaze

1 (12-ounce) package whole cranberries
½ cup honey
¼ cup water
2 tablespoons grated orange rind
2 teaspoons chopped crystallized ginger

Combine all ingredients in a medium saucepan; place over medium-high heat, and bring to a boil. Reduce heat, and simmer 10 minutes, uncovered, stirring occasionally. Yield: 1½ cups (30 calories per tablespoon).

□ *0.1 gram protein, 0 grams fat, 8.3 grams carbohydrate, 0 milligrams cholesterol, 1 milligram sodium, and 4 milligrams calcium.*

BAKED QUAIL WITH MUSHROOM GRAVY

8 quail, cleaned and skinned
Vegetable cooking spray
¼ teaspoon salt
¼ teaspoon pepper
½ teaspoon paprika
½ pound fresh mushrooms, sliced
½ cup chopped onion
1 (10½-ounce) can no-salt-added chicken broth
3 tablespoons instant nonfat dry milk
1 tablespoon all-purpose flour
½ teaspoon chicken-flavored bouillon granules
¼ cup water
½ teaspoon browning-and-seasoning sauce

Place quail on rack coated with cooking spray; place rack in a shallow roasting pan. Sprinkle quail with salt and pepper; coat with cooking spray, and sprinkle with paprika. Broil quail 3 minutes on each side or until golden. Transfer quail to a 13- x 9- x 2-inch baking dish coated with cooking spray.

Coat a nonstick skillet with cooking spray; place over medium-high heat until hot. Add mushrooms, and sauté until tender; drain and set aside. Add onion to skillet, and sauté until tender. Combine onion and remaining ingredients in container of an electric blender or food processor; process until smooth. Pour broth mixture into a small saucepan, and cook over medium heat, stirring constantly, until thickened and bubbly. Stir in mushrooms; spoon over quail. Cover and bake at 350° for 1 hour. Yield: 8 servings (200 calories per quail with ¼ cup gravy).

□ *29.3 grams protein, 6.5 grams fat, 4.2 grams carbohydrate, 0 milligrams cholesterol, 136 milligrams sodium, and 41 milligrams calcium.*

Holiday Dinners

Set Two Places For Dinner

If the number of people at your holiday dinner is two, here's just the menu you need. It makes an elaborate three-course meal, but it won't keep you in the kitchen all day.

For starters, offer Mixed Greens With Blue Cheese Vinaigrette as a separate salad course, followed by Stuffed Chicken Breasts with Glazed Sweet Potatoes and Lemon Green Beans.

For dessert choose Pots de Crème for Two or Grasshopper Tarts, two rich desserts that need to be made ahead of time.

**Mixed Greens
With Blue Cheese Vinaigrette
Commercial breadsticks
Stuffed Chicken Breasts
Glazed Sweet Potatoes
Lemon Green Beans
Pots de Crème for Two
or
Grasshopper Tarts**

MIXED GREENS WITH BLUE CHEESE VINAIGRETTE
(pictured on page 259)

¼ cup vegetable oil
1½ tablespoons white wine vinegar
1 ounce blue cheese, crumbled
½ teaspoon dried whole oregano
⅛ teaspoon salt
⅛ teaspoon freshly ground pepper
1 cup torn radicchio
1 cup torn Bibb lettuce

Combine first 6 ingredients in a jar; cover tightly, and shake vigorously. Chill at least 1 hour.

Place salad greens in a bowl. Toss greens with vinaigrette dressing just before serving. Yield: 2 servings.

STUFFED CHICKEN BREASTS
(pictured on page 258)

2 large chicken breast halves (about ⅔ pound), skinned and boned
¼ cup chopped onion
3 tablespoons chopped green pepper
1 small clove garlic, minced
2 tablespoons butter or margarine, melted
⅔ cup herb-seasoned stuffing mix
⅓ cup water
⅛ teaspoon salt
⅛ teaspoon pepper
2 tablespoons butter or margarine, melted
½ cup cream of chicken soup, undiluted
2 tablespoons dry white wine
1 tablespoon herb-seasoned stuffing mix
Chopped fresh parsley (optional)

Place each piece of chicken between 2 sheets of wax paper; flatten to ¼-inch thickness, using a meat mallet or rolling pin. Set aside.

Sauté onion, green pepper, and minced garlic in 2 tablespoons butter. Stir in ⅔ cup stuffing mix, water, salt, and pepper.

Spread stuffing mixture evenly on each chicken breast, leaving a ½-inch margin on all sides. Fold short ends of chicken over stuffing; roll up, beginning with one unfolded side. Secure with wooden picks.

Brown chicken in 2 tablespoons butter. Place in a 9-inch pieplate.

Combine soup and wine; pour over chicken. Sprinkle with 1 tablespoon herb-seasoned stuffing mix. Cover with aluminum foil, and bake at 325° for 50 minutes or until done. Garnish with chopped parsley, if desired. Yield: 2 servings.

GLAZED SWEET POTATOES
(pictured on page 258)

1 large sweet potato (about ¾ pound)
2 tablespoons butter or margarine
2 tablespoons brown sugar
2 tablespoons flaked coconut
2 tablespoons maple syrup
2 tablespoons slivered almonds, toasted

Peel potato; cut into ⅓-inch slices. Arrange in a large skillet; cover with water, and bring to a boil. Cover, reduce heat, and simmer 10 minutes or until tender. Drain potatoes, remove from skillet, and set aside.

Melt butter in skillet; stir in brown sugar, coconut, and syrup. Return potatoes to skillet, and cook until thoroughly heated; turn potatoes to coat with mixture. Arrange potatoes in a serving dish; sprinkle with almonds. Yield: 2 servings.

*Marty Petrilla
Bradenton, Florida*

LEMON GREEN BEANS
(pictured on page 258)

½ pound fresh green beans
2 tablespoons minced onion
2 tablespoons butter or
   margarine, melted
1 tablespoon lemon juice
¼ teaspoon salt
⅛ teaspoon pepper

Wash beans, and remove strings. Cut beans into 1½-inch pieces, if desired. Cook, covered, in a small amount of boiling water 12 to 15 minutes or until crisp-tender. Drain and set aside. Keep warm.

Sauté onion in butter until tender. Stir in lemon juice, salt, and pepper. Add beans; cook 1 minute or until thoroughly heated, stirring constantly. Yield: 2 servings.

POTS DE CRÈME FOR TWO
(pictured on page 259)

½ (4-ounce) package sweet
   baking chocolate
2 tablespoons egg substitute
2 teaspoons sugar
¼ cup whipping cream
¼ teaspoon vanilla extract
Whipped cream (optional)
Chocolate curls (optional)

Place chocolate in top of a double boiler; bring water to a boil. Reduce heat to low; cook until chocolate melts. Combine next 3 ingredients; gradually stir into melted chocolate. Cook in double boiler over low heat, stirring constantly, 5 minutes or until thickened. Remove from heat; stir in vanilla.

Spoon mixture into serving containers. Cover and chill at least 3 hours. If desired, garnish with whipped cream and chocolate curls. Yield: 2 servings.

GRASSHOPPER TARTS

⅔ cup chocolate wafer crumbs
1 tablespoon butter or margarine,
   melted
½ cup marshmallow cream
1 tablespoon green crème de
   menthe
½ cup whipping cream, whipped

Combine chocolate wafer crumbs and butter; press onto bottom and sides of 6-ounce freezerproof ramekins. Chill 1 hour.

Combine marshmallow cream and crème de menthe, stirring well. Set aside 2 tablespoons whipped cream; fold remaining whipped cream into marshmallow mixture.

Spoon into prepared crusts; top with reserved whipped cream. Cover loosely, and freeze at least 8 hours. Yield: 2 servings.

Throw Off The Chill With Soup

Welcome merrymakers this holiday season with a bowl of soup. Each of these soups readily lends itself to a rib-sticking menu, especially when served alongside a tossed salad or crusty bread.

Chicken-and-Sausage Gumbo is traditionally served over rice. Or you can pack cooked rice into greased custard cups or timbales, and invert the rice into bowls of gumbo.

Estimate the number of servings of these soups you'll need, and double or triple the recipe accordingly. Because these are main-dish soups, figure on at least 1 cup of soup per serving.

CHICKEN-AND-SAUSAGE GUMBO

1½ pounds smoked sausage or
   andouille
1 (3½- to 4-pound) broiler-fryer,
   cut up and skinned
¼ cup vegetable oil
½ cup all-purpose flour
2 large onions, minced
1 large green pepper, minced
1 cup minced celery
3 cloves garlic, minced
2 quarts water
2 teaspoons Creole seasoning
⅛ teaspoon hot sauce
½ cup chopped green onions
¼ cup minced fresh parsley
Hot cooked rice

Cut sausage lengthwise into 4 pieces; cut pieces into ½-inch slices. Brown in a Dutch oven; drain, reserving drippings. Set aside. Brown chicken in drippings; drain.

Combine oil and flour in Dutch oven; cook over medium heat, stirring constantly, until roux is the color of chocolate (about 30 minutes). Add minced onion and next 3 ingredients; cook until vegetables are tender. Add water; bring to a boil. Reduce heat, and simmer, uncovered, 45 minutes. Add chicken, Creole seasoning, and hot sauce; cook, uncovered, 1 hour.

Remove chicken, and set aside to cool. Add green onions and parsley to gumbo. Bone chicken, and coarsely chop. Add chicken and sausage to gumbo; heat thoroughly. Ladle gumbo into bowls; pack cooked rice into greased custard cups and invert into bowls of gumbo, or serve gumbo over rice. Yield: about 3 quarts.

Note: To remove fat from surface of gumbo, cover and refrigerate 8 hours. Remove fat; reheat gumbo, and serve. For a more traditional gumbo, leave chicken pieces intact.

Yolanda Trahan
Houma, Louisiana

CALDO DE REZ (MEXICAN BEEF STEW)

1 medium cabbage
1½ pounds stew meat
⅓ cup chopped onion
⅓ cup chopped green pepper
⅓ cup chopped celery
1 teaspoon dried parsley or cilantro
1 (14½-ounce) can stewed tomatoes, undrained
Salt and pepper to taste
4 potatoes, peeled and cubed
Commercial spicy hot tomato salsa (optional)

Cut cabbage into wedges. Combine cabbage, stew meat, and next 6 ingredients in a large Dutch oven. Bring to a boil; cover, reduce heat, and simmer 1 hour. Add potatoes; cover and simmer 30 minutes or until potatoes are tender. Serve with salsa, if desired. Yield: 6 servings.

Rachel Perez
Brownfield, Texas

CHEESE-AND-BROCCOLI SOUP

6 cups water
1 (10-ounce) package frozen chopped broccoli
1 medium onion, chopped
1 (8-ounce) loaf process cheese spread, cubed
2 teaspoons pepper
½ to ¾ teaspoon salt
½ teaspoon garlic powder
1 cup milk
1 cup half-and-half
¼ cup butter or margarine
½ cup all-purpose flour
½ cup cold water

Bring 6 cups water to a boil in a 3-quart Dutch oven; add broccoli and onion. Reduce heat, and simmer, uncovered, 10 minutes. Add cheese and seasonings, stirring until cheese melts. Stir in milk, half-and-half, and butter; cook over low heat until thoroughly heated.

Combine flour and cold water, stirring until smooth. Gradually add to broccoli mixture, stirring constantly; cook over medium heat until thickened, stirring occasionally. Yield: 2½ quarts.

Edith Shaver
Statesville, North Carolina

Salads Easy On The Cook

When you use these recipes, making salads should be easy. All of them were selected for their ease of preparation as well as for the variety of flavors they offer. When putting together special menus, you'll find these salads add a festive touch.

MARINATED MIXED VEGETABLES

1 pound fresh broccoli, cut into flowerets
1 large cauliflower, cut into flowerets
2 yellow squash, cut into thin strips
2 cups sliced carrot
1 large green pepper, cut into thin strips
Dressing (recipe follows)

Combine vegetables in a large bowl. Pour dressing over vegetables; toss gently. Cover and chill 8 hours. Drain vegetables before serving. Yield: 12 to 14 servings.

Dressing

¾ cup vegetable oil
¼ cup plus 2 tablespoons red wine vinegar
2 teaspoons sugar
1 teaspoon salt
1 teaspoon dry mustard
1 teaspoon dried whole basil
½ teaspoon pepper
⅛ teaspoon ground nutmeg
2 cloves garlic, crushed

Combine all ingredients in a jar. Cover tightly, and shake mixture vigorously. Yield: 1 cup.

Mrs. M. B. Tankersley
Waverly, Tennessee

HEARTS OF PALM SALAD
(pictured on page 257)

1 cup olive oil
½ cup white vinegar
½ cup finely chopped celery
¼ cup finely chopped sweet red pepper
¼ cup finely chopped onion
¼ cup finely chopped dill pickle
6 ripe olives, finely chopped
2 cloves garlic, pressed
¼ teaspoon capers
1 (16-ounce) can hearts of palm, drained and cut into ½-inch pieces
6 cups torn romaine lettuce

Combine first 9 ingredients; chill at least 8 hours. To serve, arrange hearts of palm on bed of lettuce on individual salad plates; top with dressing. Yield: 6 servings.

Yolanda Trahan
Houma, Louisiana

FRUIT SALAD WITH CREAM DRESSING

1½ teaspoons grated orange rind
½ teaspoon grated lemon rind
1½ tablespoons orange juice
1 tablespoon lemon juice
2 tablespoons sugar
1 egg yolk, beaten
1½ teaspoons butter or margarine
½ cup whipping cream
2 large red apples, cored and cubed
2 pears, cored and cubed
1 pound seedless green grapes

Combine first 7 ingredients in top of a double boiler. Place over boiling water; cook, stirring constantly, 10 to 12 minutes or until thickened. Remove from boiling water; cool.

Beat whipping cream until soft peaks form; fold into cooled mixture. Serve immediately, or cover and chill up to 3 hours. Combine fruit, and serve with dressing. Yield: 6 to 8 servings.

Mrs. Ben L. McKinley, Jr.
Dallas, Texas

LAYERED FRUIT SALAD

2 medium apples, unpeeled and diced
1 (17-ounce) can apricot halves, drained and sliced
1 (16-ounce) can pear halves, drained and sliced
1 (16-ounce) can sliced peaches, drained
1 (20-ounce) can unsweetened pineapple chunks, drained
½ cup orange juice
1 teaspoon lemon juice
1 (21-ounce) can cherry pie filling
3 bananas, sliced
1 cup flaked coconut, toasted

Layer apples, apricots, pears, peaches, and pineapple in a large bowl. Combine orange juice and lemon juice; pour over fruit. Spread cherry pie filling on top; cover and chill 2 hours.

Arrange bananas over pie filling; sprinkle with coconut. Serve immediately. Yield: 14 to 16 servings.

Mrs. George Lance
Madison, Tennessee

FRUIT SALAD

1 small banana, sliced
1 orange, peeled, seeded, and sectioned
1 small apple, unpeeled and diced
1 (8-ounce) can unsweetened pineapple chunks, drained
¼ cup frozen orange juice concentrate, thawed and undiluted
Lettuce leaves

Combine fruit in a large bowl. Add orange juice concentrate; toss gently. Cover and chill. Serve on lettuce leaves. Yield: 6 servings.

Pam Bryant
Monroe, Louisiana

CRANBERRY HOLIDAY SALAD

1 (12-ounce) package fresh cranberries
2 cups sugar
1 pound seedless red grapes, halved
1 cup chopped pecans, toasted
1 cup whipping cream, whipped

Position knife blade in food processor bowl; add cranberries. Cover with top; process 20 seconds or until cranberries are coarsely chopped. Combine cranberries and sugar in a bowl; cover and chill 8 hours.

Drain cranberries for 2 hours, reserving liquid for other uses. Combine cranberries, grapes, and chopped pecans; fold in whipped cream. Yield: 8 servings.

Glenna Morgan
Corpus Christi, Texas

CRANBERRY-APPLE MOLD

1 (3-ounce) package raspberry-flavored gelatin
¾ cup boiling water
1 (8-ounce) can crushed pineapple, drained
1 (16-ounce) can whole-berry cranberry sauce
1 Red Delicious apple, unpeeled and coarsely grated
1 tablespoon grated orange rind
⅛ teaspoon salt
⅛ teaspoon ground cinnamon
Dash of ground cloves
Lettuce leaves
Fresh cranberries (optional)
Orange rind strips (optional)

Dissolve raspberry-flavored gelatin in boiling water, and let cool. Stir in pineapple and next 6 ingredients, and spoon into a lightly oiled 4-cup mold. Cover and chill until firm.

Unmold onto lettuce leaves. If desired, garnish salad with fresh cranberries and orange rind strips. Yield: 8 servings.

Alice McRae
De Funiak Springs, Florida

CONGEALED CHERRY SALAD

1 (16-ounce) can pitted dark
    sweet cherries, undrained
1 (11-ounce) can mandarin
    oranges, undrained
1 (8-ounce) can crushed
    pineapple, undrained
1 (6-ounce) package
    cherry-flavored gelatin
1 cup cold water
½ cup chopped pecans

Drain all fruit, combining and reserving enough juice to measure 1½ cups. Set fruit aside. Bring reserved juice to a boil. Dissolve gelatin in boiling juice. Add cold water; chill until the consistency of unbeaten egg white.

Fold in fruit and pecans. Pour mixture into a lightly oiled 6-cup mold; cover and chill until firm. Yield: 10 to 12 servings.
Lorene Carlisle
Columbus, Georgia

FROSTY PINEAPPLE SALAD

2 cups sour cream
¾ cup sugar
2 tablespoons lemon juice
⅛ teaspoon salt
3 large bananas, mashed
1 (20-ounce) can crushed
    pineapple, undrained
½ cup chopped pecans
¼ cup maraschino cherries,
    quartered

Combine first 4 ingredients in a large bowl, stirring well. Add banana and remaining ingredients; stir until blended. Spoon mixture into paper-lined muffin cups. Cover and freeze up to 1 month. Yield: 20 servings.
Laura C. Blanton
Huntsville, Alabama

WALDORF SALAD

3 medium-size Red Delicious
    apples, unpeeled and diced
½ cup chopped celery
½ cup seedless red grapes,
    halved
½ cup chopped walnuts
¼ cup mayonnaise or salad
    dressing
1½ teaspoons sugar
½ teaspoon lemon juice
¼ cup whipping cream, whipped
Ground nutmeg

Combine first 4 ingredients in a medium bowl; set aside. Combine mayonnaise, sugar, and lemon juice. Fold in whipped cream, and pour over fruit mixture, stirring gently. Sprinkle with nutmeg. Yield: 6 servings.
Chris Bryant
Johnson City, Tennessee

Vegetables That Suit Holiday Menus

Although entrées are the main attractions of holiday meals, it's the side dishes that bring the meal together. These recipes will give you ideas for adding color and flavor to your menu.

Snap Peas and Pearl Onions, flavored with mint, is an interesting addition to any meal. Sugar Snap peas are a cousin to snow peas and have been growing in popularity throughout the South. Be careful not to overcook them as this will soften the pods and destroy the flavor.

BRUSSELS SPROUTS

1¼ pounds fresh brussels sprouts
2 cups water
1 (8-ounce) can sliced water
    chestnuts, drained
1 (10¾-ounce) can cream of
    mushroom soup, undiluted
¼ cup milk
1 cup (4 ounces) shredded sharp
    Cheddar cheese
⅛ teaspoon salt
⅛ teaspoon pepper
½ cup slivered almonds, toasted

Wash brussels sprouts thoroughly, and remove discolored leaves. Cut off stem ends, and slash bottom of each sprout with a shallow X.

Place brussels sprouts and water in a saucepan. Cook over medium-high heat until water comes to a boil; cover, reduce heat, and simmer 8 to 10 minutes or until brussels sprouts are tender. Drain.

Place sprouts in a lightly greased 1½-quart casserole; layer water chestnuts over sprouts.

Combine soup and next 4 ingredients in a saucepan; cook over medium heat until cheese melts, stirring occasionally. Pour soup mixture over water chestnuts. Sprinkle with almonds. Yield: 6 to 8 servings.

Note: Two (10-ounce) packages frozen brussels sprouts cooked according to package directions may be used for fresh brussels sprouts.
Elizabeth B. Schadt
Galveston, Texas

Tip: *The key to cooking brussels sprouts is to cook them only until done. Overcooking results in flavor change and loss of color.*

BROCCOLI BAKE

1½ pounds fresh broccoli
5 eggs, beaten
1 cup cream-style cottage cheese
2 tablespoons all-purpose flour
½ teaspoon baking powder
½ teaspoon salt
4 slices bacon, cooked and
    crumbled
½ cup (2 ounces) shredded
    Cheddar or Swiss cheese

Trim off large leaves of broccoli, and remove tough ends; wash thoroughly. Cut tops into flowerets and stalks into ½-inch pieces; cook flowerets and pieces, covered, in a small amount of boiling water 8 minutes. Drain. Arrange broccoli in a lightly greased 10- x 6- x 2-inch baking dish.

Combine eggs and next 5 ingredients, stirring well; pour evenly over broccoli. Bake, uncovered, at 350° for 20 minutes; sprinkle with cheese, and bake an additional 5 minutes. Let stand 5 minutes. Yield: 6 servings.
Ernestine Elder
Gainesville, Texas

CAULIFLOWER SOUFFLÉ

1 large head cauliflower
½ cup milk
4 eggs, separated
¼ cup all-purpose flour
¼ cup butter or margarine,
    softened
½ teaspoon salt
½ teaspoon white pepper
½ cup grated Parmesan cheese
¼ cup cracker crumbs

Remove and discard large outer leaves of cauliflower; wash and break into flowerets. Cook, covered, in a small amount of boiling water 10 minutes or until tender; drain.

Place cauliflower and milk in container of an electric blender or food processor; process until pureed. Add egg yolks, flour, butter, salt, and pepper to cauliflower mixture; process until smooth.

Beat egg whites (at room temperature) until stiff peaks form. Gently fold egg whites and cheese into cauliflower mixture.

Butter the bottom of a 1½-quart soufflé dish. Pour cauliflower mixture into dish; sprinkle with cracker crumbs. Bake at 350° for 1 hour and 10 minutes or until golden brown. Serve immediately. Yield: 6 servings.
Gwen Louer
Roswell, Georgia

CELERIED POTATO PUFFS

1 cup minced celery
2 tablespoons butter or
    margarine, melted
¼ cup minced shallots
2 pounds potatoes, peeled and
    quartered
½ cup half-and-half
1 tablespoon butter or margarine
¼ teaspoon salt
⅛ teaspoon pepper
3 egg yolks, beaten
½ cup grated Parmesan cheese
Celery leaves (optional)

Sauté celery in 2 tablespoons butter until crisp-tender; add shallots, and sauté 2 minutes. Set aside.

Cook potatoes in boiling, salted water 15 minutes or until tender; drain and mash.

Combine half-and-half and 1 tablespoon butter in a saucepan; heat until butter melts, stirring occasionally. Gradually stir into mashed potatoes; add salt and pepper. Gradually stir about 1 cup potatoes into egg yolks; add to remaining potatoes. Stir in celery mixture and Parmesan cheese.

Spoon potato mixture into 5 lightly greased 6-ounce custard cups. Set custard cups in a 13- x 9- x 2-inch pan; pour hot water to a depth of 1 inch into pan. Bake at 450° for 30 minutes or until a knife inserted in center comes out clean. Unmold onto a serving platter. Garnish with celery leaves, if desired. Yield: 6 servings.
Virginia B. Stalder
Nokesville, Virginia

SWEET POTATO CASSEROLE

3 cups grated uncooked sweet
    potato
1 cup sugar
1 cup milk
¼ cup butter or margarine,
    melted
4 eggs, slightly beaten
3 tablespoons all-purpose flour
¼ teaspoon ground allspice
¼ teaspoon ground cinnamon
¼ teaspoon ground nutmeg
¼ teaspoon salt

Combine all ingredients; stir well. Spoon into a greased, shallow 2-quart baking dish. Bake, uncovered, at 350° for 30 minutes; stir and bake an additional 15 minutes or until a knife inserted in center comes out clean. Yield: 6 to 8 servings.
Sandra H. Pichon
Slidell, Louisiana

SNAP PEAS AND PEARL ONIONS

1 pound Sugar Snap peas
18 pearl onions, peeled
2 tablespoons butter or
    margarine, melted
1 tablespoon minced fresh mint
    leaves or 1 teaspoon mint
    flakes
½ cup water
½ cup salted cashews

Wash pea pods, and remove strings and ends.

Sauté onions in butter in a large saucepan. Add peas, mint, and water. Bring to a boil; cover, reduce heat, and simmer 5 to 8 minutes or until crisp-tender. Remove from heat; add cashews. Serve immediately. Yield: 4 to 6 servings.

Aimee Goodman
Corryton, Tennessee

COMPANY SPINACH

2 (10-ounce) packages frozen
    chopped spinach, thawed
⅓ cup chopped green onions
2 eggs, beaten
¼ cup butter or margarine,
    melted
½ teaspoon garlic powder
½ teaspoon dried whole thyme,
    crushed
3 medium tomatoes, peeled and
    cut into 12 slices
½ teaspoon garlic salt
¼ teaspoon freshly ground pepper
¼ cup fine, dry breadcrumbs
⅓ cup grated Parmesan cheese

Press uncooked spinach between layers of paper towels. Combine spinach and next 5 ingredients; stir well, and set aside.

Arrange tomato slices in a lightly greased 12- x 8- x 2-inch baking dish; sprinkle with garlic salt and pepper. Spoon spinach mixture over tomatoes. Combine breadcrumbs and Parmesan cheese; mix well, and sprinkle on top. Bake at 350° for 30 minutes. Yield: 6 to 8 servings.

Velma Kestner
Berwind, West Virginia

CREAMED SPINACH IN PASTRY SHELLS

8 (3-inch) unbaked pastry shells
1 (10-ounce) package frozen
    chopped spinach
1 (10¾-ounce) can cream of
    chicken soup, undiluted
1 clove garlic, minced
1 tablespoon all-purpose flour
2 teaspoons grated onion
⅛ teaspoon salt
¼ teaspoon pepper
Hard-cooked egg slices (optional)
Spinach leaves (optional)

Bake pastry shells at 375° for 12 minutes; set aside.

Cook frozen spinach according to package directions; drain well. Combine cooked spinach and next 6 ingredients; spoon into baked pastry shells. Bake at 375° for about 15 minutes. If desired, garnish with egg slices and spinach leaves. Yield: 8 servings.

Note: To make decorative hard-cooked egg slices, cut slices with a flower-shaped cookie cutter.

Betty Rabe
Plano, Texas

Flavor With A Sauce Or Topping

Many cuisines are enhanced by a variety of sauces and toppings. We think you'll adopt the ones here. Most of them are quite easy—in no time at all you'll be pouring the sauce over a waiting plate of vegetables, fruit, or pasta.

TANGY VEGETABLE SAUCE

1 cup mayonnaise or salad
    dressing
¾ teaspoon prepared mustard
¾ teaspoon Worcestershire sauce
¾ teaspoon hot sauce
2 hard-cooked eggs, finely
    chopped

Combine all ingredients, stirring well. Serve over cooked broccoli or green beans. Yield: 1⅓ cups.

Sandy Foster
Clarkston, Georgia

PESTO SAUCE

1 cup chopped fresh parsley
¾ cup grated Parmesan cheese
¼ cup minced walnuts
2 cloves garlic, crushed
1 tablespoon dried whole basil
1 teaspoon salt
⅛ teaspoon white pepper
⅓ cup olive oil
2 tablespoons butter or
    margarine, softened
2 tablespoons boiling water

Combine all ingredients in a bowl, mixing with a fork until well blended. Serve over noodles. To store sauce, place in an airtight container, and refrigerate up to one week or freeze up to six months. Yield: 1⅓ cups.

Patricia Cairns
Elmore, Alabama

DESSERT FONDUE

1 (14-ounce) can sweetened
   condensed milk
1 (6-ounce) package butterscotch
   morsels
4 (1-ounce) squares unsweetened
   chocolate
1 (7-ounce) jar marshmallow
   cream
½ cup milk
½ cup flaked coconut
1 teaspoon vanilla extract

Combine all ingredients in top of a double boiler; bring water to a boil. Reduce heat to low, and cook until chocolate melts, stirring constantly. Pour into fondue pot; place over fondue burner. Thin fondue with additional milk, if necessary. Serve with pound cake cubes and assorted fruits as dippers. Yield: 3½ cups.

Carolyn Look
El Paso, Texas

GOLDEN FRUIT SAUCE

1 teaspoon butter or margarine
¼ cup orange juice
¼ cup pineapple juice
1 tablespoon lemon juice
⅓ cup sugar
3 egg yolks, beaten
½ cup whipping cream, whipped
Fresh mint leaves (optional)
Orange rind strips (optional)

Melt butter in a small saucepan; add orange juice and next 3 ingredients. Cook, uncovered, over low heat until sugar dissolves. Gradually stir about one-fourth of hot mixture into yolks; add to remaining hot mixture, stirring constantly. Cook over medium heat until mixture is thickened (about 5 minutes). Chill. Fold in whipped cream before serving. Serve over fruit or pound cake. If desired, garnish with mint leaves and orange rind strips. Yield: 1¼ cups. *Pearl Lakey*
Seymour, Missouri

CINNAMON-HONEY BUTTER

1 cup butter, softened
3 tablespoons honey
½ teaspoon ground cinnamon

Cream butter until light and fluffy. Add honey and cinnamon, beating until well blended. Serve with pancakes, waffles, or toasted bagel slices. Yield: 1 cup. *Marcia Luzier*
Dublin, Virginia

After-Hours Entertaining

Entertaining on a weeknight is still an option during this busy time of year, especially if you plan ahead. This easy menu is perfect to serve after shopping with friends or even after a hectic day at work.

Just follow our easy plan for preparing the meal, including entrée, salad, and bread. You might want to pick up a pie or cake from the bakery for dessert.

The night before: Slice and butter bread; wrap in foil, and refrigerate. Make salad dressing, and prepare salad ingredients; refrigerate.

Before guests arrive: Prepare chicken. (It will take 30 minutes.) Bake bread, and toss salad.

Creamy Almond Chicken
Dijon Spinach Salad
Garlic Bread
Iced tea   Coffee

CREAMY ALMOND CHICKEN

⅔ cup sliced almonds
¼ cup butter or margarine,
   divided
6 chicken breast halves, skinned
   and boned
⅛ teaspoon salt
⅛ teaspoon pepper
1½ cups whipping cream
1 tablespoon Dijon mustard
2 tablespoons orange marmalade
⅛ teaspoon red pepper
Hot cooked rice

Sauté almonds in 1 tablespoon butter in a skillet; set almonds aside.

Place chicken between 2 sheets of heavy-duty plastic wrap; flatten to ¼-inch thickness, using a meat mallet or rolling pin. Sprinkle chicken with salt and pepper.

Melt remaining 3 tablespoons butter in skillet over medium-high heat. Add chicken, and cook about 1 minute on each side or until golden brown. Reduce heat to medium; add ½ cup almonds, whipping cream, and next 3 ingredients, stirring well. Cook about 10 minutes or until sauce thickens. Sprinkle with remaining almonds; serve with rice. Yield: 6 servings.

Hazel Sellers
Albany, Georgia

DIJON SPINACH SALAD

1 pound fresh spinach, torn
6 slices bacon, cooked and
  crumbled
2 hard-cooked eggs, chopped
1 cup sliced fresh mushrooms
¼ cup vegetable oil
¼ cup olive oil
2 tablespoons lemon juice
1 tablespoon white wine
  vinegar
½ teaspoon Dijon mustard
¼ teaspoon salt
¼ teaspoon pepper

Combine spinach, crumbled bacon, chopped eggs, and sliced mushrooms in a large salad bowl; toss gently.

Combine vegetable oil and remaining ingredients in a jar; cover tightly, and shake vigorously. Pour dressing over spinach mixture; toss gently, and serve. Yield: 6 servings.
Ginny Whitt
Campbellsville, Kentucky

GARLIC BREAD

1 (16-ounce) loaf unsliced French
  bread
½ cup butter or margarine,
  softened
1 clove garlic, crushed
3 tablespoons grated Parmesan
  cheese
¼ teaspoon pepper
Dash of red pepper

Slice French bread diagonally into 1-inch slices. Combine remaining ingredients, stirring well; spread butter mixture between bread slices. Place loaf on an ungreased baking sheet, and sprinkle with a few drops of water. Bake at 350° for 10 minutes or until bread is thoroughly heated. Yield: 1 loaf.
Charlotte Pierce
Greensburg, Kentucky

MICROWAVE COOKERY

Microwave Magic For Chopped Ham And Turkey

If your ham or turkey yields more than enough to feed the family, take advantage of the extra meat with these recipes designed for the microwave oven. Each will stretch the leftovers into entrées for several more meals, with the speed and convenience you'll appreciate at this time of year.

CRUNCHY TURKEY CASSEROLE

3 cups chopped cooked turkey
1 cup chopped celery
¼ cup chopped onion
2 (10¾-ounce) cans cream of
  mushroom soup, undiluted
1 (8-ounce) can sliced water
  chestnuts, drained
1 (2-ounce) jar diced pimiento,
  drained
1 (2-ounce) package slivered
  almonds
½ cup Chinese noodles

Combine all ingredients except noodles; spoon mixture into a lightly greased 12- x 8- x 2-inch baking dish. Cover with heavy-duty plastic wrap; fold back a small corner of wrap to allow steam to escape. Microwave at HIGH 12 to 15 minutes or until thoroughly heated, stirring after 6 minutes. Sprinkle with Chinese noodles, and serve immediately. Yield: 6 servings.
Sue Clark
Athens, Alabama

Cooking the Meat

We get lots of calls each year about whether you can cook the holiday ham or turkey in your microwave oven. Some of these meats are best cooked conventionally; others work well in the microwave.

We recommend using your conventional oven when cooking a full-size turkey. Most turkeys are so large that little time is saved when they are cooked in the microwave. Also, you might miss the familiar brownness or crispness that comes from conventional cooking.

Some types of ham work well in the microwave oven and offer significant time reductions and the same juicy tenderness you expect from the conventional oven. For the microwave, we recommend using hams labeled "fully cooked." With these you won't have to worry about the doneness of the ham if your thermometer reading is off or if the ham cooks unevenly. Select only ham halves so that the meat will cook more evenly.

HEARTY STUFFED POTATOES

4 large potatoes (about 2 pounds)
1 cup chopped fresh or frozen
  broccoli
1 small onion, chopped
1 cup chopped cooked ham or
  turkey
1 (2-ounce) jar diced pimiento,
  drained
Yogurt Sauce

Rinse potatoes, and pat dry. Prick each potato several times with a fork. Arrange potatoes in a circle, leaving 1 inch between each, on a layer of microwave-safe paper towels in microwave oven. Microwave, uncovered, at HIGH 14 to 17 minutes, turning and rearranging potatoes halfway through cooking time. Let stand 5 minutes.

Place broccoli and onion in a 1-quart glass bowl. Cover with heavy-duty plastic wrap; fold back a small edge of wrap to allow steam to escape. Microwave at HIGH 4 minutes or until tender. Drain. Add ham and pimiento, and microwave at HIGH 2 to 3 minutes. Stir in Yogurt Sauce, and microwave at MEDIUM (50% power) 2 to 4 minutes or until mixture is thoroughly heated. (Do not boil.) Cut potatoes lengthwise, and top with mixture. Yield: 4 servings.

Yogurt Sauce

1 (8-ounce) carton plain low-fat yogurt
¼ cup mayonnaise or salad dressing
1 tablespoon tarragon vinegar
2 teaspoons cornstarch
1 teaspoon soy sauce
½ teaspoon dried whole thyme
½ teaspoon dry mustard
¼ teaspoon dried whole oregano
⅛ teaspoon garlic powder

Combine all ingredients, stirring until blended. Yield: 1¼ cups.

Tip: *Don't be tempted to increase the amount of seasonings called for in a microwave recipe. You can easily overdo it because there's usually less liquid to reduce their flavor; you can add more seasoning after tasting.*

CHUNKY VEGETABLE SOUP

2 (14½-ounce) cans ready-to-serve chicken broth, undiluted and divided
1 (10-ounce) package frozen lima beans
1 (10-ounce) package frozen whole-kernel corn
1 large carrot, thinly sliced
1 small onion, chopped
1 (16-ounce) can tomatoes, undrained and chopped
1½ cups chopped cooked turkey
½ cup cubed cooked ham
¼ teaspoon pepper
⅛ teaspoon dried whole basil

Combine 1 can broth and next 4 ingredients in a deep 3-quart casserole. Cover with heavy-duty plastic wrap; fold back a small edge of wrap to allow steam to escape. Microwave at HIGH 16 minutes, stirring after 8 minutes. Add remaining can of broth, tomatoes, and remaining ingredients; cover and microwave at HIGH 10 minutes or until thoroughly heated. Yield: 8½ cups.

Appetizers To Make Ahead

When you're preparing dinner for friends and run short of time, the appetizer is often the first item cut from the menu. With these make-ahead recipes, however, that situation should never happen to you.

For a cold appetizer, consider Four-Cheese Pâté or Cajun Shrimp; both can be made ahead and chilled until you need them. And Almond-Ham Rollups will keep conveniently in the freezer up to a month.

CURRIED CHUTNEY SPREAD

2 (8-ounce) packages cream cheese, softened
¾ cup finely chopped pecans
½ cup commercial chutney
½ teaspoon curry powder

Combine all ingredients in a small mixing bowl; beat at medium speed of an electric mixer until blended. Spoon into serving container. Cover and chill at least 8 hours. Serve with crackers. Yield: 2½ cups.
Marian F. Parsons
Hurricane, West Virginia

CAJUN SHRIMP

4 quarts water
1 large lemon, sliced
5 pounds unpeeled large fresh shrimp
2 cups vegetable oil
¼ cup hot sauce
1 tablespoon olive oil
1 tablespoon minced garlic
1½ teaspoons salt
1½ teaspoons seafood seasoning
1½ teaspoons dried whole basil
1½ teaspoons dried whole oregano
1½ teaspoons dried whole thyme
1½ teaspoons minced fresh parsley
Leaf lettuce

Bring water and lemon to a boil; add shrimp, and cook 3 to 5 minutes. Drain well; rinse with cold water. Peel and devein shrimp; place in a large bowl.

Combine remaining ingredients except lettuce; beat with a wire whisk. Pour over shrimp; toss. Cover; chill 8 hours. Drain shrimp; serve in a lettuce-lined bowl. Yield: 25 appetizer servings.
Shirley M. Draper
Winter Park, Florida

SAUSAGE-MUSHROOM-PHYLLO BITES

1 pound mild bulk pork sausage
2 pounds fresh mushrooms, minced
¼ cup sliced green onions
¼ cup plus 2 tablespoons butter or margarine, melted
2 tablespoons vegetable oil
1 (8-ounce) package cream cheese
1 (3-ounce) package cream cheese
1 teaspoon freshly ground pepper
1 (16-ounce) package frozen phyllo pastry, thawed
Butter-flavored vegetable cooking spray or 1 cup butter or margarine, melted

Cook sausage in a Dutch oven until browned, stirring to crumble. Drain well, and set aside.

Sauté mushrooms and green onions in ¼ cup plus 2 tablespoons butter and oil in Dutch oven until all liquid evaporates. Stir in cream cheese, pepper, and sausage.

Cut sheets of phyllo lengthwise into 3½-inch strips. Coat each phyllo strip with cooking spray, or brush with butter. Keep remaining strips covered. Fold down narrow end of strip about 3 inches. Place 2 teaspoons sausage mixture at base of folded end; fold the right bottom corner over it into a triangle. Continue folding triangle back and forth to end of strip. Repeat process with remaining phyllo and filling. Keep finished triangles covered before baking.

Place triangles, seam side down, on greased baking sheets. Coat triangles with cooking spray, or brush with melted butter. Bake triangles at 400° for 20 minutes or until golden brown. Drain on paper towels; serve hot. Yield: 8 dozen.

Note: These may be frozen before baking. Do not thaw; bake as directed. *Martha Jewels*
Silver Spring, Maryland

ALMOND-HAM ROLLUPS

1 (8-ounce) package cream cheese, softened
2 tablespoons mayonnaise or salad dressing
1 teaspoon instant minced onion
1 teaspoon Worcestershire sauce
¼ teaspoon dry mustard
¼ teaspoon paprika
⅛ teaspoon pepper
⅛ teaspoon hot sauce
1 tablespoon finely chopped almonds, toasted
1 (12-ounce) package thinly sliced boiled ham

Combine all ingredients except ham, stirring until blended. Spread 1 tablespoon mixture on each ham slice. Roll up jellyroll fashion, starting at short end; wrap in plastic wrap, and freeze up to 1 month.

Thaw at room temperature 1 hour before serving. Cut each roll into ¾-inch slices. Yield: 5 dozen.
Polly Garrett
Jefferson City, Tennessee

FOUR-CHEESE PÂTÉ
(pictured on page 1)

1 (8-ounce) package cream cheese, softened
2 tablespoons milk
2 tablespoons sour cream
¾ cup chopped pecans, toasted
2 (8-ounce) packages cream cheese, softened
1 (4½-ounce) package Camembert cheese, softened
1 (4-ounce) package crumbled blue cheese, softened
1 cup (4 ounces) shredded Swiss cheese, softened
Pecan halves (optional)
Red and green apple wedges

Line a 9-inch pieplate with plastic wrap; set aside. Combine first 3 ingredients in a small mixing bowl; beat at medium speed of an electric mixer until smooth. Spread into pieplate; sprinkle with chopped pecans.

Combine remaining cream cheese, Camembert cheese (including rind), blue cheese, and Swiss cheese in a small mixing bowl; beat at medium speed of electric mixer until smooth. Spoon into pieplate, and spread to edge. Cover with plastic wrap, and chill up to 1 week. To serve, invert onto a serving plate; carefully peel away plastic wrap. Garnish pâté with pecan halves, if desired. Serve with apple wedges. Yield: 4½ cups.
Traci Vann
Birmingham, Alabama

CHAFING DISH CRABMEAT

2 cups mayonnaise
2 tablespoons capers
1 tablespoon prepared horseradish
1 teaspoon grated lemon rind
1 teaspoon Worcestershire sauce
½ teaspoon garlic powder
2 dashes of hot sauce
1 pound fresh crabmeat, drained and flaked
Melba toast or toast points

Combine first 7 ingredients in a saucepan. Gently stir in fresh crabmeat. Stir gently over low heat until mixture is hot. (Do not boil.) Pour hot crabmeat mixture into a chafing dish. Serve with melba toast. Yield: 3½ cups.

Note: To prepare this appetizer ahead, stir ingredients together; cover and chill up to one day ahead. Heat mixture just before serving.
Brenda Daniel
Richmond, Virginia

Uncommon Ways With The Common Mushroom

Some care must be taken with mushrooms. Handle them gently, and store them unwashed in the refrigerator until ready to use. Because mushrooms are porous and absorb water rapidly, they should never be soaked; they will lose nutrients, and their texture will change. Instead, clean with a damp cloth or rinse quickly in cold water, and pat dry.

HOT MUSHROOM TURNOVERS

1 (8-ounce) package cream
  cheese, softened
½ cup butter or margarine,
  softened
1½ cups all-purpose flour
¼ pound fresh mushrooms,
  minced
1 medium onion, minced
1½ tablespoons butter or
  margarine, melted
2 tablespoons sour cream
1 tablespoon all-purpose flour
½ teaspoon salt
⅛ teaspoon dried whole thyme
1 egg, beaten

Combine cream cheese and ½ cup butter in a medium bowl, stirring well. Add 1½ cups flour, stirring until smooth. Shape dough into a ball, and cover with plastic wrap. Chill dough 1 hour.

Sauté mushrooms and onion in 1½ tablespoons butter in a heavy skillet over low heat until tender, stirring frequently. Remove from heat, and stir in sour cream and next 3 ingredients. Set aside.

Roll pastry to ⅛-inch thickness on a lightly floured surface. Cut with a 3-inch cookie cutter. Place ½ teaspoon mushroom mixture in center of each circle. Brush edges of circle with egg, and fold dough in half, pressing to seal edges. Crimp edges, and prick tops with a fork; brush tops with remaining egg.

Place turnovers 1 inch apart on ungreased baking sheets. Bake at 450° for 12 minutes or until golden brown. Serve immediately. Yield: 3 dozen turnovers.

Note: Turnovers may be frozen baked or unbaked. Allow baked turnovers to cool completely before freezing. To reheat, bake frozen turnovers at 450° for 6 to 8 minutes. To freeze unbaked turnovers, place in freezer on baking sheets until firm; remove from sheets, and place in freezer containers. Bake frozen turnovers at 450° for 15 to 20 minutes or until golden brown.

Diane W. Lang
Joppa, Maryland

MUSHROOM QUICHE

1 (9-inch) refrigerated piecrust
2 cups whipping cream
4 eggs
½ pound fresh mushrooms, sliced
¼ cup minced green onions
¼ cup butter or margarine,
  melted
¼ teaspoon salt
⅛ teaspoon pepper

Line a 9-inch quiche dish with pastry. Prick bottom and sides of pastry with a fork. Bake at 400° for 3 minutes; remove from oven, and gently prick with a fork. Bake crust an additional 5 minutes.

Combine whipping cream and eggs in a medium bowl; stir with a wire whisk until well blended. Set aside.

Sauté mushrooms and green onions in butter in a heavy skillet over low heat about 5 minutes or until tender, stirring frequently. Stir in salt and pepper. Add mushroom mixture to whipping cream mixture, stirring well.

Pour mixture into pastry shell. Bake at 425° for 15 minutes; reduce heat to 325°, and bake 35 minutes or until set. Let stand 10 minutes before serving. Yield: one 9-inch quiche.
Pamela Debardeleben
Birmingham, Alabama

MUSHROOMS À LA KING

3 cups sliced fresh mushrooms
3 tablespoons butter or
  margarine, melted
3 tablespoons all-purpose flour
1 cup sliced celery
½ cup sliced pimiento-stuffed
  olives
¼ cup (1 ounce) shredded
  Cheddar cheese
2 hard-cooked eggs, chopped
1 cup milk
½ cup water
1 (10-ounce) package frozen patty
  shells, baked

Sauté mushrooms in butter in a heavy skillet over low heat about 5 minutes or until tender, stirring frequently. Add flour, and stir until well blended. Add celery and next 5 ingredients, stirring well. Simmer, uncovered, 15 to 20 minutes or until thickened. Spoon filling into patty shells. Yield: 6 servings.
Irene R. Smith
Covington, Georgia

Rice–Rising To New Heights

Hidden beneath a rich puddle of gravy or under a generous helping of beans, rice is often undervalued as a dish that can stand on its own. But in these spectacular recipes for the holidays, the year-round grain comes out on top.

ORANGE-HERB RICE

2 tablespoons chopped onion
2 tablespoons butter or
  margarine, melted
2 cups water
½ teaspoon grated orange rind
½ cup orange juice
1 teaspoon salt
⅛ teaspoon dried whole marjoram
⅛ teaspoon dried whole thyme
1 cup uncooked long-grain rice

Sauté onion in butter in a large saucepan until tender. Add water and next 5 ingredients; bring to a boil. Add rice, and stir well. Cover and bring to a boil; reduce heat, and simmer 20 minutes. Yield: 4 to 6 servings.
Stacey Wilson
Reidsville, North Carolina

EASY MUSHROOM RICE

1½ cups uncooked long-grain rice
1 (10¾-ounce) can cream of
  mushroom soup, undiluted
1 (2-ounce) jar diced pimiento,
  drained
1 egg, slightly beaten
¼ teaspoon pepper
½ cup slivered almonds, chopped
1 cup (4 ounces) shredded sharp
  Cheddar cheese, divided

Cook rice according to package directions, omitting salt. Combine all ingredients except ¼ cup cheese; mix well. Spoon mixture into a lightly greased 1½-quart casserole. Bake at 350° for 30 minutes; sprinkle with remaining ¼ cup cheese, and bake an additional 10 minutes. Yield: 6 to 8 servings.
Alice McNamara
Eucha, Oklahoma

SAVANNAH RED RICE

5 slices bacon
1 large onion, chopped
½ cup chopped celery
½ cup chopped green pepper
1 cup uncooked long-grain rice
1 (16-ounce) can chopped whole
  tomatoes, undrained
½ cup water
½ teaspoon salt
¼ teaspoon pepper
¼ teaspoon red pepper
⅛ teaspoon hot sauce

Cook bacon in a skillet until crisp; remove bacon, reserving drippings, crumble, and set aside. Add onion, celery, and green pepper to drippings; sauté until vegetables are tender. Stir in rice and remaining ingredients. Spoon into a lightly greased 1½-quart baking dish. Cover and bake at 350° for 25 minutes or until rice is tender, stirring after 15 minutes. Yield: 4 to 6 servings.

Whole wheat flour, rye flour, and all-purpose flour give Heartland Loaves an interesting flavor and texture. The recipe makes two loaves.

A tasty orange filling is spread onto the dough and on top of Speedy Orange Rolls. In addition, they rise only 30 minutes before baking.

RICE PILAF

1½ cups uncooked long-grain rice
2 cups water
⅓ cup dry white wine
1 (10¾-ounce) can condensed
  chicken broth, undiluted
1 (1.25-ounce) envelope onion
  soup mix
1 teaspoon dried whole basil
⅛ teaspoon pepper
2 tablespoons lemon juice
1 teaspoon butter or margarine

Combine all ingredients in a lightly greased 12- x 8- x 2-inch baking dish, stirring well. Cover and bake at 350° for 1 hour and 15 minutes or until rice is tender and liquid is absorbed. Yield: 8 servings.
Brenda K. Welch
Chickasaw, Alabama

Highlight Dinner With Homemade Bread

The aroma of fresh dinner rolls and yeast breads coming from the kitchen is as much a part of the holiday season as traditional cakes, candies, and pies. For many, it's the homemade breads that are remembered throughout the rest of the year.

Whole wheat flour, rye flour, and all-purpose flour give Heartland Loaves an interesting flavor and texture. The recipe makes two loaves.

A tasty orange filling is spread onto the dough and on top of Speedy Orange Rolls. In addition, they rise only 30 minutes before baking, making them quicker to make than most yeast rolls.

EASY POTATO ROLLS

⅔ cup shortening
⅔ cup sugar
2½ teaspoons salt
1 cup cooked, mashed potato
2 eggs
2 packages dry yeast
1⅓ cups warm water (105° to
   115°), divided
6 to 6½ cups all-purpose flour

Cream shortening; gradually add sugar, beating until fluffy. Add salt, potato, and eggs; beat until smooth.

Dissolve yeast in ⅔ cup warm water. Add yeast mixture and remaining ⅔ cup warm water to creamed mixture; beat until smooth. Gradually stir in enough flour to make a soft dough. Cover and let rise in a warm place (85°), free from drafts, 1½ hours or until dough is doubled in bulk.

Punch dough down; turn out onto a floured surface. Knead lightly 3 or 4 times. Divide dough into thirds. Shape one portion into 15 balls, and place in a well-greased 9-inch round cakepan.

Repeat procedure with remaining portions. Cover and let rise in a warm place, free from drafts, 1 hour or until doubled in bulk. Bake at 375° for 20 to 25 minutes or until browned. Yield: 45 rolls.

Note: Dough may be refrigerated for up to 4 days before shaping. To freeze rolls, prepare and bake as directed; let cool. Wrap in aluminum foil; freeze. To serve, let rolls thaw; then bake in foil at 375° for 12 to 15 minutes or until thoroughly heated.
Velma Kestner
Berwind, West Virginia

SPEEDY ORANGE ROLLS

1 package dry yeast
½ cup warm water (105° to 115°)
2 to 2¼ cups all-purpose flour,
   divided
2 tablespoons butter or
   margarine, softened
1 tablespoon sugar
1 teaspoon salt
1 egg, beaten
Orange Filling

Dissolve yeast in warm water in a large mixing bowl; let stand 5 minutes. Add 1 cup flour, butter, sugar, salt, and egg. Beat at medium speed of electric mixer until smooth. Stir in enough remaining flour to make a soft dough.

Turn dough out onto a lightly floured surface; knead until smooth (about 2 minutes). Cover and let rest 15 minutes.

Roll dough to a 14- x 7-inch rectangle; spread with half of Orange Filling, leaving a 1-inch margin on long sides. Roll dough, jellyroll fashion, starting at long side. Pinch seam to seal (do not seal ends). Cut into 12 equal slices; place slices, cut side down, in greased muffin pans. Cover and let rise in a warm place (85°), free from drafts, 30 minutes.

Bake rolls at 400° for 16 to 18 minutes. Remove from oven, and spread remaining Orange Filling over tops of rolls. Yield: 1 dozen.

Orange Filling

1½ cups sifted powdered sugar
½ tablespoon grated orange
   rind
3 tablespoons butter or
   margarine, melted
2 tablespoons orange juice

Combine all ingredients in a small mixing bowl, stirring well. Yield: about ½ cup.   *Shirley A. Ray*
Pampa, Texas

HEARTLAND LOAVES

2 cups boiling water
½ cup cornmeal
⅓ cup firmly packed brown sugar
2 teaspoons salt
2 packages dry yeast
½ cup warm water (105° to 115°)
¼ cup vegetable oil
¾ cup whole wheat flour
½ cup rye flour
4½ to 5 cups all-purpose flour

Combine first 4 ingredients in a large mixing bowl; cool to 105° to 115°.

Dissolve yeast in warm water; let stand 5 minutes. Stir yeast mixture and oil into cornmeal mixture. Add wheat and rye flours, stirring well. Gradually add enough all-purpose flour to make a stiff dough.

Turn dough out onto a floured surface, and knead until smooth and elastic (about 8 minutes). Place in a well-greased bowl, turning to grease top. Cover and let rise in a warm place (85°), free from drafts, 1 hour or until doubled in bulk.

Punch dough down, and divide in half; shape each portion into a loaf. Place in two well-greased 9- x 5- x 3-inch loafpans. Cover and let rise in a warm place, free from drafts, 30 to 40 minutes or until doubled in bulk. Bake at 350° for 45 minutes or until loaves sound hollow when tapped. Cover with aluminum foil the last 15 minutes of baking, if necessary, to prevent excessive browning. Remove loaves from pans, and let cool on wire racks. Yield: 2 loaves.
L. L. Walther
East Palatka, Florida

Tip: *When a recipe calls for a "greased pan," be sure to grease the pan with solid shortening or an oil unless specified.*

BUTTERHORN ROLLS

1 package dry yeast
1½ cups warm water (105° to 115°), divided
½ cup sugar
1 egg, beaten
¼ cup butter or margarine, melted
1 teaspoon salt
4½ to 5 cups all-purpose flour
3 tablespoons butter or margarine, softened and divided

Dissolve yeast in ½ cup warm water in a large bowl; let stand 5 minutes. Add remaining 1 cup water and next 4 ingredients, stirring well. Add enough flour to make a soft dough.

Turn dough out onto a floured surface, and knead until smooth and elastic (about 4 minutes). Place in a well-greased bowl, turning to grease top. Cover and let rise in a warm place (85°), free from drafts, 1 hour or until doubled in bulk.

Punch dough down, and divide into thirds. Roll each portion to a 10-inch circle on a floured surface; spread evenly with 1 tablespoon butter. Cut each circle into 12 wedges; roll up each wedge, beginning at wide end. Place on greased baking sheets, point side down.

Cover and let rise in a warm place, free from drafts, 45 minutes or until doubled in bulk. Bake at 375° for 15 minutes or until browned. Yield: 3 dozen.
Nina Lanphear
Weatherford, Texas

Tip: *Freshen dry, crusty rolls or French bread by sprinkling with a few drops of water, wrapping in aluminum foil, and reheating at 350° for about 10 minutes.*

ONION TWIST ROLLS

1 cup sour cream
1 (0.25-ounce) package instant onion soup mix
1 package dry yeast
⅓ cup warm water (105° to 115°)
2 tablespoons butter or margarine, melted
1 tablespoon sugar
½ teaspoon salt
1 egg
2 to 2½ cups all-purpose flour
1 egg, slightly beaten
1 tablespoon water
Sesame seeds

Combine sour cream and soup mix; set aside.

Dissolve yeast in warm water in a large bowl; let stand 5 minutes. Add ⅔ cup sour cream mixture, butter, sugar, salt, and 1 egg; beat at medium speed of an electric mixer until well blended. Gradually stir in enough flour to make a stiff dough.

Turn dough out onto a lightly floured surface, and knead until smooth and elastic (about 8 minutes). Divide dough in half. Roll half to a 12- x 6-inch rectangle; spread half of remaining sour cream mixture evenly onto rectangle. Fold rectangle in half lengthwise, and cut into 1-inch strips. Twist each strip of dough, and place on greased baking sheets. Repeat procedure.

Combine slightly beaten egg and 1 tablespoon water; brush over rolls, and sprinkle with sesame seeds.

Cover and let rise in a warm place (85°), free from drafts, 1 to 1½ hours or until doubled in bulk. Bake at 375° for 12 to 15 minutes. Yield: 2 dozen.
Rublelene Singleton
Scotts Hill, Tennessee

Allspice—Warm With Tradition

Allspice is at home in the Southern cupboard, its pungent flavor a sure indicator that the harvest season has arrived. It flavors more than fall vegetables, fruits, and baked goods, however; it often enhances tomato dishes, such as Spicy Tomato Aspic. And many folks say a Bloody Mary just isn't the same without it. Meats, especially pork, benefit from its strong, distinctive flavor.

SPICY TOMATO ASPIC

2 envelopes unflavored gelatin
½ cup cold water
2 cups tomato juice
½ cup white vinegar
⅓ cup sugar
½ teaspoon ground allspice
¼ teaspoon ground cloves
¼ teaspoon salt
⅛ teaspoon pepper
Dash of hot sauce
1 small green pepper, diced
1 tablespoon grated onion
Lettuce

Sprinkle gelatin over cold water; let stand 1 minute.

Combine tomato juice and next 7 ingredients in a large saucepan. Bring to a boil over medium heat. Add gelatin to hot tomato juice mixture; stir until gelatin dissolves. Chill until mixture is the consistency of unbeaten egg white.

Fold in green pepper and onion; pour into a lightly oiled 4-cup mold. Cover and chill until firm. Unmold onto a lettuce-lined serving plate. Yield: 6 servings.

SWEET POTATO PIE

2½ cups cooked, mashed sweet
  potatoes
¼ cup sugar
½ teaspoon salt
½ teaspoon ground allspice
¼ teaspoon ground nutmeg
¼ teaspoon ground cinnamon
1 tablespoon butter or margarine,
  melted
3 eggs
¾ cup milk
⅔ cup maple-flavored syrup
1 teaspoon vanilla extract
1 unbaked 9-inch pastry shell
Whipped cream (optional)

Combine first 7 ingredients in a large
mixing bowl; stir well, and set aside.
Beat eggs; gradually add milk, syrup,
and vanilla, stirring until blended.
Gradually stir egg mixture into sweet
potato mixture, and pour filling into
pastry shell.

  Bake at 425° for 10 minutes; reduce heat to 325°, and bake 1 hour
and 5 to 10 minutes or until a knife
inserted in center comes out clean.
Let cool; serve with whipped cream,
if desired. Yield: one 9-inch pie.
Carolyn Kerr
Tampa, Florida

SPICE-MOLASSES COOKIES

¾ cup shortening
1 cup sugar
1 egg
¼ cup molasses
2 cups all-purpose flour
1 teaspoon baking soda
1 teaspoon baking powder
¼ teaspoon salt
1 teaspoon ground ginger
1 teaspoon ground cinnamon
½ teaspoon ground nutmeg
¼ teaspoon ground cloves
¼ teaspoon ground allspice
Sugar

Cream shortening; gradually add 1
cup sugar, beating well at medium
speed of an electric mixer. Add egg
and molasses; mix well:

  Combine flour and next 8 ingredients; mix well. Add about one-
fourth of flour mixture at a time to
creamed mixture, beating until
smooth after each addition. Chill
dough 1 hour.

  Shape dough into 1-inch balls, and
roll in sugar. Place 2 inches apart on
ungreased cookie sheets. Bake at
375° for 9 to 11 minutes (tops will
crack). Cool on wire racks. Yield: 4
dozen.
Marie Bilbo
Meadville, Mississippi

Bring On
The Beverages

When decking the halls this season,
bring out your finest glassware and
china because these beverages call
for the best.

RED VELVET PUNCH

1 (12-ounce) can frozen cranberry
  juice concentrate, thawed and
  diluted
1 (7.5-ounce) bottle frozen lemon
  juice, thawed
1 (6-ounce) can frozen orange
  juice concentrate, thawed and
  diluted
1 (6-ounce) can frozen pineapple
  juice concentrate, thawed and
  diluted
2 cups brandy
2 (750-milliliter) bottles
  champagne, chilled

Combine first 5 ingredients, stirring
until blended. Chill mixture. To
serve, pour mixture into punch bowl,
and add champagne. Add an ice ring
or ice, if desired. Yield: 5 quarts.
Gladys Poe
Dandridge, Tennessee

CRICKET

½ cup crème de cacao
¼ cup brandy
1 pint vanilla ice cream
Ice cubes

Combine first 3 ingredients in container of an electric blender; process
until smooth. Add enough ice cubes
to bring mixture to 3-cup level, and
blend until smooth. Serve immediately. Yield: 3 cups.   *Dolores Cruz*
Pomona Park, Florida

HOLIDAY WASSAIL

1 orange
1 lemon
1½ teaspoons whole cloves
3 (3-inch) sticks cinnamon
½ cup sugar
1 gallon apple cider
2 cups orange juice
1 cup lemon juice

Peel orange and lemon, being careful
to keep rinds intact; insert cloves in
each strip of rind.

  Combine rinds, cinnamon, sugar,
and apple cider in a large Dutch
oven; bring to a boil. Cover, reduce
heat, and simmer 10 minutes. Remove from heat; let cool completely.
To serve, add orange and lemon
juices to mixture, and cook until
thoroughly heated. Yield: about 5
quarts.   *Sandra Russell*
Gainesville, Florida

Holiday Ice Ring

The day before serving your punch, prepare a pretty ice ring with citrus roses. Boil about 7 cups of water 1 minute; let cool at room temperature. (This eliminates cloudiness in the ice ring that water straight from the tap can cause.) Pour 3 cups of the water into a 6-cup ring mold; freeze. Set remaining water aside.

For each citrus rose, cut a thin slice from the bottom of a lemon, lime, or orange, using a sharp paring knife; discard. Beginning at the top, peel a continuous strip ½- to ¾-inch wide. Starting with the first portion cut, shape the strip like a rose. Coil tightly at first to form the center, gradually coiling more loosely to form the outer petals.

Slice lemons, limes, or oranges, and cut slices in half. Arrange citrus roses, sliced citrus halves, and mint leaves on top of ice in the ring. Slowly fill the mold to the top with remaining water. Citrus roses will float to the top, but mint leaves must be submerged to stay fresh. Freeze.

To unmold, let the mold sit at room temperature 5 minutes or until loosened. Carefully float ice ring in punch.

COLONIAL COFFEE

6 cups brewed coffee
¾ cup Kahlúa or other
    coffee-flavored liqueur
½ cup brandy
Whipped cream
Ground cinnamon

Combine coffee, Kahlúa, and brandy in a large container, stirring well. Pour into 8 coffee cups. Top with a dollop of whipped cream, and sprinkle with cinnamon. Serve immediately. Yield: 8 servings.

Sandra H. Pichon
Slidell, Louisiana

SPICED CRANBERRY PUNCH

1 cup sugar
1 cup water
¼ cup whole cloves
3 (3-inch) sticks cinnamon
2 quarts cranberry juice cocktail,
    chilled
1 (46-ounce) can orange-grapefruit
    juice, chilled
1 (46-ounce) can pineapple juice,
    chilled
½ cup lemon juice
2 quarts ginger ale, chilled

Combine first 4 ingredients in a saucepan; bring to a boil. Reduce heat, and simmer 10 minutes. Remove from heat; let cool completely. Strain, discarding cloves and cinnamon sticks.

To serve, combine sugar mixture, fruit juices, and ginger ale in a large punch bowl. Yield: 7 quarts.

Peggy H. Amos
Martinsville, Virginia

Tip: *Don't wear long, flowing sleeves or blouses with bows or scarves when cooking. These clothing items can touch a burner and ignite quickly.*

Liqueurs Lend Flavor

During the holidays many cooks embellish desserts with a touch of liqueur. Recipes for soufflés enhanced with orange-flavored liqueur, pound cake topped with brandy glaze, and ice cream churned with Frangelica and hazelnut brittle will entice you to try these desserts.

GRAND MARNIER SOUFFLÉS

Butter
1 tablespoon sugar
1 cup milk
¼ cup butter
¼ cup all-purpose flour
4 egg yolks
2 tablespoons Grand Marnier or
    other orange-flavored liqueur
¾ cup sugar
2 tablespoons cornstarch
5 egg whites
1 tablespoon sugar
Custard Sauce

Lightly butter six 6-ounce custard cups; coat bottom and sides of cups with 1 tablespoon sugar. Set aside.

Heat milk in a heavy saucepan. Cover and set aside.

Melt ¼ cup butter in a large saucepan over low heat; add flour, stirring until smooth. Cook, stirring constantly, 1 minute. Gradually stir in milk, and cook, stirring constantly, until mixture thickens and begins to leave sides of pan.

Remove from heat, and let cool about 15 minutes. Add egg yolks to sauce mixture, one at a time, beating after each addition. Stir in Grand Marnier; set aside.

Combine ¾ cup sugar and cornstarch; set aside. Beat egg whites (at room temperature) until foamy. Slowly add sugar mixture; beat until stiff but not dry. Gradually stir about one-fourth of sauce mixture into egg whites; gently fold into remaining sauce mixture.

Spoon into prepared custard cups; sprinkle tops of custards with 1 tablespoon sugar. Place cups in a large shallow pan. Pour hot water to a depth of 1 inch into pan. Bake at 400° for 10 minutes.

Reduce oven temperature to 350°, and bake 20 to 25 minutes or until tops are golden brown. Remove custard cups from water. Serve immediately with Custard Sauce. Yield: 6 servings.

Custard Sauce

½ cup sugar
2 tablespoons cornstarch
4 egg yolks
1 cup milk
2 tablespoons Grand Marnier or other orange-flavored liqueur
½ cup half-and-half
½ cup whipping cream, whipped

Combine sugar and cornstarch in a medium saucepan; add egg yolks, and stir until smooth. Set aside. Heat milk in a heavy saucepan. Gradually stir hot milk into egg mixture, stirring until smooth. Cook over medium heat, stirring constantly, about 10 minutes or until mixture thickens and thermometer reaches 165°. Remove from heat, and let cool. Stir in Grand Marnier and half-and-half. Fold in whipped cream. Cover and chill. Yield: 1¾ cups.   *John Feagin, Jr. Birmingham, Alabama*

FROZEN CHOCOLATE PIE WITH PECAN CRUST

6 (1-ounce) squares semisweet chocolate
½ teaspoon instant coffee granules
2 eggs, beaten
3 tablespoons Kahlúa
¼ cup powdered sugar
¾ cup whipping cream
1 teaspoon vanilla extract
Pecan Crust
¾ cup whipping cream
1 tablespoon Kahlúa
Grated chocolate

Place chocolate squares and coffee granules in top of a double boiler; bring water to a boil. Reduce heat to low; cook until chocolate melts. Gradually stir about one-fourth of melted chocolate into eggs, mixing well; add to remaining chocolate in double boiler. Gradually stir in 3 tablespoons Kahlúa and powdered sugar. Cook, stirring constantly, until mixture reaches 165°. Cool to room temperature. Beat ¾ cup whipping cream until soft peaks form; fold into chocolate mixture. Stir in vanilla. Spoon into Pecan Crust. Cover and freeze. Transfer pie from freezer to refrigerator 1 hour before serving.

Beat ¾ cup whipping cream in a medium mixing bowl until foamy; gradually add 1 tablespoon Kahlúa, beating until stiff peaks form. Pipe or dollop whipped cream around edge of pie. Sprinkle with grated chocolate. Yield: one 9-inch pie.

Pecan Crust

2 cups coarsely chopped pecans
⅓ cup firmly packed brown sugar
3 tablespoons butter or margarine, melted
2 teaspoons Kahlúa

Combine all ingredients, mixing well. Firmly press mixture evenly over bottom and up the sides of a 9-inch pieplate. Bake at 350° for 10 to 12 minutes. Press sides of crust with back of spoon. Cool. Yield: one 9-inch crust.

FRANGELICA CREAM

⅔ cup hazelnuts or slivered almonds
¾ cup sugar
1¾ cups milk
½ cup sugar, divided
5 egg yolks
¼ cup Frangelica or other hazelnut-flavored liqueur
1 cup whipping cream

Place hazelnuts in a shallow pan, and bake at 350° for 15 minutes; cool. Remove loose skins by rubbing nuts together. Chop nuts, and set aside.

Place ¾ cup sugar in a heavy saucepan; cook over medium heat, stirring occasionally, until caramelized (sugar melts and turns golden brown). Remove from heat, add nuts, and stir. Immediately pour into a buttered jellyroll pan. Cool 1 hour. Break into small pieces.

Combine milk and 2 tablespoons sugar in a heavy saucepan; cook over medium heat until mixture boils.

While milk is heating, beat egg yolks and remaining sugar at medium speed of an electric mixer until thick and lemon colored. Gradually stir about one-fourth of milk mixture into yolks; add to remaining milk mixture, stirring constantly. Add Frangelica. Cook over low heat 5 minutes or until mixture reaches 165° (it does not thicken). Do not boil. Chill. Add whipping cream and brittle. Pour into freezer can of a 2-quart hand-turned or electric freezer. Freeze according to manufacturer's instructions. Yield: 6 cups.   *Marie Barrett Berry Louisville, Kentucky*

BRANDIED POUND CAKE

1 cup golden raisins
1 cup chopped pecans, toasted
¼ cup all-purpose flour
1 cup butter or margarine,
    softened
3 cups sugar
6 eggs
2¾ cups all-purpose flour
¼ teaspoon baking soda
1 (8-ounce) carton sour cream
3 tablespoons brandy
1 teaspoon vanilla extract
Glaze (recipe follows)

Dredge raisins and pecans in ¼ cup flour; set aside.

Cream butter; gradually add sugar, beating well at medium speed of an electric mixer. Add eggs, one at a time, beating after each addition.

Combine 2¾ cups flour and soda; add to creamed mixture alternately with sour cream, beginning and ending with flour mixture. Mix until blended after each addition. Stir in brandy, vanilla, raisins, and pecans.

Pour batter into a greased and floured 10-inch tube pan. Bake at 325° for 1 hour and 30 minutes or until a wooden pick inserted in center comes out clean. Cool in pan 10 minutes; remove from pan, and let cool 30 minutes. Spread glaze on top and sides of cake. Cool completely. Yield: one 10-inch cake.

Glaze

2 cups sifted powdered sugar
3 tablespoons brandy
2 tablespoons milk

Combine all ingredients; mix well. Yield: about 1 cup.   *H. W. Asbell*
Leesburg, Florida

Shape The Bread For Canapés

When you have the urge to serve fancy canapés, don't settle for ordinary bread bases. Add style to the dainty open-faced sandwiches by shaping and baking your own special party bread.

Whether plain or toasted, the bread serves as a display platform for tasty spreads and attractive garnishes that give the appetizers their appeal. Use your imagination to come up with your own choice of topping combinations, or gather some new ideas from the boxed material on the following page.

Making the Bread

It's easy to duplicate this recipe for tasty Canapé Bread. First, stir up the simple yeast dough, flavoring it as directed with your choice of whole wheat, all-purpose, or rye flour.

Let rise; then carefully roll the dough, and tuck it into specially shaped canapé bread pans. As it bakes, the bread takes its shape from the pans. After cooling, just slice the bread thinly, and top it as desired.

Served just after cooling, the bread has a tender texture but is firm enough to hold substantial toppings. Brown the bread in the oven as directed, and it takes on the character of commercial melba toast, offering a crisp crust for any of its accompaniments.

Many kitchen shops and mail-order companies sell sets of three pans in flower, star, and heart shapes. Or substitute 16-ounce vegetable cans or 8½- x 4½- x 3-inch loafpans to make the bread round or rectangular.

If you make the bread ahead of time, store it in an airtight container at room temperature for a couple of days, or freeze it up to three months for longer storage. To keep the bread its freshest, slice it only as you use it.

Topping the Canapés

Bread bases can be topped with any food that spreads easily and is not runny. Choices can be as simple as melted cheese or as elaborate as multicolored caviar atop cream cheese. Garnishes can range from chopped green onions to a tiny rose shaped from salmon slices.

Assemble canapés on an assembly-line basis to speed the process. If using untoasted bread, spread the topping as soon as the loaf is sliced to prevent the bread from drying out. Once assembled, cover and chill canapés up to two hours prior to serving. If chilled longer, they might become soggy. On toasted bread add the spread at the last moment to keep the bread crisp.

CANAPÉ BREAD

1 package dry yeast
⅓ cup warm water (105° to 115°)
1 cup warm milk (105° to 115°)
2 tablespoons butter or
    margarine, melted
3¼ to 3¾ cups all-purpose flour,
    divided
2 teaspoons sugar
1 teaspoon salt

Dissolve yeast in warm water in a large bowl; let stand 5 minutes. Add milk and butter to yeast mixture. Combine 2½ cups flour, sugar, and salt, and stir well. Gradually stir flour mixture into yeast mixture. Gradually stir in enough remaining flour to make a soft dough.

Turn dough out onto a lightly floured surface, and knead until smooth and elastic (about 5 minutes). Place dough in a well-greased bowl, turning to grease all sides. Cover and let rise in a warm place (85°), free from drafts, 45 minutes or until doubled in bulk.

Punch dough down, and divide in half. Roll each portion to a 7-inch log. Insert dough into greased 9-inch canapé pans, and close lids. Do not let dough rise. Bake at 400° for 50 to 55 minutes or until bread is golden brown. Remove bread from pans immediately; cool on a wire rack.

To make melba toast, slice bread about ³⁄₁₆-inch thick; place slices in a single layer on a baking sheet, and bake at 300° for 20 to 30 minutes or until toasted. Yield: 2 loaves.

Note: Bread may also be baked in two 8½- x 4½- x 3-inch loafpans. Divide dough in half, shape each half into loaves, and place in greased pans. Bake at 375° for 45 minutes or until bread is done.

Bread may also be baked in 4 (16-ounce) vegetable cans. Divide dough into 4 equal portions, and place in greased cans. Bake at 375° for 40 to 45 minutes or until bread is done.

Rye Canapé Bread: Substitute 1½ cups rye flour for 1½ cups of the all-purpose flour, and add ¾ teaspoon fennel seeds with the salt.

Whole Wheat Canapé Bread: Substitute 1½ cups whole wheat flour for 1½ cups all-purpose flour.

On Top of the Canapé

The spread and garnishes for canapés not only offer the bulk of the flavor for these appetizers, but they also add color, texture, and visual interest. Almost any type of food can become the makings for a spectacular topping. Just keep in mind how the spreads and toppings work together.

Depend on soft toppings, such as cheese spreads and flavored butters, to hold chopped or sieved garnishes in place. If used on a canapé topped with pepperoni, loose and tiny garnishes would fall off easily.

Firm, dry toppings, such as pepperoni, need large, flat garnishes that will firmly balance on top. Thin slices of fruits or vegetables usually team well with this type of topping. If large garnishes tend to fall off, secure them to the base with dabs of butter or mayonnaise.

To make eye-catching canapés, be creative with the ways garnishes are applied. Arrange them in triangles, circles, and other geometric shapes to draw attention to them. Be sure to pick garnishes that are compatible with the spreads with which they are teamed, in terms of color, texture, and taste.

The following are some suggestions for teaming spreads and garnishes that work well together. Use your own favorite recipes for the familiar spreads and toppings, or purchase them from a deli for convenience.

■ Arrange thin slices of red grapes like a flower on a canapé topped with chicken salad.

■ Top tuna salad spread or other spreads with pimiento strips and ripe olive slices.

■ Roll thin slivers of smoked salmon to look like a rose, and place on bread spread with softened cream cheese. Put a caper in the center of the rose, and add a sprig of parsley as a leaf.

■ Spread a piece of bread with guacamole, and top with cooked, crumbled bacon and alfalfa sprouts as a garnish.

■ Top bread slices with softened commercial chive-flavored cream cheese, and garnish with cucumber-slice wedges. Dip the edges of the cucumber wedge in paprika for added color.

■ Add 2 tablespoons commercial pesto to an 8-ounce carton of whipped cream cheese, and spread atop a bread slice. Pipe extra spread to dress the edges, and nestle a red pepper cutout into parsley on top.

■ Stir 2 tablespoons tomato paste into an 8-ounce carton of whipped cream cheese, and spread or pipe it on the bread. Add little pieces of pimiento and parsley to complement the flavor and contrast the color.

All Boxed Up And Someplace To Go

In the desperate search for Christmas gifts special friends will truly enjoy, look no farther than your own kitchen. Home-baked treasures are fun to both give and receive, and an afternoon spent in the kitchen baking can be a memorable holiday activity.

Here we offer ideas for scrumptious cookies to share—and lots of them! Perfect for cookie-swap parties, the recipes make from 6 dozen to 16 dozen, and the cookies can be baked ahead of time to fit into your busy holiday schedule.

These selections can be stored at room temperature up to one week and frozen for one month. An airtight container keeps Frosted Chocolate-Cherry Cookies soft, while Orange-Slice Cookies and Christmas Trees will stay crisp stored in a container with a loose-fitting lid.

FROSTED CHOCOLATE-CHERRY COOKIES

1½ cups butter or margarine, softened
1½ cups sugar
2 eggs
1 tablespoon vanilla extract
3¼ cups all-purpose flour
½ teaspoon baking powder
½ teaspoon baking soda
¼ teaspoon salt
⅔ cup cocoa
1 (10-ounce) jar maraschino cherries
Chocolate-Cherry Frosting

Cream butter in a large mixing bowl; gradually add sugar, beating at medium speed of an electric mixer. Add eggs and vanilla, beating well.

Combine flour and next 4 ingredients; add to mixture, and mix well.

Shape dough into 1-inch balls; place about 2 inches apart on ungreased cookie sheets. Press thumb in center of cookie leaving an indentation. Drain cherries, reserving juice. Cut cherries in half, and place, cut side down, in indentation of cookie. Bake at 350° for 8 minutes. Cool; drizzle with Chocolate-Cherry Frosting. Yield: 6 dozen.

Chocolate-Cherry Frosting

1 (1-ounce) square unsweetened chocolate
1 tablespoon butter or margarine
1 cup sifted powdered sugar
5 to 6 tablespoons cherry juice

Combine chocolate and butter in a heavy saucepan; cook over low heat, stirring constantly, until chocolate melts. Remove from heat. Add powdered sugar and half of cherry juice; beat until mixture is smooth. Add juice to desired consistency; stir well. Yield: ¾ cup.

Note: Cookies may be frozen up to 1 week. Place in single layers in zip-top plastic bags. *Mrs. Billie Taylor Wytheville, Virginia*

Tip: *For perfectly shaped round cookies, pack homemade refrigerator cookie dough into clean 6-ounce juice cans (don't remove bottoms) and freeze dough. Thaw cookie dough about 15 minutes; then open bottom of can and push up, using the top edge as a cutting guide.*

ORANGE-SLICE COOKIES

2 cups shortening
2 cups firmly packed brown sugar
1 cup sugar
3 eggs
3 cups all-purpose flour
1½ teaspoons baking soda
1¼ teaspoons baking powder
3 tablespoons water
3 cups quick-cooking oats, uncooked
1 (3½-ounce) can flaked coconut
20 candy orange slices, finely chopped

Cream shortening in a large mixing bowl; gradually add sugars, beating at medium speed of an electric mixer. Add eggs, beating well.

Combine flour, soda, and baking powder; add to creamed mixture, and mix well. Stir in water, oats, coconut, and candy. Chill dough at least 1 hour.

Drop dough by teaspoonfuls onto greased cookie sheets. Bake at 325° for 12 minutes or until browned. Cool. Yield: 16 dozen.
Mrs. M. J. Keener
San Angelo, Texas

CHRISTMAS TREES

1½ cups butter or margarine, softened
1 cup sugar
1 (3-ounce) package lime-flavored gelatin
1 egg
1 teaspoon vanilla extract
4 cups all-purpose flour
1 teaspoon baking powder
Red and green sugar crystals (optional)

Cream butter in a large mixing bowl; gradually add sugar and gelatin, beating at medium speed of an electric mixer. Add egg and vanilla; beat well. Combine flour and baking powder; add to creamed mixture, and mix well.

Use a cookie gun to shape dough as desired, following the manufacturer's instructions. Place cookies on ungreased cookie sheets, and garnish with sugar crystals, if desired. Bake at 350° for 12 to 15 minutes. Cool on wire racks. Yield: about 9½ dozen.

Patsy Black
Edgemoor, South Carolina

Cakes, Pies, And Cookies With Lots Of Spice

After being outside on a crisp winter day, there's nothing like walking into a kitchen filled with the aroma of freshly baked holiday sweets flavored with the spices of the season—cinnamon, cloves, and nutmeg.

WALNUT SPICE KISSES

¼ cup sugar
1 teaspoon ground cinnamon
⅛ teaspoon ground nutmeg
1 egg white
Pinch of salt
1 cup finely chopped walnuts

Combine sugar, cinnamon, and nutmeg; set aside.

Beat egg white (at room temperature) and salt at high speed of an electric mixer 1 minute. Gradually add sugar mixture, 1 tablespoon at a time, beating until stiff peaks form. Fold in walnuts.

Drop by teaspoonfuls onto lightly greased cookie sheets. Bake at 250° for 35 to 40 minutes. Yield: 2½ dozen.

Edith Askins
Greenville, Texas

SWEET POTATO CAKE

⅔ cup butter or margarine, softened
2 cups sugar
4 eggs, separated
1 cup mashed cooked sweet potatoes
2 cups all-purpose flour
1 teaspoon baking soda
½ teaspoon salt
2 tablespoons cocoa
1 teaspoon ground allspice
1 teaspoon ground cinnamon
1 teaspoon ground cloves
1 teaspoon ground nutmeg
1 cup buttermilk
1 teaspoon vanilla extract
1½ cups raisins
2 cups chopped pecans
Powdered sugar (optional)

Cream butter; gradually add 2 cups sugar, beating well at medium speed of an electric mixer. Add egg yolks, one at a time, beating well after each addition. Add sweet potatoes to mixture, mixing well.

Combine flour and next 7 ingredients; add to creamed mixture alternately with buttermilk, beginning and ending with flour mixture. Mix after each addition. Stir in vanilla, raisins, and pecans. Beat egg whites (at room temperature) until stiff peaks form; fold into batter.

Spoon batter into a greased and floured 10-inch tube pan. Bake at 325° for 1 hour and 25 minutes or until a wooden pick inserted in center comes out clean. Cool in pan 10 minutes; remove from pan, and let cool completely on a wire rack. Sprinkle with powdered sugar, if desired. Yield: one 10-inch cake. *Faye Hicks*
Charleston, West Virginia

CAROLINA SWEET POTATO PIE

1 (17-ounce) can sweet potatoes, drained and mashed
1 cup firmly packed brown sugar
⅔ cup milk
⅔ cup whipping cream
3 eggs
3 tablespoons bourbon
1 tablespoon butter or margarine, melted
1 teaspoon ground cinnamon
½ teaspoon ground nutmeg
½ teaspoon ground ginger
¼ teaspoon salt
1 unbaked 9-inch pastry shell
Whipped cream (optional)

Combine first 4 ingredients in a large bowl; beat at low speed of an electric mixer until smooth. Add eggs, one at a time, beating well after each addition. Add bourbon and next 5 ingredients; beat just until blended.

Pour mixture into pastry shell. Bake at 375° for 50 to 55 minutes or until filling is set. Cool. Garnish with whipped cream, if desired. Yield: one 9-inch pie. *Shirley Livingston*
Sebring, Florida

APPLESAUCE SPICE CAKE

¾ cup butter or margarine,
　softened
2 cups sugar
3 eggs
3 cups all-purpose flour
1½ teaspoons baking soda
1 teaspoon baking powder
¾ teaspoon salt
2 tablespoons cocoa
½ teaspoon ground cinnamon
½ teaspoon ground cloves
½ teaspoon ground nutmeg
1 (16-ounce) can applesauce
1½ cups raisins
1 cup finely chopped pecans
Panocha Frosting
½ cup chopped pecans

Cream butter; gradually add sugar, beating well at medium speed of an electric mixer. Add eggs, one at a time, beating well after each addition.

Combine flour and next 7 ingredients; add to creamed mixture alternately with applesauce, beginning and ending with flour mixture. Stir in raisins and 1 cup pecans.

Pour batter into 3 greased and floured 9-inch round cakepans. Bake at 350° for 25 to 30 minutes or until a wooden pick inserted in center comes out clean. Cool in pans 10 minutes; remove from pans, and let cool completely on wire racks.

Spread Panocha Frosting between layers and on top and sides of cake. Sprinkle ½ cup pecans on top of cake. Yield: one 3-layer cake.

Panocha Frosting

½ cup butter or margarine
1 cup firmly packed dark brown
　sugar
½ cup plus 1 tablespoon
　half-and-half
¼ teaspoon salt
4 cups sifted powdered sugar

Combine first 4 ingredients in a heavy saucepan. Cook over medium heat until mixture comes to a boil, stirring constantly. Boil 2 minutes. Remove from heat, and cool mixture to 160°. Stir in powdered sugar. Yield: enough for one 3-layer cake.

Charlotte Watkins
Lakeland, Florida

Refreshing Finale

Lemon pie lovers take heart, Heather Riggins of Nashville, Tennessee, has a recipe for Lemon Meringue Cake that is sure to become a family favorite.

LEMON MERINGUE CAKE
(pictured on page 264)

¼ cup butter or margarine,
　softened
½ cup sugar
2 eggs, separated
1 egg
1 cup all-purpose flour
1 teaspoon baking powder
⅓ cup milk
½ teaspoon vanilla extract
2 eggs, separated
1 cup water
¾ cup sugar
⅓ cup all-purpose flour
½ teaspoon grated lemon rind
¼ cup lemon juice
1 tablespoon butter or margarine
½ teaspoon cream of tartar
½ cup sugar

Cream ¼ cup butter; gradually add ½ cup sugar, beating at medium speed of an electric mixer. Add 2 egg yolks and 1 egg to creamed mixture; mix well.

Combine 1 cup flour and baking powder; add to creamed mixture alternately with milk, beginning and ending with flour mixture. Mix after each addition. Stir in vanilla.

Pour batter into a greased and floured 9-inch round cakepan. Bake at 350° for 28 to 30 minutes or until a wooden pick inserted in center comes out clean. Cool in pan 10 minutes. Remove from pan; cool completely on a wire rack.

Combine 2 egg yolks and water; set aside. Combine ¾ cup sugar and ⅓ cup flour in a heavy saucepan; add egg yolk mixture and lemon rind. Cook over medium heat, stirring constantly, until mixture thickens and comes to a boil. Boil 2 minutes. Remove from heat. Stir in lemon juice and 1 tablespoon butter. Cover with wax paper, and cool. Place cake layer on baking sheet. Spoon filling onto cake.

Beat 4 egg whites (at room temperature) and cream of tartar at high speed of an electric mixer 1 minute. Gradually add ½ cup sugar, 1 tablespoon at a time, beating until stiff peaks form and sugar dissolves (2 to 4 minutes). Spread over lemon filling. Bake at 350° for 12 to 15 minutes or until meringue peaks are lightly browned. Yield: one 9-inch cake.

Right: *Stuffed Turkey Breast (page 322) includes a filling of spinach, sweet red pepper, and spices.*

Pages 298 and 299: *Crunchy Green Salad, Pepper Pasta, and Herb Green Beans offer an array of colors to complement Roquefort Chicken. (Recipes begin on page 320.)*

Right above: *Shrimp Soufflé Roll (page 320) stars as an appetizer for this menu, but it also offers other serving options.*

Right below: *A special occasion deserves a regal finale, such as Creamy Bombe With Raspberry Sauce (page 322).*

Above: *Roast Pork With Spiced Cherry Sauce (page 324) relies on a rolled boneless pork loin roast for pleasing shape and easy preparation. Garnished with lemon wedges and purple kale, it makes a colorful entrée.*

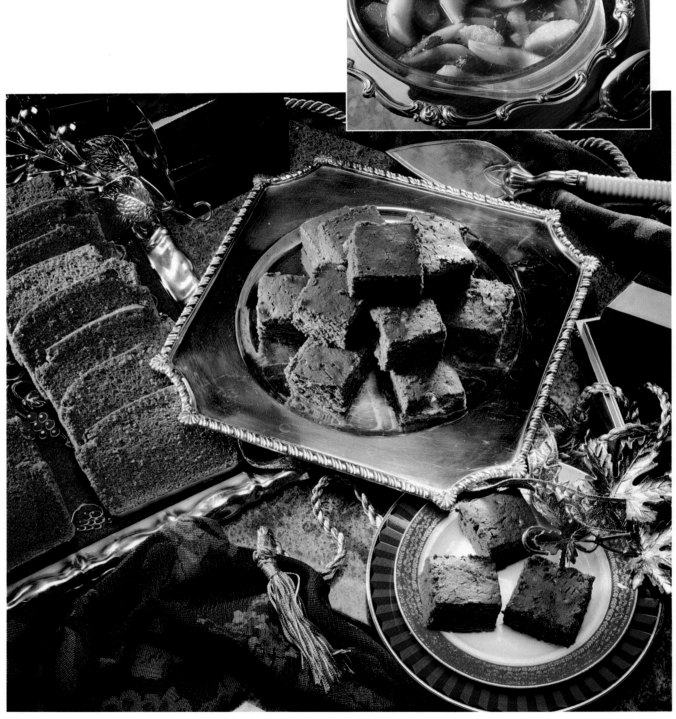

Far right: *Southerners of all backgrounds enjoy (clockwise from top) Polish Sugar Cake, Apple Strudel, and Sopaipillas. (Recipes begin on page 267.)*

Right: *Spicy Pears and Oranges (page 305) features fresh fruit baked in a cranberry sauce mixture.*

Above: *Satisfy chocolate cravings with Chocolate Pound Cake (page 325) or Chocolate-Walnut Brownies (page 325) without sacrificing healthy eating. In both recipes, calories have been trimmed to create light desserts.*

Delicate cocoa crêpes enfold strawberries and kiwifruit in Fruit-Filled Chocolate Crêpes (page 325). A rich chocolate glaze tops off this special dessert.

Freshen Menus With Fruit

For a refreshing change from the usual vegetable side dishes, why not give cooked fruits a try? Here readers share their favorite recipes using canned fruit.

SPICY PEARS AND ORANGES
(pictured on page 302)

1 (16-ounce) can whole-berry
  cranberry sauce
⅓ cup sugar
1 tablespoon lemon juice
¼ teaspoon ground cinnamon
¼ teaspoon ground ginger
6 medium pears, peeled and
  sliced
2 oranges, peeled and sectioned

Combine first 5 ingredients in a heavy saucepan. Bring mixture to a boil over medium heat, stirring often; remove from heat.

Combine pears and oranges in a 2½-quart casserole; pour cranberry mixture over fruit. Cover and bake at 350° for 40 minutes or until pears are tender. Serve warm with a slotted spoon. Yield: 8 servings.

Kay Swanner
Montgomery, Alabama

SPICED PEARS

4 (8½-ounce) cans pear halves,
  undrained
¾ cup cider vinegar
¾ cup sugar
¼ teaspoon red food coloring
1 tablespoon mixed pickling
  spices

Drain pears, reserving juice; place pears in a 2-quart bowl, and set aside. Combine reserved juice, vinegar, sugar, and food coloring in a saucepan. Tie pickling spices in a cheesecloth bag; add spice bag to liquid mixture, and bring to a boil. Reduce heat, and simmer 10 minutes. Pour mixture over pears. Cover and chill several hours. Discard spice bag before serving. Yield: 8 servings.

Mrs. Guy C. Palmer
Wagoner, Oklahoma

CHAFING DISH FRUIT

1 (16-ounce) can apricot halves in
  extra-light syrup
1 (16-ounce) can peach halves in
  extra-light syrup
1 (16-ounce) can pear halves in
  extra-light syrup
1 (20-ounce) can unsweetened
  pineapple slices
1 tablespoon grated orange rind
1 teaspoon grated lemon rind
⅔ cup orange juice
1 tablespoon lemon juice
⅔ cup pitted dates, halved

Drain fruit, reserving juices. Combine reserved juices, orange rind, lemon rind, and orange juice in a Dutch oven. Bring mixture to a boil. Simmer, uncovered, 15 minutes or until mixture is reduced to about 2½ cups. Add lemon juice and reserved fruits; bring to a boil, reduce heat, and simmer 10 minutes. Add dates; simmer an additional 5 minutes. Spoon into a chafing dish, and serve hot. Yield: 8 to 10 servings.

Gracie Moore
Winchester, Tennessee

BAKED SPICED FRUIT

1 (17-ounce) can apricot halves
1 (16-ounce) can peach halves
1 (16-ounce) can pear halves
1 (15¼-ounce) can pineapple
  chunks
1 cup orange juice
⅓ cup firmly packed brown sugar
1 tablespoon lemon juice
1 (3-inch) stick cinnamon
4 whole cloves
⅛ teaspoon mace
Dash of salt

Drain fruit, reserving syrup for other uses. Cut apricot, peach, and pear halves in half. Combine fruit in a 12- x 8- x 2-inch baking dish. Combine orange juice and remaining ingredients in a saucepan; bring to a boil, reduce heat, and simmer 2 minutes. Pour orange juice mixture over fruit. Bake at 350° for 30 minutes. Cool. Cover and chill 8 hours.

Remove cinnamon stick and whole cloves before serving. Serve cold or hot. Yield: 8 to 10 servings.

Kay Culton
Northport, Alabama

Fruit Tips

■ It is best to store most fruit in the refrigerator. Allow melons, avocados, and pears to ripen at room temperature; then refrigerate. Berries should be sorted to remove imperfect fruit before refrigerating; then wash and hull just before serving.

■ If only drained fruit is called for in a recipe, use quarters and halves rather than the more costly whole fruit. Reserve the juice for use in other recipes.

Kiwi, A Southern Fruit?

You'll probably be surprised to learn that the "exotic," fuzzy, brown kiwifruit is now grown in the South. "We were the first to plant kiwi for commercial production in the Southeast," Julian Holmes of Stately Oaks Farms in Johnston, South Carolina, boasts. "That was in 1970. Now there are approximately 300 acres of kiwi orchards in South Carolina, Georgia, and Alabama.

"We harvest the fruit in October and November when it's mature yet firm. It is imperative that kiwi be ripe to enjoy its luscious sweet flavor," Julian explains. "A ripe kiwi is spongy soft, yielding slightly to gentle pressure." To ripen it, simply leave the fruit at room temperature for several days.

Or to speed up the ripening process of kiwifruit, place the kiwi, along with an apple or banana, in a plastic bag or ripening bowl. Check the fruit every day. When the kiwi is ripe, seal it in a plastic bag and refrigerate; it should keep for three to four weeks.

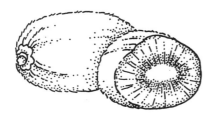

SABAYON GLACÉ

6 egg yolks
Dash of salt
⅔ cup sugar
1 cup whipping cream
½ cup Chablis or other dry
    white wine
⅔ cup Chambord
2 cups whipping cream,
    whipped
3 to 4 kiwifruit, peeled and
    sliced
Kiwifruit slices (optional)
Fresh raspberries (optional)
Fresh mint sprigs (optional)

Combine egg yolks and salt in a large bowl; beat at high speed of an electric mixer until blended. Gradually add sugar, 1 tablespoon at a time, beating until mixture is thick and lemon colored (about 5 minutes).

Heat 1 cup whipping cream, Chablis, and Chambord until hot, but not boiling. With mixer running on low speed, slowly pour hot cream mixture into beaten egg mixture. Transfer mixture to the top of a double boiler; place over boiling water, and cook, stirring constantly, 20 minutes. (Mixture will thicken only slightly.) Remove from heat. Place top of double boiler with mixture over ice water, and stir until mixture is completely cold. Fold in whipped cream. Chill thoroughly.

Up to 4 hours before serving, fold glacé gently. Arrange sliced kiwifruit around sides of compotes; spoon glacé into compotes. Chill until ready to serve. If desired, garnish with kiwifruit slices, raspberries, and mint. Yield: 8 servings.
Lou Baughman
Fort Walton Beach, Florida

KIWIFRUIT PIZZA

1 (14-ounce) can sweetened
    condensed milk
½ cup sour cream
½ cup lemon juice
1 teaspoon vanilla extract
½ cup butter or margarine,
    softened
¼ cup firmly packed brown sugar
1 cup all-purpose flour
¼ cup regular oats, uncooked
¼ cup finely chopped walnuts
3 to 4 kiwifruit, peeled and
    thinly sliced
1 (8-ounce) can sliced pineapple,
    drained
1 (11-ounce) can mandarin
    oranges, drained
4 to 6 strawberries, halved

Combine first 4 ingredients in a small bowl, stirring well. Chill.

Cream butter; gradually add sugar, beating well at medium speed of an electric mixer. Add flour, oats, and walnuts; mix well. Press mixture into a greased 12-inch pizza pan. Prick dough with a fork, and bake at 350° for 12 minutes or until crust is browned. Cool.

Spread condensed milk mixture evenly over crust. Arrange fruit over condensed milk mixture. Yield: one 12-inch pie.
Shirley Golden
Kingsport, Tennessee

TROPICAL FRUIT SALAD

1 ripe mango, peeled (optional)
1 papaya, peeled and seeded
2 ripe avocados, peeled
4 kiwifruit, peeled and sliced
3 bananas, sliced
Dressing (recipe follows)
¼ cup flaked coconut, toasted
¼ cup slivered almonds, toasted

Slice mango, if desired, papaya, and avocados into wedges, and arrange on a large serving plate. Combine kiwifruit and banana; spoon into center of arranged fruit. Drizzle fruit with about one-third of dressing. Combine coconut and almonds; sprinkle over salad. Serve with remaining dressing. Yield: 10 servings.

Dressing

⅓ cup orange juice
3 tablespoons vegetable oil
2 tablespoons brown sugar
1 tablespoon light rum
¼ teaspoon salt
½ teaspoon paprika

Combine all ingredients in a jar. Cover tightly, and shake vigorously. Chill 1 hour. Yield: ⅔ cup.
Kathleen Stone
Houston, Texas

Recipes Kids Can Make

The season for making treats for your children's homeroom classes is here. Wouldn't it be great if this year your kids helped? It's easy with these recipes that are simple to mix and require minimal cooking. They may even inspire your kids to take more interest in cooking.

These recipes were tested and approved by two novice cooks (10 and 12 years old) and several moms. Besides learning about measuring and stirring, the young cooks also learned about cleaning up!

PEANUT BARS

4 cups corn flakes cereal
2 cups puffed corn cereal
1 cup salted Spanish peanuts
1 cup sugar
1 cup dark corn syrup
1 cup creamy peanut butter
1 teaspoon vanilla extract

Combine corn flakes cereal, puffed corn cereal, and peanuts in a large mixing bowl; set aside.

Combine sugar and corn syrup in a small saucepan, and bring to a boil over medium heat. Stir in peanut butter and vanilla. Pour syrup mixture over corn flake mixture, and mix well. Press mixture into a buttered 13- x 9- x 2-inch baking pan. Cool. Cut into bars. Yield: 2 dozen.
Chris Bryant
Johnson City, Tennessee

EASY CINNAMON-PECAN ROLLS

⅓ cup chopped pecans
⅓ cup firmly packed light brown sugar
¼ teaspoon ground cinnamon
1 (8-ounce) package refrigerated crescent dinner rolls
Butter-flavored vegetable cooking spray or 2 tablespoons melted butter or margarine

Combine chopped pecans, brown sugar, and cinnamon in a small bowl; set aside.

Separate rolls at perforations, and spray one side with cooking spray or brush with butter. Sprinkle rolls with sugar mixture, and roll into crescents according to package directions. Place on a lightly greased baking sheet. Bake at 400° for 10 to 12 minutes. Yield: 8 servings.

CRUNCHY APRICOT BALLS

¾ cup nutlike cereal nuggets
¾ cup graham cracker crumbs
¾ cup finely chopped dried apricots
½ cup chopped pecans
½ cup sifted powdered sugar
¼ cup light corn syrup
1 tablespoon orange juice
Additional sifted powdered sugar

Combine first 5 ingredients in a large bowl. Combine corn syrup and orange juice; pour over apricot mixture, and stir until blended. Shape into 1-inch balls; roll in additional powdered sugar. Yield: 3 dozen.
Mrs. Roy Nieman
Dunnellon, Florida

PEANUT BUTTER FUDGE

¼ cup butter or margarine
⅓ cup milk
1 teaspoon vanilla extract
1 (16-ounce) package powdered sugar
½ cup cocoa
¼ teaspoon salt
½ cup chunky peanut butter

Melt butter in a medium saucepan; remove from heat, and add milk and vanilla.

Sift powdered sugar, cocoa, and salt together; gradually add to milk mixture, stirring until blended. Stir in peanut butter. Press mixture into a buttered 8-inch square pan.

Chill and cut into pieces. Yield: about 2 dozen.

Tip: *Peanut butter will keep its quality longer and taste fresher if stored in the refrigerator.*

DATE CANDY

2 (8-ounce) packages pitted dates
½ cup raisins
1 cup chopped pecans
½ cup flaked coconut

Position knife blade in food processor bowl; slowly drop half each of dates and raisins through food chute with processor running. Remove date mixture; repeat procedure with remaining dates and raisins.

Turn date mixture out onto wax paper; knead in pecans. Shape into a 12-inch log, and roll in coconut. Chill thoroughly, and thinly slice. Yield: one 12-inch log. *Mrs. Bruce Fowler Woodruff, South Carolina*

There's Grapefruit In The Cake

When fresh citrus is at its peak flavor this time of year, Louise B. Mosley of Leesburg, Florida, knows it's time to pull out her recipe for Fresh Grapefruit Cake. The tangy fruit adds an especially refreshing flavor to each bite.

FRESH GRAPEFRUIT CAKE

⅔ cup butter or margarine, softened
1¾ cups sugar
2 eggs
3 cups sifted cake flour
2½ teaspoons baking powder
½ teaspoon salt
½ cup grapefruit juice
¾ cup milk
1 teaspoon grated grapefruit rind
1½ teaspoons vanilla extract
Grapefruit Frosting

Cream butter; gradually add sugar, beating well. Add eggs, one at a time, beating well after each addition.

Combine flour, baking powder, and salt; add to creamed mixture alternately with grapefruit juice, beginning and ending with flour mixture. Gradually add milk. Stir in grapefruit rind and vanilla extract; mix well.

Pour batter into 2 greased and floured 9-inch round cakepans. Bake at 350° for 25 minutes or until a wooden pick inserted in center comes out clean. Cool in pans 10 minutes; remove from pans, and cool completely on wire racks. Spread Grapefruit Frosting between layers and on top and sides of cake. Yield: one 2-layer cake.

Grapefruit Frosting

1½ cups sugar
2 egg whites
1 tablespoon light corn syrup
⅛ teaspoon salt
⅓ cup grapefruit juice
1 tablespoon grated grapefruit rind
2 teaspoons vanilla extract

Combine first 5 ingredients in top of a double boiler. Beat at low speed of an electric mixer 30 seconds or just until mixed.

Place over boiling water; beat constantly at high speed 7 minutes or until stiff peaks form. Remove from heat. Add grapefruit rind and vanilla; beat 1 to 2 minutes or until frosting is thick enough to spread. Yield: 3¾ cups or enough for one 2-layer cake.

Citrus Tips

■ Deep green, yellow, and orange fruit and vegetables are good sources of vitamin A. Common sources of vitamin C are citrus fruit, deep green vegetables, and potatoes.

■ For a delicious and simple dessert, pour cream sherry over chilled grapefruit.

■ If stored at room temperature, grapefruit will keep for a day or two; when refrigerated, they will keep up to four months.

■ Whenever a recipe calls for both the rind and the juice of citrus fruit, wash and grate before juicing.

■ Roll lemons, oranges, and grapefruit on a counter before cutting to soften; you will get more juice.

■ Store lemon, orange, and grapefruit rinds in the freezer; grate as needed for pies, cakes, and cookies. Or use candied for the holidays.

Turkey Breast, Fast And Flavorful

Turkey has gained prominence for more than just a special-occasion entrée. And thank goodness for turkey breasts that cook in less time than a whole turkey.

SAVORY SEASONED TURKEY BREAST AND GRAVY

1 tablespoon olive oil
1½ tablespoons lemon juice
1 teaspoon garlic salt
1 to 2 teaspoons freshly ground pepper
1 teaspoon dried whole rosemary
1 teaspoon dried whole thyme
1 (5- to 5½-pound) turkey breast
1 medium onion, quartered
1 stalk celery, cut into 3-inch lengths
½ cup white wine
Browning-and-seasoning sauce
¼ teaspoon browning-and-seasoning sauce
1 tablespoon all-purpose flour
2 tablespoons milk

Combine olive oil and lemon juice; set aside. Combine garlic salt and next 3 ingredients; set aside.

Rinse turkey breast; pat dry. Pull skin back without detaching, and brush breast with olive oil mixture. Sprinkle with herb mixture. Pull skin back over breast. Place onion and celery in a 4-quart baking dish.

Place breast, skin side down, over vegetables; add wine. Cover tightly with heavy-duty plastic wrap; fold back a small corner of plastic wrap to allow steam to escape. Microwave at HIGH 20 minutes, giving dish a quarter-turn after 10 minutes.

Uncover turkey; turn skin side up. Brush with browning-and-seasoning sauce; cover turkey and microwave at MEDIUM-HIGH (70% power) 30 to 35 minutes or until juices run clear when turkey is pierced with a fork, basting and giving dish a quarter-turn at 10-minute intervals. Let stand 10 minutes.

When turkey is done, a microwave meat thermometer should register 175° when placed in thickest portion of turkey breast. Microwave temperature is higher than conventional temperature.

Remove skin and herb mixture from turkey breast, if desired.

Strain pan drippings, reserving vegetables and discarding fat. Add ¼ teaspoon browning-and-seasoning sauce to broth. Brush turkey breast with broth mixture.

Measure 1 cup broth. Combine broth and reserved onion and celery in container of an electric blender; process until smooth.

Combine flour and milk, stirring well; add to broth mixture in a 4-cup glass measure. Microwave at HIGH 3 to 4 minutes or until thickened, stirring at 1-minute intervals. Yield: about 12 servings.

Conventional Directions: Combine olive oil and lemon juice; set aside. Combine garlic salt and next 3 ingredients; set aside.

Rinse turkey breast; pat dry. Pull skin back without detaching, and brush breast with olive oil mixture. Sprinkle with herb mixture. Pull skin back over breast.

Place onion and celery in a 4-quart casserole. Place turkey, skin side up, on vegetables; add wine. Insert meat thermometer in meaty portion of breast, making sure it does not touch bone. Cover and bake at 325° until thermometer registers 170° (about 2 hours); baste frequently with pan drippings.

Remove skin and herb mixture from turkey; brush with browning-and-seasoning sauce, if desired.

Strain pan drippings, reserving vegetables and discarding fat. Add ¼ teaspoon browning-and-seasoning sauce to broth. Brush turkey breast with broth mixture.

Measure 1 cup broth, adding water if necessary to equal 1 cup. Combine broth and reserved onion and celery in container of an electric blender; process until smooth.

Combine flour and milk, stirring well; add to broth mixture in a small saucepan. Bring to a boil, reduce heat, and simmer 5 minutes, stirring frequently.

QUICK! Broil An Entrée

Broiling involves direct, intense heat and is a simple, healthy way to prepare many foods.

Small, uniform cuts of meat work best. All of these recipes require the food to be 4 inches from the heat source—that's usually the first rack from the top in your oven. Use vegetable cooking spray to lightly grease racks or pans without adding an excessive amount of calories.

HAMBURGERS TERIYAKI

1½ pounds ground beef
1 tablespoon soy sauce
1 tablespoon honey
1 clove garlic, crushed
½ teaspoon salt
¼ teaspoon ground ginger

Shape meat into 4 patties. Combine remaining ingredients in a small bowl, stirring well; brush on patties. Place patties on lightly greased rack of a broiler pan; broil 4 inches from heat about 15 minutes on each side or to desired degree of doneness. Yield: 4 servings.
Lisa Conner
Powder Springs, Georgia

RIB-EYE STEAKS WITH ROQUEFORT GLAZE

2 (3-ounce) packages Roquefort cheese, crumbled
2 tablespoons cream cheese, softened
1 teaspoon Worcestershire sauce
1 teaspoon commercial steak sauce
¼ teaspoon garlic powder
2 drops of hot sauce
4 small (¾- to 1-pound) rib-eye steaks

Combine first 6 ingredients; beat at medium speed of an electric mixer until smooth. Spread a thin layer over top of each steak. Place on lightly greased rack of a broiler pan; broil 4 inches from heat 4 to 6 minutes on each side or to desired degree of doneness. Yield: 4 servings.
Marge Killmon
Annandale, Virginia

BROILED CHICKEN BREAST TARRAGON

2 chicken breast halves, skinned and boned
⅛ teaspoon salt
¼ teaspoon pepper
1 tablespoon mayonnaise or salad dressing
1 teaspoon dried whole tarragon, crushed
1 teaspoon Dijon mustard

Place chicken breasts between two sheets of heavy-duty plastic wrap; pound to ½-inch thickness, using a meat mallet or rolling pin. Place chicken on lightly greased rack of a broiler pan, and sprinkle with salt and pepper.

Combine mayonnaise and remaining ingredients; spread half of mayonnaise mixture on chicken breasts. Broil 4 inches from heat 4 minutes. Turn and spread with remaining mayonnaise mixture; broil 4 minutes. Yield: 2 servings.
Donna Kay Carlson
Paducah, Kentucky

PEACHY PORK CHOPS

4 (1-inch-thick) pork chops
¼ teaspoon seasoned salt
¼ teaspoon onion powder
1 (16-ounce) can sliced peaches, undrained
2 tablespoons brown sugar
¼ teaspoon dried whole basil
2 tablespoons butter or margarine

Place pork chops on a lightly greased rack of broiler pan. Sprinkle with seasoned salt and onion powder. Broil 4 inches from heat approximately 7 minutes on each side.

Combine peaches and remaining ingredients in a small saucepan, stirring well. Cook, uncovered, over low heat 10 minutes, stirring often. Arrange chops on a platter. Pour sauce over chops. Yield: 4 servings.
Gail Smith
Pine Bluff, Arkansas

BROILED FLOUNDER

4 (3-ounce) flounder fillets
1 tablespoon lemon juice
¼ cup grated Parmesan cheese
⅛ teaspoon salt
2 tablespoons butter or margarine, softened
1½ tablespoons mayonnaise or salad dressing
1½ tablespoons chopped green onion tops
Dash of hot sauce
Green onion strips (optional)
Lemon wedges (optional)

Place fillets on a lightly greased 15- x 10- x 1-inch baking pan. Brush with lemon juice.

Combine cheese and next 5 ingredients, mixing well. Set aside.

Place fillets on lightly greased rack of a broiler pan; broil 4 inches from heat 6 to 8 minutes. Spread cheese mixture evenly over fish; broil 2 to 3 minutes or until fish flakes easily when tested with a fork. If desired, garnish with green onion strips and lemon wedges. Yield: 4 servings.
Adelaide H. Middaugh
Charleston, South Carolina

A Light Buffet For Special Occasions

Health-conscious cooks, like all good cooks, want to pull out all the stops for special occasions. We've created a lavish, yet light, menu that proves good taste doesn't have to be sacrificed for healthy dining.

These delectable and imaginative dishes are suitable for almost any special occasion, especially the holiday season. The menu serves 16, but most recipes can be halved easily for smaller gatherings.

Hot Cranberry Cocktail
Zucchini-Shrimp Appetizers
Spinach-Stuffed Tenderloin
Light Scalloped Potatoes
Orangy Carrot Strips
Chinese Cabbage Slaw
Dinner Rolls
Lemon Cake Roll

HOT CRANBERRY COCKTAIL

1 tablespoon whole cloves
2 teaspoons whole allspice
1 (32-ounce) bottle cranberry juice cocktail
3 cups unsweetened pineapple juice
1 cup water
16 (3-inch) sticks cinnamon (optional)

Tie cloves and allspice in a cheesecloth bag. Combine cranberry juice cocktail, pineapple juice, water, and spice bag in a Dutch oven; bring to a boil. Cover, reduce heat, and simmer 5 minutes.

Discard spice bag. Serve with cinnamon stick stirrers, if desired. Yield: 8 cups (61 calories per ½-cup serving).

☐ *0.2 gram protein, 0.2 gram fat, 15.3 grams carbohydrate, 0 milligrams cholesterol, 4 milligrams sodium, and 14 milligrams calcium.*

ZUCCHINI-SHRIMP APPETIZERS

2 cups water
½ pound unpeeled small fresh shrimp
Vegetable cooking spray
⅓ cup diced green pepper
1 tablespoon all-purpose flour
¼ cup skim milk
¼ cup diced green onions
1 tablespoon lemon juice
3 drops of hot sauce
¼ teaspoon salt
⅛ teaspoon white pepper
1 (2-ounce) jar diced pimiento, drained
4 zucchini (1½ pounds)
Fresh parsley sprigs (optional)

Bring water to a boil; add shrimp, and cook 3 to 5 minutes. Drain well, and rinse with cold water. Chill. Peel and devein shrimp. Chop shrimp, and set aside.

Coat a nonstick skillet with cooking spray; place over medium-high heat until hot. Add green pepper; sauté until tender. Add flour; cook 1 minute, stirring constantly. Add milk; cook over medium heat until thickened, stirring constantly. Add green onions and next 5 ingredients. Stir in shrimp, and refrigerate.

Cut each zucchini into 8 slices. Scoop out center of each slice with a melon ball scoop; discard pulp. Fill center of slices with shrimp mixture. Garnish with parsley sprigs, if desired. Serve chilled. Yield: 16 servings (20 calories per 2 appetizers).

☐ *2.6 grams protein, 0.2 gram fat, 2.2 grams carbohydrate, 18 milligrams cholesterol, 62 milligrams sodium, and 16 milligrams calcium.*

SPINACH-STUFFED TENDERLOIN

½ pound fresh spinach
Vegetable cooking spray
¼ pound fresh mushrooms, diced
¼ cup grated Parmesan cheese
¼ cup egg substitute
½ teaspoon fennel seeds
½ teaspoon ground sage
½ teaspoon salt
½ teaspoon freshly ground pepper
1 (4½-pound) beef tenderloin, well trimmed
3 cloves garlic, crushed
¾ teaspoon fennel seeds
1 teaspoon freshly ground pepper

Remove stems from spinach, and wash leaves thoroughly. Drain. Place spinach in a nonstick skillet; cover and cook over medium heat just until spinach wilts, about 3 minutes, stirring once. Remove from heat; uncover and let cool. Chop spinach; drain well, pressing spinach between layers of paper towels. Set chopped spinach aside.

Coat a nonstick skillet with cooking spray; place over medium-high heat until hot. Add mushrooms, and sauté until tender and liquid evaporates. Remove from heat; stir in chopped spinach, Parmesan cheese, and next 5 ingredients.

Trim excess fat from beef tenderloin. Cut tenderloin lengthwise to within ½ inch of each end, leaving bottom of tenderloin intact.

Combine crushed garlic cloves, ¾ teaspoon fennel seeds, and 1 teaspoon pepper, and rub over entire surface of tenderloin. Spoon spinach mixture into opening of tenderloin. Press gently to close. Tie tenderloin securely with heavy string at 1-inch intervals.

Place stuffed tenderloin on rack coated with cooking spray; place rack in a roasting pan. Insert meat thermometer into thickest portion of tenderloin. Place tenderloin in a 500° oven; immediately reduce temperature to 350°. Cook 50 to 55 minutes or until meat thermometer registers 140° (rare) or 160° (medium).

Remove stuffed tenderloin from oven. Cover loosely with aluminum foil, and let stand 10 minutes before slicing. Yield: 16 servings (201 calories per 3 ounces tenderloin and 1 ounce stuffing).

☐ *25 grams protein, 10.1 grams fat, 1.3 grams carbohydrate, 74 milligrams cholesterol, 164 milligrams sodium, and 43 milligrams calcium.*

LIGHT SCALLOPED POTATOES

Vegetable cooking spray
2 cloves garlic, minced
⅓ cup diced onion
1½ tablespoons all-purpose flour
1 (12-ounce) can evaporated skimmed milk
1½ cups skim milk
1 teaspoon salt
½ teaspoon crushed red pepper
¼ teaspoon freshly ground pepper
9 cups thinly sliced unpeeled red potatoes (about 4 pounds)
¾ cup (3 ounces) shredded Gruyère cheese
⅓ cup freshly grated Parmesan cheese

Coat a Dutch oven with cooking spray; place over medium-high heat until hot. Add garlic and onion; sauté until tender. Add flour; cook 1 minute, stirring constantly. Add evaporated milk and next 4 ingredients; cook over medium heat, stirring constantly, until mixture boils. Add potatoes, and return to a boil, stirring occasionally. Layer half each of potatoes, Gruyère cheese, and Parmesan cheese in a 13- x 9- x 2-inch baking dish coated with cooking spray. Repeat layers.

Bake at 350° for 45 minutes or until bubbly and golden brown. Let stand 30 minutes before serving. Yield: 16 servings (138 calories per ½-cup serving).

☐ *7.2 grams protein, 2.5 grams fat, 22.3 grams carbohydrate, 8 milligrams cholesterol, 240 milligrams sodium, and 183 milligrams calcium.*

ORANGY CARROT STRIPS

8 cups thin carrot strips
2 teaspoons grated orange rind
¾ cup orange juice
2 tablespoons honey
1 tablespoon cornstarch
¼ cup water

Combine first 4 ingredients in a Dutch oven. Bring to a boil; cover, reduce heat, and simmer 8 to 10 minutes or until carrots are crisp-tender.

Combine cornstarch and water; stir into carrots, and bring to a boil, stirring constantly. Cook 1 minute, stirring constantly. Yield: 16 servings (46 calories per ½-cup serving).

☐ *0.8 gram protein, 0.1 gram fat, 11.1 grams carbohydrate, 0 milligrams cholesterol, 25 milligrams sodium, and 21 milligrams calcium.*

CHINESE CABBAGE SLAW

1 tablespoon sugar
⅓ cup cider vinegar
1 tablespoon sesame oil
10 cups shredded Chinese cabbage (about 2 pounds)
1 tablespoon sesame seeds, toasted

Combine sugar, vinegar, and sesame oil in a small bowl; pour over cabbage, and toss gently. Cover and chill 8 hours.

Before serving, toss gently, and sprinkle with sesame seeds. Yield: 8 cups (20 calories per ½-cup serving).

☐ *0.8 gram protein, 1.3 grams fat, 2.1 grams carbohydrate, 0 milligrams cholesterol, 28 milligrams sodium, and 47 milligrams calcium.*
Patsy Bell Hobson
Liberty, Missouri

DINNER ROLLS

1 package dry yeast
1½ cups warm water (105° to 115°)
2 tablespoons sugar
1 teaspoon salt
¼ cup plus 2 tablespoons reduced-calorie margarine, softened
4 to 4¼ cups all-purpose flour, divided
Vegetable cooking spray

Dissolve yeast in warm water in a large mixing bowl; let stand 5 minutes. Add sugar, salt, margarine, and 1 cup flour; beat at medium speed of an electric mixer 2 minutes. Gradually stir in enough remaining flour to make a soft dough.

Turn dough out onto a lightly floured surface, and knead until smooth and elastic (about 10 minutes). Place in a bowl coated with cooking spray, turning to grease top. Cover and let rise in a warm place (85°), free from drafts, one hour or until doubled in bulk.

Punch dough down, and divide into thirds; shape each portion into 12 rolls. Place in three 8-inch baking pans coated with cooking spray. Cover and let rise in a warm place, free from drafts, 45 minutes or until doubled in bulk. Bake at 375° for 25 to 30 minutes or until golden brown. Yield: 3 dozen (74 calories per roll).

☐ *1.8 grams protein, 1.4 grams fat, 13.2 grams carbohydrate, 0 milligrams cholesterol, 84 milligrams sodium, and 3 milligrams calcium.*
Mrs. Donald C. Vanhoy
Salisbury, North Carolina

Tip: *Sifting flour, with the exception of cake flour, is no longer necessary. Simply stir the flour, gently spoon it into a dry measure, and level the top. Powdered sugar, however, should be sifted to remove the lumps.*

LEMON CAKE ROLL

Vegetable cooking spray
5 egg whites
¾ cup sugar
1½ teaspoons lemon juice
1½ teaspoons lemon extract
⅛ teaspoon salt
¾ cup sifted cake flour
2 tablespoons sifted powdered sugar
Lemon Filling
Fresh mint sprigs (optional)
Lemon twists (optional)

Coat a 15- x 10- x 1-inch jellyroll pan with cooking spray, and line with wax paper. Coat wax paper with cooking spray; set aside.

Beat egg whites (at room temperature) at high speed of an electric mixer until foamy. Gradually add sugar, 1 tablespoon at a time, beating until stiff peaks form and sugar dissolves (2 to 4 minutes). Add lemon juice, lemon extract, and salt; beat well. Gently fold flour in. Spread batter evenly in prepared pan. Bake at 350° for 8 to 10 minutes.

Sift powdered sugar in a 15- x 10-inch rectangle on a towel. When cake is done, immediately loosen from pan, and turn out onto sugared towel. Peel off wax paper. Starting at narrow end, roll up cake and towel together; cool on a wire rack, seam side down.

Unroll cake; remove towel. Spread Lemon Filling on cake, leaving a 1-inch margin around edges; reroll cake. Place on a plate, seam side down. If desired, garnish with mint and lemon twists. Yield: 16 servings (98 calories per ¾-inch slice).

Lemon Filling

½ cup sugar
1½ tablespoons cornstarch
1 egg yolk, beaten
¼ cup lemon juice
¼ cup orange juice
¼ cup water
1 tablespoon grated lemon rind

Combine first 6 ingredients in a heavy saucepan. Cook over medium heat, stirring constantly, until mixture boils. Boil 1 minute; stir in lemon rind, and let cool. Yield: enough filling for 1 cake roll.

☐ *1.6 grams protein, 0.4 gram fat, 21.7 grams carbohydrate, 17 milligrams cholesterol, 34 milligrams sodium, and 5 milligrams calcium.*

Microwave Puddings For Fall

Introduce your family and friends to these puddings from the microwave. Each takes advantage of fresh fall produce and lends itself to being served fancifully with swirls of whipped cream in ramekins.

PUMPKIN PUDDING

½ cup pecans, divided
¾ cup vanilla wafer crumbs
2 tablespoons sugar
1 teaspoon grated orange rind
2 tablespoons butter or
    margarine, melted
1 (3-ounce) package cream
    cheese, softened
½ cup firmly packed brown sugar
3 eggs
⅓ cup orange juice
1 teaspoon grated orange rind
½ teaspoon ground cardamom
1 cup cooked mashed pumpkin
Whipped cream (optional)
Vanilla wafers (optional)
Orange rind (optional)

Spread pecans in a single layer in a pieplate. Microwave at HIGH 2 minutes, stirring after 1 minute. Chop pecans; set aside.

Combine ¼ cup chopped pecans and next 4 ingredients, mixing well.

Divide mixture into 8 (6-ounce) greased custard cups or ramekins. Press crumb mixture evenly in bottom of custard cups. Microwave at HIGH 2 minutes; set aside.

Beat cream cheese at medium speed of an electric mixer until light and fluffy; gradually add brown sugar, mixing well. Add eggs and orange juice, mixing well. Add 1 teaspoon orange rind, cardamom, and pumpkin; mix until smooth. Pour into prepared custard cups.

Arrange custard cups in a circle in oven. Microwave, uncovered, at MEDIUM HIGH (70% power) 6 to 7 minutes or until pudding is set, rearranging cups halfway through cooking time. Garnish with remaining ¼ cup chopped pecans and, if desired, whipped cream, vanilla wafers, or orange rind. Serve warm or chilled. Yield: 8 servings.

BUTTERNUT SQUASH PUDDING

1 medium butternut squash
    (about 2½ pounds)
2 eggs, beaten
½ cup half-and-half
⅓ cup sugar
2 tablespoons butter or margarine
½ teaspoon ground cinnamon
⅛ teaspoon ground nutmeg
½ teaspoon grated lemon rind
2 teaspoons lemon juice
Sweetened whipped cream

Pierce squash 6 or 8 times with a fork. Place squash on paper towels in microwave oven. Microwave, uncovered, at HIGH 16 to 18 minutes, turning squash after 8 minutes. Let stand 5 minutes.

Cut squash in half, and remove seeds. Scoop out pulp, and set aside; discard shell.

Combine squash pulp, eggs, and next 7 ingredients in a mixing bowl; beat at medium speed of an electric mixer until smooth. Spoon squash mixture into an 8-inch square baking dish. Microwave, uncovered, at

HIGH 15 minutes; stir. Microwave at MEDIUM (50% power) 5 minutes. Let stand 5 minutes. Serve with sweetened whipped cream. Yield: 4 to 6 servings.

Just Open A Can Of Vegetables

At this time of year when there isn't much fresh produce, depend on canned vegetables for side dishes. Your choice of vegetables is virtually unlimited, and most recipes require little more than opening a can.

MOSAIC SALAD

1 (8.5-ounce) can tiny English
    peas, drained
1 cup chopped celery
1 cup grated carrot
1 envelope unflavored gelatin
¼ cup plus 1 tablespoon cold
    water
1 cup mayonnaise or salad
    dressing
1 teaspoon white vinegar
½ teaspoon grated onion
½ teaspoon salt
½ teaspoon prepared mustard
Lettuce leaves

Combine first 3 ingredients in a large bowl; set aside.

Sprinkle gelatin over cold water in a small saucepan; let stand 1 minute. Stir in mayonnaise and next 4 ingredients. Cook over low heat, stirring constantly, until gelatin dissolves and mixture is thoroughly heated (do not boil). Pour over vegetables; stir gently. Spoon into 6 lightly oiled individual molds; chill until firm.

Unmold onto lettuce-lined salad plates. Yield: 6 servings.

Nancy Roberts
Burleson, Texas

MARINATED BEAN SALAD

1 (16-ounce) can red kidney
  beans, rinsed and drained
1 (15-ounce) can garbanzo beans,
  drained
½ cup thinly sliced carrot
¼ cup chopped onion
3 tablespoons chopped sweet
  pickle
¼ cup vegetable oil
3 tablespoons white vinegar
1 tablespoon honey
½ teaspoon dry mustard
¼ teaspoon salt
¼ teaspoon pepper

Combine first 5 ingredients in a bowl.
Combine oil and remaining ingredients in a jar. Cover tightly, and
shake vigorously. Pour over vegetable mixture, stirring gently. Cover
and chill at least 8 hours, stirring
occasionally. Yield: 6 to 8 servings.
Mrs. E. Foreman
Lake Charles, Louisiana

SWEET-AND-SOUR BEETS

3 (16-ounce) cans sliced beets,
  undrained
½ cup sugar
2 tablespoons cornstarch
½ cup white vinegar
3 tablespoons catsup
1 teaspoon vanilla extract
6 whole cloves

Drain beets, reserving 1½ cups liquid; set beets aside.
  Combine 1½ cups beet liquid,
sugar, and remaining ingredients in a
large saucepan, stirring with a wire
whisk until cornstarch dissolves.
Cook over medium heat, stirring constantly, until mixture boils. Boil 1
minute. Remove cloves, and stir in
beets. Beets may be served warm or
chilled. Yield: 8 servings.
Ruth Welch
Paris, Texas

TANGY GREEN BEANS

4 slices bacon, cut into ½-inch
  pieces
½ cup chopped onion
2 (16-ounce) cans whole green
  beans, drained
¾ cup water
3 tablespoons white vinegar
½ teaspoon beef-flavored bouillon
  granules
¼ teaspoon pepper

Cook bacon in a large skillet until
lightly browned. Stir in onion, and
cook until tender. Add beans and remaining ingredients; cook until thoroughly heated. Yield: 6 servings.
Audrey Donahew
Elm Mott, Texas

Spruce Up Your Menu With Cabbage

Festive Potato Salad or one of these
cooked cabbage options may be just
what you need to jazz up a menu.
Smoked sausage, bacon, and fresh
tomatoes embellish Cabbage Supper.

CABBAGE SUPPER

1 pound smoked sausage, sliced
1 large onion, coarsely chopped
3 stalks celery, cut into 1-inch
  pieces
1 medium cabbage, coarsely
  chopped
3 large tomatoes, peeled and
  quartered
1 teaspoon Worcestershire sauce
¼ teaspoon seasoning blend
¼ teaspoon salt
⅛ teaspoon pepper
¼ teaspoon hot sauce
4 slices bacon, cooked and
  crumbled

Cook sausage, onion, and celery in a
large Dutch oven until sausage is
browned; drain. Add cabbage; cover
and cook over low heat 20 minutes.
Add tomatoes and next 5 ingredients,
tossing gently; cook 3 minutes.
Sprinkle with crumbled bacon. Yield:
4 to 6 servings. *Ann Sturdivant*
McComb, Mississippi

SWEET-AND-SOUR CABBAGE SOUP

1½ pounds beef stew meat
3 cups water
½ teaspoon salt
7 cups water
1 small cabbage, shredded (6
  cups)
3 stalks celery, cut into ½-inch
  pieces
1 (6-ounce) can tomato paste
¼ cup firmly packed light brown
  sugar
2 tablespoons lemon juice
¾ teaspoon lemon-pepper
  seasoning
1¼ to 1½ teaspoons salt

Combine stew meat, 3 cups water,
and ½ teaspoon salt in a Dutch oven;
bring to a boil. Cover, reduce heat,
and simmer 2 hours or until tender.
Remove meat from broth, and shred.
Return to broth. Add remaining ingredients; bring to a boil. Reduce
heat, and simmer, uncovered, 30
minutes. Yield: 3 quarts. *Sue Syers*
Louisville, Kentucky

SKILLET CABBAGE

⅔ cup chopped onion
1 clove garlic, minced
1½ teaspoons grated fresh ginger
2 tablespoons butter or
  margarine, melted
4 cups coarsely shredded cabbage
½ cup coarsely grated carrot
2 teaspoons soy sauce
¼ teaspoon freshly ground pepper
⅛ teaspoon paprika

Sauté onion, garlic, and ginger in butter in a large skillet 2 minutes. Add cabbage and carrot; stir-fry over medium heat about 5 minutes or until vegetables are crisp-tender. Stir in soy sauce, pepper, and paprika. Yield: 4 to 6 servings. *Carol Schulz Crossville, Tennessee*

APPLE COLESLAW

¼ cup sour cream
¼ cup mayonnaise or salad dressing
½ teaspoon celery seeds
1 teaspoon sugar
Dash of salt
1½ teaspoons lemon juice
2½ cups shredded cabbage
1 apple, unpeeled and sliced

Combine sour cream, mayonnaise, celery seeds, sugar, salt, and lemon juice in a small bowl; stir well.

Combine cabbage and apple in a large bowl, tossing lightly. Pour salad dressing over cabbage mixture; toss lightly to coat. Yield: 4 to 6 servings. *Janie Wallace Seguin, Texas*

FESTIVE POTATO SALAD

3 cups diced potatoes (about 3 large)
2 tablespoons vegetable oil
1 tablespoon white vinegar
1 teaspoon salt
1½ cups finely shredded cabbage
½ cup sliced ripe olives
½ cup coarsely grated carrot
¼ cup chopped dill pickle
2 tablespoons diced pimiento
2 tablespoons chopped green pepper
⅔ cup mayonnaise or salad dressing
2 teaspoons grated onion
1 teaspoon prepared mustard
⅛ teaspoon pepper

Cook potatoes in water to cover 10 minutes or until tender; drain. Combine potatoes, oil, vinegar, and salt in a large bowl; toss gently. Cover and refrigerate.

Add cabbage and next 5 ingredients to potato mixture; set aside.

Combine mayonnaise and last 3 ingredients; add to potato mixture, tossing gently. Yield: 6 to 8 servings. *Daisy Cook Tyler, Texas*

Waycross Burns For Chili

John and Linda Zechmann of Waycross, Georgia, have discovered that nothing heats a conversation or fuels a party quite like chili. And Linda's idea for a chili fest, complete with judging, ballots, and lots of guests, came from her brother, who hosts a party each year in Minnesota. Linda hated missing out on all the fun and decided to host her own chili party, Southern style.

You may want to plan a chili fest and invite your guests to enter into the fun, or simply borrow one of these recipes to create a sensational one-dish meal.

■ **Michelle and Mark Mooneyhan** built a set complete with a dancing pig to promote their winning Best Non-Chili Appetizer.

SAUSAGE PARTY RYES

1 pound ground beef
1 pound bulk pork sausage
1 (16-ounce) loaf process cheese spread, cut into small cubes
1 teaspoon dried whole oregano
2 (8-ounce) loaves party rye bread, toasted

Cook ground beef and sausage in a large skillet until meat is browned, stirring to crumble meat; drain. Stir in cheese and oregano. Cook until cheese melts; remove from heat.

Spread 1 tablespoon meat mixture on each bread slice. Place slices in a single layer on large baking sheets; freeze. When slices are frozen, place in plastic bags, and keep frozen until slices are needed.

To serve, thaw and place on baking sheets. Bake at 400° for 8 minutes. Yield: 5 dozen.

■ **Carol and Vince Richardson** were runners-up in the race for Best Wimpy Chili with their truly delicious Chili-i-Cious.

CHILI-I-CIOUS

1½ pounds ground beef
1½ pounds lean bulk pork sausage
2 large onions, chopped
1 green pepper, chopped
3 cloves garlic, crushed
3 (14-ounce) cans whole tomatoes, undrained and chopped
1 (18-ounce) can tomato paste
1 (14-ounce) can ready-to-serve beef broth
2 cups water
½ cup catsup
3 tablespoons chili con carne seasoning
1 tablespoon chili powder
1 tablespoon sugar (optional)
2 teaspoons ground cumin
¼ teaspoon red pepper
1 (14-ounce) can pinto beans, undrained

Combine beef and sausage in a large Dutch oven. Cook until browned, stirring to crumble; drain.

Add onion and remaining ingredients except beans; stir well. Cover and simmer over low heat 2½ hours, stirring frequently. Stir in pinto beans, and cook an additional 30 minutes. Yield: 3½ quarts.

■ **Patti White** won Most Serious Competitor award for her chili display with train, tracks, and song.

CHOO-CHOO CHILI

3 pounds ground beef
1 large onion, chopped
1 green pepper, chopped
2 (14.5-ounce) cans Italian-style stewed tomatoes, undrained
1 (15½-ounce) can chili beans, undrained
1 (15-ounce) can tomato sauce
2 (15-ounce) cans barbecued pork
1 (8-ounce) can tomato paste
1 (1¾-ounce) package chili seasoning mix
2 tablespoons chili powder
2 tablespoons hickory-flavored barbecue sauce
½ teaspoon garlic powder
¼ teaspoon onion powder

Combine first 3 ingredients in a Dutch oven. Cook until beef is brown; drain. Add tomatoes and remaining ingredients; stir well. Bring to a boil; cover, reduce heat, and simmer 1½ hours, stirring occasionally. Yield: 4 quarts.

■ **Cheryl and Moi Monroe, III** won Best Original Name with their spoof on the Florida Lottery.

HOTTO LOTTO CHILI

1½ pounds ground beef
½ pound lean bulk pork sausage
½ clove garlic, minced
1 (16-ounce) can whole tomatoes, undrained and sliced
1 (15.5-ounce) can red kidney beans, undrained
1 (15.5-ounce) can pinto beans, undrained
1 (6-ounce) can tomato juice
¼ cup dry red wine
2 tablespoons chili powder
1 teaspoon sugar
¾ teaspoon salt
1 bay leaf
Chopped onion
Shredded Cheddar cheese

Combine first 3 ingredients in a Dutch oven. Cook until beef and sausage are browned, stirring to crumble; drain. Add tomatoes and remaining ingredients except onion and cheese; bring to a boil. Cover, reduce heat, and simmer 1 hour, stirring occasionally. Remove and discard bay leaf. Ladle chili into serving bowls; top with onion and cheese. Yield: about 2 quarts.

■ **Laura and Mike Miller** won Best Peppy Chili, the category for chilis that tingle the taste buds.

LOLLY'S POP CHILI

5 pounds link sausage
1 pound lean ground beef
1 large onion, chopped
1 large green pepper, chopped
2 (28-ounce) cans tomatoes, undrained and chopped
1 (30-ounce) can hot chili beans
1 (4-ounce) can sliced mushrooms, undrained
1 (11-ounce) can Cheddar cheese soup, undiluted
1 (6-ounce) can tomato paste
1 (8-ounce) can tomato sauce
2 cups tomato juice
⅔ cup sliced canned jalapeño peppers
1 teaspoon garlic powder
½ teaspoon pepper
2 to 4 tablespoons hot sauce
3 cups (12 ounces) shredded Cheddar cheese

Cook sausage in a large heavy skillet until browned, turning often; drain on paper towels. Cut sausage into ½-inch slices; set aside.

Cook ground beef, onion, and green pepper until meat is browned, stirring to crumble meat; drain.

Combine sausage, beef mixture, and remaining ingredients except cheese in a large Dutch oven. Bring to a boil; reduce heat, and simmer, uncovered, 1½ to 2 hours, stirring occasionally. Top each serving with shredded cheese. Yield: 6 quarts.

■ **Roy McDonald** used a variety of hot peppers, both pickled and fresh, to win the Hottest Chili title.

ROY'S BEFORE-AND-AFTER BURNER

1 (16-ounce) package dried pinto beans
6 cups water
1½ teaspoons chili powder, divided
5 to 10 hot pickled chiles, chopped
⅓ cup chopped green pepper
6 fresh jalapeño peppers, seeded and chopped
2 pounds ground beef
1 medium onion, chopped
1 (18-ounce) can tomato paste
1 (16-ounce) can pork and beans, undrained
1 (15.5-ounce) can red kidney beans, undrained
1 (14½-ounce) can stewed tomatoes, undrained
1 cup water
1 (1¾-ounce) package chili seasoning mix
⅛ teaspoon salt
⅛ teaspoon pepper

Chili Tips

■ Cook dried beans over very low heat since a rolling boil may cause them to break or burst.

■ Store spices in a cool place and away from any direct source of heat, as the heat will destroy their flavor. Red spices will maintain flavor and retain color longer if refrigerated.

■ When buying garlic, select firm, plump bulbs that have dry, unbroken skins. Store in a cool, dry place that is well ventilated. The flavor will remain sharp up to four months.

Sort and wash dried beans; place in a Dutch oven. Cover with water 2 inches above beans; allow beans to soak 8 hours.

Drain beans. Add 6 cups water, 1 teaspoon chili powder, and pickled chiles to beans. Bring to a boil; cover, reduce heat, and simmer 2 hours. Add green pepper, jalapeños, and remaining ½ teaspoon chili powder; cover and simmer 3 hours. Let bean mixture chill 8 hours.

Cook ground beef and onion until meat is browned, stirring to crumble meat; drain. Add beef-onion mixture to bean mixture. Add tomato paste and remaining ingredients to bean mixture. Bring to a boil; cover, reduce heat, and simmer 1½ to 2 hours. Yield: 5 quarts.

■ **Betsy Lindsay** won the coveted Best Wimpy Chili award with one that is gentle to the palate. Her recipe features the tender meat from short ribs, along with ground beef.

CAMPECHE BAY RIB-TICKLING STEW

5 pounds lean short ribs
4 quarts water
1½ teaspoons salt
2 cups dried pinto beans
1½ pounds ground beef
1 medium onion, chopped
1 (28-ounce) can tomato sauce
1 tablespoon ground cumin
1 tablespoon paprika
2 teaspoons chili powder
1 teaspoon garlic powder
1 teaspoon cornmeal
½ teaspoon dried whole oregano
½ teaspoon ground red pepper

Place ribs, water, and salt in a large Dutch oven. Bring to a boil; cover, reduce heat, and simmer 1 hour or until meat is tender. Remove ribs from broth, reserving broth. Cool ribs. Remove meat from bone; chop meat, and store in refrigerator. Refrigerate broth 8 hours; remove fat.

Sort and wash beans; place in a large Dutch oven. Cover with water 2 inches above beans; soak 8 hours. Drain well.

Combine beans and broth; bring to a boil. Cover, reduce heat, and simmer 1½ hours or until beans are tender.

Cook ground beef until browned, stirring to crumble; drain. Add browned meat and remaining ingredients to beans; bring to a boil. Cover, reduce heat, and simmer 1½ hours. Yield: about 3 quarts.

A Piece Of The Past

About this time each year as the trees come ablaze with their amber and scarlet jewels, Brigitta Tinsley's thoughts turn to autumn in her native Germany. It is then that she celebrates her heritage by baking Covered Apple Cake, a family favorite from her homeland. For Brigitta, this old-world touch to her Girardeau, Missouri, residence puts the "sweet" in home, sweet home. It's a sweet your family will enjoy, too.

COVERED APPLE CAKE

Almond Pastry
3 tablespoons butter or
   margarine, melted
6 or 7 cooking apples, peeled and
   sliced
¼ cup sugar
3 tablespoons dry white wine
½ cup chopped walnuts
½ cup golden raisins
2 teaspoons quick-cooking tapioca
Whipped cream (optional)

Press two-thirds of Almond Pastry into bottom and 2 inches up sides of a 9-inch springform pan.

Combine butter and next 3 ingredients in a Dutch oven. Cook over medium heat until apples are tender, stirring occasionally. Stir in walnuts, raisins, and tapioca. Spoon mixture evenly into prepared pastry shell.

Roll remaining pastry to ⅛-inch thickness; transfer to top of pie. Trim excess pastry along edges; seal and flute. Use extra pastry to shape decorative apple cutouts. Cut slits in top crust for steam to escape.

Bake at 350° for 40 to 45 minutes or until cake is golden brown. Serve with whipped cream, if desired. Yield: 10 to 12 servings.

Almond Pastry

1 (3½-ounce) package soft almond
   paste
3 cups all-purpose flour
1 teaspoon baking powder
1 teaspoon ground cinnamon
½ cup sugar
1 cup butter or margarine,
   softened
1 egg, beaten
1 tablespoon lemon juice
Dash of rum flavoring

Combine first 5 ingredients in a large mixing bowl; cut in butter with a pastry blender until mixture resembles coarse meal. Add egg, lemon juice, and rum flavoring; stir with a fork until dry ingredients are moistened. Shape dough into a ball; chill. Yield: pastry for one double-crust 9-inch pie.
                    Brigitta Tinsley
                    Cape Girardeau, Missouri

Tip: *Always measure ingredients accurately. Level dry ingredients in a cup with a knife edge or a spoon handle. Measure liquids in a cup so that the fluid is level with the top of the measuring line. Measure solid shortening by packing it firmly in a graduated measuring cup.*

Passion For Pralines

Full of nuts and caramel flavor, pralines are typically eaten out of hand. But save a few of the crunchy rounds from your next batch to flavor desserts and pastries. It's a clever way to carry the rich flavor of pralines one step further.

Pralines are not difficult to make, but they do require precision in technique. There are two key variables in preparation: when to remove the candy mixture from the heat and when to stop beating the candy and start spooning it onto wax paper.

Using a candy thermometer takes the guesswork out of the first variable; cook the mixture to 234°. Knowing when to stop beating the mixture and start spooning, however, may take a little practice.

Beat the mixture just until the syrup begins to thicken. If you stop beating and start spooning too soon, the candy will spread too thinly and will not hold its round shape. If this happens, just beat the mixture a little longer, and try again. Take care not to beat too much, however, as the candy will harden.

Once you determine the ideal point for spooning, do so quickly because the mixture hardens fast. Often the last few pralines that you spoon will be thicker and less perfectly shaped than the first.

OLD-FASHIONED PRALINES
(pictured on page 263)

1 cup sugar
1 cup firmly packed brown sugar
2 cups coarsely chopped pecans
¾ cup buttermilk
2 tablespoons butter or margarine
Dash of salt
½ teaspoon baking soda
1 tablespoon vanilla extract

Combine first 6 ingredients in a large, heavy saucepan. Cook over low heat, stirring gently, until sugar dissolves. Cover and cook over medium heat 2 to 3 minutes to wash down sugar crystals from sides of pan. Uncover and cook to soft ball stage (234°), stirring constantly. Remove from heat, and stir in soda and vanilla. Beat with a wooden spoon just until mixture begins to thicken. Working rapidly, drop by tablespoonfuls onto greased wax paper; let stand until candy is firm. Yield: 1½ to 2 dozen.

Microwave Directions: Combine first 6 ingredients in a 4-quart casserole, stirring well. Microwave at HIGH 12 to 13 minutes, stirring every 4 minutes. Stir in soda. Microwave at HIGH 1 to 1½ minutes. Stir in vanilla. Beat with a wooden spoon just until mixture begins to thicken. Working rapidly, drop by tablespoonfuls onto greased wax paper; let stand until firm.

PRALINE PASTRIES
(pictured on page 263)

½ (17¼-ounce) package frozen puff pastry
1 egg, separated
⅓ cup ground pralines
1 teaspoon water
¾ cup sifted powdered sugar
1 tablespoon milk

Defrost pastry according to package directions. Place on a lightly floured surface; roll out to a 12-inch square. Cut pastry into 3-inch squares.

Combine egg yolk and ground pralines. Spoon about ½ teaspoon mixture in a strip down center of each square. Combine egg white and water; brush one side of each square with egg white mixture. Fold over opposite side, and press gently to seal. Make even ¾-inch cuts into pastry along sealed edge, about ¼ inch apart; spread to form a comb. Place pastries on a lightly greased baking sheet. Brush remaining egg white mixture over pastries. Freeze 10 minutes. Bake at 425° for 12 to 15 minutes or until puffed and golden brown. Transfer to a wire rack.

Combine powdered sugar and milk; drizzle mixture over hot pastries. Yield: 16 servings.

PRALINE ICE CREAM
(pictured on page 263)

2¼ cups sugar
⅓ cup all-purpose flour
½ teaspoon salt
3 eggs, beaten
5 cups milk
1 quart whipping cream
1½ tablespoons vanilla extract
3½ cups coarsely chopped pralines

Combine sugar, flour, and salt in a Dutch oven. Add eggs, and stir until smooth. Stir in milk, and cook over medium heat until thermometer reaches 165°, stirring constantly. Remove from heat, and let cool slightly; chill 2 hours.

Combine whipping cream and vanilla in a large bowl; add chilled custard, stirring with a wire whisk. Pour mixture into freezer can of a 1-gallon hand-turned or electric freezer. Freeze according to manufacturer's instructions.

Remove paddle; fold in pralines, and let ripen 1 hour before serving. Yield: 1 gallon.

DECEMBER

As you give your home a holiday glow, plan meals to fit the season. To spark your imagination, this chapter presents recipes, menus, and ideas for impressive Christmas entertaining. Our special company menu is a three-course dinner spotlighting Roquefort Chicken and Pepper Pasta. If you're looking for a traditional entrée, try the golden roast turkey pictured on the cover. Round out your meals with festive side dishes and top them off with scrumptious desserts, all served up with the colors of Christmas.

A Dinner Menu For Company

Why not have friends over for dinner during the holidays? Our menu offers several options to suit your schedule and your tastes.

If you think serving several courses is too fussy and formal, then try serving the entrée and side dishes buffet style. To streamline the menu, just serve salad, chicken, pasta, and dessert.

Only the appetizer and dessert demand advance and lengthy preparation. The chicken and side dishes can be made and served immediately; they don't require marinating or standing time. For an easier appetizer, substitute one of the ideas in our "Quick!" story on page 327. And serve the raspberry sauce over commercial ice cream or sherbet.

Shrimp Soufflé Roll
Roquefort Chicken
Pepper Pasta   Herb Green Beans
Crunchy Green Salad
Creamy Bombe
With Raspberry Sauce

SHRIMP SOUFFLÉ ROLL
(pictured on page 300)

¼ cup plus 2 tablespoons
  all-purpose flour
1½ cups milk
3 egg yolks
¾ teaspoon salt
⅛ teaspoon white pepper
⅛ teaspoon ground nutmeg
4 egg whites
Shrimp Filling
Boiled shrimp (optional)
Fresh parsley sprigs (optional)

Grease bottom and sides of a 15- x 10- x 1-inch jellyroll pan with vegetable oil. Line pan with wax paper, allowing paper to extend beyond ends of pan; grease and flour wax paper. Set aside.

Combine flour and ½ cup milk in a small saucepan. Stir in remaining milk, and cook over medium heat, stirring constantly, until thickened. Beat egg yolks in a small mixing bowl at high speed of an electric mixer until thick and lemon colored. Gradually stir about one-fourth of hot mixture into yolks; add to remaining hot mixture, stirring constantly. Stir in seasonings; transfer to large bowl, and cool.

Beat egg whites (at room temperature) until stiff, but not dry; fold into sauce mixture. Spread evenly in prepared pan; bake at 375° for 20 to 25 minutes or until lightly browned.

Remove from oven; loosen edges of soufflé with a metal spatula. Immediately cover pan with a dampened cotton towel, and invert pan and towel together, turning soufflé out onto towel. Carefully peel off wax paper. Cover with a clean piece of wax paper, and starting at long side, roll up soufflé, wax paper, and towel together. Cool completely on a wire rack; chill 3 to 4 hours.

Carefully unroll soufflé; spread with Shrimp Filling. Roll up tightly without wax paper or towel; wrap in plastic wrap. Chill 3 hours or until thoroughly chilled. Remove plastic wrap; using an electric knife, cut into ½-inch slices. Yield: 9 appetizer servings (3 slices each).

Shrimp Filling

1½ cups water
½ pound unpeeled medium-size
  fresh shrimp
2 (3-ounce) packages cream
  cheese, softened
2 tablespoons sour cream
1 teaspoon prepared horseradish
2 or 3 drops hot sauce
Dash of garlic powder
Dash of salt
2 tablespoons chopped green
  onions

Bring water to a boil; add shrimp, and cook 3 to 5 minutes. Drain well; rinse with cold water. Peel, devein, and chop shrimp; set aside.

Combine cream cheese and remaining ingredients except green onions. Beat at medium speed of an electric mixer until smooth; stir in chopped shrimp and green onions. Yield: 1½ cups.   *Janet Marett*
Birmingham, Alabama

ROQUEFORT CHICKEN
(pictured on pages 298 and 299)

1 cup fresh sourdough
  breadcrumbs
1 (1½-ounce) can grated
  Parmesan cheese
¼ teaspoon salt
¼ teaspoon freshly ground pepper
1¼ teaspoons dried whole thyme
3 tablespoons butter or
  margarine, melted
3 tablespoons olive oil
¼ cup milk
1 tablespoon white wine
  Worcestershire sauce
8 chicken breast halves, skinned
  and boned
Roquefort Sauce
Crumbled Roquefort cheese
  (optional)
Fresh thyme (optional)

Combine first 5 ingredients in a pie-plate. Combine butter, oil, milk, and Worcestershire sauce. Dip each chicken breast in milk mixture, and dredge in crumb mixture. Arrange chicken in a lightly greased 15- x 10- x 1-inch jellyroll pan. (If desired, cover and chill for 1 day. Let stand at room temperature 30 minutes before baking.) Bake at 350° for 30 to 35 minutes or until tender. Serve with Roquefort Sauce drizzled over chicken. If desired, garnish with crumbled cheese and fresh thyme. Yield: 8 servings.

Roquefort Sauce

1 shallot, chopped
1 stalk celery with leaves, chopped
2 tablespoons butter or margarine, melted
½ cup white wine
1 (10¾-ounce) can condensed chicken broth, undiluted
1 cup whipping cream
2 tablespoons crumbled Roquefort or blue cheese
1 tablespoon chopped fresh chives

Sauté shallot and celery in butter in a medium saucepan until tender. Add wine and chicken broth. Bring to a boil, and cook over medium heat, stirring frequently, until liquid is reduced to about 1 cup (about 15 minutes). Strain. Return broth mixture to saucepan. Add whipping cream, and return to a boil; reduce heat, and simmer about 15 minutes or until mixture is reduced to about 1 cup, stirring frequently. (If desired, cover and chill for 1 day. Reheat and proceed as directed.) Remove from heat; add cheese, and stir until cheese melts. Stir in chopped chives. Yield: 1 cup.

Tip: *When cooking for a crowd, plan your menu so that you can utilize several cooking appliances rather than just your oven. Don't forget to use the stove top, microwave, electric skillet, and toaster oven.*

PEPPER PASTA
(pictured on pages 298 and 299)

¼ cup butter or margarine, melted
3 tablespoons olive oil
4 cloves garlic, minced
1 teaspoon grated lemon rind
½ teaspoon crushed red pepper
1 (14½-ounce) can ready-to-serve chicken broth
3 tablespoons lemon juice
½ teaspoon salt
½ teaspoon freshly ground pepper
16 ounces uncooked fettuccine
2 sweet red peppers, cut into strips

Heat butter and oil in a medium saucepan; add garlic, lemon rind, and crushed red pepper, and cook over low heat 2 minutes, stirring occasionally. Add chicken broth and lemon juice, and simmer over medium heat until reduced to about 1¼ cups (about 25 minutes). Add salt and pepper.

Cook fettuccine in a large Dutch oven according to package directions; drain. Return fettuccine to Dutch oven; add red pepper strips and broth mixture. Cook over low heat 1 minute or until thoroughly heated, tossing gently. Serve immediately or, if desired, spoon into a lightly greased 13- x 9- x 2-inch baking dish; cover and chill. Remove from refrigerator, and let stand at room temperature 1 hour. Bake, covered, at 350° for 30 minutes. Yield: 8 servings.
Marilyn Darby
Tunica, Mississippi

HERB GREEN BEANS
(pictured on pages 298 and 299)

2 pounds fresh green beans
1 small onion, sliced
1 clove garlic, minced
1 tablespoon olive oil
¾ cup water
½ teaspoon sugar
½ teaspoon salt
½ teaspoon pepper
¼ teaspoon dried whole tarragon

Wash beans, and remove strings. Leave beans whole or cut in half, if desired.

Sauté onion and garlic in oil in a Dutch oven. Add beans, water, and remaining ingredients. Bring to a boil; cover, reduce heat, and simmer 20 minutes or until tender. Add additional water, if necessary. Yield: 8 servings.

Note: Beans may be cooked a day ahead and reheated.

CRUNCHY GREEN SALAD
(pictured on page 298)

1 cauliflower
⅓ cup vegetable oil
⅓ cup olive oil
¼ cup orange juice
¼ cup white wine vinegar
2 teaspoons grated orange rind
2 teaspoons sugar
1 teaspoon salt
1 teaspoon dry mustard
1 teaspoon dried whole basil
½ teaspoon freshly ground pepper
2 heads Bibb lettuce
2 carrots, grated
⅓ cup sliced green onions

Break cauliflower into flowerets; slice flowerets.

Combine vegetable oil and next 9 ingredients in a jar; cover tightly, and shake vigorously. Pour mixture over sliced cauliflower; cover and chill at least 1 hour.

Arrange lettuce leaves on 8 salad plates. Remove cauliflower from dressing with a slotted spoon, and place on lettuce. Sprinkle carrots and green onions on lettuce; spoon dressing over each serving. Yield: 8 servings.
Pam Lee
Birmingham, Alabama

CREAMY BOMBE
WITH RASPBERRY SAUCE
(pictured on page 300)

1 (16-ounce) package frozen
    unsweetened sliced peaches,
    thawed and drained
1 (8-ounce) carton sour cream
½ cup grenadine
½ gallon vanilla ice cream,
    softened
Vegetable cooking spray
Raspberry Sauce
Fresh raspberries (optional)
Fresh mint sprigs (optional)

Position knife blade in food processor
bowl; add peaches. Top with cover;
process until smooth. Add sour
cream and grenadine; process until
well blended.

Combine peach mixture and ice
cream in a large mixing bowl; beat at
low speed of an electric mixer until
well blended. Pour mixture into an
11-cup mold that has been coated
with cooking spray; cover and freeze
8 hours or until mixture is firm.

Two hours before serving, using
tip of a knife, loosen edges of ice
cream from mold. Invert mold onto a
chilled serving plate. Wrap a warm
towel around mold for 30 seconds.
Remove towel, and firmly hold plate
and mold together. Shake gently, and
slowly lift off mold. Immediately return bombe to freezer.

If desired, garnish with raspberries
and mint. To serve, cut bombe into
slices, and top with Raspberry
Sauce. Yield: 12 servings.

Raspberry Sauce

1 (16-ounce) package frozen
    unsweetened raspberries,
    thawed and undrained
¾ cup light corn syrup
¼ cup Grand Marnier

Position knife blade in food processor
bowl; add raspberries. Top with
cover; process 1 minute or until
raspberries are pureed.

Strain raspberries, and discard
seeds. Stir in syrup and Grand Marnier. Yield: 2 cups. *Anita Cochran*
Nashville, Tennessee

Fancy Turkey Roll

For those who prefer boneless turkey, here's an entrée that may highlight your menu. It's stuffed with a
savory filling of spinach, sweet red
pepper, and spices.

And when it comes time to serve
this elegant entrée, garnish it with
kale and red pepper strips or slices.
Then place a single green onion on
top of your fancy turkey roll.

STUFFED TURKEY BREAST
(pictured on page 297)

1 (5-pound) turkey breast, boned
    and skinned
1½ cups chopped sweet red
    pepper
1 cup chopped purple onion
1 (8-ounce) can water chestnuts,
    drained and chopped
1 tablespoon olive oil
½ teaspoon poultry seasoning
½ teaspoon dried whole savory
½ teaspoon salt
½ teaspoon pepper
1 (10-ounce) package frozen
    chopped spinach, thawed and
    drained
½ cup dry white wine
Vegetable cooking spray
¼ cup olive oil
¼ cup dry white wine
Kale (optional)
Sweet red pepper strips (optional)
Green onion (optional)
White Wine Gravy

Trim fat from turkey; remove ten-
dons. Place outer side of turkey
breast on heavy-duty plastic wrap.
Starting from the center, slice horizontally through thickest part of each
side of the breast almost to, but not
through, the outer edges. Flip cut
pieces over to enlarge breast. Place
heavy-duty plastic wrap on turkey;
pound to a more even thickness,
using a meat mallet (place loose
pieces of turkey over thinner portions). Set aside.

Sauté red pepper, purple onion,
and water chestnuts in 1 tablespoon
olive oil until tender; add poultry seasoning and next 5 ingredients. Cook,
stirring constantly, 2 minutes or until
liquid is evaporated.

Spread spinach mixture in center
of turkey breast within 2 inches of
sides; roll up turkey breast, jellyroll
fashion, starting with short side, to
an 11- x 6-inch roll. Secure at 1½-
inch intervals, using heavy string.
Place seam side down on rack in
shallow pan coated with vegetable
cooking spray.

Combine ¼ cup olive oil and ¼
cup white wine; stir well. Brush over
turkey roll. Bake, uncovered, at 325°
for 2 hours, basting often. Let stand
15 minutes.

Transfer turkey to a platter. Remove strings; if desired, garnish with
kale, red pepper strips, and green
onions. Serve with White Wine
Gravy. Yield: 10 to 12 servings.

White Wine Gravy

½ cup dry white wine
1 to 1½ cups chicken broth
½ teaspoon salt
½ teaspoon pepper
2 tablespoons cornstarch
¼ cup water

Spoon drippings from roasting pan
into a 2-cup measure. Add ½ cup
wine and enough chicken broth to
make 2 cups. Combine broth mixture, salt, and pepper in a small
saucepan.

Combine cornstarch and ¼ cup
water in a small bowl; add to mixture. Bring to a boil over medium
heat, and boil 1 minute, stirring constantly. Yield: 2 cups.

Note: If you've never boned a turkey breast before, you may want the
butcher to do it for you.

Holiday Entrées

For many Southerners, the holidays are not complete until the family says grace and the turkey is carved. Familiar menus of turkey and ham flanked by an array of side dishes also require a perfect dressing—not too moist and not too dry.

ROAST WILD DUCK WITH ORANGE GRAVY

¼ cup butter or margarine, divided
2 (1½- to 2-pound) wild ducks, dressed
¼ teaspoon salt
¼ teaspoon pepper
4 slices bacon
1 tablespoon all-purpose flour
Orange Gravy

Place 1 tablespoon butter in cavity of each duck; sprinkle each cavity with ⅛ teaspoon salt and pepper. Place ducks, breast side up, in a 13- x 9- x 2-inch pan. Melt remaining 2 tablespoons butter, and brush over ducks. Place 2 strips bacon over each duck. Bake at 400° for 30 to 35 minutes, basting frequently with drippings. Remove bacon, and sprinkle ducks with flour; baste well. Bake an additional 5 minutes. Transfer ducks to serving platter; serve with Orange Gravy. Yield: 4 servings.

Orange Gravy

1 small onion, sliced
1 tablespoon butter or margarine, melted
1 cup chicken broth
4 (2- x ¼-inch) orange rind strips
¼ cup white wine
2 tablespoons orange juice
⅛ teaspoon pepper
⅛ teaspoon red pepper
2 teaspoons cornstarch
1 tablespoon water

Sauté onion in butter in a small saucepan until tender; add broth and orange rind. Bring to a boil; reduce heat, and simmer 10 minutes. Strain broth mixture, discarding onion and rind. Combine broth mixture, wine, orange juice, pepper, and red pepper, mixing well.

Combine cornstarch and water, mixing well; stir into broth mixture. Cook over medium heat, stirring constantly. Bring to a boil, and boil 1 minute. Yield: ¾ cup.

Rublelene Singleton
Scotts Hill, Tennessee

SMOKY TURKEY BREAST

1 (5- to 6-pound) turkey breast
1 teaspoon seasoned salt
1 teaspoon crushed red pepper
1 tablespoon seasoned salt
1½ teaspoons dried whole basil
1 teaspoon paprika
Vegetable cooking spray

Rinse turkey breast with cold water; pat dry. Slit breast through center so it will be flat on grill. Combine 1 teaspoon seasoned salt and red pepper; sprinkle inside turkey breast.

Combine 1 tablespoon seasoned salt, basil, and paprika; sprinkle on outside of turkey breast. Spray turkey with cooking spray.

Prepare charcoal fire in one end of grill; let burn 15 to 20 minutes. Spread coals to one side of grill. Soak hickory chips in water 15 minutes; place hickory chips on coals. Insert meat thermometer into breast, making sure it does not touch bone. Place turkey breast on grill opposite hot coals, and cook 2½ to 3 hours or until meat thermometer reaches 170°. Yield: 12 servings.

Note: To smoke turkey, prepare charcoal fire in meat smoker; let burn 15 to 20 minutes. Soak hickory chips in water 15 minutes; place hickory chips on coals. Place water pan in smoker; add hot water until liquid reaches fill line on pan. Place turkey on rack. Cover with smoker lid; cook 4 to 5 hours or until meat thermometer reaches 170° when inserted into the thickest part of the turkey breast. If necessary, refill water pan, and add more charcoal as needed during cooking time.

James Toney
Columbus, Georgia

A Quick Primer On Meats

What is the major difference between a rolled pork loin roast and a boneless pork loin roast?

The two cuts of meat are actually the same—only packaged differently. A boneless roast is usually one slim (or thin) pork loin offered by itself. A rolled roast, however, is two pieces of loin packaged together. The butcher may tie them with string or netting. Both can be cooked as a whole unit or stuffed. They may also be halved, pounded, spread with a stuffing, and rolled up.

Is there a difference in cooking methods for a frozen turkey and a fresh turkey?

The cooking method and time for frozen and fresh turkeys are basically the same. Both are cooked to an internal temperature of 185°. A frozen turkey must be thawed in the refrigerator before cooking. A 9- to 12-pound turkey takes 1½ to 2 days to thaw; a 12- to 20-pound turkey takes 2 to 3 days.

Why is it so important to use a meat thermometer?

The shape and fat content of meat makes a difference in cooking time; thus, it's essential to check the temperature at the early end of the range listed and keep on checking until correct internal temperature is reached.

ROAST TURKEY AND CORNBREAD DRESSING
(pictured on cover)

2 cups finely chopped celery
1 small onion, finely chopped
½ cup butter or margarine, melted
5 cups crumbled cornbread
2 cups herb-seasoned stuffing mix
2 teaspoons rubbed sage
3 eggs, beaten
1 (14½-ounce) can ready-to-serve chicken broth
1 (12- to 14-pound) turkey
Vegetable oil
Orange slices (optional)
Celery leaves (optional)
Fresh sage (optional)

Sauté celery and onion in butter until tender. Combine next 3 ingredients. Add celery mixture, eggs, and broth; stir until cornbread is moist.

Remove giblets and neck from turkey; reserve for other uses. Rinse turkey thoroughly inside and out with cold water; pat dry. Lightly pack dressing into body cavities of turkey. Tuck legs under flap of skin around tail, or close cavity with skewers, and truss. Tie ends of legs to tail with cord. Lift wingtips up and over back, and tuck under turkey.

Place turkey on a roasting rack, breast side up; brush entire bird with oil. Insert meat thermometer in meaty part of thigh, making sure it does not touch bone. Bake at 325° for 4 to 4½ hours or until meat thermometer registers 185°. If turkey starts to brown too much, cover with aluminum foil. When two-thirds done, cut cord or band of skin holding drumstick ends to tail to ensure that thighs are cooked internally. Turkey is done when drumsticks are easy to move up and down. Let stand 15 minutes. If desired, garnish with orange slices, celery leaves, and sage. Yield: 20 to 24 servings.

Note: Dressing may be baked in a 13- x 9- x 2-inch dish at 350° for 20 to 30 minutes. Cook unstuffed turkeys 5 minutes less per pound than stuffed.   *Faith Lehman*
Rocky Mount, North Carolina

ORANGE-GLAZED HAM

1 (7- to 8-pound) smoked fully cooked ham half
1 cup orange juice
1 cup ginger ale
½ cup firmly packed brown sugar
2 tablespoons vegetable oil
1 tablespoon white vinegar
2 teaspoons dry mustard
½ teaspoon ground ginger
¼ teaspoon ground cloves

Trim skin away from ham, leaving no more than a ¼-inch border of fat. Place ham in a large roasting bag. Combine remaining ingredients, and pour over ham. Tie bag tightly. Place in a large bowl, and refrigerate 8 hours, turning occasionally.

Remove ham from marinade, reserving marinade. Place ham on a rack in a shallow roasting pan; insert meat thermometer, making sure it does not touch fat or bone. Bake at 325° for 2 to 2½ hours or until meat thermometer registers 140° (18 to 24 minutes per pound), basting with reserved marinade every 20 minutes. Yield: 14 servings.   *Judy Grimes*
Brandon, Mississippi

ROAST PORK WITH SPICED CHERRY SAUCE
(pictured on page 301)

1 (3- to 4-pound) rolled boneless pork loin roast
1 teaspoon salt
1 teaspoon pepper
1 teaspoon rubbed sage
1 (16-ounce) can pitted sour red cherries
12 whole cloves
1 (3-inch) stick cinnamon
1½ cups sugar
¼ cup white vinegar
¼ cup cornstarch
1 tablespoon lemon juice
1 tablespoon butter or margarine, melted
3 or 4 drops red food coloring
Purple and green kale (optional)
Lemon wedges and rind (optional)

Sprinkle roast with seasonings. Place roast, fat side up, on rack in a shallow roasting pan. Insert meat thermometer into thickest part of meat. Bake at 325° for 1½ to 2 hours or until meat thermometer registers 160° (30 to 35 minutes per pound).

Drain cherries; reserve liquid, and add water to make ¾ cup, if necessary. Tie cloves and cinnamon in a cheesecloth bag. Combine ½ cup cherry liquid, sugar, vinegar, and spice bag in a saucepan. Bring to a boil; reduce heat, and simmer, uncovered, 10 minutes. Remove spice bag. Combine cornstarch and remaining ¼ cup cherry liquid; stir into hot liquid. Cook over medium heat, stirring constantly, 1 minute or until thickened and bubbly. Stir in cherries, lemon juice, butter, and red coloring.

Place roast on a platter; if desired, garnish with kale and lemon wedges and rind. Serve with sauce. Yield: 6 to 8 servings.   *Alice McRae*
Huntsville, Alabama

ON THE LIGHT SIDE

Light Chocolate Desserts

Chocolate, the essence of indulgence, doesn't have to be banned from healthy eating. Using unsweetened cocoa instead of chocolate products made with cocoa butter, you can trim saturated fat and calories without sacrificing flavor.

Limiting saturated fats in the diet is as important as limiting cholesterol. In fact, saturated fat can increase cholesterol in the body.

The latest research on one of the saturated fats found in chocolate, stearic acid, indicates that it doesn't seem to boost cholesterol levels the way other saturated fats do. But chocolate contains other saturated fats that may cancel out the positive effects of stearic acid.

In addition to being low in saturated fat, unsweetened cocoa also has fewer calories than other forms of chocolate. And it blends readily with other ingredients.

FRUIT-FILLED CHOCOLATE CRÊPES
(pictured on page 304)

½ cup all-purpose flour
1 tablespoon sugar
1 tablespoon unsweetened cocoa
½ cup evaporated skimmed milk
¼ cup egg substitute
1 tablespoon reduced-calorie margarine, melted
Vegetable cooking spray
¾ cup sliced strawberries
2 medium kiwifruit, sliced
Chocolate Glaze
2 tablespoons sliced almonds, toasted

Combine first 6 ingredients in container of an electric blender; process until smooth. Let stand in refrigerator 2 hours. (This allows flour particles to swell and soften so that the crêpes are light in texture.)

Coat bottom of a 6-inch crêpe pan or heavy skillet with cooking spray; place over medium heat until just hot, not smoking. Pour 2 tablespoons batter into pan; quickly tilt pan in all directions so that batter covers pan in a thin film. Cook 1 minute or until lightly browned.

Lift edge of crêpe to test for doneness. Crêpe is ready for flipping when it can be shaken loose from pan. Flip crêpe, and cook about 30 seconds on other side. (This side is usually spotty brown and is the side on which the filling is placed.)

Place crêpes on a towel to cool. Stack between layers of wax paper to prevent sticking. Repeat until all batter is used.

Arrange sliced strawberries and kiwifruit in chocolate crêpe. Place on a serving dish, and drizzle each filled crêpe with 1 tablespoon Chocolate Glaze. Sprinkle each crêpe with toasted almonds. Yield: 8 servings (166 calories per crêpe with 1 tablespoon Chocolate Glaze).

□ *3.7 grams protein, 4.3 grams fat, 29.1 grams carbohydrate, 1 milligram cholesterol, 72 milligrams sodium, and 67 milligrams calcium.*

Chocolate Glaze

2 tablespoons reduced-calorie margarine
2 tablespoons unsweetened cocoa
2 tablespoons water
½ teaspoon vanilla extract
1 cup sifted powdered sugar

Melt margarine in a small saucepan. Add cocoa and water; stir until smooth. Cook over low heat until mixture begins to thicken (do not boil.) Remove from heat; add vanilla and powdered sugar, and stir until mixture is smooth. Yield: ½ cup (77 calories per 1 tablespoon).

□ *0.1 gram protein, 2 grams fat, 154 grams carbohydrate, 0 milligrams cholesterol, 28 milligrams sodium, and 4 milligrams calcium.*

CHOCOLATE POUND CAKE
(pictured on page 302)

Vegetable cooking spray
1¾ cups sifted cake flour
2 teaspoons baking powder
¼ teaspoon salt
3 tablespoons unsweetened cocoa
¼ teaspoon ground cinnamon
¾ cup sugar
½ cup vegetable oil
½ cup evaporated skimmed milk
1 tablespoon vanilla extract
4 egg whites, stiffly beaten

Coat the bottom of an 8½- x 4½- x 3-inch loafpan with cooking spray; dust with flour, and set aside.

Combine flour and next 5 ingredients in a large bowl. Add oil, milk, and vanilla; beat at medium speed of an electric mixer until batter is smooth (batter will be thick). Add one-third of egg whites, and stir gently; fold in remaining egg whites.

Pour batter into prepared pan. Bake at 350° for 45 minutes or until a wooden pick inserted in center comes out clean. Cool in pan 10 minutes; remove from pan, and cool on a wire rack. Yield: 16 servings (151 calories per ½-inch slice).

□ *2.3 grams protein, 7.1 grams fat, 19.4 grams carbohydrate, 0 milligrams cholesterol, 96 milligrams sodium, and 54 milligrams calcium.*

CHOCOLATE-WALNUT BROWNIES
(pictured on page 302)

⅔ cup reduced-calorie margarine, softened
⅔ cup sugar
½ cup egg substitute
3 tablespoons evaporated skimmed milk
1 teaspoon vanilla extract
⅔ cup all-purpose flour
⅓ cup unsweetened cocoa
½ teaspoon baking powder
¼ teaspoon salt
3 tablespoons diced walnuts
Vegetable cooking spray

Cream margarine; gradually add sugar, 1 tablespoon at a time, beating well at medium speed of an electric mixer. Add egg substitute, milk, and vanilla; beat well.

Combine flour, cocoa, baking powder, and salt; add to creamed mixture, and mix well. Stir in walnuts. Spoon into an 8-inch square pan coated with cooking spray. Bake at 325° for 30 minutes or until a wooden pick inserted in center comes out clean. Cool on a wire rack; cut into squares. Yield: 16 servings (114 calories per brownie).

□ *2.1 grams protein, 6 grams fat, 13.9 grams carbohydrate, 0 milligrams cholesterol, 134 milligrams sodium, and 25 milligrams calcium.*

CHOCOLATE WHIP

1 envelope unflavored gelatin
⅓ cup sugar
⅓ cup unsweetened cocoa
2 (12-ounce) cans evaporated skimmed milk
3 egg whites
⅛ teaspoon salt
2 tablespoons sugar
¼ teaspoon ground cinnamon
1 teaspoon vanilla extract

Combine first 4 ingredients in a heavy saucepan; let stand 1 minute. Cook over medium heat, stirring constantly, until gelatin dissolves. Pour mixture into a 13- x 9- x 2-inch pan; freeze. Remove from freezer; break into chunks.

Beat egg whites (at room temperature) and salt in a small bowl at high speed of an electric mixer until foamy; gradually add 2 tablespoons sugar, beating until stiff peaks form. Fold in cinnamon and vanilla.

Gradually add frozen mixture to beaten egg whites, beating at high speed of an electric mixer until smooth. Return to pan; freeze until firm. Yield: 8 servings (131 calories per ¾-cup serving).

☐ 8.8 grams protein, 0.6 gram fat, 22.5 grams carbohydrate, 4 milligrams cholesterol, 154 milligrams sodium, and 261 milligrams calcium.

CHOCOLATE BAVARIAN PIE

1 envelope unflavored gelatin
½ cup cold water
⅔ cup sugar
¼ cup unsweetened cocoa
1 cup evaporated skimmed milk
¼ cup egg substitute
1 teaspoon vegetable oil
1½ teaspoons vanilla extract
½ teaspoon chocolate flavoring
3 egg whites
⅛ teaspoon cream of tartar
Graham cracker crust (recipe follows)

Sprinkle gelatin over water; let stand 1 minute.

Combine sugar and next 4 ingredients in a heavy saucepan. Cook over medium heat, stirring constantly, until smooth and thickened. Remove from heat; stir in vanilla extract and chocolate flavoring. Add gelatin mixture; stir until gelatin dissolves. Chill until the consistency of unbeaten egg white.

Beat egg whites (at room temperature) and cream of tartar at medium speed of an electric mixer until stiff peaks form. Fold into chocolate mixture. Spoon filling into Graham Cracker Crust. Cover and chill until pie is firm. Yield: 8 servings (163 calories per slice).

☐ 6 grams protein, 3.5 grams fat, 27.4 grams carbohydrate, 1 milligram cholesterol, 151 milligrams sodium, and 109 milligrams calcium.

Graham Cracker Crust

¾ cup graham cracker crumbs
2 tablespoons reduced-calorie margarine, melted

Combine graham cracker crumbs and margarine, mixing well; firmly press mixture evenly over bottom and up sides of a 9-inch pieplate. Bake at 350° for 7 to 9 minutes; chill. Yield: one 9-inch crumb crust.

Here's Just The Salad You Need

Year-round, variety is common in salads served throughout the South, but during the holidays salads take a predictable turn. Choices for Christmas menus frequently contain cranberries or gelatin, such as this assortment of recipes sent to us by our readers.

Cooks who prefer gelatin salads will enjoy Sweet Cherry Salad. It's a simple but tasty combination that contains only four ingredients if you don't include the garnish.

Count on Congealed Mandarin Orange Salad for something a little more unusual. It's a colorful blend of gelatin, fruit, and nuts that's sinfully dressed with a rich sauce.

SWEET CHERRY SALAD

2 (16-ounce) cans pitted dark sweet cherries, undrained
1 (6-ounce) package cherry-flavored gelatin
¾ cup port or other sweet red wine
⅔ cup chopped pecans
Lettuce leaves
Mayonnaise or salad dressing

Drain cherries, and reserve liquid. Cut cherries in half, and set aside. Add enough water to liquid to measure 2½ cups. Bring liquid to a boil; remove from heat. Add gelatin, and stir until gelatin dissolves. Stir in port wine. Chill until the consistency of unbeaten egg white. Fold in cherries and pecans.

Spoon mixture into a lightly-oiled 6-cup mold; cover and chill until firm. Unmold onto a lettuce-lined plate; serve with mayonnaise. Yield: 10 servings. *Margaret DuBard* *Birmingham, Alabama*

CONGEALED MANDARIN ORANGE SALAD

1 (15¼-ounce) can crushed pineapple, undrained
1 (11-ounce) can mandarin oranges, undrained
1 (6-ounce) package orange-flavored gelatin
1½ cups hot tea
1 (8-ounce) can water chestnuts, drained and chopped
Leaf lettuce
Dressing (recipe follows)
Carrot strips (optional)

Drain pineapple and oranges, and reserve juices; add enough water to juices to measure 1½ cups.

Dissolve gelatin in hot tea. Add 1½ cups reserved liquid, and chill until mixture is the consistency of unbeaten egg white.

Fold pineapple, oranges, and water chestnuts into gelatin mixture. Spoon mixture into a lightly-oiled 6-cup ring mold; cover and chill until congealed ring is firm.

Unmold onto a lettuce-lined plate. Line center of ring with lettuce; spoon small portion of dressing into center, and top with carrot strips, if desired. Serve remaining dressing on the side. Yield: 8 to 10 servings.

Dressing

½ cup mayonnaise
¼ cup whipping cream
1 tablespoon grated orange rind
1 teaspoon sugar
¼ teaspoon ground mace

Combine all ingredients, stirring well. Yield: ¾ cup. *Yvonne M. Greer* *Greenville, South Carolina*

QUICK!
Offer An Appetizer

Eliminate hours of preparation with these easy-to-make appetizers. Serve one or two of these choices as hors d' oeuvres for a dinner party, or take them to office and church holiday gatherings.

During the holiday season, it's also a good idea to keep ingredients for one of these recipes on hand to make for drop-in company.

SWEET-AND-SOUR KIELBASA

2 (12-ounce) packages kielbasa, cut into ¼-inch slices
1 (12-ounce) bottle chili sauce
¾ cup red currant jelly
2 teaspoons prepared mustard
1 teaspoon lemon juice
1 (20-ounce) can pineapple chunks, drained

Cook sausage over low heat in a large skillet 8 to 10 minutes; drain. Set aside.

Combine chili sauce and next 3 ingredients in large skillet; stir well. Add kielbasa and pineapple chunks; simmer 15 minutes, stirring occasionally. Serve in a chafing dish. Yield: 24 appetizer servings. *Marie Wiker* *Gaithersburg, Maryland*

NUTTY CREAM CHEESE SPREAD

2 (8-ounce) packages cream cheese, softened
½ cup sour cream
1 (0.4-ounce) package ranch-style salad dressing mix
1 (2-ounce) package pecan chips

Combine first 3 ingredients, stirring until blended. Chill 10 minutes.

Shape mixture into a 6- x 1-inch patty; lightly coat top and sides with pecans. Serve with crackers. Yield: 2½ cups. *Janet Bain* *Ohatchee, Alabama*

CURRY DIP AND VEGETABLE PLATTER

1 cup mayonnaise or salad dressing
1 tablespoon curry powder
1 tablespoon lemon juice
1 (14-ounce) can artichoke hearts, drained and quartered
1 (14-ounce) can hearts of palm, drained and cut into 1-inch pieces
Lettuce leaves
Lemon slices (optional)

Combine first 3 ingredients. Arrange artichoke hearts and hearts of palm on lettuce leaves; garnish with lemon slices, if desired. Serve with dip. Yield: 6 to 8 servings.

Nancy Seamon *Hilton Head, South Carolina*

Tip: *Add marinated vegetable salads to your next dinner party. They can be prepared in advance and chilled until serving time—an important bonus for the busy cook.*

CHILI-AND-CHEESE DIP

1 pound ground turkey
1 (15½-ounce) can chili with beans
1 (8-ounce) loaf process cheese spread with peppers
⅓ cup milk

Cook turkey in a medium saucepan until meat is browned, stirring to crumble. Drain well. Add remaining ingredients, and cook over medium heat, stirring until cheese melts.

To serve, transfer dip to a chafing dish; serve warm with tortilla chips. Yield: 1 quart.

Microwave Directions: Crumble turkey into a 2-quart casserole. Cover tightly with heavy-duty plastic wrap; fold back a small edge of wrap to allow steam to escape.

Microwave at HIGH 5 to 6 minutes or until meat is no longer pink, stirring every 2 minutes. Drain. Stir in remaining ingredients; cover and microwave at HIGH 3 minutes or until thoroughly heated.

Linda Parker
Huntsville, Alabama

SWEET FRUIT DIP

1 (7-ounce) jar marshmallow cream
1 (8-ounce) package cream cheese, softened
1 (8-ounce) carton sour cream
1 (14-ounce) can sweetened condensed milk

Combine all ingredients in container of an electric blender; blend until smooth, stopping to scrape down sides, if necessary. Chill at least 1 hour. Serve with assorted fruits. Yield: 4 cups.
Dale Kiffe
Lockport, Louisiana

Moms And Daughters Bake Cookies

With 60 dozen cookies on the menu for the cookie swap hosted by Judy Gould and her daughter Lauren in Wake Forest, North Carolina, it's no wonder the mothers and daughters team up to bake them. Their recipes and ideas for a cookie swap may spark some new holiday plans for you and your daughter (or niece or young friend).

■ Daughters Cate and Sarah help Kerry Dearstyne with several techniques in preparing Praline Thumbprint Cookies. Their favorite part is making the thumbprints, but they've found a melon ball scoop that is more exact at making the prints than an actual thumb.

PRALINE THUMBPRINT COOKIES

1 cup butter or margarine, softened
1 cup sifted powdered sugar
2 cups all-purpose flour
1 cup finely chopped pecans
1 tablespoon vanilla extract
Praline Filling

Cream butter; gradually add powdered sugar, beating well at medium speed of an electric mixer. Add flour, mixing well. Stir in chopped pecans and vanilla.

Shape dough into 1-inch balls; place about 2 inches apart on ungreased cookie sheets. Press thumb in center of each cookie to make an indentation. Bake at 375° for 15 to 17 minutes; do not brown. Cool on wire racks. Spoon about ½ teaspoon Praline Filling into each cookie indentation. Yield: about 3 dozen.

Praline Filling

½ cup butter or margarine
1 cup firmly packed brown sugar
Dash of salt
½ cup evaporated milk
2 cups sifted powdered sugar
½ teaspoon vanilla extract

Melt butter in a medium saucepan. Add brown sugar and salt; bring to a boil. Boil 2 minutes, stirring constantly. Remove from heat; stir in milk. Bring mixture to a boil, and let boil 2 minutes or until 232°.

Remove praline mixture from heat. Cool to lukewarm. Stir in powdered sugar and vanilla; beat with a wooden spoon until mixture is smooth. Yield: about 1½ cups.

■ Pinky Cooke has baked Crispy Oatmeal Cookies for the last 10 Christmases, and she's thrilled that daughter Sydney has gotten old enough to help. Sydney is in charge of chopping the nuts and grating the orange rind.

CRISPY OATMEAL COOKIES

½ cup butter or margarine, softened
½ cup firmly packed brown sugar
½ cup sugar
1 egg
1½ teaspoons grated orange rind
½ teaspoon vanilla extract
¾ cup all-purpose flour
½ teaspoon baking soda
½ teaspoon salt
1½ cups quick-cooking oats, uncooked
½ cup chopped pecans

Cream butter; gradually add sugars, beating well at medium speed of an electric mixer. Add egg, orange rind, and vanilla, mixing well.

Combine flour, soda, and salt in a small bowl; add to creamed mixture, mixing well. Stir in oats and pecans. (Dough will be soft.) Divide dough in half. Spoon each half of dough onto a large piece of wax paper, and shape dough into a 10-inch log. Roll in wax paper, and freeze.

Cut frozen dough into ¼-inch slices (an electric knife works well), and place slices on ungreased cookie sheets. Bake slices at 350° for 10 minutes or until lightly browned. Let cookies cool 1 minute on cookie sheets, and loosen with spatula. Let cookies cool completely on cookie sheets. Yield: 5 dozen.

■ Erin Styles is old enough to measure and mix the ingredients for Orange Sugar Cookies, but Juanita helps her daughter roll and cut the cookies because that's a more difficult technique. Juanita says rolling the dough on a pastry cloth simplifies the process.

ORANGE SUGAR COOKIES

½ cup shortening
¾ cup sugar
1 egg
½ teaspoon vanilla extract
1½ teaspoons grated orange rind
2 cups all-purpose flour
½ teaspoon baking powder
½ teaspoon baking soda
¼ teaspoon salt
3 tablespoons milk
Green sugar crystals

Cream shortening; gradually add sugar, beating well at medium speed of an electric mixer. Add egg, and beat well. Add vanilla and orange rind; mix well.

Combine flour, baking powder, soda, and salt; add to creamed mixture alternately with milk, mixing well after each addition.

Roll dough to ⅛-inch thickness on a lightly floured surface. Cut with a 3-inch cookie cutter, and place on lightly greased cookie sheets. Sprinkle tops evenly with sugar crystals. Bake at 375° for 7 to 8 minutes or until cookies are lightly browned. Let cookies cool on wire racks. Yield: about 5 dozen.

■ Judy and Lauren Gould contribute one of their favorites, Chocolate Snowflake Cookies, to the event. Lauren isn't old enough to actually mix up the ingredients, but she's a great help shaping the balls and rolling them in powdered sugar.

CHOCOLATE SNOWFLAKE COOKIES

2 cups sugar
½ cup vegetable oil
4 (1-ounce) squares unsweetened chocolate, melted
4 eggs
2 teaspoons vanilla extract
2 cups all-purpose flour
2 teaspoons baking powder
½ teaspoon salt
¾ cup sifted powdered sugar

Combine sugar, vegetable oil, and melted chocolate in a large mixing bowl; beat at medium speed of an electric mixer until blended. Add eggs and vanilla, mixing well.

Combine flour, baking powder, and salt in a medium bowl. Add about one-fourth of dry mixture at a time to chocolate mixture, mixing after each addition. Cover and let chill at least 2 hours.

Shape dough into 1-inch balls, and roll in powdered sugar. Place cookies 2 inches apart on lightly greased cookie sheets. Bake at 350° for 10 to 12 minutes. Cool on wire racks. Yield: 8 dozen.

■ It takes a lot of chopped fruit and nuts to prepare Candied Fruit Drops. Lauren Gadd does most of the chopping herself, according to mother Sally. She also garnishes each one with a candied cherry half.

CANDIED FRUIT DROPS

1 cup chopped red candied cherries
1 cup chopped candied pineapple
1 cup chopped pecans
1 (8-ounce) package whole pitted dates, chopped
3½ cups all-purpose flour, divided
¾ cup butter or margarine, softened
1¾ cups firmly packed brown sugar
2 eggs
1 teaspoon baking soda
1 teaspoon salt
⅔ cup buttermilk
45 red candied cherries, halved

Combine first 4 ingredients; add ½ cup flour, tossing to coat fruit mixture. Set aside.

Cream butter in a large mixing bowl; gradually add brown sugar, beating well at medium speed of an electric mixer. Add eggs, mixing well. Combine remaining 3 cups flour, soda, and salt; add to creamed mixture alternately with buttermilk, beginning and ending with flour mixture. Mix after each addition. Stir in fruit mixture.

Drop dough by tablespoonfuls onto greased cookie sheets; press a candied cherry half on top of each cookie. Bake at 375° for 12 to 15 minutes or until cookies are lightly browned. Cool cookies on wire racks. Yield: 7½ dozen.

■ "Now that Jennifer, Lori, and Stephanie are older, they each bake a batch of Toffee Treats by themselves for the cookie swap," explains Linda Neeb. "It gets pretty messy with four cooks in the kitchen!"

TOFFEE TREATS

1 cup butter or margarine, softened
1 cup firmly packed brown sugar
1 egg yolk
1 teaspoon vanilla extract
2 cups all-purpose flour
¼ teaspoon salt
5 (1.65-ounce) milk chocolate bars, broken
¾ cup chopped pecans, toasted

Cream butter; gradually add brown sugar, and beat well at medium speed of an electric mixer. Add egg yolk and vanilla; beat well. Combine flour and salt; gradually add to creamed mixture, mixing well.

Spread batter in a lightly greased 13- x 9- x 2-inch pan. Bake at 350° for 25 to 30 minutes (crust will be soft). Remove pan from oven, and immediately arrange pieces of chocolate on hot crust. Let stand until chocolate softens; then spread evenly over crust with a spatula. Sprinkle chopped pecans on top; let cool slightly. Cut into squares while warm. Let squares cool completely in pan. Yield: 3 dozen.

■ Judy prepares bright-green Christmas Punch for the girls and their mothers at her cookie swap. This festive punch recipe relies on lime-flavored gelatin for its color. The pineapple-grapefruit juice provides a tasty kick that everyone can enjoy.

CHRISTMAS PUNCH

3 (3-ounce) packages lime-flavored gelatin
2 cups boiling water
1 (46-ounce) jar pineapple-grapefruit juice
1 (12-ounce) can frozen lemonade concentrate, thawed and undiluted
1 (12-ounce) can frozen orange juice concentrate, thawed and undiluted
3½ quarts water
2 (10-ounce) bottles ginger ale, chilled

Combine gelatin and boiling water; stir until gelatin dissolves. Add next 4 ingredients. Divide mixture in half. Freeze half of juice mixture; chill remaining half.

To serve, partially thaw frozen mixture; place in punch bowl, and break into chunks. Stir in chilled juice mixture and ginger ale. Yield: 7 quarts.

Mixes To Make And Give

Here we present mixes for all kinds of foods that will keep beyond the busy season or help you with holiday food preparation.

TURKEY-NOODLE SOUP MIX

1 cup uncooked fine egg noodles
1 tablespoon instant minced onion
2½ tablespoons chicken-flavored bouillon granules
1½ teaspoons pepper
¼ teaspoon dried whole thyme
⅛ teaspoon celery seeds
⅛ teaspoon garlic powder
1 bay leaf

Combine all ingredients in a small zip-top plastic bag, and store in a cool, dry place. (To ensure even distribution of seasonings, each recipe of soup mix must be mixed individually.) Yield: 1 cup.

Directions for recipe gift card: Combine soup mix, 8 cups water, and 1 carrot, diced, in a Dutch oven. Bring to a boil; cover, reduce heat, and simmer 15 minutes. Discard bay leaf. Stir in 3 cups cooked, diced turkey; simmer an additional 5 minutes. Yield: 2 quarts.

CHEESE-AND-PEPPER MUFFIN MIX

2½ cups all-purpose flour
¼ cup yellow cornmeal
¼ cup sugar
1 tablespoon baking powder
1 teaspoon baking soda
½ teaspoon salt
¼ teaspoon red pepper
½ cup grated Parmesan cheese
⅓ cup cultured buttermilk powder
1 tablespoon dried shredded green onions
1½ to 2 teaspoons dried red pepper flakes

Combine all ingredients; store in an airtight container in a cool, dry place. Yield: 4 cups.

Directions for recipe gift card: Place muffin mix in a large bowl; make a well in center of mixture. Combine 2 eggs, 1½ cups water, and ¼ cup vegetable oil; add to dry ingredients, stirring just until moistened. Spoon into greased muffin pans, filling three-fourths full. Bake at 400° for 20 minutes. Remove from pans immediately. Yield: 2 dozen.

Side Dishes To Please

If you'd like to add a little fanfare to plain potatoes, beans, or peas, these recipes may be just what you need.

Scrape carrots, and cut into thin slices. Sauté carrots and onion in butter in a large skillet 4 minutes; stir in wine and next 4 ingredients. Cover, reduce heat, and simmer 15 minutes or until carrots are tender. Discard bay leaf. Stir in broccoli, whipping cream, and pecans; cook until thoroughly heated. Yield: 8 servings.

Sandra Russell
Gainesville, Florida

FRUITED STUFFING MIX

1 (8-ounce) package
  herb-seasoned stuffing mix
1½ cups chopped mixed dried
  fruit
½ cup chopped pecans
¼ cup raisins or currants
1 tablespoon dried orange rind

Combine all ingredients; store in an airtight container or plastic bag. Yield: 6 cups.

Directions for recipe gift card: Combine 3 cups Fruited Stuffing Mix, ½ cup apple juice, and 2 tablespoons melted butter or margarine. Spoon mixture into desired meat or poultry; bake. Yield: enough for 1 pork crown roast or 6 Cornish hens.

Note: To stuff a turkey, use 6 cups Fruited Stuffing Mix, 1 cup apple juice, and ¼ cup melted butter or margarine.

SAUTÉED PEAS AND BACON

4 slices bacon
2 (10-ounce) packages frozen
  English peas
3 stalks celery, chopped
¼ cup sliced green onions
½ teaspoon salt
¼ teaspoon dried whole thyme
Dash of pepper

Cook bacon in a large skillet; remove bacon, reserving 1 tablespoon drippings in skillet. Drain and crumble bacon, and set aside.

Break up frozen peas with a fork. Add peas and remaining ingredients to drippings in skillet; cook over medium heat 12 to 15 minutes, stirring often. Spoon pea mixture into a serving dish, and sprinkle bacon over top. Yield: 6 to 8 servings.

Maureen Murphy
Charlottesville, Virginia

BROCCOLI-CARROT SUPREME

6 carrots
¼ cup chopped onion
2 tablespoons butter or
  margarine, melted
½ cup dry white wine
1 teaspoon salt
1 teaspoon dried whole thyme
⅛ teaspoon pepper
1 bay leaf
1 (16-ounce) package frozen cut
  broccoli, cooked and drained
¼ cup whipping cream
¼ cup chopped pecans

SWEET POTATOES WITH APRICOT GLAZE

6 medium-size sweet potatoes
  (about 2¾ pounds)
½ cup firmly packed brown sugar
½ cup apricot nectar
¼ cup butter or margarine
1 teaspoon grated orange rind
½ teaspoon grated lemon rind
½ teaspoon ground cinnamon
½ cup chopped pecans
Orange-rind rose and curls
  (optional)
Pecan halves (optional)

Cook sweet potatoes in boiling water to cover 45 minutes or until tender. Let cool to touch; peel and cut into ⅓-inch slices. Arrange in a lightly greased shallow 2-quart baking dish; set aside.

Combine brown sugar and next 5 ingredients in a small saucepan; bring to a boil, and boil 1 minute. Drizzle half of apricot mixture over potatoes; bake at 325° for 15 minutes. Drizzle with remaining apricot mixture, and sprinkle with chopped pecans. Bake an additional 15 minutes or until thoroughly heated. If desired, garnish with orange rind and pecan halves. Yield: 8 servings.

Billie Taylor
Fork Union, Virginia

TANGY GREEN BEANS

1 (10-ounce) package frozen cut
   green beans
½ cup water
2 slices bacon, chopped
¼ cup chopped onion
¼ cup white vinegar
1 tablespoon sugar

Combine green beans and water in a
saucepan. Bring to a boil; cover, reduce heat, and simmer 8 minutes.

Cook bacon and onion in a heavy
skillet until bacon is crisp. Remove
mixture with a slotted spoon; drain
and set aside. Pour off drippings
from skillet.

Combine vinegar and sugar in skillet; bring to a boil. Add beans and
bacon mixture. Cook over medium
heat until thoroughly heated. Yield: 3
servings. *Ruth Sherrer*
Fort Worth, Texas

CHEESY POTATO SOUFFLÉ

3 medium-size red potatoes (1½
   pounds), peeled and sliced
½ cup sour cream
4 eggs, separated
⅔ cup (2.6 ounces) shredded
   Cheddar cheese
¼ cup diced onion
2 teaspoons chopped chives
¼ teaspoon pepper
⅛ teaspoon baking powder

Cook potatoes in boiling salted water
to cover 8 minutes or until tender.
Drain and mash potatoes. Add sour
cream; beat at medium speed of an
electric mixer until smooth.

Beat egg yolks until thick and
lemon colored. Add yolks, cheese,
onion, chives, and pepper to potato
mixture; stir well.

Beat egg whites (at room temperature) and baking powder until stiff
peaks form; fold into potato mixture.
Spoon into a buttered 1½-quart soufflé dish; bake at 350° for 50 minutes
or until set. Serve immediately.
Yield: 6 servings. *Maggie Cates*
Greenville, Texas

Taco Salad
For Two

Taco salad is a popular item found on
restaurant menus. This recipe for
Taco Salad is just the right amount
for two. The meat is served in a
sunburst-shaped taco shell. Top this
flavorful salad with commercial picante sauce rather than the usual
salad dressing.

TACO SALAD

2 (9-inch) flour tortillas
Vegetable oil
½ pound ground beef
½ cup water
2 tablespoons taco seasoning mix
2 tablespoons chopped green
   onions
½ medium head iceberg lettuce,
   shredded
1 small tomato, chopped
¼ cup ripe olives, sliced
1 small avocado, sliced
Additional chopped tomatoes,
   shredded Cheddar cheese,
   sliced ripe olives, and sour
   cream (optional)
Commercial picante sauce

Cut tortilla into sunburst design,
using scissors. Pour oil to a depth of
3 inches into a medium saucepan 1 to
1½ inches smaller than the diameter
of the tortilla; heat to 375°. Push
tortilla into oil, using ladle, and press
down in center. Cook 45 to 60 seconds or until golden brown. Drain.
Cook ground beef in a skillet until
meat is browned, stirring to crumble;
drain. Return meat to skillet; add
water and taco seasoning. Simmer 10
minutes; stir in onions.

Layer half each of lettuce, tomato,
olives, and avocado on serving
plates. Fill tortilla cups with meat
mixture, and, if desired, garnish with
additional tomatoes, cheese, olives,
and sour cream. Serve with picante
sauce. Yield: 2 servings.

A Lesson
On Poaching Fish

Poaching is an excellent low-fat cooking method for most firm-fleshed
fish. It preserves the delicate texture
of the fish and enhances its deep flavor. Immerse the fish completely in
the poaching liquid so that an ex-
change of flavors between the fish
and the cooking liquid will take place.

Large fish are most easily cooked
in a fish poacher. Or they can be cut
in half crosswise so that they will fit
in a smaller container. A large skillet,
saucepan, or small turkey roaster can
be used to poach smaller fish, fish
steaks, and fillets.

To poach fish, wrap in cheesecloth
so that it can be removed from the
poaching liquid without breaking.
Lower the fish into simmering poaching liquid; reheat to barely simmering
for cooking. Poach 10 minutes per
inch of thickness, turning halfway
through the cooking time. Fish is
done when the flesh becomes opaque
and flakes easily with a fork.

POACHED FISH
WITH VEGETABLES

2 quarts water
2 cups dry white wine
1 (8-ounce) bottle clam juice
3 medium onions, sliced
2 carrots, cut into 1-inch lengths
3 celery stalks with leaves, cut
   into 1-inch pieces
2 teaspoons salt
Bouquet garni (recipe follows)
1 (3½-pound) dressed red snapper
1 pound baby carrots, steamed
1 pound snow pea pods, steamed
1 pound new potatoes, steamed
1 pound fresh green beans,
   steamed
1 pint cherry tomatoes
½ pound fresh mushrooms
Mustard Sauce

Combine first 8 ingredients in a fish poacher; bring to a boil. Cover, reduce heat, and simmer 30 minutes. Cool to room temperature; strain. Discard vegetables and bouquet garni. Return liquid to poacher.

Wrap fish in cheesecloth; tie ends with string. Place fish in poaching liquid; add water to cover fish 1 to 1½ inches. Cover and bring to a slow simmer; simmer 15 minutes. Remove from heat, leaving fish in liquid 15 minutes. Remove fish from liquid, and remove cheesecloth. Remove skin, and place on a large platter. Arrange steamed vegetables around fish. Serve with Mustard Sauce. Yield: 6 servings.

Bouquet Garni

4 fresh parsley sprigs
1 fresh tarragon sprig
1 fresh thyme sprig
2 bay leaves
10 peppercorns

Tie all ingredients in a cheesecloth bag. Yield: 1 bouquet garni.

Mustard Sauce

⅔ cup mayonnaise or salad
  dressing
2 tablespoons Dijon mustard
¾ teaspoon minced fresh tarragon

Combine all ingredients, stirring well; cover and chill. Yield: ¾ cup.
Judy McFarlin
Potomac, Maryland

Tip: *You should not thaw fish at room temperature or in warm water; it will lose moisture and flavor. Instead, place the fish in the refrigerator to thaw. Keep in mind that you should allow 18 to 24 hours for thawing a 1-pound package. Of course, you should never refreeze thawed fish.*

From Our Kitchen To Yours

Garnished with cranberries, orange wedges, and endive, baked ham makes a stately holiday entrée. This traditional and easily prepared favorite complements any menu and usually yields leftovers for soups or casseroles.

Whether you choose a fully cooked or a cook-before-eating ham in natural juices or with water added, preparation can be almost effortless. A fully cooked ham is ready to serve; however, baking improves the flavor and texture. If the ham is labeled "water added," a seasoned water solution, which doesn't exceed 10% of the fresh meat weight, has been injected. And when cooked, this ham tends to be very moist. A whole ham is usually 10 to 14 pounds, but you can also buy the meaty butt end or the flavorful shank end. A boneless ham is less flavorful because the external and internal fat has been trimmed. Although the price is usually higher, a boneless ham is often the best buy because there is little waste and the meat is leaner. Whatever kind of ham you select, be sure the meat is not discolored, and the liquid in the wrapping is clear. A canned ham is always boneless and fully cooked during the canning process; a small amount of unflavored gelatin is added before sealing to absorb the natural juices as the ham cooks.

Preparation

Most packaging gives preparation instructions and a date by which the ham should be eaten or sold. If cooking instructions are not on the label, follow these general guidelines. For more flavor from a fully cooked ham, bake at 325° for 15 to 20 minutes per pound or until a meat thermometer registers an internal temperature of 140°. A cook-before-eating ham is baked at 325° for 18 to 22 minutes per pound or until the internal temperature registers 160°.

You can also achieve moist, tender ham by cooking it in your microwave oven. Select a fully cooked ham half, weighing not more than 3 pounds, so you won't have to be concerned about the safety of the ham if it cooks unevenly. When cooking ham, the upper cut edge cooks faster than the center. Shielding this area with a 1½-inch-wide strip of aluminum foil reduces the energy received and slows the cooking process. Fold the foil smoothly over the ham's cut edge, and be sure the ham is placed at least 3 inches from the oven walls. If an arc (spark of electricity) occurs, flatten the foil and continue microwaving. However, some older microwave oven models can be

Tips for Mail-Order Gifts

■ Fresh or cooked meat, poultry, or fish should arrive frozen or with ice crystals in the middle. If never frozen, it should be cold to the touch. If the product is warm or has an off odor, do not eat it.

Many country hams are coated with mold. Scrub or cut off the mold as soon as the ham is received. Rinse ham with a mixture of equal parts of vinegar and water. Hang in a cool place to store; if mold reoccurs, repeat process.

■ Smoked, cured, cooked turkey can be stored in the refrigerator up to seven days or frozen up to six months.

■ Summer sausage should arrive cold and be placed in the refrigerator; some hard, dry sausages (pepperoni and hard salami) need no refrigeration.

■ Torn vacuum packaging could allow bacteria to grow; check packages carefully.

■ A whole cooked turkey should not be reheated; reheat serving-size pieces.

damaged by the use of foil, so be sure to check the manufacturer's directions before shielding.

When microwaved at a high setting, sugar used in curing ham attracts microwaves and can cause overcooking or uneven cooking. Place the ham, fat side up, on a rack in a 12- x 8- x 2-inch baking dish. Insert a microwave-safe meat thermometer, making sure it does not touch bone or fat. Shield the upper, cut edge with an aluminum foil strip, and cover the entire dish with heavy-duty plastic wrap. Microwave the ham at MEDIUM for 8 to 10 minutes per pound or until the thermometer registers 140°, turning the ham over halfway through the cooking time and rearranging the foil strip. Let stand 10 minutes before slicing.

Storage

Cured hams, whether cooked or uncooked, keep refrigerated up to one week. Before storing canned ham, check the label; some canned hams must be refrigerated, while others have been sterilized and can be stored with other canned goods for up to one year. Refrigerated, unopened canned hams keep six to nine months, but once opened, use within a week.

Ham can be frozen, but you may be disappointed with the results; frozen ham tends to lose flavor and texture. To freeze ham, wrap large portions in plastic wrap and then in foil, and freeze up to 1 month. Don't freeze canned hams, because the expansion during freezing may damage the can's seams.

Try Versatile Lemon Curd

Freshly grated lemon rind and freshly squeezed juice gives this Lemon Curd a rich, fresh-as-fruit flavor.

LEMON CURD

¼ cup grated lemon rind
⅔ cup lemon juice
2 cups sugar
1 cup butter or margarine
4 eggs, slightly beaten

Combine first 4 ingredients in top of a double boiler. Cook over simmering water, stirring constantly, until butter melts. Gradually stir about one-fourth of hot mixture into eggs; add to remaining hot mixture, stirring constantly. Cook over simmering water, stirring constantly, until mixture thickens and coats a spoon (about 15 minutes). Remove from heat; cool. Cover and refrigerate.

Serve Lemon Curd with pound cake, gingerbread, or as a filling for tarts. Yield: 3½ cups.

Note: Lemon Curd may be chilled in a tightly covered glass container up to 2 weeks. For tart filling or pudding, fold in ½ cup whipped cream to 1 cup Lemon Curd.

Merle R. Downs
Tryon, North Carolina

MICROWAVE COOKERY

What's All The Fuss About Wattage?

Here are some of the most frequently asked questions about microwave oven wattage and the difference it makes in cooking.

What is wattage? Does it make a difference? Wattage is another term for power output. In a microwave oven, the higher the power output, the quicker the food cooks. Most of the large or full-size microwave ovens offer 600 to 700 watts of power. Compact, subcompact, or low-wattage microwave ovens offer 400 to 500 watts of power. In general, the larger the oven, the faster it will cook.

How much difference in cooking time does the lower wattage make? A low-wattage microwave oven generally takes about 30% longer than a full-size oven to cook the same food.

Why would I purchase a low-wattage oven? These ovens are often low in price (around $100), require a small amount of space, and are simple to use. They work well in dorms, second homes, and recreational vehicles. The 400- to 500-watt microwave ovens are best used for light cooking, reheating small amounts of food (under four servings), and some defrosting.

What are some advantages of a high-wattage oven? Instructions on some packaged foods tell consumers NOT to cook the food in a low-wattage microwave. The recipes in our magazine and cookbooks are tested in 600- to 700-watt microwave ovens. The higher watt ovens also tend to cook food faster than lower watt ovens. The 600- to 700-watt ovens usually offer more options, such as automatic defrost, sensors, temperature probes, and varying power levels. These ovens tend to be best for someone who cooks frequently and makes recipes of four servings or more. Not all baking dishes will fit in the smaller ovens, and some recipes require various power levels to be successful.

Can I microwave popcorn in a low-wattage oven? Some brands of popcorn are labeled as "safe for all microwaves, low watt and compact." Some manufacturers advise against microwaving popcorn in 400- to 500-watt ovens. For the best results, check your use and care manual, and then look at the package directions. Always stay with the popcorn while it's popping, regardless of the wattage of the oven.

Cakes For Giving

This is the season of parties, goodies at the office coffeepot, and club get-togethers. It's that time to remember shut-ins, and special friends.

Why not surprise them with a cake? Each of these cakes will delight the recipients, and they're easy to make. They're also sturdy enough to travel well.

FIG PRESERVES CAKE

¾ cup butter or margarine, softened
2 cups sugar
4 eggs
3 cups all-purpose flour
⅛ teaspoon salt
1½ teaspoons ground allspice
1 teaspoon ground cinnamon
1 teaspoon baking soda
1 cup buttermilk
2 cups commercial fig preserves
2 cups chopped pecans
1 teaspoon vanilla extract

Cream butter; gradually add sugar, beating at medium speed of an electric mixer until light and fluffy. Add eggs, one at a time, beating after each addition.

Combine flour, salt, and spices. Combine soda and buttermilk, stirring well. Add flour and milk mixture alternately to creamed mixture, beginning and ending with flour mixture. Stir in preserves, pecans, and vanilla.

Pour batter into a greased and floured 10-inch tube pan. Bake at 350° for 1 hour and 15 to 20 minutes or until a wooden pick inserted in center comes out clean. (If necessary, shield cake the last 20 minutes to prevent excessive browning.) Cool cake in pan 10 minutes; remove from pan, and let cool completely on a wire rack. Yield: one 10-inch cake.

Aladine Standish
Houston, Texas

CHOCOLATE-TOFFEE CAKE

1 teaspoon instant coffee granules
¼ cup boiling water
1 (18.25-ounce) package devil's food cake mix with pudding
3 eggs
½ cup water
½ cup sour cream
⅓ cup firmly packed brown sugar
2 tablespoons vegetable oil
4 English toffee-flavored candy bars
¼ teaspoon instant coffee granules
1 (1-ounce) square unsweetened chocolate, melted
1 tablespoon water
1 cup sifted powdered sugar
½ teaspoon vanilla extract

Dissolve 1 teaspoon coffee granules in boiling water. Combine coffee, cake mix, and next 5 ingredients at low speed of an electric mixer just until ingredients are moistened. Beat at high speed for 2 minutes. Coarsely chop candy bars; set aside 2 tablespoons, and stir remaining candy into batter.

Spoon batter into a greased and floured 10-inch Bundt pan. Bake at 350° for 45 minutes or until a wooden pick inserted in center comes out clean. Cool cake in pan 10 minutes; remove from pan, and let cool completely on a wire rack.

Dissolve ¼ teaspoon coffee granules in chocolate, stirring until granules dissolve. Add 1 tablespoon water and remaining ingredients, stirring until smooth. Add extra water, if needed, for desired consistency.

Drizzle glaze over cake, and sprinkle reserved 2 tablespoons chopped toffee-flavored candy bars over glaze. Yield: one 10-inch cake.

Camilla C. Hudson
Denton, Texas

AMBROSIA CAKE ROYALE

2¼ cups all-purpose flour
1 teaspoon baking powder
1 teaspoon baking soda
¼ teaspoon salt
1 cup sugar
1 cup chopped pecans
1 cup flaked coconut
½ cup pineapple tidbits, drained
½ cup maraschino cherries, drained and coarsely chopped
2 tablespoons grated orange rind
2 eggs, beaten
1 cup buttermilk
¾ cup vegetable oil
Hot Ambrosia Sauce

Combine first 5 ingredients in a large mixing bowl. Add pecans and next 4 ingredients, tossing to coat.

Combine eggs, buttermilk, and oil. Add to fruit mixture; stir until blended. Spoon into a greased and floured 10-inch Bundt pan; bake at 350° for 45 to 50 minutes or until a wooden pick inserted in center comes out clean. Cool cake in pan 10 minutes; remove from pan, and let cool completely on a wire rack.

Serve with Hot Ambrosia Sauce. Yield: one 10-inch Bundt cake.

Hot Ambrosia Sauce

1 (11-ounce) can mandarin oranges, drained
½ cup chopped pecans
½ cup pineapple tidbits, drained
¼ cup maraschino cherries, drained and coarsely chopped
½ cup flaked coconut
1¼ cups sugar
¼ cup plus 2 tablespoons milk
¼ cup butter or margarine
Pinch of baking soda

Combine first 5 ingredients in a mixing bowl; set aside.

Combine sugar, milk, and butter in a heavy saucepan; bring to a boil, and cook 3 to 4 minutes, stirring constantly. Remove from heat; stir in soda. Pour over fruit mixture; stir well. Yield: 2½ cups. *Larry Miller*
Ashland, Kentucky

Appendices

EQUIVALENT WEIGHTS AND MEASURES

Food	Weight or Count	Measure or Yield
Apples	1 pound (3 medium)	3 cups sliced
Bacon	8 slices cooked	½ cup crumbled
Bananas	1 pound (3 medium)	2½ cups sliced, or about 2 cups mashed
Bread	1 pound	12 to 16 slices
	About 1½ slices	1 cup soft crumbs
Butter or margarine	1 pound	2 cups
	¼-pound stick	½ cup
Cabbage	1 pound head	4½ cups shredded
Candied fruit or peels	½ pound	1¼ cups chopped
Carrots	1 pound	3 cups shredded
Cheese, American or Cheddar	1 pound	About 4 cups shredded
cottage	1 pound	2 cups
cream	3-ounce package	6 tablespoons
Chocolate morsels	6-ounce package	1 cup
Cocoa	1 pound	4 cups
Coconut, flaked or shredded	1 pound	5 cups
Coffee	1 pound	80 tablespoons (40 cups perked)
Corn	2 medium ears	1 cup kernels
Cornmeal	1 pound	3 cups
Crab, in shell	1 pound	¾ to 1 cup flaked
Crackers, chocolate wafers	19 wafers	1 cup crumbs
graham crackers	14 squares	1 cup fine crumbs
saltine crackers	28 crackers	1 cup finely crushed
vanilla wafers	22 wafers	1 cup finely crushed
Cream, whipping	1 cup (½ pint)	2 cups whipped
Dates, pitted	1 pound	3 cups chopped
	8-ounce package	1½ cups chopped
Eggs	5 large	1 cup
whites	8 to 11	1 cup
yolks	12 to 14	1 cup
Flour, all-purpose	1 pound	3½ cups
cake	1 pound	4¾ to 5 cups sifted
whole wheat	1 pound	3½ cups unsifted
Green pepper	1 large	1 cup diced
Lemon	1 medium	2 to 3 tablespoons juice; 2 teaspoons grated rind
Lettuce	1 pound head	6¼ cups torn
Lime	1 medium	1½ to 2 tablespoons juice; 1½ teaspoons grated rind
Macaroni	4 ounces (1 cup)	2¼ cups cooked
Marshmallows	11 large	1 cup
	10 miniature	1 large marshmallow
Marshmallows, miniature	½ pound	4½ cups
Milk, evaporated	5.33-ounce can	⅔ cup
evaporated	13-ounce can	1⅝ cups
sweetened condensed	14-ounce can	1¼ cups
Mushrooms	3 cups raw (8 ounces)	1 cup sliced cooked
Nuts, almonds	1 pound	1 to 1¾ cups nutmeats
	1 pound shelled	3½ cups nutmeats
peanuts	1 pound	2¼ cups nutmeats
	1 pound shelled	3 cups
pecans	1 pound	2¼ cups nutmeats
	1 pound shelled	4 cups

Food	Weight or Count	Measure or Yield
walnuts	1 pound	1⅔ cups nutmeats
	1 pound shelled	4 cups
Oats, quick-cooking	1 cup	1¾ cups cooked
Onion	1 medium	½ cup chopped
Orange	1 medium	⅓ cup juice; 2 tablespoons grated rind
Peaches	2 medium	1 cup sliced
Pears	2 medium	1 cup sliced
Potatoes, white	3 medium	2 cups cubed cooked or 1¾ cups mashed
sweet	3 medium	3 cups sliced
Raisins, seedless	1 pound	3 cups
Rice, long-grain	1 cup	3 to 4 cups cooked
pre-cooked	1 cup	2 cups cooked
Shrimp, raw in shell	1½ pounds	2 cups (¾ pound) cleaned, cooked
Spaghetti	7 ounces	About 4 cups cooked
Strawberries	1 quart	4 cups sliced
Sugar, brown	1 pound	2⅓ cups firmly packed
powdered	1 pound	3½ cups unsifted
granulated	1 pound	2 cups

HANDY SUBSTITUTIONS

Ingredient Called For	Substitution
1 cup self-rising flour	1 cup all-purpose flour plus 1 teaspoon baking powder and ½ teaspoon salt
1 cup cake flour	1 cup sifted all-purpose flour minus 2 tablespoons
1 cup all-purpose flour	1 cup cake flour plus 2 tablespoons
1 teaspoon baking powder	½ teaspoon cream of tartar plus ¼ teaspoon soda
1 tablespoon cornstarch or arrowroot	2 tablespoons all-purpose flour
1 tablespoon tapioca	1½ tablespoons all-purpose flour
2 large eggs	3 small eggs
1 egg	2 egg yolks (for custard)
1 egg	2 egg yolks plus 1 tablespoon water (for cookies)
1 (8-ounce) carton commercial sour cream	1 tablespoon lemon juice plus evaporated milk to equal 1 cup; or 3 tablespoons butter plus ⅞ cup sour milk
1 cup yogurt	1 cup buttermilk or sour milk
1 cup sour milk or buttermilk	1 tablespoon vinegar or lemon juice plus sweet milk to equal 1 cup
1 cup fresh milk	½ cup evaporated milk plus ½ cup water
1 cup fresh milk	3 to 5 tablespoons nonfat dry milk solids in 1 cup water
1 cup honey	1¼ cups sugar plus ¼ cup water
1 (1-ounce) square unsweetened chocolate	3 tablespoons cocoa plus 1 tablespoon butter or margarine
1 tablespoon fresh herbs	1 teaspoon dried herbs or ¼ teaspoon powdered herbs
¼ cup chopped fresh parsley	1 tablespoon dried parsley flakes
1 teaspoon dry mustard	1 tablespoon prepared mustard
1 pound fresh mushrooms	6 ounces canned mushrooms

EQUIVALENT MEASUREMENTS

3 teaspoons...............	1 tablespoon		2 cups.....................	1 pint (16 fluid ounces)	
4 tablespoons.............	¼ cup		4 cups.....................	1 quart	
5⅓ tablespoons.............	⅓ cup		4 quarts	1 gallon	
8 tablespoons.............	½ cup		⅛ cup........................	2 tablespoons	
16 tablespoons.............	1 cup		⅓ cup........................	5 tablespoons plus 1 teaspoon	
2 tablespoons (liquid).....	1 ounce		⅔ cup........................	10 tablespoons plus 2 teaspoons	
1 cup......................	8 fluid ounces		¾ cup........................	12 tablespoons	

CHEESE SELECTION GUIDE

Cheese	Flavor, Texture, and Color	Used For	Goes With
American	Very mild; creamy yellow	Sandwiches, snacks	Crackers, bread
Bel Paese (Italy)	Mild; spongy; creamy yellow interior	Dessert, snacks	Fresh fruit, crusty French bread
Brie (France)	Sharper than Camembert; soft, creamy, with edible crust	Dessert, snacks	Fresh fruit
Blue (France)	Piquant, spicy; marbled, blue veined, semisoft; creamy white	Dessert, dips, salads, appetizers, cheese trays	Fresh fruit, bland crackers
Brick (United States)	Mild; semisoft; cream-colored to orange	Sandwiches, appetizers, cheese trays	Crackers, bread
Camembert (France)	Mild to pungent; edible crust; creamy yellow	Dessert, snacks	Especially good with tart apple slices
Cheddar (England) (United States)	Mild to sharp; cream-colored to orange	Dessert, sandwiches, salads, appetizers, cheese trays; use as an ingredient in cooking	Especially good with apples or pears
Chèvre (French)	Goat cheese; very pungent; creamy	Relishes, appetizers, sauces	Crackers, fruit
Cottage Cheese (United States)	Mild; soft, moist, large or small curd; white	Appetizers, fruit salads, snacks; use as an ingredient in cooking	Canned or fresh fruit
Cream Cheese (United States)	Mild; buttery, soft, smooth; white	Dessert, sandwiches, salads; use as an ingredient in cooking	Jelly and crackers
Edam (Holland)	Mild; firm with red wax coating	Dessert, appetizers, cheese tray	Fresh fruit
Feta (Greece)	Salty; crumbly, but sliceable; snow white	Appetizers; use as an ingredient in cooking	Greek salad
Fontina (Italy)	Nutty; semisoft to hard	Dessert, appetizers, sandwiches	Fresh fruit, crackers, bread
Gjetost (Norway)	Sweetish; firm, smooth; caramel-colored	Appetizers	Crackers
Gouda (Holland)	Mild, nutty; softer than Edam, with or without red wax coating	Dessert, appetizers	Fresh fruit, crackers
Gruyère (Switzerland)	Nutty; similar to swiss; firm with tiny holes	Dessert, appetizers	Fresh fruit
Jarlsberg (Norway)	Mild, nutty; firm	Sandwiches, snacks	Fresh fruit, bread
Havarti (Denmark)	Mild; rich and creamy	Snacks, sandwiches	Crackers, bread, fresh fruit
Liederkranz (United States)	Robust; texture of heavy honey, edible light-orange crust	Dessert, snacks	Fresh fruit, matzo, pumpernickel, sour rye, thinly sliced onion
Limburger (Belgium)	Robust, aromatic; soft, smooth; creamy white	Dessert	Fresh fruit, dark bread, bland crackers
Monterey Jack (United States)	Mild; semisoft; creamy white	Snacks, sandwiches, sauces, casseroles	Bread, crackers
Mozzarella (Italy)	Delicate, mild; semisoft; creamy white	Pizza; use as an ingredient in cooking	Italian foods
Muenster (Germany)	Mild to mellow; semisoft	Sandwiches, cheese trays	Crackers, bread
Parmesan (Italy)	Sharp, piquant; hard, brittle body; light yellow	Use grated as an ingredient in cooking; table use: young cheese, not aged	Italian foods; combine with Swiss for sauces
Pineapple Cheese (United States)	Sharp; firm, pineapple-shaped	Dessert, appetizers, salads, snacks	Fresh fruit
Port Salut (France)	Mellow to robust, fresh buttery flavor; semisoft	Dessert, appetizers, cheese trays	Fresh fruit, crackers

CHEESE SELECTION GUIDE *(continued)*

Cheese	Flavor, Texture, and Color	Used For	Goes With
Provolone (Italy)	Mild to sharp, usually smoked, salty; hard; yellowish-white	Dessert, appetizers; use as an ingredient in cooking	Italian foods
Ricotta (Italy)	Bland but semisweet; soft; creamy white	An ingredient in main dishes, filling, or pastries	Fresh fruit
Romano (Italy)	Sharp; hard, brittle body; light yellow	Use grated as an ingredient in cooking; table use: young cheese, not aged	Italian foods, salads, sauces
Roquefort (France)	Sharp; semisoft, sometimes crumbly; blue veined	Desserts, dips, salads, appetizers	Bland crackers, fresh fruit, demitasse
Stilton (England)	Semisoft; slightly more crumbly than blue; blue veined	Dessert, cheese trays, dips, salads	Fresh fruit, bland crackers
Swiss (Switzerland)	Sweetish; nutty with large holes; pale yellow	Dessert, cheese trays, salads, sandwiches, appetizers, use as an ingredient in cooking	Fresh fruit, squares of crusty French bread

WINE SELECTION GUIDE

Type of Wine	Specific Wine	Serve With	Temperature	When to Serve
Appetizer	Sherry (dry), Port Vermouth (dry)	Appetizers, nuts, cheese	Chilled, room temperature, over ice	Before dinner
Table Wines (white)	Rhine, Chablis, Sauterne, Light Muscat, Riesling, White Chianti	Fish, seafood, poultry, cheese, lamb, veal, eggs, lighter foods, pork (except ham)	Chilled	With dinner; any time, with or without food
Table Wines (red)	Rosé	Curry, patio parties, Chinese food, any food	Slightly chilled	With dinner; any time, with or without food
	Claret	Game, Italian food, beef, Hawaiian food	Slightly chilled	With dinner
	Chianti	Red meat, cheese, roasts, game, Italian food	Slightly chilled	With dinner
	Burgundy	Cheese, Italian food, game, ham, heartier foods, roasts, steaks	Slightly chilled	With dinner; any time, with or without food
Sparkling Wines	Champagne, dry	Appetizers, fish, seafood, poultry, main courses, desserts, cheese, any festive meal	Chilled	Any time, with or without food
Dessert Wines	Port, Muscatel, Tokay, Champagne (sweet), Sherry (cream), Madeira (sweet), Sauterne, Marsala, Malaga	Desserts, fruit, nuts, cheeses, cakes, pastries	Cool or room temperature	After dinner with dessert

Recipe Title Index

An alphabetical listing of every recipe by exact title
All microwave recipe page numbers are preceded by an "M"

Month-by-Month Index

An alphabetical listing within the month of every food article and accompanying recipes
All microwave recipe page numbers are preceded by an "M"

General Recipe Index

A listing of every recipe by food category and/or major ingredient
All microwave recipe page numbers are preceded by an "M"

Favorite Recipes

Record your favorite recipes below for quick and handy reference

Recipe	Source/Page	Remarks

Recipe	Source/Page	Remarks

Make Meal Planning Worry Free With SEASONINGS!

It's easy! We've done the work for you in our new monthly newsletter of menus-by-the-day designed exclusively for *SOUTHERN LIVING* 1989 ANNUAL RECIPES.

SEASONINGS features an at-a-glance calendar with menu suggestions for each day of the month so you know what's best to serve with what—what looks good together, tastes great together. We've tasted and tested this with that—that with the other—to take every bit of the worry, the indecision out of planning balanced meals for your family and exciting meals for your guests!

Here's what you get:

- One complete meal every day, nutritionally balanced and planned to perfection
- Quick-to-fix weekday menus— extra special fare for weekends and holidays
- EZ-to-read format, just right for the front of the 'fridge
- Useful tips and comments on menus for the month from Jean Liles, Senior Foods Editor
- Special "family favorite" recipes from the personal collections of the SOUTHERN LIVING foods staff

To receive SEASONINGS monthly for only $12.00 per year, simply write to:

Southern Living®

P.O. Box 830624
Birmingham, AL 35283-0624
Or call us toll-free:
1-800-366-4712
in Alabama 1-800-292-8667